LONDON

A HISTORICAL COMPANION

LONDON

A HISTORICAL COMPANION

KENNETH PANTON

TEMPUS

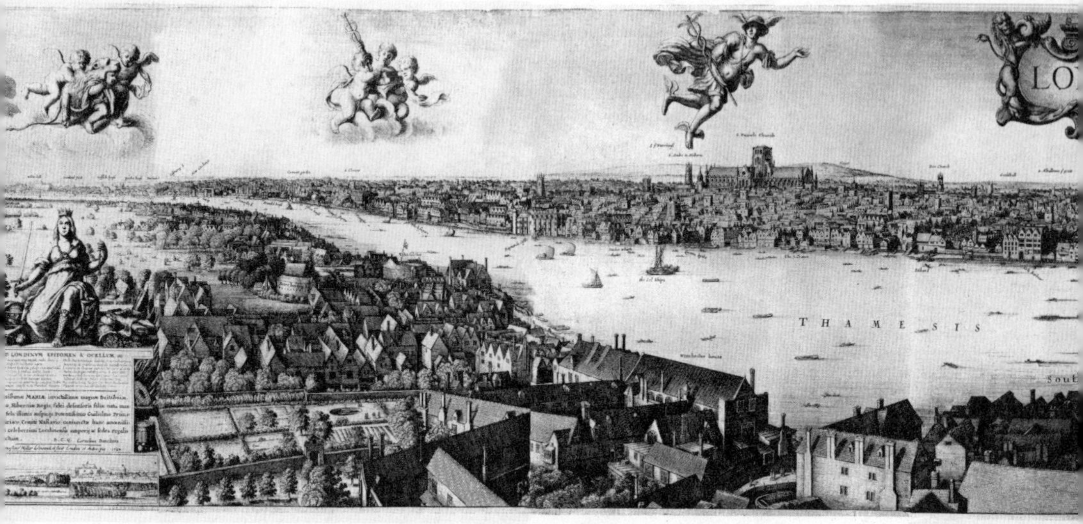

London in 1647 by Hollar.

First published 2001

This illustrated and expanded edition first published 2003,
by arrangement with Scarecrow Press.

Tempus Publishing Limited
The Mill, Brimscombe Port,
Stroud, Gloucestershire, GL5 2QG
www.tempus-publishing.com

British Library Cataloguing in Publication Data.
A catalogue record for this book is available from the British Library.

ISBN 0 7524 2577 3

Typesetting and origination by Tempus Publishing Limited
Printed in Great Britain by Midway Colour Print, Wiltshire

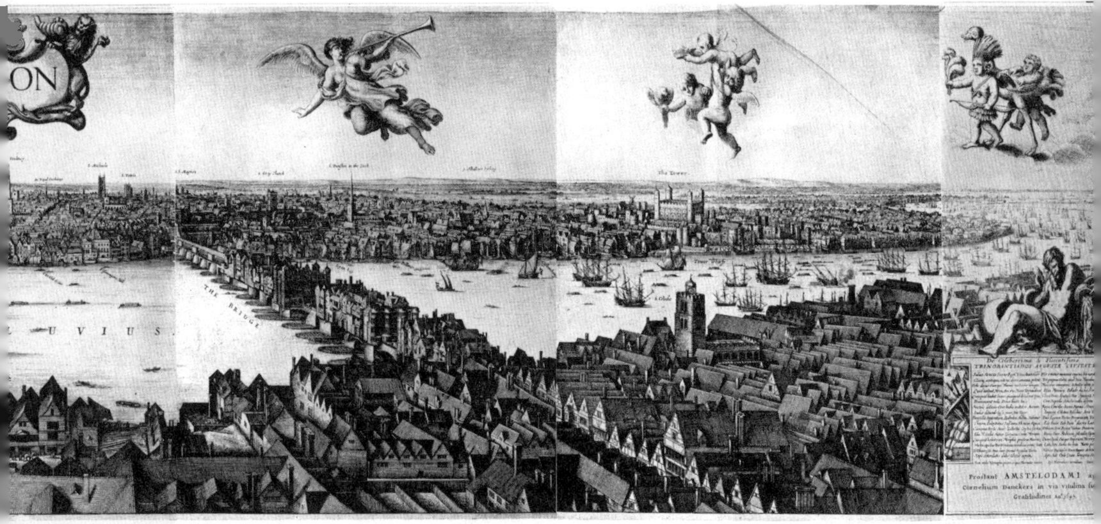

CONTENTS

INTRODUCTION 7

THE DICTIONARY 19

APPENDICES 428

- Historical Events
- Lord Mayors of London
- Chairmen of Greater London Council
- Chairmen of London County Council

ACKNOWLEDGEMENTS 477

LIST OF ILLUSTRATIONS 479

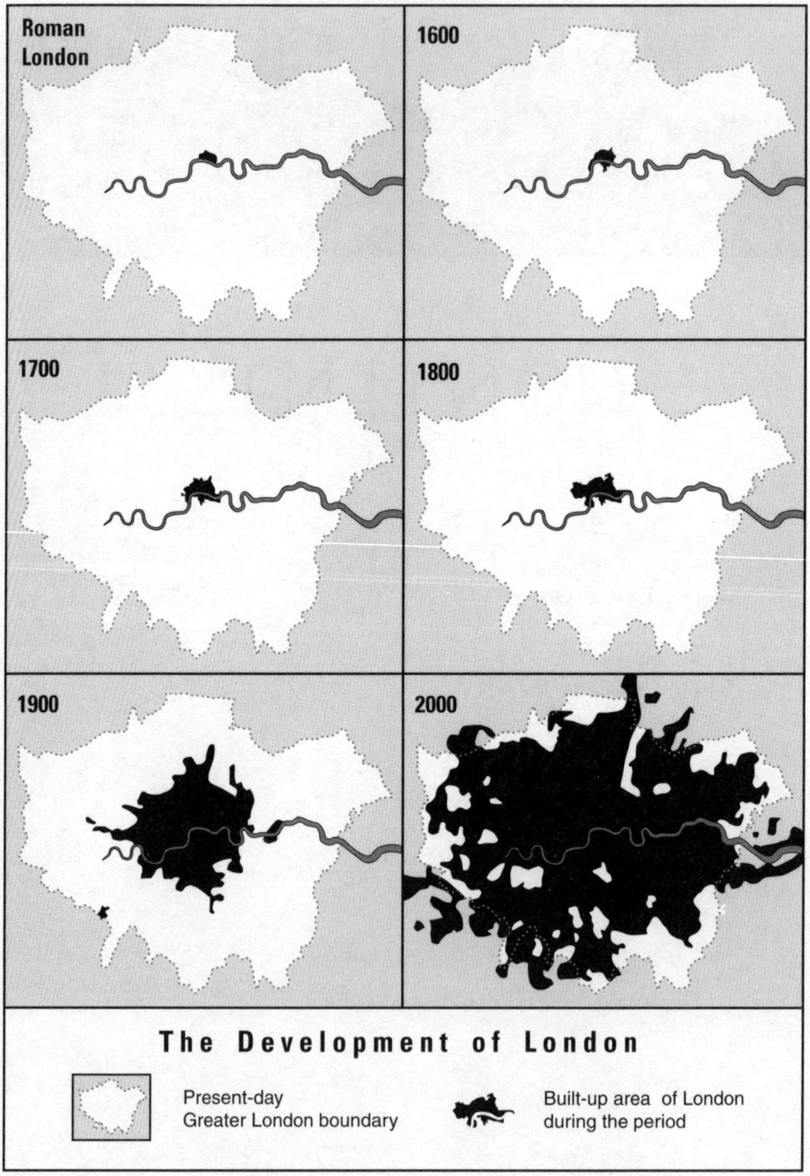

The development of London from Roman times to the present.

INTRODUCTION

London, like other cities, is part bricks, part mortar, part state of mind. Too large and complex for any individual to comprehend, it is often described as a collection of villages, each with its own personality. The working-class East End is only four miles, but a cultural universe, away from aristocratic Belgravia. Bangladeshi Spitalfields has little in common with West Indian Brixton except that it is part of the same urban area. Financiers rub shoulders, often uneasily, with civil service mandarins as they pass from the complex of government offices in Whitehall to the banks, insurance companies and money exchanges of the City of London.

PHYSICAL GEOGRAPHY

The metropolitan area lies in the south-east of the United Kingdom at latitude 51 degrees 30 minutes north and (at Greenwich) on the prime meridian of longitude. Most of the built-up area is on the north bank of the River Thames, which meanders eastwards to the North Sea across the London Basin, a structural downfold known to geologists as a syncline. The underlying rock is chalk, initially formed in oceanic conditions then buckled by the same tectonic forces that created the Alpine mountain chain in southern Europe some 40 million years ago, during the mid-Tertiary period. Later, the chalk was covered by a complex of sands, gravels, pebbles, and clays, which reach over 400 feet in depth and reflect changing environmental conditions.

Under natural conditions, the soils would be covered by deciduous woodland (notably beech, oak and alder), with marshes along the waterways, but apart from a few remnants (as at Epping Forest) the trees and sedges have been replaced by concrete and tarmac. The climate is mild, with January temperatures in the central city averaging about 5 degrees Celsius (42 degrees Fahrenheit) and July temperatures about 18 degrees Celsius (65 degrees Fahrenheit). Suburban areas are a few degrees cooler at all seasons because lower building densities and greater provision of parkland facilitate dissipation of heat. Annual rainfall totals vary from about 635 millimetres (25 inches) on the east of the metropolitan area to about 787 millimetres (31 inches) on higher parts of the urban fringe, such as the Chiltern Hills and the North Downs. Most of the precipitation is cyclonic in origin, with an autumn maximum and spring minimum.

EARLY SETTLEMENT

Although archaeological studies indicate that prehistoric communities used the Thames as a source of wildfowl and fish, London's history really begins with the Romans. These invaders from the Mediterranean arrived in AD 43 and, utilizing patches of stable sediment, built a bridge across the waterway in order to facilitate the movement of troops and supplies. A settlement known as Londinium developed at the northern bridgehead and, despite pillaging by Boadicea's Icenian followers in AD 61 and damage by fire about AD 120, grew into a substantial city.

Modern excavations have revealed that a basilica, the largest north of the Alps, was built at the site now occupied by Cornhill and connected to the bridge over the Thames by a road that followed the line of modern Gracechurch Street. Fortifications were constructed in the north-west (the area now known as Cripplegate) about AD 100 and a protective wall completed by AD 140.

Secure in the knowledge that they were technically superior to the indigenous peoples and that their frontier was moving north and west, thus making Londinium increasingly secure from attack, the Romans built a thriving commercial centre that, according to some scholars, may have housed as many as 100,000 citizens during the third century. Places of worship, administrative buildings, baths and meeting places were erected to meet religious, recreational and organizational needs.

The clays of the London Basin provided few sources of stone, so most of these early structures were fashioned from timber, with thatched roofs, and have long since decayed. However, evidence of occupation remains in remnants of the defensive wall (as at Noble Street), the outline of the Temple of Mithras (off Queen Victoria Street), and the lines of routes that led to the city gates (for example, Cannon Street and Cheapside adopt the same routes as the Roman streets built some 2,000 years ago). Excavations of cemeteries and finds of weapons and pottery have added further knowledge of changing military, social and economic life as Londinium became the capital of the new province, with increasingly complex financial institutions and a burgeoning port trading with continental Europe.

However, during the fourth century the power of the Roman Empire declined. In 410 BC, the legions marched off to defend the Holy City and Londinium was left to the mercies of Anglo-Saxon migrants from the North German Plain. Until recently, many scholars believed that these newcomers, essentially agricultural peoples lacking a tradition of urban life, simply allowed the city to decay because archaeologists had found no convincing evidence of building before the middle of the ninth century. On the other hand, some writers claimed that there must have been a considerable urban population during what was once known as the Dark Ages because St Augustine had ordained Mellitus as the settlement's first bishop in 604 BC and Bede (writing in 730 BC) had described 'Lundenwic' as a town trading with many nations.

Since 1985, the story has been clarified as a result of archaeological work carried out largely by teams from the Museum of London, who have discovered evidence of a significant settlement between the site of Whitehall and the banks of the River Fleet, beyond the Roman walls. Moreover, coins and other artefacts suggest that, for most of the period from 670 until 870 BC, the area was part of the Kingdom of Mercia, which had strong commercial links with continental Europe. For fifteen years from 871 BC, there was a lengthy period of political instability, when the city was ruled by Danish invaders, but in 886 BC King Alfred regained the territory and laid out a new town stretching from just east of the site of St Paul's Cathedral to London Bridge (between the modern Cheapside and Thames Street, and inside the area of Londinium).

Significantly, documents dating from the late eighth and early ninth centuries refer to London as Lundenburh, the *-burh* suffix indicating that it had become a fortified settlement, but it is not known whether the defences were simply the old Roman walls or whether these were augmented by new construction. Resources were certainly devoted to other forms of construction because quays were erected along the north bank of the Thames to facilitate trading, and there is documentary evidence of a significant trade in farm produce, timber and textiles.

The Scandinavians returned in 1016 and demanded, from London's citizenry, an annual tribute that amounted to one-eighth of the entire payment from the whole English realm, an indication of the city's wealth and importance at the time. The tribute undoubtedly had a serious impact on the economy, but the invaders remained only until 1042, when Edward the Confessor assumed the English throne and built a church and palace on the site of a former monastery at Westminster. Although undoubtedly born of piety, the decision was to have a long-lasting political impact because it established, away from the Roman city, a focus of urban growth that evolved into the nation's centre of political power as the church grew into Westminster Abbey and the location became the site of the Houses of Parliament.

Edward, however, had little time to make a real impact on London. He died in January 1066, just a week after his new church was consecrated and only months before the Normans changed the landscape of England. William the Conqueror, with an invading force technically superior to anything the Anglo-Saxon peoples could muster, was well aware that he would have to take command of London's wealth and trade in order to exert his influence over the remainder of the British Isles. His first attempt to enter the city failed but civic leaders, accepting that defeat was inevitable, eventually surrendered, acknowledging William as king at a coronation ceremony in Westminster Abbey on Christmas Day 1066.

The arrival of the Normans emphasized the city's importance. It was the largest town in the country, with an established system of courts administering justice and maintaining law and order within urban boundaries. Strategically, it controlled movements along the Thames and, therefore, influenced naval and commercial transport to the interior of England and to the European mainland. However, the new regime had comparatively little effect on London's social and economic institutions because the new monarch confirmed rights of male inheritance, placed London's citizens under his protection, and agreed to maintain the laws that were in place during Edward's rule. As a result, commerce experienced no serious long-term interruption, and civic government remained largely unchanged. The physical fabric was also little altered, the most significant innovation being a considerable strengthening of the settlement's defences, partly because of fear of attack but also to remind a subjugated people that the invaders were in charge. In particular, work began on the Tower of London; initially a wooden structure but, from 1078, rebuilt in stone, it was greatly enlarged over succeeding centuries to become the principal fortress in the capital.

The Norman peace, uneasy though it was at times, brought a prosperity that encouraged trade, the spread of services and urban expansion. By the end of the twelfth century, the city had 126 churches, many of the streets were paved, and stone was overtaking wood as a building material for the homes of richer merchants as well as for public structures, such as the replacement for London Bridge begun in 1176. Harbour facilities were spreading further along the riverside, and goods were arriving from regions as far apart as Scandinavia and the eastern Mediterranean. Guilds (now known as livery companies) were forming to represent the interests of manufacturers and traders, sheriffs presided over the courts, a lord mayor was accepted as head of local government by at least 1189, and immigrants were arriving from all over Europe to seek a future in one of the most powerful kingdoms in the known world.

THE MEDIEVAL CITY

During the thirteenth century, the City of London used its financial might to manipulate, and sometimes even oppose, monarchs. In return for payments to royal coffers (particularly during the reigns of kings, such as John, who engaged in lavish spending or needed funds to support large armies), the lord mayor and his advisory committee of aldermen were able to negotiate privileges that enhanced the wealth of individuals and confirmed the community's commercial supremacy in England. Thus, about 1130 (the exact date is not known), Henry I issued a charter giving London the right to conduct its financial affairs without fear of intervention from the Crown and granting Londoners the freedom to trade throughout England without paying tolls or taxes. Such favoured status inevitably facilitated the growth of a sizeable and affluent merchant class, which vied with courtiers as the richest in the realm.

Moreover, as the royal household spent increasingly lengthy periods of time in London dealing with the financiers, Parliament met in the city more and more frequently, and a plethora of courts and offices was created to meet its needs. Specialist administrators, lawyers and accountants were drawn to Westminster, and London increasingly became the pivot of national affairs, its development shaped as much by matters of state as by local conditions.

As a capital city, London had considerable strategic advantages. It was far from the frontiers with the warring Scots and Irish and was readily defended against European invaders, who would have to brave the might of a growing Navy in the Thames estuary or fight their way through 50 miles of forest and marsh from landings on the English Channel coast. The main threat came from internal uprisings, but those that did occur, such as the Peasants' Revolt of 1381, were limited in scale and duration. As a result, the city operated in a more stable economic climate than other towns, so it was better able to maximise trading advantages and ride out recession.

The wealth generated was evident in the extent and opulence of the urban fabric. The size of the medieval St Paul's Cathedral (one of the largest buildings in the country), the Gothic splendour of the Guildhall (built in 1411–39 as the focus for local government), and the mansions of men such as Sir John de Pulteney (who made a fortune as a draper) bear testimony to years of successful commerce. But the citizens who lived in material comfort and had funds to spend on fine buildings, luxurious furnishings and donations to religious charities were, in fact, a small proportion of the city's population. Most people lived in cramped, overcrowded homes that doubled as workshops and where infection spread easily. Rats fed on garbage left to decay in the streets because concepts of hygiene and knowledge of the causes of disease were limited. Water supplies were increasingly scarce as rivers were polluted with sewage, and fire spread rapidly through the timber buildings in which most of the poor were housed.

For the most deprived, Roman Catholic religious houses were a major source of food, health care and comfort. Benedictines, Carthusians, Cistercians, Dominicans, Franciscans and others owned large tracts of land in, and close to, the city, benefiting from the gifts of wealthy patrons hoping to buy themselves a place in Heaven. That source of succour vanished, however, when Henry VIII reformed the Church of England, removing it from Vatican jurisdiction and dissolving the monasteries. In London, Holy Trinity Priory (founded during the twelfth century by secular followers of St Augustine) was the first to go, Parliament approving its acquisition by the monarch in 1532. Within a decade, all the others had disbanded, their inhabitants scattered to the four winds and their estates transferred to private ownership. Some buildings (like the chapel at Holy Trinity) were demolished to provide stone for new structures, some were granted to followers from whom the king wanted continued support (Sir Edward North, Chancellor of the Court of

Augmentations, received Charterhouse, for instance), and much land eventually fell into the hands of entrepreneurs, who laid out housing for a growing population (as at Covent Garden).

The demise of the monasteries was a disaster for the indigent, who became an increasingly common sight on the streets of Elizabethan London. The City Fathers helped by distributing grain at times of famine, introduced measures for relief of the poor in 1547, and provided medical care in new facilities. Also, wealthy private citizens made a contribution by building almshouses, schools and hospitals, but, even so, the problems were sufficiently great to convince aldermen that continued urban expansion might lead to widespread hunger and that, in turn, could result in civil disorder, threatening the stability of the city (and, of course, their own sources of income). Their response, from 1580, was a series of attempts to control suburban growth, but those efforts failed to stem the tide.

Deprived of charitable support, the poor increasingly congregated in the East End, employed in dirty, noisy trades that were considered a nuisance by city merchants and therefore unwelcome in the urban core. Suburbs such as Whitechapel (a centre of metalworking, including bell-making) and Wapping (with a variety of waterfront activities) grew larger and acquired reputations as rough, drunken, crime-ridden communities – reputations they were to carry, in many cases, into the twenty-first century. Also, many tradesmen found employment at Woolwich and Deptford, on

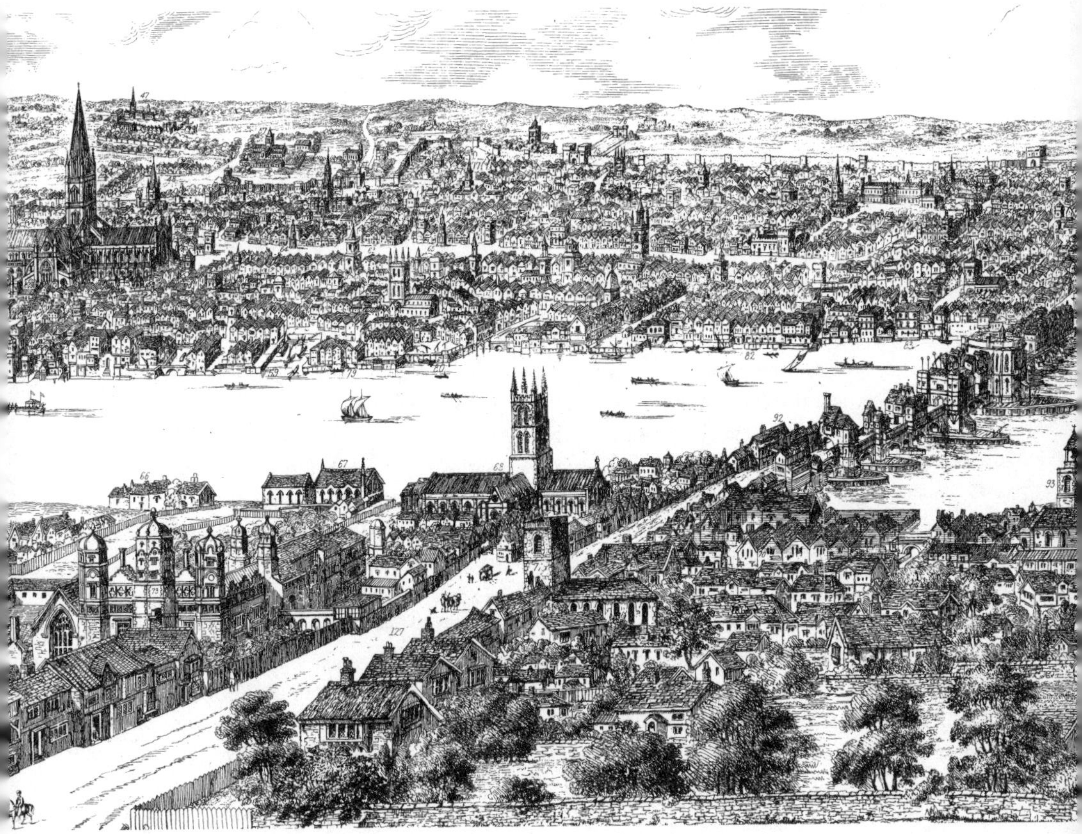

Southwark in 1543 by Wyngaerde.

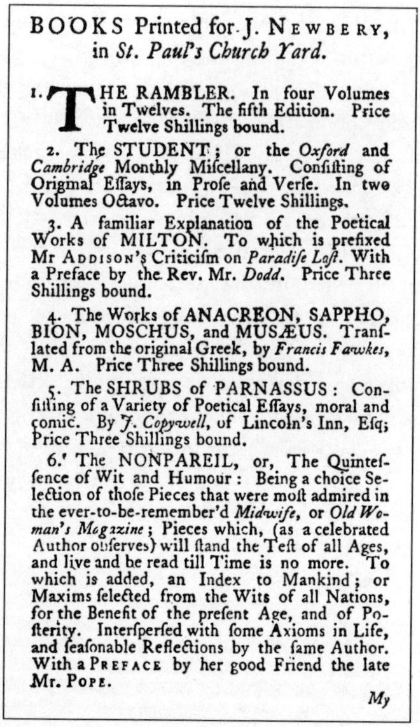

BOOKS Printed for J. NEWBERY,
in *St. Paul's Church Yard.*

1. THE RAMBLER. In four Volumes in Twelves. The fifth Edition. Price Twelve Shillings bound.

2. The STUDENT; or the *Oxford* and *Cambridge* Monthly Miſcellany. Conſiſting of Original Eſſays, in Proſe and Verſe. In two Volumes Octavo. Price Twelve Shillings.

3. A familiar Explanation of the Poetical Works of MILTON. To which is prefixed Mr ADDISON's Criticiſm on *Paradiſe Loſt.* With a Preface by the Rev. Mr. *Dodd.* Price Three Shillings bound.

4. The Works of ANACREON, SAPPHO, BION, MOSCHUS, and MUSÆUS. Tranſlated from the original Greek, by *Francis Fawkes,* M. A. Price Three Shillings bound.

5. The SHRUBS of PARNASSUS: Conſiſting of a Variety of Poetical Eſſays, moral and comic. By *J. Copywell,* of Lincoln's Inn, Eſq; Price Three Shillings bound.

6. The NONPAREIL, or, The Quinteſſence of Wit and Humour: Being a choice Selection of thoſe Pieces that were moſt admired in the ever-to-be-remember'd *Midwife,* or *Old Woman's Magazine;* Pieces which, (as a celebrated Author obſerves) will ſtand the Teſt of all Ages, and live and be read till Time is no more. To which is added, an Index to Mankind; or Maxims ſelected from the Wits of all Nations, for the Benefit of the preſent Age, and of Poſterity. Interſperſed with ſome Axioms in Life, and ſeaſonable Reflections by the ſame Author. With a PREFACE by her good Friend the late Mr. POPE.

My

A 1760 advertisement for a book publisher based in St Paul's courtyard.

the south bank of the River Thames, as the Royal Dockyards (originally established in 1512 and 1513 respectively) expanded, creating a second industrial focus. On the other side of the financial quarter, developers laid out Lincoln's Inn Fields and other prestigious residential estates, providing the beginnings of the fashionable West End.

The continued commercial expansion fuelled immigration, and the newcomers brought skills that established new trades (and thereby caused further expansion). Silk, glass, novel forms of pottery (such as majolica ware) and other manufactured goods were produced outside the city walls and therefore beyond the control either of local government officials or of the livery companies, which restricted entry into trades and controlled their activities. Moreover, that same spirit of economic freedom encouraged the growth of service provision, as at Bankside, on the south side of the Thames in Southwark, which emerged as London's main entertainment center during the late sixteenth century because theatres, such as the Rose and the Globe, could operate without fear of censorial interference by the City Corporation.

This new competitive ethos was accompanied by a growth in materialism at the expense of religious commitment. Church building declined (in fact, the nave of St Paul's Cathedral became a market place and its courtyard a crowded hive of print shops and book publishers). On the other hand, building for mercantile interests provided a constant stream of jobs as Thomas Gresham funded the construction of the Royal Exchange (which opened as London's first meeting place for traders in 1568), and the Muscovy Company (founded in 1555), the East India Company (created by royal charter in 1600) and other powerful concerns established imposing headquarters.

At the same time, the Tower of London was losing its status as a royal residence. Henry VIII converted York Place into Whitehall Palace and a former leper hospital into St James's Palace, moving the court out of the City of London into the suburbs beyond. Initially, the departure of the royal family seemed to cause little resentment: most Londoners remained loyal to Henry's successors, even forming local troops to help repel a Spanish invasion anticipated in 1588. However, the reign of Charles I proved more difficult because, shortly after succeeding to the throne in 1625, he was involved in a series of confrontations with city leaders, threatening to overturn many of their long-standing rights and privileges. Naturally, the merchants resisted and threw their lot in with the Parliamentarian cause when the civil war began in 1642, using their considerable financial resources to reject a royal authority they greatly disliked.

Even so, rejection of the individual was not rejection of the concept of monarchy and, as Oliver Cromwell's Puritan supporters closed more and more places of entertainment, public sympathy for the king returned, so news of his restoration on terms that allowed Parliament to control his excesses was received with much rejoicing in 1660. However, the concentration on political matters had diverted attention from growing infrastructural problems that were to alter the face of the city radically within a few years.

THE EMERGENCE OF MODERN LONDON

In the middle of the seventeenth century, London had a population of about a half a million inhabitants, more than any other settlement in Europe and some fifteen times greater than the port of Bristol, which, with 30,000 people, was the next largest settlement in England. That created opportunities for the acquisition of wealth but was an enormous threat to public health and safety because the unsanitary conditions were favourable breeding grounds for rats. These, in turn, provided the ideal environment for fleas infested by *Yersinia pestis*, the bacillus that causes plague.

Plague was no stranger in London. In the middle years of the fourteenth century, it may have killed as many as 100,000 citizens (half the resident population), and in 1625 it wiped out 40,000. In the autumn of 1664 it returned, appearing first in St-Giles-in-the-Fields then sweeping through Clerkenwell, Cripplegate, Shoreditch, Stepney and Westminster – the poorest, most overcrowded sectors of the urban area – but sparing no class or neighbourhood. Over the next eighteen months, at least 70,000 people died and business activity was devastated.

Then, from 2–5 September 1666, the weakened economy was further crippled by the worst fire in the city's history. Flames gained a foothold in the timber-framed bakery that made bread for the king and spread rapidly along the narrow streets, leaping across alleys from one thatched roof to another. The blaze raged for four days, destroying eighty per cent of the urban area (all but parts of the west and north-east); 13,200 houses, eighty-nine churches, and most major public and commercial structures (including the Guildhall and the Royal Exchange) were destroyed or seriously damaged.

The effects can hardly be overestimated. Concepts of insurance for buildings and belongings were rudimentary so many people became homeless, with neither funds nor welfare payments to help them recover. Merchants lost their stores and their records, manufacturers lost their workshops and factories, printers lost their presses, and livery companies lost their halls. But rebuilding began immediately. King Charles and the City Corporation each appointed three architects to draw up plans for reconstruction, with a specification that housing densities should be lower than those of earlier years.

Hollar's engraving of the Great Fire of 1666.

Inevitably, the renewal plans were compromised by political and financial realities but, even so, the new London looked very different from the old. Brick replaced wood as the primary building material for all social groups. Confined streets and tortuous lanes were replaced by wide roads designed to prevent the spread of fire. Markets were moved and expanded, new places of worship were erected for expanded parishes, harbour facilities were improved, and the Fleet River was canalized. The churches, in particular, helped to tie the new city together because over fifty of them (including a rebuilt St Paul's Cathedral) were designed by Christopher Wren, who was appointed surveyor general for London in 1669.

The Great Fire also proved a spur to physical expansion. Many of the estimated 100,000 residents who lost their homes and workplaces relocated outside the city walls in formerly independent settlements such as Clerkenwell, binding them into the built-up area. In addition, it allowed commercial and administrative communities to restructure and innovate. The Bank of England was founded in 1694 and, within fifty years, had helped re-establish the city as England's major financial centre. Over the same period, investment in harbour facilities confirmed the port's status as the largest in the country.

Also, the union of the Scottish and English Parliaments in 1707 added to Westminster's prestige as the fulcrum of national government and gave administrative emphasis to the growing civil service in nearby Whitehall. Burgeoning interest in the arts made London the literary capital of Europe during the eighteenth century. The Royal Academy of Arts, founded in 1768, boasted painter Joshua Reynolds as its first president. Dr Samuel Johnson, lionized by James Boswell, his sycophantic biographer, was lauded in the drawing rooms of Piccadilly and Pall Mall. David Garrick attracted throngs of playgoers to see his performances at Drury Lane, and the piano was heard for the first time in public at the Royal Opera House in 1767.

Fashionable Georgians lounged in city coffee houses, traveled to business in sedan chairs, and bought their goods at high-class stores such as Dodsley's bookshop and Vulliamy's clock workshop in Pall Mall. In Bloomsbury and Mayfair, speculative builders laid out gracious squares lined by houses that were adorned with colonnades and porticos reminiscent of ancient Greece and Rome. In the process, they shifted the city's centre of gravity westward as affluent residents deserted the formerly desirable Soho and Covent Garden for newer, more spacious properties.

But the darker side of urban life remained. Coal fires polluted the air, and sewage polluted water supplies. Open rivers, such as the Fleet, were blocked with garbage, and the poor, crammed into overcrowded hovels, sought refuge from their sorrows in gin. Conditions were made worse by an influx of immigrants, who helped raise London's population from an estimated 670,000 in 1700 to 959,310 at the time of the first official census in 1801. Many of these new residents came from abroad: for example, Soho had a growing French population, filling the homes abandoned by the rich, and Heneage Lane had significant numbers of Spanish and Portuguese residents. But many came from rural areas of the British Isles, where agricultural change, and notably the enclosure of fields, had produced an army of landless, homeless labourers who drifted to the towns to find work. Many of them, not surprisingly, headed for London and found homes with family or friends who had travelled before them. Thus, ethnic neighbourhoods became common, and services were founded specifically to meet their needs (a charity school for children of Welsh immigrants was founded at Clerkenwell in 1737, for instance).

Immigrant numbers continued to rise throughout the nineteenth century, driven by events such as the Irish potato famines of the 1840s and a growing industrialization, which concentrated manufacturing jobs in urban areas. As the first industrial society, Britain benefited from the creation of jobs in engineering, road construction, port industries, and the services that supplied them. All of these were labour-intensive and the limited transport systems of the time required workers to live near their work; thus, in the East End, businesses and homes jostled for space in a smoky, grimy environment that lacked any provision for personal privacy or any semblance of green space. The combined rigours of long hours in an exhausting job, a poor diet and a lack of living space took their toll, some research studies suggesting that life expectancy in Bethnal Green during the 1840s was as low as sixteen years.

It is arguable that individual deprivation was part of the price to be paid for London's metamorphosis from an important but nonetheless regional trading city to the capital of the largest empire the world has ever known. Colonial expansion was driven as much by business opportunities as by desire for political status, and the wealth created by that new commerce helped subsidize demand for the expensive homes built by John Nash at Regent's Park, by Thomas Cubitt in Belgravia, and by other developers in north, west and south London. It also provided funds for a great range of educational and scientific institutions, such as the British Museum (which moved to its present headquarters in stages from 1826 to 1881), London Zoo (opened in 1828), and the complex of facilities (including the Victoria and Albert Museum) at south Kensington.

On the other hand, public awareness of the plight of the poor was being raised by the works of writers such as Charles Dickens and the social commentator Henry Mayhew. Some individuals, including Thomas Barnardo (founder of a chain of children's homes) and William Booth (who created the Salvation Army), devoted most of their lives to improving living conditions in the East End and providing opportunities for the indigent to raise their living standards through access to education, vocational training and better diets. Also, growing numbers of philanthropists, following the example of American-born George Peabody, invested in housing provision in return for reasonable rents.

In one sense, the railways exacerbated the problems, pushing their way through the most crowded areas of London on their way to the city centre because it was easier to dispossess the poor than to move the rich. In another, they alleviated it by breaking the vice that bound dwelling place to workplace. From the 1840s, people could live in the suburbs and journey to office or factory by train, so employment opportunities widened and businesses could relocate closer to sources of labour. Then, from 1863, the expanding tentacles of the underground railway system widened the transport network further. As a result, inner-city populations began to decline and slums were replaced by stores, banks and other services.

The growing wealth of London's residents, coupled with the redistribution of population, allowed local government to invest in projects designed to increase quality of life within the city. In 1855, a Metropolitan Board of Works was created and appointed Joseph William Bazalgette to build a new, and much needed, system of sewers. Embankments were erected along the River Thames to contain the high tides, which sometimes caused flooding, and new streets, including Charing Cross Road and Shaftesbury Avenue, were driven through the core of the metropolis to improve communications.

As these improvements were being made, other ventures helped make London a safer and more pleasant environment. Streets were first lit by the Gas Light and Coke Company in 1807. The Metropolitan Police was formed in 1829, replacing a multitude of independent law enforcement agencies with a single unit. A citywide fire service was established in 1833 and an ambulance service in 1867. In 1870, a London School Board was formed, providing education for children aged five to thirteen, and in 1888 the Metropolitan Board of Works was replaced by a London County Council, which was given greater powers than its predecessor to demolish substandard properties, build homes for the working classes, and lay out parkland.

By the end of the century, London had increased its population fivefold and radically altered its physical structure, engulfing formerly independent villages, such as Hampstead, under planning policies prepared by new and more democratic forms of local government. A framework of emergency services was in place, young people were increasingly literate and numerate, and provision for the poor was improving. Essentially, the city had taken its modern form.

LONDON SINCE 1900

In 1901, London was the world's largest city, with a population of some 6.5 million, compared with 4 million in New York and 2.7 million in Paris. However, despite the advances of previous decades, it still faced enormous social problems, largely related to poor housing and a lack of national welfare policies directed at low earners and the unemployed. London County Council responded by building the Boundary Street Housing Estate in the East End, providing homes for over 5,500 Shoreditch slum dwellers at a density of 200 people to the acre and supplying medical and educational facilities. The five-storey buildings were built of good-quality brick, with high gables, and are claimed by some critics to be among the most outstanding legacies of the Arts and Crafts movement. Elsewhere, notably in Hampstead Garden Suburb, private developers were attempting to relieve the monotony of paved roads by designing neighbourhoods that incorporated parks, hedges and trees, with as few as eight houses to the acre.

The First World War did little to curb urban expansion, and the 1920s and 1930s brought continued growth as the private car made commuting ever more easy. Industry, too, contributed to the outward spread as Handley Page built an aircraft manufacturing plant at Cricklewood, Hoover erected a new factory in Western Avenue, Guinness constructed a brewery at Park Royal, and other businesses took advantage of the growing pool of labour London was able to offer.

In 1938, fearing the consequences of uncontrolled metropolitan incursion into the countryside, national and local politicians promoted the establishment of a Green Belt – a broad ring of farmland that would contain the city through strict building controls and would also provide recreational amenities for urban residents. However, before the measure had much impact, the Second World War intervened, bringing devastation to the dockland areas of the East End in particular. From 7 September 1940, central London was bombed on fifty-seven consecutive nights, and over the eight-month period of the Blitz, from then until May 1941, more than 15,000 people were killed, an estimated 3.5 million homes destroyed or made uninhabitable, and many major public buildings (such as the Houses of Parliament) seriously damaged.

The end of hostilities in 1945 heralded a lengthy period of reconstruction accompanied by the gradual reorientation of the economy to peacetime conditions and a national austerity relieved only by the Festival of Britain, which was held in 1951 on the south bank of the River Thames and included construction of a major arts complex in an attempt to raise public spirits. In 1956, the Clean Air Act introduced smokeless zones to London and put an end to the 'pea-soup' fogs that had previously plagued the city, particularly during early winter. Then, in the 1960s, a new age of affluence, coupled with greater independence for young people, ushered in an era during which 'swinging London' was the pop capital of the world. Condemned by many residents as a time of permissiveness and decadence, it nevertheless promoted the establishment of countless small businesses as the clothes boutiques and cafés of Carnaby Street and King's Road attracted thousands of visitors.

Local government, too, changed to meet new post-war conditions. The London Government Act of 1963 swept the London County Council away and replaced it with a Greater London Council responsible for comprehensive planning over a much enlarged area. It was clear that large-scale measures were necessary to deal with the traffic congestion generated by increasing leisure and business travel within the city, the growing number of visitors arriving by air and the decaying docks. The last of these posed particularly intractable problems as, one after another, port facilities closed down from 1967, unable to contend with crowded sites and competition from more modern facilities on the European mainland and around the British coast.

Eventually, in 1981, the London Docklands Development Corporation was created to manage the world's largest urban regeneration scheme. The result was a major investment of public and private funds, which led to new housing and commercial development programmes, the creation of a marina at St Katharine's Dock (near the Tower of London), and the transfer of many city offices to new sites at Canary Wharf on the Isle of Dogs.

The Greater London Council also promoted the construction of new road arteries (designed, in part, to enhance access to the Docklands from the city centre) and the movement of inner-city residents to purpose-built new towns such as Crawley and Basildon, beyond the urban fringe. However, from 1979, it was more and more evident that the council, led by left-wing politicians, and Prime Minister Margaret Thatcher's Conservative government did not see eye to eye on economic and social reform. National policies, the council members claimed, inflicted unnecessary hardship on Londoners by creating unemployment and limiting the local authority's freedom to raise income through property taxes.

In many ways, the protests were justified. In the thirty years from 1945 to 1975, London's adult male unemployment rate had rarely exceeded 1 per cent. By 1984, after Mrs Thatcher's first five years in office, it had risen to over 10 per cent and the lack of jobs was felt most sorely by the immigrant communities, undoubtedly contributing to street violence experienced in Brixton and elsewhere. Mrs Thatcher, however, was unmoved. In 1986, exasperated by the failure of London's leaders to accept her view of the world, she abolished the council and created a complex of thirty-three independent local government units with identical statutory responsibilities. In a stroke, comprehensive planning had been eliminated and, for fourteen years, individual areas of the city went their own way.

The result was a boom in office building but a lack of investment in public infrastructure and social welfare, which led to maintenance problems on the London Underground, an increase in begging, and greatly reduced programmes of house building for the low paid. By the mid-1990s, it was evident to all political parties that continued absence of funding, combined with a lack of strategic planning, would lead to serious problems, which might discourage private investment in the city. In 1997, the newly elected Labour government announced plans for a London Assembly, headed by a mayor, to reintroduce citywide schemes for educational provision, transportation, sewage control and other services. The members were elected three years later, with Ken Livingstone (a socialist politician running as an independent candidate) winning the mayoral poll by a considerable majority over official representatives of the Conservative, Labour, and Liberal Democrat parties. For city residents, the new leadership brought hope that their voice would be heard in the corridors of power and that steps would be taken to ensure that London could continue to attract the economic and human capital necessary to retain its position as one of the world's pre-eminent financial, commercial and cultural capitals.

LONDON'S POPULATION GROWTH, 1801–2001

Year	London (millions)	Greater London (millions)
1801	0.959	1.096
1811	1.139	1.303
1821	1.379	1.573
1831	1.655	1.878
1841	1.949	2.207
1851	2.363	2.651
1861	2.808	3.188
1871	3.261	3.840
1881	3.830	4.713
1891	4.227	5.571
1901	4.536	6.506
1911	4.536	7.160
1921	4.484	7.386
1931	4.397	8.110
1951	3.347	8.193
1961	3.200	7.992
1971	3.031	7.452
1981	2.497	6.713
1991	2.627	6.890
2001	2.750	7.170

Notes: Data for 1801-1991 are taken from a table in Ben Weinreb and Christopher Hibbert's The London Encyclopaedia, *published by Macmillan in 1993. Data for 2001 are taken from official census returns. No census was held in 1941.*

A

ABBEY ROAD

Abbey Road, which runs north-west for just under a mile from ST JOHN'S WOOD towards KILBURN, was made famous in the 1960s by the Beatles, who named one of their albums after the street, where the EMI recording studios were located. In medieval times, it was a country lane leading to a convent but, during the nineteenth century, it was gradually built up as affluent Londoners constructed villa homes with large gardens. Most of these houses are now subdivided into flats or have been replaced by apartment blocks.

ABBEYS

See ABBEY WOOD; BARKING; COVENT GARDEN; DULWICH; EPPING FOREST; HYDE PARK; MONASTERIES; REGENT'S PARK; ST MARYLEBONE; STRATFORD; STREATHAM; WESTMINSTER; WESTMINSTER ABBEY; WOODFORD.

ABBEY WOOD

A working-class residential area consisting largely of former local authority HOUSING built during the 1950s, Abbey Wood lies in the LONDON BOROUGH OF GREENWICH on the south-eastern fringes of the city. Originally marshland, which was first reclaimed by the monks of Lesnes Abbey during the thirteenth century, it became a testing ground for armaments manufactured at nearby Woolwich Arsenal (see ROYAL ARSENAL) in the 1700s and 1800s. The railway arrived during the last years of the nineteenth century, and construction of homes began with the development of the Bostall Estate in the years prior to the outbreak of the First World War, but significant areas of recreational open space remain, notably at Bostall Woods and Lesnes Abbey PARK.

ABERCROMBIE PLAN (1943–1944)

In 1941 LONDON COUNTY COUNCIL (LCC), worried about the impact if proposals to limit the city's economic growth were implemented, invited Sir Patrick Abercrombie to co-operate with their architect, J.H. Forshaw, in the preparation of a plan for the redevelopment of the city. Abercrombie (a past president of the Town Planning Institute and a member of the BARLOW COMMISSION (1937–1939)) responded by producing two sets of proposals. In his County of London Plan (1943), he forcefully supported the ideals expounded by Barlow, arguing that some 600,000 people should be moved out of the city, most of them from such overcrowded, BLITZ-damaged areas as the EAST END. In addition, much of the industry located along the banks of the RIVER THAMES could be removed, especially if it made no use of the waterway. With the pressures on land alleviated, some parts of London could be zoned for housing, with densities carefully controlled, and space could be made available for PARKS. The SOUTH BANK could become a focus for cultural activities and a series of new ring roads would facilitate movement around the metropolitan area.

In a Greater London Plan (1944), Abercrombie identified four rings of population. The inner, densely populated, ring would lose residents. Beyond that, a suburban ring would remain relatively stable. Further out, in a GREEN BELT ring some 5 miles in breadth, urban expansion would be strictly controlled and countryside recreation would be promoted. Finally, in an outer country ring, the inner-city residents would be re-housed in existing settlements that could be 50 miles and more from London.

By these means, Abercrombie argued, community development could be promoted, housing standards could be improved, traffic congestion could be limited and open space could be provided. His views, along with those of the Barlow Commission, influenced the capital's planners for the next three decades. For example, when the LCC published its post-war Development Plan in 1951, the proposals were based securely on his foundations, designating nine Areas of Comprehensive Redevelopment, including the South Bank (where the focus was to be on cultural activities such as theatre and music), large parts of the East End (such as STEPNEY, which was badly damaged by German bombs during the BLITZ and where new housing was to be built at densities well below pre-Second World War levels), and ELEPHANT AND CASTLE (where offices and retail facilities would take precedence over other land uses). However, Abercrombie's scheme of ring roads was dropped because of the high construction costs, and provision of PARKland was less generous than he had advocated. (See also GREATER LONDON DEVELOPMENT PLAN (1969).)

ACTON

Formerly an agricultural settlement lying some 5 miles west of MARBLE ARCH, Acton became a suburb of London as the city expanded during the late nineteenth and early twentieth centuries. A centre of royalist support during the Civil War (1642–9), it developed a reputation as a spa during the Georgian period and, as a result, attracted affluent visitors seeking health and recreation. Many of these visitors built homes in the area, seduced by the rural environment and the proximity to the capital (the Rothschild family – one of the wealthiest in the country – bought the medieval mansion at GUNNERSBURY PARK in 1835, for example). However, the idyll was destroyed by industrialization during the reign of Queen Victoria as brick-making companies and engineering firms transformed both the economy and the landscape, aided by a developing TRANSPORT infrastructure, which included the PADDINGTON Canal (opened in 1801), the RAILWAYS (which arrived in 1839) and an increasingly dense network of roads. Rows of terraced housing were built to accommodate the influx of workers, even covering the golf course in 1920. Now forming the eastern fringe of the LONDON BOROUGH OF EALING, Acton is a predominantly working-class area, providing local employment in manufacturing and service companies and relatively cheap accommodation for inner-city workers. Its name is probably derived from the Old English *actun*, meaning 'the settlement among the oak trees'. (See also CHARING CROSS HOSPITAL; PICCADILLY LINE.)

ADAM, ROBERT (1728–1792)

Widely considered the leading neoclassical architect in Georgian Britain, Adam was responsible for the design (or redesign) of a large number of country mansions (notably KENWOOD HOUSE, OSTERLEY HOUSE and SYON HOUSE in London) but also for many smaller-scale works, such as the screen in front of THE ADMIRALTY building in WHITEHALL. Born in Kirkcaldy (Fife), Adam learned the basic elements of his trade from his father, William, who was Master Mason to the Ordnance in north Britain and designer of such important homes for Scottish gentry as Hopetoun House and House of Dun. He was educated at Edinburgh High School and Edinburgh University then, in 1754, went to Italy, where he studied classical ARCHITECTURE at Rome, Florence, Naples, Vicenza and Split, and cultivated the friendship of wealthy English travellers who, he felt, might provide him with commissions.

Soon after his return to Britain in 1758, Adam established a business in London, where the combination of an affable personality, contacts in aristocratic society and the successful publication of his book *The Ruins of the Palace of the Emperor Diocletian at Spalatro in Dalmatia* (1764) made him the most sought-after architect in the city. In 1761 (jointly with Sir WILLIAM CHAMBERS, a great rival), he was appointed architect to George III, but royal acceptance did not prevent him from undertaking visionary projects. In 1768, along with his brothers James and John (also architects) and William (a financier), he leased a slum property, south of the STRAND and north of the RIVER THAMES, from the Duke of St Albans and set about turning it into an area of fashionable residences. The development, known as ADELPHI (from the Greek *adelphoi*, meaning 'brothers'), consisted of a main terrace with two groups of eleven brick houses built back to back and a single house at each end. All were tall, thin structures typical of the period, but no expense was spared on the decoration. The steep slope to the river was counteracted by a series of arches, topped by streets. Unfortunately for the Adams, the government refused to hire the vaults as storage space for gunpowder because they flooded at high tide. Also, because of their remoteness from the fashionable WEST END, the finished houses were difficult to sell (though DAVID GARRICK took No. 5). The resultant financial problems threatened completion of the project but, in 1773, Parliament passed an act permitting the brothers to hold a lottery that offered the homes as prizes, and the work was finished soon afterwards. Most of Royal Terrace, the centrepiece, was demolished just before the outbreak of the Second World War, so few houses remain, but the concept was replicated by the more conservative chambers at nearby SOMERSET HOUSE, which was begun in 1776.

At the time of the Adelphi project, Adam was at the height of his powers. He went on to design many other London buildings, such as Apsley House (constructed between 1771 and 1778 and now known as the WELLINGTON MUSEUM) and the homes in PORTLAND PLACE (*c.* 1774–80) before his death on 3 March 1792. He was buried in WESTMINSTER ABBEY, close to several monuments constructed to his own drawings. (See also CHELSEA HOSPITAL; ST JAMES'S SQUARE; SIR JOHN SOANE'S MUSEUM.)

ADDINGTON PALACE

From 1808 until 1897, Addington Palace was the official residence of the Archbishop of Canterbury. Located at the eastern edge of the LONDON BOROUGH OF CROYDON, the three-storey building was built during the sixteenth century but redesigned and refurbished between 1773 and 1779 by Robert Mylne for Barlow Trecothick, LORD MAYOR of London. In 1807, the 3,500-acre estate was purchased by the Church of England and, through most of the nineteenth century, occupied by six successive primates. However, in 1897, Archbishop Frederick Temple decided that the cost of occupying the property was too great and opted to base himself in Canterbury. The building and grounds were bought by Frederick English, a South African millionaire who had made his fortune as a diamond merchant, and remodelled internally at the considerable cost of £70,000. During the First World War, the house was put to use as a HOSPITAL, then, when hostilities ended, was converted to a country club. In 1951 it was purchased by the local authority, which leased it to the Royal School of Church Music until 1996, when it was converted into a country club and conference centre. The gardens, laid out by Capability Brown, have been converted to golf courses.

ADELPHI

See ADAM, ROBERT.

ADMIRALTY, THE

The site of the Admiralty building at the north-west end of WHITEHALL, has been used for some 400 years as a base for conducting naval business. At the beginning of the seventeenth century, it was occupied by Wallingford House, home of George Villiers, first Duke of Buckingham and Lord High Admiral of England. In 1694, however, the structure was damaged in a fire and replaced by an edifice, designed by CHRISTOPHER WREN, which provided accommodation for the First Sea Lord (the head of the Royal Navy's administrative staff) and his principal officers, but had only a single meeting room and limited office space. Between 1722 and 1726, that was demolished and the present brick building, designed by Thomas Ripley, erected in its place. The screen, topped by seahorses, which hides it from the street, was designed by ROBERT ADAM and built in 1759–61. In 1786–8, Admiralty House, a new home for the First Lord of the Admiralty (a senior government post held by statesmen such as WINSTON CHURCHILL and Arthur Balfour) was added to the south, and in 1894–95 an extension (now known as the New Admiralty) was constructed to the rear during a period of extensive public works in the city. With the exception of the Adam screen, the buildings are considered architecturally undistinguished by most critics, but the fireplace in the Board Room is decorated with outstanding woodcarvings (possibly by GRINLING GIBBONS) that incorporate nautical instruments as well as flowers and fruits. Bomb damage to the property during the Second World War and a fire in 1955 necessitated much reconstruction, which was completed in 1958. In 1964, the Board of Admiralty, formerly responsible for the management of British naval affairs, was merged with the Air Ministry and the War Office to form the Ministry of Defence, which still uses offices in the building. (See also ADMIRALTY ARCH.)

ADMIRALTY ARCH

Admiralty Arch, built in 1906–11 as part of a national memorial to Queen Victoria, forms the eastern entrance to THE MALL, separating the relative quiet of ST JAMES'S PARK and the approach to BUCKINGHAM PALACE from the turmoil of TRAFALGAR SQUARE. Designed by Sir Aston Webb, it is a stolid structure of three deep arches that takes its name from THE ADMIRALTY building to the south. The arches are fitted with wrought iron gates, the central arch being opened only to allow ceremonial processions to pass through. Rooms within the structure were vacated by the Ministry of Defence in 1994, but two years later John Major vetoed a proposal by Michael Portillo to sell the arch to a private contractor who might develop its office potential.

AIR POLLUTION

Complaints about the quality of London's air have a long history, dating from as early as the thirteenth century, when the lime industry burned large quantities of coal during the production process. From the late 1700s, the city's physical expansion (due to the combined effects of the Industrial Revolution, the growth of overseas trade and the increasing number of administrative tasks carried out in the nation's capital) compounded the problems as more people and more firms consumed more fuel. Smog (combinations of smoke and fog) became increasingly common and, for many people, proved lethal; in December 1873, for instance, a week of breathing polluted air caused 700 more deaths than expected in London for the time of year, with the elderly and people suffering from respiratory diseases particularly affected. Several pressure groups formed (such as the Coal

Smoke Abatement Society in 1881) in an attempt to force companies to introduce smoke treatment policies, but successes were limited until after the Second World War.

The City of London (Various Powers) Act of 1946 allowed local authorities to create smokeless zones, which now cover about 90 per cent of the built-up area, but failed to prevent a four-day smog, from 5 to 9 December 1952, which resulted in 4,700 more deaths than anticipated for the period. That episode prompted further action and culminated in Parliament's approval of the 1956 Clean Air Act – legislation that introduced tighter controls on emissions and affected, in particular, domestic fires, producing an 80 per cent reduction in smoke levels by the late 1990s. Faced with the stringent laws, consumers switched increasingly from coal to ELECTRICITY, gas and oil, with the result that, during the second half of the century, transport superseded industry and private households as the major source of air pollution; vehicles with petroleum engines became the major cause of high carbon monoxide levels in the atmosphere, and planes landing at the city's five AIRPORTS added nitrogen compounds and hydrocarbons. Moreover, as smoke levels decreased, the amount of sunlight reaching London rose, increasing photo oxidation of pollutants (particularly the nitrogen gases) and causing photochemical smog. Most authorities now argue that further improvements in air quality will only be achieved through a combination of technical improvements (which would limit emissions from vehicles) and legislation that would encourage travellers to use public rather than private transport. (See also ALBERT MEMORIAL; BATTERSEA POWER STATION; EAST END; KENSINGTON PALACE; CUBITT, THOMAS (1788–1855); LONDON PLANE; REGENT'S PARK; WATER POLLUTION; WEST END; WHITEHALL PALACE.)

AIRPORTS

London is served by five major airports – Gatwick, Heathrow, London City, Luton and Stansted. The first civil aerodrome in the United Kingdom, designated in 1919, was located at the western edge of the city on HOUNSLOW Heath and provided a daily service to Paris. The following year, however, it was closed and facilities developed at CROYDON, which had been built in 1915 as a base for the aerial defence of southern England during the First World War. On 2 May 1928, Croydon was formally named London Airport, but the title passed to the twin runways at Heathrow on 31 May 1946, when the first direct scheduled passenger service left for the United States. Six years later, as air traffic increased, the Conservative government approved the development of Gatwick, on the farmlands of Sussex some 25 miles south of CHARING CROSS, and, on 9 June 1958, it was opened by the queen. Croydon, increasingly hemmed in by urban encroachment, was closed the following year and its flat land converted into a factory site.

In 1966, the British Airports Authority assumed responsibility for the administration of both Heathrow and Gatwick, initiating programmes of expansion and improvement. During the 1970s, the Gatwick runway was lengthened and a second terminal building constructed, increasing the airport area to nearly 1,900 acres. In 1977, the PICCADILLY LINE of the LONDON UNDERGROUND was extended to Heathrow, offering the prospect of speedy transport between the airport and the central city for the first time (during the first twenty-two years of its existence, passengers had to make the 15-mile journey in buses or cars on roads clogged by other traffic). Then, in 1986, a fourth terminal was added to the three that had served Heathrow for nearly forty years.

Despite these improvements, the increasing demand for air travel in south-east England encouraged the government to seek a site for a third London airport. In 1985, after considerable heart-searching, it designated Stansted, about 30 miles north-east of the city centre.

Two terminals were opened and, by 1998, it had become Britain's fourth largest airport with 6.8 million passengers and twenty-four airlines serving sixty-five scheduled destinations. In the expectation of continued expansion in passenger numbers, a programme of improvements involving extensions to the terminal buildings and the construction of additional departure gates was begun in 1999.

Luton's airport, 32 miles north of central London, opened in 1938, two years after aircraft production began in the area, but has developed largely since the 1980s. It is a private concern, owned by Luton Borough Council, and has proved popular with tour companies using charter flights (Britannia, the world's largest charter airline, is based there). In 1997, it announced a ten-year expansion programme, at an estimated cost of £170 million, which would involve new administrative arrangements, a new terminal and a new RAILWAY station, allowing it to handle up to 8.5 million passengers a year.

London City Airport, the youngest and smallest of the city's air foci, was built by the John Mowlem construction company as part of the development of DOCKLANDS, opening in 1987. Although only 6 miles east of the CITY OF LONDON and the heart of Britain's business community, it suffered from poor accessibility until a road link was opened in 1993. In addition, the cramped urban site limits the size of the aircraft that can use the single runway. In 1995, Mowlem sold the airport to Dermot Desmond, a flamboyant Irish businessman, for £14.5 million, less than a third of the £50 million it is estimated to have spent on the project. That combination of new management and better access appeared to improve fortunes because, by 2000, ten airlines were operating scheduled services to twenty-six destinations in the United Kingdom and Europe.

In 1999–2000, Heathrow was the busiest of the five centres, with 63.6 million passengers. Gatwick had 31.3 million, Stansted 11.2 million, Luton 5.5 million and London City 1.5 million. In 1999, the British Airports Authority, which wants to build a fifth terminal at Heathrow, forecast that combined annual demand at London's airports would rise to 138 million passengers within a decade, far outstripping the capacity of existing facilities. Four years later, a government consultation paper argued that the best way to solve the problem would be to build two new runways at Gatwick and one at Heathrow, projects which would cost £7 billion but generate economic benefits worth £25 billion. In addition, up to three new runways could be constructed at Stansted. Environmental groups, however, fiercely oppose any expansion. (See also AIR POLLUTION; BIGGIN HILL; HENDON; JUBILEE LINE.)

AIR RAIDS

During the First and Second World Wars, London suffered greatly as a result of air raids, which caused much loss of life and damage to property. The first attack was made by a Zeppelin airship, which flew over the EAST END on 31 May 1915, in full moonlight, and dropped 120 high-explosive bombs, killing seven people. A further eleven Zeppelin incursions over the next twenty-nine months, all at night, were supported by daytime bombing raids, which began on 6 May 1916 and continued until 19 May 1918. Some Londoners sought refuge in the stations and tunnels of the TUBE system, others left the city altogether, but even so, the German bombardment killed 670 people, injured 1,960 and caused damage estimated at £2 million. The most lethal raid was on 13 June 1917, when bombs dropped by fourteen Gotha biplanes caused the deaths of 160 East Enders, including seventeen children who were sheltering in the basement of a POPLAR school.

The first aerial assault on London during the Second World War occurred on 24 August 1940, when German pilots lost their bearings and dumped explosives on the inner city. The

Royal Air Force retaliated by bombing Berlin, and the German leader Adolf Hitler, who claimed that such attacks on his capital city could never happen, responded by ordering reprisals. The period from 7 September 1940 until 11 May 1941 (when 320 bombers attacked the city, supported by over 600 fighter aircraft) became known as the BLITZ. Within five months, over 250,000 people were homeless, and by the end of the barrage over 15,000 Londoners were dead (some scholars suggest that the true figure was closer to 30,000). On the very last raid (during the night of 10–11 May 1941), the chamber of the HOUSE OF COMMONS (see PALACE OF WESTMINSTER) was destroyed, along with ST CLEMENT DANES CHURCH on the STRAND, the medieval TEMPLE CHURCH and Queen's Hall (home of the Henry Wood Promenade Concerts (see PROMS, THE)). The BRITISH MUSEUM, LAMBETH PALACE, MANSION HOUSE, the CENTRAL CRIMINAL COURT, ST JAMES'S PALACE and WESTMINSTER ABBEY were all badly damaged.

Sporadic attacks occurred over the following months, but the city was spared further serious raids until 12 June 1944, when a V1 flying bomb killed six people at BETHNAL GREEN. The V1s (the V stood for *Vergeltung*, German for 'vengeance') caused considerable fear because they were pilotless, flew at 470 miles an hour and carried a one-ton warhead. Known as buzz bombs and doodlebugs because of their noise ('doodlebug' was first used as a term for a cheap, noisy automobile), they were arriving at the rate of about sixty a day in mid-June, killing some 1,600 people and causing significant damage in suburbs south of the River Thames, such as GREENWICH and LAMBETH. After the Allied troops invaded the European mainland, the V1 launch sites were destroyed and, from the middle of August, the raids declined in number and destructiveness, but they were replaced by the threat of V2 rockets, which first reached CHISWICK and Epping on 7 September 1944. These new missiles carried explosives no greater than the V1, and their capacity to inflict damage was limited because they hit the ground with great speed, forming large craters rather than causing widespread destruction. Nevertheless, they were dreaded because they were launched from mobile pads, could not be tracked by radar and were difficult to stop in the air. A total of 518 hit London between September 1944 and March 1945, most crashing down on the East End, which had suffered so much in earlier bombardments. An estimated 2,511 people died. (See also AVERY HILL; BIG BEN; CABINET WAR ROOMS; CENTRAL LINE; CHURCHILL, WINSTON SPENCER; CLEOPATRA'S NEEDLE; CRAYFORD; GUILDHALL; IMPERIAL WAR MUSEUM; LONDON LIBRARY; ROYAL LONDON HOSPITAL; ST JAMES'S CHURCH, PICCADILLY.)

ALBERT, PRINCE (1819–1861)

Prince Albert, husband to Queen Victoria for twenty-one years, was never widely popular with Londoners, who distrusted his Germanic background and intellectual interests, but he used his influence to contribute enormously to the city's development. The second son of Ernest, Duke of Saxe-Coburg-Gotha, and Princess Louise of Saxe-Gotha-Altenburg, he was born in Rosenau on 26 August 1819 and christened Franz Albrecht August Karl Emmanuel. He first met Victoria when he was visiting Great Britain in 1836 and wrote to her regularly thereafter. In October 1839, during a second visit, Victoria proposed marriage, he accepted and the wedding was held on 10 February the following year.

A hard-working consort, Albert invested considerable effort in finding out about his adopted country and had a growing influence on the queen, as she learned to depend on his diplomatic skills and organizational abilities. He also took great interest in the arts, encouraging CHARLES BARRY and AUGUSTUS WELBY NORTHMORE PUGIN to decorate the walls of the rebuilt PALACE OF WESTMINSTER with frescoes depicting great scenes from British history and literature. He also lent his patronage to sculptor Thomas Thorneycroft, who worked for fifteen years on the statue of BOADICEA and her daughters, which stands at the north end of WESTMINSTER BRIDGE, and served as President of the Society for the Encouragement of Arts, Manufactures and Commerce (see ROYAL SOCIETY OF ARTS) for eighteen years from 1843.

His major impact on London stemmed from his enthusiastic support for the GREAT EXHIBITION of 1851. The idea of an event celebrating Britain's position as the greatest industrial power the world had ever seen was the brainchild of civil servant Henry Cole, an assistant keeper at the PUBLIC RECORD OFFICE, but it would never have happened without Albert's belief that it was the country's mission, duty and interest 'to put herself at the head of the diffusion of civilization and the attainment of liberty'. Overcoming the objections of critics, who believed that such an exhibition would merely stimulate competition from other nations, he persuaded Prime Minister Lord John Russell to appoint a Royal Commission that he would preside over and that would raise money for the project. A CRYSTAL PALACE was built for the exhibits in HYDE PARK, attracting over 6 million visitors, many of whom also patronized the stores in KNIGHTSBRIDGE and OXFORD STREET, thereby helping to establish the WEST END as a fashionable shopping area. The popular appeal of the venture generated a profit of £186,000, which the prince and his committee used to purchase 87 acres of land in south KENSINGTON as a location for a complex of institutions that would extend 'the influence of Science and Art upon productive industry'. The result was the construction of buildings for some of the nation's principal museums, educational institutions and learned societies, including the NATURAL HISTORY MUSEUM, the ROYAL COLLEGE OF MUSIC and Imperial College (now part of the University of London).

Albert, however, did not live to see the site fully developed. In 1861 he contracted typhoid during a visit to Cambridge and died on 14 December. His monuments in London include the Albert Embankment (see BAZALGETTE, JOSEPH WILLIAM), the ALBERT BRIDGE, the ALBERT HALL, the ALBERT MEMORIAL, the VICTORIA AND ALBERT MUSEUM and some fifty Albert Roads, Mews, Terraces and Closes. (See also LANCASTER HOUSE; NATIONAL PORTRAIT GALLERY; PADDINGTON STATION; RAILWAYS; ROYAL HORTICULTURAL SOCIETY.)

ALBERT BRIDGE

One of several London landmarks named in honour of PRINCE ALBERT (1819–61), husband of Queen Victoria (see, for example, ALBERT HALL and ALBERT MEMORIAL), the bridge links CHELSEA (on the north bank of the RIVER THAMES) with BATTERSEA (on the south). An ornamented mixture of cantilever and suspension designs, with three spans, it was designed by R.M Ordish, opened in 1873 and strengthened in 1973 so that it could cope with the increasing volume and weight of traffic. (See also BRIDGES; TRANSPORT.)

ALBERT HALL

In 1852, at the suggestion of PRINCE ALBERT (1819–61), Queen Victoria's consort, profits from the GREAT EXHIBITION were used to purchase a site in south KENSINGTON that could be developed as a focus of MUSEUMS and educational institutions. The prince proposed a hall with LIBRARIES, exhibition rooms and lecture facilities as a centrepiece of the complex, but nothing was achieved until, in 1863, Henry Cole (chairman of the Society of Arts) suggested that money for a building could be raised by selling 999-year leaseholds of seats. The scheme proved attractive (over 1,300 were purchased at £100 each). Queen Victoria laid the foundation stone on 20 May 1867 and formally opened the building, which had been designed by Captain Francis Fowke and Lieutenant-Colonel Henry Darracott Scott, on 29 March 1871 (in the process, she surprised her audience by adding Royal Albert to the proposed name of Hall of Arts and

Sciences). An oval structure, it is 272 feet long, 238 feet wide and more than 150 feet high, with a roof of glass and iron. On the exterior, a frieze by students of the South Kensington School of Art illustrates 'The Triumph of Arts and Sciences'.

The auditorium, which can house audiences of 8,000 people, produced an echo, which made listening to music a form of purgatory (for many years, it was said that the Albert Hall was the only place where a British composer could be sure of hearing his work twice), but despite that, it became one of London's major concert venues. Organist and composer Anton Bruckner (1824–96) played at the opening event, Richard Wagner (1813–83) conducted orchestras playing his own operatic works in 1877, and in 1886 a dance floor was laid. Since 1941, the Sir Henry Wood Promenade Concerts (see PROMS, THE) have been held there every summer (with the audience's enjoyment much enhanced by saucer-shaped objects hung from the ceiling in 1968 to improve the acoustics). The facilities are also much used for other activities (boxing matches began in 1919, for example).

In 2000 the Hall management began a £66 million refurbishment programme that included new foyers, a restaurant, improved seating and an air conditioning system.

ALBERT MEMORIAL

A 175-foot-high structure located at the southern edge of KENSINGTON GARDENS, opposite the ALBERT HALL, the memorial commemorates PRINCE ALBERT (1819–61), the husband of Queen Victoria. A public appeal (which attracted less than the trustees had anticipated) raised funds for the edifice, which was designed by George Gilbert Scott, erected between 1863 and 1876, and decorated in multicoloured stonework, gilding, mosaics and statuary with typical Victorian exuberance. The corners are adorned with large marble representations of Europe, Asia, Africa and America. Agriculture, manufactures, commerce and engineering – the foundations of Britain's nineteenth-century industrial might – decorate the podium, and 169 life-sized figures of prominent scientists and artists form a frieze around the pedestal. A statue of Albert himself sits under a canopy, holding a copy of the catalogue of the GREAT EXHIBITION (which he supported with much enthusiasm) and surrounded by statues of the sciences (such as Chemistry and Astronomy), the arts (such as Poetry and Sculpture) and the personal qualities expected of Victorian Britons (such as Fortitude and Temperance). A flight of steps, 121 feet wide, leads from street level to the base. During the early 1990s, there was much debate about the future of the memorial, which had been seriously affected by the weather and AIR POLLUTION. Some critics recommended demolition because of the cost involved in making repairs to the stonework, but the conservationist argument prevailed and an £11.2 million refurbishment programme was completed in 1998.

ALDERMAN

Aldermen are elected by the people of the CITY OF LONDON to carry out duties related to the keeping of law and order (presiding over certain courts, for example), the administration of the LIVERY COMPANIES and certain ceremonial responsibilities (such as signing the documents that proclaim a new monarch). References to Aldermen (or elder men) date from Saxon times. In 1200, during the reign of King John, a Court of Aldermen was formed in THE CITY; for the next 500 years, it acted as the centre of local government, but gradually that role has been taken over by the COURT OF COMMON COUNCIL. Now, each WARD elects one Alderman, who can remain in office until the age of seventy (from 1377 until 1975, they held office for life). Candidates must have previously received the FREEDOM OF THE CITY and be approved by the Aldermanic Court. Aldermen act as Justices of the Peace (that is, as lay judges presiding over the lower courts),

A late seventeenth-century engraving of the Lord Mayor and the Court of Aldermen.

serve on CORPORATION OF LONDON committees, act as school governors, carry out duties as trustees of HOSPITALs and perform other civic services in addition to their ceremonial commitments. On official occasions, they wear either a scarlet gown trimmed with sable or an indigo gown trimmed with bear fur. (See also LORD MAYOR; RECORDER OF LONDON.)

ALDERSGATE

Although it was the site of one of the northern entrances to the Roman city (see LONDON WALL), *Aldersgate* is a corruption of the Saxon *Ealdred's Gate.* In 1603, James I entered London by this route as he arrived from Scotland to claim the English throne, and SAMUEL PEPYS records that he saw the legs of traitors hung on the walls in 1660. It was damaged in the GREAT FIRE of 1666, repaired four years later but demolished in 1761. Aldersgate Street, which ran past the entry, survives (the gate stood opposite No. 62).

ALDGATE

Situated at the eastern edge of the CITY OF LONDON, Aldgate was the point at which the road from the Roman port of Camulodunum (now Colchester) entered the capital, and gets its name from the Saxon *Ealdgate,* meaning 'old gate'. It was rebuilt during the first half of the twelfth century and, from 1374 until 1385, a room in the walls above it was occupied by Geoffrey Chaucer while he earned a living as a customs officer. Reconstruction work was carried out in 1606–9, but it was eventually demolished in 1761. During the 1980s and 1990s, the neighbourhood experienced much office development as financial institutions built new premises close to London's traditional business area. (See also CIRCLE LINE; EAST LONDON LINE; LONDON WALL; METROPOLITAN LINE.)

ALDWYCH

Alfred the Great granted the Aldwych area, now located at the eastern edge of the CITY OF WESTMINSTER, to the Vikings as an area for settlement during the late ninth century (ST CLEMENT DANES CHURCH, which stands nearby, may have been founded at the same period). By the late nineteenth century it was a complex of narrow alleys, but one of the last of the Victorian urban renewal schemes cleared the 28 acres of slum housing to make way for a new crescent that would improve access between the STRAND and Kingsway. At the recommendation of George Gomme, the LONDON COUNTY COUNCIL's historian, the street was called Aldwych so that the traditional name would be retained. The Aldwych THEATRE, designed by W.G.R. Sprague, opened in 1905 and became well known between 1925 and 1933 for its run of Aldwych Farces. Most of them written by Ben Travers, the plays included *A Cuckoo in the Nest*, *Rookery Nook* and *Thark* and starred the same cast – Mary Brough, Robertson Hare, Ralph Lynn, Winifred Shotter and Tom Walls. From 1960–82 the theatre was the London base of the Royal Shakespeare Company. The Strand Theatre, also designed by Sprague and built as a twin of the Aldwych, was previously known as the Waldorf (1905–8), the Strand (1909–10) and the Witney (1911–2). During the BLITZ, despite bomb damage to the dressing rooms, it presented lunchtime productions of Shakespeare's plays and, after the Second World War, it offered a series of popular dramas, including *Arsenic and Old Lace, A Funny Thing Happened on the Way to the Forum* and *No Sex Please, We're British*. The nearby Waldorf HOTEL, designed by A.G.R. Mackenzie and opened in 1908, has 292 rooms, recently refurbished in Edwardian style. It is now part of Le Méridien group. The name, Aldwych, is probably derived from the Old English *ald* (meaning old) and *wic* (a town) but possibly also from the Norse *vic* (meaning inlet). (See also BRITISH BROADCASTING CORPORATION (BBC); DRURY LANE; PICCADILLY LINE.)

ALEXANDRA PALACE

Standing on MUSWELL HILL, overlooking an extensive PARK some 6 miles north of central London, Ally Pally (as it is known to local people) was built in 1873, named after the Princess of Wales and intended to rival the CRYSTAL PALACE as an exhibition centre. Sixteen days after it was opened, it was burned to the ground when some coal fell out of a workman's brazier, but it was immediately rebuilt to a design by architects Meeson and Johnson, with an auditorium, concert room, theatre, reading rooms and office space. Commercially it was not a success, even though it provided a focus for a variety of events, including musical performances, dog shows, horticultural competitions and various sports. During the First World War, the 7-acre complex was converted into a camp for refugees from Belgium, then for German prisoners of war (who were put to work landscaping the 480-acre PARK). In 1936, a section of the building was acquired by the BRITISH BROADCASTING CORPORATION, which built the world's first television transmitter on the site; the first programme (*Here's Looking at You*, a variety show) was broadcast on 26 August 1936 and regular transmissions began on 2 November. Most of the studios were moved to SHEPHERD'S BUSH in 1956 and much of the structure was unused before being destroyed by another fire in July 1980. Following restoration it reopened eight years later and now functions as a sports, exhibition and leisure centre administered by the LONDON BOROUGH OF HARINGEY. It is also the best natural viewpoint in London. (See also FINSBURY PARK.)

ANCHOR INN

Located in BANKSIDE, south of the RIVER THAMES close to LONDON BRIDGE, the Anchor is one of the most popular of London's older PUBLIC HOUSES. Built in the late eighteenth century on a site overlooking the water, where there had been an inn for at least 300 years, it still has a minstrels' gallery and nooks where runaways from the CLINK PRISON could hide. An exhibition of artefacts dating from the reign of Elizabeth I, which were found during renovations, is on display, as is a model of the original GLOBE THEATRE, which stood nearby. A raised terrace outside provides views across London to ST PAUL'S CATHEDRAL and is the ideal place to drink a pint of English beer on a warm July evening.

ANGEL, THE

Located at the junction of Goswell Road and St John Street, ISLINGTON, where travellers from the north diverged as they headed either for the finance houses of the CITY OF LONDON or the butchers' businesses at SMITHFIELD MEAT

MARKET, The Angel flourished as a coaching inn from the early seventeenth century. It was rebuilt in 1819 and again in 1899, when it was converted to Lyons' Corner House, but closed in 1960 and was unoccupied until it was refurbished as a bank in 1981–2. The area is still a focus of routeways into London (five major thoroughfares meet at the site, a major traffic bottleneck despite repeated attempts by planners to improve the flow) and has experienced much rebuilding in recent years.

ARCHITECTURE

Although most of London's urban fabric dates from no earlier than the eighteenth century, parts of the Roman wall (completed by the second century of occupation) can still be seen and all periods from the time of the Norman invasion in 1066 are represented. The Normans brought the Romanesque to Britain, employing it in St John's Chapel in the TOWER OF LONDON. By the late twelfth century, however, Gothic architecture was becoming more fashionable, with vaults, flying buttresses and increasingly elaborate floor plans. In its initial form (known as Early English), it was characterized by a lack of decoration (the Lady Chapel at SOUTHWARK CATHEDRAL is a much-quoted example), but, as builders experimented and became more confident, the plainness was superseded by intricate tracery work, such as that of the west window at ST ETHELDREDA'S CHURCH in HOLBORN. Then, from about 1350, new designs led to more robust structures (a phase known as the Perpendicular); ST OLAVE'S CHURCH in Hart Street was typical of the period and Henry VII's Chapel in WESTMINSTER ABBEY is one of its finest legacies.

During the sixteenth century, Renaissance (also known as Classical and Palladian) influences from Italy began to shape building styles, but they had a major impact on the urban skyline only after INIGO JONES completed the QUEEN'S HOUSE at GREENWICH in 1635. The success of that commission led to further patronage by courtiers and, in particular, to the planning of the Earl of Bedford's estate at COVENT GARDEN. However, much of the CITY OF LONDON's domestic architecture and most of its Gothic parish churches were destroyed in the GREAT FIRE of 1666, leaving the residents with a major rebuilding project. New regulations, intended to prevent a repeat of the tragedy, required replacement houses to be erected in brick and stone (rather than wood) and to have tiled (rather than thatched) roofs. CHRISTOPHER WREN was given the task of redesigning ST PAUL'S CATHEDRAL and planning some fifty other churches, using a rich imagination to make the most of awkward and confined sites. Forty years later, NICHOLAS HAWKSMOOR (Wren's assistant) left his own, baroque, mark with six individualistic designs for places of worship, notably CHRIST CHURCH, SPITALFIELDS, but, by then, fashions were changing again and Palladianism reappeared, initially in CHISWICK HOUSE then in the work of ROBERT ADAM. At the same time, there was a growing vogue for medieval styles, a trend that was later to be known as the Gothic Revival (or neo-Gothic). Although difficult to date, it is normally considered to have begun with writer Horace Walpole's conversion of STRAWBERRY HILL and include, as one of its finest examples, the rebuilding of the PALACE OF WESTMINSTER by CHARLES BARRY and AUGUSTUS WELBY NORTHMORE PUGIN.

The late eighteenth century brought a period of planned expansion that allowed squares and crescents to be designed as units (see, for example, BEDFORD ESTATES). Essentially, these were constructed on the conveyor-belt principle, with standard railings, window sashes and other fittings for the houses. That principle was extended following the Industrial Revolution by builders such as THOMAS CUBITT, who erected suburban terraces for the middle class, and then by a legion of entrepreneurs who covered the countryside with concrete as the RAILWAYS expanded, allowing a burgeoning workforce to live at the urban fringe and commute to clerical jobs in the city centre. One of the consequences was the growth, around the inner city and in the EAST END, of a large slum population living in conditions that were only alleviated following the introduction of welfare state policies in the 1940s and 1950s; local authorities undertook comprehensive redevelopment programmes, housing many of the least affluent Londoners in skyscraper blocks on cleared land and moving others to estates on the fringe of the built-up area. However, attempts to keep expenditure down, perhaps inevitable at a time of post-war economic reconstruction, resulted in poor-quality buildings and poor-quality design, which successor authorities had to correct at a much greater cost. More recently, although some plans have aroused controversy and others have been criticized as unimaginative (see, for example, BARBICAN), greater freedom from planning restrictions has encouraged architects to return to the earlier practice of designing buildings as individuals. As a result, the modernist jostles with the traditional, as at the DOCKLANDS, where new buildings (such as the CANARY WHARF tower) mix with converted nineteenth-century warehouses. (See also BANQUETING HOUSE; BRIDGES; BURLINGTON ARCADE; BURLINGTON HOUSE; CHAMBERS, WILLIAM; CHELSEA; GIBBS, JAMES; DANCE, GEORGE (1700–1768); DANCE, GEORGE (1741–1825); KENWOOD HOUSE; LANCASTER HOUSE; MANSION HOUSE; MARBLE ARCH; MARBLE HILL HOUSE; NASH, JOHN; OSTERLEY HOUSE; PUTNEY; RENNIE, JOHN (1761-1821); ROYAL EXCHANGE; ST DUNSTAN-IN-THE-WEST CHURCH, FLEET STREET; ST MARTIN-IN-THE-FIELDS CHURCH, TRAFALGAR SQUARE; ST STEPHEN WALBROOK CHURCH; SCOTT, GILES GILBERT; SELFRIDGE'S; SURBITON; SYON HOUSE.)

ARCHWAY

The viaduct by which Hornsey Lane (running from east to west) crosses Archway Road (running from south to north) solved a serious transport problem. The main road from the CITY OF LONDON to the towns of northern Britain had a steep inclination in order to pass Highgate Hill, straining horses that dragged wagons and coaches. In 1809, Parliament approved the construction of a 750-foot-long tunnel that would allow traffic to avoid the gradient, but, on 13 April 1812, it collapsed after only about 130 feet had been built. A cut was suggested as an alternative but necessitated construction of a bridge that would carry Hornsey Lane across the gap. JOHN NASH prepared plans for the structure, whose four arches resembled those of a Roman aqueduct. Archway Road opened in 1813 but the scheme was not completed until 1829, after Scottish engineer Thomas Telford had prepared a satisfactory drainage system. Storyteller Hans Christian Andersen, on a visit to CHARLES DICKENS, saw 'the great world metropolis mapped out in fire' when he looked from Nash's viaduct, which was replaced in 1897 by a cast-iron arch designed by Sir Alexander Binnie.

ARSENAL FOOTBALL CLUB

In 1886, a group of employees at the ROYAL ARSENAL ordnance factory in WOOLWICH formed a football club, naming it Dial Square FC after one of their workshops. The enthusiasm generated by a 6-0 victory in their first game, against Euston Wanderers, led to a second meeting in the Royal Oak PUBLIC HOUSE on Christmas Day, when the club's title was changed to Royal Arsenal (the regal prefix was dropped in 1914). Fred Beardsley, a leading member of the group, had played in goal for Nottingham Forest and used his northern contacts to secure the donation of a set of red jerseys: Arsenal has played in red ever since (the white sleeves were added in the 1920s).

Arsenal joined the Second Division of the Football League in 1893 but, by 1910, after a series of poor performances, was almost bankrupt. It was then taken over by Henry Norris (who was later to become a Conservative MP and receive a knighthood). Norris proposed a merger with FULHAM FOOTBALL CLUB, which he also owned, but the plan was turned down so, in 1913, he moved the club north of the RIVER THAMES to HIGHBURY in search of greater attendances. In 1919, when the League was reorganized at the end of the First World War, Arsenal was given a place in the First Division at the expense of local rivals TOTTENHAM HOTSPUR and it has remained there ever since. Under Herbert Chapman, who was appointed manager in 1925, it dominated English football in the inter-war years, winning the FA Cup twice and taking the League Championship on five occasions. Chapman's entrepreneurial mind also persuaded the transport authorities to rename the local LONDON UNDERGROUND station after the club.

The 1950s and 1960s were a barren period and despite a short-lived renaissance from 1968 until 1971 – when the club won the FA Cup (1968), the European Fairs Cup (1970), and the League and Cup double (1971) – it was not until George Graham became manager in 1986 that there was a further lengthy period of success. Although Graham was sacked for financial misconduct in 1994, he sowed seeds that led to major achievements in the last years of the twentieth century and the early years of the twenty-first. By 2002, Arsenal had won the European Cup Winners' Cup (1994) and achieved a further two League and Cup doubles (1998 and 2002). In the 2001/02 season, under manager Arsène Wenger, it scored in every league match and was undefeated away from home (the only other team to complete its away fixtures undefeated was Preston North End in 1888/89, when they played only eleven games). The club has won the League Championship on twelve occasions, the FA Cup on eight and the League Cup on two. It is planning to build a new stadium at Ashburton Grove, just east of its present Highbury base, at a cost of £400 million. (See also WEST HAM UNITED FOOTBALL CLUB.)

ASSOCIATION OF LONDON AUTHORITIES (ALA)

The ALA was founded in 1983, when thirteen Labour-dominated authorities withdrew from the LONDON BOROUGHS ASSOCIATION (LBA) following that body's recommendation to the national government that the left-wing GREATER LONDON COUNCIL (GLC) should be abolished. The disagreement was particularly bitter because, until the rift, the LBA had functioned as a politically non-partisan organization representing the LONDON BOROUGHS in negotiations with the government and other parties. As a result, mutual antipathy initially inhibited co-operation between the two bodies, although their interests were similar (both declared that their objectives were to protect and promote the interests of the boroughs). Also, there was an added undercurrent of animosity because the ALA acted as an avowedly Labour grouping whereas the LBA claimed that, because its membership was open to all boroughs, whatever their political leanings, it was more truly representative of the whole city. Initially, the ALA proved to be more radical than its parent, campaigning on social issues such as domestic violence, but, during the second half of the 1980s and the early 1990s, as Conservative Party supporters became increasingly disenchanted with the administrations led by Margaret Thatcher (1979–90) and John Major (1990–97), common concerns led to more numerous contacts between the organizations' officials and ultimately to joint activity on a range of issues. As the antagonism decreased, the case for re-merger strengthened, and in 1995 the ALA and the LBA reunited as the ASSOCIATION OF LONDON GOVERNMENT. (See also LONDON HEALTH EMERGENCY (LHE); LONDON PRIDE PARTNERSHIP.)

ASSOCIATION OF LONDON GOVERNMENT (ALG)

The ALG was formed in 1995 through the merger of the ASSOCIATION OF LONDON AUTHORITIES and the LONDON BOROUGHS ASSO-

CIATION, providing a forum in which representatives of the thirty-two LONDON BOROUGHS and the CORPORATION OF LONDON (the local authority for the CITY OF LONDON) could discuss matters of common interest. Also, it acts as a pressure group, attempting to win funds and policy concessions from bodies such as the national government and the European Union. Following the election of the GREATER LONDON ASSEMBLY in 2000, the organization was restructured to include (in addition to the local government representatives) members of the Greater London Employers' Association (which advises boroughs on policies relating to training and job creation), the London Boroughs Grants Committee (which contributes some £28 million a year to the funds of voluntary bodies in an attempt to reduce poverty), the London Housing Unit (a pressure group advocating improved housing conditions), and the Transport Committee for London (which facilitates the use of public transport by the elderly and disabled). It has a staff of about 150 people.

ATHENAEUM, THE

Among London's GENTLEMEN'S CLUBS, The Athenaeum has a reputation as a meeting place for the city's intellectuals. It was founded in 1824 at SOMERSET HOUSE by John Wilson Croker, who called it The Society and encouraged scientists, artists and writers to join. Six years later, it moved to the premises that it still occupies at 107 PALL MALL and renamed itself after the centre for the study of literature and science which Hadrian, Emperor of Rome, established *c.* AD 135. The rooms, designed by Decimus Burton and built of Bath stone, incorporate a frieze based on decoration of the Parthenon in Athens and (above the Doric entrance porch) a gilt statue of Pallas Athena, goddess of wisdom. An attic was added in 1899. Members in the twentieth century have included prime ministers and other politicians as well as senior figures from London's literary establishment. In 2001 the club voted to admit women to membership.

AVERY HILL

In 1902, the LONDON COUNTY COUNCIL (LCC) purchased a private estate in the south-eastern section of the city, some 9 miles from CHARING CROSS. The 86 acres of open space were turned into a public recreation area, known as Avery Hill PARK, and the mansion house, built in 1889, which became a teacher training college, is now used by the University of Greenwich. A conservatory, damaged by a flying bomb during the Second World War, was restored in 1962 and houses an outstanding collection of plants, complementing exotic tree species that adorn the rest of the site.

B

BAGNIGGE WELLS

During the Georgian period it was fashionable to visit spas, either to bathe or to drink waters believed to have therapeutic properties. In London, Bagnigge Wells, in King's Cross Road, was one of the most popular because of its accessibility and facilities. It developed during the late 1750s after Thomas Hughes, a local tobacconist, discovered that his best efforts to grow garden flowers were being undermined by the iron content of the ground water. That water proved to be an efficient purgative, and Hughes, cashing in on the leisure activities of the age, opened his property to the public, charging three pence for entry. The morning was devoted to those wanting to taste the water alone, the afternoon to those preferring tea. Games such as skittles and bowls were made available and concerts provided regular entertainment. In *Bon Ton* (1775), DAVID GARRICK suggests that the well-to-do enjoyed 'Drinking tea on summer afternoons, at Bagnigge Wells with china and gilt spoons,' but, increasingly, the lower classes infiltrated the gardens and, by the early nineteenth century, the affluent had deserted them. The venture went bankrupt in 1813; attempts to resurrect it were only partially successful, so it closed its doors for the last time in 1841. The site was quickly developed for other, more urban, purposes, but a plaque at 61–63 King's Cross Road marks the location of Bagnigge House.

BAKERLOO LINE

The Bakerloo Line was the first UNDERGROUND RAILWAY to cross London from south to north. Part of CHARLES TYSON YERKES' empire, it opened in 1906, providing services from BAKER STREET to ELEPHANT AND CASTLE via the main line stations at CHARING CROSS and WATERLOO (the name Bakerloo, a corruption of Baker Street and Waterloo, was considered by some critics to be a brash Americanism). The following year, the northern end of the route was extended to Edgware Road and, by 1917, it had reached Watford. The Stanmore branch of the METROPOLITAN LINE was added to the Bakerloo network in 1939 but transferred to the JUBILEE LINE in 1979. Services between Stonebridge Park and Watford were withdrawn in 1982 but reinstated as far as HARROW and Wealdstone two years later. Most of the rolling stock dates from 1972 and is serviced in depots at Stonebridge Park and London Road. In 2003, maintenance of the line's infrastructure was franchised to Metronet, a consortium of private businesses, but LONDON UNDERGROUND remained responsible for providing the services. (See also TUBE.)

BAKER STREET

Famed largely because of its associations with SHERLOCK HOLMES, Baker Street runs northwest for about ⅔ mile from OXFORD STREET (in the heart of the city's retail area) to REGENT'S PARK. Its housing was originally developed by builder William Baker on land leased from the Portman Estate in 1755. Holmes, the fictional detective created by Sir Arthur Conan Doyle, lived at No. 221B, a site now occupied by the Abbey National Bank, which employs a full-time member of staff to reply to letters addressed to its illustrious predecessor and erected a statue in Holmes's honour outside Baker Street's LONDON UNDERGROUND station during 1999. Nearby, at 239 Baker Street, there is a Sherlock Holmes Museum (which calls itself 221B Baker Street). During the nineteenth century, the road was a fashionable part of the city (Prime Minister William Pitt the Younger lived at No. 120 in 1802–6 and actress Sarah Siddons at No. 27 in 1817–31), but many of the houses have since been demolished or converted into shops and offices. (See also BAKERLOO LINE; JUBILEE LINE; MADAME TUSSAUD'S WAXWORKS; METROPOLITAN LINE; YERKES, CHARLES TYSON.)

BALHAM

A traditionally working-class suburb of Victorian and early twentieth-century housing, Balham probably emerged as a Saxon hamlet on Stane Street, a Roman road leading to London from the port at Chichester (some 65 miles to the south-east). It remained an agricultural area until, in the late eighteenth and early nineteenth centuries, it attracted wealthy London businessmen, who built large houses at which they could entertain their friends in the countryside. The potential for an affluent market encouraged the RAILWAY developers to open a station in 1856 and, after that, the area was transformed. Ease of access to jobs made the area desirable to workers who could not afford the high cost of central-city accommodation, so the green fields and woodlands quickly disappeared under bricks and mortar. Shops and other services were established for the newcomers as the developed area spread outwards and ultimately merged with neighbouring settlements, such as CLAPHAM (to the north) and TOOTING (to the south). As a result, the district suffers from a lack of PARKland and other recreational space. The rich businessmen have long gone and their former homes have been subdivided into flats, many of which are rented rather than owned, but in recent years, some gentrification has occurred. Much of the housing built in the past sixty years is on sites damaged by bombs during the BLITZ. The area's name may be derived from the Old English *bealg* and *hamm*, meaning 'rounded enclosure'.

BALTIC EXCHANGE

The Baltic Exchange is the world's largest shipbroking market, accounting for more than half of global business in ship sales and 60 per cent in wet bulk cargo. In addition, the 600 or so members have a growing influence on the organization of air-passenger charter flights. It is located in St Mary Axe, a street on the north-east edge of the CITY OF LONDON named after a church that housed an axe used by Attila the Hun when, according to legend, he slaughtered 11,000 virgin women who waited on the daughter of the king of England. In the early Georgian period, tallow (used to make candles, soap and lubricants) was an important commodity shipped from the Baltic states, and traders who had goods to transport to northern Europe knew that in THREADNEEDLE STREET, at the Virginia and Maryland COFFEE HOUSE (which renamed itself the Virginia and Baltick in 1744), they could meet captains looking for cargoes that would fill their holds during the return journey. In 1810, the premises had become so crowded that dealers moved to the nearby Antwerp Tavern (which became known as the Baltic Coffee House), then, in 1823, as Britain's world trading connections expanded, a formal association – the Baltic Club – was founded, with standardized trading regulations. In 1900, the club merged with the London Shipping Company (which had been founded in 1891 specifically to serve

The Bank of England in the eighteenth century.

the growing ocean liner industry) as the Baltic and Mercantile Shipping Exchange Limited and, in 1903, occupied a new granite-faced building on the site of St Mary Axe Church, which had been destroyed by fire twelve years earlier. By 1920 the brokers (whose word was considered binding when deals were made) represented nearly all the world's ship-owners and cargo interests. Moreover, the concentration of interests led to the formation of related organizations, such as the Institute of Chartered Shipbrokers. In 1987, the CORN EXCHANGE also occupied the building. On 10 April 1992, a bomb, planted by the IRA, caused much damage to the structure but had little effect on trading. The Exchange moved temporarily to LLOYD'S OF LONDON, in Lime Street, while repairs were carried out, then moved back to its former base. In 1994, however, it transferred next door to new premises – an art deco building internally refurbished for trading in the computer age.

BANK OF ENGLAND

As the central bank of the United Kingdom, the Bank of England is responsible for designing, printing and issuing currency notes circulated in England and Wales (and used throughout the country, though the Scottish and Northern Irish banks also issue notes). It also advises the Chancellor of the Exchequer on the impact of proposed government policies, attempts to maintain stability in domestic markets and intervenes in foreign exchange dealings to protect sterling. It was given a royal charter, entitling it to operate, on 27 July 1694, after William Paterson and Michael Godfrey, wealthy merchants, had suggested that a bank should be created to help William III fund a war against France by lending its share capital to the government. A total of 1,268 individuals subscribed £1.2 million, which was loaned to the state at an interest rate of 8 per cent per annum, with an additional £100,000 payable for expenses each year. The new bank was given permission to issue notes based on the security of the loan, but its early days were not easy. London's goldsmiths resented it because it stole much of their trade, rival institutions were established, and the government pressed it to supply more and more capital. However, legislation in 1708 prohibited companies with more than six partners from issuing notes, thereby greatly reducing the competition and enabling it to become banker to government departments. The management of government securities was added to its duties in 1717 and, in 1751, it assumed responsibility for administering the national debt.

The last two decades of the century brought new problems. In 1780, during the GORDON RIOTS, the Bank of England was attacked by a mob, which was beaten back by clerks who melted their inkwells to make bullets. (After that incident, the government sent guards to maintain security every night; known as the Bank Picquet, they acted as watchmen until 1973, when the bank replaced them with its own employees.) Then there was a run on funds as investors panicked during the French Revolution (which began in 1789) and, in 1797, reacted to rumours that a French force had invaded Wales. Regulations were passed to prevent cash withdrawals of more than £1 and Spanish dollars, taken from captured vessels, were circulated to meet the public's need for coinage.

The Bank of England during the nineteenth century was, in effect, the Bank of the British Empire, meeting the needs of a country expanding its commitments abroad whilst experiencing major social and economic upheaval through industrialization. In 1833, its promissory notes became legal tender (that is, they had to be accepted in payment of a debt) and, eleven years later, the Bank Charter Act allowed it to issue notes up to a total value of £14 million; issues over that sum had to be backed by gold. By the end of the century, all commercial banks had considerable deposits. These could be withdrawn on demand in the form of gold, at the Bank of England, which therefore became the keeper of the nation's gold reserve and, as a result, responsible for the control of credit.

Changing conditions after the First World War led Britain to abandon the gold standard in 1928 and, in 1946, to the institution's conversion from private to public ownership. A new royal charter provided for a governor, deputy governor and sixteen directors, all appointed by the Crown on the advice of the prime minister. In 1979, further legislation made the bank responsible for supervising all

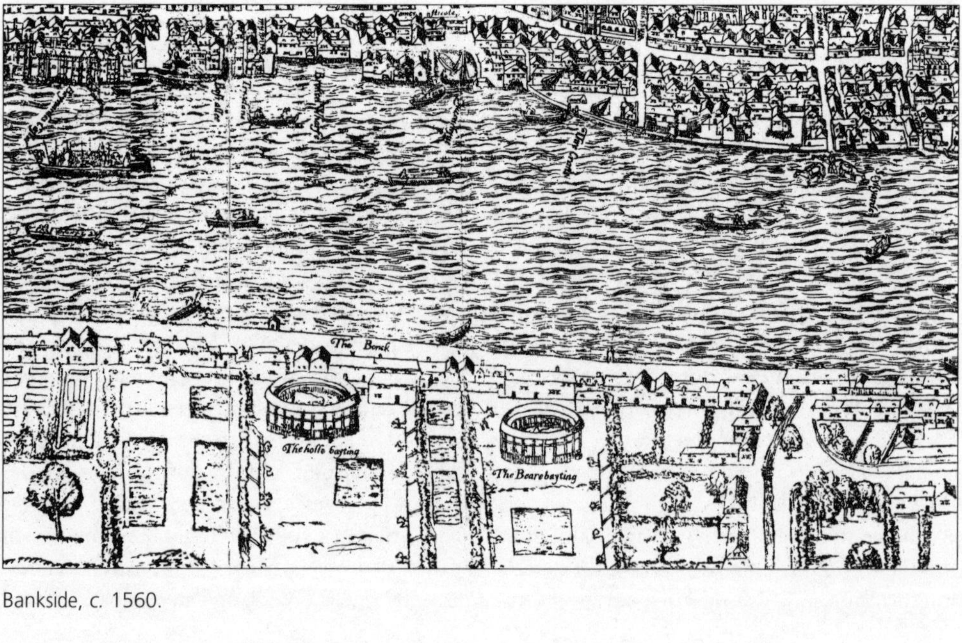

Bankside, c. 1560.

banks operating in the United Kingdom so that depositors would be protected and, in 1997, it was given sole authority to alter interest rates, a task formerly reserved for government ministers.

The Bank of England's first premises were at Mercers' Hall in CHEAPSIDE, but it stayed there for only a few months before moving to Grocers' Hall in Princes Street. In 1734 it transferred to THREADNEEDLE STREET, in the heart of the CITY OF LONDON, and it has remained there for more than 250 years, on a site covering 3.5 acres. Much reconstruction work was carried out in the 1780s and 1790s to designs by Sir John Soane (see SIR JOHN SOANE'S MUSEUM), but only the outer wall remains. The present building dates from 1925–39 when it was re-planned by Sir Herbert Baker. Its nickname – The Old Lady of Threadneedle Street – probably dates from a late eighteenth-century James Gillray cartoon, entitled 'Political Ravishment, or the Old Lady of Threadneedle Street in Danger', which mocks government attempts to affect the Bank of England's decision-making processes (an outline of the old lady is sculpted on the façade of the bank entrance). Visitors are not allowed beyond the entrance hall, but the bank maintains a MUSEUM, in Bartholomew Lane, which contains examples of modern banking technology and offers a video presentation explaining its functions and day-to-day operations. (See also MOORGATE; WATERLOO AND CITY LINE.)

BANKSIDE

During the late sixteenth and the early seventeenth centuries, Bankside, at the northern tip of SOUTHWARK on the bank of the RIVER THAMES, was the centre of London THEATRE and one of the most dissolute parts of the city. In 1988, archaeologists discovered the site of the Rose, the first of the playhouses, built in 1586–7 and still remembered in the street name Rose Alley. The Swan opened in 1596 and, according to John de Witt, who made a

Bankside was a den of iniquity in the 1640s, so the puritanical Oliver Cromwell closed the many pleasure palaces that littered the area in an attempt to eradicate the squalid atmosphere.

sketch of the building, could hold audiences of over 3,000 people. At the same time, WILLIAM SHAKESPEARE was treading the stage at the GLOBE THEATRE, originally built in 1598–9 and demolished in 1644 but now reconstructed on its original site. Actors, writers and theatre managers all lived in the area and helped to support other forms of entertainment, such as bear baiting. There were also many brothels, with rules of conduct and opening hours regulated by the Bishops of Winchester, whose London palace estate included Bankside. After the pleasure palaces were closed by Oliver Cromwell and his morally strict, Sabbath-observing Puritans during the 1640s and 1650s, much of the land was devoted to gardens, but these were gradually replaced by small industrial premises, notably BREWERIES, glassmaking works, dyers' yards and small foundries. PUBLIC HOUSES, such as the ANCHOR

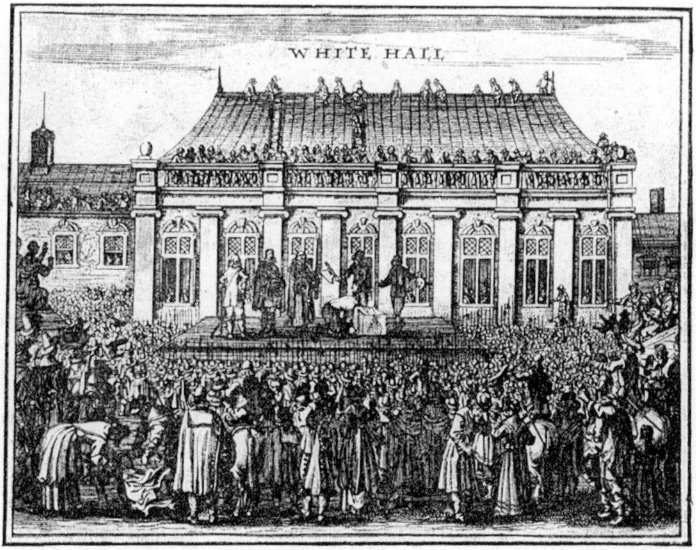

Execution of Charles I in 1649 in front of the Banqueting House, Whitehall.

INN, were established to serve thirsty workers, and wharves and warehouses were built along the RIVER THAMES, providing facilities for ships trading with other parts of Britain and with Europe. The area is now dominated by the tall chimney of Bankside Power Station, designed by GILES GILBERT SCOTT, opened in 1963, decommissioned in 1981 and refurbished to provide a home for part of the TATE GALLERY's collection of modern art in 2000. As part of the development, a new footbridge (known as the MILLENNIUM BRIDGE) was built across the Thames, linking Bankside to the CITY OF LONDON and ST PAUL'S CATHEDRAL. (See also CLINK PRISON; HENSLOWE, PHILIP.)

BANQUETING HOUSE

Considered by critics to be one of the finest examples of Renaissance ARCHITECTURE in Britain, the Banqueting House was designed by INIGO JONES and built at the command of James I as part of a planned extension of WHITEHALL PALACE. Opened in 1622 with a performance of BEN JONSON's play *Masque of Angers*, it stands on the east side of WHITEHALL, on a site occupied by earlier structures built in 1572, 1581 and 1608. Originally, the exterior was masonry brought from Northampton and Oxford but, in 1829, it was faced with more durable PORTLAND STONE. Inside, spectators could watch events from a gallery under a ceiling that was commissioned by Charles I in 1635 and painted by Peter Paul Rubens, who depicted the advantages of James's rule in nine allegorical settings. The hall was used for varied functions, including royal feasts, the reception of foreign dignitaries and state ceremonies (William of Orange and his wife, Mary, were formally offered the throne by an assembly of aristocrats and commoners who met in the building on 13 February 1689). After a fire destroyed much of the interior in 1698, the Banqueting House was converted into a chapel royal, designed by CHRISTOPHER WREN. For twenty years from 1809, it was the Horse Guards chapel, then, from 1829 until 1890, it reverted to its status as a chapel royal before becoming the Museum of the Royal United Services Institute for Defence Studies. In 1962 it was reclaimed by the government, which redecorated it in its original colour scheme and returned it to its initial use as a setting for state functions.

BARBICAN

Although it is largely occupied by a controversial post-Second World War development, the Barbican area gets its name from the medieval fortifications that surrounded London (a *barbican* is a watchtower projecting over a gate in a city's defensive wall). During the sixteenth and seventeenth centuries, it was a fashionable part of the city (the poet John Milton lived there from 1645 until 1649, for example, probably writing *L'Allegro* and *Comus* while in residence), but in the 1700s it became more working class and by the end of the Victorian period it was a run-down mix of houses and small businesses. In 1940 and 1941 it suffered greatly from German bombs (see BLITZ), so it was ripe for new construction as London rebuilt after the conflict ended. Rather than simply allow offices to take over the site, however, Duncan Sandys (Minister of Housing and Local Government in the Conservative government) appealed, in 1956, for planners to design 'a genuine residential neighbourhood, incorporating schools, shops, open spaces and amenities, even if this means foregoing a more remunerative return on the land'.

In part, Sandys' view reflected a widely held fear that a flight of middle-class groups from Britain's inner cities would take retail and related services with it, leaving the poor behind and creating problems similar to those that had evolved in the United States. His plea, therefore, fell on receptive ears and, in 1958, the site was bought by the CITY OF LONDON through a compulsory purchase order. The architectural firm of Chamberlin, Powel and Bon was commissioned to prepare plans and designed a complex that included 2,100 apartments for over 6,500 people (some of them in three skyscrapers over 400-foot high, taller than any other in Europe at the time). In addition, there were shops, offices, the MUSEUM OF LONDON, a new GUILDHALL SCHOOL OF MUSIC AND DRAMA, accommodation for two City LIVERY COMPANIES, a girls' school and an arts centre. The dense concentration of buildings was, in some ways, reminiscent of Europe's medieval walled cities, but the homes were designed to maximise privacy and many have small gardens. Open space and water features were also built into the plan in an attempt to alleviate the harshness of the masonry and feelings of confinement.

Opinions about the development were sharply divided, some critics praising its imaginative provision of homes on a confined site in the inner city, others repelled by the functionalism of the rough-tooled concrete ARCHITECTURE. Many of the complaints were directed at the Barbican Centre for Arts and Conferences. Opened in 1982, it cost £153 million, covers 20 acres and has ten levels. Inside, there is an art gallery, three cinemas, a library, restaurants, conference facilities, a 2,026-seat concert hall and a 1,166-seat theatre with rehearsal rooms. The LONDON SYMPHONY ORCHESTRA uses the Centre for performances, as did the Royal Shakespeare Company until 2001, when it moved out following actors' complaints about the subterranean auditorium, the 'concrete jungle' design and its distance from London's theatre heartland in the WEST END.

BARBICAN CENTRE FOR ARTS AND CONFERENCES

See BARBICAN.

BARINGS BANK

In 1762, John and Francis Baring established a merchant bank in Queen Street, trading internationally in the commodity markets. Forty-three years later, the business moved to Bishopsgate, then, in 1890, it became a limited company. By the late twentieth century, it was the oldest merchant bank in the CITY OF LONDON, with interests in corporate finance and investment management. However, in 1994–5, Nick Leeson, who managed its futures trading operation in Singapore, took excessive risks with the firm's funds. Betting that the Tokyo stocks would rise, he invested heavily and, when the market fell in the wake of an earthquake at Kobe, doubled his commitments. Faced with mounting losses, he fled to Europe on 23 February 1995. Barings collapsed four days later, with debts of £830 million, and was purchased by the Internationale Nederlanden Groep (ING) for £1. Leeson, arrested at Frankfurt Airport, returned to Singapore, where he received a six-and-a-half-year jail sentence after facing trial for fraud and forgery. Following a BANK OF ENGLAND inquiry, which concluded that Barings had failed to supervise its Far Eastern operations properly, several of the firm's senior staff were disqualified from holding posts as company directors. In 2001, ING sold Barings, which it had used as the American end of its investment banking operations, to rival ABNAMRO for US$275 million.

BARKING

A largely working-class suburb on the eastern edge of London, Barking is bounded by the RIVER THAMES in the south, the Roding River in the west, the community of ILFORD in the north and DAGENHAM in the east. It originated as a Saxon settlement (its name is derived from the Old English *Berecingum*, which means 'Berica's people'), developed on marshy land around Barking Abbey, which was founded by St Erkenwald around AD 666. By the time of its dissolution by Henry VIII in 1539, the abbey, located at the head of Barking Creek (which forms the mouth of the Roding), had became the largest Benedictine nunnery in England, and its inhabitants provided local people with a ready Roman Catholic market, as did the relatively large population of London, so, unsurprisingly, a considerable fishing industry developed. By the mid-nineteenth century, some 4,000 people and about 220 vessels were employed, with, in addition, others involved in tasks such as processing and distribution of the catch.

During the second half of the century, the fishing fleet moved to Great Yarmouth, in Norfolk, and Barking's economy became increasingly industrial, particularly after the RAILWAY arrived in 1854. Green fields were speedily replaced by buildings as the population more than tripled between 1901 (when it totalled 21,547) and 1951 (when it reached 78,170). One of the largest ELECTRICITY generating stations in Europe was built in 1926, providing jobs for employees with the considerable number of construction and engineering companies that flourished in the area. In addition, extensive areas were earmarked for local authority housing, including the 27,000-home Becontree estate, which straddled Barking, Dagenham and Ilford, and, when it opened in the 1920s, was one of the largest public residential developments in Europe. Many of Barking's citizens work at the Ford Motor Company's Dagenham works, in distribution companies located along the main road between London and Tilbury, in chemical and pharmaceutical firms (such as Rhone Poulenc), or with manufacturing concerns such as the GPT telephone cable business. In addition, over 2 miles of riverfront along Barking Creek are being redeveloped for a mixture of commercial, recreational and residential purposes. In 1965, part of Barking was merged with East Ham as the new LONDON BOROUGH OF NEWHAM. The remainder was united with its eastern neighbour as the LONDON BOROUGH OF BARKING AND DAGENHAM. (See also HAMMERSMITH AND CITY LINE; METROPOLITAN LINE.)

BARKING AND DAGENHAM, LONDON BOROUGH OF

In 1965, the formerly independent councils of BARKING and DAGENHAM, located on the marshy north bank of the RIVER THAMES some 10 miles east of the city centre, were merged into a single authority as part of a wide-ranging reorganization of London's local government (see GREATER LONDON COUNCIL; LONDON

BOROUGHS). It covers some 14 square miles and has a population of about 164,000 (2001). Since its creation, the largely working-class population has ensured consistent Labour Party control of the council even though substantial numbers of skilled manual workers flirted with Margaret Thatcher's Conservative Party during the 1980s. Economically, the area is dominated by manufacturing businesses such as the Ford Motor Company (which began production at Dagenham in 1931 but announced early in 2000 that it intended to close much of its plant, retaining only the engine-making facility) and the Rhone Poulenc chemical and pharmaceutical group. Service employment is limited, although Coral (a betting firm that has diversified successfully into other branches of the leisure industry) has its headquarters in the area. About half of the housing is rented from the local authority or from a housing association, most of it built between the two world wars in the form of long terraces. The Borough Council, based at a civic centre in Dagenham, operates through eight departments that carry out statutory responsibilities, including town planning, provision of education (the borough has fifty-three primary and eight secondary schools) and maintenance of social services.In 2003 the government announced that the former DOCK areas in the south of the borough would be the site of 15,000 new homes to be built by 2016 in an attempt to alleviate the housing shortage in south-east England.

BARLOW COMMISSION (1937–1939)
London's relative prosperity during the national economic depression of the 1920s and 1930s led some commentators to argue that the city's success in attracting manufacturing industry was a cause of poverty and unemployment in other regions of the United Kingdom. In 1937 the government appointed a Royal Commission on the Distribution of the Industrial Population, chaired by Sir Montague Barlow, to examine the social and economic impact of growth in the metropolis. In their report, published late in 1939 (a few months after the beginning of the Second World War), the members were unable to present convincing evidence that expansion of industrial capacity in London had caused recession elsewhere. However, they warned that over-concentration of manufacturing activity in the south-east was unwise because the area was easily attacked from the European mainland and because excessive expansion in London would cause the country's best commercial brains to leave other cities and concentrate there. Moreover, more factories would mean more traffic congestion, more urban sprawl, longer journeys to work and more limited access to the countryside for residents. As a result, they recommended that measures should be taken to promote new industrial development at sites outside south-east England. The report greatly influenced such post-war reconstruction policies as the movement of population and jobs to New Towns and the granting of financial aid to firms willing to locate in the North of England, Scotland and Wales. (See also ABERCROMBIE PLAN (1943–1944); GREATER LONDON DEVELOPMENT PLAN (1969)).

BARNARDO, THOMAS JOHN (1845–1905)
The founder of a nationwide network of homes for abandoned and poor children, Barnardo was born in Dublin on 4 July 1845. The ninth son of a German father and an Irish mother, he was raised as a Roman Catholic but converted to Protestantism in 1862 and became an evangelical preacher. In 1866, he travelled to London, intending to study medicine before undertaking missionary work in China. However, while based at the London Hospital (see ROYAL LONDON HOSPITAL), in the city's EAST END, he became deeply involved in attempts to improve the lot of homeless young people, initially founding a juvenile mission (1867) then (with financial help from Lord Shaftesbury) opening a boys' home at MILE END in 1870. Three years later, he bought an inn at

LIMEHOUSE, converting it into a headquarters for his charity work, a church and a meeting place for labourers in the nearby DOCKS. In 1874, he began to provide facilities for girls, ensuring that vocational training was made available for both sexes so that young people could break the cycle of poverty by finding steady jobs. Barnardo's insistence that the children in his care should be brought up according to the tenets of the Protestant faith plunged him into frequent conflict with Roman Catholic authorities, but his homes met a real need in a city that had a high proportion of lowly paid manual workers, many of whom suffered from long spells of unemployment and had large families. Working on the principle that no destitute youngster should ever be turned away, he probably helped about 250,000 individuals before he died at SURBITON on 19 September 1905. In 1899, his properties became the responsibility of the National Incorporated Association for the Reclamation of Destitute Waif Children, but they have always been popularly known as Dr Barnardo's homes. In recent years, the charity he founded has placed increasing emphasis on care in the community, rather than on residential provision, in order to meet changing social needs.

BARNES

Lying south of the RIVER THAMES, about 6 miles south-west of CHARING CROSS, Barnes was considered remote from the CITY OF LONDON before the nineteenth century because the village's only access was by water or by traversing the marshy common land that separated it from PUTNEY, its eastern neighbour. However, a road linked the settlement to HAMMERSMITH in 1827 (see HAMMERSMITH BRIDGE) and the RAILWAY arrived in 1846, making the area attractive to businessmen wanting a substantial suburban home in keeping with their status. The demand led to much housing development but the large green and its pond survived, as did the common (though it was drained during the second half of the century). Brewing (see BREWERIES) was once a significant local industry, but the area is now essentially a middle-class dormitory suburb. The railway crossing of the Thames west of Barnes is the oldest BRIDGE over the river downstream of RICHMOND. Erected for the London and South-Western Company and opened in 1849, it is made of cast iron. A wrought-iron structure was added on the eastern side in 1891–5. The area's name may be derived from the Old English *bereaern* and mean 'the place by the barns'. (See also LONDON WETLANDS CENTRE.)

BARNET, LONDON BOROUGH OF

When London's local government was reorganized in 1965, Barnet was created through the amalgamation of the formerly independent boroughs of HENDON and FINCHLEY, with the addition of Chipping Barnet, East Barnet and Friern Barnet, all of which previously had urban district status. The authority covers some 34 square miles in the north-west of the city and had a population of 314,600 in 2001. Although there is some light industry in the west, the area is largely residential, with the protected land of the green belt helping to keep house prices in northern neighbourhoods high and attracting wealthy families. The communities around MILL HILL and Hendon have relatively high proportions of council accommodation and a significant Asian presence, whereas the south (which includes the HAMPSTEAD GARDEN SUBURB) is heavily dominated by non-manual workers and Jewish IMMIGRANTS (at the 2001 census, 14.8 per cent of the borough's residents reported themselves as Jewish). The affluence of the borough is reflected in the number of retail establishments (Barnet has more shops than any other part of the city except the CITY OF WESTMINSTER and the LONDON BOROUGH OF CAMDEN). Several major office developments (including the British headquarters of McDonald's) provide important sources of employment, as do such educational institutions as Middlesex University and the Police

Training Centre at Hendon. (See also CRICKLEWOOD; EDGWARE; GOLDERS GREEN.)

BARNSBURY

The Barnsbury area of the LONDON BOROUGH OF ISLINGTON, some 2 miles north of CHARING CROSS, developed around Bernesbury Manor. Until the early nineteenth century, it was a rural community, dependent largely on dairy farming and market gardening. However, from about 1820 fields were dug up for clay by the brick-making companies and built over by developers. Initially, the new houses were acquired by skilled working-class and lower middle-class families but, by the beginning of the twentieth century, these groups had taken advantage of the growing network of RAILWAY lines to move farther into the suburbs. Their homes were subdivided to provide rented flats for single people seeking cheap accommodation close to the city centre so, by the end of the Second World War, many properties were shabby and poorly maintained. Since then, local authorities have undertaken improvement schemes, demolishing older premises to make way for council estates and small open spaces. In addition, new owner-occupiers have refurbished many of the terraces.

BARRY, CHARLES (1795-1860)

Although Barry is best known as the architect of the HOUSES OF PARLIAMENT (see PALACE OF WESTMINSTER), he was also responsible for the design of several other important buildings in London and was a major influence on the growth of the Gothic Revival movement in English ARCHITECTURE. The son of a stationer, he was born in Bridge Street, WESTMINSTER, on 23 May 1795, and began his career at the age of fifteen as a trainee with Middleton and Bailey, a firm of surveyors and architects based in Paradise Row, LAMBETH. In 1815, his father died, leaving Barry an inheritance that he used to finance a three-year tour of the Mediterranean lands, including France, Italy, Greece, Turkey, Egypt and Cyprus. On his return, he set up his own business in ELY PLACE, HOLBORN, and made a successful living by designing churches for the rapidly expanding populations of London and other cities. In 1829–32, he prepared plans for the Travellers' Club in PALL MALL; the first London building to be erected in the style of an Italian Renaissance palace, it is two storeys high with a plain stucco façade and an entrance set to one side. Next door, his even grander REFORM CLUB (1837–41) is constructed of PORTLAND STONE, with the rooms gathered around a central cloistered courtyard.

Barry also built several private homes, the most notable of which is Bridgewater House (1845–54) in Queen's Walk on the eastern edge of GREEN PARK. Outside London, he designed King Edward VI School, Birmingham (1833–7), the Royal Institution of Fine Arts, Manchester (1824–35) and Halifax Town Hall (opened in 1863). While working in Birmingham, he made the acquaintance of AUGUSTUS WELBY NORTHMORE PUGIN, who was to collaborate with him on the rebuilding of the PALACE OF WESTMINSTER. After the palace had been destroyed by fire on 16 October 1834, architects were invited to compete for the commission to erect a replacement on the same site, with the stipulation that the new building must be designed in either Elizabethan or Gothic style. Barry, eschewing his Italianate past, won, his proposals greatly enhanced by Pugin's meticulous drawings. The palace was officially opened by Queen Victoria in 1852 and Barry was knighted shortly afterwards. However, the stress generated by a project of such size took its toll. Worn out, he died at his home beside CLAPHAM COMMON on 12 May 1860 and was buried in WESTMINSTER ABBEY. (See also ALBERT, PRINCE; LIVERPOOL STREET STATION; TRAFALGAR SQUARE; TREASURY BUILDINGS; WESTMINSTER BRIDGE.)

BARTHOLOMEW FAIR

In 1133, Henry I gave St Bartholomew's Priory, at Smithfield, a charter entitling it to hold an annual fair for three days from St Bartholomew's Eve (24 August). Very quickly, the event evolved into the largest cloth fair in England, but by 1604, when the CORPORATION OF LONDON became responsible for its organization, it had become better known for its fire-eaters, theatre groups and other entertainers than for the goods on sale. During the nineteenth century, it gained a reputation for drunkenness and disorder, so the authorities closed it down in 1855, but it was resurrected on a small scale in 2000 as a means of raising money for the Butchers and Drovers Charitable Institute. (See also SMITHFIELD MEAT MARKET.)

BATTERSEA

Located on the SOUTH BANK of the RIVER THAMES some 3 miles south-west of CHARING CROSS, Battersea has been settled on since prehistoric times (the evidence includes a magnificently decorated Iron Age shield, found in 1857 and now in the BRITISH MUSEUM). It is mentioned in a charter of AD 693 which acknowledges that *Batrices Ege* (or Badric's Island) was owned by the Abbess of Barking, has been served by St Mary's Church since before England's conquest by the Normans in 1066, but retained its distinctiveness throughout the Middle Ages because the river and its marshes made access difficult. Fertile soil led to the growth of a market gardening industry, selling produce to the ever-increasing London population and, from the seventeenth century, local industries developed, notably copper-making, lime production, DOCKyard activities and pottery (from 1753 to 1756, John Brooks perfected the art of printing transfers on china at his premises in York House, selling the products as Battersea Enamels). However, the transfer from agricultural to urban settlement stemmed largely from the opening of the London and Southampton RAILWAY's terminus at NINE ELMS, on the eastern fringe of the area, in 1838. The station and its associated engine repair facilities provided jobs in numbers that greatly exceeded the limited local labour supply, so houses had to be built for incoming workers and services were established to meet their needs. In addition, ancillary industries (such as candle-making, chemical production and gas manufacture) sprang up, attracting additional migrants.

Between 1801 and 1901, Battersea's population increased from just over 3,000 to nearly 170,000 lowly paid and ill-educated manual workers and their families. Much of the formerly open land was covered in rows of terraced housing, as large estates in the south of the area were sold off to developers and the fields and market gardens in the north were snapped up by builders. As a result, little of the older, pre-industrial Battersea remains apart from St Mary's Church (built in 1775–7 but incorporating elements of its predecessors, such as the seventeenth-century glass in the east window and the pre-Reformation bells). During the twentieth century, the area has retained its reputation as a working-class community, but local authorities have made considerable improvements to the housing stock and provided more extensive community services, including LIBRARIES. The area is now part of the LONDON BOROUGH OF WANDSWORTH. (See also BATTERSEA BRIDGE; BATTERSEA DOGS' HOME; BATTERSEA PARK; BATTERSEA POWER STATION; HARDIE, JAMES KEIR.)

BATTERSEA BRIDGE

The first bridge over the RIVER THAMES at BATTERSEA, linking the small settlement to CHELSEA (on the north bank of the river), was a wooden structure erected in 1771–2 to Henry Holland's plans. As the only road crossing between PUTNEY and WESTMINSTER, it attracted a considerable volume of traffic but proved difficult to navigate, so it was demolished in 1881. Its cast-iron replacement, built in 1886–90, had five arches and was designed by JOSEPH WILLIAM BAZALGETTE, better known for his considerable contribution to London's nineteenth-century SEWAGE DISPOSAL system.

Houseboats have congregated at the northern end, some of them fetching as much as small apartments in neighbouring areas when they are placed on the market. The wrought-iron RAILWAY bridge (sometimes known as the West London Extension Bridge), which also connects the two communities, was erected a few yards upriver in 1861 to allow the West London Railway to run services into the station at CLAPHAM JUNCTION.

BATTERSEA DOGS' HOME

A charitable organization originally founded by Mary Tealby in 1860, the Home is London's main rescue centre for unwanted dogs and cats. It was initially based in HOLLOWAY but generated so much noise that Mrs Tealby had to move her 200 animals to a more accommodating site at BATTERSEA in 1871. Thirteen years later, the Prince of Wales became the institution's patron, setting a precedent for royal support, which was followed by Queen Victoria (1885) and Queen Elizabeth II (1956). Critics scoffed at the concept of an institution dedicated to the care of strays, but through high health standards and sustained publicity it has done much to shape a more responsible approach to pet ownership. As a result, it has some 500 dogs and cats to offer to visitors every day at its premises in Battersea Park Road.

BATTERSEA PARK

During the early nineteenth century, the common lands along the SOUTH BANK of the RIVER THAMES at BATTERSEA earned a raffish reputation. Fairs attracted thousands of visitors who lost their money gambling, drank too much at the Red House Tavern and patronized dubious fortune-tellers. Fights were common (the Duke of Wellington and Lord Winchilsea fought a duel there in 1829), so the government was eventually forced to take action and, in 1846 (following a suggestion from THOMAS CUBITT), encouraged Parliament to pass legislation establishing a PARK on the site. Under James Pennethorne's direction, a total of 198 acres was laid out then opened to the public in 1853. Seven years later, a lake was added and, in 1864, a subtropical garden was created. An oasis of green space in a predominantly working-class area, the grounds were immediately popular. They were redesigned by Osbert Lancaster for the FESTIVAL OF BRITAIN in 1951 and now include tennis courts, a running track, playing fields and a pagoda built in 1985 by Buddhist monks.

BATTERSEA POWER STATION

One of London's best-known landmarks, the coal-fired ELECTRICITY generating plant on the SOUTH BANK of the RIVER THAMES little more than a mile south-west of the HOUSES OF PARLIAMENT (see PALACE OF WESTMINSTER) was designed by GILES GILBERT SCOTT (who was also responsible for the repair work to the GUILDHALL after the Second World War). It opened in 1933, with one 300-foot-high chimney at each end, but doubled in size during the 1940s, when two additional chimneys were built. In an attempt to limit AIR POLLUTION, sulphur and other contaminants were removed before the smoke issued into the atmosphere, but, even so, local residents suffered much inconvenience from the large industrial site on their doorsteps. The plant closed in 1983, superseded by more efficient means of producing power, and was taken over by the Roche Consortium, a development company that intended to convert it into a theme PARK but ran out of funds in 1991. In 2000, however, the LONDON BOROUGH OF WANDSWORTH approved plans by Parkview Holdings to redevelop the 35-acre site as a restaurant and leisure complex at an estimated cost of £500 million.

BAYSWATER

The area bounded by KENSINGTON GARDENS and HYDE PARK (to the south) and PADDINGTON (to the north) takes its name from Bayard's Watering Place, a spring where riders allowed their horses to drink. It developed as London expanded during the early nineteenth century, with wealthy City workers buying large houses with adequate room for servants and family. However, after the First World War, economic circumstances changed and the more affluent social groups moved to smaller homes in suburban locations. Many of their former properties in Bayswater were demolished to make way for tower blocks or townhouses, others converted for use as guest houses and small HOTELS or subdivided into rented apartments. (See also DEPARTMENT STORES.)

BAZALGETTE, JOSEPH WILLIAM

(1819–1891)

Bazalgette, engineer to the METROPOLITAN BOARD OF WORKS, was responsible for providing the framework of the SEWAGE DISPOSAL system, which still serves central London. Born in ENFIELD on 28 March 1819, he was the son of Joseph William Bazalgette (whose father had arrived from France twenty-five years earlier) and his wife, Theresa. Educated privately, he became a pupil of civil engineer John McNeill in 1836 then established his own business in WESTMINSTER in 1842. He was appointed Assistant Surveyor to the Metropolitan Commission of Sewers in 1849, promoted to Engineer in 1852 and employed by the Metropolitan Board of Works in 1856 with responsibility for street improvements and lighting, river bridges, tunnels, road building and FLOOD CONTROL over 117 square miles of London. The board's principal concern at the time was public health, so plans to deal with the growing problem caused by sewage had a high priority (Bazalgette reported to a Royal Commission in 1888 that effluent 'kept oscillating up and down the river, while more filth was being constantly added to it, until the Thames became absolutely pestilential'). Despite the difficulty of constructing pipelines in a densely populated area, 80 miles of brick intercepting sewers were laid (with a fall of 2 feet per mile from west to east) and connected to outfall sewers attached to pumping stations. Work began in 1859 and was completed south of the river in 1864, but the system on the more urbanized north bank was not fully operational until 1875.

Bazalgette was also responsible for the Albert, CHELSEA and Victoria Embankments. Construction of the Victoria Embankment, which runs for 1¼ miles along the river eastwards from WESTMINSTER BRIDGE to BLACKFRIARS Bridge, was preceded by tortuous negotiations with coal wharf operators, railway authorities, the City Gas Company and other interests. The building process (which began in 1864) was complex, involving incorporation of a low-level sewer, difficulties in acquiring granite for facing stone and problems with contractors (who were unwilling to use material dredged from the Thames as fill behind the new wall) but was completed in 1870. On the south side of the river, the 1-mile Albert Embankment, between Westminster Bridge and Vauxhall Bridge, was begun in 1865 and finished three years later, with the project producing sufficient reclaimed marshland to provide a site for ST THOMAS'S HOSPITAL. The ¾-mile Chelsea Embankment, between CHELSEA BRIDGE and BATTERSEA BRIDGE, was built between 1871 and 1874, covering the main sewer for the area. In addition, Bazalgette supervised work on twelve river BRIDGES bought by the board from private owners from 1877 and designed replacement crossings at BATTERSEA, PUTNEY and HAMMERSMITH. Also, he worked with architects to plan new roads: Queen Victoria Street (opened in 1871), Northumberland Avenue (1876), SHAFTESBURY AVENUE (1886), CHARING CROSS ROAD (1887) and several other important thoroughfares, still much used, greatly facilitated travel in the growing metropolis.

In addition to his commitments in London, Bazalgette also contributed to improvements in other cities, reporting on drainage at Oxford, Glasgow and other centres, as well as preparing plans for schemes at Odessa (in

Ukraine) and Port Louis (Mauritius). A man with great technical ability and considerable diplomatic skill, he was made a Companion of the Bath in 1871, awarded a knighthood in 1874 and elected President of the Institution of Civil Engineers in 1884. He retired in 1889 and died at his home in WIMBLEDON on 15 March 1891.

BECKENHAM

A predominantly middle-class residential area lying to the north-west of the LONDON BOROUGH OF BROMLEY, Beckenham derives its name from the Old English *Beohha* (probably one of the individuals who farmed the land) and *ham* (meaning 'village'). Although the thirteenth-century lychgate at St George's Church is claimed to be the oldest in England, most of the buildings were erected during the nineteenth and twentieth centuries, as RAILWAYS, BUSES and automobiles enabled workers to commute to jobs in the inner city. Local employment is largely in service industries, including local government, education, retail provision and professional concerns (such as those of accountants, lawyers and realtors). (See also BEDLAM.)

BECKTON

In 1870, the Gas Light and Coke Company built a new plant, intended to serve the whole of London, on the north bank of the RIVER THAMES some 10 miles east of CHARING CROSS. The site was named after the company's Governor, Simon Adams Beck, who had a distinctively humane view of employer/employee relationships, building a village with two churches and a meeting hall for his workers. Within a few years, a sizeable manufacturing complex had developed, converting the by-products of gas production into fertilizer, ammonia and other commodities. Further construction took place after the opening of the Royal Albert DOCK in 1881 (the new estate was called Cyprus to commemorate Britain's capture of that Mediterranean island in 1878), but residential development was restricted because most of the land was used for industrial purposes by the PORT OF LONDON AUTHORITY. However, after the introduction of natural GAS had caused the closure of the town gas plant in 1969 and the Royal Albert Dock had followed twelve years later as harbour services were rationalized, the London Docklands Development Corporation (see DOCKLANDS), formed in 1981, prepared plans for additional homes and improved TRANSPORT infrastructure, as well as two secondary schools. The major source of employment now is sewage treatment (the Beckton plant is one of Europe's largest). (See also DOCKLANDS LIGHT RAILWAY.)

BEDFORD ESTATES

During the sixteenth century, the Russell family was given title to the earldom of Bedford. In succeeding centuries, it acquired extensive estates in London, notably at COVENT GARDEN (which was gifted to John, the first earl, in 1552 in return for services to Edward VI) and BLOOMSBURY (which was acquired through marriage in 1669). The former was sold in 1914 and the latter was greatly reduced as educational institutions (such as the BRITISH MUSEUM and the University of London) bought or leased the land from 1755, but the owners are remembered in many of the street names (Bedford Place, for example, links Bloomsbury Square with RUSSELL SQUARE). Bedford Square is one of the city's finest Georgian designs. Laid out by builders William Scott and Thomas Crewer in 1755–80, and probably planned by Thomas Leverton, it consists largely of brick houses, but the central building on each side is emphasized by its stucco finish. Residents have included two Lord Chancellors (Lord Loughborough at No. 6, 1787-96, and Lord Eldon at the same address, 1804-19) and former Prime Minister Herbert Asquith (at No. 44, 1921-4). Most of the former homes have now been converted into office space.

BEDLAM

During the late fourteenth century, the HOSPITAL at St Mary Bethlehem Priory, outside the BISHOP'S GATE, began to provide accommodation for the mentally ill (that provision was basic and hardly humane by modern standards; patients were chained to walls and whipped when they caused problems). In 1547, following the dissolution of the English MONASTERIES, the CORPORATION OF LONDON bought the buildings (by that time known as Bedlam) from Henry VIII, converting them into an asylum for lunatics. The hospital moved to Moorfields in 1557 and proved a popular attraction for city residents, who strolled along walkways as they viewed inmates housed in cages. Donations from the visitors provided the institution with a large proportion of its funds until 1770, when changing public attitudes encouraged the management to provide greater privacy for the people in their care. In 1800, the structure of the old hospital was declared unsafe so, fifteen years later, the 122 patients were transferred to newly constructed premises in LAMBETH. Provision for the criminally insane was added in 1816, then in 1835 the building was extended again, but changing medical standards led to further moves, after the First World War, to suburban sites. The Royal Bethlehem is now located at BECKENHAM, at the south-eastern edge of London, and is linked to the nearby Maudsley Hospital, founded in 1916 and now the United Kingdom's major centre of psychiatric research. The IMPERIAL WAR MUSEUM occupies part of the former Lambeth site. (See also LIVERPOOL STREET STATION; PUGIN, AUGUSTUS WELBY NORTHMORE.)

BEEFEATER

Although the men who guard the TOWER OF LONDON are formally termed Yeomen Warders of the Tower, they are usually known as Beefeaters. Founded by Edward VI in the mid-sixteenth century, they still wear the red uniform that distinguished them in Tudor times. Their popular name may derive from a partiality for roast beef, but some writers have suggested other sources for the word. For example, 'eater' (derived from the Old English *oeta*) was employed as a synonym for 'servant' fifty years after the corps was established; beefeater may have been a derogatory term used with reference to well-fed members of the royal household who performed menial duties. Now, all appointees are former warrant officers in the Army or the Royal Air Force and modern security systems have rendered their duties largely ceremonial. (See also CEREMONY OF THE KEYS.)

BEEFSTEAK CLUB

In 1735, John Rich (founder of the COVENT GARDEN theatre now known as the ROYAL OPERA HOUSE) and George Lambert (a scenery painter) formed a society for twenty-four gentlemen of noble birth. From November until June, they met every Saturday for a beefsteak dinner and convivial conversation. The society disbanded in 1866 but was succeeded by a club that intended to keep the name alive. It formed on 11 March 1866 and moved to its present home (one room above a shop in Ingram Street) thirty years later. Members include representatives of politics, the arts and education. As they arrive for their meal, they sit at a single long table in the order in which they appear. All the waiters are called Charles.

BELFAST, HMS

At 11,000 tons, the *Belfast* was the largest cruiser ever built for the Royal Navy. Launched in 1938, she saw service during the Second World War guarding Arctic convoys, took part in the Battle of North Cape on 26 December 1943 (when the German battle cruiser *Scharnhorst* was sunk) and assisted at the D-Day landings on the Normandy beaches in 1944. Her last action was in the Korean War (1950–3). After being taken out of service, she was berthed on the RIVER

THAMES at Symon's Wharf (upstream of TOWER BRIDGE) in 1971 and opened to the public, the first naval vessel to be preserved since the *Victory*, Horatio Nelson's flagship at the Battle of Trafalgar in 1805. She was refitted at Portsmouth in 1999.

BELGRAVIA

An affluent residential area between VICTORIA and HYDE PARK, Belgravia was developed by the Grosvenor family (see GROSVENOR ESTATE), taking its name from Belgrave, their Leicestershire home. Construction began during the 1820s, with development regulated by THOMAS CUBITT, who erected rows of terraced houses focusing on Belgrave Square at the same time as JOHN NASH was building BUCKINGHAM PALACE immediately to the east. By the second half of the nineteenth century, the suburb was extremely fashionable with wealthy Londoners, a status that has been retained despite the incursion of embassy buildings and conversion of some dwellings to offices for bodies such as the Country Landowners' Association and the Royal College of Veterinary Surgeons. Belgravia forms part of the CITY OF WESTMINSTER.

BELSIZE PARK

The Belsize Park suburb lies south-east of HAMPSTEAD, some 4 miles north of CHARING CROSS, on land that in medieval times was part of Belassis Manor. In 1663, Daniel O'Neill, a supporter of the Royalist cause during the Civil War, acquired the estate and rebuilt the manor house for his wife Catherine, Countess of Chesterfield. The property remained in the family's hands for nearly 150 years but changed use several times. In the early eighteenth century it was a pleasure garden patronized by royalty, then, from 1740, it was rented to affluent families such as that of Spencer Perceval, who lived in the building from 1798 until 1807, and who became Prime Minister in 1809. The house was demolished in 1853 and the land was developed as a residential neighbourhood (Belsize Avenue follows the line of the old estate's main drive). The arrival of the UNDERGROUND'S NORTHERN LINE in 1907 encouraged further building and by the early twentieth century the area was absorbed within the metropolis. In the 1930s, it earned a reputation as a centre for the arts, primarily through the influence of the artist Ben Nicholson and sculptors Barbara Hepworth and Henry Moore, who worked at Mall Studios in Belsize Place. When London's local government was reorganized in 1965, Belsize Park became part of the LONDON BOROUGH OF CAMDEN.

BERKELEY SQUARE

Lying in the heart of MAYFAIR, the square takes its name from Lord Berkeley of Stratton, a supporter of Charles II who acquired land to the north of PICCADILLY after the English monarchy was restored in 1660. It was laid out from 1739 as a quadrilateral, rather than a square, preserving the views from Berkeley House, which had been built seventy years earlier. During the twentieth century, however, the architectural integrity of the Georgian development was destroyed. The buildings on the east side were removed and replaced by a car showroom. The gardens of Lansdowne House, to the south, are now an office block, and much of the north side is also commercial accommodation. A glimpse of the original setting is gained only in the west (where No. 44 was described by architectural historian Nikolaus Pevsner as 'the best terraced house of London) and in the centre, which is dominated by thirty fine LONDON PLANE trees planted in 1789. There is no recent record of a nightingale's song.

BERMONDSEY

Bermondsey forms the northern part of the LONDON BOROUGH OF SOUTHWARK, stretching along the banks of the RIVER THAMES from LONDON BRIDGE (in the west) to ROTHERHITHE (in the east). Settlement began in 1082, when

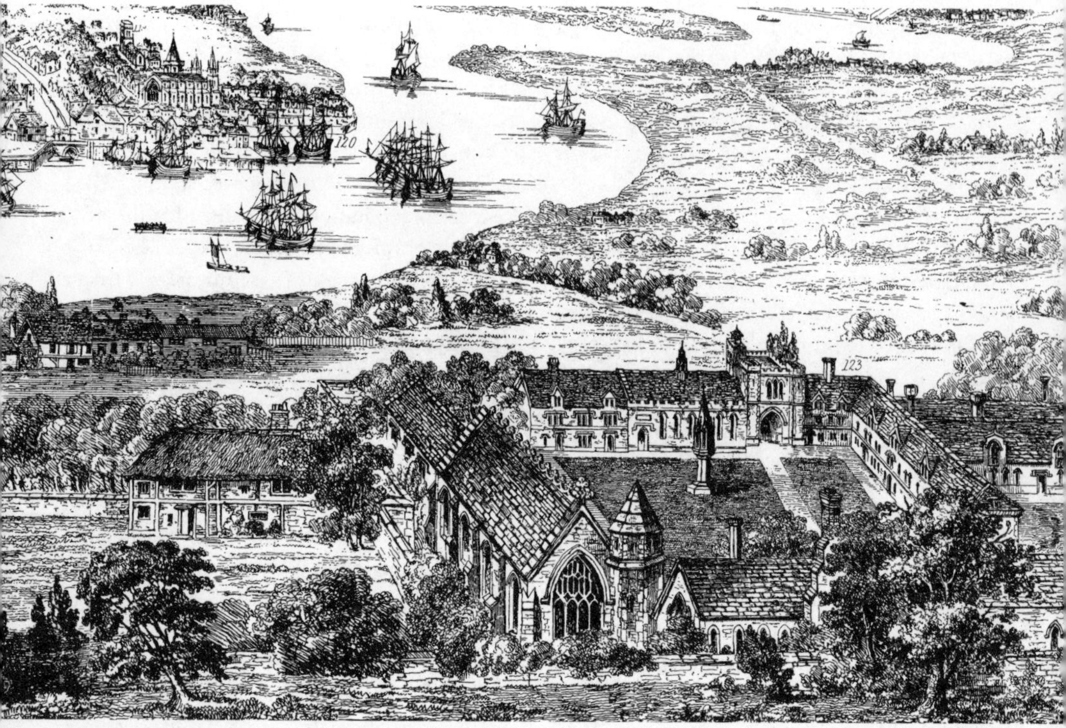

View of Bermondsey monastery in 1543.

a priory, dedicated to St Saviour, was founded amidst the marshlands. The Cluniac monks built embankments to prevent the river from flooding, grew crops on the reclaimed land, established a monastic school, and cared for the needy, so, by 1536, when Henry VIII began to close the English MONASTERIES, a sizeable community had developed. During the seventeenth century, pleasure gardens were laid out, then, in 1770, the discovery of a chalybeate spring with allegedly health-giving properties led to the development of a spa, but, within half a century, the area was totally transformed by the growing DOCK trade, which converted it into a warren of industrial premises, including BREWERIES, warehouses and manufacturers of leather goods. In 1836, the first RAILWAY line in the metropolis opened, running from Bermondsey to DEPTFORD on a 4-mile viaduct with 878 arches. A branch to CROYDON was completed three years later, emphasizing the district's importance as a transport focus. After the Second World War, however, the harbour activities declined, allowing public and private concerns to initiate major land use changes, with offices, retail facilities and housing replacing the nineteenth-century slums. The modern complex – known as London Bridge City – incorporates Hay's Wharf, the oldest in the POOL OF LONDON, where the dock has been filled in, creating a piazza that is covered by a glass roof and lined with restaurants, specialty stores and wine bars. A pier has been built to facilitate passenger transport along the river, and HMS *BELFAST* and the LONDON DUNGEON provide foci for tourists. The name of the area probably means 'Beormund's island' and is derived from the personal name and the Old English *eglond*. (See also TOWER BRIDGE.)

BETHLEHEM ROYAL HOSPITAL

See BEDLAM.

BETHNAL GREEN

Bethnal Green is the archetypal EAST END suburb – working class, with a high proportion of local authority housing and heavy dependence on social services. At the beginning of the eighteenth century, it was largely agricultural land, but the growth of the textile industry (expanding from its base in SPITALFIELDS) initiated a process of urbanization, so by 1743 there was an estimated population of 15,000 weavers, dyers and their families. Incomes were low (after a visit in 1777, John Wesley, founder of the Methodist faith with his brother Charles, wrote of 'such poverty as few can conceive without seeing it'). As a result, the declining demand for silk from about 1840 caused much distress, leading CHARLES BOOTH to allege, in 1889, that 45 per cent of the inhabitants were living in circumstances below subsistence level. Victorian philanthropists attempted to alleviate the worst effects by building blocks of apartments that could be let at affordable rents, providing educational facilities (see, for example, BETHNAL GREEN MUSEUM OF CHILDHOOD) and introducing recreational facilities, such as VICTORIA PARK. Major improvement, however, did not begin until the LONDON COUNTY COUNCIL initiated a slum clearance project shortly after its creation in 1888, beginning with the construction of the Boundary Street Estate in the area known as Old Nichol, which was notorious for both its high CRIME rate and its poor living conditions. Over the next century, local authority building programmes replaced the substandard nineteenth-century properties and the population declined as residents were moved to new homes on the outskirts of the city. Since the 1970s, there has been a process of gentrification, as the older properties that remain have been improved and purchased by young people or by others looking for relatively inexpensive accommodation close to central London. Bethnal Green is now part of the LONDON BOROUGH OF TOWER HAMLETS, but incomes are still low, so family spending power is limited and retail services reflect the lack of wealth. Some authorities claim that the area's name is derived from *Blitha*, an Anglo-Saxon personal name, and the Old English *halh*, meaning 'a nook of land'. Others claim that it may be derived from *Blithe*, a stream name from the same period, which means 'the gentle one'. (See also AIR RAIDS; CENTRAL LINE; DANCE, GEORGE (1700–68).)

BETHNAL GREEN MUSEUM OF CHILDHOOD

The museum – one of the largest of its kind in the world – contains model trains, dolls (some straight from the box, others clearly much loved), dolls' houses (the earliest dating from 1673), teddy bears and some 4,000 other playthings. In addition, there are displays focusing on changing fashions in children's clothes, books (there are over 100,000 examples) and educational toys. The exhibits (which form part of the VICTORIA AND ALBERT MUSEUM's collections) are housed in a prefabricated iron structure originally erected at south KENSINGTON in 1856 but moved to the EAST END a decade later and clothed in brick. For the next century, its galleries emphasized agricultural products and art works but, since 1974, it has concentrated solely on aspects of childhood. (See also BETHNAL GREEN.)

BEXLEY, LONDON BOROUGH OF

When local government within the metropolitan area was reorganized in 1965, Bexley was created from the formerly independent boroughs of Bexley and ERITH, along with CRAYFORD and parts of Chislehurst and Sidcup, all of which were previously in the County of Kent. Covering 23 square miles, it had a population of some 218,300 in 2001. The north of the borough, fronting the RIVER THAMES, is dominated by industrial sites and the large THAMESMEAD housing development, which was built on reclaimed marshland from 1967 and planned by the GREATER LONDON COUNCIL as an integrated community with schools, shops and businesses, as well as homes. Crayford, too, has a large working-class community, with chemical works and plastics factories forming an important element of the local economy, but the rest of the borough is relatively affluent, with large numbers of professional workers and high rates of home ownership. Major road and RAILWAY links from central London to the Kent coast connect the east and west of the borough but transport from north to south is slower, limiting communication.

BIG BANG

In the autumn of 1986, a series of reforms radically altered the operation and structure of financial institutions in the CITY OF LONDON. For some time, the City had been experiencing a relative decline in its securities trade compared with New York and Tokyo. Moreover, Margaret Thatcher's government was concerned that restrictive practices in the major money markets and computerized dealing was threatening the tradition of face-to-face transactions on the STOCK EXCHANGE. The Financial Services Act of 1986 introduced legislation that altered the United Kingdom's system of regulating investment business, increasing competition and allowing foreign interests greater access to British commerce. Although many of the new ways of working were introduced gradually, most became effective from 27 October. On that date, the Stock Exchange converted to electronic dealing from the offices of member firms, which, for the first time, could be owned by outside corporations, enabling them to build a larger capital base. Fixed-rate commissions were abolished (thus enabling dealers to compete with one another), the distinction between brokers (who bought and sold shares on behalf of clients) and jobbers (who acted as middlemen between brokers) ended and banks were permitted to buy stock-broking firms. The impact on employees' duties and lifestyles was considerable, but, for the firms and their customers, the overall effect was beneficial. The market expanded smoothly, average commissions lowered and securities firms were considerably strengthened by an influx of funds. As a result, by the mid-1990s, London was clearly the major centre of European investment banking, although many of its major institutions were wholly, or partly, controlled from abroad.

BIG BEN

Although the nickname 'Big Ben' is usually given to the 320-foot-high clock tower at the eastern end of the PALACE OF WESTMINSTER, it is more properly applied to the 13.5-ton bell that is housed inside the tower. The clock, designed by E.J. Dent and completed in 1854, has a six-hundredweight pendulum regulated by an escape wheel weighing just one-quarter of an ounce. Each of the four dials is 23 feet in diameter, with figures 2 feet high. The hour hands are 9 feet long and the minute hands 14 feet long. The bell, cast at WHITECHAPEL in 1858 after an earlier attempt by Warner of Stockton-on-Tees had proved unsatisfactory, is decorated with the Royal Arms and the Portcullis of Westminster. An inscription around the rim reads, 'This bell was cast by George Mears of Whitechapel for the clock of the HOUSES OF PARLIAMENT under the Direction of Edmund Becket Denison QC in the 21st year of the reign of Queen Victoria in the year of our Lord MDCCCLVIII.' There is some controversy about the means by which it got its name. Some writers claim that, during a debate on the naming of the bell in the HOUSE OF COMMONS, Sir Benjamin Hall (Chief Commissioner for Works) was speaking when an MP shouted out, 'Why not call it Big Ben?' The story is attractive but, unfortunately, there is no corroborating evidence in *Hansard,* the official record of Parliamentary proceedings. A second theory suggests that it is named after the 250-pound prize fighter Benjamin Caunt, who retired at the time the bell was being made.

The clock was started on 31 May 1859, but the bell developed a crack after only a few months and had to be fitted with a smaller hammer. Automatic winding gear was installed in 1913 (until then, it took two men thirty-two hours to wind it manually) and the operating mechanism was overhauled in 1956, when three of the faces were re-glazed. It has proved remarkably accurate; even the AIR RAID that destroyed much of the Parliament building on 10 May 1941 knocked it awry by only one and a half seconds.

BIGGIN HILL

Located on the south-east fringe of London, about 15 miles from CHARING CROSS, Biggin Hill is an indirect result of the invention of the airplane. During the first decade of the twentieth century, there was little urban development in the area, so John Westacott, a local farmer, allowed pilots to land aircraft on one of his fields. However, when the First World War began, the strip was commandeered for emergency landings, a wireless testing station was built and courses in telegraphy were established. As a result, the strategic importance of the aerodrome was enhanced, necessitating improved road access and housing for employees. Further expansion was undertaken in the 1920s, causing the settlement to increase both in extent and in population, but, although Royal Air Force Spitfires and Hurricanes based at Biggin Hill played a prominent role in the Battle of Britain (1940), most of the planes left after the Second World War ended in 1945. The aerodrome still operates, primarily for private flights, although there are some scheduled services to France, and the community (now housing many commuters who work in central London) has experienced significant growth as a result of public and private investment since the 1950s. The settlement's name may be derived from the Middle English *bygging* (which means 'a building') and the Old English *hyll* ('hill'). (See also AIRPORTS.)

BILLINGSGATE FISH MARKET

In the early ninth century, fishing boats were tied up at the Billingsgate quays, on the north bank of the RIVER THAMES just downstream from LONDON BRIDGE, and captains sold their catch on the street. More than a millennium later, despite the importance of the market, facilities amounted to little more than a series of sheds, where wholesalers and retailers could inspect the fish and strike deals. However, growing sales, fuelled by rapidly increasing

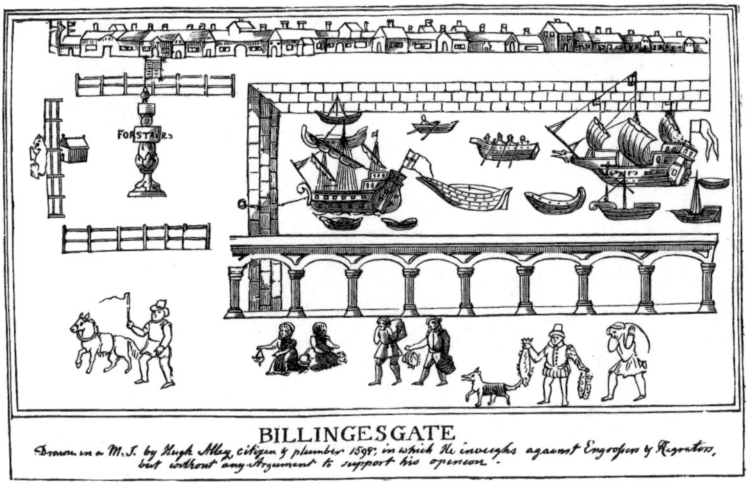

Billingsgate, *c.* 1598.

urban populations, required better premises so, in 1877, the CORPORATION OF LONDON opened a trading hall (designed by Horace Jones) on the site. It was never satisfactory. During the twentieth century, commercial conditions became increasingly difficult because the large refrigerated lorries that took the fish throughout Britain had problems negotiating the confined streets in the CITY OF LONDON, closely packed buildings made expansion of parking space impossible, the pervasive smell annoyed owners of nearby businesses, and the colourful language of the porters offended many workers commuting to the finance houses in the SQUARE MILE. As a result, in January 1982 the market was moved to a 13.5-acre site on the ISLE OF DOGS and the old brick building, with its arcades of cast-iron pillars, was bought by the London and Edinburgh Investment Trust for conversion into offices. The market has been open to visitors, as well as commercial interests, since 1698, when an Act of Parliament put an end to control of sales by a small group of retailers. Its name is said to derive from Beling, a king of the Britons. Beling's Gate was the entry to a DOCK alongside the Thames. When he died, his ashes were placed in an urn at the entrance.

BIRDCAGE WALK

With buildings on one side only, Birdcage Walk runs along the southern edge of ST JAMES'S PARK in central London, getting its name from the aviaries that James I maintained on the site. Until 1828, the only person, apart from members of the royal family, who could use the street was the Duke of St Albans, Hereditary Grand Falconer to the monarch. Much of the southern side is occupied by Wellington Barracks (home of the Foot Guards); the remainder is largely garden space at the rear of the eighteenth-century houses in Queen Anne's Gate. (See also CHANGING OF THE GUARD.)

BISHOP'S GATE

One of the northern entrances to the Roman city of LONDINIUM, Bishop's Gate was the

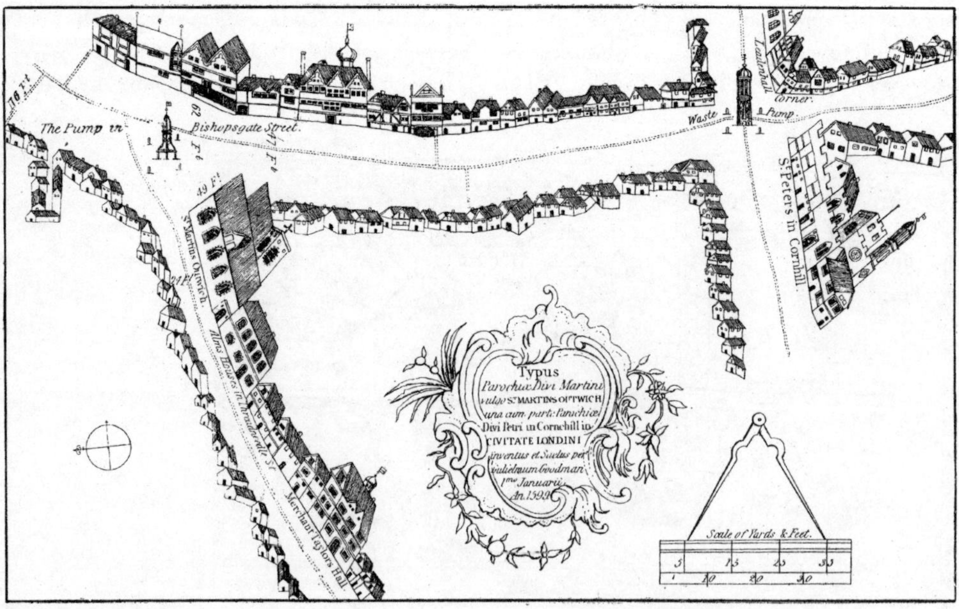

Bishopsgate, 1599.

point at which Ermine Street, one of the invaders' principal routes to their British frontier, left the settlement. It stood where the modern road that bears its name meets Camomile Street, just south of LIVERPOOL STREET STATION, and gets its appellation from Eorconweald, Bishop of London, who rebuilt it during the seventh century. In the fifteenth and sixteenth centuries, the area around the gate was a fashionable neighbourhood for wealthy merchants, but the structure was demolished in 1760 and the traders' homes were replaced, over the next 200 years, by offices and shops. (See also LONDON WALL.)

BLACK DEATH

From 1347 until 1351, much of Europe was ravaged by an epidemic of bubonic plague, which took a toll of life greater than that in any previous outbreak of disease (or war) on the Continent. The illness was caused by a bacillus (*Yersinia pestis*) carried in the bloodstream of rats. Fleas that fed on the rats transferred the infection to humans, who suffered swellings (known as buboes), fever, thirst, haemorrhages and delirium before dying. The plague reached London during the late summer of 1348 and spread rapidly through the city's overcrowded, densely packed homes, where sanitation was primitive. In January 1349, meetings of Parliament were cancelled because of the danger that members would fall ill, and by February the burial grounds were full. However, from the middle of the year, mortality levels decreased and, by the early 1350s, the epidemic had run its course (though there were recurrences in 1361 and 1368–9). Scholars have produced varying estimates of the death toll, with figures ranging from 50,000 to 100,000 people (as much as half of the city's total population); in many cases, whole families were wiped out, along with many members of religious foundations who had tried to help the sick (all but one of the monks and nuns in the Hospital of St James died, for example, as did the abbot and twenty-seven monks at the Monastery of Westminster). The impact of the disease was profound, affecting labour supply, wage structures and food availability as well as the demography of the population. (See also GREAT PLAGUE; HAMPSTEAD; PEASANTS' REVOLT.)

BLACKFRIARS

The Blackfriars area of the CITY OF LONDON, lying about a mile east of CHARING CROSS, takes its name from the Dominican monks who, in 1221, established a MONASTERY in Shoe Lane. For more than three centuries, the settlement benefited from the patronage of royalty and, frequently, was the setting for events that shaped the history of England (Parliament met there in 1311, 1450 and 1529, for example, and, in 1382, a council summoned by the Archbishop of Canterbury convened at Blackfriars to consider the allegedly heretical teachings of John Wycliffe, who had argued that there was no biblical basis for the Pope's authority over the Roman Catholic Church). In 1538, however, the monastry was dissolved during Henry VIII's campaign to establish a Church of England free of Catholic influences and most of the buildings were demolished. (Part of the site is now occupied by an art nouveau-style PUBLIC HOUSE – the Black Friar – which was built in 1875; the bars are decorated with marble and with bronze figures of the monks at work). In 1577, a THEATRE opened in Playhouse Yard, attracting the city's literati, so, by the early seventeenth century, the area had acquired a reputation as a fashionable place to live (BEN JONSON and WILLIAM SHAKESPEARE had homes there, as did the artist Anthony van Dyke).

Puritan zealots, more Calvinist and less tolerant of lax lifestyles, put an end to the entertainments in 1642, initiating a lengthy period during which industrial and commercial activities increasingly dominated residential uses (in *David Copperfield*, published in 1850, CHARLES DICKENS describes the miserable conditions in which boys washed and labelled bottles in a Victorian warehouse in

The building of Blackfriars Bridge, July 1766.

Blackfriars). Those land uses, in turn, attracted growing amounts of traffic and led to the evolution of a significant route focus. In 1760, work started on a BRIDGE, only the third to link the north and south banks of the river thames in the immediate vicinity of London. It opened to traffic in 1769 but was replaced exactly a century later by the present wrought iron structure, faced with cast iron and standing on piers of Aberdeen granite, which was designed by Joseph Cubitt. In 1864, a wrought-iron RAILWAY bridge carried the London, Chatham and Dover Company's lines across the river to meet the Metropolitan Railway at Blackfriars. A second was built a few yards downriver for the Holborn Viaduct Station Company in 1886 and a terminus, originally known as St Paul's but renamed Blackfriars in 1937, was opened by the London, Chatham and Dover the same year and substantially remodelled in 1977. In 1982 Papal banker Roberto Calvi hanged himself from the road bridge during the financial scandals that followed the death of Pope John Paul I four years earlier. Doubt has always surrounded the initial verdict of suicide and, in light of further evidence, British police opened a murder enquiry in September 2003. (See also PRINTING HOUSE SQUARE; RENNIE, JOHN; *TIMES, THE*.)

BLACKHEATH

Lying south of GREENWICH PARK, Blackheath straddles the main road from London to the cathedral city of Canterbury and the port of Dover. It derives its name either from the colour of the soil or from a corruption of *bleak heath*. Because of its strategic location, it has a long history of settlement and of involvement in national affairs; the Romans and the Saxons built bases in the area, the Danes had an encampment during the early eleventh century, Wat Tyler assembled his supporters there at the start of the PEASANTS' REVOLT, Henry VIII welcomed Anne of Cleves (his fourth wife) to England at the heath in 1540, England's first golf club was formed on the heath in 1608 (after James I had brought the sport from Scotland five years earlier), Charles II was hailed when he returned from the

Continent at the end of the period of Commonwealth rule in 1660, and John Wesley held many of his Methodist meetings here during the seventeenth century. Blackheath Football Club (the oldest public Rugby Union club in London) was formed in 1858. Urban development did not really begin until the RAILWAY arrived in 1849 and was primarily residential in nature, with wealthy Victorians acquiring large houses for their families and servants close to the open space and woodland. Schools, a Literary Institution, a roller skating rink, a concert hall and other social facilities followed, promoted by an educated population willing to support community growth. During the twentieth century many of the bigger homes have been converted into flats, but the area has retained its reputation as a relatively affluent suburb, with local interest groups (such as the Blackheath Preservation Trust) providing effective lobbies for the conservation both of the heath and of the buildings that surround it. The suburb is part of the LONDON BOROUGH OF GREENWICH. (See also LONDON MARATHON.)

BLACKWALL

A district of the LONDON BOROUGH OF TOWER HAMLETS, Blackwall is located on the north bank of the RIVER THAMES some 5 miles east of CHARING CROSS. A harbour was established by the late sixteenth century, proving popular because it afforded easy road access to the CITY OF LONDON, allowing travellers to avoid the lengthy journey around the ISLE OF DOGS in a sailing vessel. In 1606, the Virginia Settlers (led by Captain John Smith) left the port to found the first permanent English colony in North America; in 1661, the EAST INDIA COMPANY established a small wet DOCK (the first with gates to the Thames) to refit its fleet of trading vessels; and, in 1841, a RAILWAY augmented traffic by carrying passengers from London to the new steamer berths. In 1897, a 4,000-foot-long tunnel was opened under the river, connecting Blackwall to the SOUTH BANK (seventy years later, a counterpart was built a few yards downstream so that north-bound and south-bound traffic could be separated), then, during the last two decades of the twentieth century, road access was further improved. However, the passenger pier was removed in 1956 to make way for an ELECTRICITY generating station (demolished in 1991), and the docks were closed in 1980. The people who live in the area are almost entirely manual workers, although a few employees from Reuters news agency and other offices located nearby in the Isle of Dogs have found homes close to their work.

BLITZ

From 7 September 1940 until 11 May 1941, an estimated 18,800 tons of explosive were dropped on London by German bombers. According to conservative estimates, over 15,000 people were killed and 3.5 million homes damaged during the attacks, which became known as the Blitz. Some historians suggest that the number of deaths was closer to 30,000. The areas worst affected were industrial sectors of the city (such as the EAST END and the DOCKS), transport nodes and locations that had a psychological significance to the British people (including BUCKINGHAM PALACE, which was hit on the night of 15–16 October).

Many children were evacuated to temporary homes in the countryside for the duration of the raids. At the sound of the sirens that signalled the start of an attack, those who stayed behind took refuge in communal shelters or in the LONDON UNDERGROUND system. For most of the time, they were safe, but occasionally bombs penetrated the defences with devastating effect, as at Bank station in January 1941, when more than 100 people died. The economic and social impact of the bombing was enormous, with gas and ELECTRICITY supplies disrupted, transport services at a standstill, offices demolished and industrial premises destroyed, but the common experience bound

Londoners together, promoting a sense of unity that helped to overcome the disasters. In 1999, the Queen Mother unveiled a memorial in the churchyard of ST PAUL'S CATHEDRAL in honour of civilians who died in the Blitz (when the bomb struck Buckingham Palace, she responded with a comment that at least now she could look the East End in the face). (See also ABERCROMBIE PLAN (1943–44); AIR RAIDS; ALDWYCH; BALHAM; BARBICAN; BIG BEN; BLACKFRIARS; BRITISH BROADCASTING CORPORATION (BBC); CANNON STREET STATION; CHARTERHOUSE; CHELSEA; CHURCHILL, WINSTON SPENCER; CLEOPATRA'S NEEDLE; COLE ABBEY CHURCH, DISTAFF LANE; CORN EXCHANGE; CRAYFORD; CROYDON; DEPTFORD; ELEPHANT AND CASTLE; GREYFRIARS MONASTERY; GUILDHALL; HOLLAND HOUSE; HOXTON; IMPERIAL WAR MUSEUM; KNIGHTS HOSPITALLER; LANGHAM HOTEL; LEYTON; MADAME TUSSAUD'S WAXWORKS; MILE END; PALACE OF WESTMINSTER; PROMS, THE; PUGIN, AUGUSTUS WELBY NORTHMORE; ST ALFEGE'S CHURCH, GREENWICH; ST ANDREW'S CHURCH, HOLBORN; ST BRIDE'S CHURCH, FLEET STREET; ST CLEMENT DANES CHURCH, STRAND; ST ETHELDREDA'S CHURCH, HOLBORN; ST JAMES'S CHURCH, PICCADILLY; ST MARY ABCHURCH CHURCH; ST OLAVE'S CHURCH, HART STREET; SHAFTSBURY AVENUE; SHEPHERD'S BUSH; STEPNEY; STOCKWELL; TEMPLE CHURCH; WALWORTH; WATERLOO.)

BLOOMSBURY

In 1545, Thomas Wriothesley, Lord Chancellor of England, purchased the Manor of Blemonsbury (located just outside the western walls of the CITY OF LONDON). His descendant – the fourth Earl of Southampton – rebuilt the manor house in 1660, then laid out a square (now known as Bloomsbury Square) to the south. Gradually, the urban area spread as other large properties were constructed nearby. Bloomsbury became a fashionable place in which to establish a home, with access to the court and business community but also with views of the countryside. By the early eighteenth century, the land had been acquired by the Russell family, who also owned COVENT GARDEN and had an entrepreneurial approach to its estates. Wide routeways (such as Great Russell Street, Bedford Square and Gower Street) were constructed and lined with homes for the wealthy, but narrower roads, with smaller houses, provided links between them, attracting writers, musi-

A 1787 engraving of Bloomsbury Square.

cians and artists who enjoyed the sense of intimacy (see, for example, BLOOMSBURY GROUP). Lawyers, too, were attracted to the area because of its proximity to the INNS OF COURT. However, the BRITISH MUSEUM was established in Montague House in 1759, the buildings of University College began to rise above Gower Street in 1827 and Bedford College opened its doors to women students in 1849. The gradual encroachment of institutions encouraged most affluent residents to seek homes elsewhere, leaving their houses to be converted into small HOTELS, restaurants, bookshops and educational facilities. During the twentieth century, many of the Georgian buildings were demolished to make way for purpose-built academic premises, so the ARCHITECTURE of Bloomsbury is an often ill-matched mixture of styles. (See also BEDFORD ESTATES; PUGIN, AUGUSTUS WELBY NORTHMORE; RUSSELL SQUARE.)

BLOOMSBURY GROUP

In 1904, the Stephen family – Vanessa (who married art critic Clive Bell), Thoby, Virginia (who married socialist writer Leonard Woolf) and Adrian – moved into 46 Gordon Square, BLOOMSBURY. They became the core of a group of artists, authors and others who earned a reputation for their bohemian lifestyle and radical approach to philosophical issues. The underlying ethic, outlined by G.E. Moore, was that 'by far the most valuable things … are … the pleasures of human intercourse and the enjoyment of beautiful objects … It is they … that form the rational ultimate end of social progress.' Members of the clique (most of whom had studied at Cambridge University) included novelist E.M. Forster, biographer Lytton Strachey, economist John Maynard Keynes and artist Duncan Grant. For a quarter of a century, they met to discuss agnosticism, the nature of beauty and other philosophical issues but, by the 1930s, they had merged with London's literary mainstream and lost their identity. The Bloomsberries, as they were nicknamed, did not form a distinct school but were significant because of the high number of richly talented individuals involved.

BLUE PLAQUES

Many London buildings bear a blue plaque, erected to commemorate some significant individual or event associated with the property. The first, mounted by the Society for the Encouragement of Arts, Manufactures and Commerce (see ROYAL SOCIETY OF ARTS) to honour poet Lord Byron, appeared in 1866, but English Heritage (funded by the government) now assumes responsibility for their erection. About 400 individuals have been deemed worthy of recognition, including inventor John Logie Baird (who first demonstrated television transmissions at 22 Frith Street), CHARLES DICKENS (who lived at 48 Doughty Street), ISAMBARD KINGDOM BRUNEL (who lived at 98 Cheyne Walk, CHELSEA) and WINSTON CHURCHILL (whose home was at 28 HYDE PARK Gate). In 1971, the GREATER LONDON COUNCIL approved recognition of foreigners, allowing plaques to be placed on 28 Dean Street and 23 Tedworth Square, the houses of Karl Marx and Mark Twain respectively. The only criteria for commemoration are that an individual must have been dead for twenty years and that the building must still exist but, even so, the names on the 800 plaques are dominated by those of politicians and writers.

BOADICEA

Boadicea (or Boudicca) was Queen of the Celtic Iceni tribe, which occupied much of East Anglia during the first century AD. When her husband, King Prasutagas, died in AD 60, he left part of his estate to Nero, the Roman emperor, hoping that the bequest to his imperial master would ensure protection for his family. That gesture was in vain because the Romans publicly flogged Boadicea and raped her two daughters, provoking a revolt. The

Iceni pillaged the countryside and marched on LONDINIUM, from which Suetonius Paullinus, the governor, withdrew his armies in the face of overwhelming numbers, leaving the settlement and its residents to their fate. Wreaking revenge for her humiliation, Boadicea led her people on an unrestrained rampage, killing 30,000 citizens and burning the city (modern archaeologists have identified a layer of reddish soil, over a foot thick, which consists of debris from the fires). The victory celebrations were short-lived, however. Gathering his forces, Suetonius pursued Boadicea northwards and, at an as yet unidentified site named Mandessum, destroyed 80,000 of her followers in battle. According to Tacitus, the Roman historian, Boadicea poisoned herself rather than submit to the enemy. A bronze of the queen, standing in a chariot, her daughters beside her, was cast by Thomas Thorneycroft and erected at the north end of WESTMINSTER BRIDGE in 1902.

BOAT RACES

See DOGGETT'S COAT AND BADGE RACE; UNIVERSITY BOAT RACE.

BOND STREET

Housing some of the most expensive shops in London, Bond Street crosses MAYFAIR from north to south. Old Bond Street, between PICCADILLY and Burlington Gardens, was developed during the late seventeenth century as a speculative development funded largely by Sir Thomas Bond, from whom it gets its name. The rest of the street (known as New Bond Street) was built while London was experiencing a period of considerable westward expansion in the 1720s. Mayfair's growing population attracted jewellers, art dealers, auctioneers, hosiers, tobacconists and a chocolatier, all selling luxury goods to an affluent clientele, as well as such distinguished residents as essayist JAMES BOSWELL, Emma Hamilton (Horatio Nelson's mistress) and Victorian actor Sir Henry Irving. Much rebuilding and reconstruction has taken place during the twentieth century, but the narrow road has retained its fashionable status with Asprey's (founded in 1781) selling gold and silver at 165–166 New Bond Street, the Fine Arts Society (established in 1876) specializing in British paintings at 147 New Bond Street, H.M. Rayne (in business since 1889) offering handcrafted shoes at 16 Old Bond Street, and Truefitt and Hill (wigmakers to George IV) cutting gentlemen's hair at 23 Old Bond Street.

BOODLE'S

Founded as an apolitical GENTLEMEN'S CLUB by Edward Boodle in 1762, Boodle's now has a membership consisting largely of non-Londoners who visit the city on business. Its first premises were in PALL MALL but, in 1783, it moved to its present premises in St James's Street. Members have included dandy Beau Brummell, anti-slavery campaigner William Wilberforce and Prime Ministers William Pitt the Elder and William Pitt the Younger. (See also WHITE'S.)

BOOTH, CHARLES (1840–1916)

During the second half of the nineteenth century, writers and political activists voiced growing concern about the condition of London's poor (see, for example, THOMAS JOHN BARNARDO, WILLIAM BOOTH and GEORGE PEABODY). The force of their arguments was given added strength by the work of Charles Booth, who combined detailed observation with sound statistical methodology to present a depressing picture of the living conditions of the city's most destitute residents. Booth was born in Liverpool on 30 March 1840, the third son of corn merchant Charles Booth and Emily (his first wife). He was educated at the Royal Institution School then, in 1862, joined Alfred, his eldest brother, as a partner in a steamship company. Over the next fifty years, his business affairs flourished, giving him both the wealth and the time to pursue an interest in the impact of the Industrial Revolution on the British labour force. Although opposed to socialism because it implied that commercial transactions would not be 'tried in the court of profit and loss,' he was deeply concerned about the welfare of his employees, so, during the 1880s, he began a study of people in the DOCK area of London's EAST END.

The fruits of Booth's efforts were the seventeen volumes of *Life and Labour of the People in London*, which were published between 1889 and 1903. Relying partly on visits to deprived communities, partly on official data and partly on information from charitable organizations, he attempted to demonstrate 'the numerical relation which poverty, misery and depravity bear to regular earnings and comparative comfort,' using a series of coloured maps to show the extent of poverty street by street. The work was essentially descriptive, making little attempt to identify the causes of poverty or to advance an agenda for reform, but its detail provided fuel for proponents of change, such as Beatrice Webb (a cousin of Booth's wife, Mary). His scientific contributions were rewarded with the presidency of the Royal Statistical Society (1892–4) and a Fellowship of the ROYAL SOCIETY (1899). Also, he was made a Privy Councillor in 1904 and appointed to the Royal Commission on the Poor Law in 1905 (becoming a strong advocate of the introduction of pensions for the elderly). Booth died at his home in Whitwick (near Leicester) on 23 November 1916.

BOOTH, WILLIAM (1829–1912)

During the second half of the nineteenth century, several social reformers were attempting to improve the standard of living of London's poor (see, for example, THOMAS JOHN BARNARDO and GEORGE PEABODY). Booth was one of that group, motivated by Christian principles to alter social and moral conditions through the foundation of a Salvation Army. Born in Nottingham on 10 April 1829, the only son of an unsuccessful pawnbroker, he received little schooling but was much affected by the oratory of Methodist preachers who delivered sermons in local halls and chapels. In 1844, he committed himself to the Christian faith and, two years later (still only seventeen years old), began to organize services. His religious activities brought no financial reward so, in 1849, he moved to London, where he found a job at a WALWORTH pawnshop. Booth hated the work, arguing that it exploited those people least able to help themselves, but he used the income to support his mother and sisters and his free time to study for the ministry. In 1855, he married Catherine Mumford, who persuaded him to become an itinerant evangelist. Working from a base in WHITECHAPEL, where he established a mission in 1865, he held tent meetings in an attempt to reach the 'unchurched' masses. The success of his fiery oratory forced him to create an administrative structure for his growing band of volunteers, whom, in 1878, he described as a Salvation Army (a phrase that became popular and led – despite Booth's objections – to the adoption of military titles for the leadership and a distinctive uniform for members). Recruits were ridiculed, assaulted and jailed for preaching their Gospel but appeared to meet a genuine need.

In 1890, along with W.T. Stead (a campaigning journalist), Booth published *In Darkest England and the Way Out* – a radical agenda for social reform that advocated programmes of house building, provision of training centres for the unemployed, introduction of legal aid for the poor, construction of residential accommodation for abused women and other measures that gained widespread public acceptance. Other countries provided similar support and so, by the end of the century, the movement was international, expanding from London's EAST END to the European mainland, the United States, Australia and South Africa.

Despite his campaign for change, Booth was, in many ways, an unremitting Conservative; he had a narrow set of religious convictions, condemned the acquisition of wealth (although he cultivated the acquaintance of gamblers and millionaires in order to obtain funds for his missionary work), fulminated against study of the sciences and opposed sports such as cricket. But he was a highly gifted orator, who was deeply affected by the degradation in which many of London's children were forced to live, and he was instrumental in altering attitudes towards the poor.

Towards the end of his life, he was much affected by family dissension over the way the Salvation Army was run and by his declining eyesight, but he received many accolades, including an invitation to the coronation of Edward VII in 1902. He died in London on 20 August 1912, handing over the organizational reins to his son, Bramwell. The Army's Whitechapel headquarters was destroyed by German bombs in 1941 but replaced, twenty-two years later, by a purpose-built building in Queen Victoria Street (in the CITY OF LONDON). It also has training bases in south London, at DENMARK HILL and Sydenham Hill, and co-ordinates work in over ninety countries around the world. (See also BURIAL GROUNDS).

BOROUGH MARKET

Some researchers have suggested that the Borough Market in the LONDON BOROUGH OF SOUTHWARK is the oldest fruit and vegetable market in the city. A map of 1542 shows it was established by that time and documents dating from 1671 confirm its trading boundary. In 1754, it was causing such traffic congestion that it was moved from Borough High Street to its present location in Stoney Street, near SOUTHWARK CATHEDRAL. (See also MARKETS; STREET MARKETS.)

BOSWELL, JAMES (1740–1795)

Boswell's *Life of SAMUEL JOHNSON, LL.D.*, published in 1791, provides scholars with a colourful picture of manners and personalities in late eighteenth-century London society. The son of advocate Alexander Boswell and Euphemia, his first wife, Boswell was born in Edinburgh on 29 October 1740. In 1760, after attending the Universities of Edinburgh and Glasgow (but graduating from neither), he travelled to London, eager to share in 'the happiness of the *beau monde* and the company of men of genius' (*Letters Between the Honourable Andrew Erskine and James Boswell, Esq.*, 1763). The city lived up to expectations. A sociable, high-spirited young man who enjoyed the company of ladies (and was clearly attractive to them), he spent much time drinking and womanizing, catching, in the process, gonorrhoea, which was to plague him for the rest of his life. Although under pressure from his father and friends, he was forced to go back to Edinburgh after only twelve months to attempt to qualify as a lawyer, he nursed an affection for the south that was 'as violent as the most romantic lover ever had for his mistress' (*Letters*, 1763). Returning in 1762, he found lodgings in DOWNING STREET and, on 16 May the following year, met Johnson at the COVENT GARDEN premises of the actor and bookseller Thomas Davies.

Initially, Johnson was cool but the friendship ripened and survived Boswell's exile to Utrecht, where he studied civil law in order to pacify his father, who, driven to distraction by his son's hedonistic lifestyle (which included the siring of an illegitimate son to a servant girl), had threatened to disinherit him. He studied through the winter and spring then moved on to Berlin, Geneva, Naples and Corsica before returning to Scotland, where he was admitted to the Faculty of Advocates on 26 July 1766. For the next twenty years he practised law in Edinburgh, but made regular trips south to meet Johnson and his cronies. In 1773, he was elected to The Club, a group of well-known literary figures, and spent three months travelling the west coast of Scotland with Johnson. By the end of the decade, however, he was suffering from self-doubt; an attempted entry into politics was unsuccessful, his legal practice was not flourishing as he had hoped, his debts were mounting, his wife (Margaret Montgomerie, a first cousin, whom he had married in 1769) was pregnant and ill with tuberculosis, and he believed himself susceptible to a range of diseases. He consoled himself with several women, asserting that he could 'unite little fondnesses with perfect conjugal love' (*Letters of James Boswell to the Revd W.J. Temple*, 1857), and attempted to forget the quarrels with his father by drinking 'a large quantity of strong beer' (*ibid.*).

A few months after Johnson died, on 13 December 1784, Boswell published the diary of their Scottish tour as a first instalment of a biography of his friend. *Journal of a Tour of the Hebrides, With Samuel Johnson, LL.D.* was enormously successful but made the author a laughing stock because it emphasized his weaknesses (including his vanity) without making any mention of his strengths. *The Life of Samuel Johnson, LL.D.* followed in 1791 and was similarly received; 1,200 copies sold in the twelve weeks after the two-volume work appeared, but Boswell became the target of society jokes because he lionized his friend to an absurd degree, reporting personal rebuffs without quoting rejoinders, and exuded pride in his own arrogance. Moreover, after the work appeared, he found that people became less talkative when he was around, fearing that their gossip would be reported in future publications. However, because of Boswell, Johnson's witticisms are widely known, a new standard was set for biographical writing and scholars have a rich set of descriptions of London society in the last years before the Industrial Revolution changed it utterly.

Boswell moved permanently to London in 1786 but, although called to the bar that year, failed to establish a legal practice. He was grief-stricken when his wife died in 1789 and financial difficulties added to his woes. He complained constantly of depression, was knocked down and robbed while drunk in 1793 and died at his home in Great Portland Street on 19 May 1795. For over a century it was believed that his papers were destroyed after his death, but they were found at Malahide Castle (near Dublin) during the 1920s and 1930s then acquired by Yale University, which initiated a publication programme. (See also STRAND; WESTMINSTER BRIDGE.)

BOUDICCA

See BOADICEA.

BOW

An EAST END suburb, Bow developed as a bridging point where the main road from London to Essex crossed the RIVER LEA, some 5 miles east of CHARING CROSS (the bridge looked like a bow, hence the name). Before the days of surfaced roads, goods could be more easily transported by water than by land, so a small harbour grew up at the site, allowing grain to be unloaded. Industries, such as flour milling and dye works, were established close to the port, providing the basis for a small manufacturing complex. From about 1860, the pace of that industrialization increased, with soap-makers, rubber producers and others building factories. The largest plant was erected by Bryant and May, who, in 1875, employed over 5,600 workers (most of them female) to make matches: in 1888, the 'match girls' withdrew their labour and brought production to a halt – the first British attempt to organize women in trade union activity. In 1902, the LONDON UNDERGROUND arrived, expanding horizons by providing local residents with an opportunity to commute to work in the city centre. During the twentieth century, the area experienced much redevelopment as many of the older factories closed (for example, the Bryant and May plant shut down in 1979 and was converted into flats), but the essentially working-class nature of the community has not changed. (See also LANSBURY, GEORGE.)

BOW BELLS

A COCKNEY is defined as 'a person born within the sound of Bow bells', probably because, in the fifteenth century, a curfew was rung at 9 p.m. each night on the bells of St Mary-le-Bow Church (also known as the Church of Sancta Maria de Arcubus) in CHEAPSIDE. The church was burned down during the GREAT FIRE of 1666 but rebuilt seven years later by CHRISTOPHER WREN, who modelled the new structure on the Basilica of Maxentius in Rome. In 1941, it was greatly damaged by German bombs, which destroyed the peal, but it reopened in 1962. During the Second World War, the BRITISH BROADCASTING CORPORATION (BBC) regularly broadcast the sound of Bow bells to occupied Europe in order to boost morale by assuring listeners that Britain had not succumbed to Nazi armies. (See also COURT OF ARCHES; WHITTINGTON, RICHARD 'DICK'.)

BOW STREET RUNNERS

In 1748, novelist Henry Fielding (who had trained as a barrister) was appointed magistrate at the Bow Street courts. In order to supplement the efforts of the local constables, he established a squad of six thief catchers, who, by the end of the century, were known as the Bow Street Runners. John Fielding (Henry's blind half-brother) continued to support the group after he took over the magistrate's post in 1751, but the Runners were eventually disbanded in 1839, ten years after the creation of the Metropolitan Police.

BRENT, LONDON BOROUGH OF

When London's local government was reorganized in 1965, Brent was created through the amalgamation of the formerly independent boroughs of WEMBLEY and WILLESDEN. It covers 17 square miles, had a population of some 263,500 in 2001, and takes its name from the small River Brent, which separates the two communities. Ethnically, it is one of the most diverse local authorities in the United Kingdom, with about 18 per cent of its residents from the Indian subcontinent, 10 per cent from the Caribbean, 8 per cent from Africa and 7 per cent from the Republic of Ireland. Paul Boateng, MP for Brent South, was the first non-white Cabinet minister. The south is typical of inner-city environments, with high rates of deprivation (as measured by indicators such as overcrowding and unemployment) but, farther north, the proportion of citizens in professional and managerial posts is well above the national average. Although the number of manufacturing jobs in the borough declined markedly from 1981, industry still plays a significant role in the local economy; commercial giants such as the Guinness brewing company, the Heinz food processing firm and United Biscuits provide much employment, notably at industrial estates in Alperton and PARK Royal. (See also BRONDESBURY; CRICKLEWOOD; ETHNIC GROUPS; IMMIGRANTS; KENSAL GREEN; KILBURN; NEASDEN.)

BRENTFORD

Legend has it that Julius Caesar crossed the RIVER THAMES at Brentford when he brought his Roman armies to Britain in 55 BC, but there is no evidence to support the story. The settlement developed at a point where the land route from London to the west of England crosses the River Brent some 8 miles west of CHARING CROSS. It is mentioned in records (as Breguntford) by 705 BC and, in 1016, was the site of a battle between Edmund Ironside (leader of the native forces) and Cnut (king of the invading Danes). In 1642, there was further conflict when royalist forces defeated parliamentarian troops and advanced, albeit temporarily, on London. During the nineteenth century, the settlement experienced considerable industrialization, with a GAS works built in 1821, RAILWAYS spreading their tentacles in the middle years of the period, a water pumping station opened in 1835 and a fruit and vegetable market established in 1893. During the past hundred years, these have all closed but, although many of the sites have been built over (much of the railway yard was replaced by housing and a marina, for example), the area remains rich in Victorian industrial archaeology. In particular, the water-works (located near Kew Bridge) was converted into a MUSEUM in 1975; its steam engines (which were installed in 1820, supplied west London until 1944 and never needed a replacement part) are on display, along with a working forge. (See also BRENTFORD FOOTBALL CLUB.)

BRENTFORD FOOTBALL CLUB

BRENTFORD was founded in 1889 when members of the local rowing club decided they needed some activity with which to occupy themselves during the winter (by eight votes to five, football proved more popular than RUGBY). They soon became known as 'The Bees' because some Borough Road College staff, who lived nearby, supported them with a cry of 'Buck up, Bs', a chant derived from the shouts of spectators at College games and applied to Brentford because of the initial letter in the team name. 'Bs' soon became 'Bees'.

In the 1899/1900 season, the club, supposedly amateur, was fined for paying its players so it turned professional and, three years later, moved to the Griffin PARK ground, in Braemar Road, which is still its home. Despite mediocre results, it was elected to the Third Division (South) of the Football League in 1920 then, after the arrival of Harry Curtis in 1926, became a force to be reckoned with, winning all its home games in 1929 and gaining promotion to the First Division in 1935. Income from crowds of up to 30,000 at home games was invested in improvements to the stadium but, after the Second World War, fortunes waned and by 1962 Brentford was propping up English football in the League's Fourth Division.

By 1967, QUEENS PARK RANGERS, another London club, was considering the possibility of a takeover. Adverse public reaction and an interest-free £104,000 loan from the businessman Ron Blundell secured the team's future but a shoestring budget and a pool of only fourteen players hardly guaranteed major achievements. Nevertheless, the economies allowed the club to repay the loan after only four years, and the re-establishment of a youth side in 1987 brought returns as Brentford reached the quarter finals of the FA Cup in 1988/89 then won the Third Division championship in 1991/92 and was rewarded with a place in Division One of a restructured League the following season. Relegation followed after only a year, however, and the side has played in Divisions Two and Three ever since.

BREWERIES

Brewing has a long history in London. An Association of Brewers was in existence by 1292 and, by the early fifteenth century, had become one of the LIVERY COMPANIES. The Industrial Revolution of the nineteenth century initiated a series of amalgamations and the second half of the twentieth century brought closures as new technology and the need for increased accessibility led many firms to seek sites beyond the city limits (for example, the Albion Brewery in Whitechapel Road closed in 1979 after 171 years of production, the Anchor Brewery in Mile End Road shut its gates in 1975 after 218 years and the Stag Brewery in VICTORIA was sacrificed to urban redevelopment in 1959 after 318 years). Only two big producers survive – Fuller, Smith and Turner at the Griffin Brewery in CHISWICK (where beer has been produced since the days of Elizabeth I), and Young and Company in WANDSWORTH. However, since the 1980s, there has been growth in the popularity of microbreweries – tiny producers making small amounts of beer, sometimes as an addition to running a single PUBLIC HOUSE. (See also BARNES; BERMONDSEY; SPITALFIELDS.)

BRIDEWELL

In 1515–20, Henry VIII erected a brick palace beside the River Fleet, close to BLACKFRIARS,

Bridewell Prison and the entrance to the Fleet River as they appeared in 1660.

naming it Bridewell in recognition of a nearby holy well dedicated to St Bride. The CITY OF LONDON accepted the building as a gift from Edward VI in 1553, converting it into a PRISON for people found guilty of minor offences. Most were punished by public flogging, but, given the standards of the day, treatment was relatively humane; a doctor was appointed to tend to the prisoners' medical needs in 1700 (seventy-five years before any other London prison made similar provision), straw was provided for their beds from 1788 and flogging of women was abolished in 1791. The premises were burned down by the GREAT FIRE of 1666, rebuilt the following year, closed when inmates were transferred to the new accommodation at HOLLOWAY PRISON in 1855 and demolished eight years later. The site is now occupied by an office block.

BRIDGES

London's principal bridges straddle the RIVER THAMES between KINGSTON UPON THAMES (in the west) and Dartford (in the east). LONDON BRIDGE, the first of the twenty road bridges, was erected between AD 100 and 400 and, until the eighteenth century, remained the only means of crossing the river in the immediate vicinity of the city, other than by ferry (although KINGSTON BRIDGE, 12 miles to the south-west, had been opened by 1193). WESTMINSTER BRIDGE, built in 1738–50, reflected the growth of the western edge of the settlement and was followed by others over the next two centuries. However, despite the DOCK's industrial importance, TOWER BRIDGE, which first carried traffic between the CITY OF LONDON and BERMONDSEY in 1894, was the most easterly crossing until 1991, when the Queen Elizabeth II Crossing was constructed some 20 miles downriver in an effort to alleviate congestion at the Dartford Tunnel. The eleven RAILWAY bridges were all built between 1846 and 1889 as lines spread from the city centre to the suburbs and surrounding countryside. Barnes Bridge, erected in 1846–9 for the London and

South-Western Railway, was the first, bringing services from the west into CLAPHAM JUNCTION and WATERLOO, but direct access by train to central London was not possible before the construction of the Grosvenor Bridge (also known as Victoria Bridge) by the London, Chatham and Dover Railway. Opened in 1860, it served the station at VICTORIA. There are only three Thames bridges in London designated solely for pedestrians, one (built in 1884) at Teddington, a second attached to the Hungerford Railway Bridge (which was completed in 1864) and the third (opened in 2000) linking THE CITY to BANKSIDE (see MILLENNIUM BRIDGE). London's other major bridges include the cast-iron ARCHWAY viaduct (completed in 1897) and the 1,400-foot-long HOLBORN viaduct, which crossed the valley of the River Fleet in 1869. (See also ALBERT BRIDGE; BATTERSEA BRIDGE; BAZALGETTE, JOSEPH WILLIAM; BLACKFRIARS; CANNON STREET STATION; CHELSEA BRIDGE; CHISWICK BRIDGE; HAMMERSMITH BRIDGE; KEW; LAMBETH BRIDGE; PUTNEY BRIDGE; RENNIE, JOHN (1761–1821); RICHMOND BRIDGE; SERPENTINE; SOUTHWARK BRIDGE; TWICKENHAM; VAUXHALL; WANDSWORTH BRIDGE.)

BRITISH ACADEMY

At the end of the nineteenth century, the ROYAL SOCIETY was Britain's leading association of scholars, but its activities focused very strongly on the natural sciences so, in 1902, the British Academy was founded to accommodate those whose interests lay in the humanities. Initially, meetings were held at the BRITISH MUSEUM but, in 1926, WINSTON CHURCHILL (at that time Chancellor of the Exchequer) facilitated a move to MAYFAIR's Burlington Gardens. The organization transferred to BURLINGTON HOUSE in 1968 and then to Cornwall Terrace (REGENT'S PARK) in 1982. The membership consists of up to 350 resident Fellows elected because of their distinction in the arts or social sciences (past recipients of the honour include philosopher Bertrand Russell, archaeologist Mortimer Wheeler and socialist writer Beatrice Webb). A further 250 individuals who live overseas are designated Corresponding Fellows. Much of the Academy's work is concerned with administration of schools and institutes abroad, presentation of a lecture series, awards of medals to those who have made outstanding contributions to knowledge and, through the publication of its *Proceedings*, dissemination of academic knowledge.

BRITISH BROADCASTING CORPORATION (BBC)

The BBC was founded in 1922, with Lord Reith as its first Director-General. In 1926, it became a public service corporation financed by licence fees paid by listeners. The first radio transmissions were made from Savoy Hill (near Waterloo Bridge) on 14 November 1922 but, in 1932, the organization moved to larger premises at Broadcasting House in Langham Place. Although the corporation very quickly outgrew its new home, opening ancillary studios in other parts of London and in provincial cities, Broadcasting House was identified by the British public as the heart of the BBC because of its importance as a source of information during the Second World War. As a result, it was a prime target for German attacks during the BLITZ and, on 15 October 1940, was struck by a bomb that killed seven people; undeterred, Bruce Belrage continued to read the nine o'clock news to the nation while the building disintegrated around him. The World Service, much threatened by financial cuts in recent years, broadcast from Bush House (in ALDWYCH), a 1930s building that the BBC first occupied in 1940. However, late in 2000, the corporation announced that it would vacate the property and base all its journalists at Broadcasting House. The first television programmes were transmitted from ALEXANDRA PALACE in 1936 but, in 1956, operations were transferred to a 3.5-acre site (known as Television Centre) at SHEPHERD'S BUSH. In 2000 the Centre was bombed by the Real IRA but damage was limited and only one person was injured. (See also BOW BELLS; GOLDERS GREEN; LANGHAM HOTEL; PROMS, THE.)

BRITISH EMPIRE EXHIBITION

As Britain recovered from the austere conditions of the First World War (1914–9), the government considered plans for a great exhibition that would boost morale and celebrate the glories of an empire on which the sun never set. A 219-acre site was chosen at WEMBLEY, a new sports stadium was erected as a centrepiece and hundreds of pavilions, devoted largely to industry and commerce, were built amidst flower beds and fountains to designs representing the architectural traditions of the dominions and colonies. When the event was opened on 23 April 1924, George V's speech was heard around the country on radio, the first time that a sovereign had addressed his people using the new technology. Over the next eighteen months, a total of 27,102,498 visitors viewed the exhibits. Some of the buildings survived into the late twentieth century as industrial warehouses, notably the Palace of Arts (which told the story of art over the previous 200 years) and the Palace of Industry (which displayed products as different as cotton and chemicals).

BRITISH LIBRARY

In 1973, the British Museum Library, the National Central Library and the National Lending Library for Science and Technology were merged to create a single British Library. It is divided into four units – a Reference Division (which has some 10 million printed books as well as newspapers, maps, government papers, sheets of music, stamps and other documents), a Science Reference Library (the major British repository of current scientific literature), a Lending Division (which supplies books to other institutions) and a Bibliographical Division (which prepares catalogues and other records of published material). For most of its existence, the library had had no central home, operating from various locations in London, but from 1995 its collections were moved to a site close to ST PANCRAS. Initially, the new building was intended to hold 18 million books and documents, but cost increases resulted in a scaling down of the project, so about one third of the library's stock is stored 200 miles away in Yorkshire. The brick structure itself also proved controversial. Prince Charles likened it to 'an academy for secret police,' and the architect, Colin St John Wilson, claimed that, as a result, he lost so much business he had to close his practice. (See also LIBRARIES.)

BRITISH MUSEUM

The foundations of the United Kingdom's major MUSEUM were laid by physician HANS SLOANE, who suggested that, when he died, his library and natural history collections should be purchased by the nation for £20,000, less than half their true worth. Following his death in 1753, the necessary funds were raised by a lottery, Montague House (in BLOOMSBURY) was adapted to hold the exhibits and the displays were opened to the public in 1759 (though only to those people who applied for permission in writing). Other purchases and gifts augmented the Sloane exhibits, including a collection of manuscripts amassed by Robert Harley, Earl of Oxford, and his son, Edward. George II presented books accumulated by monarchs of England since Tudor times, Sir William Hamilton's Greek vases were bought in 1782, sculptures removed from the Parthenon by Lord Elgin were added in 1816, and George III's library was donated by his son (George IV) in 1820.

As distinguished eighteenth-century figures made large donations (actor DAVID GARRICK handed over a collection of plays, for example, and Captain James Cook offered material he had brought home from his explorations of the Pacific Ocean islands), the available space dwindled and temporary structures were erected around the main galleries to display exhibits. In 1823, however, work began on a new building, designed by Robert Smirke. Initially, it had a central courtyard but, during the 1850s, that was roofed over.

The transfer of the natural history collections to south KENSINGTON in 1881 (see NATURAL HISTORY MUSEUM) and of the newspaper library to Colindale in 1904–5, the building of the Edward VII galleries in 1914, the addition of the North Library in 1937, the construction of the West Gallery (for the Parthenon sculptures) in 1938, the opening of a gallery for horological material in 1975 and the move of the BRITISH LIBRARY to ST PANCRAS from 1995 have also relieved congestion, but the museum still has much more material than it can put on display. Currently, more than 4 million exhibits are presented on the 14-acre site, including coins, medals, prints and Egyptian, Greek, Roman and Japanese antiquities. Important additions during the twentieth century included the Sutton Hoo treasure (buried in a ship on England's East Coast as a memorial to a seventh-century Anglo-Saxon ruler), a hoard of Roman silver found at Mildenhall (near Cambridge) and a Roman pavement discovered (in almost perfect condition) in Devonshire. The former British Library reading room was redesigned by architect Norman Foster and reopened as the Great Court (the largest covered square in Europe) in 2000. The following year new galleries, financed by the Sainsbury family, allowed the African exhibits to be displayed more effectively. Over 5 million people visit the museum every year. (See also LONDON LIBRARY; MUSEUM OF MANKIND.)

BRITISH TELECOM TOWER

One of London's tallest buildings, the tower, located in the city centre, west of Tottenham Court Road, rises to 620 feet above ground level (including the 40-foot mast that supports a radar aerial). Formerly known as the Post Office Tower and the London Telecom Tower, it was designed by Eric Bedford and built in 1963–6. Its primary purpose is to enable radio and television waves to travel effectively above surrounding buildings in the city centre, but it also serves as a very effective landmark. A viewing platform and revolving restaurant were closed in 1975 following a bomb incident.

BRIXTON

The Brixton area, lying some 3 miles south of CHARING CROSS, consisted largely of sparsely settled, uncultivated land until the early nineteenth century. The construction of a bridge over the RIVER THAMES at VAUXHALL proved the spur to development, improving access to the CITY OF LONDON from 1816. Initially, the buildings housed middle-class and professional families with their servants, but, after the RAILWAY arrived during the 1860s, smaller homes were constructed for less wealthy commuters and the older premises were subdivided for use as apartment blocks or lodging houses. Many of the rented rooms were acquired by MUSIC HALL entertainers and THEATRE performers, attracted by low prices, local concert rooms and easy access to the WEST END (former Prime Minister John Major, son of a trapeze artist, spent part of his childhood in Brixton). From 1948, Caribbean IMMIGRANTS began to settle in the area, initially in Somerleyton Road, close to the LONDON UNDERGROUND station. At that time, local authorities were attempting to improve the housing stock by replacing old buildings with modern structures, but, in doing so, they broke up communities, contributing to feelings of insecurity and unrest that were manifested in tension with incomers.

By the 1970s, the LONDON BOROUGH OF LAMBETH had adopted policies of housing improvement (rather than demolition and rebuilding), but continued expansion of the ethnic population contributed to the growth of a self-assertive black community with a distinctive lifestyle; many young people adopted the outward trappings of Rastafarianism (though only a small proportion fully accepted the religious tenets of the movement), reggae music was popular and specialty shops opened to meet the demands of the expanding Jamaican population. Riots in 1981 sparked off similar violence in other English inner-city locations, forcing Prime Minister Margaret Thatcher to appoint a committee of enquiry, chaired by Lord Scarman. Since that time, Brixton has become less of a focus for London's black citizens and race relations have improved. Tourists as well as local people visit the STREET MARKET, which is centred on Electric Avenue (opened in 1888 as one of the first shopping streets in the city to be lit by the new power source) and consists of a colourful array of stalls selling a range of goods, with those in Granville Arcade concentrating on Caribbean foods, African clothes and Jamaican music. The area also houses a PRISON, opened in 1820 and designed for criminals sentenced to hard labour. Concerns about its security were voiced in 1972, when twenty prisoners escaped, and again in 1980, when another three (including an alleged IRA terrorist) disappeared. The building now houses about 1,000 men awaiting trial or serving short sentences.

The name of Brixton may be derived from the Old English *stan* (meaning 'stone') and *Beorhstige* (a personal name). (See also DEPARTMENT STORES; MORRISON, HERBERT STANLEY; VICTORIA LINE.)

BROADCASTING HOUSE

See BRITISH BROADCASTING CORPORATION (BBC).

BROMLEY, LONDON BOROUGH OF

When local government in the metropolitan area was reorganized in 1965, several communities previously in the County of Kent were incorporated within the London Borough of Bromley. Covering some 59 square miles, the new authority (the largest in the GREATER LONDON COUNCIL area) was created by the merger of the boroughs of BECKENHAM and Bromley, the urban districts of ORPINGTON and Penge, and parts of Chislehurst and Sidcup. Although largely residential, there is a significant concentration of light industry towards the north-east in the valley of the River Cray (a tributary of the Darenth, which meets the RIVER THAMES at Dartford) and open farmland in the GREEN BELT to the south-east. The population of about 296,000 (2001) is heavily concentrated in professional and managerial families, with many workers commuting daily to jobs in THE CITY. Over 76 per cent of homes are privately owned (compared with a London average of 57 per cent) and unemployment rates tend to be lower than for the city as a whole. (See also BIGGIN HILL.)

BROMPTON

The Brompton area, lying south of KENSINGTON, was one of the last extensive areas of present-day central London to be covered with urban development, primarily because, from the seventeenth century, it developed a considerable reputation for its market gardens and plant nurseries. That semi-rural landscape eventually attracted wealthy businessmen (who built large homes for their families) and institutions such as the Brompton HOSPITAL, which was established in 1842 to care for patients with chest and lung diseases. From the 1850s, much land was acquired for educational buildings (the VICTORIA AND ALBERT MUSEUM occupies a large part of the 100-acre site formerly used by the Brompton PARK Nursery, for example). Also, in 1880–4, the baroque Brompton Oratory was built as a church for the priests of the Institute of the Oratory, established by St Philip Neri in Rome in 1575 and introduced to London in 1848. The area's name may be derived from the Old English words *brom* (meaning 'broom') and *tun* ('homestead'), indicating that it was a place where the yellow-flowered broom once grew.

BRONDESBURY

Brondesbury lies 4 miles north-east of CHARING CROSS at the fringe of the inner city. Its name, derived from Old English, suggests that it was once the manor of a man named Brand. By the Middle Ages, the forested, hilly land was part of the estate owned by ST PAUL'S CATHEDRAL and it remained undeveloped until well into the nineteenth century. By the 1860s, however, the spreading tentacles of the RAILWAYS were encouraging builders to erect homes for wealthy merchants and, in 1866, Christ Church (designed by Charles Baker King) became the focus of a new parish for the growing population. The following decade brought an influx of Jews, some from the EAST END of London, some from Eastern Europe. Initially, these IMMIGRANTS worshipped at ST JOHN'S WOOD and HAMPSTEAD but in 1902, largely due to the influence of a Polish-born businessman, Solomon Barnett, they erected their own synagogue. The twentieth century brought further improvements to the transport infrastructure (Brondesbury Park station was opened in 1908, for example) and, as several of the more affluent residents (including many Jewish families) moved to more suburban locations, large homes were subdivided into flats for a more transient population. When local government in the metropolitan area was reorganized in 1965, Brondesbury was included within the LONDON BOROUGH OF BRENT.

BROWN'S HOTEL

Located in Dover Street (near PICCADILLY), Brown's is one of London's most exclusive HOTELS. It was established in 1837 by James Brown (who had worked as a manservant) and his wife, Sarah (a maid in Lady Byron's household). Alexander Graham Bell made the first telephone call in England from the building in 1876 and, in 1905, Franklin Roosevelt (President of the United States, 1933–45) and Eleanor (his wife) spent their honeymoon there. Other former patrons include statesman Cecil Rhodes and Rudyard Kipling. In 2003 Sir Rocco Forte bought the hotel (for the second time) at a cost of £51.5 million.

BRUNEL, ISAMBARD KINGDOM

(1806–1859)

The designer of the first transatlantic steamship and a versatile railway engineer, Brunel was born in Portsmouth on 9 April 1806, the only son of Marc Brunel (a French-born industrial inventor) and his wife Sophia. He was educated in Caen and Paris then returned to Britain in 1822 to work with his father. In 1825, he was appointed resident engineer on Marc Brunel's project to drive a tunnel under the RIVER THAMES from WAPPING (in the north) to ROTHERHITHE (in the south). By all accounts, Isambard Brunel was a hard taskmaster (if a brick came loose, he would fire the man who laid it) but he accepted his share of manual work and, in 1828, narrowly escaped death when the tunnel flooded.

Brunel's other major work in London was the design of PADDINGTON STATION, the terminus of the Great Western Railway, of which he was chief engineer. Drawing on the CRYSTAL PALACE as a model, he built a roof of glass and wrought iron, supported by cast-iron pillars and with a central aisle 102 feet across. The track was broad gauge (7 feet ½ inch) rather than the more normal standard gauge (4 feet 8½ inches). He also planned the route of the railway line from London to Bristol and made considerable contributions to marine transport. His *Great Western* (which made her maiden voyage in 1838) was the world's first successful transatlantic steamship, the *Great Britain* (1845) was the world's first large iron-hulled screw steamer and the *Great Eastern* (1858) had paddles and screw propulsion as well as an innovative double hull.

However, although Brunel was a brilliantly creative engineer, he lacked management skills. Unable to delegate work to subordinates, he found that long hours and increasing strain took their toll on his health. He died on 15 September 1859 and was buried in KENSAL GREEN cemetery. The house at 98 Cheyne Walk, CHELSEA, where he lived as a child, still stands (and is marked by a BLUE PLAQUE) but his office at 8 Duke Street has been demolished. The engine house at the south end of the Thames Tunnel is now a MUSEUM and there are statues of Brunel in Temple Place and at Paddington Station. Brunel UNIVERSITY is named in his honour. (See also EAST LONDON LINE; HANWELL; HUNGERFORD BRIDGE.)

BUCKINGHAM PALACE

Buckingham Palace, at the western end of THE MALL, has been the principal residence of the royal family since Queen Victoria succeeded to the throne in 1837. In 1702–5, John Sheffield, Duke of Buckingham, built a residence on a site at the western end of ST JAMES'S PARK. The building was purchased by George III in 1762, but his eldest son, who succeeded to the throne as George IV in 1820, decided that a more imposing London home was needed for Britain's royal family. Moreover, he insisted that JOHN NASH should be responsible for the design. Parliament, although unhappy about the projected costs, allocated £200,000 to the project, and Nash produced plans for a courtyard enclosed on all sides except the east. George, however, demanded Carrara marble, Bath stone and other expensive building materials, which pushed up the expense of construction, so the architect was twice called before HOUSE OF COMMONS committees to explain why the bills were three times greater than funds apportioned. In the end, the government's patience ran out. When the king died in 1830, Nash was dismissed and Edward Blore was commissioned to complete the work.

When Victoria moved in, the place was hardly fit for the servants let alone a queen. Bells would not ring, doors would not close, windows would not open and many fittings (such as sinks) had not been installed. Nevertheless, by 1843 she was able to write, 'I have been so happy here,' a sentiment echoed by all later monarchs with the exception of Edward VIII, who hated the place and spent only a few nights there during his short reign. In 1913, the eastern frontage was replaced by a façade of PORTLAND STONE designed by Sir Aston Webb. In addition, considerable renovation and refurbishment were carried out after the Second World War (when parts of the structure, including the chapel, were badly damaged by bombs).

The present building has about 600 rooms, most of which are used as offices or as accommodation for staff. Elizabeth II and the Duke of Edinburgh occupy twelve rooms in the north wing, facing the 40-acre gardens. The State Apartments (including the Ballroom, Music Room and Throne Room) are reserved for events such as banquets, honouring foreign dignitaries and ceremonies conferring knighthood on the great and the good. Since 1993, they have been open to the public from August until early October (while the royal family is at Balmoral, in Scotland); the admission charges contribute towards the rebuilding of the rooms at Windsor Castle, which were damaged by fire in November 1992. Charles, Prince of Wales, was born in Buckingham Palace (1948), as were his brothers Andrew (1960) and Edward (1964). Their sister – Anne – was born in CLARENCE HOUSE in 1950. In 1998, the palace authorities announced plans to double the size of the Queen's Gallery so that more of the royal art collection could be placed on display to the public. (See also CHANGING OF THE GUARD; CUBITT, THOMAS; ROYAL MEWS.)

BUNHILL FIELDS

From 1658 until 1855, Bunhill Fields, lying just outside the northern boundary of the CITY OF LONDON, was a principal BURIAL GROUND for nonconformists (that is, Protestants who adhered to sects other than the Church of England). Under the terms of an 1867 Act of Parliament, the City Corporation is responsible for managing the cemetery, which contains the graves of John Bunyan (who published *The Pilgrim's Progress* in 1678), Daniel Defoe (who wrote *Robinson Crusoe* in 1719), poet William Blake, hymn writer Isaac Watts (remembered for *When I Survey the Wondrous Cross*) and Susanna Wesley (mother of Charles and John, founders of the Methodist Church). George Fox, who formed the Society of Friends, lies in the adjacent Quaker graveyard. The proximity of the cemetery may indicate that 'Bunhill' is a corruption of 'bone hill'.

BURIAL GROUNDS

By the seventeenth century, space to bury London's dead was in short supply. The grounds of the churches had nearly filled so graves were being dug only a few inches apart and bodies were interred under the floors of chapels, causing an unbearable stench in hot weather. In order to alleviate the problem, some parishes obtained land at the edge of the city and used it as burial grounds, which remained in use until about 1850 (since then, many have been converted into public PARKS and gardens). These were replaced by seven large commercial cemeteries (authorized by government legislation during the 1830s and 1840s and located in a ring around the major residential area), but it was clear by the mid-century that they, too, would quickly run out of space. Conscious of an increasing demand for non-profit-making burial grounds, Parliament made provisions for the establishment of locally elected Burial Boards charged with obtaining land for funerals.

Since then, most of London's 3,000 acres of cemetery have been managed by local authorities. Many have become tourist attractions, sometimes because of their ARCHITECTURE (see, for instance, HIGHGATE CEMETERY) but often simply because pilgrims (and the curious) are attracted to the graves of the famous. Members of the Salvation Army visit Abney PARK Cemetery in STAMFORD HILL, where WILLIAM BOOTH (founder of the movement) is buried. ISAMBARD KINGDOM BRUNEL and Wilkie Collins lie in KENSAL GREEN, sculptor Jacob Epstein in Putney Vale, and Henry Bessemer (who invented the process for making steel from cast iron) in West Norwood. However, the problem of finding space for burials remains. Although over 70 per cent of the 60,000 Londoners who die each year are cremated, it was estimated, in 2000, that within eight years all the ground available for interments would be filled. (See also BROMPTON; BUNHILL FIELDS; GREEN PARK; GOLDERS GREEN; HUGUENOTS; MANOR PARK; ST BOTOLPH'S CHURCH, ALDGATE; ST JAMES'S CHURCH, PICCADILLY; STANMORE; WILLESDEN.)

BURLINGTON ARCADE

A precursor of the modern shopping mall, the arcade houses seventy-two small but exclusive shops along a covered passageway between PICCADILLY and Burlington Gardens. It was constructed in 1815–9 as a means of preventing passers-by from throwing rubbish into Lord Cavendish's garden and, although much altered, remains a classic piece of Regency ARCHITECTURE. Liveried beadles patrol the passageway and have authority to apprehend anybody who runs, whistles, sings or carries an open umbrella.

BURLINGTON HOUSE

The last survivor of the noblemen's mansions that once lined the north side of PICCADILLY, Burlington House was partly built in 1664–5 by architect John Denham as his London residence. Before it was completed, it was acquired in 1667 by the first Earl of Burlington, who finished the construction. In 1715, the third earl commissioned JAMES GIBBS to erect baroque colonnades at the edges of the forecourt but then changed architectural tack and, in 1717, employed Colem Campbell to redesign the building in Palladian style. When Burlington died in

1753, the house was inherited by Charlotte, his only child and wife of the Duke of Devonshire. In 1813, it was bought by Lord Cavendish, who carried out considerable internal modification, including the installation of a grand staircase. The government purchased the property in 1854 and, after much heart-searching, converted it into a headquarters for the ROYAL ACADEMY OF ARTS, the ROYAL SOCIETY and other learned organizations. (See also SAVILE ROW.)

BURNT OAK

During the 1920s, LONDON COUNTY COUNCIL promoted the establishment of a community on sparsely settled agricultural land at Burnt Oak (some 9 miles north-west of CHARING CROSS) in an attempt to alleviate housing pressures in the inner city. A RAILWAY link to ST PANCRAS was completed in 1925 and residents from ISLINGTON arrived three years later to homes constructed of metal, wood and brick. By 1931, over 40,000 houses and flats were available, attracting further immigrants who pushed the resident population up to some 20,000 by the outbreak of the Second World War. Initially, there was some friction between the working-class incomers (who had brought their inner-city customs, including an open air MARKET, with them) and families in nearby middle-class areas, but the two cultures learned to coexist, with the white-collar groups drawing on blue-collar skills. Since the 1950s, the expansion of the urban area has turned Burnt Oak into a metropolitan suburb close to the M1 motorway.

BUSES

The precursors of the familiar red double-decker London bus were the horse-drawn carriages with which, on 4 July 1829, George Shillibeer introduced a service transporting up to twenty passengers at a time from PADDINGTON to THE CITY. By 1851, a two-deck version of the wagon had appeared. Passengers on the roof sat back to back, exposed to all that the weather could throw at them, but, even so, the new conveyances proved popular with businessmen travelling to and from their offices. For some years, competition became increasingly fierce as more and more operators tried to attract customers, but from 1855 a French firm – the Compagnie Générale des Omnibus de Londres – bought up existing businesses so rapidly that three years later, when the directors registered in Britain as the London General Omnibus Company, it controlled most of the 800 vehicles on the streets. By the end of the century, commuting had become an accepted way of life for many Londoners and the 3,500 horse buses were the chief form of public road TRANSPORT. However, motorized vehicles became increasingly common from 1897 and the internal combustion engine challenged the dominance of the horse, which finally disappeared from the streets in 1916, superseded by the mass-produced B-type double-decker (affectionately known as Old Bill).

The years between the two world wars (1919–39) brought further technological and administrative developments. Pneumatic tyres, introduced in 1925, resulted in a more comfortable ride for customers, as did the roofs over the upper deck, which became common at the same time. Then, in 1933, the whole system was taken into state control, along with the LONDON UNDERGROUND and the TRAMS, presenting possibilities for a co-ordinated route network within the capital (see LONDON TRANSPORT). For the next fifty-two years, investment was shaped by income from fares and government subsidies. Diesel engine vehicles went into service in 1949, to be followed in the mid-1950s by 2,800 Routemaster buses. Wider and lighter than their predecessors, they carried more passengers but also, because they had a door at the front, allowed the driver to collect fares, making conductors redundant and therefore reducing operating costs.

In 1985, London Transport created a subsidiary company – London Buses Ltd – to run the services. That company was required to compete against private contractors for the right to operate along specified routes and found the going hard because large garages, expensive to maintain, and restrictive work practices pushed costs beyond those of small local firms. London Buses responded by subdividing into thirteen area-based units, each responsible for its own budget and able to compete against both the private sector and sister units. In 1994, all were privatized through management and employee buyouts or sales to outside interests. London Transport (renamed Transport for London in 2000) acts as a contracting agency but owns none of the 5,000 public service vehicles that, every day from Monday to Friday, carry 1.2 million passengers along the 700 routes it offers for tender.

In addition to the transport within the metropolitan area, there are bus connections to all major regions of the United Kingdom from Victoria Coach Station, which is managed by London Transport but used by independent firms. Services to and from the city were deregulated in 1985, introducing a free market (any operator can apply for a license to run buses between centres even though the route is identical to that used by an existing service). (See also CONGESTION CHARGES; OLD KENT ROAD; YERKES, CHARLES TYSON.)

BUSH HOUSE

See BRITISH BROADCASTING CORPORATION (BBC).

BUSHY PARK

The 1,100 acres of Bushy (sometimes spelt Bushey) Park and neighbouring Hampton Court PARK, in the LONDON BOROUGH OF RICHMOND UPON THAMES, were enclosed as a hunting forest by Henry VIII in 1538. Access to the public has been available since his death, nine years later. Bushy Park's outstanding feature is an avenue of 274 chestnut trees, flanked by lime trees, which were planted during the seventeenth century by CHRISTOPHER WREN and stretch for a mile over the grass. A statue, believed to be of Diana the huntress, stands at the southern end and the eighteenth-century Bushy Park House near the northern end (Lord North occupied the premises while he was Prime Minister in the 1770s). Towards the western edge of the PARK, 100 acres have been converted into a woodland garden alongside the Longford River (an artificial inlet cut by command of Charles I in 1639 in order to draw water from the River Colne). Hampton Court Park (separated from Bushy Park by Hampton Court Road) is more formally laid out because of its proximity to HAMPTON COURT PALACE. In addition to the landscaped areas, the parks have sports pitches, horse riding facilities, a swimming pool and a pond for sailing model boats. The land is still owned by the Crown and is managed by the ROYAL PARKS Agency.

Henry VIII created Bushy Park as a hunting forest. Drawing by Hans Holbein.

C

CABINET WAR ROOMS

In 1938, as conflict between the United Kingdom and Germany seemed increasingly likely, civil service buildings at Clive Steps, off King Charles Street, were adapted for use by the British government during hostilities. Between 1940 and 1945, while the Second World War raged, Prime Minister WINSTON CHURCHILL directed operations from the Map Room, accompanied by his Chiefs of Staff. When AIR RAIDS made travel in London dangerous he slept in a nearby room, from which he broadcast several of his radio addresses to the nation. His Cabinet congregated in a meeting place soundproofed to keep out the noise of enemy attacks and close to an anteroom containing a telephone with a direct link to the President of the United States. The remainder of the 3-acre facility consisted of a canteen, a HOSPITAL, a shooting range and tiny sleeping quarters for the 528 workers. The rooms are now open to the public, looking much as they did in the 1940s, with coloured pins sticking into the wall-maps and the Cabinet Room arranged as if ministers were expected for a meeting.

CABLE STREET

Cable Street, built in London's industrial EAST END in the late eighteenth century, was originally 200 yards long (the length of a cable) and lined by rope manufacturing companies. It has since been extended from the CITY OF LONDON in the west to LIMEHOUSE in the east and now has a variety of commercial buildings. On 5 October 1936, it formed part of the route chosen for a march by supporters of the fascist movement, led by Sir Oswald Mosley. Left-wing opponents and local residents built barricades that would disrupt the procession but became involved in scuffles with the police, who were attempting to dismantle the obstacles and preserve the movement's right of assembly. As the struggles became more frequent, Fenner Brockway (Secretary of the Independent Labour Party) was injured by a police horse and, realizing that there would be serious violence if the fascists and their opponents confronted each other, telephoned government officials. Mosley was ordered to cancel the demonstration but, over the next week, many Jewish properties in the area suffered damage as the thwarted marchers took their revenge.

CAFÉ ROYAL

In 1865 Daniel Nicolas Thévenon opened a café at 15–17 Glasshouse Street, near PICCADILLY CIRCUS. The business was successful, expanding into property in REGENT STREET and, by the turn of the century, attracting the fashionable members of London's bohemian artistic set (including Oscar Wilde, Aubrey Beardsley and Augustus John) as well as nobility such as brothers David and Bertie – as they were known by their family – Windsor (later Edward VIII and George VI). Most met amid the red velvet seats and marble tables of the domino room, but there was also a billiard room, a lunch bar and space for private meetings. Although the property was rebuilt in 1923–4 to Sir Henry Tanner's designs, it retained its attraction for writers into the 1930s (T.S. Eliot and J.B. Priestley were frequent visitors). The main entrance is now at 68 Regent Street, where the rococo decoration in the grill room preserves the opulent atmosphere.

CAMBERWELL

In the eighteenth century, Camberwell (which lies east of BRIXTON and about 2½ miles south-east of CHARING CROSS) was a country village best known as the place where the now extinct Camberwell Beauty butterfly was first identified in 1748. Development began about 1820, with buildings constructed along the main roads for wealthy men who wanted a rural home for their families but daily access to their offices in the CITY OF LONDON. In 1844, a new cathedral-like church was built to replace the twelfth-century stone chapel destroyed by fire three years earlier; designed by George Gilbert Scott and dedicated to St Giles, it has a remarkable east window planned by John Ruskin. In 1868, William Rossiter founded an art gallery in Peckham Road. Then, in 1896, a technical school was established to teach design skills to local apprentices. Rossiter's gallery flourished; now known as the South London Art Gallery, it houses over 300 works by Victorian artists (including John Everett Millais, founder of the Pre-Raphaelite Brotherhood). In addition, since 1953 (using funds provided by the local council in celebration of the coronation of Elizabeth II) it has built up a significant collection of paintings by such twentieth-century artists as Duncan Grant (a member of the BLOOMSBURY GROUP) and John Piper. The technical school, which is located next door, has been renamed Camberwell College of Art and has concentrated on teaching the fine arts, as well as design, since 1908. However, Camberwell Green, site of a fair that survived until 1855, is a busy road junction devoid of any trace of the rural peace that Felix Mendelssohn discovered when he visited in 1842 and, moved by the tranquillity, wrote *Spring Song* (which was originally titled *Camberwell Green*).

The origin of the area's name is uncertain but it may be derived in part from the Old English *wella*, which means 'stream' or 'spring'.

CAMDEN, LONDON BOROUGH OF

When the GREATER LONDON COUNCIL replaced the LONDON COUNTY COUNCIL in 1965, the pattern of local government in the city was transformed as authorities were merged to form larger units. Camden was a product of the reorganization, created by the amalgamation of the boroughs of HAMPSTEAD, HOLBORN and ST PANCRAS. Covering an area of 8 square miles, it had a population of 198,000 at the time of the census in 2001, an increase of 17,300 since the survey a decade earlier. It takes its name from Charles, Earl Camden, whose family owned much of the land during the eighteenth and nineteenth centuries. The south has a large working-class population, who find jobs in nearby city centre commercial firms (Camden has more square feet of shop and office space than any borough other than the CITY OF WESTMINSTER), with institutions such as London University or with the TRANSPORT industries, though a few neighbourhoods (such as CAMDEN TOWN) are popular with young professionals and many properties are rented to students. Further north, Hampstead and HIGHGATE retain their image as foci for artists and writers with an affluent lifestyle. Levels of owner-occupation are low (35 per cent of households own their own home, compared with 56 per cent in

London as a whole), rates of overcrowding are high (17 per cent of the city's households live in overcrowded conditions but in Camden the proportion rises to 30 per cent), and there is a considerable ethnic mix, with Irish residents in KILBURN, Asian communities around EUSTON STATION, Greek Cypriots in Camden Town and a growing black presence off Camden High Street. The Holborn area has a particularly heavy concentration of educational, legal and religious organizations, including the BRITISH MUSEUM, SIR JOHN SOANE'S MUSEUM, Lincoln's Inn (one of the INNS OF COURT) and ST ETHELDREDA'S CHURCH (the oldest Roman Catholic church in the country). (See also BEDFORD ESTATES; BELSIZE PARK; BLOOMSBURY; CAMDEN TOWN; CHALK FARM; DICKENS' HOUSE MUSEUM; GOSPEL OAK; HAMPSTEAD GARDEN SUBURB; HAMPSTEAD HEATH; KEATS' HOUSE; KENTISH TOWN; KING'S CROSS; LINCOLN'S INN FIELDS; PRIMROSE HILL; SPANIARDS, THE; SWISS COTTAGE.)

CAMDEN TOWN

The area north of EUSTON STATION takes its name from the first Earl Camden, who acquired the land by marriage in 1749. Although the earl gave developers permission to build 1,400 houses in 1791 and the Veterinary College of London (now the Royal Veterinary College) was founded during the same year, there was little urban encroachment until the second decade of the nineteenth century. In 1816, the construction of the REGENT'S CANAL (designed to link the RIVER THAMES to the Grand Junction Canal at PADDINGTON) introduced coal companies and other small industries to the area. Then, in 1837, the opening of Euston Station added to the pressures on land so that by the end of the century, farms had given way to uniform rows of terraced houses. Irish IMMIGRANTS began to move in around 1880, taking advantage of the relatively low rents, and they were followed from about 1930 by Greek Cypriots, who set up small businesses in the catering and textile industries. (In 1948, the Cypriot community acquired the vacant All Saints Church, converting it for use by Greek Orthodox worshippers, but became involved in controversy eight years later when Kallinikos Macheriotis – one of the priests – was deported for supporting armed resistance to British rule in Cyprus.)

After the Second World War, much of the area east of Camden High Street was redeveloped, attracting a growing number of middle-class families to what had been a predominantly blue-collar area. From the 1960s, Camden Passage developed as an important antique market and Camden Lock as a centre for more general bric-a-brac, both attracting significant numbers of tourists. Camden Town also has important associations with the arts. CHARLES DICKENS lived at 16 Bayham Street in 1823–4 and drew on his expertise of the area when he depicted the homes of characters such as Bob Cratchit in *A Christmas Carol* (1843) and Mr Micawber in *David Copperfield* (1850). Also, in 1911 a coterie of painters (including Augustus John, Wyndham Lewis and Walter Sickert, the last of whom, some writers claim, was JACK THE RIPPER) formed a Camden Town Group whose work consisted largely of informal portraits, north London street scenes and nude figures in depressing apartments. It merged with others two years later to form a London Group, which thrived until the Second World War.

CANARY WHARF

The development of Canary Wharf, on the ISLE OF DOGS, has been marred by controversy ever since plans were first proposed in 1985. Initially, a consortium of banks backed the major urban renewal project, attracted by a package of government concessions that included relative freedom from planning controls and a ten-year moratorium on property taxes. However, the group's suggestions for a complex of offices, shops and HOTELS, based in three high towers, did not meet with universal acclaim, critics pointing out that other buildings in the EAST END were low rise, that the TRANSPORT infrastructure was limited and that the towers would block the view across the river to GREENWICH PARK. Faced with opposition and national financial recession, several of the partners withdrew but, in 1987, Olympia and York (owned by the Canadian Reichman Brothers) took charge of the scheme. Appointing architects Cesar Pelli and I.M. Pei as design consultants, they constructed a single 850-foot tower (the tallest in the United Kingdom) and incorporated a concert hall and a railway station on the 71-acre site. Local authorities tackled problems of access by preparing plans for the extension of the JUBILEE LINE of the LONDON UNDERGROUND, road improvements and the extension of the DOCKLANDS LIGHT RAILWAY to provide a direct link with THE CITY. Despite Olympia and York's collapse in 1992, the development proceeded, with Paul Reichman finding new sponsors and buying control back from the banks for a reputed £800 million three years later. With 4.7 million square feet of commercial space available, a further 8.8 million planned and rental costs lower than those in the City, the venture stimulated office decentralization from central London, led by *The Daily Telegraph* newspaper and such finance houses as Barclays Bank and Morgan Grenfell. On 19 February 1996 the IRA bombed the tower, killing two people and injuring a hundred, but the incident had no effect on the Wharf's attraction for investors. However, by 2003 difficult trading conditions were affecting financial and other service companies and several major tenants (including London Underground) were indicating that they might have to exercise options to give up office space in order to cut operating costs.

CANNING TOWN

From 1846, when a RAILWAY station was opened, Canning Town developed on the north bank of the RIVER THAMES some 6 miles east of CHARING CROSS. The new settlement, probably named after Lord Canning (Governor General of India), housed manual workers from the Royal Victoria DOCK (which was completed in 1855), the Thames Ironworks and Shipbuilding Company (which built naval vessels at its base on Bow Creek from 1846 until 1912), the coal wharves and other industrial premises that lined the waterways. It was one of the most deprived areas in London's EAST END during the late nineteenth and early twentieth centuries, then suffered greatly from bombing during the BLITZ. After 1945, however, successive local authorities implemented major regeneration plans that included the demolition of much low-quality Victorian housing, and construction of homes with modern amenities (as at the KEIR HARDIE estate). TRANSPORT improvements included provision of integrated interchange facilities for passengers on the BUSES, the DOCKLANDS LIGHT RAILWAY and the LONDON UNDERGROUND. The new Underground station was erected on the site of the Thames Ironworks, where HMS *Warrior*, Britain's first iron-hulled battleship, was built in 1859. Employees from the works formed what was to become WEST HAM UNITED in 1895, hence the name hammers, from the hammering of steel.

CANNON STREET STATION

The RAILWAY station in Cannon Street, which opened in 1866, is located on a site of considerable historical importance. Excavations have revealed a sizeable Roman building, with reception rooms, private apartments and painted walls, suggesting that the governor of the province built his principal base there between AD 80 and 100. During the Middle Ages, the Hanseatic League's STEELYARD, headquarters of its trading empire, dominated the area and candle-makers sold their products nearby (the street's name – *Cannon* – is derived from 'candlewick'). The station, designed by John Hawkshaw and opened in 1866, was built as the terminus of the South Eastern Railway at the southern edge of the CITY OF LONDON. Due to the steep slope of the shoreline, the tracks, brought over the RIVER THAMES on a five-span bridge with cast-iron Doric piers, required a 60-foot-high viaduct, built of 27 million bricks, to carry them onto the platforms. The station was a cavernous structure covered by a 680-foot-long roof, which formed a single arch reaching a height of 106 feet at its highest point. Twin towers dominated the riverfront entrance and a HOTEL to accommodate travellers was erected facing Cannon Street. The building, badly damaged during the BLITZ, was extensively renovated during the 1960s, when the roof was replaced and shops, office accommodation and a walkway were incorporated. Since then, further commercial facilities have been added but the original walls, and the towers, remain. Much of the Victorian ornamentation on the bridge, which was also designed by Hawkshaw (along with John Wolfe-Barry), was removed when the structure was upgraded in 1979.

CANONBURY

Now part of the LONDON BOROUGH OF ISLINGTON, the area acquired its name because the canons of St Bartholomew's Priory (see SMITHFIELD MEAT MARKET), held the land from 1253 until the dissolution of the MONASTERIES by Henry VIII in 1536–41. Some early development focused on the tower built by Prior William Bolton in the early sixteenth century and the mansion erected by Sir John Spencer (a cloth merchant and later LORD MAYOR of London) in 1593–7 but, by the late 1700s, the economy was still essentially agricultural. In 1820, however, Henry Leroux obtained a building lease for 19 acres and laid out Canonbury Square, hoping that it might evolve into a second BLOOMSBURY. Further urban expansion occurred to the east during the 1840s and 1850s as the Marquess of Northampton developed Canonbury PARK, encouraging further construction of villas and substantial homes for relatively wealthy citizens. During the early part of the twentieth century, the area was engulfed by the expansion of the inner city but, though it became a little shabby, it retained its attraction for some middle-class groups (George Orwell lived at 27 Canonbury Square in 1945, for example). After the Second World War, considerable regeneration work was undertaken (both by local authorities and by private interests) to repair bomb damage and upgrade housing standards. As part of that process, the tower has been restored and converted into a THEATRE.

CARDBOARD CITY

During the 1970s, homeless people began to congregate in the network of subways outside Waterloo station. By the mid-1980s, over 200 men and women slept there regularly, building homes with discarded boxes and earning the area the nickname 'Cardboard City'. Although the noisome assembly, many of whom were mentally disturbed, made some passers-by nervous, the police and social services tolerated the shanty town until 1991, when it was discovered that residents' fires were damaging the fabric of the tunnels. A concerted effort to clear the area was partially successful, but many of those who moved filtered back after repair work was finished, so the community re-formed, albeit with fewer members. In 1997, however, the British Film Institute began construction of a seven-storey IMAX cinema (the largest in Europe) on the site and, the following year, the LONDON BOROUGH OF LAMBETH won a High Court order compelling the remaining thirty-five or so occupants to leave.

CARLTON CLUB

The Carlton has been the social headquarters of the Tory, then Conservative, Party since the time of the Great Reform Act of 1832. As a prelude to the introduction of the Act, which laid the foundations for universal adult suffrage in the UK, the Tory Party, which was opposed to reform, had been all but wiped out in the 1830 election. Tories anxious to rebuild their strength leased rooms at 2 Carlton House Terrace, forming an association that would admit no more than 700 like-minded individuals. Membership was much sought after, so much so that the limit was increased to 900 in 1857, by which time the Tory Party had relabelled itself the Conservative Party following Robert Peel's *Tamworth manifesto*. The club is now based at 68 St James's Street. (See also GENTLEMEN'S CLUBS.)

CARLYLE'S HOUSE

From 1834 until his death in the drawing room on the first floor in 1881, Thomas Carlyle lived at 5 (now 24) Cheyne Row, one of a row of brick properties built in 1708. During that time, he wrote *The French Revolution* (3 volumes, 1837), *On Heroes, Hero-Worship and the Heroic in History* (1841) and *The History of Friedrich II of Prussia, Called Frederick the Great* (6 volumes, 1857–65) while entertaining other leading authors, including John Ruskin, CHARLES DICKENS, Charles Kingsley and Alfred Lord Tennyson. The house, now maintained by the National Trust, is much as Carlyle left it; his hat perches on a peg, the pictures are those he owned and Nero, his dog, lies buried in the garden.

CARNABY STREET

During the 1960s, Carnaby Street (one of a maze of small, narrow streets east of REGENT STREET) was as much a part of swinging London as the Beatles and Mick Jagger. John Stephen, John Vince and Andreas Spyropoulos had opened a boutique selling men's clothes in 1957 and their success attracted similar retailers to the site. Within a decade, the road was lined with shops catering to both sexes in an era when fashion focused on colourful, outrageous garments. Businesses emphasized the arcade-like atmosphere by laying bright paving and erecting ornamental arches but, by the 1970s, young people's tastes had changed and stores were sold, so there is now little evidence of the area's considerable influence on popular culture. The street takes its name from Karnaby House, which was erected on its east side in the late seventeenth century.

CATFORD

Catford, located some 6½ miles south-east of CHARING CROSS, is a residential area of the LONDON BOROUGH OF LEWISHAM. Until the middle of the nineteenth century, it was little more than a hamlet with an economy based almost entirely on agriculture, largely because of the distance from London and the problems caused by regular flooding when the water level rose in the River Ravensbourne. However, the arrival of the RAILWAY in 1857 encouraged builders to erect homes for commuters and, within a few years, the fields had been replaced by rows of houses. In half a century, the village was transformed into a metropolitan suburb. Since the end of the Second World War, redevelopment has resulted in the demolition of many older properties (including the original Town Hall, completed in 1875, and St Laurence's Church, opened in 1886) to make way for office accommodation and retail facilities. Catford is now a busy shopping and administrative centre, with the headquarters of the Borough Council and regionally important recreational facilities at the ABC Cinema, Lewisham Theatre and the greyhound racing stadium. Its name may be derived from the Old English words *catt* and *ford*, meaning 'the ford frequented by wildcats'.

CATO STREET CONSPIRACY

In 1820, a group of political dissidents met in a stable loft at 6 Cato Street (near MARBLE ARCH) to plot the death of the entire British Cabinet while the members were dining at Lord Harrowby's GROSVENOR SQUARE resi-

The Cato Street conspirators surprised. A contemporary drawing by George Cruikshank.

dence on 23 February. They planned to behead Lord Sidmouth (the Home Secretary) and Lord Castlereagh (one of his allies) but were betrayed, probably by George Edwards. On the day set for the killing, a detachment of Coldstream Guards, accompanied by policemen, broke into the loft and arrested several of the dissidents. Others (including Arthur Thistlewood, who killed one of the policemen with his sword) escaped. Thistlewood was taken into custody the next day and, on 1 May, was hanged at NEWGATE PRISON, along with John Brunt, William Davidson, James Ings and Richard Tidd. Five of their colleagues were exiled to penal colonies overseas. Public sympathy for the men was considerable – so much so that the executioner was attacked in the street and narrowly escaped castration. Cato Street was renamed Horace Street in 1827 but reverted to its original appellation early in the twentieth century. It has been redeveloped to provide apartment dwellings but the loft has been incorporated into No. 1A.

CAVENDISH SQUARE

The square, laid out by John Prince, was the first urban development on land owned by Edward Harley, Earl of Oxford, on the north side of OXFORD STREET. It was named in honour of his wife, Lady Henrietta Cavendish Holles. Building began in 1717 and (although it proceeded in fits and starts for financial reasons) provided a focus for other construction as a gridiron pattern of streets was built around it, each named after a member of the Oxford family, one of their titles or one of their estates. In 1741, the property was inherited by the earl's daughter, Margaret, who married William Bentinck, Duke of Portland (see PORTLAND PLACE), and, by 1800, was almost entirely developed. Distinguished residents have included Horatio Nelson (see TRAFALGAR SQUARE) in 1791 and H.H. Asquith from 1895 until his appointment as Prime Minister in 1908. During the twentieth century, the substantial homes have been replaced by offices and apartments and, in 1971, a parking garage was built under the garden in the centre of the square. (See also ST MARYLEBONE.)

CEMETERIES

See BURIAL GROUNDS.

CENOTAPH

The United Kingdom's memorial to servicemen and women of the British Empire and

Commonwealth who were killed during the First and Second World Wars stands in the middle of WHITEHALL. Designed by Sir Edward Lutyens, it is built of PORTLAND STONE and was erected in 1919–20. The dedication to those who fell during the Second World War was added in 1946. A simple structure, it carries no religious motif and is decorated only by the flags of the Army, the Merchant Marine, the Royal Air Force and the Royal Navy. At 11 a.m. on the morning of the Sunday closest to 11 November (the hour and date on which hostilities ceased at the end of the First World War) a remembrance service is held, with the royal family and leaders of the major political parties in attendance. The word *cenotaph* is derived from the Greek *kenos* (meaning 'empty') and *taphos* ('tomb').

CENTRAL CRIMINAL COURT

The trials of people from the London area accused of major CRIMES are normally held at the Central Criminal Court in the CITY OF LONDON. The first courthouse on the site was built in 1539 beside NEWGATE PRISON in a street named Old Bailey. The present structure, designed by Edward Mountford, was erected in 1902–7. Faced with PORTLAND STONE, it is surmounted by a 12-foot-high gilded statue of Justice holding a sword in one hand and a set of scales in the other. An extension was added in 1970–2, allowing nineteen hearings to take place simultaneously. On the first two days of every session, the judges carry posies of flowers, a reminder of the stench associated with the old prison. Those tried at the court (which is commonly known as the Old Bailey) include Oscar Wilde (found guilty of homosexuality in 1895), William Joyce 'Lord Haw Haw' (condemned to death as a traitor in 1945 for broadcasting in support of Nazi Germany), poisoner Hawley Harvey Crippen (1910) and multiple murderers John Reginald Halliday Christie (1953, see RILLINGTON PLACE) and Peter Sutcliffe (1981). (See also COMMON SERJEANT; KRAY TWINS; RECORDER OF LONDON.)

CENTRAL HALL

The headquarters of the Methodist Church in England were opened in 1912 on a site in Storey's Gate (near ST JAMES'S PARK). The main hall, which can hold a congregation of 2,700 people, hosts concerts and public gatherings as well as church services. In 1946, it was used for the first meeting of the General Assembly of the United Nations.

CENTRAL LINE

Plans to develop an UNDERGROUND railway link between OXFORD STREET and the CITY OF LONDON were proposed as early as 1866 but were not implemented until 1900, when the Prince of Wales (later Edward VII) inaugurated the Central London RAILWAY's services between SHEPHERD'S BUSH and CORNHILL. A flat fare of 2d (which led the *Daily Mail* to nickname the line 'The Twopenny TUBE') helped attract passengers and, by 1920, extensions had been completed westwards to EALING Broadway (a station opened at Wood Lane to serve the new exhibition halls at the WHITE CITY in 1908) and eastwards to LIVERPOOL STREET STATION (where the route connected to the main line terminus of the Great Eastern Railway). Construction work for further expansion was interrupted by the outbreak of the Second World War but the tunnels were used as bomb-proof factories and air-raid shelters (on 3 March 1943 over 170 people died at BETHNAL GREEN station when a crowd seeking refuge after an AIR RAID siren had sounded panicked on hearing the noise of anti-aircraft fire). In the late 1940s the track was extended to West RUISLIP in the west and to Hainault and Ongar in the east. A major upgrading of facilities began in 1988 then, in 1995, trains became one-man operated.

Services between Epping and Ongar were discontinued in 1994 but, even so, the Central Line is still the longest in the LONDON UNDERGROUND system, stretching for 46 miles, passing through forty-nine stations and using seventy-two trains to provide a rush-hour service. The major service work is carried out at a depot in West Ruislip but engines and carriages are also serviced at Hainault and at White City. In 2003 maintenance of the line's infrastructure was franchised to Metronet, a consortium of private businesses, but LONDON UNDERGROUND remained responsible for providing the services.

CEREMONY OF THE KEYS

Every night, the TOWER OF LONDON is closed with a 700-year-old ritual known as the Ceremony of the Keys. A BEEFEATER, accompanied by an escort, locks the West Gate, the Middle Tower and the Byward Tower (the main entrance). At the Bloody Tower, challenged by a sentry, he replies that he brings Queen Elizabeth's keys. The Chief Warder raises his hat with a shout of 'God preserve Queen Elizabeth,' and the guard responds with 'Amen' just before the clock strikes 10 p.m., then a bugler sounds the Last Post before the Chief Warder carries the keys to the Resident Governor for safekeeping until the tower is opened the next day.

CHALK FARM

The suburb of Chalk Farm lies some 3 miles north of CHARING CROSS, sandwiched between HAMPSTEAD HEATH (to the north) and REGENT'S PARK (to the south). The first part of the name is derived from the Old English *ceald* and *cot* and refers to 'cold cottages' (the words were corrupted to 'Chalcot' and then, in the eighteenth century, to 'chalk'). The land was given to Eton College by Henry VI and was used primarily for farming until the 1820s, when the school began to lay out streets, giving them names such as Eton Avenue and Fellows Road. The RAILWAY arrived in 1837, providing a link to EUSTON STATION, and other transport improvements quickly followed (for example, the Round House THEATRE stands on the site of the turntable at the London and Birmingham Company's rail terminus, opened in 1851). The improved accessibility led to further urban development so, by the early twentieth century, the area was engulfed by metropolitan expansion, with flats and terraces filling the spaces between the original villas. In 1965, when the city's local government was reorganized, Chalk Farm became part of the LONDON BOROUGH OF CAMDEN.

CHAMBERS, WILLIAM (1723–1796)

Chambers, architectural rival of ROBERT ADAM, and designer of the ornamental buildings (including the pagoda) at the ROYAL BOTANIC GARDENS in KEW, was born in Göteborg (Sweden) on 23 February 1723, the son of a merchant of Scottish descent. The family moved to England in 1728. After leaving school at the age of sixteen, he found work as a supercargo (the officer on a merchant ship in charge of the cargo) with the Swedish East India Company, collected material for a book on *Designs of Chinese Buildings* (published in 1757) during a voyage to Canton and, after only two years, gave up his career at sea to study ARCHITECTURE, initially in Paris and later in Rome. When he returned to Britain in 1755, he established himself in London's Poland Street (close to SOHO) and was given a commission to design a villa for Lord Bessborough at ROEHAMPTON (now known as Manresa House, the building is used as a training centre for Jesuit priests). Through mutual acquaintances, he was introduced to Augusta, Princess Dowager of Wales, who invited him to design gardens for her palace at Kew, where he used his knowledge of the Orient to construct replicas of a Chinese temple (1760), a Turkish mosque (1761) and a 163-foot-high pagoda (also 1761), only the last of which survives. The project was well received by the royal family, resulting in Chambers' appointment (jointly with Adam) as Architect of Works to George III in 1772. The success also led to other commissions for distinguished individuals and organizations, notably for the building of Melbourne House (now The

Albany) in PICCADILLY (1770–4) and SOMERSET HOUSE (1776–86), and for alterations to Marlborough House in THE MALL (1770–2).

As Chambers' fame grew, he moved from Poland Street to Berners Street (north of OXFORD STREET), then to Norton (now Bolsover) Street in Marylebone and associated with the great artists and writers of the day, including actor DAVID GARRICK, poet Oliver Goldsmith and painter Joshua Reynolds. In 1768, he helped to found the ROYAL ACADEMY OF ARTS and, in 1770, was dubbed a Knight of the Polar Star by King Adolphus Frederick of Sweden. He died on 8 March 1796 and was buried in WESTMINSTER ABBEY. A pillar of the London establishment, he was an architectural conservative (criticizing ADAM's ADELPHI scheme, for example) but, even so, took the prevailing Palladian fashion and remoulded it in a way that influenced building design on an international scale. (See also COCKFOSTERS; OSTERLEY HOUSE.)

The Coronation procession of Edward VI passing Charing Cross on its way from London to Westminster.

CHANCERY LANE

Chancery Lane, which connects High Holborn and FLEET STREET, got its name in 1377, when Edward III acquired a property for the Keeper of the Rolls of Chancery. That building was demolished in 1896, but the street still houses several public buildings, notably the former PUBLIC RECORD OFFICE and the Law Office (the principal professional organization for solicitors in England and Wales). The entrance to Lincoln's Inn (see INNS OF COURT) is on the west side of the road and that to the Royal Commission on Historical Manuscripts in Quality Court, an alley on the east side. When a new sovereign ascends the throne, Chancery Lane is one of the places where a formal announcement of the succession is made by heralds.

CHANGING OF THE GUARD

The ceremony of changing the guard at BUCKINGHAM PALACE is one of London's most popular tourist attractions. The guard is normally mounted by one of the five regiments of Foot Guards in the HOUSEHOLD DIVISION. At 11.27 a.m., the new guard marches from Wellington Barracks and, accompanied by bandsmen, makes its way along BIRDCAGE WALK to the palace forecourt, where it relieves the old guard. The ceremony is held every day from April until mid-August and every other day for the rest of the year. The mounted guards at HORSE GUARDS PARADE are also ceremonially changed at 10 a.m. on Sundays and 11 a.m. during the remainder of the week. At both locations, less formal changes of personnel take place throughout the day.

CHARING CROSS

When Eleanor, wife of Edward I, died at Harby (Nottinghamshire) in 1290, she was carried to London for burial. At each place where her coffin rested en route, her husband erected a cross in her memory, the last being built at Charing Cross, now a busy junction where the STRAND and WHITEHALL meet, close to TRAFAL-

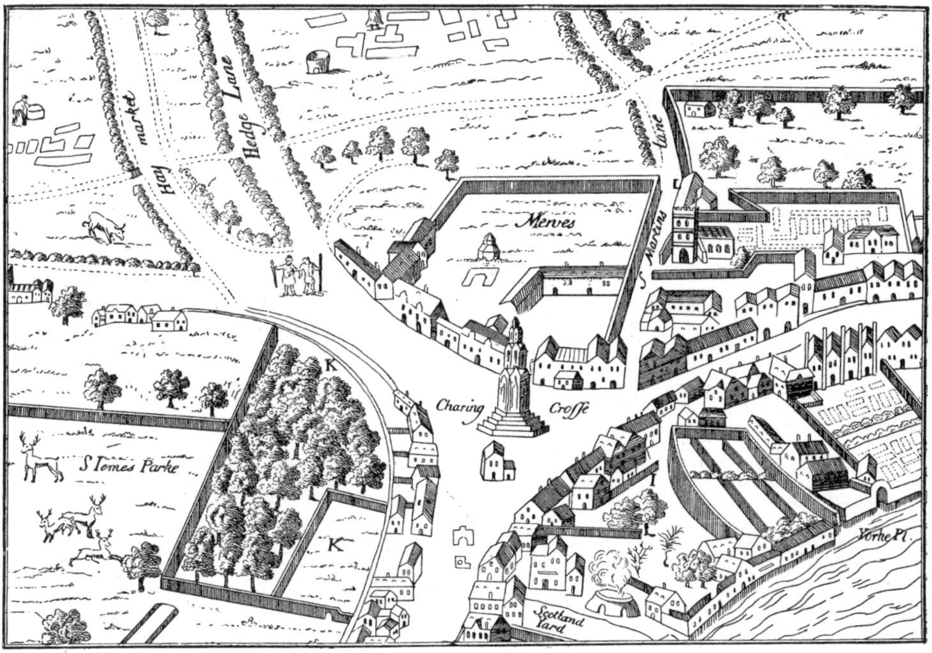

Plan of the Charing Cross area, *c.* 1554.

GAR SQUARE, in the heart of London. (Some authorities claim that the area's name is derived from the French *chère reine*, which means 'dear queen', others that it comes from *cierran,* the Old English word for 'turn', and refers to a bend in the road on the northern shore of the RIVER THAMES). Edward's cross, suffering from the ravages of weather, was demolished in 1647, by which time Charing Cross had become a bustling community (during the eighteenth century, SAMUEL JOHNSON remarked that 'the full tide of human existence' was to be found there). In 1823, Benjamin Golding established a small HOSPITAL in Villiers Street (see CHARING CROSS HOSPITAL), but eleven years later it was superseded by a larger building, designed by Decimus Burton and funded by subscriptions that included donations from the Duchess of Kent (mother of Queen Victoria). During the 1860s, the South-Eastern RAILWAY built a BRIDGE across the Thames in order to bring trains into the heart of London (see HUNGERFORD BRIDGE) and constructed a station (designed by John Hawkshaw) on the site of the Hungerford fruit, vegetable and meat MARKET. Above the terminus, a lavishly furnished HOTEL (one of the first buildings in the city to be faced with artificial stone) was erected to plans prepared by E.M. Barry, and a replica of the Eleanor Cross was placed in front of it. The hospital moved to more spacious accommodation at FULHAM in 1973, but the station survives, bringing commuters from Kent and the boroughs of south-east London to jobs in the city centre. LONDON UNDERGROUND stations at Embankment and Trafalgar Square, along with the frequent BUSES, make the area one of the most important traffic hubs in the modern metropolis. All road measurements to London are traditionally based on the distance to Charing Cross. The area forms part of the CITY OF WESTMINSTER. (See also BAKERLOO LINE; JUBILEE LINE; NORTHERN LINE; REGENT STREET; VICTORIA LINE.)

CHARING CROSS BRIDGE

See HUNGERFORD BRIDGE.

CHARING CROSS HOSPITAL

Charing Cross Hospital was founded in 1818 by Dr Benjamin Golding, who, as a medical student, had devoted much of his spare time to providing medical care for the poor. Initially, the sixteen-bed unit, known as the West London Infirmary and Dispensary, was based in Suffolk Street but in 1823 it moved to Villiers Street and four years later it assumed its present name. Then, with the support of the Duchess of Kent and other members of the royal family, funds were raised for the construction of a new building, which was designed by Decimus Burton and erected in Agar Street. It opened in 1834 and was extended several times during the nineteenth and twentieth centuries. By the end of the Second World War, however, it was evident that the cramped central London site was increasingly unsuitable and, in 1973, the hospital moved to FULHAM Palace Road. The training of medical students began in 1822 (David Livingstone, the explorer and missionary, learned many of his treatments on the wards) and in 1911 the school became a college of the University of London. It merged with WESTMINSTER HOSPITAL medical school in 1984, then became part of the Imperial College School of Medicine when it was formed in 1997. In 1994, Charing Cross Hospital united with the ACTON, HAMMERSMITH and Queen Charlotte and CHELSEA Hospitals to form the Hammersmith Hospitals National Health Service Trust. It is now the principal site in west London for the treatment of serious injuries and has important cancer, neurological and renal facilities.

CHARING CROSS ROAD

During the 1880s, a thoroughfare was constructed between CHARING CROSS and BLOOMSBURY in an attempt to improve traffic flow in the city centre. The work (planned by JOSEPH WILLIAM BAZALGETTE and George Vulliamy, engineer and architect, respectively, of the METROPOLITAN BOARD OF WORKS) involved the widening of Crown and Castle Streets and the demolition of some of the worst slums in the city. Architecturally, the road has little to commend it, but it is a busy route lined with shops, restaurants and THEATRES. Foyle's (which claims to be the largest bookshop in the world) is at Nos 119–125. In 1949, Helen Hanff began a twenty-year correspondence with another bookshop – Marks and Co.; the letters, published in one volume under the title *84 Charing Cross Road* (1970), became a bestseller but the shop is now closed, replaced by a café-bar.

CHARING CROSS STATION

See CHARING CROSS.

CHARLTON

Charlton, in the LONDON BOROUGH OF GREENWICH, has managed to maintain some semblance of its former village atmosphere despite its absorption into the city during the nineteenth century. There is evidence of settlement in the area from pre-Roman times and of the existence of a village when William the Conqueror carried out his DOMESDAY BOOK survey of England in 1085–6. Since 1612, the principal building has been Charlton House, built by Adam Newton and considered to be one of the best examples of Jacobean ARCHITECTURE in the country. Constructed of red brick, with white stone dressings and quoins, it is owned by the borough, which uses it as a community centre and library. The green close to the mansion was the site of Charlton Horn Fair on 18 October each year. The origins of the event are unclear, but the local tradition is that John I (who ruled from 1199–1216) granted land to a miller as compensation when the monarch seduced his wife during a hunting expedition. Horns are the emblem of a wronged husband. Other writers have suggested that the name may be derived from pictures of St Luke in a preliterate, God-fearing society (18 October is dedicated to the saint, who is often depicted riding beside a cow and an ox). At its height during the eighteenth and nineteenth centuries, the fair attracted thousands of visitors (many of whom wore horn headbands), but allegations of drunkenness, violence and indecency caused the authorities to close it down in 1872. During the twentieth century, much former open space in the area has been covered with houses and industrial estates, but areas of PARKland (including Horn Fair PARK) have been preserved as a recreational resource. Charlton's name is probably derived from the Old English *ceorl* and *tun* and means 'the freeman's homestead'. (See also CHARLTON ATHLETIC FOOTBALL CLUB.)

CHARLTON ATHLETIC FOOTBALL CLUB

One of the less fashionable of London's major clubs, Charlton was founded in 1905 by members of East Street Mission, Charlton Reds and other local sides. After playing on pitches at WOOLWICH Common (1907-08), Pound PARK (1908–13) and Horn Lane (from 1913), it moved to The Valley, its present ground, in 1919 (the team is known as 'The Addicks' after a nearby fish and chip shop). It was elected to the Third Division (South) of the Football League in 1920 and experienced its most successful years under manager Jimmy Seed, a former TOTTENHAM HOTSPUR player, on either side of the Second World War. After winning the Third Division (South) championship in 1935 (two years after Seed arrived), the club went on to become runners-up in the First Division (1937), runners-up in the FA Cup (1946) then winners of the FA Cup in 1947 (while celebrating the victory, Seed broke the cup's lid: since then, the lid has been tied on with ribbons at all cup finals). Crowds of up to 75,000 at home games allowed Charlton to invest in ground improvements at the former chalk pit site but relegation to the Second Division in 1956, then to the Third in 1971, seriously affected funds.

In 1982, an attempt to regenerate spectator interest by signing Allan Simonsen, a former European Footballer of the Year, from Barcelona did not pay off (Simonsen played just seventeen games before returning to his native Denmark). By the following year, funds had almost dried up and the business was near to bankruptcy. The new chairman (John Fryer) owned the club but not the freehold to the ground so, for seven years, Charlton was itinerant, playing its games from 1985–91 at Selhurst PARK (the home of CRYSTAL PALACE FOOTBALL CLUB) and in 1991/92 at Upton Park (the home of WEST HAM UNITED). Supporters were incensed and formed the Valley Party, which contested local elections and ultimately inspired a return to the traditional home in December 1992. Since then, heavy investment has resulted in major improvements (most recently, the construction of a 9,000-seat East Stand in 2001/02) so the stadium now holds only 26,500 spectators – far fewer than in its heyday – but supporters watch games in far greater comfort than their predecessors enjoyed. The return to old haunts appeared to inspire the side. Charlton was promoted to the Premier League in 1998 and has remained there ever since apart from the 1999/2000 season, when, following relegation, it won the Division One championship.

CHARTERHOUSE

In 1348, when the BLACK DEATH was ravaging London and corpses lay for days awaiting burial, Sir Walter Manny bought 13 acres of land in CLERKENWELL and donated it to the CITY OF LONDON for use as a cemetery. A chapel was built on the site of what is now Charterhouse Square so that Masses could be said for the souls of the dead. Twenty-two years later, the pious Sir Walter founded a Carthusian MONASTERY on the site, converting the chapel for use as the foundation's place of worship. It thrived until 1536, when six of the monks were hanged at TYBURN for refusing to accept Henry VIII as head of the Church of England. The monarch assumed control of the property, which passed through a succession of aristocratic owners before being acquired, in 1611, by Thomas Sutton (reputedly the richest commoner in England). Sutton had no children, so he used his wealth to establish Charterhouse as a school for forty boys and a hospital for eighty poor gentlemen. The school flourished, becoming one of England's most prestigious educational institutions and numbering essayist Joseph Addison and preacher John Wesley among its old boys. It moved to Godalming (Surrey) in 1872, turning its buildings over to Merchant Taylors' School, which occupied them until it ran out of space and transferred to more commodious premises at Sandy Lodge (Middlesex) in 1933. The buildings suffered badly from incendiary bombs dropped by German planes on the night of 10–11 May 1941, but they were sympathetically restored by Lord Mottistone and Paul Paget. A medical school for ST BARTHOLOMEW'S HOSPITAL was erected on the site of the Great Cloister in 1949, but elderly pensioners to this day occupy rooms in the older part of the complex.

CHEAM

Cheam, an outer London suburb located 11 miles south-east of CHARING CROSS, was probably settled by Saxon migrants during the sixth century. It developed an important pottery industry during the Middle Ages but remained primarily agricultural until the 1920s, when an increasing demand for houses close to the rural fringe encouraged developers to line spacious streets with detached homes for affluent office workers. The focus of the community is a Tudor Revival-style shopping area, with black and white timbered stores, built just before the Second World War, but several eighteenth-century houses survive as reminders of the old village. The area was included in the LONDON BOROUGH OF SUTTON when local government in the metropolitan area was reorganized in 1965. Its name may be derived from the Old English *ceg* (meaning 'tree stumps') and *ham* ('farmstead').

CHEAPSIDE

During the early Middle Ages, Cheapside was the CITY OF LONDON's largest MARKET (its name is derived from the Old English word *ceap*, which means 'to barter'). Country people crowded into the town to sell their wares, each in their own sector of the retailing area – the poulterers were in Poultry, the bakers in Bread Street and the dairymen in Milk Street, for example. Those found guilty of attempting to cheat customers were put into stocks (in 1382, for instance, one man was found guilty of selling a rotten conger eel and was clamped while the fish was burned in front of his face). However, during the thirteenth century, a competing market was established on the site of the present MANSION HOUSE. From then, trade declined. Most buildings were made of wood so the GREAT FIRE of 1666 ravaged the area, but properties were speedily rebuilt in stone and, by the early nineteenth century, the district was known for its trade in precious metals and linens. For much of the Victorian period, Cheapside was an important shopping area but, over the past 100 years, offices and warehouses have replaced many of the stores. Few of the older buildings survive, but the market's legacy is evident in the number of LIVERY COMPANY headquarters that cluster around the street. (See also BANK OF ENGLAND; BOW BELLS; JONSON, BEN; LONDINIUM.)

CHELSEA

Chelsea lies on the north bank of the RIVER THAMES some 2 miles south-west of CHARING CROSS. The origins of the settlement are obscure but it was certainly in existence by AD 787, when Offa, King of Mercia, held a

The Lord Mayor's procession in 1761 passing down Cheapside.

Early seventeenth-century Cheapside before the Great Fire of 1666.

synod at the site. By the sixteenth century, it had become a popular haunt of the aristocracy, with Henry VIII, the Duke of Norfolk, the Earl of Shrewsbury and others owning residences in the area. In 1528, Sir Thomas More (who was to become Henry's Lord Chancellor) rebuilt the south chapel of Chelsea Old Church, which was founded by at least 1157. (The church, previously known as All Saints, was badly damaged during the BLITZ in 1941 but restored by Walter Godfrey after the Second World War; it contains some of England's finest Tudor monumental ARCHITECTURE and, in work by Hans Holbein the Younger, the earliest Renaissance architecture in the country.) CHELSEA HOSPITAL, established by Charles II in 1682 as a home for elderly soldiers, spurred further development, then, in 1745, a porcelain works (founded by Nicholas Sprimont) introduced manufacturing activity and attracted artists seeking commissions to decorate the china. Over the years, the artistic colony grew, so, by 1891 (when Frank Brangwyn and James Abbott McNeill Whistler were local residents), it was able to constitute itself as a club and rent premises in KING'S ROAD. One of its principal events was an annual Chelsea Arts Ball, which was held at the ALBERT HALL but became so riotous that it was discontinued after 1959. During the late nineteenth and early twentieth centuries, population increased as a result of the opening of an army barracks (designed for 1,000 infantrymen) in 1861, the South-Western Polytechnic (later Chelsea College) in 1891, CHELSEA FOOTBALL CLUB in 1905 and other institutional and public employers.

Chelsea was made a metropolitan borough within the LONDON COUNTY COUNCIL structure in 1900 but amalgamated with KENSINGTON in 1965 to form the ROYAL BOROUGH OF KENSINGTON AND CHELSEA. Since then, there has been much redevelopment, but the Chelsea Society, an influential group of local residents, exerts pressure to retain the best of the older buildings and promote a sense of identity.

The origins of the suburb's name are obscure. Some authorities claim that the first element is derived from the Old English *caelic* (which means 'chalice'), others that it is from *cealc*, a word for 'chalk' from the same period. The second element may be from *hyth*, the Old English word for 'landing place'. Alternatively, as the settlement is located beside the river, the name may be a corruption of the Old English *chesil*, meaning 'shingle'. (See also BATTERSEA BRIDGE; BRUNEL, ISAMBARD KINGDOM; CARLYLE'S HOUSE; CHARING CROSS HOSPITAL; CHELSEA BRIDGE; CHELSEA FLOWER SHOW; CHELSEA PHYSIC GARDEN; DOGGETT'S COAT AND BADGE RACE; NATIONAL ARMY MUSEUM; WESTMINSTER HOSPITAL.)

CHELSEA BRIDGE

In 1851–8, a BRIDGE, designed by Thomas Page and incorporating cast-iron towers, was built across the RIVER THAMES to improve access between CHELSEA and BATTERSEA. Weapons uncovered during the building work revealed evidence of a battle fought between the Roman invaders and native Britons at the site. The present bridge dates from 1934.

CHELSEA FLOWER SHOW

The Royal Horticultural Society was formed in 1804 (as the Horticultural Society of London) by a group of botanists and gardeners led by John Wedgwood (son of Josiah Wedgwood, who founded the pottery firm at Stoke-on-Trent). In 1821, it leased 33 acres of land at CHISWICK and, ten years later, held its first exhibition. Financial problems during the 1850s were solved by the intervention of PRINCE ALBERT (husband of Queen Victoria), who became president in 1858 and persuaded the Commissioners of the Great Exhibition to provide the organization with access to their south KENSINGTON property. By 1882 expenses had become prohibitive, forcing the society to abandon its London gardens, but in 1903, it was gifted an extensive area at Wisley (Surrey) and established its main nurseries there. The following year, it opened a new headquarters in Vincent Square, then, in May 1913, held the first of its annual shows in the grounds of CHELSEA HOSPITAL. The gold medals awarded to exhibitors are highly prized and the show is undoubtedly the highlight of Britain's horticultural year, but increasing numbers of visitors (including members of the royal family) place great pressures on the limited exhibition space. The society has also organized the annual flower show at HAMPTON COURT PALACE since 1993 and hosts regular events at its Vincent Square site and its hall in nearby Greycoat Street. Its collection of some 50,000 books forms one of the world's leading horticultural LIBRARIES.

CHELSEA FOOTBALL CLUB

In 1896, building contractor Gus Mears and his brother, J.T. Mears, bought the Stamford Bridge athletic ground, and an adjacent market garden, in west London. After turning down an offer from the Great Western RAILWAY, which wanted to build sidings for its freight wagons, the men embarked on a project to develop the site as a football stadium. The facilities were offered to FULHAM FOOTBALL CLUB but rejected because the rent (£1,500 a year) was considered too high, so local financier F.W. Parker suggested that a completely new team should be created and that its ground should be the best in the country. The CHELSEA Football and Athletic Company was formed in 1905 and joined the Second Division of the Football League, playing in a vast stadium capable of holding 100,000 spectators and consisting largely of great banks built from debris accumulated during the extension of the LONDON UNDERGROUND.

The club was promoted after only two seasons but for forty years its success was limited as it moved back and forth between the two divisions. Then, in 1955, they won the First Division Championship (helped by the keen eye of scout Jimmy Thompson, who brought several talented youngsters to the club's apprenticeship scheme) and, from 1963 to 1972, inspired by manager Tommy Docherty, they finished in the top ten for nine years in a row (though a second Championship eluded them). A team awash with such stars as Charlie Cooke and Peter Osgood, they also won the League Cup (1965), the FA Cup (1970) and the European Cup-Winners Cup (1971) but the success did not last. A decision to convert the elderly ground into a 50,000 all-seat stadium proved more expensive than expected, forcing the club to the edge of bankruptcy. The transfer of leading players helped reduce the overdraft but led to relegation and, in order to repay funds, the directors decided to sell Stamford Bridge to property developers.

The freehold was regained, after a lengthy battle led by Chairman Ken Bates, when the developers went out of business in 1992 and appeared to spur renewed success. The FA Cup was won in 1997, the League Cup and the European Cup Winners Cup in 1998, and the FA Cup again in 2000. Stadium redevelopment reduced capacity to 42,449 but added hotels, restaurants, conference rooms and other facilities. In 2003 Russian businessman Roman Abramovich bought Bates' controlling interest in the club and immediately embarked on a multi-million pound spending spree in an attempt to strengthen the playing staff.

CHELSEA HOSPITAL

Established in 1682 and formally known as the Royal Hospital because it was founded by Charles II, CHELSEA Hospital was established to provide accommodation for soldiers no longer able to undertake military duties. The brainchild of Sir Stephen Fox (England's first Paymaster General), who modelled it on French and Irish provision, it was designed by CHRISTOPHER WREN and completed in 1689, when 476 'pensioners' took up residence. Their home, planned around three courtyards, has changed little over the past three centuries apart from a series of minor works carried out, under the supervision of ROBERT ADAM, in 1765–82 and a stable block added by Sir John Soane (see SIR JOHN SOANE'S MUSEUM) in 1814. Pensioners dine in the Great Hall, where the Duke of Wellington (who commanded British troops during the Napoleonic Wars) lay in state after his death in 1852. The panelled hall contains a large mural, by Antonio Verrio, of Charles II on horseback and a painting of one pensioner who married for the third time at the age of 100. A nearby chapel is decorated with flags captured during battle and a painting by Sebastiano Ricci that shows Christ's resurrection. Most resident pensioners (who number about 420) are over sixty-five years of age, though men up to ten years younger may be admitted if they are unable to work. Divided into six companies, each under an officer, they receive board, lodging, clothing, a weekly allowance and medical care. Everyday dress is a navy blue uniform with a peaked cap bearing the initials R.H. but, on ceremonial occasions, required dress is a scarlet frock coat and three-cornered hat. Many out-pensioners receive financial help from the hospital. In May each year, the CHELSEA FLOWER SHOW is held in the grounds. (See also GIBBONS, GRINLING; HAWKSMOOR, NICHOLAS.)

CHELSEA PENSIONER

See CHELSEA HOSPITAL.

CHELSEA PHYSIC GARDEN

The garden was established in 1676 by the Apothecaries' Company (one of the LIVERY COMPANIES) so that its members could conduct research into the properties of medicinal plants. Although initially the land was leased, the property (in Swan Walk on the north bank of the RIVER THAMES) was gifted to the company in 1722 by HANS SLOANE. In 1732, seed sent to James Oglethorpe in Georgia stimulated the growth of the cotton industry in North America. There is, in addition to the herb garden, a wide range of shrubs and trees (the first cedars in England were planted at the site in 1684).

CHESSINGTON

Located at the southern tip of the BOROUGH OF KINGSTON UPON THAMES, Chessington is a predominantly residential area that developed, between the First and Second World Wars, around a medieval village core. Although the thirteenth-century church of St Mary the Virgin is of interest to architectural historians, the community's major attraction is the World of Adventures theme PARK, an extension of a zoological garden that opened in 1931 and was, for a time, the largest privately owned collection of animals in the world. In 1997, the park was bought for a reported £377 million by Charterhouse Development in a deal that also involved the purchase of MADAME TUSSAUD'S WAXWORKS. The suburb's name may be derived in part from the Old English *dun* and mean 'Cissa's hill' or 'Cissa's down'.

CHIEF COMMONER

In the CITY OF LONDON, the leader of the COURT OF COMMON COUNCIL acts as chairman of the CORPORATION OF LONDON's City Lands and Bridge House Estates Committee, which was formed in 1592 and administers many of the corporation's accounts. Because of the importance of the chairmanship, the individual holding the post became known, in nineteenth-century parlance, as the Chief Commoner, a title that gradually entered official records of office-bearers.

CHIGWELL

Although Chigwell is part of the county of Essex, it lies well within the M25 MOTORWAY, which many people consider to be the real boundary of London, and parts of it were included within the LONDON BOROUGH OF REDBRIDGE when local government in the metropolitan area was reformed in 1965. Located in the valley of the River Roding, it developed as a forest hamlet frequented by the nobility, who regularly hunted the woods in medieval times, but is now a dormitory suburb providing homes for workers who commute to city offices. Partly because of the lack of industry, many older buildings remain, including the seventeenth-century King's Head PUBLIC HOUSE, which Charles Dickens used as a model for The Maypole in *Barnaby Rudge*. Because of its upmarket reputation, Chigwell was chosen as the home of Essex girls Sharon and Tracey in the BBC television series *Birds of a Feather* though the filming was done elsewhere. The major employer is the David Lloyd Tennis Centre, a private sports complex.

CHILTERN HILLS

The Chilterns form the north-west rim of the LONDON BASIN, stretching for some 60 miles from the RIVER THAMES at Goring to the

Luton area of Bedfordshire. They reach a maximum height of only 974 feet (at Walbury Hill in Berkshire) but culminate in a chalk escarpment that dominates the low plains of central England. Large sections of the hills are covered with beech woods, which once provided the basis of a local furniture industry, but are now more important as recreational space for city dwellers.

CHILTERN HUNDREDS

Elected Members of Parliament are not permitted to resign their seats. However, they are also barred by law from holding an office of profit under the crown, so MPs wishing to leave the HOUSE OF COMMONS normally apply for the Stewardship of the Chiltern Hundreds, a position which carries a nominal salary. The 'Hundreds' are the former administrative districts of Stoke, Burnham and Desborough in the Chiltern Hills area of Buckinghamshire.

CHINATOWN

During the Second World War, a number of Chinese restaurants opened in the Gerrard Street area, south of SHAFTESBURY AVENUE, to cater to servicemen who had acquired a taste for East Asian food while serving abroad. Property was cheap and rents low, so, as Britain returned to peacetime conditions in the 1950s, several striptease clubs were established and the Chinese community (most of its members from Hong Kong) capitalized on visitors by opening shops selling foods, crafts, music, herbal medicines and other goods. From 1973, annual New Year celebrations have generated considerable tourist interest and local authorities have deliberately emphasized the Far Eastern imagery by erecting oriental arches and placing Chinese characters on street signs. As a result, the area is busy with shoppers, particularly on weekends, when Chinese people from all over south-east England arrive to stock up with foods not readily available elsewhere. (See also LIMEHOUSE.)

CHINGFORD

Chingford lies on the north-east edge of London, some 10 miles from CHARING CROSS. Saxon immigrants established a settlement in the marshes along the sides of the Bourne River but, by the twelfth century, the community had moved to nearby hillsides and was clearing the oak and beech forest to provide pastureland and timber. Although brick-makers and potters provided employment during the medieval period, the economy was essentially agricultural until, in 1873, the arrival of the Great Eastern RAILWAY encouraged urban development. The impact of the builders was more restricted than in other parts of the city, however, because, in 1878, the CORPORATION OF LONDON took control of EPPING FOREST in order to maintain it as recreational space. Also, during the first half of the twentieth century, the Metropolitan Water Board (see WATER SUPPLY) built a series of dams in the valley of the RIVER LEA, forming a string of reservoirs and preserving much of the marshland. Chingford was included within the LONDON BOROUGH OF WALTHAM FOREST, created in 1965, primarily because many of its residents commute to work in the city centre. Its name may be derived from the Old English *cingel* and *ford* and mean 'shingle crossing place'.

CHISWICK

A predominantly residential area lying 6 miles west of CHARING CROSS, Chiswick evolved at a point on the north bank of the RIVER THAMES where the currents facilitated development of a small quay and where it was possible to ford the waters to the southern shore. Until the RAILWAY arrived in 1849, it was essentially a village that focused on several large estates (see, for example, CHISWICK HOUSE) and on the production of fresh fruit and vegetables for the London market. The new transport system, however, attracted commuters wanting to work in the city but live in the countryside. The estates were sold, subdivided and built over as developers raised flats and terraced

A view of Chiswick, c. 1750, from an old print.

homes to meet the needs of the incomers (in the 1920s and 1930s, the Duke of Devonshire's lands, south of Chiswick High Road, were the last to succumb). After the Second World War, much of the area was the focus of regeneration and improvement programmes that incorporated office development, local authority housing and upgrading of the A4 road, leading to the M4 motorway and the West of England. Chiswick was included in the LONDON BOROUGH OF HOUNSLOW when that authority was created in 1965. Its name probably derives from the Old English *ciese* and *wic*, and indicates that it is the location of a farm where cheese was made. (See also AIR RAIDS; ROYAL HORTICULTURAL SOCIETY.)

CHISWICK BRIDGE

The road bridge connecting CHISWICK (on the north bank of the RIVER THAMES) to MORTLAKE (on the south) was opened in 1933. Its three concrete arches, faced with PORTLAND STONE, are the finishing point for the annual boat race between Oxford and Cambridge Universities. (See also UNIVERSITY BOAT RACE.)

CHISWICK HOUSE

In 1714–5 and in 1719, Richard Boyle, the third Earl of Burlington, made lengthy visits to Italy. A gifted architect, he was much influenced by the building styles he saw there and modelled Chiswick House (erected in 1725–9) on one of Andrea Palladio's villas near Vicenza. His friend, William Kent, was responsible for the interior and for the garden (which departed from the tradition of formal topiary by adopting a more natural look). The structure (two suites of apartments around an octagonal-domed saloon) proved highly influential, sparking a revival of interest in the classical style and influencing ROBERT ADAM'S work. However, Burlington never lived in it, preferring to use it as a gallery for his art collection and for entertaining his friends, who included Alexander Pope, Jonathan Swift and George Frideric Handel. In 1892, it was converted for use as a mental HOSPITAL and in 1928 was purchased by the Middlesex County Council in order to prevent the land from being acquired by developers. The property is now managed by English Heritage, the government's conservation agency.

CHOLERA

See SNOW, JOHN.

CHRIST CHURCH, NEWGATE STREET

See GREYFRIARS MONASTERY.

CHRIST CHURCH, SPITALFIELDS

Considered by many critics to be one of architect NICHOLAS HAWKSMOOR's masterpieces, Christ Church was consecrated in 1729. Representing a brief flirtation with the baroque building style before the flowering of Palladianism (see CHISWICK HOUSE), it has four pillars to mark the entrance, which is surmounted by a tower and spire. The interior is spacious, with Corinthian columns and aisles overlooked by two tiers of gallery. However, after over two centuries of use, it was declared unsafe in 1957 and closed to worshippers. Planners proposed demolition in order to allow new development in the area but a campaign led by John Betjeman and T.S. Eliot forced them to back down. During the 1990s, Friends of Christ Church, SPITALFIELDS, obtained grants from English Heritage and from the National Lottery to enable a start on renovations, which included restoration of the organ and replacement of features destroyed by the Victorians.

CHRISTIE'S

One of the leading auction houses in London, Christie's was established in 1766 by James Christie, a former midshipman in the Royal Navy, who sold a wide range of goods from his base in PALL MALL. In 1823, his son (also James) transferred the business to 8 King Street, where it has remained ever since (although the premises were reconstructed following bomb damage during the Second World War). During the twentieth century, the firm became renowned for its Eton-educated experts, whose social contacts with wealthy families sustained a flow of art to the salerooms. The 1980s and 1990s, in particular, were marked by high-profile auctions, including a bid of £24.75 million for Vincent Van Gogh's *Sunflowers* in 1987. In 1997, worldwide sales exceeded £1.2 billion, surpassing those of arch rival SOTHEBY'S for the first time since 1954. The following year, Frenchman François Pinault bought the firm for a sum of over £900 million, taking it out of British control. Sales are held on five days each week from October until July.

CHRIST'S HOSPITAL

See GREYFRIARS MONASTERY.

CHURCHILL, WINSTON SPENCER

(1874-1965)

Churchill was born at Blenheim Palace (Oxfordshire) on 30 November 1874, the elder son of Lord Randolph Churchill and his wife Jennie. He studied at HARROW School (his letters home suggest he felt that his parents were not paying him enough attention) and the Royal Military Academy Sandhurst then, in 1895, joined the 4th Queen's Own Hussars as a second lieutenant and went with the regiment to India (1896) and Egypt (1898). After resigning his commission in 1889, he covered the Boer War for the *Morning Despatch* and entered Parliament as the Conservative MP for Oldham in 1900. He later represented Manchester and Dundee constituencies as a Liberal before returning to the Conservative fold and, in 1924, winning the marginal seat at Epping (later renamed WOODFORD) in 1924, holding it for the rest of his career in the HOUSE OF COMMONS.

After he became Prime Minister in 1940, Churchill directed the country's Second World War effort from No. 10 DOWNING STREET, the CABINET WAR ROOMS (a former Board of Trade building overlooking ST JAMES'S PARK), and a disused LONDON UNDERGROUND station at the corner of PICCADILLY and Down Street (near HYDE PARK CORNER). Aware of the growing German threat during the 1930s, he had spoken frequently of London's vulnerability to air attack (in 1934, for example, he referred to the city as 'the greatest target in the world, a kind of tremendous, fat, valuable cow tied up to attract the beast of prey') and, during the BLITZ, he encouraged anti-aircraft gunners to keep firing even when they couldn't see anything because he felt that was better for Londoners' morale than cowering in the quiet of their homes and AIR-RAID shelters waiting for bombs to fall. Frequently, too, he would climb up to attic windows and roofs to watch the action then, wearing his hat and smoking his cigar, he attempted to keep up the spirits of those who had lost family, friends and homes by touring the damaged sites. In 1944, as the V1 bombs fell, he assured Josef Stalin that the attacks had 'no appreciable affect upon the ... life of London' while, in private, he considered the options for reprisals.

In 1945, with the war over, the country voted a Labour government into power and Churchill was reduced to leadership of the opposition. He became Prime Minister again in 1951 but was never as effective in peace as in war. In 1955, he resigned. He died on 24 January 1965. Following a state funeral, he was buried beside his father in the graveyard of St Martin's Church, close to Blenheim Palace.

Although Chartwell, in the Kent countryside, was undoubtedly Churchill's favourite base, he had several homes in London (apart from his official residences). The most notable were 29 St James's Place (1880-3), 35A Great Cumberland Street (1883-1900), 105 Mount Street (his first bachelor apartment, in which he lived from 1900 until 1905), 12 Bolton Street (1905-9), 33 Eccleston Square (1909-13 and 1916-7), 41 Cromwell Road (1915-6), 16 Lower Berkeley Street (1918), 1 Dean Trench Street (1919-20), 2 Sussex Square (1920-4), 11 Morpeth Mansions (1932-9) and 28 Hyde PARK Gate (1945-65). (See also ADMIRALTY, THE; BLUE PLAQUES; BRITISH ACADEMY; CARLTON CLUB; MADAME TUSSAUD'S WAXWORKS; ST MARGARET'S CHURCH, WESTMINSTER; SIEGE OF SIDNEY STREET.)

CHURCH OF THE IMMACULATE CONCEPTION, WESTMINSTER

The church, in Farm Street, is the English headquarters of the Jesuit movement. Built to plans prepared by J.J. Scoles and opened in 1849, it has a nave flanked by red granite pillars and a high altar designed by AUGUSTUS WELBY NORTHMORE PUGIN. After 1963, when it was made a parish church, it became very fashionable and hosted many society weddings.

CIRCLE LINE

Buoyed by the success of London's first UNDERGROUND RAILWAY, which ran its inaugural services in 1863, Parliament approved proposals to extend the track into a loop connecting the main line stations north of the RIVER THAMES. The Metropolitan RAILWAY was given powers to complete part of the work and a second company – the Metropolitan District Railway – was formed to do the rest. Unfortunately, the relationship between the firms proved acrimonious so construction was not finished until 1884, and even then only pressure from powerful financial interests in the CITY OF LONDON ensured the building of the final link from ALDGATE to MANSION HOUSE. For nearly half a century both railways ran services along the route as branches of other services but in 1933, when the LONDON PASSENGER TRANSPORT BOARD took the capital's transport services into public ownership, the Circle Line was given its individual identity. A circuit of the 37 miles of track, stopping at each of the twenty-seven stations, takes about fifty minutes. Trains (and maintenance depots) are shared with the HAMMERSMITH AND CITY LINE. In 2003 maintenance of the line's infrastructure was franchised to Metronet, a consortium of private businesses, but LONDON UNDERGROUND remained responsible for providing the services. (See also EAST LONDON LINE; VICTORIA.)

CITY AND GUILDS OF LONDON INSTITUTE

The institute, based in Giltspur Street, was founded in 1878 by the LIVERY COMPANIES and the CORPORATION OF LONDON to promote technical and scientific education, with an

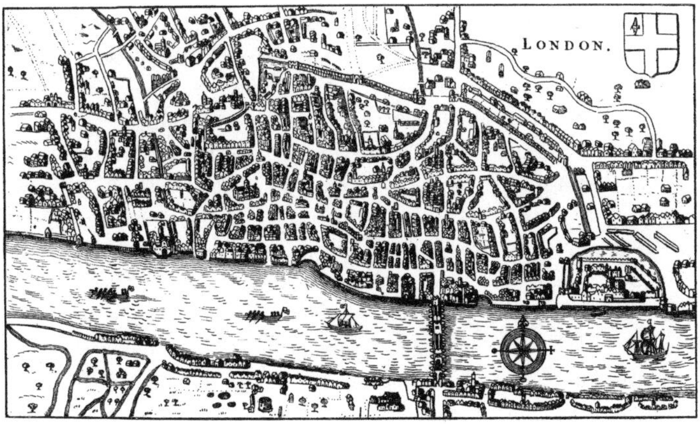

A plan of the City of London in the time of the Tudors.

emphasis on technology and on fine art as applied to industry and commerce. It has become England's principal examining body for craft skills, testing students in over 400 subjects as disparate as communications, flour confectionery and radio operation. In addition, it provides a consultancy, research and training service.

CITY CHAMBERLAIN

The Chamberlain, whose post dates from 1237, is the CORPORATION OF LONDON's principal finance officer.

CITY CORPORATION

See CORPORATION OF LONDON.

CITY LIVERY COMPANIES

See LIVERY COMPANIES.

CITY OF LONDON

The City covers 677 acres (or slightly over 1 square mile) at the heart of the capital and has a permanent population of only about 7,200 people (2001), most of whom are residents in the BARBICAN development or security workers in offices. The date of the earliest settlement is unknown but excavations clearly indicate that the Romans established a substantial community during the first century AD, maintaining a presence until AD 410 (see LONDINIUM). The Saxons arrived during the fifth century (Ethelbert, the first Christian king of Kent, founded ST PAUL'S CATHEDRAL in AD 604) and ruled through ALDERMEN, a system that was retained after the Norman Conquest in 1066. In 1067, William the Conqueror, the Norman leader, granted the City a charter recognizing the rights and privileges it had enjoyed under Saxon rule (but cannily built the TOWER OF LONDON just outside the eastern wall so that the citizens were constantly reminded who was in charge). During the medieval period, the accumulation of wealth and prestige associated with the presence of royalty made London the richest city in England, an affluence that often resulted in funds being loaned to monarchs so that they could pursue military campaigns (or other policies) both at home and abroad. Astute civic leaders used that financial dependence to win concessions from the Crown, ultimately developing a unique system of local government (see CORPORATION OF LONDON), with a LORD MAYOR, attended by SHERIFFS, supported by the weekly Court of Husting (composed of the Aldermen) and, from 1285, advised by groups of respected residents who became known as the COURT OF COMMON COUNCIL.

Financial dealings have remained the principal economic activity and a major (albeit declining) source of employment in the City, which has become one of the world's leading trading centres. During the early 1970s, some 500,000 men and women commuted, every weekday, from suburbs to the offices that line the narrow streets, virtually excluding all other businesses except those (such as the PUBLIC HOUSES) that serve them. By the early twenty-first century, however, the tide had lessened, with only about 280,000 people arriving each day, a reflection of changing technology (notably the introduction of computers) and changing employment practices (particularly a trend towards working at home). About 75 per cent of the employees work for financial concerns and about 40 per cent for foreign companies (there are some 560 non-British banks in the City).

In terms of domestic and foreign earnings, the influence of the 'SQUARE MILE' is enormous. City-based banks invest more capital abroad than those of any other country, accounting for about 18 per cent of global foreign loans. The foreign exchange market is by far the world's largest, with a daily turnover in 1996 of US$464 million, more than that of New York and Tokyo combined (nearly twice as much trading in the dollar takes place in London as in the United States). Also, the City is the world's largest insurance market, accounting for nearly 30 per cent of world marine insurance and nearly 40 per cent of aviation insurance. In addition, it is the global centre for forward trading in gold and (through the LONDON METAL EXCHANGE) sets world prices for non ferrous metals. (See also BALTIC EXCHANGE; BANK OF ENGLAND; BARBICAN; BEDLAM; BIG BANG; BLACKFRIARS; BRIDEWELL; CANNON STREET STATION; CENTRAL LINE; CHEAPSIDE; CIRCLE LINE; CITY CHAMBERLAIN; CITY MARSHAL; CITY REMEMBRANCER; COLE ABBEY CHURCH, DISTAFF LANE; COMMON CRYER AND SERJEANT-AT-ARMS; COMMON HALL; COMMON SERJEANT; COMPTROLLER AND CITY SOLICITOR; CORN EXCHANGE; CORNHILL; CUSTOM HOUSE; DOCKLANDS LIGHT RAILWAY; EASTCHEAP; FINSBURY PARK; FLEET STREET; FREEDOM OF THE CITY; GREATER LONDON AUTHORITY; GREAT FIRE; GREAT PLAGUE; GUILDHALL; HOUNDSDITCH; INTERNATIONAL PETROLEUM EXCHANGE (IPE); LEADENHALL MARKET; LIVERY COMPANIES; LLOYD'S OF LONDON; LOMBARD STREET; LONDON ASSEMBLY; LONDON BRIDGE; LONDON FIRST; LONDON INTERNATIONAL FINANCIAL FUTURES AND OPTIONS EXCHANGE (LIFFE); LONDON INTERNATIONAL INSURANCE AND REINSURANCE MARKET ASSOCIATION (LIRMA); LONDON METAL EXCHANGE (LME); MANOR PARK; MANSION HOUSE; NEWGATE; NEWGATE PRISON; METROPOLITAN LINE; METROPOLITAN POLICE; MOORGATE; NORTHERN LINE; RECORDER OF LONDON; ST ANDREW UNDERSHAFT CHURCH, LEADENHALL STREET; ST BARTHOLOMEW'S HOSPITAL; ST BARTHOLOMEW-THE-GREAT CHURCH, SMITHFIELD; ST BENET'S CHURCH, PAUL'S WHARF; ST BOTOLPH'S CHURCH, ALDGATE; ST BRIDE'S CHURCH, FLEET STREET; ST DUNSTAN-IN-THE-WEST CHURCH, FLEET STREET; ST ETHELBURGA-THE-VIRGIN-WITHIN-BISHOPSGATE CHURCH, BISHOPSGATE; ST ETHELDREDA'S CHURCH, HOLBORN; ST MARY ABCHURCH CHURCH, ABCHURCH LANE; SOUTHWARK BRIDGE; STOCK EXCHANGE (LSE); SWORDBEARER; TEMPLE BAR; TEMPLE OF MITHRAS; THREADNEEDLE STREET; TOWER BRIDGE; WALBROOK; WALWORTH; WARD; WARDMOTE; WATERLOO AND CITY LINE; WATLING STREET; WHITEFRIARS.)

CITY OF LONDON POLICE

See METROPOLITAN POLICE.

CITY MARSHAL

The City Marshal is the second most senior of the LORD MAYOR's three principal personal staff, who are known as the Esquires. The post dates back to 1589 and the holder's original task was to maintain law and order in the CITY OF LONDON. Nowadays, in addition to ceremonial duties, he must ensure that the Lord Mayor's public engagements are efficiently organized. (See also COMMON CRYER AND SERJEANT-AT-ARMS; SWORDBEARER.)

CITY PRIDE INITIATIVE

See LONDON PRIDE PARTNERSHIP.

CITY REMEMBRANCER

The Remembrancer, whose office dates from the reign of Elizabeth I, is a senior law officer of the CORPORATION OF LONDON. The holder of the post, who is elected by the COURT OF COMMON COUNCIL, advises the corporation on Parliamentary matters, communicates its views to the government and the monarch, and organizes ceremonial occasions at the GUILDHALL.

CLAPHAM

A largely working-class suburb some 3 miles south-east of CHARING CROSS, Clapham was probably founded during the Anglo-Saxon period (its name may be a corruption of the Old English *clopeham*, which means 'the homestead on the hill'). Londoners, in 1664–6, seeking to avoid the GREAT PLAGUE and the GREAT FIRE settled in the area, then, in 1690, a coach service was established to Gracechurch Street, giving regular access to the ROYAL EXCHANGE and other trading institutions. Wealthy citizens, such as SAMUEL PEPYS and Percy Bysshe Shelley, set up homes as the village became increasingly fashionable during the eighteenth and early nineteenth centuries, but the arrival of the RAILWAY in 1838, and industrial development in nearby BATTERSEA, wrought changes to the social structure as workers in the new candle factories, GAS works and chemical manufactories encouraged developers to build properties more in keeping with their employees' limited means. Although these sources of income are gone, much of the Victorian character remains in the rows of closely packed terraces that still characterize the neighbourhood. In 1965, Clapham was incorporated into the new LONDON BOROUGH OF LAMBETH. (See also CLAPHAM COMMON; CLAPHAM JUNCTION; CLAPHAM SECT; DOMESDAY BOOK; LONDON TRANSPORT MUSEUM.)

CLAPHAM COMMON

Until the early eighteenth century, Clapham Common (about 4 miles south-west of CHARING CROSS) was undeveloped, frequented only by highwaymen who preyed on the stage coaches carrying travellers to the CITY OF LONDON. From 1722, however, the boggy areas were drained and the land improved, so by 1855 William Makepeace Thackeray was able to claim in *The Newcomers* (1853–5) that 'of all the pretty suburbs that adorn our metropolis there are few that exceed in charm Clapham Common.' Many of the houses that line the edge of the 200-acre open space were built by wealthy merchants and writers (SAMUEL PEPYS died at his home on North Side in 1703 and historian Lord Macaulay was born at 5 The Pavement) but the only building on the open space itself is a PUBLIC HOUSE (The Windmill) where drinkers lounge on the grass through long summer evenings. Clapham Common, unlike some of the more staid city centre PARKS, is a regular site for circuses, evangelist campaigns, reggae festivals and other boisterous events. (See also BARRY, CHARLES.)

CLAPHAM JUNCTION

Britain's busiest RAILWAY junction lies close to the industrial communities of BATTERSEA and CLAPHAM at a point where tracks from VICTORIA Station and WATERLOO Station converge. From Monday to Friday, about 1.4 million travellers and over 2,000 trains arrive every day. The first services were routed through the area in 1838, then, in 1863, a station was built. Commuters bought homes nearby and facilities were established to serve them as the community grew. Also, because of its accessibility, the area developed a reputation as an entertainment and shopping centre with MUSIC HALLS, THEATRES, cinemas and a large DEPARTMENT STORE. By the beginning of the twenty-first century, Clapham Junction had evolved into the commercial heart of Battersea, with a shopping centre located alongside the station, which was the scene of a major accident on 12 December 1988, when two passenger trains collided, killing thirty-five people. (See also BATTERSEA BRIDGE; BRIDGES.)

CLAPHAM SECT

In the early nineteenth century, a group of wealthy evangelical Anglicans (including William Wilberforce, the anti-slavery campaigner) argued that commitment to the Christian faith must be evidenced by efforts to improve the situation of the poor and oppressed. Most lived close to CLAPHAM COMMON, where they worshipped at Holy Trinity Church, so they were christened the Clapham Sect. As well as organizing financial help for the needy, they placed much stress on the importance of education as a means of improving living standards, supported missionary work at home and abroad, and founded *The Christian Observer* to propagate their views. Several members had seats in the HOUSE OF COMMONS, where they worked for prison reform and the suppression of cruel sports. The focus of activity was the Thornton family, who provided hospitality as well as encouragement; one of its principal members is commemorated in the name of Henry Thornton School in South Side, near Clapham Common.

CLARENCE HOUSE

The south-west suite of state rooms in ST JAMES'S PALACE is joined by a passage to Clarence House, designed by JOHN NASH and built for William Duke of Clarence (later William IV). The original construction work was completed in 1828, but an additional storey was added in 1873 and much restoration undertaken following bomb damage incurred during the Second World War. Although for much of the war the building was the headquarters of the Red Cross and St John's Ambulance Brigade, it has been used primarily as a residence for members of the royal family. Princess Elizabeth lived there from 1947 until 1950, giving birth to Princess Anne shortly before she left. In 1953, the Queen Mother moved into Clarence House following the death of her husband, George VI, the previous year. After she died in 2002, a £4.5 million refurbishment was carried out and plans were made for Prince Charles and his sons, William and Harry, to leave their accommodation in St James's Palace and move into the building.

CLARIDGE'S HOTEL

Claridge's is one of London's most exclusive HOTELS, patronized by royalty and heads of state. It was founded in 1855 when William Claridge (a butler) used his savings to purchase Mivart's Hotel in Brook Street, MAYFAIR, acquired by the Savoy Company in 1890 and rebuilt in red brick in 1895–9. A £42 million refurbishment, carried out in 1996–7, retained the best of the interior (including the art deco restaurant designed by Basil Ionides in 1926) and helped boost operating profits. In 1998, the Savoy Group was taken over by Blackstone and Colony, an American investment firm, at a cost of £520 million. The hotel's 420 staff service 198 rooms, with a single-bed apartment costing over £2,000 a night.

CLEOPATRA'S NEEDLE

A granite obelisk some 65 feet high and 186 tons in weight, the Needle was carved from a quarry at Aswan (Egypt) about 1475 BC, erected at Heliopolis, and carved with dedications to various gods. Later, it was moved to Alexandria, where it stood for hundreds of years before falling over. In 1819, it was presented to Britain by Mohammed Ali, the Turkish Viceroy of Egypt, but nobody was able to suggest a means of moving it until engineer John Dixon designed a special pontoon in 1877. It left Alexandria in September that year and, after surviving a storm in the Bay of Biscay, reached London the following January. Initially, it was destined for a site near the

HOUSES OF PARLIAMENT, but the location suffered from subsidence, so instead it was erected on the Victoria Embankment between HUNGERFORD BRIDGE and WATERLOO Bridge. A set of coins, four Bibles in different languages, a razor, a box of pins, Bradshaw's *Railway Guide* and copies of daily newspapers were buried beneath it, along with photographs of twelve of the most beautiful ladies of the time. The obelisk, which has no known connection with Cleopatra, was slightly damaged in one of the early AIR RAIDS on London during the BLITZ.

CLERKENWELL

Clerkenwell lies about 1½ miles north-east of CHARING CROSS, north of the CITY OF LONDON. It developed as a village around the Benedictine nunnery of St Mary and the Priory of St John of Jerusalem (see KNIGHTS HOSPITALLER), which were founded during the twelfth century on land gifted by Jordan de Briset. When Henry VIII dissolved the MONASTERIES between 1536 and 1541, most of the religious buildings were demolished and the land was given to aristocratic families, who are remembered in such road names as Albemarle Way and Aylesbury Street. During the sixteenth century, however, many of these wealthy groups moved to accommodation closer to the royal court and their homes were taken over by merchants and craftsmen. Clerkenwell was transformed into an industrial community, with skilled tradesmen employed in BREWERIES, gin distilleries, print works, jewellery manufacturing and clockmakers' shops. The discovery of medicinal springs brought additional sources of income, leading to the establishment of SADLER'S WELLS in 1683 and Islington Spa in 1685.

By 1740, the area was a popular recreational focus, but the urban expansion that accompanied the Industrial Revolution consumed most of the open space, replacing grassy banks with textile workshops, small metal plants and rows of cheap terraced houses. The situation was exacerbated by road and RAILWAY construction, which destroyed many of the worst slums but added to the number of homeless people. Poverty led to political unrest as Clerkenwell Green became a regular meeting place for protest groups.

During the early twentieth century, economic decay and slum clearance programmes resulted in population decline, but the national economic resurgence of the 1980s was reflected in an expansion of office accommodation and restoration of some of the best of the older housing, such as the Woodbridge Estate, originally erected in the late eighteenth century. Little of the original religious houses survives, but the MUSEUM of the Order of St John, in St John's Gate, outlines the history of the knights and their modern successors, the St John Ambulance Brigade, which has 250,000 members around the world. Some authorities claim that the area gets its name from a site, known as the Clerks' Well, where the Worshipful Company of Parish Clerks of the City of London performed mystery plays. (See also CHARTERHOUSE.)

CLIMATE

The weather experienced by the first Londoners must be inferred from archaeological and other indirect sources (see, for example, LONDON CLAY), but records of rainfall have been kept since 1697 and of wind direction since 1723. Over the past 300 years, climatic variations have followed a cyclical pattern, with cold winters during the 1740s and 1770s, and in 1809–17, 1836–45 and 1875–82. Since 1919, there has been a lengthy warming trend, with January temperatures averaging about 5 degrees Celsius (42 degrees Fahrenheit) in the 1990s and July temperatures averaging 18 degrees Celsius (65 degrees Fahrenheit). The inner city tends to be warmer in all months because of the heat retained by buildings, emitted by vehicle engines and dispersed by central heating equipment. Rain falls on an average of 165 days each year, amounting to 23 inches annually, and is spread fairly equally throughout the seasons. The prevailing wind is from the west-south-west. (See also AIR POLLUTION.)

CLINK PRISON

A small jail located south of the RIVER THAMES near the GLOBE THEATRE, Clink Prison was used during the sixteenth and early seventeenth centuries to lock up troublemakers from the brothels and drinking houses of the BANKSIDE area. Documentary evidence indicates that it was built by 1509, but that by the 1760s it housed only a few debtors. The prison was destroyed during the GORDON RIOTS in 1780 and never replaced. Its name is commemorated in Clink Street (where it was located) and in the vernacular phrase 'in the clink', meaning 'in prison'. The site now houses a MUSEUM that displays instruments of torture. (See also ANCHOR INN.)

CLUBS

See GENTLEMEN'S CLUBS.

COADE STONE

During the 1760s, Eleanor Coade improved the weatherproof qualities of terracotta by adding materials such as glass and ground quartz. Because of its resistance to the elements, Coade stone became very popular as an ornamental material on buildings and for making statues during the late eighteenth and early nineteenth centuries. The company, based in LAMBETH, went out of business in 1840, but its product can still be seen on such buildings as the ROYAL OPERA HOUSE in COVENT GARDEN and the lion at the south side of WESTMINSTER BRIDGE.

COCKFOSTERS

Cockfosters lies some 11 miles north of CHARING CROSS in the former royal hunting forest of ENFIELD Chase (the suburb's name is derived from the Middle English words for Chief Forester). In 1777, Dr Richard Jebb saved the life of the Duke of Gloucester, brother of King George III, while he was visiting Trento in the Italian Alps and, as a token of gratitude, the royal family gave him 200 acres of the Chase for his own use. Jebb commissioned the architect WILLIAM CHAMBERS to convert a lodge into a more spacious manor house on the estate, which later became known as Trent PARK, and Cockfosters gradually developed at the south-west edge of the property, initially consisting of a few cottages for agricultural workers, some larger villas for wealthier families and a PUBLIC HOUSE (known as The Cock). Growth was slow until, in 1933, the arrival of the PICCADILLY LINE fuelled residential development. By the outbreak of the Second World War the settlement was transformed, becoming part of the metropolitan area, but the establishment of the GREEN BELT prevented northward expansion of the bricks and mortar from 1938 and, although many gap sites have been filled in, local residents still have access to semi-rural areas. From 1939 until 1945, Jebb's house at Trent Park was used as an interrogation centre for German prisoners of war. Later, it became a teacher training college, which merged with Middlesex Polytechnic (now Middlesex UNIVERSITY) in 1974. The grounds were acquired by local authorities and opened to the public in 1974. When London's local government was reformed in 1965, Cockfosters was included in the LONDON BOROUGH OF ENFIELD.

COCKNEY

By tradition, a Cockney is an individual born within the sound of BOW BELLS. The term (derived from the Middle English *cokeney*, which means 'a misshapen egg' or 'cock's egg') was applied during the Middle Ages to weak or effeminate men, but by the seventeenth century was widely used as a denigrating synonym for 'Londoner'. More recently, Cockneys have been depicted, by filmmakers and novelists, in a romanticized fashion, as happy-go-lucky working-class people with a distinctive dialect (using rhyming slang such as 'plates of meat' for 'feet', for example) and an accent that makes much use of the glottal stop. (See also EAST END; LAMBETH WALK.)

COFFEE HOUSES

In 1652, Pasqua Rosee (a Greek immigrant) opened London's first coffee house in St Michael's Alley, close to the ROYAL EXCHANGE. Although the smell of coffee was sometimes considered a public nuisance, the new drink quickly became fashionable so within ten years there were eighty-two establishments in THE CITY, with other businesses serving cocoa and chocolate. The houses were important foci for gossip and transmission of news, so patrons selected the ones most suited to their business and social needs; those in PALL MALL were favoured by wealthy aristocrats, the St James's Coffee House (at 87 St James's Street) was known as the haunt of Whig supporters, Will's (at 1 Bow Street) was frequented by scholarly writers such as John Dryden, the Bedford (in COVENT GARDEN) attracted a theatrical clientele (including DAVID GARRICK) and Child's (in Warwick Lane, close to ST PAUL'S CATHEDRAL) was preferred by clergymen (and the frequently less than morally upright JAMES BOSWELL). In order to preserve their distinctiveness, and keep out unwanted guests, many coffee houses began to charge subscriptions and ultimately evolved into gaming rooms or GENTLEMEN'S CLUBS (White's, at 37–38 St James's Street, originated as White's Chocolate House, for example). Lloyd's Coffee House, originally located in Tower Street, became the insurance market now known as LLOYD'S OF LONDON.

A scene in a London coffee house, c. 1688, from a contemporary engraving.

Reductions in the tax on coffee in 1808 and 1825 led to an enormous growth in the number of coffee houses during the nineteenth century and to an increase in coffee drinking by less affluent members of the community. Fashionable society moved on to other pursuits, but the seventeenth- and eighteenth-century businesses (which also sold wine and spirits) left a legacy in the language and habits of modern PUBLIC HOUSES. The buxom, cheerful barmaid made her first appearance in early coffee houses as proprietors used her charms to attract male custom (César de Saussure noted that he was waited on by 'beautiful, neat, well-dressed and amiable, but very dangerous nymphs', and essayist Sir Richard Steele commented that 'These Idols receive all day long the admiration of the Youth'). The bar, a term now applied to a drinking establishment as well as to the counter at which drinks are sold in a pub, was the place, close to the fire, where the coffee pots were kept warm in the coffee houses. (See also BALTIC EXCHANGE; CORNHILL; HAMP-

STEAD; KNIGHTS HOSPITALLER; STOCK EXCHANGE (LSE); THEATRE ROYAL, DRURY LANE.)

COLE ABBEY CHURCH, DISTAFF LANE

After the GREAT FIRE of 1666, Cole Abbey (then known as St Nicholas Cole Abbey) was the first church to be rebuilt to designs prepared by CHRISTOPHER WREN. Its name is probably a corruption of *Coldharbour*, a Middle English term for 'shelter', but may also be derived from a moorage on the RIVER THAMES where fishermen landed their catches. The original chapel was founded at least by 1144, when it is mentioned in written records, and was the site of the first Roman Catholic Mass to be said in London after Mary I succeeded to the throne in 1553 and re-established the papal authority rejected by Henry VIII nineteen years earlier. Wren's replacement, completed in 1677, is built of red brick, with stone facing on the south side. It was damaged by bombs on 11 May 1941 (the last heavy attack of the BLITZ), but many of the furnishings (including the pulpit and font) were saved and returned to their original sites when restoration work (using Wren's plans) was completed by Arthur Bailey in 1962.

COLLEGE OF ARMS

The college, which regulates the conferment of armorial bearings throughout the United Kingdom (except Scotland) and in the Commonwealth of Nations, was founded by Richard III in 1484 and has occupied its present site in Queen Victoria Street since 1555. Its original building was destroyed by the GREAT FIRE of 1666 but replaced in 1671–8 by a structure designed by Morris Emmett, Master Bricklayer to the Office of Works. The Earl Marshal (a hereditary title held by the Dukes of Norfolk since 1672) is the chief official, responsible for organizing major state ceremonials, such as coronations. He is assisted by three kings of arms, six heralds and four pursuivants. All are members of the royal household rather than civil servants.

COMMITTEE ON HOUSING IN GREATER LONDON (1963–1965)

See MILNER HOLLAND REPORT.

COMMON CRYER AND SERJEANT-AT-ARMS

The Common Cryer carries the mace that precedes the LORD MAYOR of the CITY OF LONDON on ceremonial occasions, opens meetings at COMMON HALL and organizes the Lord Mayor's daily activities. The origin of the office is unknown but it was certainly established by 1338.

COMMON HALL

The assemblies that choose candidates for the post of LORD MAYOR and elect the SHERIFFS of the CITY OF LONDON are known as Common Hall. Traditionally, they are held on Midsummer's Day (24 June) to vote for the Sheriffs and on Michaelmas Day (29 September) to select two ALDERMEN to contest the mayoral position. The franchise is limited to members of the LIVERY COMPANIES. (See also COMMON CRYER AND SERJEANT-AT-ARMS; COMMON SERJEANT.)

COMMON SERJEANT

The Common Serjeant is one of the principal legal officers of the CORPORATION OF LONDON, second in rank to the RECORDER OF LONDON. He acts as the Recorder's deputy at the CENTRAL CRIMINAL COURT and, at COMMON HALL, submits the names of candidates at elections for LORD MAYOR and SHERIFF. His attendance is also required at ceremonial events. The position was established at least by 1319 and, until 1888, was filled by election. Since then, the job has gone to people nominated by the Crown, though the Corporation, which pays the salary, must formally approve the appointment.

COMMONWEALTH INSTITUTE

The institute, located in Kensington High Street, acts as an information centre for members of the Commonwealth of Nations, offering conference facilities for business interests, hosting art exhibitions, providing extensive library facilities for researchers and working with schools to provide material for classroom projects. Originally founded to commemorate the golden jubilee of Queen Victoria's rule in 1887 (when it was known as the Imperial Institute), it is housed in a pagoda-like building designed by Sir Robert Matthew (of Johnson-Marshall and Partners) and opened in 1962. Most of the organization's funding is provided by the British government through the Foreign and Commonwealth Office.

COMPTROLLER AND CITY SOLICITOR

A senior official of the CORPORATION OF LONDON, the Comptroller and City Solicitor is principally responsible for the conduct of the authority's legal business but also participates in many of the CITY OF LONDON's ceremonial activities and carries out other traditional duties (such as ensuring the security of the keys to the City Seal, which is used to authenticate formal documents). The duties are an amalgamation of tasks previously held by individual officers of the corporation (for example, the post of City Solicitor dates from 1545).

CONGESTION CHARGES

On 17 February 2003 KEN LIVINGSTONE, London's mayor, introduced a £5-a-day toll on vehicles driving within an 8-square-mile area of the city centre. 700 video cameras police the system by scanning the rear number plates of 250,000 vehicles which enter the area between 7 a.m. and 6.30 p.m. during the working week. Drivers can pay in advance at shops and garages, over the phone or by internet but attempts to dodge the charge can result in fines of up to £120. Much of the anticipated annual revenue of £120 million will be used to improve bus services. The tolls were introduced in an attempt to reduce congestion in the city centre (research studies show that the average speed of vehicles in central London was only 8.6 miles per hour in 2003) and the success of the experiment is being closely watched by planners in other cities which experience similar problems.

CONNAUGHT HOTEL

In 1891–3, Carlos Place was built to improve movement between GROSVENOR SQUARE and BERKELEY SQUARE in MAYFAIR. The Connaught was erected on the west side of the street in 1897, occupying a site that had provided accommodation for visitors to the city since 1815. Initially, Auguste Scorrier, the proprietor, called it 'The Coburg' but the name was changed in 1917 because of anti-German feeling in Britain. During the Second World War, it served as a headquarters for Charles de Gaulle's Free French forces. The Connaught was once known as London's home for landed families because many wealthy individuals rented permanent suites. Now part of the Savoy Group, it is one of the capital's leading HOTELS, recognized for its discreet service and outstanding restaurant.

CONSTITUTION ARCH

See HYDE PARK CORNER.

CONSTITUTION HILL

A tree-lined avenue connecting THE MALL with HYDE PARK CORNER, Constitution Hill separates the gardens of BUCKINGHAM PALACE from GREEN PARK. It was the site of unsuccessful attempts to assassinate Queen Victoria in 1840, 1842 and 1849, and the location where Sir Robert Peel (founder of the METROPOLITAN POLICE force) met his death after falling from his horse in 1850. Nobody knows how the street got its name, but some scholars suggest that Charles II exercised there in order to improve his constitution. (See also LONDON MARATHON.)

CORN EXCHANGE

London's first Corn Exchange was erected in 1747 at Mark Lane, the location of a CITY OF

LONDON market founded during the late thirteenth century. Initially, it was little more than a walled courtyard open to the elements, but extensions and improvements were made at various stages during the nineteenth and early twentieth centuries. The building was severely damaged in 1941, during the BLITZ, but reopened in 1954. In 1987, business transferred to the BALTIC EXCHANGE, where dealers trade in such commodities as fertilizer and animal feed as well as in cereals.

CORNHILL

One of eight streets that meet at the BANK OF ENGLAND, Cornhill may have got its name from the medieval grain MARKET that was held on the site. It was well-known both for its stocks, where merchants caught cheating were clamped, and (from the sixteenth to the nineteenth centuries) for the COFFEE HOUSES that flourished in its alleyways. Although the present buildings, dating from the late 1800s, are now occupied mainly by finance firms, the area once had important literary associations. Thomas Guy, who founded GUY'S HOSPITAL in 1721, had a bookshop at the junction with LOMBARD STREET and poet Thomas Gray was born in a house on the site where No. 39 now stands. Smith and Elder ran a publishing business at No. 65 (now No. 32) from 1816 until about 1868 (Charlotte and Anne Brontë caused Mr Smith much consternation when they appeared at his office in 1848 to prove that they were the authors he knew as Currer and Acton Bell) and CHARLES DICKENS' Mr Pickwick stayed on several occasions at the George and Vulture Inn in Castle Court, attended by Sam Weller. There are two churches – St Peter-upon-Cornhill and St Michael – both of which were designed by CHRISTOPHER WREN but have since been much restored. St Peter's is allegedly built on the site of the Roman basilica constructed in AD 179. (See also CENTRAL LINE; GREYFRIARS MONASTERY.)

CORPORATION OF LONDON

Local government within the CITY OF LONDON is organized by a corporation whose powers and procedures are determined as much by precedent as by statute. It consists of a LORD MAYOR (who serves for one year), two SHERIFFS (who are junior only to the Lord Mayor in status), ALDERMEN (whose responsibilities are largely administrative) and a COURT OF COMMON COUNCIL (an elected body representing residents). From the thirteenth until the eighteenth centuries, the Aldermen carried out most duties, but the Court of Common Council has been the effective governing body for the past 200 years, meeting in the GUILDHALL. Much of the work is done by committees that have specific areas of responsibility, such as the management of EPPING FOREST, educational provision and the conduct of LEADENHALL MARKET. (See also CHIEF COMMONER; CITY AND GUILDS OF LONDON INSTITUTE; CITY CHAMBERLAIN; CITY MARSHAL; CITY REMEMBRANCER; COMMON CRYER AND SERJEANT-AT-ARMS; COMMON HALL; COMMON SERJEANT; COMPTROLLER AND CITY SOLICITOR; FREEDOM OF THE CITY; GUILDHALL SCHOOL OF MUSIC AND DRAMA; LONDON PRIDE PARTNERSHIP; MANSION HOUSE; MUSEUM OF LONDON; RECORDER OF LONDON; ROYAL NAVAL DOCKYARDS; SWORDBEARER; THAMES, RIVER; THEATRE; WARD; WARDMOTE; WATERMEN; WATER SUPPLY.)

COUNTY HALL

In 1905, the LONDON COUNTY COUNCIL (LCC) decided to build a new headquarters on a site south of the RIVER THAMES opposite the HOUSES OF PARLIAMENT (see PALACE OF WESTMINSTER). Construction at the location, formerly occupied by a complex of lumber yards and small factories, began in 1909, was halted in 1916 because of the First World War and resumed in 1919. The building, designed by Ralph Knott following an international competition, was formally opened by George V on 17 July 1922 but was not fully completed for another eleven years. A six-storey structure finished in PORTLAND STONE and granite, it has a series of internal courtyards as well as office space, rooms for committee meetings and a debating chamber. Additional premises to the south (built to plans prepared by the LCC's own staff of architects) were added in 1963. County Hall became the main base of the GREATER LONDON COUNCIL in 1965 and lay empty for several years after that body was abolished in 1986. In 1993, however, it was bought by a Japanese company and converted into a family entertainment complex with HOTELS and restaurants attached. The major attractions are a large aquarium and a soccer MUSEUM.

COURT OF ARCHES

The court is the principal court of appeal for the Church of England's Province of Canterbury. It gets its name because it originally met at St Mary-le-Bow Church (see BOW BELLS), which was also known as the Church of Sancta Maria de Arcubus. From 1660 until about 1800, it stood at the centre of the ecclesiastical judicial system, handing down judgments on marriage, inheritance and moral issues, but in the nineteenth century most of its rights were transferred to the secular courts. Reports (known as Process Books) of about 10,000 of its cases are held at LAMBETH PALACE, providing historians with much information about life in southern England during the late seventeenth and eighteenth centuries.

COURT OF COMMON COUNCIL

On the first Friday in December, voters in each of the twenty-five WARDS (local electoral areas) in the CITY OF LONDON elect freemen (see FREEDOM OF THE CITY) to serve on the Court of Common Council, which, since the eighteenth century, has been the principal decision-making body in the CORPORATION OF LONDON's local government structure. Most of the candidates are members of the LIVERY COMPANIES; those who are successful are known as Common Councilmen, hold office for one year and are eligible for re-election at the end of their term. Meetings of the court are held at the GUILDHALL every third Thursday (except during the summer and Christmas holidays). The LORD MAYOR presides over debates, which are different in context from those in the council chambers of the LONDON BOROUGHS because the participants have not been elected on the basis of their allegiance to a political party. Common Councilmen form the bulk of the corporation's numerous committees, which deal with matters as distinct as management of open spaces and the conduct of MARKETS. On formal occasions, they wear a mazarine (light blue) gown with short, fur-trimmed sleeves.

COURTAULD INSTITUTE OF ART

In 1931, the institute was founded by textile manufacturer Samuel Courtauld (at the suggestion of Viscount Lee of Fareham) as a college of the University of London (see UNIVERSITIES) and a centre for the study of Western art. Both men, anxious to provide the university with facilities equivalent to the Ashmolean Museum in Oxford and the Fitzwilliam Museum in Cambridge, bequeathed their collections of paintings to it when they died in 1947. These gifts were augmented by donations from the estates of Robert Witt (1952), William Spooner (1967) and others. The Courtauld (the first educational institution in Britain to award degrees in art history) was originally based in Portman Square, with its galleries in Woburn Square, but it moved to SOMERSET HOUSE in 1990. It houses one of Europe's most important collections of impressionist and post-impressionist paintings and makes its library of 130,000 books, along with an archive of 3 million photographs, available to scholars. In addition, it supports research centres studying illuminated manuscripts and Romanesque sculpture in Britain and Ireland.

COUTTS AND COMPANY

Although Coutts is best known as Elizabeth II's banker, it can also claim the distinction of being one of the oldest finance houses in London. It was founded in 1692 by John Campbell but became particularly well established during the second half of the eighteenth century, largely through the business skills of Edinburgh brothers James and Thomas Coutts, who were made partners in the firm in 1755 and 1760 respectively. George III placed his account in their hands, a practice followed by every British monarch since. Now part of the RBS/NatWest, Coutts has fifteen branches in London, with its headquarters at 440 Strand in a building designed by Frank Gibberd and Partners and opened in 1978 (the structure retained elements of the site's early nineteenth-century developments planned by JOHN NASH). Traditions that all male employees must wear a frock coat and eschew beards are still observed.

COVENT GARDEN

Following Henry VIII's dissolution of the English MONASTERIES in 1536–41, the Covent Garden area – an open space owned by WESTMINSTER ABBEY and used by the monks to grow vegetables – was acquired by the Crown, then, in 1552, granted to John Russell, first Earl of Bedford, as a reward for his services to Edward VI (see BEDFORD ESTATES). In 1630, Francis Russell, the fourth Earl, was granted a development licence by Charles I and commissioned INIGO JONES to design one of London's first extensive planned estates. Jones drew on his knowledge of Leghorn (Italy) and Paris to prepare a scheme that incorporated a piazza (measuring 316 feet from north to south and 420 feet from east to west) with, on the west side, ST PAUL'S CHURCH, which was intended to provide a focus for the new community. The southern aspect, fronting the earl's gardens, was left open, but the northern and eastern fringes of the square were lined by tall, terraced houses more typical of continental European ARCHITECTURE than of English styles. Conservative critics voiced their opposition but, after the buildings were erected, Russell found no difficulty commanding high rents from tenants such as poet William Alexander, dramatist Thomas Killigrew and courtier Sir Edmund Verney.

The harmony of Jones's design lasted only a few decades, however. In 1670, William Russell, fifth Earl (and later first Duke) of Bedford obtained a royal charter to hold a daily fruit and vegetable MARKET in the piazza and to collect tolls from traders. With a grow-

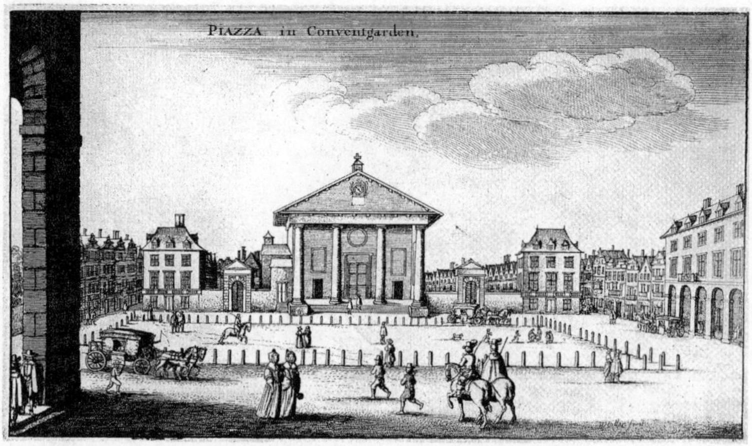

The piazza in Covent Garden, an engraving by Hollar.

ing urban population located nearby and 15,000 acres of market gardens within a radius of 10 miles, the market expanded rapidly, changing the social and economic context of the area in the process. COFFEE HOUSES, Turkish baths and brothels were opened to meet the needs of the newcomers, and the formerly patrician houses were subdivided into small apartments, many of which were taken over by actors.

In 1828, faced with increasing congestion and consistent flouting of the trading rules, Parliament approved legislation intended to reorganize the buying and selling of goods. The temporary booths were replaced, during the 1830s, by permanent halls, which were designed by Charles Fowler and described in the *Gardener's Magazine* as of 'great beauty and elegance', but which also completely obliterated Jones's piazza. In 1874–5 and 1888–9, these halls were covered by glass and iron roofs but that did nothing to reduce complaints from residents as more and more people flocked to the area and traders spread into nearby streets. In 1918, the Duke of Bedford (finding that most of the income from Covent Garden was being spent on upkeep of the buildings and regulation of trade) sold the concern to the Covent Garden Estate Company, owned by the Beecham family, then, in 1962, an Act of Parliament established the Covent Garden Market Authority to manage the complex, paying the Beechams £3.9 million for the business.

In 1974, trading transferred to a new, purpose-built site at NINE ELMS, a move that destroyed a traditional way of life in inner London, spelt the end for many small local businesses (such as PUBLIC HOUSES and newsagents) that relied on the market workers for income, and left a large city-centre site unused. As early as 1969, the GREATER LONDON COUNCIL, following the prevailing fashion for commercial development, had indicated that it intended to demolish most of the older buildings and erect office blocks in their place, but public protests were so vehement and so sustained that, in 1971, a public inquiry sent the planners and politicians back to their drawing boards. New, and more widely acceptable, proposals were prepared for conversion of the market hall into small units, primarily specialist shops, boutiques, wine bars and restaurants, with offices on the top floor. Booths now line the open areas and street entertainers provide music, juggling and puppet shows, attracting hundreds of thousands of visitors to one of London's newer tourist attractions.

Covent Garden lies within the CITY OF WESTMINSTER. (See also GARRICK CLUB; LONDON TRANSPORT MUSEUM; ROYAL OPERA HOUSE; THEATRE MUSEUM; THEATRE ROYAL, DRURY LANE.)

CRAYFORD

Crayford is located south of the RIVER THAMES at a point, some 15 miles east of CHARING CROSS, where invading Jutes defeated the Britons in AD 457 and where the main road from London to Dover crosses the River Cray. It developed as an industrial centre during the seventeenth century, when Cresheld Draper, the local landowner, established linen bleaching and textile printing processes. The manufacture of chemicals, optical instruments, carpets, bricks and knife handles was added following the Industrial Revolution, then, in 1888, Hiram Maxim introduced production of machine guns. Also, the first Wolseley cars were built at Crayford in 1903. Many of the commercial buildings were destroyed in AIR RAIDS during the BLITZ but St Paulinus's Church, which dates from the decades following the Norman Conquest in 1066, still stands, its chancel located between twin naves and its altar hidden by the piers of the arcade. Since the area was incorporated within the LONDON BOROUGH OF BEXLEY in 1965, a series of business parks have been developed, attracting such major companies as Burmah Castrol Chemicals, British Telecom and Allied Mills.

CRICKET

See ESSEX COUNTY CRICKET CLUB; LEYTON ORIENT FOOTBALL CLUB; LORD'S CRICKET GROUND; MARYLEBONE CRICKET CLUB; MIDDLESEX COUNTY CRICKET CLUB; OVAL, THE; SURREY COUNTY CRICKET CLUB.

CRICKLEWOOD

A suburb to the north-east of WILLESDEN, Cricklewood is a largely residential area that straddles Edgware Road, where most commercial development is located. The arrival of the Midland RAILWAY stimulated growth from 1868, resulting in the construction of terraces of small homes for the labour force and the building of large goods and coal sidings. The availability of TRANSPORT and a pool of skilled manual workers attracted aircraft manufacturer Handley Page to the area in 1913, then, after the First World War, motor company Armstrong Siddeley provided additional employment. However, limitations of space restricted technological change and, in 1930, these businesses moved out, leaving the land (including Handley Page's aerodrome) for conversion into playing fields, housing estates and premises for small light-engineering firms. The area's name may be derived from the Middle English words *crikeled* and *wode*, indicating 'a curved wood'.

CRIPPLEGATE

Cripplegate was built by the Romans as a northern entrance to LONDINIUM (see LONDON WALL). The derivation of its name is uncertain, some scholars claiming that cripples once begged there, others that it comes from the Old English *crepel* (which means 'covered way' and may refer to the invaders' defences), and some that lame sightseers were cured when the body of Edmund the Martyr passed through in 1010. The structure was rebuilt by the Brewers' Company (one of the LIVERY COMPANIES) in 1244 and served as a prison during the fourteenth century. Further reconstruction was carried out in 1491, but, in 1760, the gate was demolished so that improvements could be made to the road system. (See also GREAT FIRE; SHAKESPEARE, WILLIAM.)

CROWN JEWELS

The crown jewels, and other items used during the coronation of a new monarch, are permanently on display in the TOWER OF LONDON. The oldest items are an ampulla (dating from about 1399) and a spoon (dating from the twelfth century), both of which are used when a new ruler is anointed. The other elements of the regalia date from the mid-seventeenth century or later because, after the execution of Charles I in 1649, the earlier symbols of majesty were destroyed by Parliamentarians. St Edward's crown was probably fashioned from one of the older crowns for the coronation of Charles II in 1661; weighing 5 pounds, it is used for the crowning ceremony but, because of its weight, immediately replaced by the lighter Crown of State, which was made for Queen Victoria. In addition, there is a jewelled sword and golden spurs (both of which represent knighthood), an orb (symbolizing Christianity's dominance of the globe), a ring (celebrating Dignity), and a sceptre (standing for regal power and justice). All are made of precious metals and richly adorned with precious stones (the Crown of State, for example, has a frame of fine gold inset with over 3,000 jewels, mainly diamonds and pearls but including a ruby presented to the Black Prince during the fourteenth century). Other items on display include the crown made for the coronation of Queen Elizabeth (consort of George VI) in 1937; it includes the 109-carat Koh-i-Noor diamond, which is supposed to bring good luck to a woman who wears it but bad luck to a man.

CROUCH END

The Crouch End suburb lies 5 miles north of CHARING CROSS. It evolved during the medieval period as a route centre (its name is derived from the Latin *crux*, which means *cross*) and is still an important transport node. The area became built-up during the nineteenth century and is now a locally important retail and service focus in the LONDON BOROUGH OF HARINGEY.

CROYDON

A suburb lying some 10 miles south of CHARING CROSS, Croydon is located at a point where the Roman road from London to Portsmouth followed a dry valley into the NORTH DOWNS. The settlement was established by Saxon times, developed partly due to the patronage of the Archbishops of Canterbury (it was the last stop on the journey from the ecclesiastical capital of England to the nation's centre of government), and, by the seventeenth century, had become a significant market and administrative town. In 1803, the Surrey Iron RAILWAY (the world's first public rail service, provided by horse-drawn carriages) linked the town to WANDSWORTH, then the arrival of the steam railway in 1839 encouraged further urban growth and, in 1920, the local aerodrome became London's first significant civil AIRPORT. Serious bomb damage during the BLITZ allowed local authorities to undertake a wholesale reconstruction of the central business area from 1954, deliberately promoting accessibility as a means of attracting office firms and building shopping and entertainment complexes in order to encourage in-migration of labour. As a result, the modern townscape is more typical of the American central city than the British, with more than fifty skyscrapers dominating the street pattern. Croydon may have got its name from the Old English *crogen* and *denu*, which denote a long, narrow valley where saffron grows. (See also EAST LONDON LINE; EPSOM; RENNIE, JOHN.)

CROYDON, LONDON BOROUGH OF

Croydon, with 330,600 residents (2001) has the largest population of all the LONDON BOROUGHS. Covering 33 square miles, it was formed in 1965 through the amalgamation of the County Borough of CROYDON, the Rural District of Coulsdon and the Rural District of Purley. Since then, the local authority has vigorously pursued a policy of attracting commercial and retail development. As a result, central Croydon alone has some 2.7 million square feet of office space and one of the most popular shopping complexes outside the WEST END. Although many people travel by train to central London for work, the borough itself provides significant employment in financial services, the retail sector and healthcare. The south of the area is archetypal commuter land, with communities such as Cousldon and Purley living in detached and semi-detached houses close to golf courses and the open land of the GREEN BELT. Farther north, there are fewer professional and managerial workers, a larger IMMIGRANT presence and greater residential mobility, but owner-occupation rates are high and scores below average on deprivation indices. (See also ADDINGTON PALACE; AIRPORTS.)

CRYSTAL PALACE

One of the principal features of the GREAT EXHIBITION in 1851 was the structure designed by Thomas Paxton and built in HYDE PARK to house some of the principal exhibits. It took 2,000 workmen, who used 400 tons of glass, 4,000 tons of iron, 200 miles of wooden sash bars and 30 miles of guttering, to build the palace, then, when it was completed, troops of soldiers were told to jump and shout inside to make sure that it would stand up to the wear and tear of visitors. When the exhibition ended, the building was re-erected south of the RIVER THAMES on a hilltop at Sydenham, where it served as a THEATRE, concert hall and exhibition centre at the hub of an amusement PARK. On the night of 30 November 1936, however, it burned to the ground. The site was redeveloped during the 1960s to provide a National Sports Centre, with an Olympic-standard swimming pool, a dry ski slope, an athletics stadium and facilities for indoor activities. 200 acres of surrounding land were landscaped to provide PARKS, gardens and boating lakes. (See also BRUNEL, ISAMBARD KINGDOM; CRYSTAL PALACE FOOTBALL CLUB; EAST LONDON LINE.)

CRYSTAL PALACE FOOTBALL CLUB

The CRYSTAL PALACE was built to house the GREAT EXHIBITION in 1851 and was then moved to SYDENHAM, where it became the focus of a south London theme PARK. It gave its name to several sports groups which formed in the mid-nineteenth century, including a football club founded in 1861 by workers on the site. Crystal Palace was one of the fifteen teams which took part in the first FA Challenge Cup competition in 1872 and twenty cup finals were played at its ground between 1895 and 1914, with crowds of over 100,000 arriving by public transport for the games.

In 1905, the club was reformed as a professional side, playing in the Southern League. During the First World War, its ground was used by the Army so it transferred to HERNE HILL and then, in 1919, to The Nest, a site opposite the present-day Selhurst railway station. It was elected to the Third Division (South) of the Football League in 1920, won promotion after only one season and moved to Selhurst Park, a former brickfield and still its home, in 1924. For the next forty years, it had little success and, in 1956, was placed in the newly formed Fourth Division. Promotion to the Third Division followed in 1961, to the Second Division in 1964 and to the First Division in 1973 but the side was unable to maintain its advance and has see-sawed between divisions ever since. Its most successful period was in the late 1980s and early 1990s. In 1981, when local support was ebbing away and income was falling, Ron Noades (previously the owner of WIMBLEDON FOOTBALL CLUB) bought the business. Three years later, he installed Steve Coppell as manager and, under Coppell's astute eye, players, acquired free or cheaply, blended to form an effective team based on fast attacking forwards good enough to take Manchester United to a replay in the FA Cup final of 1990 and win the Zenith Data Systems Cup (for full members of the Football League) in 1991.

In the 1990/91 season, Crystal Palace finished third in the First Division and five players won international caps, but it proved difficult to hold on to the stars and financial fortunes, as well as footballing fortunes, waned again, reaching their nadir in 1998, when Mark Goldberg took over as Chairman. Within months, doubts were raised about Goldberg's finances as well as those of the club, and administration was placed in the hands of the Official Receiver amid rumours of debts amounting to as much as £22 million. Budget cuts meant that players were transferred, long-serving staff members were made redundant and employees who remained were unpaid for long periods. By 2000, however, circumstances had improved. Debts amounted only to some £4 million and the club survived. The Selhurst Park ground, which has been much renovated from 1969, now has a capacity of 26,000. (See also CHARLTON ATHLETIC FOOTBALL CLUB.)

CUBITT, THOMAS (1788–1855)

Until the early nineteenth century, anyone wanting labour to erect a building had to contract with individual craftsmen. Cubitt was the first businessman to tackle the whole task, from site clearance to interior fixtures, and so was responsible for many of the London properties that were completed during the construction boom of the Regency and early Victorian periods. The son of Jonathan Cubitt, he was born in Buxton (Norfolk) on 25 February 1788 and trained as a carpenter before setting up business on his own in 1809. Faced with the economic necessity of keeping his workforce busy, he purchased vacant land, built houses, then sold the properties – a speculative approach to commerce that was to become his hallmark. His first projects were in HIGHBURY and the ST PANCRAS area, but he realized that wealthy individuals were seeking property to the west, rather than the north, of the CITY OF LONDON and, from 1825, turned his attention to BELGRAVIA. In addition, he undertook much work for the royal family, including the construction of the east front of BUCKINGHAM PALACE. Cubitt was one of the principal advocates of the establishment of BATTERSEA PARK and of improvements in urban environmental quality (he limited the output of smoke from his Thames Bank factory, for instance). He made significant donations to educational and religious organizations and negotiated the purchase of a property for the GREAT EXHIBITION without charging any fee. He also made sure that his employees were treated fairly; when his premises were destroyed by fire in 1854, he refused to lay off any of his men and allocated finances to replace their tools. Cubitt died, a self-made millionaire, at his home near Dorking on 19 November 1855. (See also CUBITT TOWN; ISLINGTON; PIMLICO; STOKE NEWINGTON; VICTORIA.)

CUBITT TOWN

During the 1840s and 1850s, the land at the south-east of the ISLE OF DOGS was developed by William Cubitt (LORD MAYOR of London in 1860–1 and brother of builder THOMAS CUBITT) to provide an industrial complex of sawmills, brickworks, timber wharves and a cement factory as well as homes for DOCK workers. Most of these sources of employment no longer exist, but the area remains largely working class, consisting primarily of local authority housing estates, although some private homes were built along the RIVER THAMES during the 1970s in an attempt to diversify the social composition of the community.

CUPER'S GARDENS

During the late seventeenth and early eighteenth centuries, these long, narrow gardens were a popular place of recreation for middle-class Londoners. They were opened in about 1683 by Abraham Boydell Cuper, gardener to Thomas Howard, Earl of Arundel, and located on the south side of the RIVER THAMES in SOUTHWARK on a site now covered by the southern approaches to WATERLOO Bridge. During the summer months in particular, visitors arrived by boat to follow winding paths, lined with trees and shrubs, towards a landscaped lake at the west end of the property. Further attractions were added in 1738, when Ephraim Evans took over the business and established a band, which played during the evenings. Servants in livery were not allowed to enter and watchmen were employed to keep potential troublemakers out. In 1753, new legislation designed to reduce the incidence of theft resulted in the conversion of much of the area into a tea garden but in 1760 the facilities closed down and the land was developed as a vinegar distillery.

CUSTOM HOUSE

London's first centre for the collection of import and export duties was erected at Old Wool Quay, on the north bank of the RIVER THAMES near the TOWER OF LONDON, in 1273. It was rebuilt in 1378 then again in 1559 (after being burned down), 1669 (following damage in the GREAT FIRE), 1717 (three years after it was destroyed by an explosion in a nearby gunpowder store) and 1817 (after another conflagration). The present structure, in Lower Thames Street, was designed by David Laing and is located a few yards west of the thirteenth-century premises.

The name is also applied to an area of south NEWHAM near the Royal Victoria DOCK where customs were collected during the nineteenth century. It developed as an area of working-class housing close to employment in riverside industries but suffered greatly from

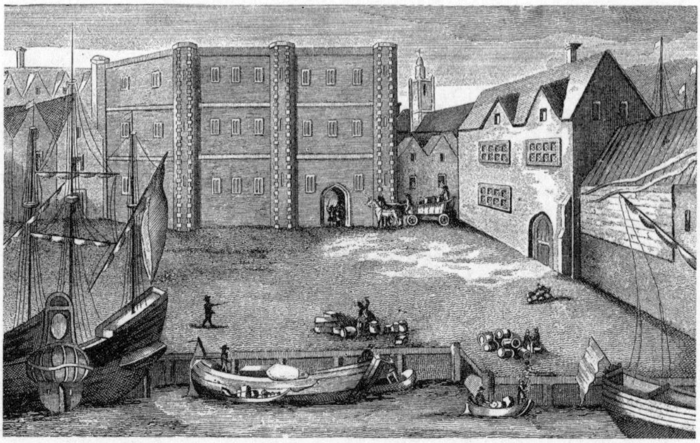

View of the Custom House, *c.* 1600.

bombing during the BLITZ and was extensively redeveloped, largely for residential purposes, after the end of the Second World War. A research unit, founded by Sir Patrick Manson at a seamen's HOSPITAL close to the Royal Albert Dock in 1890, evolved into the London School of Tropical Medicine, which is now part of the University of London (see UNIVERSITIES).

CUTTY SARK

One of the last, and one of the fastest, of the tea clippers that sailed between Britain and the Far East, the *Cutty Sark* (212 feet 5 inches long, 36 feet wide and weighing 921 tons) was built at Dumbarton (Scotland) in 1869 for John Willis, a London ship-owner. The construction work bankrupted the builders (Scott and Linton) so the final fitting was carried out by William Denny and Brothers. After a period of carrying cargoes of Australian wool, the vessel plied between Portugal and North America before undergoing a complete refit in 1922. She served as a training ship for young sailors until after the Second World War then was restored to her original state. Since 1954, she has lain in dry DOCK at GREENWICH, housing an exhibition of ships' figureheads and maritime prints. Her name is taken from Robert Burns' poem *Tam O' Shanter*, which includes a reference to a shapely young witch wearing only a cutty sark, or short shift. Alongside her lies the 54-foot-long ketch *Gipsy Moth IV*, in which Francis Chichester, then in his sixties, made a solo circumnavigation of the world from 27 August 1966 to 28 May 1967. In recognition of the achievement, Elizabeth II knighted Chichester using the sword with which Elizabeth I had conferred the same honour on Francis Drake 387 years earlier.

D

DAGENHAM

Lying on the marshy north bank of the RIVER THAMES, about 12 miles east of the city centre, Dagenham developed as a working-class suburb of London during the twentieth century. It was founded during Saxon times (its name is derived from the Old English *Deccanhaam*, which means 'Decca's home') and remained a predominantly agricultural settlement until the end of the First World War. From then, however, it became increasingly residential and industrial, with the population rising from about 9,000 in 1921 to over 114,000 in 1951. In part, the change was due to provision of local authority housing on sites away from the congested inner-city core (for example, over half of the 27,000-home Becontree Estate – the largest public development of its kind in Europe at the time – was in Dagenham). Also, industrialists found the extensive areas of flat land inviting: the Ford Motor Company began production there in 1931 and Bryant and May (makers of matches) followed three years later. Other manufacturing companies produced goods as diverse as telephone cables, armaments and popcorn. The trends continued into the second half of the century, obliterating all of the early rural settlement except parts of the medieval church and an inn dating from about 1500. In 1965, most of the community was united with BARKING, its western neighbour, in the LONDON BOROUGH OF BARKING AND DAGENHAM, although some territory in the north was incorporated within the LONDON BOROUGH OF REDBRIDGE.

DALSTON

Dalston lies in London's EAST END, some 4 miles north-east of CHARING CROSS. Probably founded in Anglo-Saxon times (the name may be derived from *Deorlaf*, a personal name, and the Old English *tun*, meaning homestead), it was an agricultural village until the 1830s, when local landowners succumbed to the financial inducements of developers and began to sell sites for housing. Market gardens that had sold fresh produce to city markets were dug up and their soil was moulded into building bricks. Many of the early properties (such as those at De Beauvoir Square, designed by R.L. Roumieu and built in 1838) housed affluent families but, with growing industrialization, the area rapidly evolved into a working-class suburb of the expanding metropolitan area. In the twentieth century, local authorities became increasingly involved in slum clearance and house-building programmes, varying from the low-rise Somerford Estate (1946-9) to tower blocks erected in the 1960s and demolished thirty years later (as at the Holly Tree Estate). Partly because housing is cheap by London standards, the area has attracted a large number of

IMMIGRANTS, initially Jews, Turks and Africans but now including significant groups of Vietnamese, Kurds and others (the variety of foods available in Ridley Road market, the commercial heart of the area, bears witness to the community's multicultural background). In recent years, some streets have experienced gentrification as young couples have bought properties and invested in improvements (Tony Blair and his wife, Cherie, made 59 Mapledene Road their first married home, for example). Dalston was included in the LONDON BOROUGH OF HACKNEY when local government in the metropolitan area was reformed in 1965. (See also EAST LONDON LINE.)

DANCE, GEORGE the Elder (1700–1768)
During the middle years of the eighteenth century, George Dance the Elder designed the MANSION HOUSE, several churches and numerous other public buildings in the CITY OF LONDON. The son of a mason, he joined his father's business in 1717 and was responsible for the refurbishment of the stonework at the South Sea Company's headquarters as well as in the Carshalton home of Sir John Fellows, its Governor. In 1732, he worked with surveyor James Gould, his father-in-law, on designs for a development at the Minories then, in 1735, was appointed Clerk of Works to the CORPORATION OF LONDON. Dance's new post carried no salary but conferred the prestige he needed in order to attract private commissions from wealthy clients and organizations. Over the next fifteen years, he prepared plans for the Mansion House (1739), St Leonard's Church, SHOREDITCH (1736), ST BOTOLPH'S CHURCH, ALDGATE (1741–4), St Matthew's Church, BETHNAL GREEN (1743–6), a new corn market in Mark Lane (1747), a headquarters for the Surgeons (one of the LIVERY COMPANIES) in 1748 and a replacement (which was never built) for NEWGATE PRISON. Then, from 1756 until 1760, he collaborated with Robert Taylor on the renovation of LONDON BRIDGE, a task that involved demolition of housing and replacement of the two arches with a single span. Although some writers have praised his ability to maximise the use of cramped sites, modern architects often consider his designs clumsy and uninspired. Dance died on 8 February 1768 and was buried at St Luke's Church, Old Street. (See also FINSBURY.)

DANCE, GEORGE the Younger (1741–1825)
The son of GEORGE DANCE THE ELDER (who designed the MANSION HOUSE), Dance was responsible for the rebuilding of NEWGATE PRISON (1770–8), the neoclassical design of All Hallows Church at LONDON WALL (1765–7), the oval layout of FINSBURY Circus (1777) and the unusual mixture of Gothic, Greek and Indian elements on the front of the GUILDHALL (1788–9). However, most of the structures were swept away in subsequent redevelopment programmes, leaving only street patterns and a few properties (such as the group of five-storey houses in The Crescent, near TOWER HILL) as a legacy. Born in Chiswell Street, Moorfields, he studied in Italy from 1758 until 1764 then trained as an architect in his father's office, eventually succeeding him as Clerk of Works to the CORPORATION OF LONDON in 1768. He was elected a Fellow of the Society of Antiquaries in 1794 and was a founding member of the ROYAL ACADEMY OF ARTS, with which he held the post of Professor of Architecture from 1798 until 1805. As he aged, he tended to forsake building design for art, contributing several chalk portraits to academy exhibitions. He died at his home in Gower Street (now No. 91) on 14 January 1825 and was buried in ST PAUL'S CATHEDRAL.

DENMARK HILL
A south London suburb, lying east of BRIXTON, Denmark Hill is named after Prince George of Denmark, whose wife (Queen Anne) had a house in the area. Development in the nineteenth century was largely resi-

dential and middle class, with writer John Ruskin living at 163 Denmark Hill from 1843 until 1872 and engineer Henry Bessemer (inventor of the steel manufacturing process that bears his name) maintaining a mansion on a site now occupied by a housing estate. During the early twentieth century, the combination of a semi-rural environment and easy access to central London attracted a number of institutional interests, notably King's College HOSPITAL (1913), Maudsley HOSPITAL (1915) and the Salvation Army's WILLIAM BOOTH Training College (designed by GILES GILBERT SCOTT and opened in 1932).

DEPARTMENT STORES

In the mid-nineteenth century, most goods in London were sold in specialist stores or in bazaars, such as that established by John Trotter at SOHO in 1816. During the 1860s and 1870s, however, William Whiteley (following trends in Paris) bought up shops in middle-class Westbourne Grove, BAYSWATER, and advertised himself as a 'Universal Provider'. HARRODS, founded in 1853 as a grocery store, followed suit in equally fashionable KNIGHTSBRIDGE, then, over the next thirty years, drapers in OXFORD STREET, REGENT STREET and PICCADILLY expanded their premises, making businesses such as Debenham's, Dickens and Jones, and Swan and Edgar household names.

The first purpose-built department store in the city was Bon Marché, opened by James Smith at BRIXTON in 1877 and backed by money he won gambling on horse races. Others followed in the early years of the twentieth century, most notably SELFRIDGE'S, which brought American sales methods to Britain. In succeeding decades, some retailers (such as Marks and Spencer) became international concerns, but by the early twenty-first century most were feeling the sharp edge of competition from low-cost discount stores and some (such as C&A) were forced to close.

DEPTFORD

Located on the SOUTH BANK of the RIVER THAMES between ROTHERHITHE and GREENWICH, Deptford was a convenient fording point across the River Ravensbourne (the first element of the settlement's name probably derives from the Old English *deop*, or 'deep'), so it became the last stop for coaches travelling from Dover to London and developed as a village with an inn serving the passengers. In 1513, however, Henry VIII established a ROYAL NAVAL DOCKYARD at Deptford Creek, transforming the small settlement into a burgeoning industrial centre and attracting ancillary services such as the victualling yard, which became the British Navy's most important supply depot. TRINITY HOUSE, which ensures that Britain's coastal waters can be navigated safely, was based at Deptford during the sixteenth century, and the EAST INDIA COMPANY, formed in 1600, developed shipbuilding facilities and warehouses on the west side of the creek. For over 300 years, the port was a major focus of Britain's maritime development – Francis Drake set sail from the harbour in 1577 on the start of his circumnavigation of the world, James Cook left to search for the continent of Terra Australis in 1768 and, in 1820, the General Steam Navigation Company became one of the first firms in the world to offer scheduled services in coal-powered vessels.

The emphasis on the sea and ships continued to flourish until 1869, when the DOCKyard closed, a victim of silting by the Thames' currents and lack of space for expansion. The victualling yard survived until 1961 but its site has since been developed as a large local authority housing estate named after SAMUEL PEPYS, who, during the seventeenth century, was Secretary to the Navy Board, which managed the docks. Little of the medieval fabric of the area remains, with the exception of the fifteenth-century ragstone tower of the parish church, dedicated to St Nicholas, the patron saint of sailors (the church itself was severely damaged by an incendiary device, dropped by German bombers in 1940, but was subsequently restored). However, Albury Street retains some early Georgian houses, with elaborately carved door cases, which were occupied by sea captains during the early 1700s. The modern community is working class and multicultural (about 20 per cent of the population is of Afro-Caribbean descent) but has suffered little from ethnic tensions. In 1992, the government provided funding for a regeneration programme designed to improve the quality of the urban area and attract new employment. The UNIVERSITY of Greenwich has a campus in the town, which forms the north-east corner of the LONDON BOROUGH OF LEWISHAM. (See also EVELYN, JOHN; GIBBONS, GRINLING.)

DESIGN MUSEUM

The MUSEUM, which opened in 1989 at a former warehouse on Butler's Wharf, was funded by the Conrad Foundation as part of the London DOCKLANDS regeneration project. It has two main galleries, one showing how design affects the way commercial products look and how they are used, the other displaying examples of contemporary design from around the world. Exhibits range from children's toys to household furniture and from kitchen appliances to artwork.

DICKENS, CHARLES (1812–1870)

Dickens used his vast knowledge of London to weave tales of city life that fascinated Victorian Britain. The eldest son of civil servant John Dickens and his wife, Elizabeth, he was born in Portsea (near Portsmouth) on 7 February 1812. The family moved to the London area two years later, settling, in 1816, at Chatham, which features in the partly autobiographical *David Copperfield* (1849–50) and other stories. John Dickens, on whom Charles modelled Mr Micawber (one of the characters in the novel), was, apparently, an affectionate father, but he had little financial sense. As a result, the family frequently suffered hard times, notably in 1824, when Mr Dickens was committed, as a debtor, to the MARSHALSEA PRISON and Charles was withdrawn from school so that he could earn an income making up parcels in a warehouse. The experience was undoubtedly humiliating for a middle-class boy, but it provided a wealth of material for his literary work; the impoverished landlady from whom he rented a room in CAMDEN TOWN was the model for Mrs Pipchin in *Dombey and Son* (1848), the Marshalsea features in *Little Dorrit* (1857) and scenes involving vulnerable young people appear frequently in other writings. In 1825, as his fortunes improved, he obtained a job as a legal clerk, then, after learning shorthand (as described in *David Copperfield*), he found employment as a reporter in the law courts before becoming a journalist specializing in Parliamentary matters.

In 1833, using Boz as a pen name, Dickens began to submit articles to periodicals. The success of these essays led to an invitation from publisher Chapman and Hall to write a narrative that would accompany a series of engravings. The result – *The Pickwick Papers* (1836–7) – was an outstanding success, largely through the creation of a kindly, streetwise COCKNEY whom Dickens named Sam Weller. On the strength of that reception, he gave up his newspaper job, wrote *Oliver Twist* (1837–9) as a series for *Bentley's Miscellany* (which he edited), then followed with *Nicholas Nickleby* (1839), *The Old Curiosity Shop* (1840–1) and *Barnaby Rudge* (1841), creating a series of humorous characters but stressing the problems of the poor and needy in nineteenth-century cities. As fame and fortune increased, he moved from 48 Doughty Street in HOLBORN (1836–9), to 1 Devonshire Terrace (1839–51), then to Tavistock House in Tavistock Square, BLOOMSBURY (1851–60) and finally to Gad's Hill, Rochester (1860–70). His output was enormous as he edited weekly periodicals, wrote stories, commented on political affairs, designed amateur theatricals and gave public readings. However, by the 1850s his spirits were at a low ebb; his marriage was crumbling and disillusionment with the politics of Viscount Palmerston's Liberal government was evident in novels such as *Bleak House* (1852–3) and *Little Dorrit* (1857), which were much less effervescent than their predecessors, with heavier symbolism and more complex characterization. After his wife left him in 1858, he turned increasingly to public appearances, undertaking lengthy tours to provincial towns, as well as to France and the United States, but the rigours of travelling, coupled with perpetual brooding, wore him down. He collapsed suddenly on the evening of 8 June 1870, after working on *Edwin Drood*, and died the following day. (See also ARCHWAY; BLACKFRIARS; CARLYLE'S HOUSE; CORNHILL; DICKENS' HOUSE MUSEUM; GEORGE INN; HAMPSTEAD HEATH; HIGHGATE CEMETERY; HOLLAND HOUSE; JACK STRAW'S CASTLE; KENSAL GREEN; NEWGATE PRISON; OLD CURIOSITY SHOP; ROOKERIES; ST DUNSTAN-IN-THE-WEST CHURCH, FLEET STREET; ST PANCRAS; SPANIARDS, THE; TWICKENHAM.)

DICKENS' HOUSE MUSEUM

The MUSEUM is based at 48 Doughty Street, the sole surviving London home of CHARLES DICKENS (1812–70). He moved in during March 1837, along with Kate (his wife) and Charles (their baby son). During his stay, he wrote *Oliver Twist* (1837–9), *Nicholas Nickleby* (1839), parts of *The Pickwick Papers* (1836–7) and *Barnaby Rudge* (1841). By 1839, however, Mrs Dickens had given birth to two daughters and the terraced house had become cramped, so, in October, the family moved to 1 Devonshire Terrace (near REGENT'S PARK). In 1924, the property was acquired by the Dickens Fellowship, which displays many first editions of the writer's work alongside such personal possessions as the velvet-covered desk he used for public readings.

DISTRICT LINE

Following the success of its first UNDERGROUND venture (the line between Farringdon and PADDINGTON, opened in 1863), the Metropolitan RAILWAY prepared proposals to extend the route into a circle which would link the overground termini north of the RIVER THAMES. However, the capital required for such a venture was considerable so a second company – the Metropolitan District Railway – was formed to build the southern section of track. Initially, it was expected that the two firms would merge, but differences between the management led to estrangement and the District (always the Cinderella of the two) sought financial success by bringing workers from south-west London to jobs in the City. It began services between South KENSINGTON and WESTMINSTER in 1868 and extended to MANSION HOUSE three years later. Then it turned to the west, reaching Kensington OLYMPIA in 1872, HAMMERSMITH in 1874, RICHMOND in 1877, EALING Broadway in 1879, HOUNSLOW in 1883 (the branch was transferred to the PICCADILLY LINE in 1964) and WIMBLEDON in 1889. Pressure from business interests in the CITY OF LONDON led to the completion of the inner circle project (now the CIRCLE LINE) in 1884 and ultimately to the extension of services eastwards to Upminster in 1902. In 1901, close to bankruptcy, the company was taken over by Charles Tyson Yerkes and four years later the line was electrified. Most trains are serviced at Ealing Common and Upminster though those on the Richmond and Wimbledon branches go to Hammersmith and NEASDEN. In 2003, maintenance of the line's infrastructure was franchised to Metronet, a consortium of private businesses, but LONDON UNDERGROUND remained responsible for providing the services. (See also VICTORIA.)

DOCKLANDS

The 8½ square miles of former DOCKS, which comprise the world's largest urban regeneration scheme, are known as Docklands. During the late 1960s, the RIVER THAMES shipping business moved downstream to Tilbury, leaving an extensive area close to the city centre derelict as port facilities closed. In 1971, initial plans to convert the area to office and commercial purposes were rejected by the Conservative government in the face of public outcry but, ten years later, the London Docklands Development Corporation (LDDC) was established to secure long-term physical, social and economic regeneration of the area by creating an attractive environment, providing housing that would enable people to live on the site and encouraging businesses to open up. By 1998, it had built over 20,000 homes, virtually doubled the population (from 39,400 to 77,000) and spent £1.75 billion of public money. The private sector had invested £6.27 billion, constructed 14.7 million square feet of office space and provided 43,000 new jobs, with major international companies such as News International and Citibank moving in. The social infrastructure also improved as eleven new primary schools were built, specialty stores opened and £116 million was spent on community programmes, health centres and other amenities. Critics complained that TRANSPORT provision was limited and that the lack of strict planning control had resulted in a disjointed landscape. Also, in times of recession, speculators had difficulty selling property but most observers felt that the benefits of change outweighed the weaknesses. In 1994, the LDDC began to wind down its activities and hand its properties and responsibilities to the LONDON BOROUGHS OF NEWHAM, SOUTHWARK and TOWER HAMLETS, finally closing its offices in March 1998. (See also DESIGN MUSEUM; DOCKLANDS LIGHT RAILWAY (DLR); EXCEL; INTERNATIONAL PETROLEUM EXCHANGE (IPE); JUBILEE LINE; LONDON COMMODITY EXCHANGE; POOL OF LONDON; PORT OF LONDON AUTHORITY (PLA).)

DOCKLANDS LIGHT RAILWAY (DLR)

Proposals to regenerate the economy of London's DOCKLANDS during the 1970s and 1980s relied on the provision of a modern TRANSPORT infrastructure which, by facilitating the movement of goods and employees, would encourage commercial and manufacturing concerns to establish offices and plant in the area. Construction of an electrified light RAILWAY, using a third rail to supply power because the London Docklands Development Corporation was opposed to unsightly overhead cables, began in 1984 and utilized existing or abandoned lines wherever possible in order to reduce costs. The initial services, which ran in 1987, linked STRATFORD to the ISLE OF DOGS and the southern edge of the City close to the TOWER OF LONDON.

Although the trains were unmanned and the stations unstaffed, the route was enormously popular, with hourly passenger numbers exceeding forecast daily totals within weeks of the line's opening and encouraging planners to extend stations, increase the length of trains and consider expansion of the system. In 1991, new tunnelling provided a link to Bank Station (and the first connections to the LONDON UNDERGROUND system) in the heart of the CITY OF LONDON. In 1998, the line was extended east to BECKTON and the following year a route was developed south of the RIVER THAMES to LEWISHAM. By 2002, thirty-two carriage units were carrying some 160,000 passengers through thirty-four stations along 17 miles of track every working day. Maintenance is carried out at depots in Beckton and POPLAR.

In 1997, the DLR was franchised to a consortium consisting of the railway management and Serco, a public company with global interests in transport and other services. Serco bought out the shares of the former management the following year and will run the services until 2006. (See also CANARY WHARF; CANNING TOWN.)

DOCKS

London's docks date at least from the days of the Romans because archaeological evidence shows that the invaders tied their galleys to posts on the north bank of the RIVER THAMES, close to their base along the Walbrook Stream. By the 1720s, according to Daniel Defoe, there were 'about two thousand sail of all sorts, not reckoning barges, lighters or pleasure boats or yachts' using the harbour facilities, which, before the end of the century, had become thoroughly congested. The commerce promoted by the Industrial Revolution added to the problems but also encouraged several companies to invest in construction schemes designed to stimulate trade. Between 1802 and 1921, a series of enclosed docks was built along both sides of the river in a 10-mile stretch from the western end of the POOL OF LONDON downstream to Gallions Reach. The most westerly was St Katharine's (opened in 1828 beside the TOWER OF LONDON) and the most easterly the 245-acre Royal Group (the largest area of impounded dock water in the world). The establishment of a PORT OF LONDON AUTHORITY in 1909 provided a means of comprehensive planning, boosting commerce significantly, so, by the early 1960s, a labour force of about 100,000 was handling over 60 million tons of cargo each year.

The period between 1965 and 1981 brought a change of fortune. Faced with competition from foreign ports, outdated equipment and a growth in container ships that required deep-water berths closer to the mouth of the Thames, dock companies located near the city centre went out of business, closing yards that were later to be redeveloped as office, leisure and housing complexes (see DOCKLANDS). The main focus of activity is now at Tilbury, some 20 miles downstream from TOWER BRIDGE. Originally opened in 1886, its wharves and warehouses have been much modernized in recent years, with new provision for containers, bulk cargoes (such as steel and grain) and roll-on, roll-off ferry traffic. The improvements have allowed London to maintain its position as Britain's largest port (and the eighth largest in Europe) in terms of annual cargo tonnage processed. In addition, a cruise terminal has been constructed to handle the growing leisure traffic. A MUSEUM outlining the social and economic history of the area opened in a converted nineteenth-century warehouse at West India Quay, Hartsmere Road, in 2003. Also that year, the government earmarked former dock areas as a site for the construction of 15,000 new homes in an attempt to reduce south-east England's housing shortage. (See also BERMONDSEY; BLACKWALL; BLITZ; BOOTH, CHARLES; CANNING TOWN; CUBITT TOWN; CUSTOM HOUSE; EAST INDIA COMPANY; LIMEHOUSE; LONDON DOCK STRIKE; MILLWALL; POPLAR; RENNIE, JOHN. Opening and closing dates for individual docks are listed in the Chronology of Historical Events, beginning on page 428.)

DOGGETT'S COAT AND BADGE RACE

In 1713, Thomas Doggett, manager of the DRURY LANE Theatre (see THEATRE ROYAL), left a will ensuring that part of his estate would provide a coat and silver badge for the winner of a boat race to take place every year on the RIVER THAMES. The oldest annual sporting event in the country, it is held on 1 August over a 4½-mile course from LONDON BRIDGE to Cadogan Pier at CHELSEA, with participants sculling against the ebb tide.

DOMESDAY BOOK

William the Conqueror defeated Harold II at the Battle of Hastings and was crowned king of England on Christmas Day 1066. In the years that followed, he extended his power over the country and, in 1085, ordered a national survey of his possessions so that he could maximise his returns from land taxes. The Domesday Book, the most comprehensive record of the time, was completed the following year but although the *Anglo-Saxon*

Chronicle claims that 'there was not a single hide nor rod of land nor … an ox, a cow, a pig … left out' there are no data on London, probably because the extent of property holding there was sufficiently well known. For historians, geographers and other researchers, however, the document provides valuable evidence about the settlements that lay outside the city in the eleventh century but which were later absorbed in the metropolitan area. For example, the first written mention of PUTNEY occurs in the Domesday Book in the form of a reference to fishery tolls. PECKHAM was known as 'Pecheha', the land on which ST JOHN'S WOOD is built was part of the estate of a lady named Eideva and CLAPHAM (listed as 'Clopeham' and held by Goisfrid de Mandeville) had assets of three hides (a hide was a measure of acreage), six ploughs and five acres of meadow. The Domesday Book gets its name because it was said to be as authoritative as the Last Judgement on Doomsday and because *dom* means 'assessment' in Old English. (See also LEWISHAM; MORTLAKE; NORTHOLT; PUBLIC RECORD OFFICE; TOTTENHAM.)

DORCHESTER HOTEL

The Dorchester, one of London's leading HOTELS, stands on the site of the former home of the Earl of Dorchester in PARK LANE. Opened in 1931, it is built of reinforced concrete and, for that reason, became General Dwight Eisenhower's British headquarters after the United States entered the Second World War in 1941. It has 244 rooms, furnished in the style of an English country house, and a ballroom, panelled in black Spanish glass, which has hosted state as well as private functions.

DOWNING STREET

In about 1680, Sir George Downing built a cul-de-sac of brick-terraced houses along a short street leading from WHITEHALL. In 1720, part of the property was acquired by the Crown and, since 1732, No. 10 has been the official residence of the Prime Minister (though early holders of the office often preferred to live in more spacious premises elsewhere). No. 12, which was purchased in 1803 and became the Judge Advocate General's residence, is now used by the government Whips, and No. 11, bought in 1805, is the home of the Chancellor of the Exchequer. All of the structures have been much altered internally since they were erected, No. 10 by William Kent in 1732–5, Sir John Soane (see SIR JOHN SOANE'S MUSEUM) in 1825 and Raymond Erith in the 1950s and 1960s. The last of these improvements revealed evidence of Roman occupation of the site, the remains of a Saxon hall and part of the WHITEHALL PALACE tennis court, built for Henry VIII in 1533. For security reasons, gates were placed across the entrance to the street in 1990, preventing public access. (See also GORDON RIOTS; TREASURY BUILDINGS.)

DRAIN, THE

The 1½-mile LONDON UNDERGROUND connection that links THE CITY to WATERLOO railway station is known affectionately as the Drain by the thousands of commuters who use it every weekday; everyone who has watched the street-level entrances swallow up the jostling, bumping flow of rush-hour humanity knows how appropriate that nickname is. The line, opened in 1898, was built by the London and South-Western RAILWAY. In 1947, it became the only UNDERGROUND link in the national rail network following nationalization of the system by the Labour government, but, in 1994, it was handed over to LONDON TRANSPORT. It carries some 12 million passengers each year. (See also WATERLOO AND CITY LINE.)

DRURY LANE

The street, which connects ALDWYCH and the STRAND to High HOLBORN, takes its name from Sir Thomas Drury, who built a house beside the roadway during the sixteenth century. It became a fashionable neighbourhood for over 100 years, with residents including the Earl of Stirling (1634–7), Oliver Cromwell (1646) and the Earl of Clare (1683). However, during the Georgian period it declined in status and, by 1900, contained some of the worst slums in the city. Road-building programmes in the early twentieth century resulted in the clearance of many properties and the construction by the Peabody Trust (see PEABODY, GEORGE) of solid homes for some 1,500 working-class Londoners. (See also THEATRE ROYAL, DRURY LANE.)

DULWICH

The former hamlet of Dulwich lies at the southern tip of the LONDON BOROUGH OF SOUTHWARK. It has a lengthy history; records show that King Edgar granted the land to one of his supporters in AD 967, the Cluniac monks at BERMONDSEY Abbey held it from the early eleventh century until the sixteenth, and Henry VIII sold it to Thomas Calton in 1544 (following the dissolution of the MONASTERIES). In 1605, it was bought by actor and theatre-owner Edward Alleyn, who used part of his fortune to endow a 'College of God's Gift in Dulwich', which provided education for twelve poor scholars and an almshouse for six poor brothers and six poor sisters. During the eighteenth century, the area developed a reputation as a spa, but development was limited until the enclosure of common land (which followed Parliamentary legislation in 1805 and 1808) allowed wealthy Londoners to acquire property and build country villas. The opening of a RAILWAY station at nearby CRYSTAL PALACE provided a spur to growth from 1856, so homes for the middle classes and for manual workers replaced woods, market gardens and farmland during the final decades of the nineteenth century. Further construction during the twentieth century made Dulwich an integral part of the metropolitan area, but sensitive planning preserved much open space. In particular, the 72 acres of Dulwich PARK attract visitors to the displays of azaleas and rhododendrons. The Alleyn Foundation now supports three educational establishments – Alleyn's School, James Alleyn's Girls' School and Dulwich College. The college also administers Dulwich Picture Gallery, Britain's oldest public art gallery. Opened in 1814, it is housed in a building designed by Sir John Soane (see SIR JOHN SOANE'S MUSEUM) and extensively refurbished by Rick Mather Associates in 1998–2000. It contains an impressive representative collection of the major periods in the evolution of painting in Europe, including William Hogarth's *A Fishing Party* (*c.* 1730), Anthony Van Dyck's *Portrait of Emanuel Philibert* (1624) and Watteau's *Le Bal Champêtre* (1714–5). Many of the works were collected by Alleyn himself; others formed a bequest by Sir Francis Bourgeois in 1811.

Dulwich's name may be derived from the Old English *dile* and *wisc*, indicating 'a marshy meadow where dill grows'.

E

EALING

The suburb of Ealing, some 9 miles from CHARING CROSS, is an important retail centre on the western side of London. It was probably founded in Saxon times but experienced little development until the eighteenth century, when it became very fashionable with aristocrats and wealthy merchants (in 1761, for example, Princess Amelia, daughter of King George II and Caroline of Ansbach, set up home in GUNNERSBURY House). These residents maintained a semi-rural environment until, in the 1870s and 1880s, builders constructed, piecemeal, terraces of middle-class housing and turned Ealing into the 'Queen of the Suburbs', with no significant industrial employment and, therefore, few manual workers except in the west at Stevens Town. The opening of RAILWAY stations from 1879 encouraged further building (particularly during the first decade of the twentieth century) but, even so, the area has retained its predominantly residential character, with commercial activity concentrated on Ealing Broadway, which formed part of the main road from London to Oxford until the 1980s. The settlement's name may be derived from an Old English personal name and *ingas*, indicating 'the settlement occupied by Gilla's family or followers'. (See also CENTRAL LINE; DISTRICT LINE; EALING STUDIOS; MIDDLESEX COUNTY CRICKET CLUB; PUGIN, AUGUSTUS WELBY NORTHMORE.)

EALING, LONDON BOROUGH OF

Ealing is a diverse collection of formerly independent villages that coalesced as the urban area expanded westwards. Merged under a single authority in 1965, they cover some 21 square miles and have a resident population of 301,000 (2001). Uxbridge Road, Western Avenue and Westway, running from east to west across the borough, attracted light industry and commercial developments that (along with job opportunities in the central city, a relatively low proportion of public sector housing and the availability of rented properties) encouraged the growth of large concentrations of IMMIGRANTS. SOUTHALL's Asian community is one of the largest in the country and there is a large Polish group in the north of the area. (See also ACTON; HANWELL; NORTHOLT.)

EALING STUDIOS

In 1904, film producer George Barker bought West Lodge at The Green in EALING, and went into business as Barker Motion Photography Ltd. The firm was bought by Union Studios in 1929 then acquired by Associated Talking Pictures, which updated the facilities and began filmmaking in 1931. In 1938, Michael Balcon took control of the company, changed its name to Ealing Studios Ltd and, until the early 1950s, made a series of highly successful movies – including *Kind Hearts and Coronets*

(1949) and *Whisky Galore* (also 1949) – which starred such distinguished actors as Alec Guinness and became known as the Ealing Comedies. The premises were sold to the BRITISH BROADCASTING CORPORATION in 1955 then, in 1992, were acquired by the National Film and Television School, which leased the stages to independent producers. In 2000, they were taken over by Fragile Films, which spent £10 million upgrading technology and announced plans for a new series of comedies.

EARL'S COURT

The Earl's Court area of west London gets its name from the Earls of Zetland, Warwick and Holland, who were Lords of the Manor during medieval and early modern times. It remained agricultural until, during the 1860s, the building of the Metropolitan RAILWAY attracted urban development that, within two decades, covered the fields with rows of houses. In the twentieth century, wealthier residents moved farther into the countryside, leaving their properties to be converted into small HOTELS or subdivided for rent to young IMMIGRANTS seeking jobs in the central city (in particular, Australians arrived in large numbers, leading outsiders to refer to the neighbourhood as Kangaroo Valley). The principal building is the Earl's Court Exhibition Hall, which, when it opened in 1937, was Europe's largest reinforced concrete structure. Designed by Chicago architect C. Howard Crane, its 450,000 square feet are used for events such as boat shows and travel fairs. A smaller hall, adding 17,000 square feet, was completed in 1992.

EASTCHEAP

Eastcheap, located to the north-east of LONDON BRIDGE, was the location of the CITY OF LONDON's meat MARKET during the medieval period. Its western end was demolished in 1829–31 to facilitate the construction of King William Street (which links the MONUMENT area to the BANK OF ENGLAND) and the roadway was widened in the mid-1870s while the Metropolitan RAILWAY was built. The street is now occupied by banks, offices and small shops. The second element of the name is probably derived from *ceap* – the Old English word for 'barter'. (See also ST CLEMENT DANES CHURCH, STRAND.)

EAST END

In the northern hemisphere, the prevailing winds blow from the west. As a result, in Britain's nineteenth-century industrial cities they carried AIR POLLUTION to the east of the built-up area. As manufacturing increased, wealthy citizens, unwilling to suffer the problems caused by dirt, soot and dust, bought

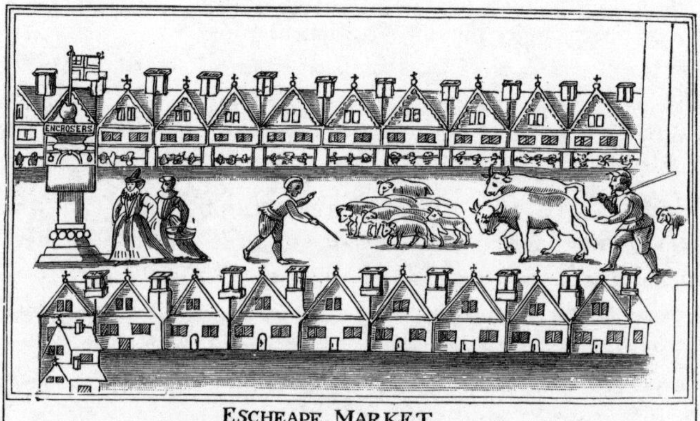

ESCHEAPE MARKET
from a very old Drawing. Vide Dr. Combe.

Eastcheap market, c. 1598.

homes in the more pleasant westerly parts of the metropolitan area, where the cleaner air supported trees, PARKS and gardens. Working-class citizens, without the funds to compete for the desirable properties, had to remain amidst the grime, particularly so because factories, mills and DOCKS increasingly congregated in the east, near the potential labour force. In some usages, London's East End stretches from the eastern boundary of the CITY OF LONDON to the metropolitan boundary with the County of Essex, a distance of some 10 miles. More frequently, the term is applied to inner-city areas such as BETHNAL GREEN, BOW and HACKNEY. In the public's imagination, these communities are characterized by deprivation – limited shopping facilities (a reflection of low incomes), high levels of local authority housing and terraced properties, and low levels of educational attainment. There is also a distinctive accent (for example, the East End is one of very few areas in Britain to use the glottal stop) and a strong family structure. In practice, however, these stereotypes have decreasing validity.

London's East End is still one of the most deprived areas of the United Kingdom, with relatively high rates of unemployment, low incomes, poor housing and limited green space for public recreation. However, standards have risen markedly as a result of concerted efforts by central and local government over the past fifty years. Reductions in AIR POLLUTION, stemming from legislation introduced in 1946 and 1956, have greatly improved the quality of the urban environment and the closure of the docks since 1965 has provided opportunities for redevelopment. Population densities have reduced as families have moved to more suburban sites (notably in Essex) and, from the late 1970s, young middle-class couples began a process of gentrification as they purchased terraced homes and used improvement grants to install bathrooms, central heating and other amenities. The CANARY WHARF scheme has attracted other incomers and local authorities have insisted that builders must construct low-cost homes on estates designed primarily for professionals. Consortia of government and private concerns have invested in job creation and are supported by the activities of philanthropic organizations, such as Quaker Social Action. The East End still lags behind the rest of London in economic development and retail facilities but the image portrayed in *EastEnders* is often misleading. In 2003 the government announced its support for a bid to hold the 2012 Olympic Games in London. If the bid is successful, most of the events would be held in the East End, providing further potential for the economic regeneration of the area. In addition, the East End is earmarked as the site for 15,000 new homes to be built by 2016 in an attempt to alleviate housing shortages in south-east England. (See also ABERCROMBIE PLAN (1943–44); BARKING; BARKING AND DAGENHAM, LONDON BOROUGH OF; BARNARDO, THOMAS JOHN; BETHNAL GREEN MUSEUM OF CHILDHOOD; BLACKWALL; BLITZ; BOOTH, CHARLES; BOOTH, WILLIAM; BOW BELLS; CABLE STREET; CANARY WHARF; CANNING TOWN; COCKNEY; DALSTON; DOCKLANDS; EAST HAM; EDMONTON; HACKNEY, LONDON BOROUGH OF; HARDIE, JAMES KEIR; ISLE OF DOGS; JACK THE RIPPER; KRAY TWINS; LANSBURY, GEORGE; LEYTON ORIENT FOOTBALL CLUB; LIMEHOUSE; MILE END; MILLWALL FOOTBALL CLUB; NEWHAM, LONDON BOROUGH OF; PEABODY, GEORGE; PETTICOAT LANE; POPLAR; POPLARISM; REGENT'S CANAL; ROYAL LONDON HOSPITAL; SIEGE OF SIDNEY STREET; STEPNEY; STRATFORD; TOWER HAMLETS, LONDON BOROUGH OF; TOYNBEE HALL; VICTORIA PARK; WEST HAM UNITED FOOTBALL CLUB; WHITECHAPEL.)

EAST HAM

An EAST END suburb some 8 miles from CHARING CROSS, East Ham was probably settled during Roman times but remained a village until the second half of the nineteenth century. Between 1851 and 1911, its population grew from 1,750 to over 133,500 as IMMIGRANTS flooded in, most of them working-class or lower-middle-class families who had skills that could be used at the DOCK on the north bank of the RIVER THAMES, the GAS works at BECKTON, or other industries on the fringes of the area. They successfully resisted incorporation within the LONDON COUNTY COUNCIL's jurisdiction in 1889, remaining in the County of Essex until 1965, when East Ham became part of the LONDON BOROUGH OF NEWHAM as the local government of the metropolitan area was reorganized. It forms a Parliamentary constituency that consistently produces majorities for Labour Party candidates and sometimes displays a radical streak, as when, in 1923, it chose Susan Lawrence, one of the first two women elected to represent Labour in the HOUSE OF COMMONS.

The second part of the settlement's name is derived from *hamm*, a common Old English element in place names with several possible meanings, including 'land within a river meander' and 'an enclosure'.

EAST INDIA COMPANY

The company was formed in 1600, when Elizabeth I granted a charter giving a group of merchants exclusive rights to trade with India and with east and south-east Asia. The prime focus of the commerce was spices, which commanded a high price in Europe, but cotton, indigo, porcelain, saltpetre (used both to preserve meat and to make explosives), silks and tea were also important. In 1661, the firm established its own DOCK at BLACKWALL, expanding them in 1806 in order to cope with the increasing volume of imports. Trade was organized from a headquarters in Leadenhall Street (in the CITY OF LONDON) and goods were stored at warehouses in Cutler Street. In addition to its business activities, the company wielded enormous political influence, acting as the government's agent and greatly extending the area absorbed within the British Empire. However, alleged maltreatment of native peoples, coupled with financial irregularities, led, in 1784, to legislation that transferred control from shareholders to a regulatory board answerable to Parliament. The monopoly rights were removed in 1813 then in 1873, sixteen years after the Indian Mutiny demonstrated that a private concern could not adequately represent British interests in the subcontinent, the company was wound up. (See also DEPTFORD; WANSTEAD.)

EAST LONDON LINE

LONDON UNDERGROUND's East London Line was originally constructed as a main-line RAILWAY and was incorporated into the TUBE system when the city's transport services were taken into public ownership in 1933 (see LONDON TRANSPORT). In 1823, construction began on a tunnel connecting WAPPING (on the north bank of the River Thames) with ROTHERHITHE (on the SOUTH BANK). Although some of the finest engineers in the land (including Marc Brunel and his son, ISAMBARD KINGDOM BRUNEL) were employed on the project, geological and other difficulties held up the work so that the link took twenty years to complete. In 1865, it was purchased by the East London Railway, which used it to develop services between LIVERPOOL STREET STATION and NEW CROSS, New Cross Gate and OLD KENT ROAD (the first services ran under the river from Wapping in 1869 and the route was completed in 1876). The trains were run by five different companies, which eventually leased the line from the East London Railway in 1884.

As the CIRCLE LINE was completed, a branch was constructed from ALDGATE to the East London Line, allowing the Metropolitan Railway and the Metropolitan District Railway to provide through services from west London to south-east London. However, these trains were discontinued during the Second World War and never reinstated.

In 1933, the route became part of the METROPOLITAN LINE but it regained its identity, as the East London Line, in 1988. It closed for three years from 1995, partly to carry out maintenance work in the Brunels' tunnel (despite conservationist claims that the treatment was unnecessary and that it would mar the tunnel's appearance). Current plans envisage its extension to FINSBURY PARK and WILLESDEN Junction (using the former North London Railway route between Broad Street and DALSTON Junction), to West CROYDON and CRYSTAL PALACE, and to WIMBLEDON, all by 2006. Repairs are carried out at a depot in New Cross and at the Metropolitan Line depot in NEASDEN. In 2003, maintenance of the line's infrastructure was franchised to Metronet, a consortium of private businesses, but London Underground remained responsible for providing the services.

EDGWARE

Edgware lies at the north-west fringe of London, astride WATLING STREET, which connected the Roman settlements of LONDINIUM and Verulamium (now St Albans). The hamlet, which is first mentioned in written records dating from AD 978, was owned by various religious interests (including the Priory of St Bartholomew, the Knights of St John of Jerusalem and All Souls College, Oxford) for much of the medieval period. Despite the arrival of the RAILWAY in 1867, it retained its rural character until extensions to the LONDON UNDERGROUND'S NORTHERN LINE connected it to the central city in 1924. It is now a residential suburb, although there have been some institutional developments, notably the North London Collegiate School (located in Canons PARK, a Georgian residence built for the Duke of Chandos) and the National Orthopaedic Hospital. Elements of Edgware's age are evident in the fifteenth-century tower of St Margaret's Church and the White Hart, a seventeenth-century coaching inn in High Street. Its name is probably derived from the Old English *wer*, meaning in full 'Ecgi's weir or fishing enclosure'.

EDMONTON

Edmonton lies on the west bank of the RIVER LEA, some 8 miles north-east of CHARING CROSS on the main road from London to Cambridge. During the eighteenth and early nineteenth centuries, the Bell Inn was a favourite PUBLIC HOUSE with city dwellers because of its attractive rural location and accessibility. The essayist Charles Lamb (who lived in Church Street) entertained visitors at the hostelry, and in *John Gilpin* (1782) poet William Cowper tells how Gilpin's wife recommended the place for a wedding anniversary celebration (with unfortunate results, because Gilpin's horse bolted). In 1872, the arrival of the Great Eastern RAILWAY changed the character of the area, attracting developers, who built low-quality housing for manual workers from the EAST END. These quickly turned into slums, most of which were replaced by higher quality local authority housing in the years after the Second World War. The suburb was incorporated within the LONDON BOROUGH OF ENFIELD in 1965. Its name may mean 'Eadhelm's *tun* (homestead)'. (See also SOUTHGATE; WOOD GREEN.)

EGHAM

Egham, administratively part of the County of Surrey, lies at the western edge of the London metropolitan area, beside the M25 MOTORWAY and only 3 miles from the end of the runway at Heathrow AIRPORT. Its name, which means 'Ecga's homestead', is probably derived from an Old English personal name coupled with the suffix *ham*. For most of its existence, the settlement was an agricultural village but its location near a bridging point on the RIVER THAMES also made it a focal point for TRANSPORT (sixty coaches a day were passing through during the early nineteenth century) and that, in turn, led to the establishment of inns and other services for travellers. In the last quarter of the nineteenth century, Thomas Holloway (who had amassed a fortune selling patent medicines) erected an ornate building, modelled on the

Château de Chambord (in the Loire valley), at a site on the outskirts of Egham and founded a college for women. Opened by Queen Victoria in 1886, it united with Bedford College (also formerly a women's institution) in 1985 and now teaches some 4,000 students as part of the UNIVERSITY of London system. At nearby Runnymede, King John signed the Magna Carta in 1215, limiting his power to raise taxes and conceding considerable political control to England's noblemen. From 1773 until 1884, the same area was a popular venue for horse races, which regularly attracted members of the royal family.

ELECTRICITY

Electricity began to challenge GAS as a source of lighting from 1882, when Parliamentary legislation authorized the use of overhead and underground cables as a means of providing power. The world's first electricity generating station was opened at Holborn Viaduct the following year, supplying energy that lit the CENTRAL CRIMINAL COURT and the Post Office, but it was quickly followed by others, so, by the outbreak of the First World War, there were over seventy in London. Competing interests installed prepayment meters and offered customers cut-price wiring, operating with little government regulation and creating a complex pattern of provision as public and private interests adopted both alternating and direct current delivered at a range of voltages. LONDON COUNTY COUNCIL made consistent attempts to reduce the confusion but, although improvements were made as small undertakings merged, rationalization was limited until 1948, when the Labour government nationalized the industry and created a London Electricity Board authorized to distribute power throughout the city. The Electricity Act of 1989 returned the industry to private hands in 1991, reintroducing competition but retaining standards of supply.

In 1890, electricity was first used on the LONDON UNDERGROUND, providing power for the line from STOCKWELL to King William Street (in the CITY OF LONDON). The innovation was extremely popular (because it eliminated the discomfort caused by smoke and dirt from coal-fired engines) and, as its use spread, led to rapidly increasing passenger numbers. (See also AIR POLLUTION; BANKSIDE; BATTERSEA POWER STATION; BRIXTON; STREET LIGHTING.)

ELEPHANT AND CASTLE

A busy road junction about 1 mile south of SOUTHWARK BRIDGE, the Elephant and Castle was an important coaching station during the eighteenth and nineteenth centuries and later became a RAILWAY terminus (see BAKERLOO LINE). Nearby properties were badly damaged by bombs during the BLITZ, but the area was redeveloped during the early 1960s to include a covered shopping mall, a cinema, a sports centre, government offices and premises for the London College of Printing. A further regeneration scheme, costing £1.5 billion, was announced by the LONDON BOROUGH OF SOUTHWARK in 2000. The origin of the area's name is unclear, but it is certainly taken from a PUBLIC HOUSE that had adopted it in 1760. Some scholars claim that it is a corruption of *L'Infanta de Castile* (a term used to describe the daughter of Philip III of Spain, with whom Prince Charles, son of James I, attempted to arrange marriage in 1623), but an elephant with a castle on its back was a relatively common feature in medieval European heraldry (possibly to emphasize strength), and the enterprising landlord may simply have copied the device onto a sign and hung it outside his inn in order to attract custom. (See also ABERCROMBIE PLAN (1943–44); WALWORTH.)

ELTHAM

The suburb of Eltham lies in the LONDON BOROUGH OF GREENWICH, some 9 miles southeast of CHARING CROSS. Archaeological excavations reveal that it was probably settled during Roman times, but its growth focused on Eltham Palace, which was presented to Prince Edward (later Edward II) by Anthony Bek, Bishop of Durham, in 1305. For 200 years, it was a favourite royal residence; according to tradition, Edward III established the Order of the Garter (the oldest knighthood in Europe) at a meeting there in 1348, and it was the site of the marriage, by proxy, of Henry VII to Joan of Navarre in 1402. However, Henry VIII preferred GREENWICH PALACE, and by the middle of the seventeenth century it had fallen into disrepair. The Great Hall, with an imposing hammer-beam, completed in 1480, was restored by Stephen Courtauld, who obtained a lease on the property in 1931, but little else remains. The proximity of the palace and the availability of rural land encouraged the establishment of other large houses, such as Eltham Lodge (a Restoration building designed by Hugh May for Sir John Shaw and completed in 1664). More recent urban expansion is largely the result of nineteenth- and early twentieth-century improvements to road and RAILWAY links with central London. Entertainer Bob Hope was born at 44 Craigton Road on 29 May 1903.

ELY PLACE

From 1290 until 1772, the Bishops of Ely retained a London mansion in Ely Place, HOLBORN. In 1327, Philippa of Hainault resided there before her wedding to Edward III and John of Gaunt (her fourth son and the real ruler of England during her husband's last years) lived in the building from 1381 until 1399. It served, during the civil wars of the 1640s, as a prison for royalist captives and a hospital for Parliamentary supporters injured in battle and then, in a state of considerable disrepair, was acquired by the Crown in 1772. The clergy moved to Dover Street and the building was demolished, but the neighbouring ST ETHELDREDA'S CHURCH, built in the late fourteenth century as a chapel for the bishops, survives. (See also BARRY, CHARLES.)

EMBANKMENTS

See BAZALGETTE, JOSEPH WILLIAM.

EMERGENCY SERVICES

See LONDON AMBULANCE SERVICE; LONDON FIRE BRIGADE; POLICE.

ENFIELD

The suburb of Enfield lies on the northern fringe of London on the west bank of the RIVER LEA some 11 miles north-east of CHARING CROSS. Utilizing the fertile alluvial soils, it developed as a significant agricultural area before the Normans invaded England in 1066 and remained rural until the Industrial Revolution stimulated economic change during the eighteenth century. Before the construction of surfaced roads, the river was the major TRANSPORT link. During the 1760s, it was canalized so that barges could be used to carry grain from Hertfordshire to London. Flour mills were built at Ponders End during the early nineteenth century and, in 1804, a small arms factory was constructed nearby; muskets were manufactured from 1816 and, in 1854, the premises were expanded to allow production of the Enfield rifle. The Edison Swan Electric Light Company (which pioneered the manufacture of valves for radios) opened in 1886, the Northmet ELECTRICITY generating station in 1903 and other manufacturing concerns following the completion of the Cambridge Road after the First World War. These sources of employment attracted workers from throughout the country, generating a building boom (particularly during the 1930s). When the GREATER LONDON COUNCIL was formed in 1965, the community united with neighbouring areas to form the LONDON BOROUGH OF ENFIELD.

The origin of the name is uncertain. The second element is predictably derived from the Old English *feld*, meaning a tract of land that has been cleared of trees. The first element could be derived from *ean*, 'lambs', or from 'Eana', a personal name. (See also COCKFOSTERS; SOUTHGATE.)

ENFIELD, LONDON BOROUGH OF

The most northerly of the LONDON BOROUGHS, Enfield was formed in 1965 by the amalgamation of the Borough of EDMONTON, the Borough of ENFIELD and the Borough of SOUTHGATE. Covering 31 square miles (about one-third of it GREEN BELT land, upon which development is strictly controlled), it has a population of 273,600 (2001). The south-west is largely residential, with a high proportion of the employed population in professional, managerial or skilled technical jobs. Elsewhere, however (and particularly in the east, along the valley of the RIVER LEA), there is more industrial activity, including chemical production, food processing and printing. In recent years, the local authority has made successful attempts to attract high-tech firms producing optical products, photographic goods and biotechnology. As a result, some 17 per cent of the workforce is employed in manufacturing and many businesses with household names – such as the Ford Motor Company and Coca-Cola Schweppes – have plants in the area. The conversion of the Lea Valley from an industrial wasteland into London's first regional PARK has also helped entice employers to the borough, as has access to good road communications with the rest of the country. (See also COCKFOSTERS; MIDDLESEX COUNTY CRICKET CLUB; SOUTHGATE.)

EPPING FOREST

A remnant of the woods that once swathed south-east England, Epping Forest covers over 9 square miles and lies about 13 miles north-east of CHARING CROSS. After the Norman invasion in 1066, England's kings used the land for hunting, often finding accommodation at nearby Waltham Abbey, which had been founded as a collegiate church of secular canons in 1030. From the late eighteenth century, however, monarchs became less attached to the chase, much of the woodland was cut down for fuel (or used as building material) and the cleared land was ploughed. The 9,000 acres of trees cleared between 1771 and 1871 left only 3,000 acres untouched, encouraging campaigners to press for legislation that would prevent further encroachment. In 1874, the CORPORATION OF LONDON won a court ruling that all enclosures of land since 1851 had been illegal. Four years later, Parliament awarded it control of 6,000 acres, enabling it, in 1882, to proclaim the forest 'an open space for the enjoyment of the people forever'. Much used for recreation by residents in the working-class areas of east London, where PARKS are relatively limited, it is now the largest hornbeam wood left in England and has a population of several hundred deer. There are MUSEUMS at Queen Elizabeth's Hunting Lodge (originally built for Henry VIII in 1543) and in Sun Street, Waltham Abbey; the former concentrates on natural history and the latter on daily life in the area from early settlement to the present day. The forest's name may be derived from the Old English *yppe* and *ingas*, indicating a community which lived on a ridge used as a lookout point. (See also LEYTONSTONE.)

EPSOM

Epsom was England's first spa town. Located 14 miles south-east of CHARING CROSS on the slopes of the NORTH DOWNS, it was settled at least by Anglo-Saxon times (its name is derived from *Ebbe* – an Old English personal name – and the suffix *ham*, which means 'homestead'). By the end of the first millennium, it was part of the estate of the Abbey of Chertsey but it remained undeveloped until the early seventeenth century, when stories spread of the curative powers of the water from the well on the common. Visitors (including SAMUEL PEPYS) arrived in ever-increasing numbers, seeking relief from all sorts of ailments and needing hotels and other accommodation while they stayed. Shops opened, assembly rooms were built and facilities for recreation were provided. In 1695, Nehemiah Grew was granted a royal patent to make Epsom Salts (which are now known to contain hydrated magnesium sulphate and are retailed around the world) but from about 1730 fashionable society moved to the new resort at Bath and local trade declined.

For many years, however, horse racing had been a popular sport on the springy turf of the Downs (Pepys' first visit to Epsom, in 1663, was spurred by a desire to see a race) and the growing popularity of the Derby, founded in 1780, brought crowds of spectators, who caused enormous traffic jams. That, in turn, encouraged the railway companies to provide local services, with lines linking the growing town to CROYDON from 1847 and to WIMBLEDON from 1859. The increased accessibility spurred residential development and, along with the relatively clean air and the rural location, encouraged LONDON COUNTY COUNCIL to build three mental hospitals, providing more employment at the beginning of the twentieth century. The town is now an important retail and service centre in the County of Surrey, with a large white-collar population, many of whom commute to work in central London. (See also NONSUCH PALACE.)

ERITH

Records show that a settlement existed at Erith, on the marshy SOUTH BANK of the RIVER THAMES 14 miles east of CHARING CROSS, as early as AD 695 (the name is probably derived from the Old English *ear* and *hythe*, which indicate a landing place of mud or gravel). During the medieval period, the community focused on Lesnes Abbey, an Augustinian foundation established in 1178 by Richard de Luci as a penance for supporting Henry II in a dispute that led to the murder of Thomas Becket, Archbishop of Canterbury. The buildings are now in ruins, but the surrounding lands have been converted into a 200-acre woodland PARK renowned for spring displays of bluebells and daffodils.

During the early sixteenth century, Henry VIII built a naval DOCKyard at Erith to fit out warships built upstream at WOOLWICH, stimulating the growth of port facilities. The combination of these industries and the transport potential of the North Kent RAILWAY (which arrived in 1849) encouraged further manufacturing growth during the second half of the nineteenth century, including the opening of the Callender Cable Company in 1880 and the Maxim-Nordenfelt Gun Company (which later became known as Vickers) in 1887. The area suffered greatly from bombing during the BLITZ and was much redeveloped after the Second World War. It became part of the LONDON BOROUGH OF BEXLEY in 1965. In 1998, archaeologists found the remains of a prehistoric forest in the mud of the Thames shoreline at Erith. The soggy remnants of alder, ash, oak and (unexpectedly) Scots pine and yew allowed specialists to refine their understanding of the natural vegetation of the river estuary 12,000 years ago, as the last Ice Age ended.

ERMINE STREET

Built by the Romans, Ermine Street ran north for over 200 miles from London to York. Some scholars suggest that it may also have extended south of the city, crossing the RIVER THAMES near the site of LONDON BRIDGE. It is named after Arminus, a Saxon leader who defeated Roman troops at Winfeld, on the River Weser in Germany, in AD 9.

EROS, STATUE OF

See PICCADILLY CIRCUS.

ESQUIRES, THE

The principal members of the LORD MAYOR's personal staff – the CITY MARSHAL, the COMMON CRYER AND SERJEANT-AT-ARMS and the SWORDBEARER – are collectively known as the Esquires. Their primary task is to ensure that official engagements run smoothly.

ESSEX COUNTY CRICKET CLUB

The Essex CRICKET club, which has played some of its matches at ILFORD since 1924, was formed at Brentwood in 1876 and was accorded first-class status by the MARYLEBONE CRICKET CLUB (MCC) in 1894. It achieved its greatest successes during the last decades of the twentieth century, winning the county championship on six occasions between 1979 and 1992, the Sunday League Championship three times (1978, 1984 and 1985), the Benson and Hedges Cup twice (1979 and 1998) and the NatWest Trophy twice (1985 and 1987). When the County Championship sides were divided into two divisions for the 2000 season, Essex was placed in the lower group and since then it has been something of a yo-yo team, failing to re-establish itself among the country's elite sides.

EUSTON STATION

One of London's principal RAILWAY stations, Euston is the terminus for trains serving north-west England and the west of Scotland. It was built by the London and Birmingham Railway in 1837, occupying a site, towards the edge of the urban area, which was dominated by market gardening businesses. In 1838, a 72-foot-high portico (designed by Philip Hardwick and incorporating four Doric columns) was erected in front of the structure, in 1839 two HOTELS were opened alongside, and then, ten years later, the concourse and waiting rooms were redesigned. Over the next century, the complex changed little, although the area around it developed a landscape of bed and breakfast establishments, PUBLIC HOUSES, restaurants and retail services catering to travellers. During the 1960s, however, British Rail demolished the Victorian edifice, despite howls of protest from conservationists who wanted the portico retained, and replaced it with a new building, which has eighteen platforms and a 30,000-square-yard piazza designed by R.L. Moorcroft to meet twentieth-century needs. Further office accommodation was opened in 1976. (See also CHALK FARM; VICTORIA LINE.)

EVELYN, JOHN (1620–1706)

Evelyn's diary, written over a period of seventy-five years, provides historians with a rich source of information about seventeenth-century London. Although less personal than the writings of SAMUEL PEPYS, it covers a much longer period and describes conditions during such major events as the Civil War (1642–9), the Restoration of the monarchy in England (1660), the GREAT PLAGUE (1664–6) and the GREAT FIRE (1666). Evelyn was born in Wotton (Surrey) on 31 October 1620, the fourth child of wealthy landowner Richard Evelyn and his wife, Eleanor. A staunch royalist, he joined the army of Charles I at the outbreak of the Civil War but left for home after only three days, noting that his continued presence with the troops would expose him to financial ruin 'without any advantage to his majesty'. In 1643, after some months spent making improvements to the family estate, he embarked on a European tour, travelling to Italy and France, then, on 27 June 1647, marrying Mary, the only daughter of Sir Richard Bourne, the king's ambassador to Paris. In 1652, he moved into his father-in-law's property in DEPTFORD, where he lived quietly throughout the period of Commonwealth government but nevertheless enjoyed the entertainments London offered. In 1657, for example, he reported seeing a bearded lady and there are details of visits to pleasure gardens, near CHARING CROSS, where 'the thickets seem to be contrived to all advantages of gallantry'.

Evelyn also corresponded with many of the educated men of the day, including scientist Robert Boyle, to whom, in 1659, he addressed a letter proposing the foundation of a college that would be dedicated to 'the promotion of experimental knowledge'. That vision eventually took practical form as the ROYAL SOCIETY, to whose council he was nominated in

1662 by Charles II. Although shocked by the conduct and lavish spending of Charles's followers after the king was restored to his throne in 1660, Evelyn was much respected by the monarch and served on several important committees, including those formed to consider improvements to London streets (1662), regulate Gresham College (see GRESHAM, THOMAS) in 1663 and repair ST PAUL'S CATHEDRAL (1666). He was also consulted regarding the foundation of CHELSEA HOSPITAL in 1681 and served as treasurer at Greenwich Hospital (see ROYAL NAVAL COLLEGE) from 1695 until 1703.

In many ways, Evelyn was typical of the gentry of the period, his religious and political opinions reflecting the prevailing loyalist landowning orthodoxy, but he was unusually curious about the world around him, conducting his own research into matters that intrigued him. He is remembered as one of the fathers of arboriculture because he advocated the planned planting of woodlands and in *Sylva, Or a Discourse of Forest-Trees, and the Propagation of Timber* (produced in 1664 for the Commissioner of the Navy and still in use during the nineteenth century), described methods of pruning, pest control and transplanting that were based on work carried out on the family lands. He also developed a new form of etching, known as the mezzotint, and wrote a moving biography of Margaret, wife of Lord High Treasurer Sidney Godolphin. Evelyn died in his home at Wotton on 27 February 1706. (See also GIBBONS, GRINLING.)

ExCEL

The ExCel conference centre, built on the site of the Royal Victoria DOCK, opened its first 65,000 square metres of space for business in November 2000. Further development will increase its size to 155,000 square metres, making it the largest building of its type in Britain. Designed as the focal point of a small waterfront town on the north bank of the RIVER THAMES, it is equipped with technology intended to attract futuristic international exhibitions and will be served by a complex of HOTELS and restaurants. Estimates suggest that by the time the project is complete it will have created about 14,000 jobs, many of them in the LONDON BOROUGH OF NEWHAM, one of the poorest parts of the city. Many jobs, however, may be at the expense of employment in older locations, such as the hall at EARL'S COURT.

EYRE REPORT In 1997, Chris Smith, Secretary of State for Culture, asked Sir Richard Eyre to chair a committee charged with preparing a report on government proposals to make the English National Opera share the ROYAL OPERA HOUSE facilities in COVENT GARDEN with the Royal Opera and the ROYAL BALLET. The document, published the following year, was a damning indictment of management at the opera house, where three chief executives, two chairmen and the entire board had resigned within a year. Alleging overspending, arrogance and elitism, Eyre proposed that a new artistic director should be appointed, that top salaries should be cut, that financial controls should be tightened and that public funding should be increased. Within weeks, the chairman was replaced and the Arts Council (the government's agency for dispensing grants to drama, literary and music groups) had promised higher levels of financial support.

F

FAIRS
Annual fairs were held regularly in England from Anglo-Saxon times, providing opportunities for larger-scale trading than was possible at weekly MARKETS. Many survived until the Victorian period, when increasing drunkenness and civil disorder encouraged local authorities to discontinue them. There are records of a two-week fair taking place in PECKHAM in late July and early August each year from the early thirteenth century until 1827. Other events were held at CROYDON, PINNER and TOWER HILL from the fourteenth century, at STEPNEY from the seventeenth and at MITCHAM from the eighteenth. A number still survive, including that on HAMPSTEAD HEATH, which takes place every August bank holiday weekend. (See also BARTHOLOMEW FAIR; CHARLTON; FROST FAIRS; ST JAMES'S FAIR.)

FENCHURCH STREET STATION
In 1841 the London and Blackwall RAILWAY opened the CITY OF LONDON's first train station at Fenchurch Street. It was replaced, in 1854, by a new terminus (also used by the London, Tilbury and Southend Railway), which was extensively redesigned in 1935. During the 1980s a £1.6 million development, known as Broadgate and financed by Stanhope Properties, integrated the station with new office premises. Rail services bring some 30,000 commuters from east London and Essex into the City each weekday.

FESTIVAL OF BRITAIN
In 1951 Clement Atlee's Labour government promoted a Festival of Britain in an effort to boost public morale at a time of food rationing and economic reconstruction following the end of the Second World War. The principal focus in London was a DOCKside area of LAMBETH, between WATERLOO BRIDGE and HUNGERFORD BRIDGE, where derelict buildings were demolished and a series of pavilions, which told the story of Britain's land and its people, were erected in their place. Murals, water sculptures and a skylon (a vertical structure that could be lit up at night) provided additional attractions. The intent was to create a relaxed, funfair atmosphere but the only structure designed to be permanent was the ROYAL FESTIVAL HALL, which became the focus for the development of an arts complex on the SOUTH BANK of the RIVER THAMES. Farther west, BATTERSEA PARK was redesigned by Osbert Lancaster and John Piper to incorporate new walks and a fountain. (See also NORTHERN LINE.)

FINCHLEY
The suburb of Finchley lies some 7 miles north-west of CHARING CROSS. Although it was settled by the Saxons, it experienced little

growth until the Great Northern RAILWAY provided a train link to central London in 1867. The increased accessibility attracted speculative builders, who erected homes for middle-class commuters, ultimately covering the fields with houses and linking formerly independent villages. The local authority has established conservation areas to protect the best of these Victorian and Edwardian neighbourhoods. Finchley was incorporated within the LONDON BOROUGH OF BARNET when London's local government was reorganized in 1965. Its name is probably derived from the Old English *finc* and *leah*, which suggest that the place was once a woodland where finches were common. (See also FINSBURY PARK; JEWISH MUSEUM.)

FINSBURY

Until the seventeenth century, Finsbury was an extensive area of moorland lying outside the northern wall of the CITY OF LONDON. Victims of the GREAT PLAGUE were buried there in communal graves in 1664–5 and refugees from the GREAT FIRE found safety on the open space beyond the flames in 1666. Building began in about 1670 and increased during the Georgian period, with the Finsbury Estate, planned by GEORGE DANCE THE ELDER (1700–1768) and laid out as a residential suburb between 1777 and 1800, and Finsbury Circus (designed by his son, GEORGE DANCE THE YOUNGER (1741–1825)) and constructed in 1815–7. Office developments appeared in the early twentieth century, so, by the end of the Second World War, the area had become an extension of London's financial district. It was incorporated within the LONDON BOROUGH OF ISLINGTON in 1965. The name is probably derived from *Finn* (an Old Scandinavian personal name) and *burh*, or fortified manor. (See also MOORGATE.)

FINSBURY PARK

The 115-acre Finsbury Park, located 5 miles north of CHARING CROSS in the LONDON BOROUGH OF HARINGEY, is a remnant of HORNSEY Woods that was saved from urban encroachment and, in 1869, dedicated as one of London's first public PARKS. Because of its importance as green space in an area otherwise devoted to commerce and housing, its name was gradually applied to the surrounding area and particularly to the suburb otherwise known as Stroud Green.

In 1861, the Great Northern RAILWAY opened a station at Seven Sisters, renaming it Finsbury Park when the new recreational resource was opened just to the north eight years later. During the late nineteenth and early twentieth centuries, the station became an important route focus as overground routes connected it to East FINCHLEY (1866) and the newly built ALEXANDRA PALACE (1873), and UNDERGROUND routes connected it to the finance houses of the CITY OF LONDON (via the NORTHERN LINE) in 1904 and to the retail and theatre district around PICCADILLY (via the PICCADILLY LINE) in 1906. Developers capitalized on the accessibility and the attraction of the park, erecting homes for relatively affluent families. However, as the metropolitan area continued to expand, middle-class groups moved further away from the city centre and their houses were subdivided for occupation by less wealthy incomers, including IMMIGRANTS from Cyprus, Algeria and Barbados. A mosque, built in 1990 to serve the sizeable Muslim community, gained a reputation as a focus for Islamic fundamentalism and the park's extensive facilities (which include a boating lake, a children's playground and London's sole American football pitch) were much vandalized. Local residents complained about the noise created by rock concerts, nuisance created by the audiences, drug dealing and violence but, in 2003, the Heritage Lottery Fund awarded the local authority a £3.4 million grant to help improve amenities. (See also EAST LONDON LINE; HOLLOWAY.)

FLEET LINE

See JUBILEE LINE.

FLEET MARRIAGES

During the first half of the eighteenth century, marriages were conducted, without proper authority, by clergymen sent to FLEET PRISON for failure to pay debts. Many of the ceremonies took place in nearby hostelries, which displayed signs showing male and female hands clasped, but Parliament declared the unions void in 1753.

FLEET PRISON

There is documentary evidence of a PRISON on the east bank of the FLEET RIVER in 1170 but some scholars suggest that it may have been erected a century earlier, soon after the Norman invasion (1066). Conditions for the inmates were appalling but, for the Keeper, very lucrative because he could claim customs dues from vessels arriving at the Fleet and fees from prisoners for lodging, food and privileges. The system was open to great abuse (many of the men who paid for a day outside the jail simply vanished), but it survived until the institution was closed in 1842. The building was demolished in 1846 and the site acquired by the London, Chatham and Dover RAILWAY in 1864. (See also GORDON RIOTS.)

FLEET RIVER

The Fleet rises in HAMPSTEAD and flows southwards to enter the RIVER THAMES east of CHARING CROSS. Although its name is probably derived from a Saxon word for 'tidal inlet', it is not mentioned in records until the twelfth century, when ships unloaded cargoes on its banks. It attracted a number of small industries, including tanneries, cutlery-makers and wharf facilities where butchers could dump waste. Nearby residents complained of the smell but, although the waterway was cleaned up in 1502 and 1606, it was inaccessible to boats by 1652, partly because of the rubbish covering its sur-

The yard at Fleet Prison, c. 1749.

View of the Fleet River, c. 1750.

face. During the eighteenth century, it was covered over and now runs underground as part of the city's SEWAGE system.

FLEET STREET

Fleet Street (named after the FLEET RIVER) extends eastwards for ⅓ mile from TEMPLE BAR to Ludgate Hill. During the medieval period, it was a major thoroughfare where senior figures in the Catholic Church built their residences. That coterie of learned citizens helped to attract booksellers and printing shops, which congregated in the area from the late fifteenth century. On 11 March 1702, the first newspaper – the *Morning Chronicle* – began to publish from premises in FLEET STREET. By the mid-twentieth century, most of the major English dailies had their headquarters there, news agencies such as Reuter's and the Press Association maintained offices, and the regional press rented rooms for London representatives. From the early 1980s, however, hot metal succumbed to computerized printing technologies and business managers became increasingly frustrated by congested inner-city conditions that prevented easy delivery of newsprint and fast distribution of papers. Most big publishers moved out (for example, News International built premises at WAPPING for *THE TIMES* and *The Sun*, and *The Daily Telegraph* relocated, with *The Guardian*, to the ISLE OF DOGS). The pubs, legal practices and other businesses that relied on the newspapers for trade suffered with the departure of customers, but most have survived, finding new clients in the offices that replaced the presses. (See also ROTHMAN'S OF PALL MALL; ST BRIDE'S CHURCH, FLEET STREET; ST DUNSTAN-IN-THE-WEST CHURCH, FLEET STREET; SWEENEY TODD; WAPPING DISPUTE.)

FLOOD CONTROL

Flooding has long been a problem in London. The *Anglo-Saxon Chronicle* reported in 1099 that the RIVER THAMES 'sprung up to such a height and did so much harm as no man remembered that it ever did before'. Records indicate that, during the sixteenth century, one incursion of water left fish dying on the floor of WESTMINSTER HALL, and SAMUEL PEPYS noted in his diary that, on 7 December 1663, 'There was last night the greatest tide that ever was remembered in England to have been in this river, all Whitehall having been drowned'. Large-scale attempts to limit damage and loss of life followed the passage of the Thames Flood Act in 1879; embankments were built along much of the river (see BAZALGETTE, JOSEPH WILLIAM), heightened between 1930 and 1935 (following a flood in 1928) and raised again in 1971–2. However, by the time of the last construction work, scientists had provided convincing evidence that the defences would have only limited effect if meteorological and marine conditions combined in a form predicted to occur once every 200 years. Troughs of low pressure moving from the western Atlantic could push surges of high water southwards through the North Sea. As those surges reached the narrow entrance to the English Channel, they would back up into the Thames estuary and be carried towards London with the high tide. When the inevitable flooding occurred, 45 square miles of the city would be inundated (including the major government offices in the vicinity of WHITEHALL), the LONDON UNDERGROUND would be unable to function, more than a million people would drown, gas and ELECTRICITY supplies would be cut off and damage to property would cost billions of pounds to repair. Moreover, according to the researchers, the likelihood of such floods was increasing every year because global warming was melting the polar ice caps, the south-east of Britain was tilting downwards at the rate of about 12 inches every century and the weight of buildings was causing the metropolis to sink into its foundation of LONDON CLAY and other sediments.

Faced with the facts, the Conservative government decided, in 1972, to authorize construction of a flood barrier across the river at WOOLWICH, where the waterway was comparatively straight and the subsurface of clay-with-flints was suitable for building. Completed in 1982, the barrier (designed by Charles Draper) is a 570-yard-long machine rather than a dam. It has ten moveable gates, four of which are wide enough to allow seagoing vessels through. In normal conditions, these gates sit on the river bed but when high water levels threaten they can be raised to stem the tide (by 2003 they had been used on more than seventy occasions). The cost of installation amounted to about £500 million, of which one-quarter was funded by the GREATER LONDON COUNCIL and the rest by government. As current conditions of sea-level rise (just under 3 feet per century), the Thames barrier is expected to protect the capital from flooding until the year 2030; at that time, new solutions will be required. Its operation is the responsibility of the National Rivers Authority, which has provided a visitors' centre on the SOUTH BANK.

FOOTBALL

The game of football has been played in Britain for centuries under a variety of local rules. Frequently, matches ended violently, so, in 1846, a nationally agreed set of regulations was negotiated then in 1863 the Football Association (now based in Lancaster Gate) was established to administer the sport. During the second half of the nineteenth century, several teams were formed in industrial areas of the city, where the game was most popular (see, for example, CANNING TOWN and ROYAL ARSENAL). The creation of an English League in 1888 furthered calls for payments to players, the growth of professionalism and, since the end of the Second World War, increasing commercialization. Of the thirteen London clubs currently playing in the four major divisions, the oldest are FULHAM (formed in 1879), LEYTON ORIENT (1881) and TOTTENHAM HOTSPUR (1882). Hundreds of other teams play in semi-professional, amateur and school leagues. (See also ARSENAL FOOTBALL CLUB; BRENTFORD FOOTBALL CLUB; CHARLTON ATHLETIC FOOTBALL CLUB; CHELSEA FOOTBALL CLUB; CRYSTAL PALACE FOOTBALL CLUB; MILLWALL FOOTBALL CLUB; OVAL, THE; QUEENS PARK RANGERS FOOTBALL CLUB; WATFORD FOOTBALL CLUB; WEMBLEY; WEST HAM UNITED FOOTBALL CLUB; WESTMINSTER HOSPITAL; WIMBLEDON FOOTBALL CLUB.)

FOREST HILL

A residential suburb in the LONDON BOROUGH OF LEWISHAM, some 6 miles south-east of CHARING CROSS, Forest Hill was largely undeveloped until the early nineteenth century, when canal and RAILWAY building brought an influx of population. During the 1880s German IMMI-

GRANTS established a community in the area, building a church in Dacres Road where theologian Dietrich Bonhoeffer (who was executed in 1945 for plotting against Adolf Hitler) was pastor from 1933 until 1935. In the twentieth century many of the Victorian homes were subdivided into flats and others made way for local authority housing developments. (See also HORNIMAN MUSEUM.)

FORTNUM AND MASON

London's best-known grocery store was founded in 1707, when William Fortnum resigned from his post as footman in Queen Anne's household and set up business as a supplier of provisions in partnership with Hugh Mason. The pair were ideally suited to commerce because Mason had a quick commercial mind (for example, he established stables near the store in order to facilitate deliveries to customers) and Fortnum was able to use his experience with the royal family to stock high-value goods he knew would appeal to the moneyed classes. In 1808–14, during the Peninsular War, British officers used Fortnum and Mason as a source for luxuries they could not find while on campaign and, in 1819, Sir William Edward Parry bought 2 hundredweight of cocoa to take on his unsuccessful attempt to find a north-west passage from the Atlantic Ocean to the Pacific Ocean. For three centuries the business has supplied groceries to reigning monarchs and it still stocks a vast range of unusual and expensive foods. Despite updating its premises at 181 Piccadilly and adding furniture, clothing and other goods to its wares, it has retained elements of the shopping experience of bygone eras by keeping chandeliers and red carpet in the food hall and insisting that sales assistants must wear morning coats.

FOUNDLING HOSPITAL

In 1739 master mariner Thomas Coram, disturbed by the number of infants abandoned on the streets by their parents, persuaded King George II to grant him a charter for the establishment of a children's hospital at Lamb's Conduit Fields. Demand for admission was so great that a ballot was instituted and strict rules were established (only the first child of an unmarried mother could be accepted, for example). William Hogarth supported the venture by encouraging other painters (including Thomas Gainsborough and Joshua Reynolds) to donate works of art that were put on display, attracting members of the public who made donations when they went to view the pictures. George Frideric Handel also contributed by holding performances of his oratorio *Messiah*. The hospital moved out of London in 1926 and the site was redeveloped but the Thomas Coram Foundation for Children (now known as Coram Family) continues its charitable work (and still displays its pictures) from offices in Brunswick Square.

FREEDOM OF THE CITY

In medieval times, as apprentices of the craft guilds (see LIVERY COMPANIES) gained experience, they had to appear before a court of their seniors in order to prove their competence. If they were successful, they were considered free of the guild and entitled to practice on their own. That status achieved, they then had to be made free of the CITY OF LONDON in order to set up business. The custom of awarding the Freedom of the City has continued into modern times and can be earned by redemption (that is, by being sponsored by two members of livery companies), by servitude (which involves completion of an apprenticeship to a Freeman) or by patrimony (children of Freemen may be awarded the Freedom of the City if they were born after their parent's admission and are over twenty-one at the time of application). Each successful candidate pays a fee, which is used to further the CORPORATION OF LONDON's educational work. Approval of applications is vested in the ALDERMEN (when the applicant is a member of a livery company) and the COURT OF COMMON COUN-

CIL (in all other cases). British nationals who have given outstanding service to the country may be awarded Honorary Freedom of the City. Formerly, Freemen had the right to certain educational and other privileges but these were largely superseded by welfare state legislation after the Second World War.

FREEMAN

See FREEDOM OF THE CITY.

FREUD'S HOUSE

In 1938 Sigmund Freud fled to London from his native Austria, where the Nazis condemned his work as being 'Jewish science'. He moved into a house at 20 Maresfield Road, in SWISS COTTAGE, and died there on 23 September the following year. Anna, his daughter and also a psychoanalyst, occupied the property until her own death forty-three years later, keeping her father's study and library as it was during his last months. The building is now a MUSEUM where visitors can see Freud's prototype couch, his letters and other personal effects.

FROST FAIRS

Until LONDON BRIDGE was demolished (and replaced by JOHN RENNIE's structure in 1823–31), its narrow arches impeded the flow of the RIVER THAMES, causing the water to freeze in particularly cold winters. Londoners seized the opportunity to hold celebrations that became known as frost FAIRS (though, technically, they were not fairs because these required a royal charter). In 1564–5, for example, archery tournaments were held on the ice and in 1683–4 (when Charles II attended with his family) an ox was roasted. Similar events took place in 1715–6, 1739–40, 1788–9 and 1813–4, with merchants setting up stalls and musicians leading dances.

FULHAM

Early in the eighth century, Bishop Tyrhtilus of Hereford granted land in Fulanhum, on the north bank of the RIVER THAMES, to Waldhere, Bishop of London. Some three centuries later, Waldhere's successors built a summer home (which became known as Fulham Palace) on the site and a small community grew around the building, with a second focus developing at a ferry landing site nearby. By 1500 the people were utilizing the fertile alluvial soils to grow vegetables for the London market, an enterprise so successful that it prevented significant urban development from encroaching until the second half of the nineteenth cen-

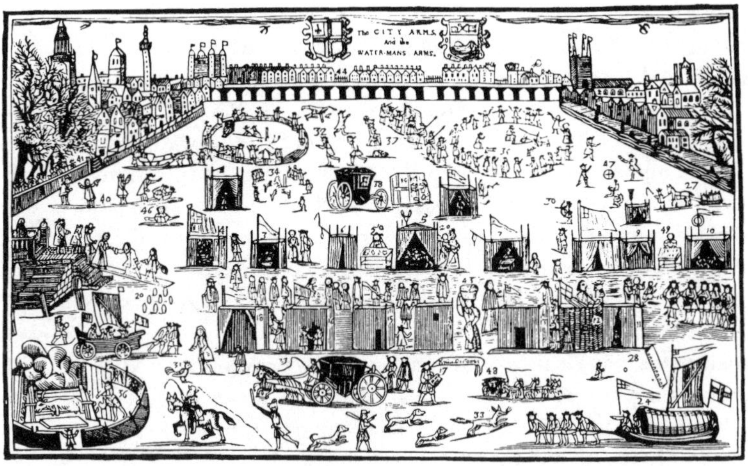

Frost Fair on the River Thames, 1683.

tury, even though the central city lies only 4 miles to the north-east (the last farm in the area was sold in 1910 and the land converted to a housing estate). Ultimately, however, the pressure from builders became too great to resist. The arrival of the RAILWAYS, the construction of a workhouse and infirmary (now the site of CHARING CROSS HOSPITAL) in 1849, the erection of a GAS plant, the provision of facilities for travellers along Fulham Palace Road (the main highway from London to the naval base at Portsmouth, on the south coast of England) and the opening of an ELECTRICITY generating station in 1936 all created compelling demands for space where workers and commuters could establish homes. The new residents, in turn, provided a market for shops, entertainments and other services, so, by 1950, Fulham's character had changed and the community had become a metropolitan suburb. In 1965, when the city's local government was reorganized, it was incorporated within the LONDON BOROUGH OF HAMMERSMITH AND FULHAM. The name, probably derives from the personal name *Fulla* and the Old English *hamm*, means 'Fulla's land within a river bend'. (See also CHARING CROSS; FULHAM FOOTBALL CLUB; HURLINGHAM CLUB; PUTNEY BRIDGE; ROYAL MARSDEN HOSPITAL; WANDSWORTH BRIDGE.)

FULHAM FOOTBALL CLUB

During the second half of the nineteenth century, as sport became more organized, many clubs were formed around workplaces, schools and other institutions. Fulham was one such. It originated as Fulham St Andrews, a church side, in 1879 and dropped the affiliation nine years later because its leaders wanted to appeal to a wider support. In 1899, it turned professional and joined the Southern League then, in 1907, it was admitted to the Second Division of the Football League. After that, its upward movement stuttered as it alternated between the League's lower divisions, winning no major trophies and distinguishing itself only by short spells in the First Division (1949–52 and 1959–68), by winning the championships of the Third Division (South) in 1932 and the Second Division in 1949, and by reaching the FA Cup final in 1975 (when it lost 2-0 to WEST HAM UNITED).

However, the club's fortunes changed in 1997, when Mohammed Al Fayed (owner of HARRODS, *Punch* magazine and the Ritz Hotel in Paris) bought the freehold of its Craven Cottage stadium (in Stevenage Road) and acquired a major shareholding in the business. Almost immediately, he installed former England captain Kevin Keegan as director of football and international player Ray Wilkins as manager. Wilkins lasted for only one season but, by the time he left, the Fulham side was radically different from the one he had inherited and was clawing its way up the ladder, winning promotion from Division Three to Division Two in 1997, then (as champions) from Division Two to Division One in 1999 and (again as champions, this time ten points ahead of the runners-up) from Division One to the Premier League in 2001. In 2002, it played in a senior European competition for the first time, qualifying for the UEFA Cup.

In his first five years as owner, Al Fayed spent over £70 million on new players and pitch improvements, winning local authority approval for a major refurbishment of the club's Craven Cottage stadium despite vociferous local opposition. In 2001, Fulham arranged a ground-sharing scheme with QUEENS PARK RANGERS which would allow the team to play home games at QPR's Loftus Road pitch during the upgrading. However, the club's losses in the 1999/2000 season amounted to £14 million and in 2000/01 to £24 million (a sum which some observers believe was the largest annual deficit ever recorded in English football). Almost inevitably, the club announced at the end of 2002 that it was scrapping the plans to redevelop its own ground and that it would seek a permanent home elsewhere. (See also CHELSEA FOOTBALL CLUB; LONDON WASPS RUGBY FOOTBALL CLUB.)

G

GARRICK, DAVID (1717–1779)
David Garrick revolutionized eighteenth-century London THEATRE, replacing a very affected style of acting with more natural characterization. He also greatly influenced other aspects of the stage, writing, producing and promoting playhouses. His entry into the world of entertainment happened by chance rather than design because his family had no background in the profession. Peter, his father, was an Army officer descended from HUGUENOT immigrants and Arabella, his mother, was the daughter of a clergyman at Lichfield Cathedral. He was born at the Angel Inn, Hereford, on 19 February 1717, while his father was on a recruiting trip, and initially educated at Lichfield Grammar School. In 1736, he transferred to the academy that SAMUEL JOHNSON had opened at Edial but that venture was unsuccessful, so, in March 1737, the two men set off to seek their fortunes in London.

Initially, Garrick intended to study law, but a legacy from an uncle allowed him to set up business as a wine merchant. The work led to contacts with the bohemian world of the theatre, in which he thrived. Turning his hand to playwriting, he drafted *Lethe, Or Esop in the Shades*, a comedy that received its first performance in the Drury Lane Theatre (see THEATRE ROYAL, DRURY LANE) in April 1740. Then, in March 1741, when the actor playing Harlequin at a theatre in Goodman's Fields fell ill, Garrick stepped in to play the part. A series of relatively minor appearances followed over the next few months, earning him a growing reputation, but in October of the same year he shot to fame when he appeared in the leading role in WILLIAM SHAKESPEARE's *Richard III* and was lauded by a public who loved his realistic portrayal of a king killed in battle. Over the next six years, theatregoers in London and Dublin flocked to see him in Shakespearean dramas, including *Hamlet* and *King Lear*, and in works by BEN JONSON, Thomas Otway and other popular writers. In 1747, in partnership with James Lacy (a failed actor but a canny businessman), he bought a lease on the Drury Lane Theatre, carrying his inventiveness into theatre organization by moving the orchestra from the gallery to the front of the stage and refusing to reduce admission prices for playgoers who arrived late. His repertoire, strongly biased towards works by Shakespeare, turned the theatre into the most successful of its time and made him a rich man, able to employ ROBERT ADAM to enlarge his country villa on the RIVER THAMES, near HAMPTON COURT PALACE, and entertaining lavishly both there and at 27 Southampton Street, his townhouse north of the STRAND.

In 1776, Garrick sold his interest in the Theatre and retired. Three years later, he became ill while celebrating the New Year with Lord and Lady Spencer at Althorpe PARK, Northamptonshire, and on 20 January, shortly after returning to London, died at his home in the Adelphi (see ADAM, ROBERT) development. He was buried at Poet's Corner in WESTMINSTER ABBEY. In 1831, the Duke of Sussex founded the GARRICK CLUB (for actors, writers, painters and other artists) in his memory. Now located at 15 Garrick Street, its membership is still heavily drawn from workers in theatre and other branches of entertainment, including television and film. Three London theatres were also named after him. (See also BAGNIGGE WELLS; BRITISH MUSEUM; CHAMBERS, WILLIAM; MIDDLESEX HOSPITAL; ST-GILES-IN-THE-FIELDS CHURCH, ST GILES HIGH STREET; STREATHAM.)

GARRICK CLUB

The Garrick Club (named after the actor DAVID GARRICK) was founded in 1831 to provide rooms where theatre people could meet men from other walks of life who shared their interests (it was very popular with writers, for example). Initially based in a converted hotel at 35 King Street, close to COVENT GARDEN, it numbered several of the aristocracy among its members. In 1864, it moved to its present premises at 15 Garrick Street, where it houses an important collection of portraits (many of them collected by Charles Mathews, a nineteenth-century comedian) and other stage memorabilia. One of the beneficiaries of the estate of the children's author A. A. Milne, the club agreed, in 1998, to sell the copyright of the Winnie the Pooh character to the Disney Corporation for a sum reported by newspapers to be about £50 million. Despite protests from those (allegedly including former Chancellor of the Exchequer Norman Lamont) who wanted the windfall to be divided between members, the club committee won approval for the money to be used partly for charity and partly to refurbish the property. The Garrick Club, which includes the Prince of Wales as a member, has received much criticism for its unwillingness to accept women except as guests. The waiting list for men is some seven years.

GAS

In 1807 Frederick Winsor presented a display of gas street lighting in PALL MALL as a celebration for the birthday of George, Prince of Wales, but its use for that purpose on a permanent basis did not begin until 1814, when the Gas Light and Coke Company provided lamps on WESTMINSTER BRIDGE. Other firms soon followed so, by 1850, major streets (such as Tottenham Court Road) were lit, as were BUCKINGHAM PALACE and the HOUSE OF COMMONS (see PALACE OF WESTMINSTER). Over the next two decades, companies divided much of the urban area among themselves so that each had a monopoly in some districts, but from 1870 the Gas Light and Coke Company increasingly dominated the north London market, providing a cheap product through underground mains from its riverside plant at BECKTON, where the coal needed for the production process arrived by barge. Gradually, it merged with its competitors to become the largest gas manufacturing company in Europe.

On the other side of the river, the South Metropolitan Gas Company was becoming similarly dominant from its base in GREENWICH. From the 1880s, both firms, threatened by the growth of ELECTRICITY supply companies, put much effort into the marketing of gas as a source of power and heat rather than light, placing an emphasis on fires and kitchen equipment in an attempt to maintain profits, but after the Second World War the Labour government eliminated competition by nationalizing supply companies and creating regional boards with responsibility for providing gas to different parts of the metropolitan area. As a result, manufacture was concentrated at a smaller number of sites and, with changing technology, converted from coal to oil-based supplies. The discovery of natural gas in the North Sea in 1965 caused further change, leading to the closure of all town gas plants by the end of the 1970s. The last gas street lamps to be lit by hand every evening survived in the Temple area (see INNS OF COURT) until 1986. (See also STREET LIGHTING.)

GATWICK AIRPORT

See AIRPORTS.

GEFFRYE MUSEUM

The MUSEUM, located in Kingsland Road, Haggerston, houses a series of furnished rooms depicting the development of interior design in London from the fifteenth until the twentieth centuries. Exhibits include Georgian shopfronts, wood panelling (which originally graced city mansions), a carpenter's shop from LIMEHOUSE and the plastered ceiling from the hall of the Company of Pewterers (one of the LIVERY COMPANIES). The building was erected in 1714 as an almshouse and paid for with funds from the estate of Sir Robert Geffrye, LORD MAYOR of London in 1865 and Master of the Ironmongers' Company (another livery organization). It was bought by the LONDON COUNTY COUNCIL and opened as a museum in 1914. A major extension was completed in 1998.

GENTLEMEN'S CLUBS

The first gentlemen's clubs in London were informal groups that met in COFFEE HOUSES or taverns to gossip during the late seventeenth century. As the gatherings increased in size, some of these groups took over entire properties (particularly in the St James's area close to PALL MALL) and paid fees to the proprietor in return for rights to dine, read newspapers and socialize. Inevitably, men associated with friends and colleagues who shared their interests, so the clubs developed distinct identities; for example, THE ATHENAEUM (formally founded in 1824) became popular with intellectuals, the GARRICK CLUB with writers, the CARLTON CLUB (1832) with the Tory Party and the Reform Club (1836) with Whigs. Many of the organizations eventually built imposing premises in central London and often had long waiting lists of potential members. During the twentieth century, they became less popular but a large number still survives, though most have now admitted women to membership. (See also BARRY, CHARLES; BEEF-STEAK CLUB; BOODLE'S; BOSWELL, JAMES; HURLINGHAM CLUB; JERMYN STREET; JOHNSON, SAMUEL; MARYLEBONE CRICKET CLUB (MCC); PICCADILLY; STOCK EXCHANGE (LSE); WHITE'S.)

GEOLOGICAL MUSEUM

The Geological MUSEUM was founded in 1837 to educate the public about Britain's mineral resources. It moved to its present building in Exhibition Road in 1935, became part of the NATURAL HISTORY MUSEUM in 1985 and now houses over a million specimens, including a reference collection of building stones that is used often by conservation workers attempting restoration projects. A £12 million refurbishment, completed in 1998, allowed the museum to develop an innovative approach to exhibitions, adopting modern technology to mount eye-catching displays of fossils and gems and to demonstrate the story of the earth's evolution. In addition, it provides offices for the British Geological Survey, formed in 1835 to prepare geological maps of Great Britain.

GEOLOGY

See CHILTERN HILLS; GEOLOGICAL MUSEUM; LONDON BASIN; LONDON CLAY; NORTH DOWNS.

GEORGE INN

There is evidence that the site where the George Inn stands in Tooley Street, south of LONDON BRIDGE, was occupied by a hostelry in 1542. The present building, dating from 1642, is the last galleried coaching inn left in London. Originally, it enclosed three sides of a courtyard, but the central and northern wings were demolished in 1899 to make way for RAILWAY developments. CHARLES DICKENS knew the place well, describing it in several of his novels, including *Little Dorrit* (1857). Scenes from his works (and from the plays of WILLIAM SHAKESPEARE) are performed in the yard during the summer.

GIBBONS, GRINLING (1648–1721)

One of the finest in a long line of London woodcarvers, Gibbons was born in Rotterdam on 4 April 1648, the son of an English emigrant. While working in DEPTFORD in 1671, he was discovered by diarist JOHN EVELYN, who introduced him to Charles II and the royal court. His finely crafted reproductions of flowers, fruits and game, carved in lime wood, were well received by wealthy aristocrats and merchants, who inundated him with commissions, many of which had to be carried out by other people, albeit to Gibbons's designs. He had considerable talent as a sculptor as well; Dalkeith House (in East Lothian) has a marble chimneypiece by Gibbons and several churches (such as Exton, in Rutland) have monuments on which he worked. In London, his versatility is clearly evident. He carved the choir stalls, thrones and organ screen for ST PAUL'S CATHEDRAL in oak and most of the exterior panels below the lower windows in stone. In ST JAMES'S CHURCH, PICCADILLY, he completed the reredos in lime and the font in marble. At ST MARY ABCHURCH, his altar screen incorporates four Corinthian pillars, which support a pediment decorated with urns. His monuments are seen in WESTMINSTER ABBEY and his statuary in the bronzes of Charles II at CHELSEA HOSPITAL and of James II in front of the NATIONAL GALLERY. Gibbons died at his home in Bow Street on 3 August 1721 and was buried in ST PAUL'S CHURCH, COVENT GARDEN. (See also ADMIRALTY, THE; ST JAMES'S PALACE.)

GIBBS, JAMES (1682–1754)

Gibbs, best known for his design of ST MARTIN-IN-THE-FIELDS CHURCH, was born on 23 December 1682 to Aberdeen merchant Peter Gibbs and his wife, Isabel. After graduating from the city's Marischal College, he studied at the Scots College in Rome, intending to train as a missionary, but turned his attention to ARCHITECTURE, with Carolo Fontana (Surveyor General to Pope Clement XI) as his tutor. In 1709, funded by John Erskine, Earl of Mar (whom he had met in Holland), he set up a practice in London and won the commission to design St Mary-le-Strand Church (1714–23), which critic Simon Jenkins describes as the finest eighteenth-century ecclesiastical building in the city. In 1719, he added two storeys and a steeple to the tower of ST CLEMENT DANES CHURCH (designed by CHRISTOPHER WREN) then, in 1722, began work on St Martin-in-the-Fields, incorporating a steeple and classical portico, which were reproduced in countless later buildings throughout Britain and North America. In addition, he was responsible for the design of several of the memorial sculptures in WESTMINSTER ABBEY, including that of John Holles, Duke of Newcastle (1723). His best-known works outside London are the Senate House in Cambridge (1722–30), All Hallows Church, Derby (1723–5) and the Radcliffe Library, Oxford (1737–49). Although never the most fashionable of architects (his Italian experiences led him to adopt elements of the baroque that were never fully appreciated by a society in love with Palladianism), Gibbs had a distinctive style that won many admirers and influenced successors for nearly a century after his death in London on 5 August 1754. (See also BURLINGTON HOUSE; ST BARTHOLOMEW'S HOSPITAL.)

GIPSY HILL

During the seventeenth century, the relatively remote area of hilly land west of present-day CRYSTAL PALACE became an increasingly popular gathering ground for the gypsy community, who earned an unsavoury reputation as troublemakers in nearby communities. Efforts to remove them proved unsuccessful until, early in the nineteenth century, Parliamentary legislation allowed landowners to enclose previously open fields with walls and hedgerows. The arrival of the RAILWAY in the mid-century completed the dispersal process, as speculative builders destroyed the last remnants of the encampments by erecting houses for middle-class commuters who had jobs in the central city but were prepared to travel to them from homes near the countryside.

GLOBE THEATRE

In 1598–9, Cuthbert and Richard Burbage built a round THEATRE at BANKSIDE, then the centre of London's entertainment district. It took its name from the sphere on its sign and (because it had no roof) was used only during the summer months. Although many writers had works performed on its stage, it has become most closely associated with WILLIAM SHAKESPEARE, many of whose plays – including *Romeo and Juliet*, *Macbeth*, *Othello*, *The Taming of the Shrew* and *The Winter's Tale* – were presented to London audiences there. The theatre was destroyed by fire in 1613, rebuilt, but closed by Puritan authorities in 1642. In 1970, Sam Wanamaker (the Chicago-born actor and film director) established a Shakespeare Globe Playhouse Trust with the intention of raising funds to build a replica. Construction began, seventeen years later, on a site some 200 yards from the location of the original theatre and was greatly aided by archaeological excavations that, in 1989, revealed details of the sixteenth-century building. The modern structure presented its first season in 1997 and forms the core of a growing artistic and educational complex, with a library, an archive of audiovisual material and other resources.

GOLDERS GREEN

Although Golders Green lies only some 5 miles north-west of CHARING CROSS, it survived as a predominantly agricultural area until the early twentieth century. The catalyst for change was the extension to the NORTHERN LINE of the LONDON UNDERGROUND system, which was tunnelled under HAMPSTEAD HEATH and opened in 1907. Its arrival greatly improved accessibility to the central city and sparked a frenzy of speculative house-building by private developers. Many of those who bought the new homes were second generation Jewish IMMIGRANTS moving from

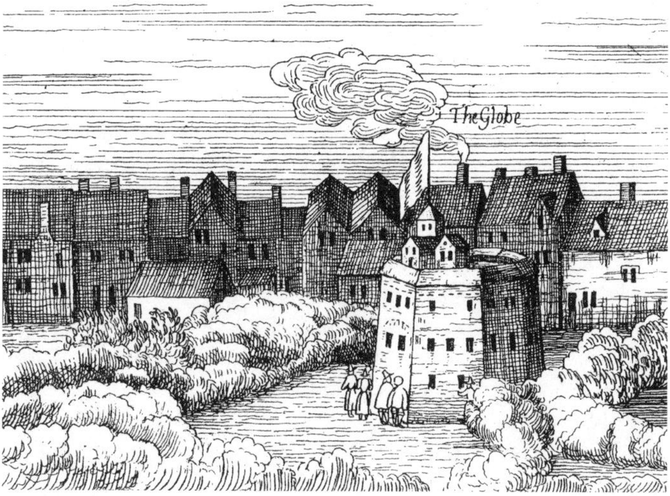

The Globe Theatre in the early seventeenth century, from Visscher's *Panorama of London*.

WHITECHAPEL and other areas of the EAST END, taking with them distinctive foods and religious practices. The Jews' College (founded in 1855) contains the largest library on Judaism in Europe, the Jewish Cemetery (opened in Hoop Lane in 1895) buries Sephardic Jews under flat stones in its eastern section and Reform Jews under upright stones in the west, and both Finchley Road and Golders Green Road have competing kosher butchers, bagel shops and booksellers. The Hippodrome THEATRE, originally opened as a MUSIC HALL in 1914, became the home of the BRITISH BROADCASTING CORPORATION's Radio Concert Orchestra in 1968 and, in 1974, Ivy House (where dancer Anna Pavlova lived from 1913 until her death in 1931) was converted into a MUSEUM of ballet. Golders Green was incorporated within the LONDON BOROUGH OF BARNET when local government in the metropolitan area was reorganized in 1965. The area's name is derived from that of the Godyere family.

GORDON RIOTS

In 1780, Lord George Gordon led a series of protests designed to coerce Lord North's Tory government into dropping its plans to repeal legislation that discriminated against Roman Catholics. On 2 June, he marched to Parliament at the head of a mob of supporters intent on presenting a petition of protest. The action provoked a week of rioting across the city. Chapels in SPITALFIELDS and Moorfields were set ablaze, jails (including FLEET PRISON and NEWGATE PRISON) were ransacked and inmates released, official government residences in DOWNING STREET were attacked and the BANK OF ENGLAND was stormed (albeit unsuccessfully). Estimates of the number of people killed range from about 250 to over 800. Gordon was tried on a charge of high treason but acquitted on the grounds that he had no treasonable intent. Twenty-one other men were hanged. (See also CLINK PRISON; LAMBETH PALACE; POLICE.)

GOSPEL OAK

A traditionally working-class residential suburb lying between KENTISH TOWN and HAMPSTEAD HEATH, some 3½ miles north of CHARING CROSS, Gospel Oak gets its name from the practice of reading passages from the Bible under a tall oak tree during the ceremonial beating of the parish boundaries just before Ascension Day (forty days after Easter) each year. Until the middle of the nineteenth century, the area was used primarily for grazing but the gradual extension of London's urban area encouraged developers to purchase land and erect rows of terraced houses, particularly after the Midland RAILWAY, the North London Railway and the Tottenham and Hampstead Junction Railway improved accessibility to other parts of the city. Brickfields, train-shunting yards, a TRAM depot and small factories provided local employment. After the Second World War, much of the poorer-quality property was demolished and replaced by large local authority housing estates, particularly in the Lismore Circus area. Gospel Oak was incorporated within the LONDON BOROUGH OF CAMDEN in 1965.

GRAND UNION CANAL

The first Grand Union Canal was opened in 1814, linking London to Leicestershire and Northamptonshire in the East Midlands of England. It was taken over, in 1894, by the Grand Junction Canal Company, which completed a second Grand Union Canal thirty-five years later by connecting REGENT'S CANAL with other waterways so that barges could travel as far as Birmingham. Management responsibility passed to the British Transport Commission in 1948 (when the Labour government placed all of Britain's canals under state control) then, in 1963, to the British Waterways Authority.

GRAY'S INN

See INNS OF COURT.

GREATER LONDON

The thirty-five LONDON BOROUGHS, along with the CITY OF LONDON, are together known as Greater London. Greater London has a total population of 7.17 million people (2001) and covers an area of 610 square miles (a population density of 11,757 people per square mile). Fourteen central authorities – the CITY OF WESTMINSTER, the CORPORATION OF LONDON, the ROYAL BOROUGH OF KENSINGTON AND CHELSEA, and the LONDON BOROUGHS OF CAMDEN, HACKNEY, HAMMERSMITH AND FULHAM, HARINGEY, ISLINGTON, LAMBETH, LEWISHAM, NEWHAM, SOUTHWARK, TOWER HAMLETS and WANDSWORTH – are collectively termed Inner London by the Office of Population Censuses and Surveys (though other bodies, such as the INNER LONDON EDUCATION AUTHORITY (ILEA) have used different groupings). Inner London has 2.77 million residents on 116 square miles (a population density of 23,846 people per square mile). The remaining authorities – the ROYAL BOROUGH OF KINGSTON UPON THAMES and the LONDON BOROUGHS OF BARKING AND DAGENHAM, BARNET, BEXLEY, BRENT, BROMLEY, CROYDON, EALING, ENFIELD, GREENWICH, HARROW, HAVERING, HILLINGDON, HOUNSLOW, MERTON, REDBRIDGE, RICHMOND UPON THAMES, SUTTON and WALTHAM FOREST – comprise Outer London. Outer London has a population of 4.4 million people on 494 square miles, a density of 8,919 people per square mile.

GREATER LONDON AUTHORITY (GLA)

The Greater London Authority was created by an act of Parliament in 1999 (see GREATER LONDON AUTHORITY ACT) in order to provide a strategic planning authority for the whole metropolitan area, including the CITY OF LONDON. Its head is the MAYOR OF LONDON, who acts as the executive officer, controlling the budget and developing plans that will improve the cultural, economic and social fabric of the city. A twenty-five-member LONDON ASSEMBLY scrutinizes the Mayor's proposals and conducts investigations into issues it considers critical to the way of life of metropolitan residents and visitors. Most of the £50 million cost is met by central government.

The GLA is based in a newly erected building, designed by Fosters and Partners, on the south bank of the RIVER THAMES beside TOWER BRIDGE. The Authority committed itself to a twenty-five-year lease, the developer met the £65 million construction costs and the government paid for the fittings.

GREATER LONDON AUTHORITY ACT (1999)

The act created a legislative body for the whole of London, with a MAYOR OF LONDON (who is responsible for decision-making), a LONDON ASSEMBLY (with powers to change the Mayor's budget and scrutinize his or her performance) and a GREATER LONDON AUTHORITY (consisting of the Mayor and the Assembly). The first elections were held on 4 May 2002 and the successful candidates took office on 3 July.

GREATER LONDON COUNCIL (GLC)

The GLC was established by the London Government Act of 1963 and met for the first time two years later when its predecessor – the LONDON COUNTY COUNCIL (LCC) – was disbanded. Its creation was essentially the result of population movements because, during the 1950s, middle-class groups had fled the city, effectively leaving the LCC permanently under the control of the Labour Party. The new authority – covering an area of about 610 square miles, more than five times that of its predecessor, and encompassing many of the affluent suburbs – would, the Conservative government believed, provide right-wing politicians with an opportunity to take over. That belief was justified; for ten of its twenty-one years' existence the Conservatives were in the majority. The council was composed of ninety-two members, each elected for four years. A Leader (the political head) was chosen by the party with the most seats and a chairman (the ceremonial head) by the whole body. Responsibilities were wide ranging (though not as wide ranging as those of the LCC), including strategic planning of road networks, traffic control, financial control of LONDON TRANSPORT, education in the central-city boroughs (see INNER LONDON EDUCATION AUTHORITY) and the administration of the LONDON FIRE BRIGADE.

Given the impact of its decisions on the day-to-day lives of Londoners (and on outsiders who commuted to work), the authority was unsurprisingly dogged by controversy. At the 1970 council elections, most areas had candidates running solely to protest about the priority given to roads over housing. In the mid-1970s, the Labour camp was divided by internecine strife stemming from disagreements about the social implications of plans to reduce the authority's £1.6 billion debt. In the late 1970s, Horace Cutler, the Conservative Leader of the Council, gained a reputation for outspoken criticism of transport workers and erratic changes of policy. When Labour gained control in 1981 and appointed a clique of left-wingers to important positions, with KENNETH ROBERT LIVINGSTONE as Leader, matters came to a head. Despite critical articles in many newspapers, Livingstone and his supporters proved to be very popular with city residents and thus provided a focus of dissent against the free-market policies of Margaret Thatcher and her followers in Parliament. Right-wing groups called for the abolition of the authority (see, for example, LONDON BOROUGHS ASSOCIATION) and Mrs Thatcher listened. Her substantial Conservative Party majority approved a HOUSE OF COMMONS bill abolishing the Greater London Council, which ceased to exist on 31 March 1986, leaving London as the world's only major metropolitan area without a citywide planning authority. Many of the GLC's responsibilities and assets were devolved to the thirty-two boroughs. Others were transferred to government-appointed bodies. (See also GREATER LONDON DEVELOPMENT PLAN (1969); LONDON AMBULANCE SERVICE; LONDON HEALTH EMERGENCY (LHE); LONDON MARATHON; LONDON RESIDUARY BODY (LRB); M25 MOTORWAY; MARBLE HILL HOUSE; THAMESMEAD.)

GREATER LONDON DEVELOPMENT PLAN (1969)

In 1969, four years after it had taken office, the GREATER LONDON COUNCIL (GLC) presented its plans for the economic and social development of the metropolitan area. The proposals included a reversal of the policies, initially mooted by the BARLOW COMMISSION and the ABERCROMBIE PLAN, which were designed to move jobs and people out of the capital. Homes for 250,000 people would be built in the GREEN BELT, the erection of tall buildings would be controlled and access would be improved by the building of new roads. Every aspect of the scheme had its critics but none more so than the suggestion that four concentric orbital routes (or ringways), totalling 400 miles in length and costing some £2 billion, should be constructed in an effort to keep cars out of residential areas. The innermost (known as the London Box or Motorway Box) would be a loop encircling the central city. The second would see the existing North and South Circular Roads upgraded. The third would be in the Green Belt and include a crossing of the RIVER THAMES at Dartford, to the east of the main built-up area. The fourth (the responsibility of the Department of Transport rather than the GLC) would be in open countryside well beyond the city's outer suburbs. The government submitted the plan to a Panel of Enquiry chaired by Frank Layfield, QC, and after 237 days of public hearings, at which 28,000 objections were considered, the committee sharply chastised the planners, claiming that there was often no link between the aims specified and policies designed to achieve those aims. Nevertheless, although the members rejected the middle ringways, they supported the Motorway Box (which was eventually abandoned as well) and the outer ring (which became the M25 MOTORWAY). The planners went back to their drawing boards and, in 1976, a revised plan, which put more emphasis on public transport provision, was approved.

GREAT EXHIBITION

The suggestion that an exhibition of achievements in the arts and the sciences should be held in London was first proposed by Henry Cole, an assistant keeper at the PUBLIC RECORD OFFICE. It was enthusiastically endorsed by Lord John Russell's Liberal Party government, which, in 1850, appointed a Royal Commission to raise money for the event. PRINCE ALBERT (Queen Victoria's husband and a staunch supporter of the project) presided over a committee consisting of such distinguished national figures as Russell himself, Robert Peel, William Gladstone (who had been President of the Board of Trade in Peel's administration) and builder THOMAS CUBITT. A site was chosen at HYDE PARK (much to the chagrin of *THE TIMES*, which forecast that the open space would disappear under 'a bivouac of vagabonds') and Joseph Paxton was invited to build a CRYSTAL PALACE to house the exhibits after a competition that attracted over 200 entries had failed to produce a satisfactory design. Most of the objects on display reflected Britain's technological expertise (including engines, textiles, domestic utensils and other products of the industrial age) but there were many other treasures to make the 6 million visitors gasp with wonder, including the Koh-i-Noor diamond (which had been brought to Britain from the Punjab in 1849 and added to the CROWN JEWELS), the largest pearl ever discovered, a bronze statue of Richard the Lionheart (King of England from 1189 to 1199) and a glass fountain 27 feet high. The success of the venture, which was opened by Queen Victoria on 1 May 1851 and ran for fourteen weeks, earned Paxton a knighthood and produced profits sufficient to purchase 84 acres of land in south KENSINGTON, which were developed as an educational complex incorporating the ALBERT HALL, the GEOLOGICAL MUSEUM, the NATURAL HISTORY MUSEUM, the ROYAL COLLEGE OF ART, the ROYAL COLLEGE OF MUSIC, the SCIENCE MUSEUM, the VICTORIA AND ALBERT MUSEUM and other institutions.

GREAT FIRE

Early in the morning of 2 September 1666, fire broke out in the premises of Thomas Farynor, the Royal Baker in PUDDING LANE, close to the RIVER THAMES. It spread rapidly through the closely packed wooden houses that lined the narrow streets of the CITY OF LONDON, raging for more than three days before it was fully extinguished. SAMUEL PEPYS records that, while he sat in an alehouse in BANKSIDE, he saw 'one entire arch of fire from this to the other side of the bridge and in a bow up the hill about a mile long'. Seeking safety for his wife and belongings, he fled to WOOLWICH but returned within hours to find Charles II trying to help soldiers put out the

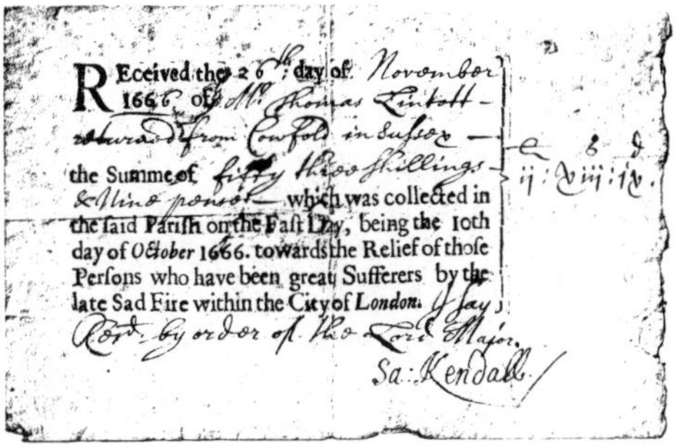
RECeived the 26th day of November 1666 of Mr Thomas Lintott
... from Cowfold in Sussex
the Summe of fifty three shillings
& nine pence which was collected in the said Parish on the Fast Day, being the 10th day of *October* 1666. towards the Relief of those Persons who have been great Sufferers by the late Sad Fire within the City of *London*.
Recd by order of the Lord Major.
Sa: Kendall

Widespread sympathy was excited throughout the country following the Great Fire of London in 1666. Within a week of the news reaching Lyme Regis in Dorset, the townspeople raised and sent to London £100 to aid those affected.

Leake's exact survey of the streets contained within the ruins of the City of London, 1669.

The Great Fire of London, 1666, from a contemporary print.

flames at CRIPPLEGATE. Only nine lives were lost (including a maid in the building where the conflagration started) but over 460 acres were blighted, with eighty-nine churches (including ST PAUL'S CATHEDRAL) burned down and more than 13,000 other structures destroyed. In the aftermath, owners had to prove title to land before they could re-erect properties, a Fire Court was established to settle disputes and new regulations required builders to use brick and stone, rather than wood, for construction. Many of the designs for new public buildings were prepared by CHRISTOPHER WREN, who was the architect of fifty City places of worship in addition to ST PAUL'S CATHEDRAL. (See also GREYFRIARS MONASTERY; GUILDHALL; HAMPSTEAD; LEADENHALL MARKET; LONDON FIRE BRIGADE; MONUMENT; MOORGATE, NEWGATE PRISON; ST BRIDE'S CHURCH, FLEET STREET; STEELYARD; THREADNEEDLE STREET.)

GREAT ORMOND STREET HOSPITAL FOR SICK CHILDREN

Even by the middle of the nineteenth century, London had few hospital facilities for children, who were excluded from most institutions caring for the sick. Determined to improve medical care for the young, Dr Charles West rented a property at 49 Great Ormond Street in 1851, providing ten beds for patients aged from two to twelve (it was felt that those under two should be treated as outpatients because they needed the care and comfort of their mother). In 1877, a larger hospital was built on the same site and in 1893 a further extension was opened, allowing doctors to look after 240 youngsters. Further rebuilding was carried out during the 1930s. The hospital became part of the National Health Service system when the Labour government introduced its programme of welfare state policies from 1946 and has undertaken extensive refurbishment in recent decades, increasing provision to 305 beds. In 1994, it converted to National Health Service Trust status in order to give its management greater control over finances and, by the end of the century, it employed 1,760 medical and administrative staff to look after 18,800 inpatients and 66,000 outpatients each year. The institution benefits significantly from J.M. Barrie's gift of the copyright of his play *Peter Pan* in 1927. Under English law, those benefits would have expired in 1987 (fifty years after Barrie's death), but a special Act of Parliament passed that year extended the rights to all royalties in perpetuity. After the Second World War, an Institute of Child Health was developed at the hospital. Now Britain's leading research centre focusing on childhood diseases, it merged with University College (part of the UNIVERSITY of London) in 1996.

GREAT PLAGUE

From the winter of 1664–5 until the spring of 1666, London suffered an epidemic of plague. The disease, carried by fleas that had fed on the blood of infected rats, was first detected in St Giles-in-the-Fields (a suburb lying west of the CITY OF LONDON) but spread quickly through the closely packed, overcrowded and unsanitary houses of the capital. Slum areas such as SHOREDITCH and STEPNEY bore the brunt of the deaths, but no section of society was spared. Charles II and his royal court fled to HAMPTON COURT PALACE on 29 June 1665, lawyers deserted the INNS OF COURT and employers closed their factories because coal boats would not call at the DOCKS. Houses whose members had fallen victim to the infection were marked with a red cross and guards were placed at the door to prevent residents from leaving for forty days after the sufferer had died or recovered. Given the high mortality rate (725 in the week before the king left, for example), BURIAL GROUNDS filled, bodies lay in piles awaiting interment and the stench of death permeated all corners of the city. The LORD MAYOR ordered that all dogs and cats should

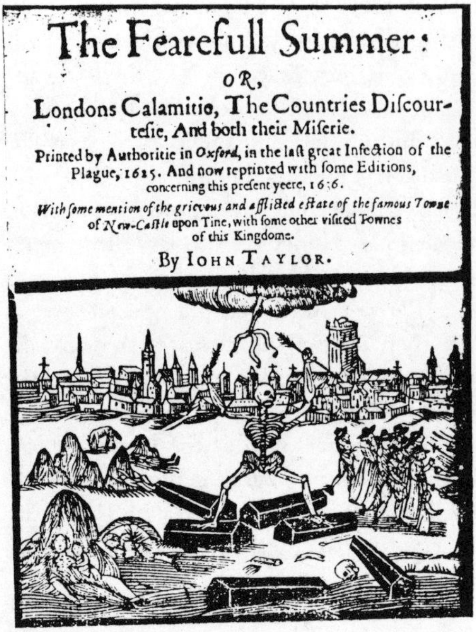
The Fearefull Summer:
OR,
Londons Calamitie, The Countries Discourtesie, And both their Miserie.
Printed by Authoritie in Oxford, in the last great Infection of the Plague, 1625. And now reprinted with some Editions, concerning this present yeere, 1636.
With some mention of the grievous and afflicted estate of the famous Towne of New-Castle upon Tine, with some other visited Townes of this Kingdome.
By IOHN TAYLOR.
A contemporary woodcut of the plague of London.

be killed because they might spread the disease; some 200,000 of the latter were destroyed, thereby removing one of the rats' most effective predators and adding to the incidence of the disease. However, in December 1665 the mortality rate fell and stayed low so, on 1 February of the following year, the court returned, encouraging other refugees to follow. The official total of people who died was 68,577 but public records were inaccurate (and probably falsified to prevent alarm) so scholars suggest that the actual number was closer to 100,000 (out of an estimated population of some 460,000). One children's nursery rhyme recalls the event:

Ring-a-ring o' roses,
A pocket full of posies,
Atishoo! Atishoo!
We all fall down.

The ring of roses is the rash that was one of the early symptoms of the illness, the posies were bunches of flowers carried to ward off the smell of decay and the 'atishoo' represents the sneezing fits that characterized the later stages of the affliction. The last line refers to the mass deaths. (See also FINSBURY; HAMPSTEAD; ST BOTOLPH'S CHURCH, ALDGATE; ST GILES-IN-THE-FIELDS CHURCH, ST GILES HIGH STREET; ST OLAVE'S CHURCH, HART STREET.)

GREAT STINK

During the exceptionally hot summer of 1858, the sewage carried by the RIVER THAMES emitted a stench that became known as the Great Stink. Pleasure boats cancelled trips and the windows of the HOUSES OF PARLIAMENT (see PALACE OF WESTMINSTER) were draped in sheets soaked in chloride of lime in an attempt to alleviate the smell. Tons of chalk lime and carbolic acid were poured into the river but had little impact, so the stink continued until cooler, wetter weather arrived in the early autumn. (See also WATER POLLUTION.)

GREEN BELT

In the period between the two world wars, politicians, academics and local authority planners voiced increasing concern that London's physical expansion might lead to a continuous sprawl of urban development as far south as the English Channel and as far north as Birmingham. The result was an Act of Parliament that, in 1938, designated a 'Green Belt' of protected land around the city. Building was restricted, preventing existing settlements from growing and stopping the encroachment of metropolitan influences. The results were not wholly satisfactory. The Green Belt undoubtedly provided an area where Londoners could escape into the countryside, particularly on weekends, but it also drove house prices higher as buyers competed for homes in environmentally attractive areas, thus preventing the young and the poor from finding places to live (for that reason, parts of the area were christened 'the gin and Jaguar belt' by the press). Also, much development simply leaped the protected area, so urban influences actually reached well beyond the city. In recent decades, population growth in south-east England has led construction firms to demand a relaxation of the building restrictions. (See also ABERCROMBIE PLAN (1943–44); COCKFOSTERS; GREATER LONDON DEVELOPMENT PLAN (1969); NORTH DOWNS.)

GREEN PARK

Green PARK gets its name from the colour of the grass and trees that dominate; traditionally, there are few flowers because the site was used as a BURIAL GROUND for lepers during the Middle Ages. Its 53 acres, which form a triangle bounded by PICCADILLY, CONSTITUTION HILL and ST JAMES'S PALACE, were enclosed by Henry VIII during the first half of the sixteenth century and converted into a ROYAL PARK during the second half of the seventeenth by Charles II, who laid out walkways and built a snow house for cooling drinks during the summer (the mound where the house stood can still be seen opposite 110 Piccadilly). During the Georgian period, the park was popular both for duelling and for ballooning. Now, it provides a green oasis, close to the heart of the city, where office workers and shoppers can relax over a picnic lunch. It is still owned by the Crown and is maintained by the ROYAL PARKS Agency. (See also BARRY, CHARLES; JUBILEE LINE.)

GREEN PARK ARCH

See HYDE PARK CORNER.

GREENWICH

The suburb of Greenwich, on the eastern edge of London south of the RIVER THAMES, dates at least from Anglo-Saxon times (its name is derived from the Old English *grone* and *wic*, meaning 'green dwelling place'). It developed, initially, as a small port close to GREENWICH PALACE and the Franciscan MONASTERY established by Edward IV in 1480 but the establishment of a ROYAL NAVAL DOCKYARD at Deptford Creek in 1513 hastened expansion, introducing craftsmen skilled in the industrial tasks of shipbuilding and repair and providing a foundation for other institutions, such as the ROYAL OBSERVATORY, which was created by royal warrant in 1675 and had close links with the Navy because navigation on the high seas depended heavily on a knowledge of the disposition of the stars. Greenwich Hospital (a home for disabled seamen, which was later converted into the ROYAL NAVAL COLLEGE) added to the complex during the 1690s and, with the other employment sources, stimulated residential development (Crooms Hill, for example, is largely Georgian). The RAILWAY, which arrived in 1878, brought the settlement within commuting range of the CITY OF LONDON, then, in 1902, a pedestrian tunnel built under the Thames allowed residents easy access to jobs in the burgeoning DOCK on the north bank of the river. Greenwich now has a flourishing tourist trade, with more than 2.5 million visitors arriving each year to look at the buildings, picnic in the PARK and scramble on to the tea clipper, *CUTTY SARK*, which is preserved in dry DOCK at King William Walk. Numbers were boosted in 1997, when the United Nations made Greenwich Britain's seventeenth WORLD HERITAGE SITE. (See also GREENWICH, LONDON BOROUGH OF; GREENWICH MEAN TIME (GMT); GREENWICH PARK; JUBILEE LINE; MILLENNIUM DOME; MILLWALL FOOTBALL CLUB; NATIONAL MARITIME MUSEUM; PRIME MERIDIAN; QUEEN'S HOUSE; RANGER'S HOUSE; ST ALFEGE'S CHURCH, GREENWICH.)

GREENWICH, LONDON BOROUGH OF

The borough was formed in 1965 through the amalgamation of the previously independent local authorities of GREENWICH and WOOLWICH. Covering 18 square miles, it has a population of some 214,400 (2001) and very contrasting environments. The south of the area, around ELTHAM, is primarily residential with some 40 per cent of residents living in public sector housing and over half working in manual posts. The north-east, too, has a high proportion of local authority homes but also provides job opportunities at industrial estates in ABBEY WOOD and in Woolwich, which has a long history of dockyard work. Elsewhere, TOURISM provides a significant income, with visitors attracted by the *CUTTY SARK*, GREENWICH OBSERVATORY, the NATIONAL MARITIME MUSEUM and related sites. Nevertheless, unemployment is higher than in many other parts of the city and, by the end of the century, with nearly one quarter of the adult population claiming social security benefits because of low incomes, problems associated with poverty were placing significant strains on local government finances. In 2003 the government announced that up to 40,000 new homes would be built in the north of the borough in an attempt to alleviate the housing shortage in south-east England. (See also AVERY HILL; BLACKHEATH; CHARLTON; PLUMSTEAD; ROYAL NAVAL DOCKYARDS.)

GREENWICH HOSPITAL

See ROYAL NAVAL COLLEGE.

GREENWICH MEAN TIME (GMT)

Since 1884, mean solar time at the PRIME MERIDIAN (0° longitude), which passes through the ROYAL OBSERVATORY at GREENWICH, has been used as the international basis for chronometry in order to avoid the confusion arising from a multiplicity of local systems. Until 1925, the start of the solar day (denoted by 00:00 hours GMT) was noon but, since then, it has occurred at midnight in order to accord with the beginning of the civil day. In 1928, the International Astronomical Union changed its nomenclature, replacing the term Greenwich Mean Time with Universal Time. The original phrase, however, is still much in use, particularly in English-speaking countries (with reference to time zones, for example).

GREENWICH MERIDIAN

See PRIME MERIDIAN.

GREENWICH PALACE

For three centuries, Greenwich Palace was a favourite residence of England's monarchs and particularly of the Tudors, who ruled from 1485 until 1603. The building, initially known as Bella Donna, was erected in 1426 by Humphrey, Duke of Gloucester and brother of Henry V, who made provision for a large LIBRARY; the first substantial collection of books to be formed by an individual rather than an institution, it became the foundation on which Oxford University created the

Greenwich Palace from Wyngaerde's *Panorama of London*, 1543.

Bodleian Library after his death. Henry VI acquired the property in 1447 and Henry VII rebuilt it in 1500–6, renaming it Placentia (meaning 'the pleasant place'). Henry VIII, born there in 1491, greatly enjoyed hunting in the extensive grounds (see GREENWICH PARK) and became very fond of the residence, adding a banqueting hall, armouries and a tilt-yard for jousting. His daughters, Mary (later Mary I) and Elizabeth (later Elizabeth I), were also born at Greenwich; Mary was never greatly enamoured of the place but Elizabeth spent many summers there after she became queen (during one visit Walter Raleigh allegedly spread his cloak over a puddle so that she would not get her dainty shoes dirty and during another she signed the warrant sending Mary, Queen of Scots, to her death after asking that it be hidden amongst other documents so that she would not know what she was doing). Following the execution of Charles I in 1649, Oliver Cromwell's Parliamentarian supporters tried to sell the palace but, in grimly Puritan England, could find no purchaser. Instead, they turned it into a biscuit factory then (in 1653–4) into a prisoner of war camp holding captives taken during the war with Holland. After the Restoration of the monarchy in 1660, Charles II undertook some rebuilding work but his successors, William III and Mary II, had little interest in the house, preferring HAMPTON COURT PALACE and KENSINGTON PALACE, so, in 1694, it was demolished and the Royal Naval Hospital (later adapted as the ROYAL NAVAL COLLEGE) was erected in its place.

GREENWICH PARK

The first of the ROYAL PARKS to be enclosed, Greenwich Park was created in 1433 by Humphrey, Duke of Gloucester and brother of Henry V, when he built walls around his residence at Bella Donna, which became GREENWICH PALACE. Henry VIII held regular sporting events at the site on May Day (and an oak tree that he danced around with Anne Boleyn, his second wife, survived until 1991, when it was blown down in a gale). In 1662, Charles II employed André Le Nôtre, the French landscape gardener renowned for his work at the Palace of Versailles, near Paris, to lay out the grounds anew, constructing tree-lined avenues and introducing a series of terraces (see ST JAMES'S PARK). In particular, he made a focal point of the QUEEN'S HOUSE, designed by INIGO JONES and erected in 1616–35 for Anne of Denmark, wife of James I. Additional trees were planted during the 1660s, then, in 1675, the ROYAL OBSERVATORY was built on a site formerly occupied by the Duke of Gloucester's castle. The public was admitted during the eighteenth century, the RAILWAY arrived at Greenwich in 1838 and steamer trips from central London began in 1854. Ready access turned the PARK into a popular recreational resource, with Londoners bringing their children on day trips, particularly on weekends and holidays, to look back at the city from Greenwich Hill. It remains popular with tourists, who visit the NATIONAL MARITIME MUSEUM (at its northern edge) and the eighteenth-century RANGER'S HOUSE (to the south-east). There are also sports pitches, a boating pond, a deer enclosure and regular puppet shows for children in the summer. The 200-acre estate is still Crown land managed by the ROYAL PARKS Agency. (See also LONDON MARATHON.)

GRESHAM, THOMAS (1519–1579)

Founder of the ROYAL EXCHANGE, Gresham was the second son of Sir Richard Gresham and Audrey, his first wife. In 1535, after a period of study at Cambridge University, he was apprenticed to his merchant uncle, Sir John Gresham (LORD MAYOR of London in 1547), who traded principally with the Levant and ensured that his nephew gained a thorough knowledge of international commerce. From 1551 until 1574, he was a royal agent, basing himself in Antwerp for much of the year while he negotiated loans for the

English Crown, providing his government with information about political conditions in Europe and arranging the provision of supplies for the Army. Gresham's trading practices were often highhanded, sometimes downright illegal (he was not averse to bribery, for example, and, at one point, prepared a scheme to smuggle currency from Holland to London in bags of pepper), but he was regarded favourably at court and, in 1559, was knighted on his appointment as Ambassador to the Court of the Duchess of Parma, Regent of the Netherlands. His activities were well rewarded financially, allowing him to purchase several fine residences (including a country home at OSTERLEY HOUSE and a town mansion in Bishopsgate Street) and to invest in schemes designed to bring benefits to London and its citizens. One of these projects was the construction, at his own expense, of a central meeting place for exchange dealers in the CITY OF LONDON. Known as the ROYAL EXCHANGE, it opened in 1568 and soon became a focal point for wealthy merchants. He also supported eight almshouses close to his city home and, in 1579, endowed Gresham College, creating seven lectureships in the arts and sciences. Gresham died suddenly on 21 November 1579 after leaving a meeting at the exchange. Allegedly the richest commoner in England, he was followed to his grave in St Helen's Church, Bishopsgate, by 200 poor men and women clothed in black gowns.

GREYFRIARS MONASTERY

In 1224, four Franciscan friars established a base at a CORNHILL property gifted to them by John Travers, SHERIFF of London. The following year, textile merchant John Ewin offered them land in Newgate Street, where they built a MONASTERY. The settlement flourished for 300 years, attracting many wealthy patrons after the heart of Queen Eleanor (wife of Edward I) was buried before the high altar of the monks' church in 1291, but was broken up in 1538 as a result of Henry VIII's anti-Catholic campaign. The church was retained, initially as a store for wine taken from captured French ships but then (renamed Christ Church) as the religious focus for a local parish. In 1553, just ten days before he died, Edward VI established a hospital and school for fatherless boys in the building, which was destroyed in the GREAT FIRE of 1666 but rebuilt in 1667–87 to CHRISTOPHER WREN's designs. The school (known as Christ's Hospital) remained on the site until 1897, when it moved out of London to Horsham (Sussex). Five years later, most of the buildings were demolished to make way for post office facilities. With the exception of the steeple, the church was destroyed by bombs during the BLITZ. (See also PUGIN, AUGUSTUS WELBY NORTHMORE.)

GROSVENOR ESTATE

In 1677, Sir Thomas Grosvenor acquired, through marriage to Mary Davies (the twelve-year-old heiress of a scrivener), 400 acres of land in BELGRAVIA and PIMLICO, with a further 100 acres in MAYFAIR. At the time, the estate lay west of the urban area of the city and was comprised mainly of underdeveloped marshland but expansion during the Georgian and Victorian periods converted it into some of the most highly valued property in the CITY OF WESTMINSTER. Building in Mayfair began in the 1720s and in Belgravia 100 years later, with development concentrating on substantial terraced houses that would appeal to the affluent. Despite suffering heavy estate taxes during the twentieth century, much of the original inheritance is still intact although large parts of the less fashionable Pimlico area have been sold. In 1979, Grosvenor Estate Holdings was formed to combine the various elements of the property (which now include land in Australia, Canada and the United States, and contribute significantly to the wealth of the Duke of Westminster, who owns the estate) under a single management group. The family name is also retained in many of the local road names, including Grosvenor Street (which links HYDE PARK to New Bond Street) and GROSVENOR SQUARE (where the UNITED STATES EMBASSY is located).

GROSVENOR SQUARE

The second largest square in London (after LINCOLN'S INN FIELDS) was built between 1725 and 1731 as the focus of the GROSVENOR ESTATE'S 100-acre development in MAYFAIR because Sir Richard Grosvenor wanted to emulate the success of Hanover Square, laid out by Richard Lumley (Earl of Scarborough) a decade earlier. The schemes for architectural symmetry were never realized (with over thirty building groups leasing sites, uniformity was always unlikely) but the area did attract high-status residents, including three Prime Ministers – the Marquess of Rockingham (who lived there from 1750 to 1782), Lord North (at various times between 1753 and 1792) and Henry Addington (1792–95). The square has a long association with the United States; John Adams (first US Ambassador to Britain and later President of the United States) lived at No. 9 from 1785 to 1788, financier John Pierpoint Morgan occupied No. 12 from 1902 to 1943, and No. 20 was the US Army's headquarters during the Second World War. However, of the original houses, none remains (the last was demolished in 1968). The UNITED STATES EMBASSY, constructed in 1958–61, occupies the west side and much of the remainder has been rebuilt in neo-Georgian style as HOTELS and offices. The Square witnessed a violent riot against the Vietnam War on the steps of the US Embassy in 1968, when some members of a crowd of 80,000 protestors clashed with police. Some 300 people were arrested and 90 policemen injured. The character of the square has changed once again following the introduction of concrete barriers and other security measures after the events of 11 September 2001 in America. (See also STREET LIGHTING.)

GRUB STREET

According to SAMUEL JOHNSON'S *Dictionary of the English Language*, published in 1775, Grub Street was 'originally the name of a street in Moorfields in London, much inhabited by writers of small histories, dictionaries and temporary poems; whence any mean production is called grubstreet'. The name (probably originally taken from a resident known as Grubbe) was changed to Milton Street in 1830 but has lingered in the English language as a general term for the world of literary hacks (some scholars attribute its first use in that sense to satirical poet Andrew Marvell, who lived at HIGHGATE and was buried at ST GILES-IN-THE-FIELDS CHURCH in 1678). Tobias Smollett describes a Grub Street dinner party in *Humphrey Clinker* (1771) and George Gissing deals with the vicissitudes of London literary life in *New Grub Street* (1891).

GUILDHALL

For nearly 900 years, the Guildhall has been the centre of local government in the CITY OF LONDON. It probably originated as the place where Saxons went to hand over their taxes (the Old English *gild* means 'payment') but there is no documentary reference to a building until 1128, when a Guildhall is included in a survey of property owned by ST PAUL'S CATHEDRAL. The present structure, begun in 1411 and largely completed by 1439. Apart from the exterior walls, it was destroyed in the GREAT FIRE but was rebuilt immediately afterwards and survived the BLITZ even though it was set on fire in an AIR RAID in December 1940. Its central feature is the Great Hall, 150 feet long and 89 feet high (one of the largest in the country and, therefore, a popular location for entertaining visiting dignitaries and mounting showpiece events). Lady Jane Grey (Queen of England for only nine days) was tried for treason there in 1553, Archbishop Thomas Cranmer defended himself (equally unsuccessfully) against a similar charge in 1555 and, in 1606,

Henry Garnet (a Jesuit priest) was found guilty of an attempt to blow up the HOUSES OF PARLIAMENT (see GUNPOWDER PLOT; PALACE OF WESTMINSTER). Today, its stained-glass windows and statues of national heroes, including Admiral Horatio Nelson and Sir WINSTON CHURCHILL, provide a setting for civic and state functions such as the LORD MAYOR's banquet. The Old Library housed a reference library and MUSEUM from 1873 until 1974, when the collections were moved to a newly constructed west wing and to the MUSEUM OF LONDON. Both now serve as reception halls. The biggest medieval crypts in London lie underneath.

Over the years, the building has been much altered to meet changing needs. Following the Great Fire, a flat roof was installed, the work probably supervised by CHRISTOPHER WREN. In 1862, the COURT OF COMMON COUNCIL decided to replace it with a hammer-beam ceiling more in keeping with the medieval style of the rest of the Guildhall, sanctioned the reconstruction of much of the interior and built a minstrels' gallery. A further roof (designed by GILES GILBERT SCOTT and with arches of stone) and new stained-glass windows were needed following an air raid in 1940 and the Lady Mayoress's Gallery (originally erected in 1910) was rebuilt in 1953. More recently, a hall for City LIVERY COMPANIES who do not have their own premises was added (again to Scott's plans) in 1957, an ambulatory giving access to offices and kitchens was built the same year, six new commemorative windows were placed in the west crypt in 1973 and the west wing was opened in 1974. In 1987–8, excavations revealed a Roman amphitheatre under the Guildhall Yard. (See also DANCE, GEORGE (1741–1825).)

GUILDHALL SCHOOL OF MUSIC AND DRAMA

The school, one of Britain's leading arts colleges, was founded by the CORPORATION OF LONDON in 1880 to promote the teaching of music (THEATRE studies was added in 1937). Classes were initially held at an unused warehouse in Aldermanbury but transferred to BLACKFRIARS in 1887 then, in 1977, to the BARBICAN, where students have access to a 300-seat auditorium, a music hall and other facilities. By the end of the twentieth century, over 700 students, from forty countries, were studying such disparate topics as early music, music therapy and technical theatre. The school's graduates (who include Ewan McGregor) find work with orchestras and in films and television drama as well as on the stage.

GUNNERSBURY

Gunnersbury lies some 7 miles west of CHARING CROSS, deriving its name from *Gunnhildr* (a Scandinavian personal name) and the Middle English *bury* (meaning 'manor house'). Some writers claim that Gunnhildr was the daughter of Canute, King of Denmark and Norway and ruler of England from 1016 until 1035. The estate has changed hands several times. From 1761 until 1786, it was the summer residence of Princess Amelia, the fourth of eleven children born to George II and Caroline of Ansbach, and in 1835 it was purchased by banker Lionel de Rothschild, whose son, Leopold, made the Japanese garden one of the most admired in the country. When Leopold died in 1917, some of the land was sold to builders then, in 1925, a further 186 acres were acquired by local councils and converted into a public PARK. Both of the houses on the land were built in the early nineteenth century. The larger of the two is now a MUSEUM of local and social history. KENSINGTON Cemetery, which occupies the south-eastern corner of the park, was opened in 1926 and contains a memorial to the Polish prisoners of war who were killed by Soviet troops in 1940 and buried in mass graves at Katyn Forest, near Smolensk, in Russia. General Tadeusz Bor-Komorowski, who led the Warsaw Uprising against German occupation

The chief conspirators of the Gunpowder Plot, 1605.

in 1944, is buried in the cemetery. (See also ACTON; KEW; EALING.)

GUNPOWDER PLOT

In 1605, a group of Roman Catholics devised a plan to kill James I, along with his advisers, by blowing up the HOUSES OF PARLIAMENT in the hope that sympathizers would seize power while the country was leaderless and give Catholics rights denied them by the government. However, Francis Trenshaw, one of the men involved, tried to save his brother-in-law, Lord Monteagle, by sending him an unsigned note warning him to stay away from the PALACE OF WESTMINSTER on 5 November. Monteagle informed the authorities, who searched the building and found Guy Fawkes (the group's explosives expert) in a cellar stacked with twenty to thirty barrels of gunpowder. Under torture in the TOWER OF LONDON, he revealed the names of his co-conspirators, all of whom were put to death (Fawkes himself was hung, drawn and quartered on 31 January 1606). The incident led to further repression of Catholicism and is still celebrated, on the anniversary of the event, by the burning of effigies of Guy Fawkes on bonfires throughout the country.

GUY'S HOSPITAL

Guy's was founded in 1721 by LOMBARD STREET publisher and bookseller Thomas Guy, who wanted to provide care for incurables. Initially, the unit had 100 beds but it expanded during the eighteenth and nineteenth centuries, adding, for example, dental facilities as early as 1799. Its staff contributed to its reputation. Distinguished medical workers based at the site included Thomas Addison (who advanced knowledge of adrenal gland disorders), Richard Bright (who carried out pioneering studies into kidney disease) and Thomas Hodgkin (who investigated enlargement of the lymphatic glands and spleen). All have diseases named after them.

Much of the hospital was rebuilt at the end of the nineteenth century and, in 1935, a private wing (funded by Lord Nuffield) was added. Two tower blocks were erected after the Second World War to provide surgical, ward and office space.

Guy's has had a long association with ST THOMAS'S HOSPITAL, partly because its founder was a governor of the older institution and partly because the two buildings originally stood opposite each other in St

Thomas's Street. In 1993 they combined, for management purposes, as a National Health Service Trust. The Trust plans to develop cancer and renal institutes at Guy's, which is one of the largest employers in the LONDON BRIDGE area.

GWYN, ELEANOR 'NELL' (1650–1687)
The most popular actress in late seventeenth-century London, Eleanor 'Nell' Gwyn (or Gwynn) was born on 2 February 1650, allegedly in an alley off COVENT GARDEN. Her father is unknown (according to tradition, he died in a debtor's prison while she was still an infant) and her mother (Helena) ran a brothel where, as a child, Nell sold brandy to patrons. At the age of fourteen, while selling oranges to audiences at the King's Theatre (on the site now occupied by the THEATRE ROYAL, DRURY LANE) she attracted the attention of actor Charles Hart, became his mistress and, through his connections, launched herself into a career on the stage. A fine dancer and singer, she was ideally suited for the female roles in Restoration dramas, starring as the King's Company's leading comedienne and appearing as Florimel in John Dryden's *Secret Love* and Mirida in James Howard's *All Mistaken*. SAMUEL PEPYS was captivated, referring to her as 'pretty, witty Nell'. In 1669, she was introduced to Charles II, who added her to his list of mistresses. For the rest of her life, she was faithful to the monarch, bearing him two sons and entertaining his aristocratic friends. Small and slender, she was greatly loved by the English public, who saw her as the antithesis of the Puritan ethos, but, by the time of the king's death in 1685, she was deeply in debt. Charles's last wish was that she should not starve and his brother, James II, respected the request, paying off her creditors and granting her a pension of £1,500 a year. In March 1687, she was stricken by apoplexy and partially paralysed. She died on 14 November and was buried, as she had asked, at ST MARTIN-IN-THE-FIELDS CHURCH, TRAFALGAR SQUARE.

H

HACKNEY

Hackney lies on the west bank of the RIVER LEA, 4 miles north-east of CHARING CROSS. The area was rural until the mid-nineteenth century, providing country homes for noble families (for example, Lady Margaret Lennox, the mother of Henry Darnley, Mary Queen of Scots' first husband, lived in Brooke House) and open spaces (such as Hackney Marshes) where less wealthy residents could enjoy hare coursing and fishing. However, as London's urban area expanded, fields and market gardens were superseded by small industries, particularly woodworking, textile manufacturing and shoemaking, so by the beginning of the twentieth century, the land was covered with terraces occupied mostly by manual workers. After the Second World War, many of these properties were demolished to make way for local authority housing estates. In 1965, Hackney was amalgamated with SHOREDITCH and STOKE NEWINGTON to form the LONDON BOROUGH OF HACKNEY. The origin of the name is uncertain. It may be derived from the Old English *eg* ('island') and *Haca*, a personal name. However, the first element may also come from *haccan* (meaning 'to kill with a sword or battleaxe'), suggesting a place of conflict. (See also WHITECHAPEL.)

HACKNEY, LONDON BOROUGH OF

The borough was formed in 1965 through the amalgamation of the borough of HACKNEY, the Borough of SHOREDITCH and the Borough of STOKE NEWINGTON. Stoke Newington, which has a common boundary with the north-eastern edge of the CITY OF LONDON, has some commercial activity, but the remainder of the area is largely residential, with pockets of industry along the RIVER LEA. The 202,800 population (2001), spread over 8 square miles of London's working-class EAST END, is one of the most deprived in the country. Over half of all families live in public-sector housing, incomes are low and unemployment is higher than average for the metropolitan area. Moreover, there is considerable ethnic diversity (40 per cent of residents are of non-white ancestry) and the quality of the urban environment is poor. During the 1990s, the local authority initiated a series of efforts to improve the quality of life, attracting over £1 billion of funding for regeneration projects from organizations such as the European Union. As a result, tower blocks on municipal estates (such as Holly Street) were replaced by more traditional homes, with local labour employed on the construction sites. Also, small PARKS were built to alleviate the urban drabness. But considerable social problems remain (Hackney Downs School was closed by the government in 1996 because of its low educational standards, for example), there are few sites suitable for large business premises and transport links are poor.

(See also CLAPTON; DALSTON; HOXTON; STAMFORD HILL; VICTORIA PARK.)

HACKNEY CABS

Hackney carriages (four-wheeled coaches) first appeared in London in 1625, taking their name from the two *haquenées* (or ambling horses) that pulled them. Their numbers grew so by the end of the seventeenth century there were 700 operating for hire in the city, and by the beginning of the nineteenth century there were over 1,000. In 1823, however, the two-wheeled *cabriolet de place* (a term which was speedily shortened to cab) was introduced from Paris and it quickly superseded the hackney, particularly after the four-wheeled version (known as the growler) was developed in the 1830s. Drawn by a single horse, the growler carried three passengers (two inside and one beside the coachman). Then, from the late nineteenth century, motorized TAXIS became increasingly common and, in 1947, the last driver of a horse-drawn hackney retired from the trade.

A seventeenth-century four-wheeled coach.

HAM HOUSE

In 1610, Sir Thomas Vavasour (Knight Marshal to James I) built a country mansion on the SOUTH BANK of the RIVER THAMES, within easy riding distance of RICHMOND PALACE. Sixty-two years later, John, Earl of Lauderdale, embarked on a reconstruction programme that turned the house into one of the most luxurious in the land, with a marble staircase, leather wall hangings, satins on the beds and furniture upholstered to co-ordinate with the decor. After that, the structure of the building was comparatively unaltered for nearly 300 years so when it was acquired by the National Trust in 1948 the VICTORIA AND ALBERT MUSEUM, managers of the property, were able to use Lauderdale's records to re-create the rooms' seventeenth-century sumptuousness and open the building to the public. In addition, the formality of the landscaped grounds has been retained, forming a contrast with the 'natural' plantings of early eighteenth-century properties.

HAMMERSMITH

Hammersmith lies on the north bank of the RIVER THAMES some 5 miles west of CHARING CROSS. The fertile alluvial soils favoured the growth of a market gardening industry, with vegetables and flowers going to the London market from the fifteenth century and urban development restricted to the main roads that traversed the area, connecting BAYSWATER to UXBRIDGE and KENSINGTON to BRENTFORD. During the second half of the nineteenth century, however, the metropolitan area's westward expansion combined with the improvements in accessibility wrought by the RAILWAY to force land prices up, encouraging owners to sell to speculative builders, who built terraces of small homes for working-class and lower-middle-class families. Partly because of the social structure of its new population, the area acquired a reputation as an entertainment complex, with cinemas, a film studio, the OLYMPIA exhibition hall (erected in 1884), QUEENS PARK RANGERS FOOTBALL CLUB (founded in 1885), the Lyric Theatre (built in 1890), the Palais de Danse (opened in 1919 and, two years later, the first British dance hall to have a jazz band on stage) and the BRITISH BROADCASTING CORPORATION's Television Centre (which produced its first programmes in 1960). The Hammersmith Odeon has been the venue for countless rock and pop concerts. In 1965, Hammersmith was united with neighbouring FULHAM to form the LONDON BOROUGH OF HAMMERSMITH AND FULHAM. Its name probably means 'a place with a hammer-forge'. (See also CHARING CROSS HOSPITAL; DISTRICT LINE; HAMMERSMITH AND CITY LINE; HAMMERSMITH BRIDGE; KELMSCOTT PRESS; METROPOLITAN LINE; PICCADILLY LINE; ROYAL COMMISSION ON LONDON TRAFFIC (1903–05).)

HAMMERSMITH AND CITY LINE

LONDON UNDERGROUND's Hammersmith and City Line links HAMMERSMITH, in west London, to BARKING, in the east. The track between PADDINGTON and Farringdon follows the route of the world's first UNDERGROUND passenger railway, opened in 1863 and a commercial success despite the fulminations of THE TIMES, which was horrified by the idea of people being 'driven amid palpable darkness through the foul subsoil of London'. Services were extended to Hammersmith in 1864 and to Moorgate in 1865, then to the main-line station at LIVERPOOL STREET (1875), to WHITECHAPEL (1884) and to Barking (1936). In 1933, when London's transport was taken into public ownership (see LONDON TRANSPORT), management responsibilities passed to the METROPOLITAN LINE but since 1990 the Hammersmith and City has had its own identity on TUBE maps. Trains are repaired at depots in Hammersmith and NEASDEN. In 2003, maintenance of the line's infrastructure was franchised to Metronet, a consortium of private businesses, but London Underground remained responsible for providing the services. (See also CIRCLE LINE.)

HAMMERSMITH AND FULHAM, LONDON BOROUGH OF

One of the smallest of the LONDON BOROUGHS, HAMMERSMITH and FULHAM houses 165,200 people (2001) on only 6 square miles. It was formed in 1965, when the two communities were united under a single local authority as part of a reorganization of local government in the metropolitan area. Good transport links to Heathrow Airport and the national motorway system have attracted major employers such as Coca-Cola and Disney, both of whom have their British headquarters on Hammersmith Broadway. There is also a large media presence, with the BRITISH BROADCASTING CORPORATION's Television Centre, record companies (such as EMI), film businesses (such as United International Pictures) and publishers (such as HarperCollins) all providing employment. As a result, property prices are high and there are pockets of considerable affluence (as in Fulham). However, amidst the wealth, the borough has some of Britain's poorest neighbourhoods, including WHITE CITY and SHEPHERD'S BUSH, which were targeted for employment and training initiatives during the 1990s. (See also HAMMERSMITH BRIDGE.)

HAMMERSMITH BRIDGE

The first suspension BRIDGE in London, Hammersmith Bridge links the LONDON BOROUGH OF HAMMERSMITH AND FULHAM (on the north bank of the RIVER THAMES) to the community of BARNES (on the south). Its 422-foot central span was completed in 1827 but replaced in 1883–7 by a new structure designed by JOSEPH WILLIAM BAZALGETTE. In 1939, the IRA attempted to blow up the bridge, but the bomb was discovered and thrown into the river by a passer-by. Improvements were made to the load-bearing girders in 1973–6, but, in January 1997, cars were banned from using the crossing, although buses, cyclists and pedestrians continued to use it.

HAMPSTEAD

The 443-foot high hill on which Hampstead has developed, some 4½ miles north of CHARING CROSS, was settled in prehistoric times and became a refuge for Londoners fleeing the BLACK DEATH of 1348–50 and the GREAT PLAGUE of 1664–6. However, it did not experience significant urban growth until after the

A woodcut of the flight of townspeople into the country to escape from the Great Plague of London.

GREAT FIRE (1666) when its trees were felled so that the CITY OF LONDON could be rebuilt. From 1701, fashionable London society arrived to sample the allegedly health-promoting waters that emerged from a chalybeate spring, encouraging entrepreneurs to open COFFEE HOUSES, a bowling green, an assembly room for concerts and other facilities for genteel entertainment on the southern slopes of the incline. By 1725, according to Daniel Defoe, Hampstead was being transformed 'from a little village almost to a city' and by 1801 (the year of the first British census) the population numbered 4,300. During the nineteenth century, the area became popular with wealthy businessmen, politicians, writers and artists who sought escape from the growing pollution of the central city and who confirmed its reputation as a high-status neighbourhood (Wilkie Collins lived in Church Row, for example, architect George Gilbert Scott in Admiral's Walk and John Keats in Wentworth Place). The literary set continued to move in during the twentieth century (even though the arrival of the TUBE in 1900 made Hampstead more attractive to commuters); poet Edwin Muir lived in Downshire Hill during the 1930s and in his autobiography, published in 1954, claimed that the flats of the day were 'filled with writing people and haunted by young poets despairing the poor and the world, but despairing together, in a sad but comforting communion'. When local government was reformed in 1965, Hampstead was absorbed by the LONDON BOROUGH OF CAMDEN, which has treated the area sensitively, preserving its essentially residential nature. Its name probably derives from the Old English *ham stede*, meaning 'homestead'. (See also BELSIZE PARK; BRONDESBURY; HAMPSTEAD GARDEN SUBURB; HAMPSTEAD HEATH; HARLEQUINS RUGBY FOOTBALL CLUB; JACK STRAW'S CASTLE; KEATS' HOUSE; NORTHERN LINE; RACHMANISM; ROYAL FREE HOSPITAL; SPANIARDS, THE.)

HAMPSTEAD GARDEN SUBURB

When, in 1907, Wyldes Farm (located immediately north-west of HAMPSTEAD HEATH) was put on the market by Eton College, Henrietta Barnett (whose husband had founded TOYNBEE HALL in 1884) suggested that some 160 acres of the land could be used to develop a residential area in which people from all social classes would live together in an integrated, stable community. A trust – the Hampstead Tenants' Association – was formed to buy the property, Raymond Unwin and Barry Parker (who had designed Letchworth Garden City a few years earlier) were invited to prepare plans for the layout, and architects such as Edward Lutyens (who thought Mrs Barnett 'a nice woman but a Philistine') were commissioned to work on individual buildings. The result was a suburb of secluded closes, roads that curved with the contours of the hillside, tree-lined streets and a mix of housing types. Flats for skilled manual workers predominated to the north of the area, semi-detached villas for the middle class to the west and large detached homes for affluent families to the south, at the edge of the Heath. The relatively high ground rents paid by the rich were intended to reduce those levied on poorer residents, with housing for vulnerable groups (such as the disabled and the elderly) built in special quadrangles amidst other residences. The First World War interrupted progress and afterwards, though the suburb was considerably extended, pressure on accommodation forced up prices. As a result, the community became increasingly middle class and the planners' ideal was never realized. Hampstead Garden Suburb has been criticized because it has no shopping facilities (and no PUBLIC HOUSE) at its core but, even so, most modern scholars consider it a good example of sensitive urban planning. In 1996, the government placed 500 of the buildings (mainly the artisans' houses) on a list of structures it considered of national architectural or historic interest, thereby limiting the extent to which they can be altered.

HAMPSTEAD HEATH

The 790 acres of Hampstead Heath, in the LONDON BOROUGH OF CAMDEN, have an element of wildness that contrasts with the carefully managed flowerbeds and lawns of central-city open spaces such as KENSINGTON GARDENS and ST JAMES'S PARK. The area first began to attract attention in 1698 as stories spread of the medicinal properties of springs bubbling to the surface in the woodlands. Authors and poets wrote of their qualities (CHARLES DICKENS, John Keats and Alexander Pope were all regular visitors) and encouraged local residents who, from 1831 to 1871, fought a long-running battle with Sir Thomas Maryon, the Lord of the Manor, to ensure that the land did not succumb to urban development. Now, as many as 100,000 people turn up on bank holidays to fly kites, enjoy the view from Parliament Hill or swim in the pools (one for men, one for women). KENWOOD HOUSE, at the northern fringe of the Heath, is a regular venue for outdoor concerts of classical music during the summer. (See also CHALK FARM.)

HAMPTON COURT PALACE

When Thomas Wolsey, Archbishop of York, began building Hampton Court Palace in 1514, he intended that it would be the finest residence in England. Located on the north bank of a meander in the RIVER THAMES, about 12 miles south-west of CHARING CROSS, it became famous throughout Europe both for the splendour of its ARCHITECTURE and the sumptuousness of its furnishings. Initially, it had about 280 rooms, but Henry VIII (to whom Wolsey gifted the property in 1529 in a vain attempt to regain the status lost by his failure to plot the monarch's divorce from Catherine of Aragon) added a library and additional kitchens as well as replacing the Great Hall and

Cardinal Wolsey began building Hampton Court Palace in 1514.

Elizabeth I was very fond of hunting at Hampton Court. In this contemporary woodcut, she is depicted with her huntsman.

refurbishing the chapel. Such was the haste to get the work done that carpenters were employed night and day, working by candle-light after darkness had fallen. Gardens were laid out, trees planted and deer introduced to the surrounding PARKland (see BUSHY PARK). Edward VI (Henry's only son) spent most of his fifteen years at Hampton Court and Mary I (Edward's half sister) pined there for four years while she hoped for a child. Elizabeth I (another half sister) conducted affairs of state at the palace but also turned it into a place for festivity and entertainment, with hunts, balls and banquets to keep her guests amused. James I, her successor, continued the tradition but also, more seriously, held a Conference of Divines in 1604 in a fruitless effort to resolve theological differences between the Puritans and the Church of England (one of the results of that meeting was the Authorized Version of the Bible in English).

Between 1651 and 1658, Oliver Cromwell lived in the palace, but his simple tastes appealed little to Charles II, who, after the monarchy was restored in 1660, set about redesigning the gardens, acquiring lavish furnishings and providing accommodation for his string of courtesans. From 1689, William III and Mary II carried out another extensive building programme, using CHRISTOPHER WREN to redesign the property in accordance with late seventeenth-century taste by building in the French Renaissance style. Construction and decoration work continued until George III came to the throne in 1760. George broke with tradition by staying away from Hampton Court (allegedly because he harboured a grudge about being chastised there while he was a child) and his successors followed suit. In 1986, fire damaged some of Wren's south wing, but it was restored over the next six years, with some of the Tudor features he had covered up being uncovered again. Since Queen Victoria's reign, the public has been allowed increasing access to the building. Modern visitors can see many of the rooms, including the state apartments (which contain works of art by Pieter Brueghel, Tintoretto and others), Henry VIII's Great Hall (with a hammer-beam roof over a chamber 97 feet long, 40 feet wide and 60 feet high) and the enormous Tudor kitchens. The grounds contain lawns and formal flowerbeds, an astronomical clock designed by Nicholas Oursian in 1540, a maze laid out for William III and a vine, planted by landscape gardener Capability Brown in 1768, which still produces grapes. (See also KENSINGTON PALACE; ROYAL HORTICULTURAL SOCIETY.)

HAMPTON COURT PARK

See BUSHY PARK.

HANWELL

The suburb of Hanwell, lying some 10 miles west of CHARING CROSS, developed during the medieval period as a bridging point where one of the principal routes out of London crossed the River Brent (a tributary of the

RIVER THAMES). Until the nineteenth century, it was little more than a hamlet, with a few houses clustered around the twelfth-century St Mary's Church and services for travellers located on the Uxbridge Road. However, in 1838 the Great Western RAILWAY improved accessibility to the metropolitan area, attracting incomers (ISAMBARD KINGDOM BRUNEL built the Wharncliffe Viaduct to take the trains over the river, giving passengers such an impressive view of the surrounding countryside that Queen Victoria regularly told her engine driver to slow down so that she could fully enjoy the crossing). St Mary's was rebuilt in 1842 and a school for poor children opened in 1856 (Charlie Chaplin was one of its pupils), providing employment in construction trades and encouraging builders to erect estates of small houses for workers. As population grew, Hanwell became increasingly urban in character but, even so, has managed to retain its village green and some semblance of former village life. It was incorporated within the LONDON BOROUGH OF EALING in 1965 and derives its name from two Old English words, *hana* and *wella*, which suggest that this was a place with a spring or stream where cocks (probably wild birds) could be found.

HARDIE, JAMES KEIR (1856–1915)

In 1892, Keir Hardie won a Parliamentary election at WEST HAM South, becoming one of the first two members of working-class political organizations to represent London in the HOUSE OF COMMONS (see PALACE OF WESTMINSTER) (the other was John Burns, who took the BATTERSEA seat at the same time). Born at Legbrannock (Lanarkshire) on 15 August 1856, he was the illegitimate son of Mary Keir, a servant girl who was later to marry carpenter John Hardie. With no schooling, he started work as a message boy at the age of seven then, after three years, turned to coal mining and earned a reputation as an agitator demanding improved conditions throughout the industry. In 1878, blacklisted by employers and unable to get a job, he opened a stationer's shop and wrote newspaper articles while developing his political activities as an official of groups devoted to miners' interests. Nine years later, he launched *The Miner* in order to give his views wider currency and in 1888 he unsuccessfully attempted to win a seat in Parliament as the member for Mid-Lanark.

Keir Hardie's election victory at West Ham South was not entirely unexpected because the constituency was located in the heart of London's working-class EAST END, but it was certainly made significantly easier by the death of the Liberal Party candidate shortly before polling. Unfortunately, he and John Burns never saw eye to eye, so their co-operation at the Palace of Westminster was limited. After Burns's election to the LONDON COUNTY COUNCIL in 1889, he helped form an alliance (known as the Progressives) between the socialists and the Liberals. Unwilling to jeopardize that sometimes uneasy association by identifying himself with Keir Hardie's hardline policies, he rejected the Scot's suggestion that a small Parliamentary grouping should be formed under Burns's leadership and later stood as a Liberal for the Battersea seat. Keir Hardie, however, continued to plough a militant furrow, earning himself the nickname 'Member for the Unemployed' as a result of his impassioned speeches supporting the rights of the jobless. In 1893, he became the first chairman of the Independent Labour Party, which had been formed through the merger of several small socialist associations, but, despite the attendant publicity, lost his West Ham seat two years later when the Liberals withdrew their support for his campaign.

For five years, he edited *The Leader* (a periodical that had developed from *The Miner*) and tried to persuade the trade unions to form a new political party that would represent working people. A Labour Representation

Committee was eventually founded in 1900 and Keir Hardie, fighting at Merthyr Tydfil, was one of two candidates to win Parliamentary seats on its behalf that year. In 1906, the organization changed its name, became the Labour Party, won twenty-six seats in the General Election and elected Keir Hardie the first chairman of the Parliamentary Labour Party. However, he had to resign from the position after only a few months as a result of failing health and, on 26 September 1915, died in Glasgow, believing himself to be a failure because he was unable to persuade workers throughout Europe to strike in an attempt to prevent the outbreak of the First World War. (See also CANNING TOWN.)

HARINGEY

Haringey and Harringay are variant spellings of HORNSEY. The first part of the name is probably derived from the Old English *Haering* (a personal name) or from *haring* (meaning 'grey wood') and the suffix from *haeg*, which means 'enclosure'. 'Haringeie' and 'Haringesheye' are both used in thirteenth-century documents. The first settlement in the area may have been established in the forest by Haering and his followers.

HARINGEY, LONDON BOROUGH OF

When local government in the metropolitan area was reorganized in 1965, Haringey was formed by the merger of the formerly independent Boroughs of HORNSEY, TOTTENHAM and WOOD GREEN. It houses a population of 216,500 (2001) on 11½ square miles, with significant communities of African, Caribbean, Cypriot, Irish and Jewish extraction, and a high proportion of homes rented from the municipal authority. The eastern area is largely residential, with Wood Green providing the major shopping facilities. Tottenham has a more industrial character. Most businesses in the borough are small (90 per cent have fewer than twenty-five employees), with retailing (and the associated wholesale distribution trade) providing more jobs than any other sector of the economy, though confectionery production, clothing manufacture and engineering are also important. Strongly working class in composition, the local authority provides consistent majorities for the Labour Party in local and Parliamentary elections. (See also ALEXANDRA PALACE; ARCHWAY; HARINGEY; MUSWELL HILL.)

HARLEQUINS RUGBY FOOTBALL CLUB

Harlequins was formed, as HAMPSTEAD Football Club, in 1866 and changed its name four years later because it was drawing players and support from a wider area than the north London suburb alone. (At the meeting to decide on the new name, the members agreed to keep the HFC monogram then pored over a dictionary until they found a word which everybody thought was suitable.) For more than four decades, it was an itinerant side, playing at fifteen different venues before being invited to settle at TWICKENHAM, the headquarters of English rugby but the site of only a few games every winter (Harlequins still play occasional matches there). It was based at Teddington from 1925–63 then acquired a 14-acre site close to its Twickenham pitch and developed the Stoop Memorial Ground, which is still its home (the stadium is named after Adrian Dura Stoop, who represented the club 182 times from 1901 to 1939, won 15 England caps and made major innovations in back play).

Most of Harlequins' major honours have been earned in comparatively recent years. They have won the RFU's knockout competition twice, beating Bristol 28-22 in 1988 and Northampton 25-13 in 1991. In 2001, they defeated the French side Narbonne in the final of the European Shield. In addition, the club has lifted the Middlesex seven-a-side trophy thirteen times (five of them in a row from 1986 to 1990) and 216 players have earned international caps, including 147 for England, 18 for Scotland, 13 for Ireland and 9 for Wales.

HARLEY STREET

Renowned as a location for doctors' surgeries, Harley Street (which runs north from Cavendish Square to the southern edge of REGENT'S PARK) was built in the second quarter of the eighteenth century as part of the development of the Portland Estate (see PORTLAND PLACE) and named for the family of the landowner, Edward Harley, Earl of Oxford and Mortimer. It was immediately fashionable; portrait painter Allan Ramsay lived at No. 67 from 1770 to 1780, J.M.W. Turner at No. 64 from 1804 to 1808, and the Duke of Wellington's wife, Kitty, at No. 11 from 1809 to 1814. Largely because of the affluent patients living nearby, the medical men moved in from around 1845 and still occupy most of the properties, offering treatments in such disparate specializations as cosmetic surgery, dentistry, dermatology, hypnotherapy, ophthalmology and testicular implantation. By the beginning of the twenty-first century, some 1,500 physicians, surgeons and dentists were based in Harley Street, along with eight private hospitals.

HARRINGAY

See HARINGEY.

HARRODS

One of the world's most famous department stores, Harrods was founded in 1853, when tea merchant Charles Harrod opened a grocery shop in KNIGHTSBRIDGE, then a village outside London. Harrod's son (also Charles) took over the business in 1861, when the WEST END was becoming increasingly fashionable and shopkeepers were attracting customers by offering a variety of goods under a single roof rather than specializing in a particular product. Within a decade, there were sixteen assistants in the store and sales were rising annually. In 1873, an extension was built, followed a year later by the acquisition of additional premises, but in December 1883 the whole shop was destroyed by fire. In the aftermath, Harrod wrote to every customer, explaining that 'in consequence of the above premises being burnt down, your order will be delayed in the execution a day or two' but adding that 'I hope, in the course of Tuesday or Wednesday next, to be able to forward it'. The letter proved to be a masterstroke, laying the foundations of a reputation for quality service. Also, the fire itself brought benefits because it allowed Harrod to build a new, five-storey, purpose-built shop with fittings designed to appeal to an affluent society (the additional space permitted an increase in the range of goods offered, allowing Harrods to boast that it could provide anything anybody asked for, from a mouse to an elephant). In 1889, the firm became a limited liability company and nine years later London's first escalator was installed (an assistant stood at the top, ready to administer smelling salts to customers who fainted as a result of using the new mode of transport). The main part of the present terracotta frontage was constructed between 1901 and 1905, with the Meat Hall decorated by art nouveau tiles depicting hunting scenes at the same time.

Harrods now has 300 departments, where 4,000 assistants serve 35,000 customers who spend over £1.1 million a day. There are eleven restaurants. The business was bought by House of Fraser in 1959 but sold to the Al Fayed brothers in 1985. Following the car crash that killed Diana, Princess of Wales, and Dodi Al Fayed in 1997, Mohamed Al Fayed (Dodi's father) claimed that the Duke of Edinburgh had planned the deaths. In 2000, the Duke withdrew his patronage from the store and Al Fayed responded by surrendering his warrants (or privileged rights) to supply goods to Elizabeth II, Queen Elizabeth the Queen Mother and Prince Charles. (See also FULHAM FOOTBALL CLUB.)

HARROW, LONDON BOROUGH OF

When London's local government was reorganized in 1965, Harrow, uniquely, retained its pre-existing boundaries (which, in fact, had changed little since the eleventh century). The borough, covering 20 square miles and housing 211,300 people (1998), is located on the north-west fringe of the metropolitan area. Although largely residential in character, it has significant office development, with strong banking, information technology and business service sectors whose growth is facilitated by good rail transport to the central city and by road links to the national motorway network and Heathrow AIRPORT. Over 75 per cent of households own their own homes, with residents heavily concentrated in the professional and managerial employment groups. There is a large Asian community, many of whom are involved in retailing and other small businesses. (See also HARROW-ON-THE-HILL; PINNER; STANMORE.)

HARROW-ON-THE-HILL

Harrow is one of three main areas of upland in north-west London (the others are HAMPSTEAD and HIGHGATE). It was settled by Anglo-Saxon times (deriving its name from the Old English *hergae*, which means 'shrine' or 'temple') and is mentioned in documents, dating from AD 767, which define a grant of land by Offa (King of Mercia) to Stidberht (Abbot of St Albans). During the medieval period, the woods surrounding the 406-foot-high hill were popular with the monarchy as hunting grounds so many of the buildings erected at the time were associated with visiting aristocrats (for example, the King's Head PUBLIC HOUSE is built on the site of Henry VIII's hunting lodge). However, because of the steepness of the slopes and the policies of the governors of Harrow School (which owns much of the land), construction since then has been limited, leaving much open space for use as sports fields. The school was founded in 1572 by John Lyon, a local farmer, and has become one of the most prestigious in the country. Former pupils include seven Prime Ministers – Spencer Perceval, Viscount Goderich, Robert Peel (Earl of Aberdeen), Lord Palmerston, Stanley Baldwin and WINSTON CHURCHILL – as well as such distinguished figures from other walks of life as Lord Byron and Second World War military commander Earl Alexander of Tunis. Modern Harrow is predominantly residential, with associated retail and administrative services. Development is restricted by conservation area legislation that protects the urban fabric,

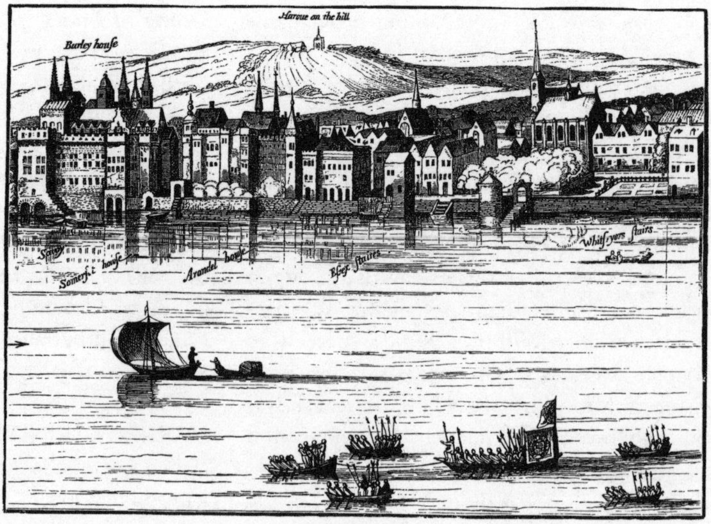

View of Harrow-on-the-Hill from the Thames, early in the seventeenth century.

notably St Mary's Church, whose fifteenth-century spire is a landmark for miles around. The suburb was included within the LONDON BOROUGH OF HARROW when local government in the metropolitan area was reorganized in 1965.

HATTON GARDEN

Hatton Garden, the street that links Holborn Circus (at the northern boundary of the CITY OF LONDON) to Clerkenwell Road (in the LONDON BOROUGH OF CAMDEN), is one of the major centres of the world diamond trade. It takes its name from Sir Christopher Hatton, Chancellor to Elizabeth I, who erected a mansion on orchard land in the area in 1576. The properties that line the roadway were popular with London's gentry during the seventeenth and eighteenth centuries (George Bate, Oliver Cromwell's physician, died there in 1688, for example) but, by the 1830s, several jewellers had established premises and, as their number increased, private residents moved out to less commercial areas. In recent years, however, depressed trading has encouraged some firms to seek other, less expensive, locations, and De Beers, the South African-based company that dominates the production and sale of rough diamonds, has been under pressure to transfer many of its London jobs to its home country, further threatening the street's dominance in the marketing of precious stones.

HAVERING, LONDON BOROUGH OF

Havering is located on the north-east fringe of the London metropolitan area, covering 46 square miles (half of which is protected by GREEN BELT legislation) and housing 224,200 residents (2001). It was formed in 1965 through the merger of the Borough of Romford and Hornchurch Urban District, taking its name from the village of Havering-atte-Bower. Romford is the principal retail and administrative centre, with a regionally important office complex and a predominantly white-collar workforce. Hornchurch and Upminster have large skilled manual groups, many of whom work at the Ford Motor plant in nearby DAGENHAM and have roots in the EAST END. Largely a commuter borough, Havering has the highest proportion of owner-occupiers of any LONDON BOROUGH (nearly 80 per cent) and a low proportion of immigrants.

HAWKSMOOR, NICHOLAS (1661–1736)

Although his reputation is overshadowed by that of his mentor, CHRISTOPHER WREN, Hawksmoor was an architect of considerable ability (albeit with a sometimes eccentric style) whose work shaped the townscape of late seventeenth- and early eighteenth-century London. Born in Nottinghamshire in 1661, he was employed by Wren as a clerk at the age of eighteen, working with him on the building of ST PAUL'S CATHEDRAL and CHELSEA HOSPITAL. He was appointed Clerk of Works at KENSINGTON PALACE in 1691, adding the King's Gallery in 1695–6. At Greenwich Hospital (see ROYAL NAVAL COLLEGE), where he became Deputy Surveyor in 1705, he was responsible for the architectural decoration of the hall and supervised the implementation of construction plans prepared by Wren and Sir John Vanbrugh. Hawksmoor also worked on such large country houses as Castle Howard (Yorkshire) and Blenheim Palace (Oxfordshire), as well as on buildings for the University of Oxford, but he is now best known for his London churches, particularly St Anne's (in Commercial Road, LIMEHOUSE), St Mary Woolnoth (in King William Street, in the CITY OF LONDON) and CHRIST CHURCH, SPITALFIELDS. He died at his home in Millbank, WESTMINSTER, on 25 March 1736. (See also ARCHITECTURE; ST ALFEGE'S CHURCH, GREENWICH.)

HAYMARKET

Haymarket, some 400 yards long, links Coventry Street to PALL MALL East in central

London. During the seventeenth century, a MARKET for straw and hay was established in the area (probably because the king's horses were stabled nearby). The Queen's THEATRE (opened in 1704) and the Haymarket Theatre (1720) attracted playgoers to the site so, when the market closed in 1830, the land was quickly colonized by other forms of entertainment, with taverns and prostitutes serving the clientele. During the twentieth century, cinemas added to the complex, making Haymarket an important component of the city's WEST END. The Queen's Theatre (now known as Her Majesty's) has had mixed commercial fortune; during the nineteenth century, it was remodelled by JOHN NASH (1816–8), burned down (1867), rebuilt (1869), closed because of debt (1881), then demolished (1891). The present building – a French Renaissance-style structure designed by C.J. Phipps – was erected in 1897 and, in recent years, has housed such successes as Andrew Lloyd Webber's musical *Phantom of the Opera* (which had its first performance in 1986). The Haymarket was rebuilt to Nash's plans in 1821 but remodelled by Phipps in 1880. Most of the other properties lining the street were erected during the twentieth century and function as shops or showrooms. (See also REGENT STREET)

HAYWARD GALLERY

Although some critics have fulminated at the Hayward's concrete façade (architectural historian Ann Saunders described it as 'of quite frightening ugliness' in 1988), the gallery has become an important venue for art exhibitions next to the concert halls on the SOUTH BANK of the RIVER THAMES near WATERLOO Bridge. Designed by Hubert Bennett and built in 1968, it was named after Sir Isaac Hayward, Leader of the GREATER LONDON COUNCIL at the time.

HEATHROW AIRPORT

See AIRPORTS.

HENDON

The suburb of Hendon is located in north-west London some 7 miles from CHARING CROSS. Although it has a long history (the land was owned by WESTMINSTER ABBEY as early as the tenth century and the fabric of St Mary's Church dates from only 300 years later), the settlement remained an agricultural village until 1911, when Claude Graeme-White converted open fields into an aerodrome that earned world renown as a centre of innovation during the early days of aircraft development (within months of its establishment, it had been the base for the first aerial postal delivery and the starting point of the first non-stop flight from London to Paris). Also, from 1920 until 1937, the Royal Air Force (RAF) mounted annual air displays, giving visitors an opportunity to see new military airplanes, demonstrating the pilots' skills and raising money for charities. TRANSPORT-related industries, including car manufacturing, were based in premises nearby, but urban encroachment ultimately limited the airfield's potential and, after the Second World War, much of it was used for building. However, several of the hangars were retained and, in 1972, converted for use as a MUSEUM showing the development of the Royal Flying Corps, which became the RAF in 1918. Displays tell the story of the Battle of Britain and outline the exploits of Bomber Command. Planes on display range from the Sopwith Camel to the Spitfire and the Hurricane. Since 1954, Church Farm House Museum, in Greyhound Hill, has housed displays dealing with local history in a seventeenth-century building where several of the rooms have been furnished in period style. In 1965, Hendon was incorporated within the LONDON BOROUGH OF BARNET. Its name may be derived from the Old English *heah* and *dun*, indicating a settlement on a high hill.

HENRY WOOD PROMENADE CONCERTS

See PROMS, THE.

HENSLOWE, PHILIP (*c.* 1550–1616)

Henslowe was the principal THEATRE owner during the late Elizabethan period, when BANKSIDE was the centre of London entertainment and BEN JONSON, INIGO JONES, WILLIAM SHAKESPEARE and others drew large crowds to masques and plays. He was born in Lindfield (Sussex), probably in 1550, to Edmund Henslowe (Master of the Game in Ashdown Forest) and his wife, Margaret. For some years, he worked as a servant of the bailiff to Viscount Montague, work that took him to SOUTHWARK by 1577. When his master died, he married the widow and, using her money, purchased property and invested in a range of businesses, pawn shops, lodging houses, inns and small industries, such as dyeing and starch making. In 1587, he built the Rose Theatre (the first at Bankside), thirteen years later he constructed the Fortune (the largest theatre of its day), then, in 1613, he erected the Hope (which was designed for bear baiting as well as plays). Henslowe kept a tight hold on finances, buying works from authors then hiring out his theatres to groups of players but keeping writers and actors indebted to him in order to retain their services. His diary (which lists details of bills for costumes, payments to authors, loans to players, names of plays performed and dates of performances) is a major source of information about the economics of late sixteenth- and early seventeenth-century theatre management. He died in London on 6 January 1616 and was buried in St Saviour's Church, Southwark.

HERNE HILL

Some authorities claim that the suburb of Herne Hill (bordering DULWICH and CAMBERWELL some 4 miles south of CHARING CROSS) derives its name from a seventeenth-century resident of the area. Others believe that the River Effra, long paved over, once had an island with a heronry and that the birds left a legacy in the name. In the later eighteenth and early nineteenth centuries, the area was semi-rural in character, with large detached houses providing homes for affluent families (in his autobiographical work, *Praeterita*, published in 1885–9, John Ruskin describes the country walks around 28 Herne Hill, where he lived from 1823 to 1842). However, in the 1860s, the arrival of the RAILWAY transformed the area as rows of cheap houses were built to house an influx of working-class groups, turning it into part of metropolitan London within two decades. The LONDON COUNTY COUNCIL and other local authorities have provided much public housing since the end of the Second World War but many neighbourhoods retain their Victorian character and the grounds of former Brockwell Hall (built in 1811–13 but largely destroyed by fire in 1990) have been converted into a public PARK with an eighteenth-century walled garden and an open-air swimming pool. Herne Hill became part of the LONDON BOROUGH OF LAMBETH in 1965. (See also CRYSTAL PALACE FOOTBALL CLUB.)

HIGHBURY

Although Highbury lies only 3 miles north-east of CHARING CROSS, it maintained an essentially rural character until the early nineteenth century, supplying London with dairy goods and other agricultural products. Speculative builders began to construct properties in 1774, but there was little growth in population until the 1820s, when THOMAS CUBITT erected a row of villas at Highbury Grove. Highbury College (a theological centre) followed in 1826, PARK Terrace in 1830, Highbury New Park in 1853–61 and Grosvenor Avenue in the 1860s, all providing homes for relatively affluent families. Meanwhile, Highbury Barn was supplying entertainment ranging from tea and cakes to circus events, open-air dances and club dinners for as many as 4,000 people at a sitting; ultimately, however, local residents complained of the noise and the facility closed in

1871. The developers' demands and competition for property by commercial concerns (such as ARSENAL FOOTBALL CLUB, which relocated from WOOLWICH in 1913) placed considerable pressure on land (the Barn vanished under bricks and mortar within twelve years) but some open space was preserved, notably the 27.5 acres of Highbury Fields, which were saved from encroachment in 1885 and 1891. Twentieth-century local authority housing provision has detracted from the Victorian character of the area, and many of the original properties are gone, but several of the early streets survive. Highbury was included within the LONDON BOROUGH OF ISLINGTON when local government in the metropolitan area was reorganized in 1965. Its name derives from the Old English words for 'high manor'. (See also NORTHERN LINE; VICTORIA LINE.)

HIGHGATE

Highgate – 5 miles north of CHARING CROSS – takes its name from the tollhouse situated on a hill close to the village during the fourteenth century. Kilns dating from the first century indicate that it was occupied by the Romans but the area remained largely undeveloped until the final decades of the sixteenth century, when affluent courtiers built grand homes overlooking London. A free school (which still survives as Highgate School) was established by Sir Roger Cholmley in 1565, and a nonconformist chapel opened in 1622 (these churches were banned within 5 miles of the CITY OF LONDON; the site in Southwood Lane lay just outside that boundary). By the late seventeenth century, wealthy merchants were building properties (or adapting the older mansions for their own use), beginning an expansion of population that was reflected in the later growth of institutions such as the Whittington Almshouses, erected by the Mercers' Company (one of the LIVERY COMPANIES) in 1822, and the Smallpox Hospital, which opened in 1850. Many of the old buildings remain (including Cromwell House, built in 1637–8 for the Sprignell family, and St Michael's Church, constructed in 1831–2), but new developments (including projects by the LONDON BOROUGH OF CAMDEN) have extended the settlement. At the junction of Highgate Hill and ARCHWAY, a stone cat sits on the pavement, allegedly at the spot where RICHARD WHITTINGTON heard BOW BELLS calling him back to London and promising him that he would serve three times as LORD MAYOR. (See also HIGHGATE CEMETERY; NORTHERN LINE.)

HIGHGATE CEMETERY

In 1839, the London Cemetery Company opened a 17.5-acre BURIAL GROUND, planned by architect Stephen Geary in collaboration with landscape gardener David Ramsay and located on the south slope of HIGHGATE West Hill. It very quickly became a fashionable place for funerals, attracting visitors who marvelled at the views of London as well as at the flamboyant Victorian decoration of the tombstones, so, in 1857, a 19.5-acre extension was added to the south-east. A century later, however, the firm's successor – the United Cemetery Company – was suffering from a cash shortage and its land had degenerated into a tangle of weeds where monuments were hidden by shrubbery and buildings were falling apart. Local people, determined to restore the area to its former glory, formed the Friends of Highgate Cemetery, a volunteer group that acquired the freehold in 1981 and began repair work. Eight years later, ownership was transferred to the Custodian of Charities. In recent years, many improvements have been made, attracting a growing stream of visitors (including a number of film companies). Some of the tombs fascinate simply because of their decoration – menagerie keeper George Wombwell is guarded by a sleeping, cross-pawed lion, for example, and the headstone at cricketer Frederick Lillywhite's grave displays a broken wicket, showing that he had completed his innings. Other vaults shelter the bones of the rich and famous (some of whom lived in nearby HAMPSTEAD); Michael Faraday (the discoverer of electromagnetic induction) rests in Highgate, as do CHARLES DICKENS and George Eliot, philosopher Herbert Spencer and bare-knuckle fighter Tom Sayers. Dante Gabriel Rossetti committed his young wife, Lizzie Siddal, to the earth then had her coffin dug up so that he could retrieve a book of manuscript poems he had buried with her. The most famous grave is that of Karl Marx, who died in 1883 and lies under a headstone as weighty as his writings.

HILLINGDON, LONDON BOROUGH OF

When metropolitan local government was reorganized in 1965, Hillingdon was created through the merger of the Borough of UXBRIDGE and the Urban Districts of Hayes and Harlington, RUISLIP and Northwood, and Yiewsley and West Drayton. It covers 43 square miles, has a population of 243,000 (2001) and takes its name from Hillingdon village, which stands close to the centre of the area. Heathrow AIRPORT, located in the southern part of the borough, is a major employer that has attracted ancillary service and manufacturing industries, aided by good road links to the nationwide motorway system. However, that transport network has also raised problems of noise pollution, illegal IMMIGRANTS and drug smuggling, which are continuing sources of discontent among local residents. Uxbridge, further north, is a prosperous commuter suburb with low unemployment levels, and Ruislip, with a high proportion of GREEN BELT land, has more in common with neighbouring rural communities than with the urban core.

HOLBORN

Holborn, located north of the STRAND, takes its name from the Holebourne stream (a tributary of the FLEET RIVER) and is first mentioned in a tenth-century document that records a grant of land by Edgar, King of England from 959 until 975, to WESTMINSTER ABBEY. Its boundary with the CITY OF LONDON (which lies immediately to the east) is marked by two stone obelisks, known as Holborn Bars, which were erected in about 1130 to identify a tollbooth. The area has given its name to a number of metropolitan landmarks, including a street called Holborn, which is known to have existed as early as the thirteenth century, when it was an important route by which wool, corn, timber and other products were delivered to city customers. Today, the road (now known for most of its length as High Holborn) links SHAFTESBURY AVENUE to the major road junction at Holborn Circus, which was constructed in 1872 as part of a traffic improvement programme. The same programme included the building of Holborn Viaduct, 1,400 feet long and 80 feet wide, across the valley of the Fleet so that Holborn could be connected to Newgate Street and the neighbourhood of ST PAUL'S CATHEDRAL. In 1874, the London, Chatham and Dover RAILWAY opened a station at the south-eastern end of the viaduct, providing commuters from the towns along the SOUTH BANK of the RIVER THAMES with easy access to the city's financial district. During the LONDON COUNTY COUNCIL's jurisdiction, Holborn was the smallest of the metropolitan boroughs. Dominated by commercial properties, it was incorporated within the LONDON BOROUGH OF CAMDEN when local government was reorganized in 1965. (See also ELECTRICITY; ELY PLACE; INNS OF CHANCERY; INNS OF COURT; METROPOLITAN DRINKING FOUNTAIN AND CATTLE TROUGH ASSOCIATION; PICCADILLY LINE; RED LION SQUARE; ST ANDREW'S CHURCH, HOLBORN; ST ETHELDREDA'S CHURCH, HOLBORN.)

HOLLAND HOUSE

In 1606, Sir Walter Cope, James I's Chancellor of the Exchequer, built a mansion in extensive grounds at KENSINGTON. Originally known as Cope Castle, it acquired its present name after it was inherited by Lady Rich (Sir Walter's daughter), whose husband was created Earl of Holland in 1624. In the late eighteenth and early nineteenth centuries, it was one of the social centres of London as such Whig politicians as Prime Minister George Canning and Earl Grey mixed with leading literary figures of the day, including CHARLES DICKENS, Richard Brinsley Sheridan and William Wordsworth (see HOLLAND HOUSE CIRCLE). From 1866, however, parts of the estate were sold to developers, then, during the BLITZ, most of the building was destroyed. The LONDON COUNTY COUNCIL bought the property in 1952, restored the east wing and converted it for use as a youth hostel dedicated to George VI. Art exhibitions are sometimes held in the Orangery and the former ice house, and the PARK (which incorporates a rose garden, an iris garden and a Dutch garden) provides an important oasis of green space in a densely populated area of west London.

HOLLAND HOUSE CIRCLE

Early in 1851, painter G.F. Watts moved into HOLLAND HOUSE as the guest of Sara Prinseps. Over the next thirty years, the rambling building became the focus of a bohemian clique as the farmland it overlooked was converted into the streets and squares now known as west KENSINGTON. Such young, talented artists as Frederick Leighton and Holman Hunt (attracted as much by Prinseps' three beautiful sisters as by Watts) set up studios nearby and were joined at Sunday afternoon soirees by writers as renowned as William Thackeray and Alfred Lord Tennyson, scientists as distinguished as astronomer John Herschel and politicians as senior as Prime Ministers Benjamin Disraeli and William Gladstone. Their relationships did not accord with modern stereotypes of Victorian rectitude (Joseph Edgar Boehm actually died in a highly compromising position whilst supposedly teaching the art of sculpture to Queen Victoria's daughter, Princess Louise) but, nevertheless, they successfully established a respected status as moral exemplars by producing patriotic and morally uplifting works. Their allegorical style is now out of fashion (partly because few houses have room for 50-foot-long canvases) but, in their day, they were regarded throughout Europe as the most gifted painters of the period and some (such as Leighton) became millionaires.

HOLLAND PARK

See HOLLAND HOUSE.

HOLLOWAY

The area between HIGHGATE and FINSBURY PARK, 4 miles north of CHARING CROSS, was owned throughout the medieval period by the Dean and Chapter of ST PAUL'S CATHEDRAL. It is first referred to as Holloway (meaning 'sunken highway') during the fifteenth century and became urbanized following the building of HOLLOWAY PRISON in 1852, the establishment of the METROPOLITAN CATTLE MARKET on the 75-acre site of a Jacobean mansion house in 1855, and the construction of roads and RAILWAYS during the third-quarter of the nineteenth century. Rows of cheap houses and small industrial premises replaced fields and hedgerows, creating a suburb that earned an unenviable reputation for shabby terraces occupied by underpaid clerical workers (the lifestyle is described in George and Weedon Grossmith's *Diary of a Nobody*, published in 1892). Since the Second World War, local authorities have improved the housing stock (partly by building on the site of the cattle market, which closed in 1963) but Holloway is still characterized by a mixture of industry and residential property. It was incorporated within the LONDON BOROUGH OF ISLINGTON in 1965. (See also BATTERSEA DOGS' HOME.)

HOLLOWAY PRISON

The first prison at HOLLOWAY was built in 1852 to house both sexes but, from 1902, accepted women only (including Emmeline Pankhurst and other campaigners for female suffrage). The present red-brick structure, the largest women's jail in Britain, was designed by Robert Matthew, Johnson-Marshall and Partners to meet modern standards and erected in 1970. The 500 inmates live in units of sixteen or thirty-two people, with bedrooms housing one or four prisoners. Each unit has its own dining area and common room, but a hospital, swimming pool and gymnasium serve the whole jail. Mothers with infant children have special facilities.

HOLMES, SHERLOCK

In 1887, Arthur Conan Doyle, unable to make ends meet as a Portsmouth doctor, turned to mystery writing in an attempt to boost his income. His first short novel – *A Study in Scarlet* – was an outstanding success, introducing amateur detective Sherlock Holmes to a middle-class public ready to suspend its disbelief and accept a romanticized world of crime in which a pipe-smoking, violin-playing, eccentric dilettante draws startlingly logical conclusions from scraps of evidence overlooked by plodding police officers. Holmes (modelled on Dr Joseph Bell, who lectured at Edinburgh University, where Conan Doyle studied medicine) lived in rooms at 221B BAKER STREET, where his adventures where chronicled by his friend Dr John Watson (whose character is drawn from that of Dr James Watson, president of the Portsmouth Literary and Scientific Society). Conan Doyle moved to London in 1890 and opened a medical practice at 2 Devonshire Place, ST MARYLEBONE, but it attracted few patients, so he returned with vigour to his writing, publishing a series of short stories featuring Holmes in *Strand* magazine. By 1893, he was bored by the character and tried to kill him off in a struggle with his archenemy, Professor Moriarty, but public demand forced him to bring the detective back to life in *The Hound of the Baskervilles*, published in 1902. Conan Doyle was knighted in the same year for his work at a field hospital in South Africa during the Boer War and died at Crowborough (Sussex) on 7 July 1930, by which time Holmes had become one of the most copied characters in crime fiction, with a cult following. Many of the tales illuminate the social history of the metropolitan area at the end of the nineteenth century, focusing on the lifestyles of different social classes and on social distinctions between town and country.

HONOURABLE ARTILLERY COMPANY

The Artillery Company claims to be the oldest military unit in the United Kingdom. It was created in 1537, when Henry VIII gave a body of citizen archers (known as the Guild of St George) the formal title of Fraternity or Guild of Artillery of Longbows, Crossbows and Handguns and made it responsible for the defence of London. The prefix 'Honourable' was first applied in 1685, though not confirmed until the nineteenth century. Initially, the company was based in Artillery Lane, Bishopsgate (see BISHOP'S GATE), but, in 1642, it moved to its present location in City Road, where, on 18 June 1774, the first major CRICKET match held in Great Britain was played between Kent and All England. Although most of their duties are now ceremonial, members saw active service during the First and Second World Wars and, as part of the modern Territorial Army, undergo regular military training.

HONOURABLE CORPS OF GENTLEMEN AT ARMS

Officially, members of the corps (originally formed by Henry VIII in 1509) act as bodyguards to the royal family but their public duties are now largely ceremonial. They dress in skirted red coats, carry battleaxes and wear helmets with white plumes at all times, even at religious services. Like the YEOMEN OF THE GUARD, they formerly served with the armed forces.

HORNIMAN MUSEUM

During his travels abroad, tea magnate Frederick J. Horniman amassed a large collection of objects that he made available to the public at his home in FOREST HILL in 1890. Eight years later, the house was demolished and replaced by a stone and brick art nouveau building designed by C. Harrison Townsend. When it was completed in 1901, the MUSEUM, along with 21 acres of PARKland and garden, was handed over to the LONDON COUNTY COUNCIL. The collection that it houses is a typically Victorian blend of natural history and ethnography, including a stuffed walrus, shrunken heads and musical instruments.

HORNSEY

Hornsey is located some 6 miles north of CHARING CROSS. It was probably founded during Saxon times as a forest settlement and was owned for much of the medieval period by the Bishops of London, who used it for hunting. Urban development began in 1850, when the Great Northern RAILWAY built a station at the eastern end of the village, allowing commuters to work in the CITY OF LONDON and return to country homes at night; within thirty years, fields and woods had been covered by housing estates, small industries and urban services. After the Second World War, many of the less sound properties were replaced by local authority residential building. In 1965, when local government within the metropolitan area was reformed, Hornsey was incorporated within the LONDON BOROUGH OF HARINGEY. The last part of the name may be derived from the Old English *haeg*, meaning 'enclosure', and the first part either from *Haering* (a personal name) or from *haring* ('a grey wood'). (See also FINSBURY PARK; HARINGEY; WOOD GREEN.)

HORSE GUARDS PARADE

Horse Guards Parade, located immediately east of ST JAMES'S PARK, is built on the former tiltyard of WHITEHALL PALACE. Horse Guards building, which lines three sides of the courtyard, stands on the site of a palace guardhouse; designed by William Kent in Palladian style, it was erected in 1750–60 under the direction of John Vardy. The entrance from WHITEHALL is guarded, between 10 a.m. and 4 p.m. each day, by two cavalrymen of the HOUSEHOLD DIVISION (the changing of the guard at 11 a.m. is one of London's principal tourist attractions). Every year, on the reigning monarch's official birthday, the ceremony of TROOPING THE COLOUR is held on the parade ground, which is marked by statues of distinguished military commanders, including Lord Kitchener (who organized the British Army at the start of the First World War with the slogan 'Your country needs you') and Lord Mountbatten of Burma (who was murdered by the IRA in 1979). (See also TREASURY BUILDINGS.)

HOTELS

Hotels were slow to develop in London, partly because wealthy male visitors to the city stayed at their clubs (see GENTLEMEN'S CLUBS) and ladies stayed in private houses. The less affluent used inns or other lodgings. Even by the early nineteenth century, most of the few establishments called hotels were hired out as whole buildings rather than as separate rooms. The spur to the development of accommodation for travellers was the expansion of the RAILWAY network, which brought people from the provinces in increasingly large numbers from the 1830s. Railway companies themselves built hotel properties at their London termini, many of them (such as the Midland's Grand Hotel at ST PANCRAS) lavishly decorated and luxuriously furnished. The success of these ventures encouraged other entrepreneurs, including Frederick Gordon, who opened the Grand Hotel, the

Metropole Hotel and the Victoria Hotel on Northumberland Avenue during the 1870s. Later, in the period between the First and Second World Wars, many aristocratic mansions, deserted by owners who had fled to the country or found the cost of upkeep too high, were demolished to make way for hotels (the Duke of Westminster's Grosvenor House in PARK LANE was replaced by the Grosvenor House Hotel in 1926–8, for example). Also, many large townhouses in areas such as BLOOMSBURY and Marylebone (see ST MARYLEBONE) were subdivided for use as bed and breakfast establishments, attracting restaurants, public houses and other services in their wake. By the later 1990s, London had over 1,000 hotels, motels, guest houses and similar businesses. Of the total 138,000 beds available each night, the majority were concentrated in inner-city localities, notably the CITY OF WESTMINSTER (48,000), the ROYAL BOROUGH OF KENSINGTON AND CHELSEA (19,400) and the LONDON BOROUGH OF CAMDEN (16,600). (See also ALDWYCH; BAYSWATER; BROWN'S HOTEL; CANARY WHARF; CANNON STREET STATION; CLARIDGE'S HOTEL; CONNAUGHT HOTEL; DORCHESTER HOTEL; EARL'S COURT; EUSTON STATION; EXCEL; GROSVENOR SQUARE; JERMYN STREET; JOHNSON'S HOUSE, DR; KENSINGTON; KING'S CROSS; LANGHAM HOTEL; LEICESTER SQUARE; LIVERPOOL STREET STATION; MAYFAIR; PIMLICO; PORTLAND PLACE; RITZ HOTEL; RUSSELL SQUARE; ST GEORGE'S HOSPITAL; SMITH, W.H., LTD; STRAND; VICTORIA.)

HOUNDSDITCH

The 300-yard-long street that connects ALDGATE to Bishopsgate (see BISHOP'S GATE) follows the line of the moat that formed part of the north-eastern defences of the CITY OF LONDON during medieval times. It may derive its name from kennels where hunting animals were kept or (according to the sixteenth-century historian JOHN STOW) from the habit of using it as a depository for 'much filth, especially dead dogges'. The population plummeted during the GREAT PLAGUE of 1664–6, when 1,100 victims were buried in a communal pit, but had recovered by the nineteenth century, when the area gained a reputation as a Jewish neighbourhood with cheap clothes and other goods. During the twentieth century, most of the properties were converted for use by banks and other financial institutions. (See also SIEGE OF SIDNEY STREET.)

HOUNSLOW

Hounslow is located on the western fringe of London, 11 miles from CHARING CROSS and directly under the flight path of planes landing at Heathrow Airport. It lies on the Roman road that ran from London to the route centre of Calleva Attrebatum (now known as Silchester) but developed from 1214, following the establishment of a priory by the Friars of Holy Trinity to provide accommodation for travellers and care for the sick. The heathland around the settlement became popular as a military training ground (James II maintained a standing army there from 1686, cavalry barracks were built in 1793 and accommodation for infantry was added in 1875). Also, in 1784, General William Roy established a base line for the mapping of Britain, which was retained until satellite imagery replaced conventional surveys during the late twentieth century.

Despite the presence of the Army, the community's prosperity relied heavily on provision of services for travellers to and from the west of England, with inns providing refreshment and rooms for coach passengers as well as facilities for changing, shoeing and stabling horses. In 1840, the opening of the Great Western RAILWAY killed the coaching trade, but TRANSPORT retained its local economic importance, with the London and South-Western Railway providing services from 1850 and the District Railway from 1883. In addition, during the early twentieth century, Hounslow became a focus of BUS routes and maintenance then, in 1919, the site of the first civil AIRPORT in Britain, with daily services to Paris (the first flight to Australia from England left in November of the same year). In 1932, the LONDON UNDERGROUND system arrived, the PICCADILLY LINE providing regular services to the city centre. These developments encouraged house building for local workers and for commuters as well as office construction for firms requiring easy accessibility, fuelling a considerable expansion both of population numbers and of the urban area as well as an increase in the community's importance as a retail and service centre. The settlement acquired Urban District Council status in 1894, became a borough in 1932 then, when London's local government was reorganized in 1965, gave its name to a new LONDON BOROUGH OF HOUNSLOW. Its name may be derived from the Old English *hlaw* (which means 'mound' or 'rising ground') and *hund*, which could mean 'hound' but which, as *Hunt*, could also be a personal name. (See also DISTRICT LINE; SIEGE OF SIDNEY STREET.)

HOUNSLOW, LONDON BOROUGH OF

The London Borough of Hounslow was created in 1965 through the amalgamation of the Borough of BRENTFORD and CHISWICK, the Borough of Heston and Isleworth, the Borough of HOUNSLOW and the Urban District of Feltham under a single local authority. It covers 23 square miles and had a resident population of 212,300 in 2001. The area has considerable ethnic and economic diversity, with a large Asian community and a mixture of manufacturing, office and service jobs. The proximity of Heathrow AIRPORT (to the west) and the Great West Road (which bisects the area and provides links to the national motorway network) attracted light industries, particularly around Brentford, Chiswick and Feltham, but recession and the movement of business to more spacious semi-rural sites resulted in higher than average rates of unemployment among manual workers during the 1990s. The Borough Council responded with a major regeneration programme, focusing on Feltham, which is designed to attract 2,500 jobs through expansion of trading estates and the development of a technology park. CHISWICK HOUSE, OSTERLEY HOUSE and SYON HOUSE help draw tourists to the east of the area but not in sufficient numbers to have a major impact on employment.

HOUSEHOLD CAVALRY

See HOUSEHOLD DIVISION.

HOUSEHOLD DIVISION

The seven regiments of the British Army's Household Division undertake numerous ceremonial tasks, including guard duties at BUCKINGHAM PALACE, HORSE GUARDS PARADE, ST JAMES'S PALACE and the TOWER OF LONDON. With the exception of the Irish Guards (established in the nineteenth century) and the Welsh Guards (formed during the First World War), all were founded during the seventeenth century. The mounted regiments that form the Household Cavalry are distinguished by their uniforms, the Life Guards wearing scarlet tunics and carrying white plumes on their headdress, the Blues and Royals blue tunics and red plumes. Bandsmen, led by trumpeters (on grey horses) and drummers (on skewbalds), are dressed in scarlet and gold. The five regiments of Foot Guards all wear red tunics and black bearskins; they have different collar badges, shoulder badges and buttons but are most readily identified by the presence or colour of the plumes on their headgear (the Coldstream Guards have red plumes, the Grenadier Guards white, the Irish Guards blue, the Welsh Guards green and white, and the Scots Guards no plume). All seven groups have distinguished records of active service and still undertake normal military duties. (See also CHANGING OF THE GUARD; KNIGHTSBRIDGE; ST JAMES'S PARK; STATE OPENING OF PARLIAMENT.)

HOUSE OF COMMONS

See PALACE OF WESTMINSTER.

HOUSE OF LORDS

See PALACE OF WESTMINSTER.

HOUSES OF PARLIAMENT

See PALACE OF WESTMINSTER.

HOXTON

Hoxton is a traditionally working-class area lying some 2½ miles north-east of CHARING CROSS. Until the seventeenth century, it was a rural village that produced vegetables and flowers for the London market but as building land in the capital became increasingly scarce its open fields attracted developers. LIVERY COMPANIES erected almshouses for their members (for example, in 1692 the Haberdashers Company constructed a property that would provide accommodation for twenty men unable to provide for themselves and schooling for the sons of another twenty) and business interests opened MUSIC HALLS to supply entertainment for the growing urban population (the Britannia Theatre, in High Street, held its first performances in 1850, catering to audiences of up to 3,000 people). By the end of the nineteenth century, the suburb was one of the poorest in the city, with infectious disease spreading readily in the overcrowded homes, but the extensive damage suffered during the BLITZ (when the Britannia Theatre was destroyed) allowed local authorities to restructure housing provision in municipal developments. Like other parts of the EAST END, Hoxton has experienced some gentrification in recent years. It was incorporated within the LONDON BOROUGH OF HACKNEY when London's local government was reformed in 1965. The name probably means 'Hoc's *tun* (homestead)'.

HUGUENOTS

In the last years of the seventeenth century, London's population was augmented by an estimated 30,000 Huguenots, who were persecuted in France because of their Protestant beliefs. Skilled silk weavers, they settled primarily in SPITALFIELDS and SOHO, earning a considerable reputation for their craftsmanship. The large windows that allowed light into their attic rooms can still be seen at Fournier Street (near CHRIST CHURCH, SPITALFIELDS), where floor joists were packed with silk waste to deaden the sound of the looms. A smaller group established a community at WANDSWORTH, where they built up a hat-making industry sufficiently respected to attract orders from the Roman Catholic clergy at the Vatican. At East Hill, many of the IMMIGRANTS were buried in a tiny cemetery close to their church. The BURIAL GROUND was closed in 1854 and converted into a public garden; many of the inscriptions on the gravestones are now too eroded to read easily but a memorial erected in 1911 lists some of the families represented. (See also MERTON; MORTLAKE; PADDINGTON; STREATHAM.)

HUNGERFORD BRIDGE

The first Hungerford BRIDGE, designed by ISAMBARD KINGDOM BRUNEL and built in 1841–5, provided access from the SOUTH BANK of the RIVER THAMES to Hungerford MARKET, which sold fruit, vegetables, meat and fish. However, the market closed in 1860, unable to compete with COVENT GARDEN, and the site was developed by the south-eastern RAILWAY as CHARING CROSS Station. Brunel's bridge was replaced by the present wrought-iron lattice-girder structure built to John Hawkshaw's design in 1864. The railway bridge (also known as Charing Cross Bridge) has a footbridge (one of only two across the Thames in central London) on its eastern side and was subject to a major overhaul in 1979, when new cross girders were installed. In 2001–2, the footbridge was upgraded and a second walkway added on the west side.

HURLINGHAM CLUB

In 1875, the rules of polo were formalized by the Hurlingham Club at its Ranelagh

Gardens premises in FULHAM. The club was formed in 1867, when Frank Heathcote leased land at Hurlingham House (built in 1760) so that members could indulge in pigeon shooting, but the organization rapidly developed into a more general association for people with sporting interests as facilities were provided for cricket, croquet, golf, lawn bowls, skittles, squash, swimming, tennis and other activities. The site on which the first polo match was played, in 1874, was converted into a municipal housing estate by the LONDON COUNTY COUNCIL in 1946.

HYDE PARK

Hyde Park covers 340 acres of central London, stretching from BAYSWATER in the north to GREEN PARK in the south and from KENSINGTON GARDENS in the west to MAYFAIR in the east. During the Middle Ages, it was owned by WESTMINSTER ABBEY but, when that MONASTERY was dissolved in 1540, the land was acquired by Henry VIII as a hunting forest. The public were admitted from the early seventeenth century and on May Day, in particular, fashionable London paraded itself in the grounds (in 1663, SAMUEL PEPYS records buying new clothes before going to Hyde Park in the hope of being noticed by Charles II). After dusk, however, it was a dangerous place, haunted by highwaymen and a popular location for settling disagreements by duel; the Duke of Hamilton and Lord Mohun killed each other in one contest there in 1712, for example. In 1730, Queen Caroline, wife of George II, added a boating lake, known as the SERPENTINE, increasing the area's recreational attractions, then, during the nineteenth century, the PARK became the setting for large public gatherings, such as the GREAT EXHIBITION in 1851. From 1860, the Victorians introduced flowerbeds, fountains and statues, formalizing, managing and taming the landscape. Modern usage reflects these traditions; protagonists disagree verbally, rather than violently, at SPEAKERS' CORNER, horse riders still use ROTTEN ROW (where William III exercised his animals), the Serpentine is popular with canoeists and young couples in paddle boats, crowds still gather for big events (the Rolling Stones have played there) and, on a summer Sunday, as many as 50,000 people will use the facilities for quiet recreation – jogging, dog walking, swimming or listening to concerts at the bandstand. The park is still owned by the Crown and maintained by the ROYAL PARKS Agency. (See also LANSBURY, GEORGE; PARKS.)

The rules of polo were formalized by the Hurlingham Club at Ranelagh Gardens.

HYDE PARK CORNER

At the south-east corner of HYDE PARK, five roads meet at one of London's busiest traffic junctions, used by more than 150,000 vehi-

The Hyde Park Corner turnpike, 1798.

cles every weekday. In the eighteenth century, the site was the location of a tollgate, where fees were charged to travellers making their way from the west into PICCADILLY. The entrance to the PARK is now marked by a three-arched classical screen designed by Decimus Burton and erected in 1825 to provide a suitably regal approach from BUCKINGHAM PALACE. Burton was also responsible for Wellington Arch (also known as Constitution Arch and Green PARK Arch), which stands at the centre of the junction. Intended as a triumphal entry to Hyde PARK, it was erected outside Apsley House in 1828 but moved to its present position in 1883 so that it would dominate the western end of CONSTITUTION HILL. The structure houses a police station (the second smallest in London after that at TRAFALGAR SQUARE) and is surmounted by *The Quadrigia*, a bronze statue (completed by Captain Adrian Jones of the Third Hussars in 1912) that shows the angel of peace descending into a chariot drawn by four horses.

Apsley House, on the north of Hyde Park Corner just east of the former tollgate, was known as No. 1 London because of its position. It was designed by ROBERT ADAM and built in 1771–8 for Lord Chancellor Henry Bathurst but, in 1817, became the home of the Duke of Wellington, who lived in it until his death in 1852. The property was presented to the nation by the seventh duke in 1947 then converted into the Wellington MUSEUM, which opened in 1952.

The interior has remained much as it was when the first Duke was in residence, with exhibits (depicting both his army and his political career) focusing on the Waterloo Gallery, where he held an annual banquet to celebrate his victory over Napoleon's army on 18 June 1815. The front of the building is marked by a bronze statue of Wellington, mounted on Copenhagen, the horse that carried him to victory at Waterloo; designed by Joseph Edgar Boehm, it was cast from captured French guns and erected in 1888. Nearby, there are memorials to men of the Machine Gun Corps and the Royal Regiment of Artillery who died in the First World War.

In 2001 English Heritage revealed plans (prepared by Kim Wilkie, one of Britain's leading landscape architects) to remodel Hyde Park Corner at a cost of £20 million. (See also CHURCHILL, WINSTON SPENCER; MAYFAIR; ST GEORGE'S HOSPITAL.)

I

ILFORD

A residential suburb lying on the east bank of the River Roding, some 9 miles north-east of CHARING CROSS, Ilford has a lengthy history, with archaeological investigations revealing evidence of an Iron Age encampment. About 1140, Adeliza, Abbess of Barking, established a leper house that was enlarged forty years later by Abbess Mary Becket in memory of her brother Thomas, who had been murdered at Canterbury Cathedral in 1170. Nearby, a village developed at the limit of navigation on the river, with commodities such as timber, gravel and coal imported and exported, but significant population growth dates from 1839, when the arrival of the RAILWAY promoted a construction boom, attracting families willing to commute to city-centre jobs in order to have ready access to semi-rural environments on weekends. The area was the home of Ilford Films, one of the major manufacturers of camera film in the UK, until the 1960s. Present-day homes date mainly from the 1930s and 1950s and are located in large local authority estates, including the 27,000-unit Becontree development, begun in 1921 by the LONDON COUNTY COUNCIL and shared with neighbouring BARKING and DAGENHAM. Ilford was incorporated within the LONDON BOROUGH OF REDBRIDGE when London's local government was reformed in 1965, becoming the new authority's principal administrative base. The name appears to be derived from Celtic and Old English roots – *Hyle* is a Celtic stream name and *ford* remains unchanged in meaning since Anglo-Saxon times. (See also ESSEX COUNTY CRICKET CLUB; MANOR PARK; WALTHAMSTOW.)

IMMIGRANTS

London's development has been shaped by immigrants. It was founded by the Romans (see LONDINIUM), developed by the Normans and influenced by people from around the world who were attracted by the city's wealth and prestige. During the nineteenth century, the expansion of sea-borne trade with a growing empire brought foreign sailors to the DOCKS along the banks of the RIVER THAMES; many settled, forming distinctive communities, such as that of the Chinese in LIMEHOUSE. In the 1920s and 1930s, significant numbers of migrants (including some professional groups, such as doctors and lawyers) arrived from the Asian subcontinent and the early years of the Second World War brought large numbers from central and eastern Europe.

The bulk of foreign immigration, however, took place from the 1950s, when organizations such as British Railways, London Transport and the National Health Service conducted recruitment campaigns in the Caribbean and Africa in an attempt to reduce labour shortages. Jamaicans, in particular, arrived in large numbers, but many of the arrivals came from other West Indian islands, and from Ghana and Nigeria. These newcomers tended to settle in different parts of the city (Anguillans in Slough, for example, and Trinidadians in NOTTING HILL), forming readily identifiable concentrations that were often the focus of racial tension. In an attempt to avoid conflict, Harold Macmillan's Conservative government passed legislation that restricted immigration from Commonwealth countries after 1 July 1963. Even more stringent measures were approved in 1968, 1971, 1981 and 1988, in an attempt to reduce the number of people admitted permanently to the United Kingdom. In recent years, asylum seekers from Eastern Europe and Middle Eastern troublespots such as Iraq, Iran and Afghanistan have added to the already diverse ethnic and cultural composition of the capital's population.

Returns from the 2001 census showed that 27.1 per cent of London's population was born outside the United Kingdom and that non-white citizens formed a majority of the residents in the LONDON BOROUGHS OF BRENT and NEWHAM (54.7 per cent in the former and 60.6 per cent in the latter). Several commentators have argued that these figures reflect the arrival of large numbers of asylum seekers and illegal immigrants since the late 1990s. Others point out that the enlargement of the European Union will attract immigrants from Eastern Europe so that a total of around 200,000 incomers could be settling in the United Kingdom each year over the next ten years, with about two-thirds of them opting to live in London and neighbouring counties. (See also BRONDESBURY; DALSTON; DEPTFORD; FINSBURY PARK; HILLINGDON, LONDON BOROUGH OF; INNER LONDON EDUCATION AUTHORITY (ILEA); LEYTONSTONE; RACHMANISM; SIEGE OF SIDNEY STREET; SOUTHALL; STOCKWELL.)

IMPERIAL WAR MUSEUM

The MUSEUM was established by Act of Parliament in 1920. Originally based at CRYSTAL PALACE, it moved to KENSINGTON in 1924 then to its present location – the Lambeth Road site of BEDLAM – in 1935. During the 1980s, it was completely rebuilt in order to improve its displays of material relating to the two world wars and to improve visitors' understanding of the conflicts. One area, for example, is designed as a First World War trench, where the sounds of battle reverberate beyond barbed wire. Elsewhere, an EAST END AIR-RAID shelter receives a severe jolt as a bomb lands nearby. The museum also has a large collection of twentieth-century British art and an extensive collection of artefacts, including tanks and fighter planes.

INNER LONDON

See GREATER LONDON.

INNER LONDON EDUCATION AUTHORITY (ILEA)

The ILEA was established in 1965 as a committee of the GREATER LONDON COUNCIL (GLC) charged with provision of EDUCATION at all levels (with the exception of the universities) in the CITY OF LONDON and twelve inner-city LONDON BOROUGHS – CAMDEN, GREENWICH, HACKNEY, HAMMERSMITH AND FULHAM, ISLINGTON, KENSINGTON AND CHELSEA, LAMBETH, LEWISHAM, SOUTHWARK, TOWER HAMLETS, WANDSWORTH and WESTMINSTER. The largest authority of its kind in the world, it wielded considerable power, arguing that providing high-quality education, with good resources for LIBRARIES and related learning facilities, could help overcome the problems created by deprived homes and neighbourhoods. In addition, it supported a research unit that made an important academic contribution to scholars' understanding of the dynamics of education in Britain's metropolitan areas, particularly among IMMIGRANT groups. The ILEA survived the GLC's abolition in 1986, becoming an elected body in its own right, but agitation among its constituent boroughs for the right to govern their own affairs led to its dismemberment on 31 March 1990.

INNER TEMPLE

See INNS OF COURT.

INNS OF CHANCERY

Although the original reason for their foundation is not clear, the Inns were probably created during the medieval period to train Chancery Clerks, who prepared writs for the English courts. By the fifteenth century, they had become schools for aspirant lawyers but, over the next 300 years, students increasingly turned for tuition to the INNS OF COURT, which had the sole right to decide whether individuals could be admitted as barristers and therefore prosecute or defend cases in the senior courts of England and Wales. The Inns of Chancery gradually became more important as meeting places for lawyers who could appear only in the lower courts but the formation of the Law Society, which began to regulate standards for these legal representatives in 1825, rendered them obsolete. During the nineteenth century, they closed down and their property was taken over by other interests. The nine principal Inns were Clifford's (founded in 1345 but closed in 1903), Thravies (formed in 1348 and dissolved during the 1760s), Staple (which survived from 1378 until 1884 and whose building in HOLBORN has been converted for use as offices), Furnival's (dissolved in 1817 and named after Lord Furnival, who rented the property to law students in 1383), Lyon's (which originated as a tavern, became an Inn of Chancery in 1420 and was dissolved in 1863), Barnard's (which was functioning by 1435 but whose dilapidated property was purchased by the Mercers, one of the LIVERY COMPANIES, in 1892), Clement's (founded by 1480 and named after ST CLEMENT DANES CHURCH, located nearby on the STRAND, its property was sold in parcels between 1868 and 1891) and New Inn (formed in 1485 but taken over by the LONDON COUNTY COUNCIL in 1899 and demolished to facilitate road improvements).

INNS OF COURT

The four Inns are legal societies that have the exclusive right to admit law students as barristers, a title that confers the right to prosecute or defend cases at the senior courts in England and Wales. Lincoln's Inn dates at least from 1422, Middle Temple from 1501, Inner Temple from 1505 and Gray's Inn from 1569, but all were probably founded in the fourteenth century to protect the rights of lawyers and teach the principles of English law (music, dancing and history were also on the curriculum so that students could be prepared for a place in the higher strata of professional society). Each Inn is independent of the others, and of central government, apart from a Council of Legal Education (established jointly in 1872 to regulate training practices) and a Senate (formed in 1974 to carry out certain administrative duties related to law reform and maintenance of standards). The term 'Inn' arose because each body provided accommodation for students and their teachers.

Lincoln's Inn is named after either Henry de Lacy (Earl of Lincoln and adviser to Edward I during the later thirteenth and early fourteenth centuries) or Thomas de Lyncoln (King's Serjeant at HOLBORN during the early 1400s). It moved to its present location on the west side of CHANCERY LANE between 1422 and 1522. The early records of the Inner and Middle Temples were destroyed during the PEASANTS' REVOLT in 1381 but it is known that both occupy sites formerly owned by the KNIGHTS TEMPLAR. The two Inns, neighbours on the south side of FLEET STREET, were given their property in perpetuity by James I in 1608 provided they maintained the TEMPLE CHURCH (which was consecrated in 1185 and is one of only five round churches in England) but the estate was not formally divided until 1732, when the Middle Temple took the west side and the Inner Temple the east. That part of the Knights' land outside TEMPLE BAR was known as Outer Temple but never had any association with the legal profession. Gray's Inn occupies the site, in Gray's Inn Road, of the London home of Sir Reginald le Grey, who died in 1308. It has extensive gardens that were laid out in 1606 by Sir Francis Bacon, a distinguished lawyer who, twelve years later, became Lord Chancellor, one of the most powerful positions in the land. (See also RED LION SQUARE.)

INTERNATIONAL PETROLEUM EXCHANGE (IPE)

The IPE, based in a redeveloped area of the DOCKLANDS at the south-eastern edge of the CITY OF LONDON, is Europe's principal energy futures and options exchange, trading over US$2 billion daily in 2003. It lists contracts for four major commodities – Brent crude (which establishes the benchmark price for two-thirds of the world's crude oil), gas oil (the price of which is used to value heating oil, diesel and aviation fuel throughout Europe), natural gas (launched in 1997 as Europe's first natural gas futures contract) and electricity (which was added in 2001). Traditionallly, trading of the first two is by 'open outcry', with dealers facing each other on the market floor (known as a pit), but natural gas and electricity negotiations were computerized. The exchange, which opened in 1981, demutualized in 2000. The following year the share capital was acquired by Intercontinental Exchange, providing IPE with a wider trading platform and presaging extended trading hours and further computerization. (See also LONDON CLEARING HOUSE (LCH).)

INTERNATIONAL UNDERWRITING ASSOCIATION OF LONDON (IUA)

The IUA was formed in 1999 through the merger of the LONDON INTERNATIONAL INSURANCE AND REINSURANCE MARKET ASSOCIATION (LIFFE) and the International Underwriting Association of London. It is the world's largest representative organization for international and wholesale insurance and reinsurance companies.

ISLE OF DOGS

Some 4 miles east of CHARING CROSS, the RIVER THAMES curves sharply south, creating a peninsula known as the Isle of Dogs. The name has never been satisfactorily explained: some writers claim that royal dogs were once kennelled in the area, others that it was once frequented by stray dogs. The marshy land lay undeveloped until, in 1802, the West India DOCKS were built in the north of the area. During the 1840s and 1850s, CUBITT TOWN and MILLWALL were established in the south, creating communities whose economic health relied largely on warehousing and shipbuilding. The declining importance of these activities during the twentieth century resulted in high rates of unemployment and consequent poverty. Following the closure of the docks in 1980 and the creation of the London DOCKLANDS Development Corporation the following year, attempts were made to revitalize the area by changing the industrial structure. BILLINGSGATE FISH MARKET was transplanted from THE CITY, printing works were built by *The Daily Telegraph* and *The Guardian*, the London Arena (a venue for major spectator events) was constructed on the site of Millwall Dock, the controversial CANARY WHARF complex included office provision for commercial concerns, road access was improved and the DOCKLANDS LIGHT RAILWAY was linked to the CITY OF LONDON. However, although the landscape was transformed, the jobs created in the new light industries were very different from those in the docks so most were taken by outsiders and the local unemployment rate remained high. In addition, the majority of workers commute from suburban homes, so the Isle's residents are mainly working class despite attempts to diversify the social structure by building homes attractive to professional groups. (See also MILLWALL FOOTBALL CLUB.)

A view of Islington in 1665, by Hollar.

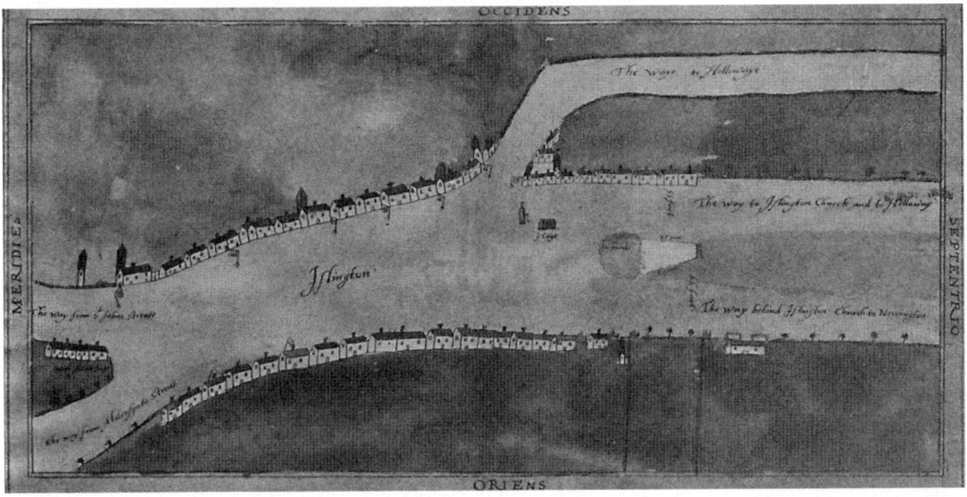

A plan of Islington in the middle of the sixteenth century.

ISLINGTON

Islington, located 2 miles north-east of CHARING CROSS, developed during the medieval period, when it passed through the hands of a series of landowners and was popular with English monarchs, who hunted in the surrounding forest (and, in the case of Henry VIII, built mansions for mistresses). Later, it became fashionable with religious nonconformists (Charles Wesley, cofounder of the Methodist Church, was educated at Charles Morton's Academy, for instance) and earned a reputation for tea gardens that, along with other recreations, attracted affluent visitors from the CITY OF LONDON during the eighteenth century. However, road building, the construction of the REGENT'S CANAL (which opened in 1820) and the arrival of the RAILWAY (in 1850) encouraged speculative developers (such as THOMAS CUBITT) to convert market gardens and other open space into housing estates. Many of these were sensitively designed to suit educated office workers but, during the first half of the twentieth century, as families moved to more suburban sites, the properties were converted for use as bed-sitters by a more transient and impoverished population. From the early 1960s, parts of the area regained their fashionable status (Tony Blair lived in Islington before taking up residence in 10 Downing Street) but parts of the area remain among the most deprived in London. In 1965, it merged with FINSBURY to form the LONDON BOROUGH OF ISLINGTON. The origin of the name is unclear, but records show that before the Norman invasion of 1066 it was known as *Gislandune*, which may mean 'Gisland's hill or down'. (See also MARYLEBONE CRICKET CLUB (MCC).)

ISLINGTON, LONDON BOROUGH OF

The borough was created in 1965 by the amalgamation of the formerly independent local government authorities in FINSBURY and ISLINGTON. Lying immediately north of the CITY OF LONDON, it forms a long strip of land that covers some 6 square miles and has a resident population of 176,000 (2001). Islington has little manufacturing industry, although there is some light engineering. TOURISM is important near the boundary with THE CITY, where finance firms and other commercial concerns also provide employment. Although some neighbourhoods (such as CANONBURY) have significant representation of professional and managerial groups, most are largely working class. The borough ranks high on most deprivation indices, with low rates of owner-occupation and car ownership and relatively high proportions of one-parent families with dependent children. (See also ANGEL, THE; BARNSBURY; BUNHILL FIELDS; CHARTERHOUSE; CLERKENWELL; HIGHBURY; HOLLOWAY; PENTONVILLE; TUFNELL PARK; VICTORIA LINE.)

J

JACK STRAW'S CASTLE

One of London's best-known PUBLIC HOUSES, the Castle, once a coaching inn, was extensively redesigned in 1964. Some writers argue that it is named after one of the leaders of the PEASANTS' REVOLT in 1381. However, although the building was certainly a rallying point for the rebels, 'Jack Straw' was also a generic name for farm workers, so the pub may simply have gained its title from the agricultural labourers who frequented it. Its historical associations and its location in North End Way, close to HAMPSTEAD, made it popular with the literary set during the nineteenth century; Wilkie Collins, CHARLES DICKENS and William Makepeace Thackeray were regular imbibers. (See also SPANIARDS, THE.)

JACK THE RIPPER

On 7 August 1888, thirty-five-year-old Martha Taylor was found murdered in a building near Whitechapel Road. Over the next three months, five other women were killed in the same area of the EAST END; all had their throats cut, all were mutilated and all but one were prostitutes. Mary Ann Nicholls was found on 31 August, Anne Chapman on 8 September, Elizabeth Stride and Catherine Eddowes on 30 September and Marie Kelly (the non-prostitute) on 9 November. The press, assuming that one person was responsible for all the deaths, nicknamed the murderer Jack the Ripper and fuelled public fascination with the case. Police investigations, conducted in the glare of publicity and taunted by letters from an individual who claimed to be responsible, involved interviews with hundreds of suspects but failed to identify a culprit. The mystery remains unsolved, but Jack the Ripper has become a minor industry, with walking tours of the square mile where the bodies were found a regular element of London's tourist season and a steady stream of books claiming to unmask the killer. The suspects include Prince Albert (Duke of Clarence) and his Cambridge University tutor, James Stephen. In recent times, Walter Richard Sickert, an artist, has emerged as the prime suspect. (See also MANOR PARK.)

JACKSON'S OF PICCADILLY

During the seventeenth and eighteenth centuries, the Jackson family established a series of businesses in London, notably candle-making and tallow merchandising. In the 1820s, Richard Jackson merged all of the enterprises into a single concern based at 190 PICCADILLY then, in 1840, opened larger premises at Nos 170–72 so that the shop could stock a wider range of goods, including fruit, game, poultry, soaps and wine. Jackson's built a considerable reputation with affluent WEST END residents but closed its retail outlet in 1980 in order to concentrate on the supply of teas (and other commodities) to stores, such as HARRODS, that have a large trade in luxury foods.

JERMYN STREET

Famed for its men's clothing shops, Jermyn Street parallels the south side of PICCADILLY for some 600 yards from HAYMARKET to St James's Street. It was built during the late seventeenth century on land owned by Henry Jermyn, Earl of St Albans, and, by Queen Victoria's reign, was lined with fashionable HOTELS. None of the early properties survive and the hotels (with the exception of the Cavendish) have closed, replaced by shirt-makers, shoe retailers and hatters, who began to infiltrate from about 1840, taking advantage of the affluent clientele in nearby residential areas and GENTLEMEN'S CLUBS. Former residents include Isaac Newton (who lived in a house on the site now occupied by No. 87) and Thomas Wall (inventor of a distinctively British form of ice cream and founder of a large food processing group), who was born at No. 113, which is now a restaurant.

JEWISH MUSEUM

The MUSEUM, founded in 1932, was based at Woburn House (in Tavistock Square) until 1995, when it moved to more spacious premises at Nos 129–131 Albert Street (north of EUSTON STATION). It owns one of the world's finest collections of Jewish ceremonial art and presents a series of exhibits detailing the history of Jews in Britain since the time of the Norman Conquest in 1066. An annex at the Sternberg Centre (a Jewish community centre at 80 East End Road, FINCHLEY) houses the organization's social history collections, including some 400 tape recordings and 12,000 photographs. In addition, displays outlining the Jews' place in London life incorporate reconstructions of a tailor's workshop and a cabinet-maker's business.

JOHNSON, SAMUEL (1709–1784)

Although Samuel Johnson would earn more than a footnote in histories of English literature because of his contributions as poet, critic, essayist and lexicographer, he is best remembered for his witticisms and his role in London social life as documented by JAMES BOSWELL. The son of bookseller Michael Johnson and his wife, Sarah, he was born in Lichfield on 18 September 1709 and educated at the local grammar school. He attended Oxford University but left in 1729 without completing his degree, took a teaching post at a school in Market Bosworth, then, in 1736, set up his own academy for young gentlemen at Edial. The venture collapsed after only a few months, encouraging Johnson to seek his fortune in London along with pupil DAVID GARRICK, who was later to achieve fame as an

The London Chronicle: N° 1

OR,

UNIVERSAL EVENING POST.

To be continued every TUESDAY, THURSDAY, and SATURDAY.

SATURDAY, JANUARY 1, 1757.

IT has been always lamented, that of the little Time allotted to Man, much must be spent upon Superfluities. Every Prospect has its Obstructions, which we must break to enlarge our View: Every Step of our Progress finds Impediments, which, however eager to go forward, we must stop to remove. Even those who profess to teach the Way to Happiness have multiplied our Incumbrances, and the Author of almost every Book retards his Instructions by a Preface.

The Writers of the *Chronicle* hope to be easily forgiven, though they should not be free from an Infection that has seized the whole Fraternity; and, instead of falling immediately to their Subjects, should detain the Reader for a Time with an Account of the Importance of their Design, the Extent of their Plan, and the Accuracy of the Method which they intend to prosecute. Such Premonitions, though not always necessary when the Reader has the Book complete in his Hand, and may find by his own Eyes whatever can be found in it, yet may be more easily allowed to Works published gradually in successive Parts; of which the Scheme can only be so far known as the Author shall think fit to discover it.

The Paper which we now invite the Publick to add to the Papers with which it is already rather wearied than satisfied, consists of many Parts; some of which it has in common with other periodical Sheets, and some peculiar to itself.

The first Demand made by the Reader of a Journal is, that he should find an accurate Account of foreign Transactions and domestick Incidents. This is always expected; but this is very rarely performed. Of those Writers who have taken upon themselves the Task of Intelligence, some have given, and others have sold their Abilities, whether small or great, to one or other of the Parties that divide us; and without a Wish for Truth, or Thought of Decency, without Care of any other Reputation than that of a stubborn Adherence to their Abetters, carry on the same Tenor of Representation through all the Vicissitudes of Right and Wrong, neither depressed by Detection, nor abashed by Confutation; proud of the hourly Encrease of Infamy, and ready to boast of all the Contumelies that Falsehood and Slander may bring upon them, as new Proofs of their Zeal and Fidelity.

With these Heroes we have no Ambition to be numbered; we leave to the Confessors of Faction the Merit of their Sufferings, and are desirous to shelter ourselves under the Protection of Truth. That all our Facts will be authentick, or all our Remarks just, we dare not venture to promise: We can relate but what we hear, we can point out but what we see. Of remote Transactions the first Accounts are always confused, and commonly exaggerated; and in domestick Affairs, if the Power to conceal is less, the Interest to misrepresent is often greater; and what is sufficiently vexatious, Truth seems to fly from Curiosity; and as many Enquirers produce many Narratives, whatever engages the publick Attention is immediately disguised by the Embellishments of Fiction. We pretend to no peculiar Power of disentangling Contradiction, or denuding Forgery. We have no settled Correspondence with the Antipodes, nor maintain any Spies in the Cabinets of Princes. But as we shall always be conscious that our Mistakes are involuntary, we shall watch the gradual Discoveries of Time, and retract whatever we have hastily and erroneously advanced.

In the Narratives of the daily Writers every Reader perceives somewhat of Neatness and Purity wanting, which at the first View it seems easy to supply: But it must be considered, that those Passages must be written in Haste, and that there is often no other Choice, but that they must want either Novelty or Accuracy; and that as Life is very uniform, the Affairs of one Week are so like those of another, that, by any Attempt after Variety of Expression, Invention would soon be wearied, and Language exhausted. Some Improvements however we hope to make; and for the rest we think, that when we commit only common Faults, we shall not be excluded from common Indulgence.

The Accounts of Prices of Corn and Stocks, are to most of our Readers of more Importance than Narratives of greater Sound, and as Exactness is here within the Reach of Diligence, our Readers may justly require it from us.

Memorials of a private and personal Kind, which relate Deaths, Marriages, and Preferments, must always be imperfect by Omission, and often erroneous by Misinformation; but, even in these, there shall not be wanting Care to avoid Mistakes, or to rectify them whenever they shall be found.

That Part of our Work by which it is distinguished from all others, is the *Literary Journal*, or Account of the Labours and Productions of the *Learned*. This was, for a long Time, among the Deficiencies of English Literature, but as the Caprice of Man is always starting from too little to too much, we have now, amongst other Disturbers of human Quiet, a numerous Body of *Reviewers* and *Remarkers*.

Every Art is improved by the Emulation of Competitors; those who make no Advances towards Excellence, may stand as Warnings against Faults. We shall endeavour to avoid that Petulance which treats with Contempt whatever has hitherto been reputed sacred. We shall repress that Elation of Malignity, which wantons in the Cruelties of Criticism, and not only murders Reputation, but murders it by Torture. Whenever we feel ourselves ignorant, we shall, at least, be modest. Our Intention is not to preoccupy Judgment by Praise or Censure, but to gratify Curiosity by early Intelligence, and to tell rather what our Authors have attempted, than what they have performed. The Titles of Books are necessarily short, and therefore disclose but imperfectly the Contents; they are sometimes fraudulent, and intended to raise false Expectations. In our Account this Brevity will be extended, and these Frauds, whenever they are detected, will be exposed; for though we write without Intention to injure, we shall not suffer ourselves to be made Parties to Deceit.

If any Author shall transmit a Summary of his Work, we shall willingly receive it; if any literary Anecdote, or curious Observation, shall be communicated to us, we will carefully insert it. Many Facts are known and forgotten; many Observations are made and suppressed; and Entertainment and Instruction are frequently lost, for Want of a Repository in which they may be conveniently preserved.

No Man can modestly promise what he cannot ascertain. We hope for the Praise of Knowledge and Discernment, but we claim only that of Diligence and Candour.

[Price Two Pence.]

The first number of *The London Chronicle*, with Johnson's introductory article.

Samuel Johnson wrote for several early newspapers and periodicals. This is the first edition of *The London Chronicle*, with Johnson's introductory article.

actor. From 1738, he contributed regularly to the *Gentlemen's Magazine* and, in 1744, published *An Account of the Life of Mr Richard Savage, Son of the Earl Rivers* (the biography described the impoverished conditions in which his poet friend lived and which Johnson knew firsthand, partly because of his own difficult circumstances and partly because he and Savage spent much time together). In 1750, he introduced *The Rambler*, a twice-weekly periodical, to London society. Published by John Payne, each of the 208 issues was a single anonymous article, 203 of which were written by Johnson himself. Most were moralistic, including themes such as *The Frequent Contemplation of Death Necessary to Moderate the Passions*, but tell much about the issues debated in mid-eighteenth-century intellectual circles.

Johnson's *Dictionary of the English Language*, published in two volumes in 1755, cemented his growing reputation. The work was not the first of its kind, but it was well received because of its polished definitions and the wide range of quotations used to demonstrate nuances in the usage of words listed. However, fame was not accompanied by fortune. Most of the income from sales of the *Dictionary* paid helpers and defrayed expenses, with neither publication of *The Idler* (a periodical reminiscent of *The Rambler*) in 1758–60 nor returns from *Rasselas, Prince of Abyssinia* (his only lengthy work of fiction, which was finished in 1759) helping to augment finances. Only in 1762, when he accepted a pension of £300 a year from the government, did his circumstances improve (ironically, in the *Dictionary*, Johnson notes that the word pension is 'generally understood to mean pay given to a state hireling for treason to his country').

In 1763, he was introduced to Boswell and formed a friendship that would last until his death. Many of the aphorisms that make Johnson probably the most quoted author after WILLIAM SHAKESPEARE are carefully noted

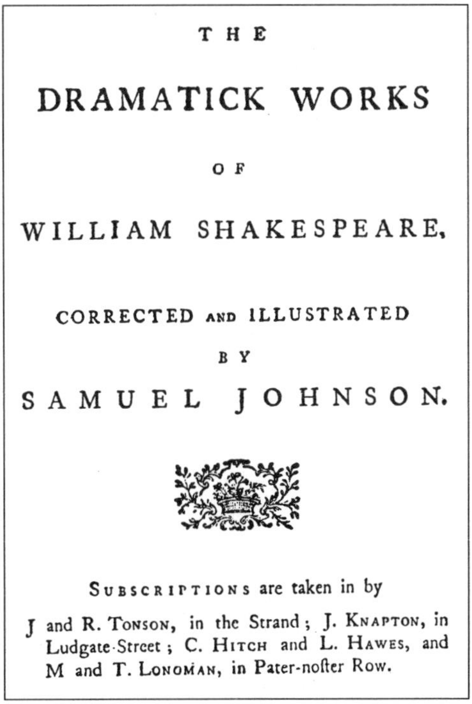

THE

DRAMATICK WORKS

OF

WILLIAM SHAKESPEARE,

CORRECTED AND ILLUSTRATED

BY

SAMUEL JOHNSON.

SUBSCRIPTIONS are taken in by

J and R. TONSON, in the Strand; J. KNAPTON, in Ludgate-Street; C. HITCH and L. HAWES, and M and T. LONGMAN, in Pater-nofter Row.

Samuel Johnson edited several editions of Shakespeare's works.

in Boswell's writings, as are his assessments of friends, acquaintances and other authors. For example, in his *Life of Samuel Johnson, LL.D.* (1791), Boswell refers to Johnson's opinion of politician Edmund Burke, with whom he had founded The Club (a group of influential figures, including artist Joshua Reynolds and writer Oliver Goldsmith) in 1764. 'In private life he is a very honest gentleman,' he says, 'but I will not allow him to be so in publick life.' The same work also includes the assertion that 'when a man is tired of London, he is tired of life; for there is in London all that life can afford.' Elsewhere, in Boswell's *Journal of a Tour of the Hebrides* (1784), Johnson remarks that 'By seeing London, I have seen as much of life as the world can shew.'

Johnson continued to publish after meeting Boswell, editing an eight-volume edition of William Shakespeare's works (1765), preparing political tracts (including one that defended the right of the British government to tax colonists in North America on the grounds that the emigrants had freely left a country where they had Parliamentary representation for a land where they had none) during the early 1770s and (1778 and 1781) writing a series of biographies of English poets. He was awarded doctorates by Trinity College, Dublin, in 1765 and Oxford University in 1775 but never referred to himself as Dr Johnson; Boswell's *Life* popularized that usage.

From his childhood, Johnson suffered from physical infirmities that affected his relationships and his behaviour. He was short-sighted, hard of hearing, frequently afflicted by depression, debilitated by chronic bronchitis and limited in mobility by dropsy (swelling of the lower limbs). He suffered a stroke in June 1783 and died on 13 December the following year. His body lies in WESTMINSTER ABBEY. (See also CHARING CROSS; GRUB STREET; JOHNSON'S HOUSE, DR; KNIGHTS HOSPITALLER; OLDE CHESHIRE CHEESE, YE; ROYAL NAVAL COLLEGE; VAUXHALL.)

JOHNSON'S HOUSE, DR

From 1748–59, SAMUEL JOHNSON lived at 17 Gough Square, near FLEET STREET. In 1750, he began to publish *The Rambler*, a twice-weekly periodical, but by the time his wife, Tetty, died in the house in 1752, he was deeply involved in the compilation of a *Dictionary of the English Language*, which had been commissioned by a consortium of booksellers. Converting his attic (which ran the whole length of the property) into a workroom, he employed six clerks (five of whom were Scots) to help with the preparation of the work, which was published in 1755 and immediately made him a household name in fashionable London. After Johnson left, the building became a somewhat shabby HOTEL, but, in 1910, it was purchased by Lord Cecil Harmsworth, who restored it and presented it to the nation three years later. Now owned by the Dr Johnson's House Trust and open to the public, it contains several of the writer's personal belongings, paintings of him and his acquaintances and a first edition of the *Dictionary.*

JOINT LONDON ADVISORY PANEL

See LONDON PRIDE PARTNERSHIP.

JONES, INIGO (1573–1652)

The spread of Palladianism in England during the early seventeenth century was largely due to Jones's influence, which was strongly felt in London. The son of an impoverished cloth worker, also named Inigo, Jones was baptized at the Church of St Bartholomew the Less in Smithfield, but further information about his early years is limited. There is some evidence that he worked for a while as a joiner's apprentice and that he showed some skill as an artist. By 1604, he had certainly visited Italy (probably financed by William Herbert, Earl of Pembroke, who had learned of his ability as a landscape painter) and attracted the patronage of Christian IV of Denmark. Christian's sister, Anne, wife of James I, introduced him to the London court, where he designed the scenery and costumes for a series of masques, the words for which were very often written by BEN JONSON. He also worked for the Earl of Salisbury, for whom he designed his first building, the New Exchange (now demolished) in the STRAND. In 1610, he was appointed Surveyor of Works to Henry, Prince of Wales, then, five years later, became Surveyor to the King.

In 1613, Jones made a second journey to Italy, where he studied the works of the country's greatest architects, including Andrea Palladio (1508–80), who had revived classical styles. When he returned to London the following year, he introduced these ideas into his plans for the QUEEN'S HOUSE at GREENWICH (1616–35) and, more particularly, at the BANQUETING HOUSE (1619–22), which is regarded as his masterpiece. Faced with PORTLAND

Inigo Jones.

STONE, which Jones introduced to London ARCHITECTURE (possibly because Palladio had used light-coloured exteriors in his Italian structures), the Banqueting House marked the beginning of the king's redesign of the WHITEHALL area and consists of a single chamber standing above a vaulted crypt. It has only two façades, suggesting that it was originally designed as part of a much larger palace.

Of Jones's other buildings, only the Queen's Chapel at ST JAMES'S PALACE remains intact, but the architect's influence is clearly evident elsewhere in the city and notably at COVENT GARDEN, where he introduced London to the formally planned town square (1630). From 1633 to 1642, he worked on ST PAUL'S CATHEDRAL; his repairs to the nave and his replacement to the west front of the church were destroyed in the GREAT FIRE of 1666 but scholars believe that the designs helped to shape CHRISTOPHER WREN's work on CITY OF LONDON churches. He died, unmarried, on 21 June 1652 and was buried in ST BENET'S CHURCH, PAUL'S WHARF, which was also destroyed in the 1666 fire. His Renaissance style dominated English building practices until the middle of the eighteenth century. (See also SYON HOUSE.)

JONSON, BEN (1572–1637)

The most important playwright of his era after WILLIAM SHAKESPEARE, Jonson is best known for his comedies, particularly *Every Man in His Humour* (1598), *Volpone* (1606), *The Alchemist* (1610) and *Bartholomew Fair* (1614). The son of a clergyman (who died two months before Jonson was born on 11 June 1572), he was educated at Westminster School, spent some months working as a bricklayer, then fought with the English forces in Flanders. By 1592, he was back in London and, by 1595, was working in the THEATRE trade. In 1597, he was writing for PHILIP HENSLOWE, the most important playhouse proprietor of the day and, in 1598, had a major success with *Every Man in His Humour*, which was given its first performance by the Lord Chamberlain's Company at the GLOBE THEATRE, with Shakespeare in the cast.

Jonson's fame was such that, in 1603, the new king, James I, commissioned him to provide entertainment for the court as it stayed at Althorpe during its journey from Edinburgh to London. Such events usually took the form of masques, relatively simple affairs in which players danced and sang for the audience. Jonson, however, made them much more extravagant, introducing dialogue and dramatic action, employing sumptuous costumes and using complicated scenic effects designed by INIGO JONES. Enticed by the novelty, people flocked to the performances and lauded the author, praising him for his characterization and his skilfully composed plots.

However, although the public acclaimed him, he was constantly in trouble. In 1597, he was imprisoned because of his involvement in a production of *The Mask of Dogs*, which the courts considered seditious. The following year, he killed actor Gabriel Spencer in a duel fought at SHOREDITCH and escaped being hanged only by pleading benefit of clergy (the ability to read the Latin Bible). He got into trouble again in 1603 when his classical tragedy, *Sojanus*, was considered treasonable and in 1604, when *Eastward Ho!*, to which he had contributed, was condemned for its anti-Scottish sentiment. Such a boisterous lifestyle, lived on the edge of the law, earned the condemnation of many upright citizens but made him a role model for young artists, particularly writers (including Robert Herrick and Richard Lovelace) who gathered at the Mermaid Tavern in CHEAPSIDE and were later to become known as the Cavalier Poets.

In 1618–19, Jonson embarked on a walking tour to Scotland and was made an Honorary Burgess of Edinburgh but, by that time, his powers and popularity were waning. Plays such as *The Staple of News* (1625), although still demonstrating his mastery of language, had only moderate success and, from 1627, the court masques were organized by other writers. In 1628, he suffered a stroke, after which he was virtually confined to his house until his death on 6 August 1637. In his last years, he was a poor man. At one point, the Dean of Westminster Abbey asked if he could help. Jonson allegedly responded by telling him that 'Six feet long by two feet wide is too much for me. Two feet by two feet will do for all I want', so he was buried upright in Poet's Corner (see WESTMINSTER ABBEY). The epitaph on his tombstone reads simply 'O Rare Ben Jonson'. (See also BANQUETING HOUSE; BLACKFRIARS.)

JUBILEE LINE

The Jubilee Line is the most recent TUBE line to appear on the map of the LONDON UNDERGROUND. It was planned in the late 1960s and 1970s, initially in an effort to relieve congestion at BAKER STREET station, where the two branches of the BAKERLOO LINE which served north-west London merged, bringing thousands of commuters into the central city during the morning rush hour. Originally known as the Fleet Line, it was renamed in 1977 to commemorate the Silver Jubilee of Queen Elizabeth II's accession to the throne.

The route from Baker Street to STANMORE was transferred from the Bakerloo Line to the Jubilee Line and a new tunnel built from Baker Street to CHARING CROSS, where the merger of STRAND and TRAFALGAR SQUARE stations allowed a connection to both the Bakerloo and the NORTHERN LINES. Services began in 1979 but, by that time, it was clear that the existing transport infrastructure in DOCKLANDS was insufficient to support the planned urban regeneration programme, so LONDON TRANSPORT decided to extend the line from GREEN PARK to WATERLOO then eastwards along the south side of the RIVER THAMES, across the river to CANARY WHARF, and on to North GREENWICH and STRATFORD. The work was finished in 1999, allowing the station at North Greenwich to serve visitors travelling to the MILLENNIUM DOME (though the rush to complete the job on time led to numerous operational problems). Trains (most of which date from 1996) are serviced at a depot near Stratford. There are long-term plans to build links to London City AIRPORT and THAMESMEAD and to convert the rolling stock to automatic operation. In 2002, maintenance of the line's infrastructure was franchised to Tube Lines, a consortium of private businesses, but London Underground remained responsible for providing the services. (See also SOUTHWARK, LONDON BOROUGH OF.)

K

KEATS' HOUSE

In 1818, John Keats was invited to move into a house at Wentworth Place, HAMPSTEAD, by fellow writer Charles Armitage Brown. During his two years there, he wrote much of his best work, including *Ode to a Nightingale*, which was inspired by a bird singing in the garden. In 1819, Fanny Brawne, Keats' fiancée, moved into the adjoining cottage with her widowed mother, but the two never married because, in 1821, the poet died, at only twenty-five years of age, of tuberculosis in Rome. Both properties were purchased in 1838–9 by Eliza Chester, a retired actress, who converted them into one unit and added a drawing room on the east end of the building. Restoration work was carried out in 1974–5 and major structural repairs in 1998. The house is open daily as a MUSEUM displaying some of Keats' personal effects, including letters.

KELMSCOTT PRESS

In 1891, William Morris founded the Kelmscott Press close to Kelmscott House, his HAMMERSMITH home. Convinced that a return to the values and practices of the past would improve society and that workers should strive for the highest standards of craftsmanship, he commissioned handmade paper such as that used in the fifteenth century and designed three new type faces (Chaucer, Golden and Troy) for use with dark inks. Books were pressed and bound by hand. Over the next seven years, Kelmscott published fifty-three titles in sixty-six volumes, the best known of which is *The Works of Geoffrey Chaucer*, which appeared in 1896. The quality of the publications greatly influenced competing printers, leading to considerable improvements in design and production. (See also WILLIAM MORRIS GALLERY.)

KENNINGTON

An inner-city suburb lying some 2 miles south-east of CHARING CROSS, Kennington benefited from royal patronage during the medieval period (Edward the Black Prince, son of Edward III, had a palace there during the fourteenth century, for example) and the Prince of Wales is still ground landlord in several parts of the area. It remained a village until well into the eighteenth century, but improvements in TRANSPORT, such as the opening of WESTMINSTER BRIDGE in 1750, led to urban development during later Georgian and Victorian times (many of the terraces built then still survive, notably in Cleaver Square, Kennington Road and Kennington PARK Road). Kennington Park, formerly a 20-acre common, was the principal place of execution for the County of Surrey (several supporters of the Second Jacobite Rebellion, in 1745–6, were hung, drawn and quartered there) and, from the seventeenth until the nineteenth centuries, it was an important meeting place for religious and political groups (John Wesley, co-founder of the Methodist Church, preached to congregations of over 50,000). From 1818, however, it was eroded by road improvements, church building and other developments; the remnant that survives provides sports and recreational facilities in a part of the city otherwise lacking such amenities. The area was incorporated within the LONDON BOROUGH OF LAMBETH when London's local government was reorganized in 1965. Its name may be derived from the Old English *cyne* and *tun*, meaning 'royal homestead'. (See also OVAL, THE; SURREY COUNTY CRICKET CLUB.)

KENSAL GREEN

The Kensal Green suburb, 5 miles north-east of CHARING CROSS, developed after the first of London's commercial BURIAL GROUNDS was laid out by J.W. Griffiths on a 54-acre site in 1833 (39 acres were allocated to adherents of the Church of England, the rest to nonconformists). Built to relieve pressure on overcrowded church properties, the burial ground became fashionable after the Duke of Sussex and Princess Sophia, son and daughter of George III, were interred in 1843 and 1848 respectively. The actor Charles Kemble (1854), ISAMBARD KINGDOM BRUNEL (1859), W.M. Thackeray (1863), Anthony Trollope (1882) and Wilkie Collins (1889) all followed over the next fifty years. Several of the terraced streets built at the time still survive, but many of the larger properties (including Kensal Lodge, where W. Harrison Ainsworth entertained fellow novelist CHARLES DICKENS and other literary figures) have been demolished. Kensal Green was incorporated within the LONDON BOROUGH OF BRENT when local government in the city was reorganized in 1965. Its name may be derived in part from the Old English *cyning* and *holt*, or 'the king's wood'.

KENSINGTON

Kensington lies about 3 miles west of CHARING CROSS on land that rises from the north bank of the RIVER THAMES. It is first mentioned as Chenesit (or Cynesige's estate) in William the Conqueror's Domesday survey of England, carried out in 1085–6. During the medieval period, the land was increasingly used for agriculture and, by the late sixteenth century, was supplying hay and vegetables to the London market. Then, from about 1600, courtiers and merchants built large mansions in the area, attracted by the advantages of large estates relatively close to the city (see, for example, HOLLAND HOUSE). After 1689, when William III instructed CHRISTOPHER WREN to convert Nottingham House into KENSINGTON PALACE, the immigration intensified, with the royal court attracting aristocratic neighbours and providing a market for local traders, but the most significant rise occurred during the nineteenth century, with the resident population leaping from 8,556 in 1801 to 176,628 in 1901 as rural estates were leased or sold to developers. In addition, land originally acquired for the GREAT EXHIBITION of 1851 was used to provide space for a variety of national educational institutions, including the VICTORIA AND ALBERT MUSEUM (established at its present site in 1857), the ROYAL COLLEGE OF ART (1863), the NATURAL HISTORY MUSEUM (1881) and the ROYAL COLLEGE OF MUSIC (1883). These, in turn, attracted numerous private schools, which have continued to flourish, and shopping facilities, along with other service-oriented businesses, which opened to cater to the newcomers. In the twentieth century the trend continued, with an important retail focus developing in Kensington High Street, former family homes converted into HOTELS and rented apartments and foreign governments purchasing properties for use as embassies. In 1901, Queen Victoria (who had been born at Kensington Palace) granted the area the title of Royal Borough, then, when local government was reorganized in 1965, it was incorporated within the ROYAL BOROUGH OF KENSINGTON AND CHELSEA. (See also ALBERT HALL; ALBERT MEMORIAL; DISTRICT LINE; GUNNERSBURY; KENSINGTON GARDENS.)

KENSINGTON AND CHELSEA, ROYAL BOROUGH OF

The borough was formed in 1965 through the amalgamation of previously independent authorities. It covers an area of about 4½ square miles, stretching from the RIVER THAMES north to the LONDON BOROUGH OF BRENT and from the LONDON BOROUGH OF WESTMINSTER in the east to the LONDON BOROUGH OF HAMMERSMITH AND FULHAM in the west. In 1901, KENSINGTON, which forms the northern half of the borough, was granted the title of Royal Borough by Queen Victoria but associations with the monarchy go back to 1689, when William III bought a country house and commissioned CHRISTOPHER WREN to convert it into KENSINGTON PALACE (where Victoria was born in 1819). Partly because it has long been populated by aristocrats, who built substantial residences, about 70 per cent of the borough is covered by conservation area legislation, which restricts redevelopment but promotes TOURISM. Some 10,000 firms provide employment in the leisure industry (including HOTELS, which provide about 14 per cent of all bed spaces available to London's visitors), manufacturing (and associated distribution facilities), pharmaceuticals, cosmetics and media services. Together, these companies generate about 86,000 jobs, of which one-quarter are filled by local people. The resident population in 2001 numbered 158,900. Some two-thirds of the adult population is unmarried and accommodation is more expensive than anywhere else in the city (in 2002, the average cost of a residential property was over £650,000, compared with £249,000 for London as a whole). The Borough Council is dominated by the Conservative Party, but there is strong minority representation by Labour Party voters both in working-class and in middle-class areas. (See also CARLYLE'S HOUSE; CHELSEA; CHELSEA PHYSIC GARDEN; COMMONWEALTH INSTITUTE; GEOLOGICAL MUSEUM; HARRODS; HOLLAND HOUSE; KENSINGTON GARDENS; NATIONAL ARMY MUSEUM: NATURAL HISTORY MUSEUM; VICTORIA AND ALBERT MUSEUM.)

KENSINGTON GARDENS

The gardens, covering 275 acres and lying immediately to the west of HYDE PARK, were originally part of the private grounds of KENSINGTON PALACE but George II (who reigned from 1727 to 1760) opened them for public use on Saturdays when the royal family was not in residence. The Round Pond (now a popular place for sailing model boats) was built in 1728, access was extended in the 1830s by William IV, a flower walk was laid out towards the southern edge of the estate in 1843, then, from the 1860s, the Victorians and Edwardians used the PARK to indulge a passion for statues. The ALBERT MEMORIAL was erected in 1863, a granite obelisk commemorating John Hanning Speke's identification of the source of the River Nile was built the following year and sculptures of Queen Victoria and William III were added in 1893 and 1907 respectively. A representation of Physical Energy (by G.F. Watts) was completed in 1904 but children (including those of advancing years) are much more likely to be captivated by George Frampton's whimsical bronze of Peter Pan (the little boy who never grew up, created by J.M. Barrie), which was placed near the SERPENTINE in 1912, and the tree trunk, carved with small animals by Ivor Innes, located in the playground at the northern end of Broad Walk in 1928. In summer, the PARK is a popular place for kite flying and puppet shows. It is also a haunt of one of Britain's endangered species – the nanny, wearing sensible shoes and conservative dress, who pushes an infant in a perambulator and trails an older brother or sister at her heels; their concentration in the park reflects the suitability of the habitat, a large diplomatic community in nearby KNIGHTSBRIDGE. The gardens are still owned by the Crown and are maintained by the ROYAL PARKS Agency.

KENSINGTON PALACE

Originally a country mansion, the palace, located in the south-west corner of KENSINGTON GARDENS, has experienced several phases of development. The first building on the site was erected early in the seventeenth century by Sir George Coppin and purchased in 1689 by William III, who instructed CHRISTOPHER WREN to supervise its extension. Following the death of his wife, Queen Mary, at the house in 1694, the king (who disliked central London, where the AIR POLLUTION exacerbated his asthmatic condition) became increasingly attached to the palace, lavishing much attention on the landscaping of the gardens. After suffering serious injuries when he fell from his horse at HAMPTON COURT PALACE in 1702, he begged to be taken back so that he, too, could die there. In 1714, Queen Anne – his sister-in-law and successor – also passed away at KENSINGTON (a result of apoplexy caused by overeating). She had treated the residence as a pleasant country escape but George I wanted greater comfort and a building more in keeping with his royal status, with new state rooms, improved kitchen facilities and additional courtyards built in 1718. George II made Kensington his main residence, but George III, who succeeded him in 1760, preferred a home nearer the corridors of power.

Since that time, no reigning monarch has lived at the palace but it has been much used by other members of the royal family. Queen Victoria was born in a ground floor room in 1819 and held her first Privy Council meeting in the Red Saloon in 1837. In 1867, Princess Mary Adelaide gave birth to a daughter, also Mary, who was to become the consort of George V, and, in recent years, Prince Charles, Diana, Princess of Wales, Princess Margaret, the Duke and Duchess of Gloucester, Princess Alice, the Duke and Duchess of Kent, and Prince and Princess Michael of Kent have all had homes there. Victoria opened the state apartments (designed by Colen Campbell and decorated by William Kent) to the public in 1889; access to further rooms (including Queen Victoria's bedroom and nursery) was granted in 1933. There is an exhibition of court dress as well as numerous mementos of Victoria's reign. (See also HAWKSMOOR, NICHOLAS.)

KENTISH TOWN

The village of Kentish Town grew around a daughter chapel of ST PANCRAS Church, which was built, in 1449, on a major route out of London to the north. Some 3 miles from CHARING CROSS and outside the urban area of the CITY OF LONDON, it developed a reputation as a healthy place to live so wealthy families erected country houses in which to entertain their friends. Around the end of the eighteenth century, however, the pace of construction accelerated and the area was transformed from a small agricultural settlement into a desirable London suburb. For seventy years, it maintained its status but, in the 1860s, the arrival of the Midland RAILWAY, with its attendant smoke and grime, encouraged most of the affluent residents to leave. The railway company bought large areas of land for sheds and sidings, craftsmen opened small industrial premises and labourers flooded in to find jobs, turning the community into a typically poor working-class district. During the twentieth century, the social composition of the area has changed little, with many properties subdivided to provide efficiency apartments for students and others needing cheap accommodation. Kentish Town was incorporated within the LONDON BOROUGH OF CAMDEN when London's local government was reorganized in 1965. Its name may be derived from the Celtic *ken* (which may be translated as 'green' or 'river') and the English *ditch*, possibly a reference to the River Fleet, which flows nearby. Alternatively, 'Kentish' may have been the personal name of a local resident in medieval times.

KENWOOD HOUSE

One of ROBERT ADAM's finest works, Kenwood lies in wooded PARKland at the northern fringe of HAMPSTEAD HEATH. The first building on the site was erected in 1616 but the present structure dates from 1764, when William Murray (Attorney General and later Lord Chief Justice) commissioned Adam, then a very fashionable architect, to remodel the property. When Murray died in 1793, the estate passed to David Murray, his nephew, who added wings (of white Suffolk brick) designed by George Saunders. The property was retained by the family until 1922, when the Kenwood Preservation Council purchased 120 acres to prevent building developments and vested the land in the LONDON COUNTY COUNCIL (LCC). In 1924, Edward, Lord Iveagh, bought the house and remaining grounds. Upon his death, three years later, the building (which housed an extensive art collection) and the PARKS also passed into LCC hands. The whole area is now managed by English Heritage, established by the government in 1983 to preserve historic buildings and enhance public enjoyment of them. The north frontage of the house is a stucco block with a portico, surmounted by a pediment, rising to the top of the building. Inside, the major architectural feature is the library, which has a tunnel-vaulted ceiling painted by Antonio Zucchi, but there is also a collection of paintings, donated by Lord Iveagh in 1927 and including works by Thomas Gainsborough, Rembrandt and Joshua Reynolds. The estate, landscaped by William Murray, includes a lakeside concert venue.

KETCH, JACK

In 1685, Jack Ketch bungled the execution of the Duke of Monmouth, failing to sever the unfortunate aristocrat's head even with five blows of his axe and ultimately sawing it off with a knife. After that incident, all London executioners were known in the vernacular as Jack Ketch.

KEW

A fashionable, middle-class suburb on the SOUTH BANK of the RIVER THAMES about 7 miles west of CHARING CROSS, Kew was probably settled before the Roman invasion of Britain in AD 43. Its status, however, dates from the sixteenth century, when its accessibility by boat and its proximity to RICHMOND PALACE made it an attractive location for the homes of the aristocracy (Mary Tudor, sister of Henry VIII, had a house there, for example). Queen Anne donated the site for St Anne's Church, which was built on Kew Green in 1710–4 (but extended in 1770, 1836 and 1884), and that encouraged further construction during the eighteenth century, as did the erection of a wooden BRIDGE across the Thames to GUNNERSBURY in 1758–9. (A structure of Purbeck stone replaced that edifice in 1784–9 and it, in turn, was superseded by the present granite bridge, opened in 1903). In 1869, the London and South-Western RAILWAY also built a link across the river, using a lattice-girder bridge set on cast-iron piers; that added to the pressures on land for development but Kew retained its essentially residential nature, partly because so much of the open space was owned by the Crown. The modern focus of the area is the ROYAL BOTANIC GARDENS, which were established by Princess Augusta (widow of Frederick, son of George II) and donated to the nation by Queen Victoria in 1841. Nearby, in a 1970s building in Ruskin Avenue, many of the documents relating to the history of Britain are stored in the PUBLIC RECORD OFFICE, which makes its archives available to researchers. The origin of the place name is unclear, partly because historical documents give a variety of spellings. The most popular explanations suggest that it may be derived from the Old English *caeg* or Middle English *key* (both of which mean 'landing place' or 'quay'), coupled with *hoh* (meaning 'a spur of land').

KEW BRIDGE MUSEUM

See BRENTFORD.

KEW GARDENS

See ROYAL BOTANIC GARDENS.

KEW PALACE

See ROYAL BOTANIC GARDENS.

KIDBROOKE

For much of the medieval period, a small village thrived at Kidbrooke, some 5 miles south-east of CHARING CROSS. However, by the end of the fifteenth century – and for reasons still unclear – it had been abandoned, its church derelict. From then until the 1930s, when suburban development spread outwards from the metropolitan area (aided by improvements in the road from central London to Dover), a small population earned a living from farming. The area, incorporated within the LONDON BOROUGH OF LEWISHAM in 1965, is now predominantly residential, with a mixture of local authority and private housing developments. Its name is said to derive from the Old English *cyta* and *broc*, meaning 'the brook where kites fly'.

KILBURN

A traditional working-class residential suburb within the LONDON BOROUGH OF BRENT, Kilburn lies some 4 miles north-west of CHARING CROSS alongside WATLING STREET, built by the Romans to connect Dubris (now Dover) with Verulamium (now St Albans). Even by the early medieval period, the well-travelled road had attracted settlement, including a priory (established in 1130), inns and lodging houses. From 1742, the Bell Tavern (which had been functioning since about 1600) capitalized on Georgian tastes by encouraging affluent Londoners to venture out and taste the bitter, milky waters diverted from a local spring into its pump room, but the establishment of a RAILWAY connection with EUSTON STATION in 1852 resulted in construction of houses for less wealthy commuters. The opening of BRONDESBURY Station (on the North London Railway) in 1860 and the arrival of the METROPOLITAN LINE (now part of the LONDON UNDERGROUND system) in 1879 added impetus to that development, increasing the population and thus fuelling demand for shops and other services along Edgware Road (which follows the line of Watling Street); the Gaumont State Cinema (built to designs, by George Coles, which included a tower and a richly decorated foyer) was the largest cinema in Europe when it opened in 1937. During the twentieth century, many of the houses were subdivided into single-room flats, which became popular with Irish IMMIGRANTS seeking cheap accommodation. The cinema, too, has changed, now serving as a bingo hall. The origins of the name are obscure, but some writers suggest this it is derived from the Old English *cu* and *burna*, meaning 'cows' stream'. (See also QUEENS PARK RANGERS FOOTBALL CLUB.)

KING'S CROSS

King's Cross lies at the edge of central London, about 1½ miles north of CHARING CROSS. Until the early nineteenth century, it was the site of a small village, known as Battle Bridge, located beside the FLEET RIVER. During the eighteenth century, the settlement was renowned as a spa, attracting hundreds of visitors every week. Also, in 1746 it became the site of a hospital for victims of smallpox, then one of the major deadly diseases in the city. In 1836, a memorial to George IV was erected at the junction of Euston Road, Gray's Inn Road, Pentonville Road and St Pancras Road. Designed by Stephen Geary, it incorporated a statue of the monarch on top of a pillar. The column, 60 feet high, stood on an octagonal base and was guarded by replicas of Britain's four patron saints (St Andrew for Scotland, St David for Wales, St George for England and St Patrick for Ireland). Initially, the base was used as a police station but later it was converted into a PUBLIC HOUSE. Public reaction to the structure was so negative that it was removed in 1842–5. In 1851–2, the Great Northern Railway built its terminus on the site of the hospital (see KING'S CROSS STATION), greatly affecting local land uses. HOTELS, cafeterias, boarding houses, small shops and other businesses were established to provide services for travellers and still dominate the local economic scene. The area was included within the LONDON BOROUGH OF CAMDEN when local government in the metropolitan area was reorganized in 1965. (See also KING'S CROSS FIRE.)

KING'S CROSS FIRE

At about 7.30 p.m. on the evening of 18 November 1987, towards the end of the rush hour, a fire broke out underneath one of the escalators connecting KING'S CROSS STATION with LONDON UNDERGROUND'S PICCADILLY LINE. The fire burned for about 15 minutes, then swelled quickly into a major conflagration, sending a ball of flame up the escalator to the ticket hall. Emergency procedures proved inadequate as escalators carried people to the heart of the blaze, trains disembarked passengers onto smoke-filled platforms, and station staff were unable to evacuate tunnels. As a result, thirty-one people died. Twenty firemen (including one who was killed) received commendations for bravery. Following the tragedy, a public inquiry heard evidence over a period of ninety-one days, concluding that the cause was probably a cigarette, dropped by a passenger, which fell on grease-impregnated dirt, spawning flames that spread to the timber of the escalator. The members made 150 safety recommendations and the UNDERGROUND banned smoking throughout the system. Litigation continued in the courts for many years: in 1996, for example, a guitarist who was unable to resume his career satisfactorily won damages totalling £650,000.

KING'S CROSS STATION

When the station was opened on the site of the Whittington Smallpox HOSPITAL at KING'S CROSS in 1852, it was the largest RAILWAY terminus in the country. Built by the Great Northern Railway, it was planned by Lewis Cubitt (younger brother of THOMAS CUBITT), who prepared a design that, he said, depended for its effect 'on the largeness of some of its features, its fitness for its purpose and its characteristic expression of that purpose'. The result was a widely admired building consisting of two train sheds (each 800 feet long and 105 feet wide) that had a yellow brick frontage at the south end. Underneath one of the platforms, there was stabling for the 300 horses that delivered goods to and from the station (the granary held 60,000 sacks of corn) and the coal stores held 150,000 tons of fuel for the steam engines. In 1973, major reconstruction work was completed on the concourse, providing modern shops and ticket offices, with improved access to the LONDON UNDERGROUND system, but the essence of the Victorian structure is still evident. Most services from the station connect London to the suburbs north of the city, the East Coast of England and Scotland. In recent years, it has gained fame for its fictional platform 9¾ from which the Hogwarts Express departs in the Harry Potter books. (See also KING'S CROSS FIRE; VICTORIA LINE.)

KING'S ROAD

King's Road runs for 2½ miles from BELGRAVIA to FULHAM, forming the main route through CHELSEA. Until 1830, it was a private thoroughfare, allowing Charles II access to HAMPTON COURT PALACE and George III to his residence at KEW (see ROYAL BOTANIC GAR-

DENS). Although some eighteenth-century residential properties remain (as at Nos 211–215, which were built during the 1720s), the street is now best known for its boutiques, PUBLIC HOUSES and restaurants. In the 1960s it earned a reputation for avant-garde fashions, which it still retains.

KINGSTON BRIDGE

The present BRIDGE connecting KINGSTON UPON THAMES (on the east bank of the RIVER THAMES) to Hampton Wick (on the west) was built of brick, faced with stone, in 1825–58. However, the crossing, some 12 miles south-west of central London, was in use at least by 1193, when William de Coventry was appointed Master of the Bridge. Because it and LONDON BRIDGE provided the only roads over the Thames until the eighteenth century, Kingston Bridge became a focus of land routes and therefore contributed significantly to the growth of settlement in the area. The remains of that medieval structure have been incorporated in the John Lewis Department Store. The London and South-Western RAILWAY constructed a cast-iron bridge a few yards downriver, in 1860–3, to provide a connection between Kingston and TWICKENHAM. It was superseded, in 1907, by a replacement made of steel.

KINGSTON UPON THAMES

Kingston lies on the east bank of the RIVER THAMES some 10 miles south-west of CHARING CROSS. It was settled during Saxon times (when it was the site of crowning ceremonies for seven monarchs, including Edward the Elder, son of Alfred the Great, in AD 900) but became particularly important in the medieval period because it provided the first crossing upriver from LONDON BRIDGE. The settlement benefited from its location close to several royal residences, such as HAMPTON COURT PALACE and NONSUCH PALACE, but also developed an important MARKET because it was a natural focus of land and river transport routes. Ancillary industries, such as boat building, brewing and milling, provided additional sources of income and diversified the local economy. When PUTNEY BRIDGE opened in 1729, Kingston lost some of its traffic but it retained its regional influence and is still a significant market town with employment in aviation, chemicals, engineering, plastics and printing. Although the central area has been redeveloped, much of the medieval street pattern has been preserved and the ARCHITECTURE dates from the fifteenth century. The name is probably derived from the Old English *cyning* and *tun*, meaning 'king's estate'. (See also KINGSTON UPON THAMES, ROYAL BOROUGH OF.)

KINGSTON UPON THAMES, ROYAL BOROUGH OF

The Borough of Kingston Upon Thames was formed in 1965 through the amalgamation of the formerly independent authorities of KINGSTON UPON THAMES, Malden and Coombe, and SURBITON, all of which were previously located in the County of Surrey. Its regal prefix, originally earned through the thirty royal charters awarded to Kingston between 1200 and 1685, was confirmed by Elizabeth II. Covering some 12 square miles, it stretches from RICHMOND PARK in the north to Ashtead Common in the south and from the RIVER THAMES in the west to Motspur PARK in the east. Although most of the land is devoted to residential uses, the construction of a relief road around Kingston in 1989 helped to reduce traffic congestion and attracted several large stores to the area. These were augmented, during the 1990s, by the expansion of the Eden Walk shopping centre into one of the largest retail complexes in south-east England. The local authority and the University of Kingston are major employers but the opening of seven business parks has attracted several multinational companies, including Samsung Electronics and Nikon, adding to the range of clerical and manufacturing jobs. In 2001, the borough had a population of 147,300, the smallest of all the London authorities. (See also CHESSINGTON; WORCESTER PARK.)

KNIGHTSBRIDGE

Knightsbridge runs for ¾ mile along the south side of HYDE PARK from Kensington Road to HYDE PARK CORNER. According to legend, it takes its name from a bridge across a tributary of the RIVER THAMES where two knights fought a duel to the death. More prosaically, it may simply be a corruption of the Old English *cniht* and *brycg* and mean 'the young men's bridge' or 'the serving boy's bridge'. It was developed during London's nineteenth-century expansion and now has a variety of land uses, including HOTELS, offices and apartments. House prices in some postal districts are among the highest in the United Kingdom. Knightsbridge Barracks are the headquarters of the Household Cavalry (see HOUSEHOLD DIVISION), with stabling for nearly 300 horses and the same number of men. The barracks was established in the late eighteenth century, but the modern buildings, designed by Basil Spence (who prepared the plans for Coventry Cathedral), were erected in 1966. The area was included in the CITY OF WESTMINSTER when London local government was reshaped in 1965.

KNIGHTS HOSPITALLER

The Hospitallers (also known as the Knights of Malta, the Knights Hospitaller of St John of Jerusalem and the Most Venerable Order of the Hospital of St John of Jerusalem) were established in the eleventh century as a religious community dedicated to caring for the sick. In London, it was based at the Priory of St John of Jerusalem in CLERKENWELL, where travellers could seek temporary shelter. The property was destroyed in 1381, during the PEASANTS' REVOLT, but re-erected shortly afterwards, incorporating a church (now known as St John, Clerkenwell), which was famed for its soaring bell tower. In 1536–41, when the MONASTERIES in England were dissolved, many of the Knights fled, leaving the church to Henry VIII, who used it to store the tents he needed when hunting. In 1547–50, much of the stone was removed to build SOMERSET HOUSE and by the eighteenth century most of the Priory had vanished. The chapel chancel survived, however, despite serving at various times as a playhouse, a private place of worship for Lord Burleigh and a nonconformist meeting hall. It was repaired in 1721–3 and became a parish church before being returned to the Hospitallers in 1929. During the BLITZ, it was damaged by German bombs but restored, under the supervision of Lord Mottistone, after the Second World War. The Priory Gatehouse, built of Kentish ragstone and erected in 1504, also escaped demolition. Its rooms provided offices for Elizabeth I's Master of the Revels in the sixteenth century, a COFFEE HOUSE during the late seventeenth century and a printing works (where SAMUEL JOHNSON was provided with writing accommodation) in the eighteenth century. It was reacquired in 1874 by the Knights and now houses a MUSEUM of exhibits describing the order's history (St John's Ambulance Brigade, founded in the Gatehouse in 1877, has more than 250,000 members around the world). The suburb of ST JOHN'S WOOD is built on formerly forested land owned by the Hospitallers prior to the Reformation. (See also KNIGHTS TEMPLAR.)

KNIGHTS OF MALTA

See KNIGHTS HOSPITALLER.

KNIGHTS TEMPLAR

The Order of the Knights Templars was formed in 1119 to defend pilgrims travelling to the Holy Land. Initially, it had provincial headquarters near CHANCERY LANE but, in 1165, it moved to a new site on the north bank of the RIVER THAMES, ¾ mile east of CHARING CROSS, where it built a circular church (some scholars claim that the design was chosen in honour of the Church of the Holy Sepulchre in Jerusalem, others that the Dome of the Rock, in the same city, was a more likely model). In the early fourteenth century, members were accused of irreligious practices, the order was dissolved (1312) and its property in London was acquired by arch rival the KNIGHTS HOSPITALLER, which leased the land to lawyers. The site is now occupied by the Inner and Middle Temples of the INNS OF COURT. (See also TEMPLE BAR; TEMPLE CHURCH.)

KRAY TWINS

During the 1960s, London's criminal underworld was organized by a small number of gangs, each of which controlled a geographical area. In the EAST END of the city, the principal figures were twins Reginald and Ronald Kray, who ran a protection racket, enforced by violence, while maintaining a public image of respectable businessmen who contributed to local charities. Police investigations of their activities were hampered by threats to potential witnesses, but, eventually, some associates agreed to give evidence in return for their own freedom. In January 1969, the Krays and several of their closest henchmen were put on trial at the CENTRAL CRIMINAL COURT. Ronnie was sentenced to life imprisonment for the shooting of George Cornell (a member of the Richardson gang, which was based in south London) at the Blind Beggar public house in WHITECHAPEL in March 1966. Reggie, found guilty of being an associate, was jailed for ten years. In addition, both were imprisoned for life (with the judge's recommendation that they serve at least thirty years) for the murder of Jack McVitie, a small-time criminal who was stabbed to death in a basement flat in STOKE NEWINGTON in October 1966. In 1979, Ronnie, a homosexual with a history of mental problems, was certified insane. He died in Broadmoor maximum security psychiatric hospital on 17 March 1995 (over 60,000 people lined the streets of east London to watch the funeral procession). His brother was released on compassionate grounds five years later, when doctors discovered that he was suffering from terminal cancer of the bladder, and passed away in his sleep at a hotel in Thorpe St Andrew, near Norwich, on 1 October 2000.

L

LAMBETH

Lambeth lies on the east bank of the RIVER THAMES between WATERLOO and CLAPHAM. In documents dating from the eleventh century, the area adjacent to the river is named Lamhytha so this may have been a place where lambs were transferred to and from ships. Until the early eighteenth century, it was largely marshland though a few industrial premises were located in the area, notably the Vauxhall plate glass works, a factory making COADE STONE and a pottery producing tin-glazed earthenware. After the opening of WESTMINSTER BRIDGE facilitated access in 1750, industrial activity increased (the Doulton and Watts porcelain company was founded in 1815, for instance) and houses were built to accommodate the inflow of workers. Following the Second World War, most of the poorer-quality residential developments were replaced by local authority housing estates and manufacturing gave way to offices. In 1965, when the capital's local government was reformed, the area gave its name to the LONDON BOROUGH OF LAMBETH. (See also BEDLAM; LAMBETH BRIDGE; LAMBETH PALACE; LAMBETH WALK.)

LAMBETH, LONDON BOROUGH OF

Formed in 1965 through the amalgamation of CLAPHAM, LAMBETH and STREATHAM, the borough covers some 11 square miles. Shaped like a trapezium, it stretches for 7 miles from the RIVER THAMES in the north to Streatham Vale in the south but at its broadest (between Streatham and West Norwood) is only 3 miles wide. Close to the Thames, commercial and administrative interests have pushed out residential land uses, with government offices, the SOUTH BANK arts complex and the transport hub of WATERLOO railway station using most of the space. Elsewhere, extensive undeveloped areas provide facilities for recreation, notably on the commons at Clapham, Streatham and Tooting Bec. Over most of the borough, however, housing dominates, much of it (in suburbs such as BRIXTON and VAUXHALL) small flats rented by individuals and families with low incomes. Deprivation levels are high: Lambeth has some of the highest rates of single-parent families, overcrowding and lack of access to private transport in the United Kingdom. In addition, about 40 per cent of the resident population belongs to an ethnic minority, mainly black Caribbean or black African. The population at the time of the 2001 census was 266,200. (See also CARDBOARD CITY; DENMARK HILL; GIPSY HILL; HERNE HILL; KENNINGTON; OVAL, THE; STOCKWELL; TULSE HILL; WANDSWORTH, LONDON BOROUGH OF.)

LAMBETH BRIDGE

The first BRIDGE to cross the river between LAMBETH (on the east bank) and WESTMINSTER

View of Lambeth, by Hollar, c. 1674.

(on the west) was opened in 1862 at a site that had been used by ferrymen from at least 1513 until 1750. The suspension design, with three 268-foot spans, was proposed by P.W. Barlow. In 1932, it was replaced by the present five-span steel arch structure, built to plans prepared by George Humphreys.

LAMBETH CONFERENCE

See LAMBETH PALACE.

LAMBETH PALACE

The palace is the official residence of the Archbishop of Canterbury, ecclesiastical head of the Church of England. One of very few domestic buildings surviving in London from the medieval period, it was originally constructed in the early thirteenth century but was extended and renovated on several occasions, notably in 1434–5 (when the Lollards' Tower was built to improve water supplies), 1486–1501 (when a gatehouse was erected), 1553 (when Queen Mary authorized a refurbishment), the 1630s (when Archbishop Laud renovated the chapel), the 1660s (when the Great Hall and the Guard Room were rebuilt) and 1828–34 (when Edward Blore added offices and redesigned the living quarters). The first primate to occupy the palace was Stephen Langton (whose consecration as archbishop in 1207 precipitated a crisis between King John and Pope Innocent III). John Wycliffe was called to the chapel to defend himself against charges of heresy in 1377, Wat Tyler's supporters burned furnishings and beheaded the archbishop during the PEASANTS' REVOLT in 1381, Thomas More was taken to the guard room and questioned about his refusal to accept Henry VIII as head of the Church in 1534 and during the GORDON RIOTS in 1780 the building was placed under siege. In 1610, Archbishop Bancroft bequeathed his books to his successors, forming the nucleus of an extensive library that includes manuscripts dating from the ninth century.

Since 1867, the Bishops of the Church of England have met at irregular intervals to debate matters of common interest at the Lambeth Conference. The 1888 convention accepted four matters of principle (known as the Lambeth Quadrilateral) to be used as the basis for discussions about union with other Christian groups; three of these (acceptance

Lambeth Palace, *c.* 1647.

of the Holy Scripture as the rule of faith, of the Apostles' and Nicene Creeds, and of the sacraments of baptism and the Lord's Supper) have caused few problems but most Protestant denominations have proved unwilling to adopt an episcopacy, as required by the fourth principle. In 1900, 9 acres of the palace grounds were donated to the LONDON COUNTY COUNCIL for use as a public PARK, providing a significant area of green space in a largely developed area of the inner city.

LAMBETH WALK

Lambeth Walk, which parallels the course of the RIVER THAMES for about ½ mile in the LONDON BOROUGH OF LAMBETH, gives its name to a dance supposedly representing the strutting of the local COCKNEYS. Performed with walking steps in march time, it was first popularized in 1937 by Lupino Lane in the musical *Me and My Gal* and, according to young people of the era, was often used in dance halls as a relatively gentle item to follow the more exhausting jitterbug. The street had a popular MARKET, established during the early nineteenth century.

LANCASTER HOUSE

The foundations of the house, in Stable Yard on the west side of ST JAMES'S PALACE, were laid in 1825 and building begun to designs prepared by Benjamin Wyatt for Frederick, Duke of York (of nursery rhyme fame). The structure (originally named York House) was still unfinished when the duke died, deeply in debt, two years later, so the government took over the mortgage and leased the property to the Marquess of Stafford (the income from the deal was used to purchase ground for VICTORIA PARK in the EAST END). When the marquess passed away in 1833 (shortly after being created first Duke of Sutherland), the building was still incomplete, so the second duke commissioned Wyatt to plan the interior, with CHARLES BARRY hired as adviser and Robert Smirke appointed to implement the proposals. The exterior of the building was plain – a three-storey rectangle of Bath stone with a simple, two-storey Corinthian portico at the entrance. The inside, however, was ebulliently decorated in the style of Louis XV of France, with a grand staircase rising to the full height of the building and lit from a clerestory. For the remainder of the century, York House was one of the pivots of London's social life, with the Sutherlands entertaining the major social reformers of the day, including Lord Shaftesbury (who promoted legislation designed to improve conditions for factory workers) and William Garrison (the American advocate for the abolition of slavery), as well as Queen Victoria (who came with PRINCE ALBERT and the Duke of Wellington to hear Frédéric Chopin play the piano in 1848). In 1912, the fourth duke sold the building to industrialist Sir William Lever (later Viscount Leverhulme), who renamed it Lancaster House after his native county and presented it to the nation. Until 1946, it housed the London MUSEUM (see MUSEUM OF LONDON) but is now used largely for government conferences and receptions.

LANGHAM HOTEL

The Langham was the first of London's luxury HOTELS. Built in PORTLAND PLACE in 1864–5, it had seven floors reminiscent of a Florentine palace, with 600 rooms decorated in scarlet and gold and mosaic flooring laid by Italian craftsmen. For eighty years, its private suites housed the rich and famous, including Emperors Napoleon III of France and Haile Selassie of Ethiopia, but in 1940, during the BLITZ, a land mine fractured its 38,000-gallon water tank and flooded the building. The BRITISH BROADCASTING CORPORATION, which provided radio services from nearby Broadcasting House, later adapted it for use as offices and studios but in 1991 it returned to its original use as the 350-room Langham Hilton.

LANSBURY, GEORGE (1859–1940)

George Lansbury led the Labour Party from 1931 to 1935, campaigning for the rights of the poor and for improvements in the living conditions of citizens in London's EAST END. The son of railwayman George Lansbury and Mary, his Welsh wife, he was born near Lowestoft (Suffolk) on 21 February 1859 but moved to the capital with his family when he was nine, eventually setting up home in WHITECHAPEL. At fourteen he left school for work in the Great Eastern RAILWAY's coal depot but, in 1890, married the daughter of a local sawmill owner and became a partner in his father-in-law's business. He was deeply influenced by Christian socialist philosophies, taking up the cause of the deprived in local politics, helping to find jobs in rural areas for the urban unemployed, and serving as a member of the Royal Commission on the Poor Laws in 1905–9. He first entered Parliament in 1910, representing BOW and Bromley for the Labour Party, but resigned after two years in order to contest the seat as an independent and draw attention to his support for women who demanded the right to vote. He failed to win re-election but continued to espouse the socialist cause, helping to found the *Daily Herald* (the Labour movement's first daily newspaper) in 1912 and defending the rights of conscientious objectors during the First World War.

A man of great charisma, he drew large crowds to hear his speeches, moving listeners with a rhetoric that emphasized the importance of brotherly love as the foundation on which all political action should be based. Turning words into deeds, he led a campaign designed to win financial support for the unemployed, ultimately serving a jail sentence as a result of his activities (see POPLARISM) but returning to the HOUSE OF COMMONS (see PALACE OF WESTMINSTER) in 1922 with great local support.

When Prime Minister Ramsay MacDonald formed his second government in 1929, Lansbury was made Commissioner of Works, approving many projects (such as the construction of the lido in HYDE PARK) that brought benefits to London citizens. Following Labour's defeat in the General Election in 1931, he was made Leader of the Party but his pacifist beliefs were increasingly at odds with the philosophies of the times and, after four years, he gave up the post, unable to approve of the use of force against Italian troops that had invaded Abyssinia. As war clouds darkened over Europe in the late 1930s, he found few who would support his belief that Britain should adopt a policy of disarmament and was politically marginalized. He died in London on 7 May 1940, three days before the fall of France.

LAW COURTS

See ROYAL COURTS OF JUSTICE.

LAYFIELD ENQUIRY

See GREATER LONDON DEVELOPMENT PLAN (1969).

LEA, RIVER

The Lea (or Lee) rises in Bedfordshire and flows southwards for 46 miles, through east London, to meet the RIVER THAMES at POPLAR. It has long been used for navigation: the Romans employed it as a means of access to Verulamium (now St Albans) and King Alfred chased an invading Danish force up it in AD 896. In 1767, a series of locks was built to improve shipping movements (particularly for vessels carrying cargoes of grain from Hertfordshire and Essex), and during the nineteenth century it was the focus for many industrial premises, including flour mills at Ponders End and a small arms factory at Enfield Lock. In 1967, a major rehabilitation scheme was introduced in an attempt to reverse the effects of pollution, resulting from centuries of use, by turning the area into a regional PARK. Local authorities have combined to clean up some 2,000 acres along 25 miles of river and construct a chain of reservoirs that supplies London with about one-sixth of its water needs as well as provides facilities for bird watching, fishing, sailing and other activities. In 2003 the government announced its support for a bid to hold the 2012 Olympic Games in London. If successful, the events would be held in the lower Lea Valley, providing the potential for regeneration of the site through provision of new homes, commercial properties and TRANSPORT infrastructure. The waterway's name may be derived fro Celtic roots. (See also LEYTONSTONE; SOUTHGATE; STRATFORD; WATER SUPPLY.)

LEADENHALL MARKET

Based on the south side of Leadenhall Street, which stretches from ALDGATE to CORNHILL, in the CITY OF LONDON, Leadenhall MARKET stands on the site of the basilica (or town hall) that marked the centre of Roman LONDINIUM. It has been offering provisions since the fourteenth century, when the Neville family allowed people from outside London to sell poultry, cheese and butter from the grounds of their lead-roofed mansion house. In 1445, a granary was built and the market widened its range of produce, adding goods such as grain and eggs. Later, wool and leather were also made available. The buildings (including the mansion) were destroyed in the GREAT FIRE of 1666 but replaced by three courtyards; one sold beef (along with leather and wool), one concentrated on veal, mutton and lamb (with fish and cheese as sidelines) and one dealt in fruit, vegetables and herbs. In 1881, these were replaced by a flamboyant, glass-roofed market designed by Horace Jones. Foodstuffs are still the most common goods on sale but, in recent years, bookshops and other stores have begun to infiltrate. The PUBLIC HOUSES are popular with office workers from nearby financial institutions, such as LLOYD'S OF LONDON.

LEE, RIVER

See LEA, RIVER.

LEICESTER SQUARE

In 1631–5, the Earl of Leicester erected a mansion on the northern side of what is now Leicester Square. By the end of the seventeenth century, the gardens laid out in front of the new building were lined on all sides by the homes of aristocrats, artists and merchants, creating a very fashionable, affluent neighbourhood. For nearly 150 years, despite

Leicester Square from an old print, *c.* 1750.

the encroachment of some commercial activity, the area retained its very desirable status but, during the 1840s, the opening of New Coventry Street brought increased traffic so the wealthy citizens moved out to quieter suburban locations. Their large homes were converted to HOTELS, shops and MUSEUMS. These, in turn, attracted other activities, particularly restaurants and THEATRES (the Alhambra playhouse opened in 1858, the Empire in 1884 and the Hippodrome in 1900). As a result, the character of the square changed radically within a few decades, becoming, by the early years of the twentieth century, a centre of London nightlife (particularly male nightlife, hence the nostalgic farewell reference in *It's a Long Way to Tipperary*, the First World War soldiers' song). Since then, it has remained at the heart of the WEST END, close to a number of London's largest cinemas, as well as the theatres. Some semblance of the earl's gardens has survived, however, largely through the efforts of Albert Grant, a larger-than-life financial speculator whose business dealings eventually took him to the bankruptcy courts but who had sufficient sensitivity to purchase the remaining open land in 1874 and refurbish the space, which has statues of three former Leicester Square residents – surgeon John Hunter (see ROYAL COLLEGE OF SURGEONS OF ENGLAND) and artists William Hogarth and Joshua Reynolds.

LEWISHAM

Lewisham lies south of the RIVER THAMES between BLACKHEATH (to the north) and CATFORD (to the south) about 6 miles from CHARING CROSS. It was settled during Anglo-Saxon times, focusing on St Mary's Church, and, for 1,000 years, survived as a small farming and industrial centre, with much of the industry (such as the mill that produced metal for armour during the sixteenth century) depending on water power supplied by the River Ravensbourne. During the seventeenth century, when the village became a fashionable place for country homes, a number of substantial houses were erected, a grammar school founded and almshouses established, then, in 1774–7, the church was rebuilt in neoclassical style to designs by George Gibson. In 1849, however, the RAILWAYS arrived and the community was transformed as builders erected terraces for commuters prepared to trade the time spent travelling to work for a residence in a semi-rural environment. By 1900, Lewisham was a middle-class residential suburb and by the end of the twentieth century most of the early properties had disappeared to make way for new developments, including a shopping centre and sports complex. In 1965, when London's local government was reorganized, the town gave its name to the new LONDON BOROUGH OF LEWISHAM. That name is used in the DOMESDAY BOOK (1086) in the form 'Levesham'. It may be derived from an Old English personal name coupled with the suffix *ham* and mean 'Leofsa's homestead'.

LEWISHAM, LONDON BOROUGH OF

Created in 1965 by the amalgamation of the previously independent authorities at DEPTFORD and LEWISHAM, the borough covers 14 square miles. It has a narrow frontage (about ⅓ mile) on the RIVER THAMES, but broadens to the south, reaching a maximum of 5 miles between Upper Sydenham and Grove PARK. Largely residential, with extensive public and private housing estates, Lewisham houses 249,000 citizens (2001) who focus on central London for employment. Incomes are generally below the urban average, reflecting relatively high rates of unemployment. Deptford, to the north, has all the social characteristics of the inner city, with fewer than two of every five homes owner-occupied and one in three of the population in a non-white ethnic group. Other areas are more typically suburban, though there is a significant concentration of light industry in the west, where the major shopping facilities are located. The borough is crossed by several major roads and rail routes, which connect London to settlements on the Thames estuary and the English Channel coast. (See also BECKENHAM; BLACKHEATH; CATFORD; DOCKLANDS LIGHT RAILWAY (DLR); FOREST HILL; KIDBROOKE; MILLWALL FOOTBALL CLUB; NEW CROSS; SYDENHAM.)

LEYTON

Leyton lies 6 miles north-east of CHARING CROSS on marshland east of the RIVER LEA. It was probably settled in Roman times and farmed by the Saxons, remaining predominantly agricultural until the Industrial Revolution. In 1840, the Eastern and Northern RAILWAY built a station at Lea Bridge and, with the Great Eastern Railway (which arrived in 1856), acquired large amounts of land for use as sidings and maintenance depots. Immigrants flooded in to seek work, turning the settlement into a working-class suburb towards the edge of the metropolitan area. Leyton suffered badly during the BLITZ and was extensively redeveloped after the Second World War. In 1965, it was incorporated within the LONDON BOROUGH OF WALTHAM FOREST when the capital's local government was reorganized. The place name may be derived from the river's name, coupled with the Old English suffix *tun*, meaning 'the homestead on the River Lea'. (See also LEYTON ORIENT FOOTBALL CLUB.)

LEYTON ORIENT FOOTBALL CLUB

Leyton Orient was an offshoot of the Glyn CRICKET Club, which in 1881 established a football team so that its members could keep fit during the winter. Two years later, the name was changed to Orient Football Club at the suggestion of one of the players, who worked for the Orient Shipping Line (clearly, too, it was an apt title for a team located in the EAST END). In 1898, Clapton was added in an effort to attract support from the then affluent nearby suburb. From 1946 until 1966, the side was known as Leyton Orient, then it reverted to Orient for twenty-one years before readopting Leyton Orient in 1987. Since then, the club title has been more stable than its finances.

The team turned professional in 1903 and joined the Second Division of the Football League in 1905. Since then, it has languished in the lower reaches of the League structure, distinguishing itself only by winning the Third Division (South) in 1956 and the Third Division in 1970. Its high point was 1962/63, when it played in the First Division, but it won only six of its forty-two games, finished in twenty-second place, and was relegated after only one season.

Lack of success on the field was accompanied by financial problems. During the 1930s, the lack of funds led to talk of mergers with other clubs (notably Thames FC, which also played in the Football League) but a fighting fund preserved the side's independence. In the mid-1960s, buckets were passed round the crowds at home games in an attempt to raise money and amalgamations were mooted again, this time with non-League Basildon FC and Romford FC. Then, in 1995, when Leyton faced bankruptcy and the Professional Footballers' Association was paying the players' wages, Barry Hearn (who had supported the side as a lad and made his fortune by promoting snooker tournaments) stepped in to buy the business. He has received much criticism (not least for allegedly racist remarks made on a radio show) but has apparently stabilized the club's finances (though without any sustained improvement in its League position).

Leyton plays at the Matchroom Stadium in Brisbane Road, a ground it has occupied since 1936. It has a capacity of just under 11,000 (more than enough to hold the average home gate of about 4,000 supporters) but if plans for improvements are completed that will fall to around 9,000 (significantly less than would be required if the club is to move up the divisions of the Football League).

LEYTONSTONE

Lying some 7 miles north-east of CHARING CROSS, Leytonstone derives the first part of its name from LEYTON, a neighbouring settlement on the banks of the RIVER LEA. The stone commemorated by the second part was probably a mile marker on a branch of the Roman road from LONDINIUM to Camulodunum (now Colchester). For most of its history, Leytonstone was little more than a hamlet, depending for its survival on farming and erecting its first church only in 1749. However, from 1856, when the Eastern Counties RAILWAY built a station and ran nine services into London each day, the population grew rapidly as developers converted the surrounding fields and pastures into housing estates. That development continued through the twentieth century, turning Leytonstone into a metropolitan suburb and sweeping away many of the older buildings in the process. Many of the new homes were provided by the local authorities but, despite its predominantly working-class background, the community has produced several well-known personalities, including the film director Alfred Hitchcock, Fanny Craddock (one of the first television chefs), former England cricket captain Graham Gooch and, most recently, football superstar David Beckham. Recent planning policies have improved access to recreational open space (as in the Lea Valley and at EPPING FOREST) and cheap rents (reflecting the somewhat run-down nature of parts of the area) are attracting a small IMMIGRANT community, including incomers from Eastern Europe. Leytonstone was included in the LONDON BOROUGH OF WALTHAM FOREST when the city's local government was reorganized in 1965.

LIBERTY'S

In 1875, Arthur Lasenby Liberty, son of a Buckinghamshire draper, opened a shop at 218A REGENT STREET, selling Indian silk to an affluent clientele. The business was an immediate success, allowing him to expand into a wider variety of oriental goods and take over additional premises. In 1924, a major redevelopment allowed the firm to acquire Nos 210–20 and build an entrance from Great Marlborough Street using timbers from the men-of-war HMS *Hindustan* (launched in

1824) and HMS *Impregnable* (launched in 1865 and the largest ship of its day). The flamboyant Regent Street frontage incorporated a 115-foot-long frieze, showing the wealth of distant lands, and a clock on which St George fights a battle with a dragon every hour. Liberty's has exerted enormous influence on the tastes of the wealthy ever since its establishment, promoting (at various times) hand-printed fabrics, art nouveau designs, pre-Raphaelite lines and countryside imagery in a range of furniture, wallpaper and jewellery as well as textiles. At the beginning of the twenty-first century, however, its sales were affected by new discount retailers and its future was in doubt. A fire in November 2000 that gutted the basement and destroyed thousands of square feet of floor space added to the uncertainties. Then, early the following year, Liberty announced plans to scrap its high-fashion ready-to-wear collection and to pull out of mail order and e-commerce business in order to concentrate on core retail activities and spend £4 million refurbishing its store. (See also MERTON.)

LIBRARIES

Although educational, religious and professional institutions such as the ROYAL COLLEGE OF PHYSICIANS OF LONDON and the ROYAL SOCIETY provided libraries for the use of their members, Londoners had no facilities for borrowing books until rising levels of literacy and changing fashions led to an increase in reading for pleasure during the eighteenth century. As demand for access to the works of writers such as Daniel Defoe, Charles Dickens and Walter Scott mounted, entrepreneurs established commercial lending libraries for the leisured middle classes, particularly during the reign of Queen Victoria. By 1900, the largest of these enterprises was Mudie's, which held a stock of nearly a million volumes on its site at the corner of New Oxford Street and Museum Street. W.H. SMITH had also acquired a considerable share of the market as a branch of its newspaper distribution and retailing business. In 1844, the LONDON LIBRARY (founded through the efforts of Thomas Carlyle, William Gladstone and John Stuart Mill) opened in PALL MALL with the aim of providing texts that could be loaned to scholars of the humanities and, in 1855, the Public Libraries Act gave local government bodies power to fund public libraries from property taxes, so by 1900 Londoners had wide access to reading material. That access increased throughout the twentieth century, particularly following the introduction of welfare state policies by the Labour government after the Second World War. As a result, the libraries in the LONDON BOROUGHS had lending stocks of about two books per resident, with extensive collections for children and ancillary newspapers, periodicals, compact discs and videos. In addition, changes in technology have led to investment in computers with Internet access as methods of information gathering focus on electronic media and reciprocal arrangements allow London libraries to meet readers' demands for the esoteric by obtaining books for short periods from other collections. (See also BARBICAN; BRITISH LIBRARY; BRITISH MUSEUM; CHARLTON; CHELSEA FLOWER SHOW; COMMONWEALTH INSTITUTE; COURTAULD INSTITUTE OF ART; FREUD'S HOUSE; GLOBE THEATRE; GOLDERS GREEN; GREENWICH PALACE; GUILDHALL; HAMPTON COURT PALACE; KENWOOD HOUSE; LAMBETH PALACE; LONDON SCHOOL OF ECONOMICS AND POLITICAL SCIENCE (LSE); NATIONAL ARMY MUSEUM; NATURAL HISTORY MUSEUM; ORPINGTON; ROYAL ACADEMY OF MUSIC; ROYAL BOTANIC GARDENS; ROYAL COLLEGE OF SURGEONS OF ENGLAND; ROYAL FESTIVAL HALL; ROYAL GEOGRAPHICAL SOCIETY; RUISLIP; SCIENCE MUSEUM; SLOANE, HANS; SWISS COTTAGE; WIMBLEDON; WOOLWICH.)

LIFFE

See LONDON INTERNATIONAL FINANCIAL FUTURES AND OPTIONS EXCHANGE (LIFFE).

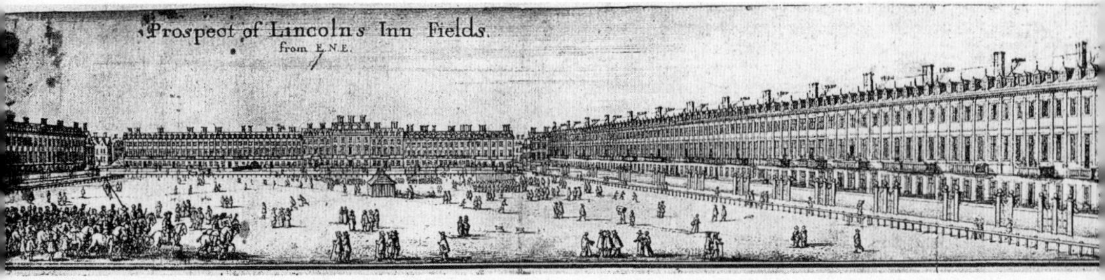

Prospect of Lincoln's Inn fields, by Hollar, c. 1657.

LIGHTERMEN

Traditionally, lightermen have had the sole right to carry goods from ship to shore on the RIVER THAMES (and, by doing so, make the ships lighter). They united with the WATERMEN in 1700 (following a dispute over the transport of passengers) and thrived until the nineteenth century, when the construction of enclosed DOCKS (where ships could berth alongside quays) greatly reduced their numbers. The progressive closure of London's harbour facilities after the Second World War caused further unemployment but a few individuals keep the trade alive, mostly as masters of waste disposal vessels and dredgers.

LIMEHOUSE

Limehouse, located on the north bank of the RIVER THAMES some 3½ miles east of CHARING CROSS, takes its name from the production of lime, which was an important industry in the area during the Middle Ages, but its economic development was more closely linked to London's rising importance as a maritime centre. During the sixteenth and seventeenth centuries, many seafarers (such as Sir Humphrey Gilbert, who established England's first North American colony at Newfoundland in 1583) acquired homes there and, by the eighteenth century, it had an important shipbuilding industry. The opening of the West India DOCKS in 1802 brought an influx of manufacturing and importing companies, stifling the former seagoing atmosphere but offering new sources of employment and tying Limehouse into the EAST END as open spaces between formerly independent communities were urbanized. Many of the new residents were from abroad, particularly Chinese sailors who arrived on EAST INDIA COMPANY ships. Relations between the incomers and the local people were often strained because British seamen claimed that Chinese mariners were undercutting their wages, so several violent clashes occurred (especially in 1908). However, the IMMIGRANTS stayed, settling in Limehouse Causeway and Pennyfields, where they were operating about thirty shops and restaurants by 1914 (and were portrayed in the somewhat sensationalist novels of Sax Rohmer, who based the evil Fu Manchu on a tall, well-dressed Chinese man he saw getting into a car in Limehouse Causeway on a foggy night in 1911). During the twentieth century, Limehouse shared in the decline of the docks and suffered in the bombing of the BLITZ. The former resulted in the closure of most of the industrial premises and the latter in large-scale rebuilding programmes by local authorities. As a result, the area is now predominantly residential, albeit still largely working class. Also, the Chinese community has vanished, dispersing during the 1950s when nearly all the buildings in Pennyfields and the Causeway were demolished and replaced by council flats. The only sign of their existence remains in road names such as Canton Street and

Peking Street. Limehouse was included within the LONDON BOROUGH OF TOWER HAMLETS when metropolitan local government was reorganized in 1965. (See also BARNARDO, THOMAS JOHN.)

LINCOLN'S INN

See INNS OF COURT.

LINCOLN'S INN FIELDS

Lincoln's Inn Fields, in HOLBORN, form central London's largest open square. Originally common land (known as Cup Field and Purse Field), they were initially used as animal pasture, then became a place of execution during the sixteenth century and were ultimately developed from 1638, when William Newton was given permission by Charles I to build houses around the perimeter (despite the objections of Lincoln's Inn). The area immediately became fashionable; Edward Montagu (Earl of Sandwich), Thomas Pelham-Holles (Duke of Newcastle), ELEANOR 'NELL' GWYN (mistress of Charles II), and Prime Ministers William Pitt the Younger, Spencer Perceval and William Gladstone all had homes there at various times over the next two centuries. Most of the early properties are gone, replaced by buildings dating from 1730 to 1960. The gardens became a public PARK in 1894. (See also SIR JOHN SOANE'S MUSEUM.)

LITTLE VENICE

See REGENT'S CANAL.

LIVERPOOL STREET STATION

The station was opened in 1874, on the site of BEDLAM, as the terminus of the Great Eastern RAILWAY. It was extended in 1891 (shortly before the Great Eastern HOTEL, designed by CHARLES BARRY, was added on the eastern side) and, with eighteen tracks, was the biggest in London until VICTORIA station was enlarged in 1908. In 1986, a major redevelopment programme was undertaken, with refurbishment of the station concourse involving improvements in shopping and restaurant facilities and the construction of the Broadgate office complex above platforms 11–18. (See also CENTRAL LINE; EAST LONDON LINE; HAMMERSMITH AND CITY LINE.)

LIVERY COMPANIES

The CITY OF LONDON's livery companies (also known as guilds) were founded as tradesmen's organizations from the twelfth century onwards and got their name because members wore a distinctive livery (or uniform). Initially, their prime purpose was to protect the interests of their crafts by supervising standards of workmanship, controlling the entry of apprentices and regulating prices. However, they also had an important welfare role, looking after members who had fallen on hard times (by arranging funerals, for instance). In the process, many became very wealthy, building opulent premises and meeting regularly for lavish meals. Rivalry was intense (in 1267, the Tailors and the Goldsmiths had a pitched battle, the Clothworkers and Cordwainers added to the mêlée, and the leading protagonists were later hanged). So, in 1514, the Court of Aldermen (see ALDERMAN) was forced to intercede and establish an order of precedence based primarily on the capital resources of the guilds, with the Mercers (dealers in high quality textiles) at the top, followed by the Grocers, Drapers, Fishmongers and Goldsmiths. The sixth rung of the ladder posed problems because the Skinners and the Merchant Tailors both claimed the position, so the LORD MAYOR, showing all the qualities of diplomacy for which Britain is renowned, decreed that the two contestants should alternate sixth and seventh place each year, a decision that led to the phrase 'at sixes and sevens' (meaning confused or unco-ordinated). The Haberdashers, Slaters, Ironmongers, Vintners and Clothworkers, respectively, were allocated the next five positions. These high-ranking organizations were known as the Great Twelve; the other thirty-six were considered minor companies.

During the seventeenth and eighteenth centuries, the companies found themselves under pressure, partly because of differences with the Crown (in 1608, for example James I forced them to finance the settlement of immigrant farmers in Ulster) and partly because changing demands for services reduced the membership of some guilds. The Industrial Revolution brought a change in fortunes, however, as craft skills increased in economic importance, and the later twentieth century has seen the establishment of a series of new companies representing modern ways of earning a living (the Launderers' Company, open to people employed in the dry cleaning business, was formed in 1960, for instance).

By the early twenty-first century, there were about 100 companies, ranging in size from groups such as the Basketmakers' Company (which was formed in 1569 and has a livery of 500) to those such as the Cooks' Company and the Fan Makers' Company (formed in 1311 and 1709 respectively and with liveries of fewer than 100). All are ruled by annually elected courts, headed by a Master, but membership criteria vary; some companies accept only individuals who have connections with their trade, some respect entry by patrimony (accepting a son born while his father was a liveryman) and some have a policy of redemption (being sponsored by two members). Although they still seek to maintain the status of their crafts and have a role in the government of the City of London (see SHERIFF, for instance), much of their modern work is charitable. The Haberdashers' Company (formed in 1327 by men who made tents and padded tunics worn under battle armour) supports schools in several parts of England, the Spectaclemakers' Company (founded in 1629) grants funds for research projects dealing with optical issues and the Clothworkers' Company (created by an amalgamation of guilds in 1528) has shown particular concern for the blind. (See also BREWERIES; CHEAPSIDE; CHELSEA PHYSIC GARDEN; CITY AND GUILDS OF LONDON INSTITUTE; COMMON HALL; COURT OF COMMON COUNCIL; CRIPPLEGATE; DANCE, GEORGE (1700–1768); FREEDOM OF THE CITY; GUILDHALL; HIGHGATE; HOXTON; NEW CROSS; ROYAL COLLEGE OF SURGEONS OF ENGLAND; ROYAL FREE HOSPITAL; ST ANDREW'S CHURCH, HOLBORN; WATERMEN.)

LIVINGSTONE, KENNETH ROBERT (1945–) In May 2000, Ken Livingstone – a politician with political views significantly to the left of Tony Blair's Labour Party – won London's first mayoral election contest despite the best efforts of the British government to engineer his defeat. The son of Robert Livingstone and his wife, Ethel, he was born on 17 June 1945 and educated at Tulse Hill Comprehensive School in south London before working as a technician at the Chester Beatty Cancer Research Institute, then, in 1973, taking a teacher's certificate at the Philippa Fawcett College of Education. He joined the Labour Party in 1969 and gained a seat on the Council of the LONDON BOROUGH OF LAMBETH two years later, serving as vice chairman of the Housing Committee in 1971–3. In 1978, he moved to the LONDON BOROUGH OF CAMDEN, sitting as a Council member until 1982 and acting as chairman of the Housing Committee in 1978–80.

It was with the GREATER LONDON COUNCIL (GLC), however, that Livingstone became a household name. First elected to represent Norwood (1973–7), he later campaigned successfully in HACKNEY North (1977–81) and PADDINGTON (1981–6). In 1981, the Labour Party, led by the politically moderate Andrew McIntosh, gained control of the Council with a nine-seat majority. Under party rules, an election for Leader of the GLC Labour group (and, by implication, of the GLC itself) had to be held immediately and Livingstone, aided and abetted by fellow left-wingers, mounted a successful challenge. As a result, London got a far more militant administration than it had bargained for. Within weeks, Livingstone was annoying Margaret Thatcher with announcements that, in order to tackle London's problems, property taxes would have to rise by 120 per cent and that the authority's multimillion-pound art collection would have to be sold. As unemployment in the city increased, he hung a giant banner chronicling the rise on COUNTY HALL, located on the SOUTH BANK of the RIVER THAMES directly opposite the HOUSE OF COMMONS (see PALACE OF WESTMINSTER) and clearly in Mrs Thatcher's view. When he invited the mother of an IRA member to tea and held a republican party on the day Prince Charles married Diana, Princess of Wales, a rash of press editorials accused him of insensitivity.

The Conservative government eventually decided that enough was enough and abolished the GLC in 1986. Livingstone remained in politics, however, winning the Brent East constituency for Labour at the 1987 General Election. In the HOUSE OF COMMONS, he specialized in economic affairs, kept a comparatively low profile and, over the next decade, acquired a reputation as a champion of London among those who regarded the early 1980s as the GLC's golden era, in which it fought a war of attrition with a Prime Minster who was driven by concepts of financial gain rather than social concern.

When plans for a GREATER LONDON AUTHORITY (GLA) were announced shortly after Labour won the 1997 General Election, Livingstone sought selection as the party representative but was rejected because of his left-wing views. Undeterred, he entered the contest as an independent and won, taking over 38 per cent of the vote (some 12 per cent more than his closest challenger). His success was hailed as a victory for the people over the Labour machine, which had done its best to derail the Livingstone campaign, expelling him from the party and issuing statements claiming that it would be a disaster for London if he topped the poll.

Livingstone has control over an annual budget of about £5 billion (more than that of many members of the United Nations) and is a good media performer, presenting Prime Minister Blair with a political opponent who has real clout and a clear mandate from the people he represents. He also speaks his mind. Shortly before his election he claimed that 'Every year, the international financial system kills more people than World War II but at least Hitler was mad', and in 2003 he told an audience of schoolchildren that the American President, George W. Bush, was a 'coward' leading a 'venal and corrupt administration'. Outside politics, he is recognized as an authority on amphibians, particularly newts, and served as vice president of the Zoological Society of London from 1991 to 1998. (See also CONGESTION CHARGES; LONDON PLAN.)

LLOYD'S OF LONDON

Lloyd's is the world's leading insurance exchange, writing about one-third of all airline insurance and reinsuring the liability risks of nearly all of the ships. It is not itself an insurance company; members have traditionally consisted of individuals and syndicates, who accept liability for the losses incurred by claims. These members are known as 'names' because, when the insurance is arranged through a syndicate, the parties sign their names to the contract. The practice of insuring ships and cargoes against loss became common during the sixteenth century. By the 1680s, Edward Lloyd's COFFEE HOUSE in Tower Street – a favoured haunt of ship masters and merchants and, therefore, a source of reliable, up-to-date information about vessel movements and cargoes – had become accepted as the best place in London to arrange an insurance deal. The business flourished but, during the 1700s, increasingly attracted speculators willing to take wild gambles so, in 1769, a new coffee house was opened in Pope's Head Alley by the more sober financiers. Five years later, by which time the group had developed formal rules of procedure and appointed a governing committee, it transferred to the ROYAL

EXCHANGE, where it remained until it moved to Leadenhall Street in 1928. By that time, its horizons had broadened well beyond the shipping industry and its importance as a centre for the insurance of nearly all types of risk was recognized abroad, particularly in the United States (which accounted for about 30 per cent of its total business by the 1990s).

In 1957, a large extension for the underwriters was opened in Lime Street but, in 1978, needing additional space, Lloyd's commissioned architect Richard Rogers to redevelop the Leadenhall site. The result was a controversial glass and steel structure, first used in 1986, which some commentators thought was more suited to Dallas than London but others felt was an imaginative break from traditional styles. The heart of the building is a large chamber (known as The Room) where trading is done. Around it rise twelve floors, including a gallery for spectators. The total space available for underwriters is about 200,000 square feet.

Lloyd's membership rose steadily from seventy-nine in 1771 to nearly 16,000 in 2003. Foreigners were admitted as names in 1968, women the following year. In 1982 an Act of Parliament (Lloyd's Act) gave its directors immunity from lawsuits and enabled it to become an entirely self-regulating body, but those principles were challenged soon afterwards when the institution's existence was threatened by cumulative losses of more than £8 billion from 1987 to 1992. The immediate cause was claims on policies involving asbestos poisoning and environmental pollution, but critics alleged that many names had taken unacceptable risks and that unsupervized expansion, coupled with poor management of trading, meant that those who ran Lloyd's had to accept some of the blame. Court cases followed in the United Kingdom and elsewhere, leading to a settlement offer that cost £3.1 billion but was accepted by 91 per cent of members in 1996. Two years earlier, corporate capital had been introduced for the first time in an attempt to shore up the market and very quickly overtook the names in underwriting Lloyd's total risk of £10 billion. In 2002, the syndicates reported a trading profit, their first for six years.

Lloyd's is managed by a council of eighteen people, including representatives of names and corporate capital as well as nominated members approved by the Bank of England. In addition, a twelve-member Regulatory Board is responsible for enforcing standards. Since 1998, the organization's activities have been subject to review by the Financial Services Authority, a non-government agency created by Parliament and charged with maintaining public confidence in Britain's financial institutions. (See also LUTINE BELL.)

LOMBARD STREET

One of eight thoroughfares that meet at the BANK OF ENGLAND, Lombard Street has been at the centre of London's banking industry since merchants arrived from Lombardy in northern Italy during the twelfth century, and now provides offices at No. 10 for the Institute of Bankers (the leading British organization training financial service workers). The wealth generated by the firms located in the buildings that line the street's 300 yards has given rise to the assertion that anyone who wagers 'All Lombard Street to a china orange' is convinced that the bet is safe. The church of St Edmund the King, on the north side of the street, was founded in the twelfth century and dedicated to an East Anglian monarch who was killed by Viking invaders for refusing to renounce Christianity. The building, destroyed in the GREAT FIRE of 1666 was replaced by a structure designed by CHRISTOPHER WREN and Robert Hooke in 1670–9. (See also GUY'S HOSPITAL.)

LONDINIUM

When the Romans arrived in Britain in AD 43, led by Aulus Plautius, they landed near the site of the modern town of Deal, in Kent, and made their way north-west. The RIVER THAMES formed a barrier to their advance, with marshlands on both shores, but the invaders were able to build a bridge at a point where a sandbar on the southern side stood opposite a gravel patch on the north. A port, known as Londinium (though no-one is sure what the name means), developed on the north bank, surviving the ravages of an attack by BOADICEA in AD 61 to become the capital of the new colony. Ultimately, the settlement expanded to over 300 acres, with city walls, the largest basilica north of the Alps built east of the WALBROOK, a Governor's Palace erected on the site of CANNON STREET STATION, baths constructed where CHEAPSIDE and Upper Thames Street now stand, and places of worship founded so that soldiers and administrators could pay homage to their gods (see, for example, TEMPLE OF MITHRAS). By the second century, when the frontier had moved far to the north, the city was a thriving commercial centre, with quays and warehouses where goods were imported and exported. However, from AD 408, Rome's defences were threatened by groups from the north German Plain and, two years later, the legions were withdrawn from Britain. It is unclear what happened to Londinium after they left, but almost certainly the population dwindled when the Anglo-Saxons (an agricultural, rather than an urban people) arrived in Britain shortly afterwards. Only fragments of the fabric remain, although the MUSEUM OF LONDON has a large collection of artefacts dating from the period. (See also ALDERSGATE; ALDGATE; BISHOP'S GATE; CITY OF LONDON; CORNHILL; CRIPPLEGATE; ERMINE STREET; GUILDHALL; HIGHGATE; LEADENHALL MARKET; LEYTONSTONE; LONDON WALL; LUDGATE; NEWGATE; WATLING STREET.)

LONDON, CITY OF

See CITY OF LONDON.

LONDON, TREATY OF

On several occasions since the mid-fourteenth century, negotiations have led to the signing of documents known as the Treaty of London.

1. Edward, the Black Prince, captured John II of France at the Battle of Poitiers on 19 September 1356 and carried him back to London, where he was forced to sign a treaty surrendering much of his land to the English monarch, Edward III. The French refused to honour the document.
2. In 1373, England and Portugal negotiated a mutual aid pact that is still in force.
3. Meetings between representatives of England and Spain in 1604 led to cessation of hostilities between the two nations after sixteen years of war.
4. In 1718, Britain, France, the Netherlands and the Holy Roman Empire (sometimes known as the Great Powers) determined that, on the extinction of the male line of the Medici family, the Grand Duchy of Tuscany would pass to Don Carlos de Bourbon (later Charles III of Spain). Also, Victor Amadeus II, Duke of Savoy and sovereign ruler of Piedmont, was forced to yield Sicily to the Hapsburg empire in exchange for Sardinia (then a Spanish possession).
5. Britain, France and Russia signed an understanding to support the Greeks' campaign for independence from Ottoman rule in 1827. The pact is sometimes known as the London Convention.
6. Five years later, the same powers allied with Bavaria to guarantee Greek independence within prescribed boundaries but retained rights of intervention and insisted that the new country should be ruled by a monarchy.
7. In 1840, Mohammed Ali, the Ottoman empire's viceroy in Egypt, forfeited his control over Syria and Adana in return for the right to pass his Egyptian sovereignty to his children. The treaty established a family dynasty that survived for over a century.
8. Prussia agreed to withdraw from Luxemburg in 1867, allowing the Grand Duchy to become an independent nation whose neutrality was guaranteed by Britain

and other European powers. Sovereignty was vested in the Nassau family.
9. The Balkan Wars were ended by a treaty signed in London in 1913. The document prescribed much-reduced boundaries for the Ottoman empire.
10. In 1914, some months prior to the outbreak of the First World War, Britain, France and Russia formed an alliance against Germany, the Austro-Hungarian empire and Turkey (often known as the Central Powers).
11. Italy joined the alliance against the Central Powers in 1915 in return for the right to control Trentino, part of the South Tyrol, Trieste, part of Dalmatia, Albania, Libya and areas of German East Africa and Asia Minor after the war. In addition, Britain agreed to pay Italy 1.25 billion lire. Under pressure from the United States, Britain and France reneged on the treaty in 1918.
12. In 1946, Transjordan was given full independence from the United Kingdom.

LONDON AMBULANCE SERVICE

London's first ambulance service was established by the Metropolitan Asylums Board, which was created in 1867 and used carriages to take sick and mentally ill patients to its hospitals. Responsibility for provision passed to the LONDON COUNTY COUNCIL in 1930 and then, in 1965, to the newly formed GREATER LONDON COUNCIL, which merged parts of nine different units to create a single London Ambulance Service. In 1974, a restructuring of health service provision transferred control to the South-West Thames Regional Health Authority and, in 1996, the service took advantage of legislation introduced by the Conservative government to convert to self-governing National Health Service Trust status, giving its managers fuller control over policy and resource allocation. Day-to-day activities are in the hands of a chief executive (assisted by a group of directors) who reports to a London Ambulance Service Trust Board consisting of a chairman, the chief executive and eight other members. The service employs about 3,700 people and accident and emergency units respond to some 2,800 calls every day. The seventy ambulance stations, with 700 vehicles (including motorbikes designed to make their way quickly through congested city traffic), are controlled from a single centre at WATERLOO.

LONDON ASSEMBLY

The Assembly was created in 1999 by the GREATER LONDON AUTHORITY ACT. Its role is to act as counterpoint to the MAYOR OF LONDON by scrutinizing his or her performance and submitting proposals designed to improve services to citizens. The Assembly also reviews drafts of the Mayor's strategic proposals and conducts investigations into matters of London-wide significance. In addition, it has the power to change the Mayor's budget (subject to a two-thirds majority). The twenty-five members serve for four years and are elected on the same day as the Mayor. The election process is complicated, taking into account votes in fourteen constituencies, party lists and other factors in an attempt to produce a distribution of seats that will reflect the votes cast across the whole city (including the CITY OF LONDON). The first elections on 4 May 2000 produced nine Labour Party representatives, nine Conservatives, four Liberal Democrats and three Green Party members.

LONDON BASIN

London lies in a geological trough drained by the RIVER THAMES and its tributaries. The sides of the syncline are formed by chalk initially laid down under the seas of the Cretaceous period (144–66.4 million years ago) then folded by later orogenic activity. They rise to just under 1,000 feet in the NORTH DOWNS (at the southern edge of the city) and to about 970 feet in the CHILTERN HILLS (to the north-west). The floor of the basin, which opens towards the east, is a complex of sands, gravels and clays deposited as the oceans advanced and retreated during the Tertiary period (66.4–1.6 million years ago). More recent alluvial materials overlie some of these sediments. Much of the material has been removed for brick-making and road infill, leaving large holes that have been utilized for refuse disposal, nature reserves and recreation such as waterskiing. London is built mainly on three gravel terraces above the Thames – the Boyn Hill terrace (which averages 100–130 feet above sea level and is the base for settlements such as RICHMOND and ISLINGTON), the Lynch Hill terrace (which averages 75–80 feet and provides a foundation for the CITY OF LONDON), and the Taplow Terrace (which at only about 30 feet above sea level, lies under TRAFALGAR SQUARE and STEPNEY). For most of their history, the low-lying lands in the basin have been liable to flooding (see FLOOD CONTROL). (See also LONDON CLAY.)

LONDON BOROUGHS

The first twenty-eight boroughs in London were created in 1898, partly in order to limit the power of the LONDON COUNTY COUNCIL (LCC), which had been established ten years earlier. Boroughs were territorial divisions of the LCC area (now essentially the inner city) and exercised responsibilities over local matters, leaving strategic planning to the citywide authority. The geographical nature of the boundaries caused problems because affluent boroughs were able to provide more extensive, and better quality, services than the poor boroughs could do. Also, in the years following the end of the Second World War, as many people left the central city for new homes in the suburbs, it was clear that many of the authorities were too small (in terms both of population and of size) to carry out their duties properly. In 1965, the system was reorganized, with the GREATER LONDON COUNCIL (GLC) replacing the LCC and covering a much wider area. Thirty-two new boroughs were established, each with an elected council charged with carrying out duties intimately affecting the daily lives of citizens, such as in refuse disposal, library provision (see LIBRARIES) and administration of certain personal social services. The twenty outer boroughs also had responsibility for state-supported EDUCATION (with the exception of UNIVERSITIES) but, in the inner twelve boroughs, that task was given to the INNER LONDON EDUCATION AUTHORITY (ILEA), operating as a committee of the GLC, which also had statutory responsibility for citywide strategic planning. Following the GLC's abolition on 31 March 1986, the outer boroughs became unitary authorities, with a statutory duty to provide all local government services. The ILEA continued to supervise inner-city education until 1990, when it, too, was disbanded and its responsibilities handed over to the constituent boroughs. (See also ASSOCIATION OF LONDON AUTHORITIES (ALA); ASSOCIATION OF LONDON

GOVERNMENT (ALG); LONDON BOROUGHS ASSOCIATION (LBA) and individual borough entries.)

LONDON BOROUGHS ASSOCIATION (LBA)

In 1964, the LBA was created as a forum in which representatives of the CORPORATION OF LONDON (the local authority for the CITY OF LONDON) and the thirty-two newly established LONDON BOROUGHS could discuss common problems, co-ordinate activities and act as a pressure group on government. It avoided internal political conflict until 1982, when its Conservative Party majority proposed that the Labour-led, and socially radical, GREATER LONDON COUNCIL (the strategic planning body for the city as a whole) should be abolished. Incensed, most of the Labour boroughs withdrew the following year to form their own organization, the ASSOCIATION OF LONDON AUTHORITIES (ALA). For the next decade, the LBA's remaining nineteen boroughs and the corporation were dominated by Conservative councillors, reflecting the political complexion of the national government, so policies tended to be reactive rather than confrontational or proactive. Five committees dealing with policy and finance, EDUCATION and training, environment, housing and social services each met five times a year and representatives had frequent discussions with Cabinet ministers, senior civil servants and trade unions in an attempt to influence decision making. Successes included concessions from the government on issues such as management of local authority housing and the financial arrangements for schools that opted out of borough control. These activities, and the salaries of the fifteen officers, were funded by the subscriptions paid by the member authorities. Increasingly, however, the lobbying was carried out in conjunction with the ALA, particularly during the early 1990s, as the LBA became disillusioned with the administrations of Margaret Thatcher and John Major. The two groups cooperated closely on the preparation of London Local Authority Bills, which allow Parliament to introduce legislation tackling specific problems common to certain boroughs (such as control over all-night cafés and powers to deal with faulty burglar alarms). They also worked together to obtain grants from the European Union's Social Fund, winning some £10 million in 1993–4. Over the years, the bitterness of the 1983 dispute faded as a sense of common purpose re-emerged and, in 1995, the two bodies reunited as the ASSOCIATION OF LONDON GOVERNMENT. (See also LONDON PRIDE PARTNERSHIP.)

LONDON BOX

See GREATER LONDON DEVELOPMENT PLAN (1969).

LONDON BRIDGE

The first BRIDGE linking the banks of the RIVER THAMES was erected by the Romans between AD 100 and 400. It was rebuilt several times but, until WESTMINSTER BRIDGE opened in 1750, remained the only direct route into the city from the south. In 1014, the wooden structure was deliberately destroyed by King Ethelred for military reasons and, in 1091, its replacement was blown away by a gale. Fire ravaged the third bridge in 1136, encouraging citizens to begin work on a stone crossing in 1176. Twenty-five years later, the new edifice was lined by houses and had room for a small chapel, dedicated to St Thomas Becket, at the centre. From then, it featured in many major episodes in English history: Simon de Montfort used it to enter London while he held Henry III captive in 1264, the head of William Wallace (the Scottish freedom fighter portrayed as Braveheart in the Mel Gibson film) was displayed on it in 1305 (initiating a singularly grisly custom that lasted until 1661), Henry V's body (accompanied by over 800 retainers) was brought back to the capital over it after he died of typhus in France in

London Bridge, *c.* 1750.

London Bridge, early seventeenth century. Note the decapitated heads on 'Bridge Gate'.

1522 and in 1660 Charles II rode back over it to reclaim his throne after the restoration of the English monarchy.

The bridge also had a significant effect on London life. Its nineteen narrow arches made navigation difficult and greatly impeded the flow of the Thames, causing the river to freeze over in winter (see FROST FAIRS) and concentrate sewage (see, for example, GREAT STINK). From 1758 to 1762, the houses were removed and the arches strengthened but, by the early nineteenth century, it was clear that a new structure was needed to meet the needs of the industrial age. Designed by JOHN RENNIE and, following his death, built by his son, also John, in 1823–31, the replacement had five arches and was sited a few yards upriver of its venerable predecessor. In 1970, it was sold to American interests for £1 and transported stone by stone to Lake Havasu City in Arizona (there is an enduring belief in London that the Americans thought they were buying TOWER BRIDGE). The present bridge, built of pre-stressed concrete and with three arches, opened in 1973; it is functional but lacks the architectural interest of the earlier crossings. *London Bridge Is Falling Down* – the children's nursery rhyme – probably dates from the days of Ethelred's demolition, though the words did not take their present form until the seventeenth century. (See also DANCE, GEORGE (1700–1768); DOGGETT'S COAT AND BADGE RACE; GUY'S HOSPITAL; MOORGATE; ST THOMAS'S HOSPITAL; TRANSPORT.)

LONDON BRIDGE CITY

See BERMONDSEY.

LONDON CITY AIRPORT

See AIRPORTS.

LONDON CLAY

A marine sediment deposited during the Eocene period (from approximately 57.8 to 36.6 million years ago), London clay underlies most of the metropolitan area, reaching a thickness of about 600 feet in places. Brown, grey or bluish in colour, it has yielded fossils of molluscs, worms, crabs, fish, brachiopods, crocodiles and other animals, along with the fruit of palm trees and conifers. That assemblage suggests that, while the clays were being laid down, the LONDON BASIN was experiencing climatic conditions similar to those of the modern tropics.

LONDON CLEARING HOUSE (LCH)

A limited company founded in 1888, the Clearing House guarantees deals struck on the INTERNATIONAL PETROLEUM EXCHANGE of London, the LONDON INTERNATIONAL FINANCIAL FUTURES AND OPTIONS EXCHANGE, the LONDON METAL EXCHANGE and Tradepoint Stock Exchange. After a contract has been agreed at one of these centres it is substituted by two new ones between LCH and each of the parties involved (a process known as novation). If one side defaults, the other is compensated from the Clearing House's default fund, to which each member contributes £150 million. In 1999 the Clearing House introduced additional over-the-counter services for the wholesale inter-bank market.

LONDON COMMODITY EXCHANGE

The Exchange was formed in 1954 through the merger of a number of organizations marketing soft commodity futures and conducted business at its premises on Mincing Lane (in the CITY OF LONDON), where Mediterranean produce had been bought and sold as early as the tenth century. In 1987, it transferred to St Katharine's DOCK (at the western end of the DOCKLANDS redevelopment area), renaming itself LONDON FOX, THE FUTURES AND OPTIONS EXCHANGE, and concentrating on cocoa, coffee, grain, potatoes, meat, rice, rubber and soybean meal. Nine years later, it was absorbed by the LONDON INTERNATIONAL FINANCIAL FUTURES AND OPTIONS EXCHANGE.

LONDON CONVENTION (1827)

See LONDON, TREATY OF.

LONDON COUNTY COUNCIL (LCC)

The LCC was the first of the city's local authorities to be directly elected by residents. It was established by the Local Government Act of 1888, replacing the METROPOLITAN BOARD OF WORKS and exercising its jurisdiction over an area of some 117 square miles covering the centre of modern London. A total of 126 councillors were elected to serve for three years. In addition, the councillors themselves elected twenty-one ALDERMEN, who held office for six years. Their duties and responsibilities were extensive and expanded during the seventy-seven years of the body's existence, covering housing, TRANSPORT, SEWAGE DISPOSAL, EDUCATION and other services that affected the daily lives of citizens.

From the LCC's inception, its policies were determined by political ideologies. The Progressives (essentially supporters of the Liberal Party) were in overall control for most of the period from 1889 until 1907 and the Moderates (allied to the Conservative Party) from 1907 until 1934, when Labour became the majority grouping. After the Second World War, middle-class families increasingly left the inner city for new homes in suburbs established by counties beyond LCC boundaries. As a result, the increasing concentration of manual groups in the inner city effectively guaranteed socialist control of the metropolitan area. That proved popular with the voters but, during the 1950s, was a constant thorn in the flesh of Conservative governments, so, in 1957, a Royal Commission, chaired by Sir Edwin Herbert, was appointed to investigate alternative forms of local provision. Its report, presented to Parliament in 1960, recommended creation of new boroughs (see LONDON BOROUGHS) exercising more limited powers than those acquired by the LCC. In addition, it envisaged a GREATER LONDON COUNCIL with responsibility for strategic planning and covering a wider territory. The proposals were welcomed by the predominantly Conservative HOUSE OF COMMONS, which passed the necessary legislation in 1963. The LCC met for the last time two years later. (See also ABERCROMBIE PLAN (1943-44); ALDWYCH; AVERY HILL; BETHNAL GREEN; BLUE PLAQUES; BURNT OAK; CHELSEA; COUNTY HALL; EAST HAM; EDUCATION; ELECTRICITY; EPSOM; GEFFRYE MUSEUM; HARDIE, JAMES KEIR; HERNE HILL; HOLBORN; HOLLAND HOUSE; HORNIMAN MUSEUM; HURLINGHAM CLUB; ILFORD; INNS OF CHANCERY; KENWOOD HOUSE; LAMBETH PALACE; LONDON AMBULANCE SERVICE; LONDON FIRE BRIGADE; LONDON SCHOOL OF ECONOMICS AND POLITICAL SCIENCE (LSE); LONDON TRANSPORT (LT); MARBLE HILL HOUSE; MORDEN; MORRISON, HERBERT STANLEY; NATIONAL WESTMINSTER TOWER; OLD VIC; POPLARISM; QUEEN ELIZABETH HALL; RANGER'S HOUSE; ROEHAMPTON; ROYAL NATIONAL THEATRE; SEWAGE DISPOSAL; TOOTING; TRAMS; WATERLOO; WATER SUPPLY.)

LONDON DISCOUNT MARKET ASSOCIATION (LDMA)

Bills of exchange (documents that merchants use to confirm that payments for goods will be made on a specified date) are marketable commodities. They are exchanged for cash, at a discount, thereby facilitating acquisition of funds that can be applied where liquid capital is needed. In London, the trades are carried out by 'bill brokers' attached to discount houses, which are members of the LDMA and were founded, in most cases, during the first half of the nineteenth century. With the volume of business amounting to several billion pounds for a single house every working day, the significance of the deals is considerable, so the firms work closely with the BANK OF ENGLAND, which uses the relationship to influence interest rates and thus shape national monetary policies.

LONDON DOCK STRIKE (1889)

On 19 August 1889, workers in London's DOCK went on strike in support of a pay rate of a 'tanner' (sixpence) an hour. Led by John Burns, Tom Mann and Ben Tillett, and buoyed by £79,000 contributed by well-wishers in Australia and Britain, they forced the port managements to accept their demand at negotiations chaired by Cardinal H.E. Manning, Archbishop of Westminster. The men returned to work on 16 September, buoyed by a success that brought more than their 'docker's tanner'. Encouraged by a victory for organized labour, unskilled labourers throughout the country formed new trade unions in the hope of improving their working conditions.

LONDON DOCKLANDS DEVELOPMENT CORPORATION (LDDC)

See DOCKLANDS.

LONDON DOCKS

See DOCKS.

LONDON DUNGEON

Located in Tooley Street, BERMONDSEY, the London Dungeon is a MUSEUM that concentrates on torture and death. Realistic life-sized exhibits show, in graphic detail, religious martyrs burning at the stake and a Jacobite supporter being hung, drawn and quartered. Instruments designed to cause mutilation are featured, along with a reconstruction of the gallows at TYBURN and a description of conditions in NEWGATE PRISON. Despite its gruesome theme, the museum is one of city's most successful tourist sites, attracting more than 600,000 visitors every year.

LONDON EYE

Also know as the Millennium Wheel, the London Eye is located beside COUNTY HALL and allows visitors a view of the city from 450 feet above the RIVER THAMES as it carries them on a 30-minute trip in thirty-two capsules, each holding twenty-five people. The £20 million project was funded by British Airways to celebrate the beginning of the twenty-first century. The conditions set by urban planners allow it to remain in place for five years.

LONDON FIRE BRIGADE

London had no organized means of defending life and property against flames until after the GREAT FIRE of 1666. That experience persuaded insurance firms that their interests would be best served by forming private fire brigades, which would only attempt to put out blazes at properties that the parent company insured. Over the years, the brigades increasingly cooperated, a process that ultimately led to their amalgamation as the Fire Engine Establishment in 1833. The resources of the new organization were frequently stretched, however, as when much of the PALACE OF WESTMINSTER was destroyed in 1834 and when, in 1861, a warehouse fire in Tooley Street took two days to extinguish. Eventually, in 1865, Parliament was persuaded that a citywide service should be provided at public expense and it approved legislation creating the Metropolitan Fire Brigade, controlled by the METROPOLITAN BOARD OF WORKS. Responsibility for the service (which formally changed its name to the London Fire Brigade in 1904) was taken over by the LONDON COUNTY COUNCIL in 1899, the GREATER LONDON COUNCIL in 1965 and the London Fire and Civil Defence Authority (which consists of one member from each of the thirty-three local authorities in the metropolitan area) in 1986. It has a staff of about 7,300 (of whom 6,100 are firemen), 114 stations and 650 engines operating from three major bases in LEWISHAM, STRATFORD and WEMBLEY, with an emergency control centre in LAMBETH. Members attend nearly 200,000 incidents annually, with the stations at BRIXTON, PADDINGTON and PECKHAM averaging over 3,000 calls every year. Much of the Brigade's work concentrates on fire prevention, rather than on firefighting, allowing it to devote an increasing amount of time to other incidents, such as rail accidents, motorway crashes and animal rescues.

LONDON FIRST

From its headquarters in Tothill Street (near the HOUSES OF PARLIAMENT (see PALACE OF WESTMINSTER)), London First co-ordinates public and private interests in an effort to promote investment in the city, improve the quality of TRANSPORT, reduce AIR POLLUTION and encourage TOURISM. Established in 1992, the organization has a membership of more than 300 businesses, whose financial contributions support a small staff and pay for project costs and is governed by a board composed of commercial and local government interests. In 1994, it established the London First Centre to provide a free consultancy service to companies interested in opening premises in the city. London First also co-chairs the LONDON PRIDE PARTNERSHIP with the ASSOCIATION OF LONDON GOVERNMENT.

LONDON FOX, THE FINANCE AND FUTURES EXCHANGE

See LONDON COMMODITY EXCHANGE.

LONDON GAZETTE

The *Gazette*, published by the British government, carries official announcements (such as the award of military decorations). It first appeared on 5 February 1666, promoted by Charles II, and is printed at premises in PRINTING HOUSE SQUARE.

LONDON HEALTH EMERGENCY (LHE)

Britain's largest pressure group dedicated to the preservation of the National Health Service (the United Kingdom's system of socialized medicine), London Health Emergency was founded in 1983 to campaign against the Conservative government's plans to close hospitals in the city. Initial funding was provided by the GREATER LONDON COUNCIL and, after that body was disbanded in 1986, by the Labour-dominated members of the ASSOCIATION OF LONDON AUTHORITIES. By the late 1990s, it had over 200 affiliated organizations (including trade unions and community groups) linked by a quarterly newspaper with a print run of over 10,000 copies. As well as providing a resource base for activists and the media, LHE carries out research and publicity work for local authorities and other bodies. It advocates abolition of the market system in healthcare and proposes the establishment of a single health authority to co-ordinate services in the capital.

LONDON INTERNATIONAL FINANCIAL FUTURES AND OPTIONS EXCHANGE (LIFFE)

LIFFE, based at Cannon Bridge in the CITY OF LONDON, opened in 1982 as a trading base for over 200 companies and individuals dealing in financial transactions involving an element of risk. In essence, traders who have contracts that depend on changing share prices, variations in interest rates or altering asset values, may transfer the risk to others willing to accept the consequences of upswings and downswings in the market. As a result, banks, insurance companies and other institutions can protect pension funds, offer fixed rate mortgages to house buyers and lend funds at specified rates to small businesses. Most trading was done by the traditional 'open outcry' method, with dealers facing each other across a 'pit' floor, but there were facilities for computerized deals in low-volume commodities, such as financial futures, options and sugar futures. A statistical service provided historical data on activities to traders, financial institutions and other bodies (such as UNIVERSITIES).

The Exchange absorbed the London Traded Options Market in 1992 and LONDON FOX, THE FUTURES AND OPTIONS EXCHANGE (see LONDON COMMODITY EXCHANGE) in 1996, by which time it was the largest of its kind in Europe, with an average daily volume of 660,000 contracts valued at £160 billion. However, it failed to respond to changes in trading methods, holding on to open outcry when others were moving to electronic trading. As a result, competitors (especially the German futures exchange in Frankfurt, which was fully automated) rapidly encroached on LIFFE's business and in 1998 the 210 members voted to computerize their dealings. The following year, a link was developed with the Chicago Mercantile Exchange, allowing traders access to business on both sides of the Atlantic. In 2001 a joint venture with NASDAQ (the North American exchange for high technology shares) aimed at forming a market for stock futures then, later in the year, LIFFE was bought by Euronext (a consortium consisting of the Belgian, Dutch and French stock exchanges). (See also LONDON CLEARING HOUSE (LCH); ROYAL EXCHANGE.)

LONDON INTERNATIONAL INSURANCE AND REINSURANCE MARKET ASSOCIATION (LIRMA)

LIRMA, based in Mincing Lane in the CITY OF LONDON, is one of the world's largest representative organizations for insurance and reinsurance companies. Formed in 1991 through the merger of a number of pre-existing groups, it has ninety-six full members located in London and the European

Economic Area, with a further eighty-seven associate members in other parts of the globe. Trading is almost exclusively in non-life business, with an emphasis on catastrophic risks such as earthquakes and hurricanes. In the mid-1990s, the Association accounted for about two-thirds of all non-marine treaty insurance business on the London market (the largest in the world) and underwrote more than £3 billion of premium income each year (most of it contributing to Britain's invisible earnings). In 1999 it merged with the Institute of London Underwriters to form the INTERNATIONAL UNDERWRITING ASSOCIATION of London.

LONDON IRISH RUGBY FOOTBALL CLUB

For most of London Irish's history, the club has been known more for its social atmosphere than for its achievements on the pitch but, in recent years, it has established itself in the top rank of English rugby. The team was formed in 1898 to provide a sporting focus for Irish exiles in the city and it has attracted many talented players. In the 1920s, George Stephenson and George Beamish both captained the national side and in the 1950s, bolstered by men of the calibre of Andy Mulligan and Tony O'Reilly, it was well represented in the British Lions, the Barbarians and other select sides. It flourished again in the mid-1960s, the early 1970s and also in the early 1990s (when Robert Saunders won the captaincy of Ireland at the age of only twenty-two).

From 1996, when Rugby Union shed its amateur status, the club made determined efforts to attract quality players, whatever their nationality, and by 2002 (the year in which it finished fourth in the Premiership table and defeated Northampton 38-7 in the Powergen Cup final) it had members who had international experience with England, Fiji, New Zealand, South Africa, Wales and Western Samoa as well as Ireland. In 2001, London Irish signed a seven-year contract to play its home games at the Madejksi Stadium of Reading Football Club, although the training grounds and administrative offices remain at its traditional home in Sunbury. Like most senior rugby sides, it fields mini, youth and junior teams and has a strong community programme.

LONDON LIBRARY

Thomas Carlyle founded the London Library as an act of revenge. Angry because he had to wait several hours while books were delivered to his desk in the BRITISH MUSEUM, he determined to establish a facility where readers could borrow books and enjoy them in their own homes. His frustrations were clearly shared by others because 500 supporters proved willing to pay a £2 subscription as well as a £6 entry fee and many of those supporters were well-known public figures. Charles Dickens was a founding member (as was philosopher John Stuart Mill), aspiring politician William Gladstone served on the first governing committee and William Makepeace Thackeray was the first auditor. From 1841 until 1845, the books were housed on the first floor at the Traveller's Club at 49 PALL MALL but since then the Library has had its own premises at the north-west corner of ST JAMES'S SQUARE. One of its most troublesome patrons, apparently, was Carlyle himself: he wrote comments on the page margins of the texts he borrowed and then refused to return the books on time.

By the outbreak of the Second World War, the collection numbered some 475,000 volumes. Many of these were destroyed when a flying bomb landed nearby in 1944 but, even so, the Library now owns over a million books, including many in languages other than English. It is strongest in the humanities (notably history and literature) but also has significant collections in the fine and applied arts, religion, topography and travel. Although a few fifteenth-century books were sold in

1970, the London Library has retained most of the stock accumulated since its foundation and is still run on a subscription basis, its policies determined by a committee elected by the subscribers. (See also LIBRARIES.)

LONDON MARATHON

The marathon was the brainchild of athlete Chris Brasher, who helped pace Roger Bannister to the first four-minute mile in 1954 and won the 3,000-metre steeplechase at the Melbourne Olympic Games in 1956. Brasher competed in the 1979 New York marathon and returned to the United Kingdom convinced that a similar event could be held in London. Helped by a business colleague, John Disley (also a distinguished runner), and Donald Trelford (editor of *The Observer*) he gained the support of the GREATER LONDON COUNCIL, the METROPOLITAN POLICE and the governing bodies of British athletics. With financial support from the Gillette company, the first race was held on 29 March 1981. (The first men home – American Dick Beardsley and Norwegian Inge Simonsen – crossed the finishing line hand in hand, staging a dead heat.) A total of 7,747 people took part and 6,255 finished. By 2003, over 80,000 applications for the event were being received annually by the organizers: some 45,000 of these are accepted and two-thirds of the starters finish.

The race has always begun at BLACKHEATH Common and GREENWICH PARK. However, the route has varied (though it always stays close to the RIVER THAMES) and the finishing line has been at CONSTITUTION HILL (1981), WESTMINSTER BRIDGE (1982-93) and THE MALL (since 1994). The event is a serious competition, attracting the world's leading long-distance runners and including a section for wheelchair athletes, but the vast majority of the participants run for fun, raising money for charity. Many wear fancy dress and some show enormous courage. In 2003, the last person to finish was the former boxer Michael Watson, who suffered brain damage in a world middleweight title fight with Chris Eubank in 1991 and had been unable to walk for ten years afterwards. He took six days to complete the 26 miles and 385 yards. (See also WHITE CITY.)

LONDON METAL EXCHANGE (LME)

The Metal Exchange, based in Leadenhall Street, in the CITY OF LONDON, is the world's largest nonferrous futures exchange. It has its origins in the ROYAL EXCHANGE, where metal dealers first met regularly during the late sixteenth century, but was formally constituted in 1877 to trade in copper and tin. Lead and zinc were added in 1920 (though they had been the subject of earlier unofficial deals), primary aluminium in 1978, nickel in 1979 and aluminium alloy in 1992. The system of buying and selling is unique. At 11.45 a.m., the trading floor (known as the Ring) opens and the metals trade in sequence for five minutes each. At 12.30 p.m., the process is repeated, with the metals in a different order. Following the announcement of the prices agreed, a period of more general trading (termed the Kerb) is held, with all seven metals on the market simultaneously. A second session of Ring trading is held between 3.20 p.m. and 5 p.m. The value of the deals, which amount to over US$2,000 billion a year, sets the global reference price for each commodity. By the late 1990s, LME had a membership of over 100 firms in five categories but only the twelve in the most senior group could trade in the Ring. In 1987, the Exchange was constituted as a limited company with a Board of Directors responsible for managing the institution and a Ring Committee ensuring that trading rules are observed. (See also LONDON CLEARING HOUSE (LCH).)

LONDON PASSENGER TRANSPORT BOARD (LPTB)

See LONDON TRANSPORT (LT).

LONDON PHILHARMONIC ORCHESTRA (LPO)

The London Philharmonic was formed in 1932 by Sir Thomas Beecham, a sometimes cantankerous conductor who railed against the standard of music in the United Kingdom. It quickly earned a reputation for high-quality performances, so, when Beecham went to the United States in 1939, it was able to continue as a self-governing group of musicians, a status that it has maintained ever since. It experienced a difficult financial period during the 1950s but survived to become the resident orchestra for the Glyndebourne opera season (from 1964), work with conductors of the calibre of Sir Adrian Boult and Sir George Solti and undertake major foreign tours (including, in 1956, the first visit to the Soviet Union by a British orchestra and, in 1973, the first to China by a Western orchestra). In 1990, the LPO was made resident symphony orchestra at the ROYAL FESTIVAL HALL. Plans for a merger with the ROYAL PHILHARMONIC ORCHESTRA were dropped in 1995 after a report by management consultants indicated that any financial savings would not justify the artistic turmoil involved.

LONDON PLAN (2002)

In 2002, KEN LIVINGSTONE, London's Mayor, announced plans for London's economic and social welfare, stressing the need to provide housing for an estimated population increase of 700,000 people by 2016, to build well-designed office space, to recycle waste and to conserve energy. The proposals included three new crossings over the RIVER THAMES, 130 new schools, an increase in the size of the METROPOLITAN POLICE force, improved public TRANSPORT and construction of 23,000 houses every year (10,000 of them for families with low incomes). Inevitably, although some bodies supported the suggested measures (the London Tourist Board liked the emphasis on the economic impact of visitors to the capital and the Royal Institute of British Architects praised the emphasis on good design, for example) there were many critics. The House Builders' Federation claimed that the requirement to include low-cost properties meant that some developments would not be built but Shelter (a charity caring for the homeless) argued that the proportion of cheaper homes was far too low to meet London's needs. Environmental groups, and the Green Party, protested that office construction, AIRPORT expansion, and new roads would put pressure on existing amenities, such as open space.

LONDON PLANE

A hybrid of *Platanus orientalis* (a native of western Asia and south-east Europe) and *Platanus occidentalis* (a North American species), the London plane tree was introduced from Virginia in 1636. It became popular as a decorative species from the mid-eighteenth century, particularly after the Industrial Revolution, because it sheds its bark and, therefore, survives in areas where AIR POLLUTION is high. It gets its name because it is common in the central city (see, for example, BERKELEY SQUARE and THE MALL.)

LONDON PLANNING ADVISORY COMMITTEE (LPAC)

LPAC is the statutory planning committee for London. Created by the same Parliamentary legislation that dissolved the GREATER LONDON COUNCIL in 1986, it advises government and the LONDON BOROUGHS on strategic planning matters and major development proposals, represents the capital's interests in discussions dealing with regional planning in south-east England and makes recommendations relating to vehicle parking policy. At the end of the 1990s, its major priorities included the balancing of housing needs with job creation and improving the quality of the urban environment (particularly along the RIVER THAMES). The Committee consists of one representative from each of the thirty-three local authorities in the city and has a staff of twenty-two.

LONDON PRIDE

The pink flowers of this saxifrage (*Saxifraga umbrosa*) light up the corners of basement patios and window boxes throughout London's inner suburbs. The plant gets its name because it survives in relatively dark conditions, where other species wither and die.

LONDON PRIDE PARTNERSHIP

In 1993, John Gummer, Secretary of State for the Environment, launched a City Pride Initiative, which invited London, Birmingham and Manchester to produce plans combining a vision for each city's future with realistic policies for achieving it. In the capital, LONDON FIRST was given responsibility for producing the documents and responded by forming a partnership of public and private organizations, including the ASSOCIATION OF LONDON AUTHORITIES, the CORPORATION OF LONDON, the LONDON BOROUGHS ASSOCIATION and the London Chamber of Commerce. The blueprint that these bodies published in 1995 identified five priorities – business growth, improved TRANSPORT, better EDUCATION and training, more good-quality housing at affordable prices and higher standards of environmental quality. It also suggested three aims – creation of a robust economy, greater social cohesion and provision of a high-quality service infrastructure. Gummer responded by inviting the consortium leaders to meet regularly with the government's Cabinet Sub-Committee for London, under the title of the Joint London Advisory Panel, to discuss issues of strategic importance to the metropolitan area and move towards implementation of the proposals.

LONDON REGIONAL PASSENGERS' COMMITTEE (LRPC)

Established by the 1984 TRANSPORT Act, the LRPC considers complaints and suggestions from individuals or groups concerned about BUS and RAILWAY services in and around London, making recommendations to LONDON TRANSPORT, the government and other bodies when necessary. In addition, it reviews objections to plans involving withdrawal of rail services and reports to the Secretary of State for Transport on any hardships likely to result from the closures. London Transport is required by law to consult with LRPC over bus service alterations, fare changes and other planning proposals. The LRPC, based in Gresham Street (in the CITY OF LONDON), consists of a chairman and up to thirty members chosen to represent a cross section of public transport users, including the disabled, ethnic minorities and commercial concerns. All of the appointments are made by the Secretary of State.

LONDON REGIONAL TRANSPORT (LRT)

See LONDON TRANSPORT (LT).

LONDON RESIDUARY BODY (LRB)

The seven-member LRB was appointed to wind up the affairs of the GREATER LONDON COUNCIL, which was abolished on 31 March 1986. The prime tasks were disposal of the authority's assets (such as COUNTY HALL) and reallocation of its responsibilities to other bodies. Following the break-up of the INNER LONDON EDUCATION AUTHORITY four years later, it carried out similar redistribution procedures. Most of the work was completed by 1994.

LONDON RING MAIN

See WATER SUPPLY.

LONDON SCHOOL OF ECONOMICS AND POLITICAL SCIENCE (LSE)

When Henry Hunt Hutchison, a left-wing sympathizer, died in 1894, he left instructions that the funds generated by his estate should be utilized for socially progressive purposes. Five trustees agreed that the finances should found an educational institution, modelled on L'École Libre des Sciences Politiques in Paris, which would be known as the London School of Economics and Political Science and would study major social problems. In 1896, LSE founded the British Library of Economic and Political Science (now one of the finest collections of social texts in the world) and, in 1900, became a college of the UNIVERSITY of London. Initially based in ROBERT ADAM'S ADELPHI development, it moved, in 1900, to a Clare Market site donated by the LONDON COUNTY COUNCIL and remained there throughout the twentieth century, building new premises and converting neighbouring properties in the 1920s, 1930s, 1960s and 1970s. It has an international reputation for academic excellence and, through consultancy work and published research, has had a major impact on economic and political decision making. (See also EDUCATION.)

LONDON SCOTTISH FOOTBALL CLUB

London Scottish was formed by a group of expatriate Scots at McKay's Tavern in Water Lane, off LUDGATE Hill, in April 1878. The football in its title was the handling code and it proved to be a focus for RUGBY-playing exiles from north of the border, providing more Scottish internationals than any other club (and including several, like Mike Campbell-Lamerton and Gavin Hastings, who captained their country and the British Lions). In particular, it earned a reputation for exciting seven-a-side teams, winning the Middlesex tournament on six occasions (five of them between 1960 and 1965) and finishing as runners-up on another six. In the days before competitive leagues were introduced, its First XV regularly figured prominently in the unofficial merit tables and in 1995 it followed the trend by turning professional. However, it was unable to find the financial backing necessary to secure its existence as a top-rank club and it folded after only one season in the Premiership, returning to its earlier amateur status. Currently, it regularly fields six sides, as well as mini, colts and youth teams, in London leagues.

LONDON STOCK EXCHANGE

See STOCK EXCHANGE (LSE).

LONDON SYMPHONIES

In 1790, Johan Peter Saloman, a violinist and impresario who presented regular concerts at rooms in Hanover Square, commissioned six symphonies and twenty other pieces from Austrian composer Joseph Haydn. Haydn arrived in London to begin work in 1791 and was so impressed (both by his reception and by the musical atmosphere) that he remained until June of the following year then returned for a second visit in 1794. During his stays, he wrote twelve symphonies (Nos 93–104), which are considered by many scholars to be the greatest of his works (particularly Symphony No. 102 in B-flat Major) and are collectively known as the London Symphonies.

LONDON SYMPHONY ORCHESTRA (LSO)

The LSO is the capital's oldest orchestra, formed when the Queen's Hall Orchestra disbanded (amidst considerable friction) in 1904. It has toured widely, worked with most major twentieth-century conductors (including Hans Richter and Edward Elgar) and made many recordings, becoming resident, in 1981, at the Barbican Centre, where it plays about eighty concerts every year. Administration is in the hands of a Board of Management, which has thirteen members, nine of whom play with the orchestra.

LONDON TEA AUCTIONS

Tea, imported from India and the Far East, was first auctioned in London during 1679. The sales became an accepted method of setting a fair price for a commodity that varied greatly in quantity but, during the twentieth century, were increasingly replaced by deals conducted over the telephone and by e-mail. The last auction was held at the Chamber of Commerce in Queen Victoria Street on 29 June 1998. Since then, major purchasing companies (such as Tetley and Unilever) have worked through brokers, who pass orders directly to consumers.

LONDON TELECOM TOWER

See BRITISH TELECOM TOWER.

LONDON TRANSPORT (LT)

Public TRANSPORT provision in London suffered from considerable managerial instability throughout the twentieth century. In 1929, faced with competition from independent operators, the managers of the city TRAMS (run by the LONDON COUNTY COUNCIL), the LONDON UNDERGROUND and the London General Omnibus Company announced that they intended to co-ordinate their services. Implementation of the plan was prevented by critics who interpreted the proposals as a scheme by Lord Ashfield, chairman of the UNDERGROUND, to enhance his personal power but, on 1 July 1933, Prime Minister Ramsay MacDonald's national government formed a London Passenger Transport Board (LPTB), taking all BUSES, trams, trolleybuses and Underground trains into public ownership in order to facilitate integration of provision. That body, like its successors, became known as 'London Transport' in popular speech. Following the outbreak of the Second World War in 1939, the government assumed control of the LPTB for strategic reasons and remained in charge until the board was replaced by the London Transport Executive (LTE) on 1 January 1948. The Transport Act of 1969 denationalized the city's transport, handing responsibility for financial control and overall policy to the GREATER LONDON COUNCIL (GLC) but leaving the LTE in charge of day-to-day management.

In 1984, however, the service was nationalized for a second time, London Regional Transport (LRT) was created as a statutory corporation answerable to the Secretary of State for Transport and a Board consisting of three full-time members, supported by part-time members with business expertise, was appointed to oversee provision. LRT organized its activities by establishing a series of wholly owned subsidiaries. Two of these (London Underground Ltd and VICTORIA Coach Station Ltd) have been retained, but London Transport Advertising and London Buses Ltd were sold to the private sector in 1994 and 1995 respectively. Also, DOCKLANDS LIGHT RAILWAY was transferred (at the government's insistence) to the London DOCKLANDS Development Corporation in 1992 and London Transport International (a consultancy company) ceased trading the same year.

The scale of London Transport's operation is enormous. Every working day, the system copes with an influx of about a million people from the suburbs between 7 a.m. and 10 a.m. and a similar exodus between 4 p.m. and 7 p.m. A workforce of over 18,000 enables 470 Underground trains to serve 267 stations located along 254 miles of rail and 5,000 buses to operate on 700 routes. Capital expenditure exceeds £1.1 billion each year. In July 2000, London Transport was renamed Transport for London. (See also DRAIN, THE; EAST LONDON LINE; JUBILEE LINE; LONDON REGIONAL PASSENGERS' COMMITTEE (LRPC); LONDON TRANSPORT MUSEUM; MORRISON, HERBERT STANLEY.)

LONDON TRANSPORT EXECUTIVE (LTE)

See LONDON TRANSPORT (LT).

LONDON TRANSPORT MUSEUM

In the years between the two world wars, the London General Omnibus Company built up a small collection of its vehicles. Following the establishment of the LONDON TRANSPORT EXECUTIVE in 1948, the MUSEUM for British Transport was opened at a disused bus garage in CLAPHAM, using that collection as a nucleus but incorporating additional paintings and models. From 1973, it was based at SYON HOUSE, where it was known as the LONDON TRANSPORT Collection. Then, in 1980, it moved to a converted flower market building at COVENT GARDEN and, renamed the London Transport Museum, concentrated on 150 years of public transport in the capital. The displays include a reconstruction of the first city omnibus, operated by George Shillibeer in 1829, and a knifeboard horse BUS, on which passengers on the roof sat back to back. In addition, there are several early steam locomotives and features showing the early days of the LONDON UNDERGROUND. (See also PICK, FRANK; TRANSPORT.)

LONDON UNDERGROUND

Initially, UNDERGROUND railways were a means of reducing road congestion and of allowing businesspeople easy access to suburban homes. The first, operated by the Metropolitan RAILWAY, opened on 10 January 1863 and ran for just under 4 miles from PADDINGTON to the CITY OF LONDON. It was successful from the start, encouraging a flurry of proposals for similar developments, including an Inner CIRCLE LINE (completed in 1884) and extensions to settlements at the urban fringe. Using a refinement of the system introduced by Marc Brunel earlier in the century, James Greathead constructed the world's first underground electric TUBE railway from King William Street (near the BANK OF ENGLAND) to STOCKWELL (south of the RIVER THAMES) in 1890. A connection between WATERLOO and THE CITY (see WATERLOO AND CITY LINE) opened eight years later and the 'twopenny tube' (which got its nickname from the flat 2d fare) followed in 1900. During the first decade of the twentieth century, much of the finance for new lines came from CHARLES TYSON YERKES, an American who funded the BAKER STREET and WATERLOO (quickly abbreviated to 'Bakerloo') Railway and the Great Northern, PICCADILLY and BROMPTON Railway, both of which introduced services in 1906. His CHARING CROSS, EUSTON and HAMPSTEAD Railway followed in 1907.

After the First World War ended in 1918, there was a further phase of activity that, by 1932, had extended the system as far afield as Watford (20 miles north-west of central London) and MORDEN (10 miles south). In 1933, the lines were nationalized and one body, formally known as the London Passenger Transport Board but always referred to as LONDON TRANSPORT, was created to provide a planning authority that could develop the underground railways as a single unit. The outbreak of the Second World War in 1939 put a temporary stop to developments (many stations were used as shelters during the BLITZ), but work very quickly resumed after the conflict, bringing extensions to the CENTRAL LINE by the end of the 1940s. In 1962, construction began on the VICTORIA LINE – the first new tube line in the inner city for fifty years – which opened in stages from 1969 until 1971. In 1977, the PICCADILLY LINE reached Heathrow AIRPORT and, in 1979, a new JUBILEE LINE (named to celebrate Elizabeth II's Silver Jubilee in 1977) linked BOND STREET to CHARING CROSS. An extension through the DOCKLANDS to STRATFORD, in the EAST END, was completed in 2000.

Technological innovation also brought changes to the rolling stock and increased comfort for passengers. The early steam trains had equipment that converted spent steam into water but, even so, were unsuitable for the deep tube lines. Greathead's electric system, therefore, greatly enhanced potential for development, though the steam engines remained in service until 9 September 1961. In 1936, technical improvements to the carriages allowed motors to be housed under the floor of compartments, adding significantly to seating capacity. Air doors replaced metal mesh gates at about the same time, making travel less hazardous, but the major improvements in safety over the past fifty years have followed harrowing accidents. On 28 February 1975, a train crashed into a wall at the end of MOORGATE Station, killing thirty-five people and injuring seventy-four; speed controls and other preventive measures were introduced soon afterwards. Also, in the aftermath of a blaze that killed thirty-one commuters and rescue workers at KING'S CROSS STATION in 1987, a major investment was made in improvements to escalators and refuse disposal arrangements (see KING'S CROSS FIRE). The Underground now operates daily services as far afield as Amersham, 27 miles north-west of the city centre. It maintains 267 stations, 254 miles of track and 470 trains that carry 2.5 million passengers every weekday. Oxford Circus (see OXFORD STREET) and VICTORIA are the busiest stations, with some 86 million travellers a year.

By the end of the century, lack of investment had resulted in considerable deterioration of the system, which used elderly carriages and needed much maintenance so, shortly after its election in 1997, the Labour government announced plans for partial privatization, with commercial interests taking responsibility for track and signalling within three years, but internal disagreements over funding led to postponements. Robert Kiley, who had redesigned the New York subway, was appointed commissioner of the newly established Transport for London body in 2000, and the following year the government agreed to invest £4 billion in the network.

In addition to operating a railway, London Underground (despite consistently difficult financial circumstances) has been a significant supporter of the arts. Its headquarters in Broadway, built in 1927–9 over ST JAMES'S PARK station, was designed by Charles Holden, who incorporated sculptures by the then controversial Jacob Epstein, Eric Gill and Henry Moore in the façade. Even earlier, in 1908, FRANK PICK had started to commission advertising posters by Graham Sutherland and other artists – a policy that London Transport still pursues. Also, since 1986, passenger compartments have featured short poems among the sales literature on the walls. The idea was the brainchild of American novelist Judith Chernaik, who wanted to take poetry to the captive audience of commuters, and has been a considerable success. (See also ARSENAL FOOTBALL CLUB; BAKERLOO LINE; BOW; BRIXTON; BUSES; CANARY WHARF; CANNING TOWN; CHELSEA FOOTBALL CLUB; CHURCHILL, WINSTON SPENCER; DISTRICT LINE; DOCKLANDS LIGHT RAILWAY (DLR); EAST LONDON LINE; EDGWARE; ELECTRICITY; FINSBURY PARK; FLOOD CONTROL; GOLDERS GREEN; HAMMERSMITH AND CITY LINE; HOUNSLOW; MERTON; MERTON, LONDON BOROUGH OF; METROPOLITAN LINE; MILL HILL; MORRISON, HERBERT STANLEY; NEWHAM, LONDON BOROUGH OF; NORTHERN LINE; OLD KENT ROAD; PICCADILLY CIRCUS; ROTHERHITHE; ROYAL COMMISSION ON LONDON TRAFFIC (1903-05); SOUTHGATE; SOUTHWARK, LONDON BOROUGH OF; SWISS COTTAGE.)

LONDON WALL

Towards the end of the second century, the Romans built a wall to protect LONDINIUM. Some 2 miles long and enclosing an area of about 330 acres, it was composed of ragstone, which had to be imported from Kent because the clays on which the settlement was located were wholly unsuitable for large-scale construction work. Entry points were provided at ALDERSGATE, ALDGATE, BISHOP'S GATE, CRIPPLEGATE, LUDGATE and NEWGATE. The structure (now known as London Wall) served as the boundary of London's urban area until the sixteenth century but was increasingly breached as the settlement spread outwards, particularly during the late eighteenth and the nineteenth centuries (in several places, it was incorporated into the foundations of the new buildings). Parts can still be seen (for example, in the small garden at the MUSEUM OF LONDON and at TOWER HILL). (See also DANCE, GEORGE (1741-1825).)

The London Wall can clearly be seen in this 1543 panorama by Wyngaerde.

LONDON WASPS RUGBY FOOTBALL CLUB

The Wasps Rugby Union club was formed in 1867 by a group of men, most of them medical students, who were regulars at the Eton and Middlesex PUBLIC HOUSE in Finchley Road (the title they chose for their club reflected the nineteenth-century fashion for naming sporting groups after birds, animals, insects and other wildlife). In 1871, when the Rugby Football Union was established, they were invited to become founding members but the team's representatives turned up at the wrong place on the wrong date and had to be admitted later.

In its early days, the side played at various locations in north London, but in 1925 it settled at the Sudbury pitch that was to be its home for the next seven decades. As there was no league structure, all games were friendlies and, although the team developed a good reputation and met with some success (it went through the 1930/31 season unbeaten, for example), it was not until after the Second World War that it became a national force, producing a series of England players (including Ted Woodward and Richard Sharp) from the late 1940s until the 1960s. The 1970s brought a downturn in fortunes until 1979, when Mark Taylor (capped ten times for New Zealand) and Roger Uttley (who won twenty-three England caps and later became the national coach) joined the club and reinvigorated the first team. Over the next ten years, seventeen players were selected to represent England and, in 1989, the national under-21 XV, the B XV and the full England XV were all captained by men from Wasps.

The introduction of a league system in 1988 and the development of professional Rugby Union from 1996 saw the club develop into one of the strongest in the country, winning the Middlesex Seven-a-Side Tournament in 1993, the League Championship in 1997, and the Tetley's Bitter Cup in 1999 and 2000. In 1997, the business was bought by Chris Wright, owner of QUEENS PARK RANGERS FOOTBALL CLUB. Wright laid a new pitch, suitable for both football codes, at QPR's Loftus Road ground and, in

2000, the Sudbury site was sold to a housing development company for £8 million. Shortly afterwards, however, FULHAM FOOTBALL CLUB reached an agreement to share QPR's pitch while its Craven Cottage stadium was being redeveloped and, in 2002, amidst vociferous opposition from local residents (who feared traffic chaos and a reduction in property values), Wasps negotiated a two-year move to Adams PARK, home of Wycombe Wanderers, another Football League side.

LONDON WELSH RUGBY FOOTBALL CLUB

The club was formed in 1885 to provide sporting and social facilities for Welsh exiles in London and developed a strong fixture list with leading English and Welsh sides. In the 1960s and 1970s (prior to the introduction of a league structure in 1988), when all games were friendlies and titles were decided on the basis of unofficial merit tables, Welsh won the English championship six times (1967, 1968, 1969, 1971, 1978 and 1979). They also took the Middlesex Seven-a-Side trophy five times (1968, 1971, 1972, 1973 and 1984). The First XV holds the record for the longest unbeaten run in the national leagues – twenty-five games from December 1993 until January 1995 – and in the 1994/95 season it scored a club record of 1,035 points but it has been less successful since the introduction of professional Rugby Union in 1996. London Welsh play at Old Deer PARK in RICHMOND.

LONDON WETLANDS CENTRE

The construction of a ring main to improve WATER SUPPLY to London homes and businesses during the 1980s and 1990s made a number of surface reservoirs redundant. At a 130-acre site close to BARNES and directly under the final approach to Heathrow AIRPORT from the west, Thames Water (which is responsible for water distribution in the city) agreed to allow the Wildfowl and Wetlands Trust to develop a nature reserve, with much of the construction work funded by Berkeley Homes in return for permission to build a series of luxury flats on some of the land. The centre, which opened in 2000, features captive wetland birds from around the world, breeding them as part of its conservation effort, but it also attracts tens of thousands of wild species including rarities such as the bittern. Many of the 150,000 annual visitors are children, who learn from such old-fashioned educational activities as pond dipping as well as from high-tech touch-screen computers.

LONDON ZOO

In 1828, the Zoological Society of London (founded three years earlier) opened its collection of animals to the public in gardens laid out by Decimus Burton at the northern end of REGENT'S PARK. The royal menagerie (previously housed at Windsor Castle) augmented the exhibits in 1830 and additional beasts were brought from the TOWER OF LONDON in 1832–4. The first chimpanzee, displayed in 1835, was an immediate sensation, as were the four giraffes that arrived the following year (these created a fashion for ladies' clothes with patterns resembling those on their skins). The world's first reptile house was opened in 1843, the first aquarium in 1853 and the first insect houses in 1881. As the number of animals increased, the zoo was redesigned and refurbished, with eminent architects preparing many of the plans for new buildings, such as the Mappin Terraces for bears and goats (designed by John Belcher and J.J. Joass, erected in 1913, and representing an important step away from cages to more natural settings for animals), the aviary (constructed under Lord Snowdon's supervision in 1963–4) and the elephant house (brainchild of Hugh Casson and opened in 1965). In the early 1990s, changing social attitudes, declining attendances and the elimination of government support threatened the institution's existence, but changes in management, coupled with large donations, ensured its survival. Much effort is now concentrated on conservation of threatened species and on education. A children's zoo opened in 1995, for example, and four years later a new building with sixty-five live animal exhibits, designed to tell visitors about the Web of Life, was added.

LORD MAYOR

The Lord Mayor is the leader of the CORPORATION OF LONDON, the local authority for the CITY OF LONDON. Records first mention a Mayor of London (Henry FitzAilwyn) in 1189, but it was not until 1215 that King John gave THE CITY a charter permitting it to elect an official of its own choice. The title 'Lord Mayor' began to be used during the sixteenth century but was never formally granted. Over 700 men and a single woman have held the post, which confers certain rights as well as a number of duties. Within the city, the holder ranks second in status only to the monarch (and therefore ahead even of the heir to the throne). The position brings membership of the Privy Council, granting the holder the right to be styled 'Right Honourable' and theoretical access to the sovereign. The Lord Mayor is elected annually from, and by, a Court of ALDERMEN, not by the city's residents, and must have previously served as a SHERIFF. The election is held on Michaelmas Day (29 September), when members of the LIVERY COMPANIES nominate two individuals for the post, one of whom will normally be the most senior alderman who has not held the position. It is that person who is usually appointed by the Court of Aldermen, but the decision requires the monarch's approval. The Lord Mayor now has no political power.

On the Friday preceding the second Saturday in November, the new Lord Mayor is admitted to office at a ceremony known as the Silent Change because the trappings of authority, including a sword and a mace, are handed from the retiring Lord Mayor to his successor without a word being exchanged by the principals or any of the attendants. The following day, he drives to the ROYAL COURTS OF JUSTICE to take the oath of office. Formerly, the procession (known as the Lord Mayor's Show) allowed citizens to present addresses along the route, but, from the sixteenth century, pageants became popular elements of the event and now participants decorate lorries according to a theme chosen by the incoming Lord Mayor (topics such as natural resources, transport and education have been featured in recent years).

Two days after being sworn in, the Lord Mayor hosts a banquet at the GUILDHALL, the Corporation of London's headquarters, in honour of his predecessor. The event has been held annually, except during wartime, for more than 400 years and is attended by senior politicians, representatives of the member countries of the Commonwealth of Nations, religious leaders and the heads of major commercial concerns. Traditionally, the Prime Minister makes a major speech surveying the United Kingdom's role in international affairs. For the next twelve months, the Lord Mayor officially resides at the MANSION HOUSE and undertakes numerous ceremonial engagements. He also acts as the Corporation's chief magistrate, chairing meetings of the Court of Aldermen and the COURT OF COMMON COUNCIL. In addition, he holds several *ex officio* appointments, such as the Chancellorship of City University, which have their own obligations. Although the Lord Mayor is paid by the Corporation of London for performing his or her duties, holders of the office meet many of their own expenses. By implication, only the affluent can aspire to the position. (See also CITY MARSHAL; COMMON CRYER AND SERJEANT-AT-ARMS; COMMON SERJEANT; ESQUIRES, THE; PEASANTS' REVOLT; RECORDER OF LONDON; SWORDBEARER; TEMPLE BAR; WARD; WHITTINGTON, RICHARD 'DICK'.)

LORD MAYOR'S BANQUET

See LORD MAYOR.

LORD MAYOR'S SHOW

See LORD MAYOR.

LORD'S CRICKET GROUND

In 1752, a group of wealthy individuals who regularly played cricket at White Conduit Fields in ISLINGTON formed the White Conduit Club. Some years later, feeling that public playing fields were beneath their dignity, they asked Thomas Lord, one of their employees, to find a place where they could enjoy their sport in private, so, in 1787, Lord took a lease on the piece of land now occupied by Dorset Square (to the south-west of REGENT'S PARK near Marylebone Road). Shortly afterwards, some of the club members reconstituted themselves as the MARYLEBONE CRICKET CLUB (they played their first match against a White Conduit team the following year, winning by eighty-three runs). In 1811, facing a rent increase, Lord moved his turf to a site at Marylebone Bank then, five years later (just before the REGENT'S CANAL was driven through the area), picked it up again and relaid it at its present location in ST JOHN'S WOOD Road.

Its association with the MCC led to the ground being recognized as the home of cricket and the most famous cricket ground in the world. A MUSEUM of cricket was established in 1865, the club acquired the freehold of Lord's ground in 1866, a new grandstand was erected the following year, and the Tavern was rebuilt the year after that. Middlesex County Cricket Club, founded in 1864, made the ground its home base in 1877. During the twentieth century, major reconstruction work turned the ground into a modern stadium, which became a regular venue for Test matches against other countries. See MARYLEBONE CRICKET CLUB (MCC).

LUDGATE

According to legend, King Lud built an entry to the western edge of London in 66 BC. Archaeological evidence suggests, however, that the original structure was erected by the Romans to allow passage through LONDON WALL to a BURIAL GROUND located near the present site of FLEET STREET. The gate was rebuilt in 1215 and 1586 but demolished in 1760.

LUTINE BELL

Traditionally, the Lutine Bell was rung at LLOYD'S OF LONDON to signal important announcements for insurance underwriters and brokers. It was originally carried by *La Lutine,* a French frigate that surrendered to Britain in 1793, became part of the Royal Navy, but was sunk off the coast of Holland in 1799, with a cargo of gold and silver bullion. Lloyd's met claims of £1 million as a result of the loss. Several salvage attempts were made, one (in 1858) recovering the ship's bell, which was hung in the underwriting room at the ROYAL EXCHANGE and sounded whenever news of overdue ships was received. Normally, when vessels were late, underwriters attempted to limit their potential loss by asking brokers to reinsure some of their liability. When reliable information was received, the bell was rung once if the news was bad (as when a ship had gone down), twice if it was good (if there had been a positive sighting, for example). The chimes eliminated the possibility of unprincipled trading by ensuring that everybody got the details at the same time. Modern communications have rendered the Lutine Bell redundant, however. Last rung to announce a lost ship in 1979 and a safe arrival in 1981, it is now used only on ceremonial occasions.

LUTON AIRPORT

See AIRPORTS.

M

M25 MOTORWAY

Proposals for an orbital route around London were voiced early in the twentieth century by W. Rees Jeffreys, who suggested to the ROYAL COMMISSION ON LONDON TRAFFIC (1903-5) that a 'boulevard' should be built, encircling the city. However, nothing was done until 1969, when the GREATER LONDON COUNCIL announced plans for alleviating traffic congestion in the metropolitan area (see GREATER LONDON DEVELOPMENT PLAN (1969)). A 118-mile ring road – now known as the M25 motorway – was an integral element of the scheme but there were many objections (a total of thirty-nine public enquiries was held) so construction was delayed for several years. The first section (the 2.7 miles from junctions 23 to 24) was completed in 1975 and the last (the 3.8 miles from junctions 22 to 23) eleven years later. The total cost was £909 million (or about £7.7 million for every mile).

The motorway – the longest urban ring road in the world – has twenty-nine junctions and connects with nine other motorways along its route; 57 miles lie to the south of the RIVER THAMES and 61 miles to the north. At the eastern extremity, the crossing of the Thames at the Dartford Tunnels and the Queen Elizabeth II Bridge is classified as an A road so that learner drivers and other road users banned from the motorways can have access between Kent and Essex.

The M25 has been congested ever since it was opened, with usage exceeding forecasts within weeks of its completion. In part, that is a result of the large number of junctions, which encourages local traffic to use the facility for only a few miles, but the lack of alternative routes also channels vehicles on to the motorway. The inevitable consequence has been additional expenditure on road widening schemes, equipment that allows different speed limits in different lanes and other efforts to improve traffic flow. For many people, the M25 forms the boundary of the Greater London area.

MADAME TUSSAUD'S WAXWORKS

As a child, Marie Groszholtz, born in Strasbourg (France) in 1761, learned the art of making wax figures from her uncle, Dr Philippe Curtius. In 1780, she was appointed art tutor to Élisabeth (sister of Louis XVI). Because of her position she was considered an enemy of the people during the French Revolution and required to make death masks of prominent individuals who died on the guillotine, including Louis and his queen, Marie Antoinette (both of whom were killed in 1793). She inherited her uncle's collection of figures in 1794 then, the following year, married engineer François Tussaud, but the relationship foundered and, in 1802, as conditions in France worsened, she moved to

Britain, taking an exhibition of her work around major cities before settling at a permanent site in BAKER STREET in 1835.

In 1884 (by which time there were 400 figures on display), her grandsons moved the galleries to their present site around the corner in Marylebone Road. Much of the material was damaged by fire in 1925 and by bombs during the BLITZ, but the casts from which the models were made survived. The oldest figure on display (known as the Sleeping Beauty) is that of Madame du Barry (mistress of Louis XV of France), which was modelled in 1765. Others, often now displayed as tableaux, include Maximilien Robespierre (architect of France's Reign of Terror in 1793–4), George III, Lord Byron, Benjamin Franklin and WINSTON CHURCHILL. Some are permanently on view to the public; others (such as entertainers) appear and disappear as fashions change. Most subjects, who are usually modelled from life, supply clothes for their figure.

In 1958, a planetarium was added to the business, built on the site of the Madame Tussaud's cinema, which had been destroyed by a bomb in 1940. Initially, the displays of star systems were accompanied by live commentaries but most are now automated in order to accommodate a range of special effects, including a virtual reality, three-dimensional journey through the cosmos. A gallery depicting the history of astronomy was opened in 1980. The complex is one of the most popular tourist attractions in London, Madame Tussaud's alone admitting over 2.7 million visitors annually. In 1998, it was acquired by Charterhouse Development from Pearson, the media group, for a reported cost of £377 million, a price that included the World of Adventures theme PARK at CHESSINGTON. The Alton Towers theme park in Staffordshire is part of the same commercial empire.

MAIDA VALE

In 1806, British troops, led by General Sir John Stuart, defeated a French force at Maida, in southern Italy. Not long afterwards, a PUBLIC HOUSE named Hero of Maida opened in north-west London near the GRAND UNION CANAL. As more and more homes were erected during the 1840s and 1850s, the area became known as Maida Hill and then as Maida Vale. By the 1860s, brick buildings were more common than the stucco mansions constructed twenty years earlier, and by the 1880s apartments had superseded individual homes. The area is still largely residential, though many of the older houses have been subdivided and local authority housing has replaced many of the poorer structures in the east of the area, as at the Mozart Estate, erected in 1975. The suburb forms part of the CITY OF WESTMINSTER.

MALL, THE

The Mall forms a processional route from ADMIRALTY ARCH to BUCKINGHAM PALACE. Just under ¾ mile long, it was originally laid out as part of a scheme of improvements to ST JAMES'S PARK shortly after Charles II was restored to the throne in 1660, replacing PALL MALL as the major location for the game from which that thoroughfare took its name and becoming, until late in the seventeenth century, a fashionable place for wealthy Londoners to promenade. In 1903–4, the line of the road was moved a few yards to the south as part of plans, prepared by Aston Webb, for a national tribute to Queen Victoria. The street was built 65 feet wide, with walkways, 25 feet broad, on either side. LONDON PLANE trees and decorated lamp-posts lined the route. The QUEEN VICTORIA MEMORIAL lies at the western end, statutes dedicated to the Royal Marines and to Captain James Cook in the east and a memorial to men of the Royal Artillery who died during the Boer War of 1899–1902 in the south-east. (See also CHAMBERS, WILLIAM; LONDON MARATHON.)

MANOR PARK

A residential suburb lying 8 miles north-east of CHARING CROSS, Manor Park is built on land formerly owned by the Hamfrith estate. The property was purchased by the East Counties RAILWAY in 1838 and rented to William Fry, son of prison reformer Elizabeth Fry. Then, in 1866, the manor house was sold to Henry (later Cardinal) Manning for conversion to a school and, from 1872, the construction of a railway station hastened the transformation from a rural to an urban environment. From the 1890s, the land to the south and east (formerly known as Little ILFORD) was sold to a developer and, gradually, the Manor Park name was applied to the whole area, of which some 175 acres are utilized by the CITY OF LONDON Cemetery, one of the largest public BURIAL GROUNDS in Europe. Designed by William Haywood and opened in 1856, the cemetery includes the graves of many former city residents who were originally interred in their local churchyards but whose remains were moved when improvements were made to the urban fabric in the second half of the nineteenth century. The graves at the site include those of Catherine Eddowes and Mary Ann Nicholls (both of whom were victims of JACK THE RIPPER) and former England football captain Bobby Moore. Manor Park was included in the LONDON BOROUGH OF NEWHAM when metropolitan local government was reorganized in 1965.

MANSION HOUSE

The official residence of the LORD MAYOR of the CITY OF LONDON was built in 1739–52 to designs by GEORGE DANCE THE ELDER. Standing opposite the BANK OF ENGLAND on a site where criminals were once clamped in the stocks, it is constructed of PORTLAND STONE in the Palladian style, with a portico of six Corinthian pilasters topped by a richly sculptured pediment. The banqueting room (known as the Egyptian Hall because it was based on a description of the home of the pharaohs published by the Roman architect Marcus Vitruvius Pollio during the first century BC) has columns on all sides, with an ambulatory separating them from the walls. Originally, a clerestory allowed light to enter from above, but it was removed in 1794–5. The apartments on the second floor include a ballroom, originally known as the Dancing Gallery. Furnishings are opulent, with ornamental wood and plaster work, a large collection of statuary depicting British historical figures and characters from English literature, paintings of London scenes, displays of gold and silver plate and the Lord Mayor's insignia of office (which include a sceptre of crystal mounted in gold and a chain of gold, onyx and diamonds). Since it was constructed, the building (which also functions as a court house) has been much altered, detracting somewhat from the sense of space generated by the original design. (See also CIRCLE LINE; DISTRICT LINE.)

MARBLE ARCH

The Arch stands on an island at the intersection of Bayswater Road, Edgware Road, OXFORD STREET and PARK LANE. Designed by JOHN NASH, it is built of marble and, like the Arch of Constantine in Rome, has three archways flanked by Corinthian columns. The reliefs on the north side are by Richard Westmacott and those on the south by Edward Baily; a statue of George IV should have crowned the parapet but was located at TRAFALGAR SQUARE instead. In 1828, the structure was erected as a gateway to BUCKINGHAM PALACE but it proved too narrow for the state coach and so was moved, in 1851, to its present position, where it sits in the middle of one of the busiest traffic junctions in the city.

MARBLE HILL HOUSE

Regarded as a classic example of an eighteenth-century English country house, Marble Hill (near TWICKENHAM) was designed by Lord Henry Herbert for Henrietta Howard (Countess of Suffolk and mistress of the Prince of Wales, who later succeeded to the throne as George II). Erected under the supervision of Roger Morris in 1724–9, it is built in Palladian style and set in PARKland (laid out by Charles Bridgman) that stretches down to the RIVER THAMES. From 1734, the Countess used the mansion to entertain her friends (who included poet and dramatist John Gay, Alexander Pope and Horace Walpole), but, following her death in 1767, it passed through a variety of hands, becoming increasingly dilapidated until it was bought by the LONDON COUNTY COUNCIL in 1902. After the Second World War, it was restored by the GREATER LONDON COUNCIL and, in 1966, opened to the public as a MUSEUM of eighteenth-century furnishings and paintings.

MARKETS

London's status as England's pre-eminent trading centre, coupled with its relatively large population, led to the growth of urban markets during the medieval period. CHEAPSIDE was the principal location, leaving a legacy of modern street names (such as Honey Lane and Bread Street), which bear testimony to the goods sold there. Livestock became increasingly concentrated at Smithfield (see SMITHFIELD MEAT MARKET), fish at BILLINGSGATE FISH MARKET, meat at EASTCHEAP and butter, cheese and poultry at LEADENHALL MARKET. As demand increased, the quality of produce grew and the range expanded. New markets, such as COVENT GARDEN, were established to meet needs and, from the 1830s, the spreading RAILWAY network allowed goods to be brought from throughout Great Britain and Europe. However, by the second half of the twentieth century, escalating rents, the problems of operating in cramped facilities and competing demands for inner-city space forced most of the big sites to move to more suburban locations (thus Covent Garden's vegetable market was relocated at NINE ELMS in 1964 and Billingsgate on the ISLE OF DOGS in 1982). Vacated premises were redeveloped as office and retail accommodation. (See also BOROUGH MARKET; BRENTFORD; BURNT OAK; CHARING CROSS; CORN EXCHANGE; CORNHILL; COURT OF COMMON COUNCIL; DALSTON; FAIRS; HAYMARKET; HUNGERFORD BRIDGE; LONDON TRANSPORT MUSEUM; METROPOLITAN CATTLE MARKET; PECKHAM: PETTICOAT LANE; PINNER; PORTOBELLO ROAD MARKET; RAG FAIR; ROYAL NAVAL DOCKYARDS; SHADWELL; SHEPHERD'S BUSH; SPITALFIELDS; STRATFORD; STREATHAM; STREET MARKETS; THEATRE MUSEUM; WHITECHAPEL.)

MARLBOROUGH HOUSE

The house, immediately east of ST JAMES'S PALACE, was designed by CHRISTOPHER WREN and built in 1709–11 for Sarah, Duchess of Marlborough, who had obtained a lease on the land from her friend, Queen Anne. Although Sarah died in 1744, the building remained in the hands of the family until 1817, when it reverted to the Crown. For over a century, until the death of Queen Mary in 1953, it was used as a residence for members of the royal family but in 1959 it was presented to the government for conversion into a Commonwealth of Nations conference centre.

MARSHALSEA PRISON

In the sixteenth century, Marshalsea PRISON in SOUTHWARK was one of London's most important jails. Its name is derived from the court convened by the Steward and Marshal of the King's Household, but the date of its foundation is unknown (though it was certainly built by 1381, when it was stormed during the PEASANTS' REVOLT). By the eighteenth century, the condition both of the structure and of the inmates, most of whom were debtors, was causing serious concern and in 1842 it was closed. In *Little Dorrit* (1857), CHARLES DICKENS (whose father was incarcerated in the cells in 1824) describes the place as 'an oblong pile of barrack building, partitioned into squalid houses standing back to back, so that there were no back rooms; environed by a narrow paved yard, hemmed in by high walls spiked at the top.'

MARYLEBONE

See ST MARYLEBONE.

MARYLEBONE CRICKET CLUB (MCC)

Marylebone Cricket Club was formed shortly after Thomas Lord leased a piece of land for a cricket pitch south-west of REGENT'S PARK in 1787 (see LORD'S CRICKET GROUND). Partly because its membership consisted largely of affluent and distinguished gentlemen, the MCC gradually became recognized as the ultimate authority on the rules of cricket and thus as the international headquarters of the sport. The MCC is now run by a committee headed by a president (currently Charles Fry, who took over from Sir Tim Rice in October 2003), who is appointed by his predecessor and holds the post for an indefinite period. Past presidents have included the Duke of Edinburgh and former prime minister Sir Alec Douglas-Home. The current president is Sir Tim Rice. In 1999, after a lengthy campaign, women were admitted as members. The current waiting time for membership is eighteen years.

MAYFAIR

Recognized for its affluence and gracious living, Mayfair is bounded by OXFORD STREET (to the north), PARK LANE (to the west), PICCADILLY (to the south) and REGENT STREET (to the east). It lies within the CITY OF WESTMINSTER and gets its name from a fair held near HYDE PARK CORNER from 1686 until 1735. From the 1660s until the 1770s, the area developed as an aristocratic suburb close to the royal court at ST JAMES'S PALACE, moving the heartland of affluent London west from COVENT GARDEN and SOHO in the process. Most of the building was undertaken by great landholders (particularly the GROSVENOR ESTATE) whose names are remembered in the roads that cut through their property – the widowed Lady Berkeley of Stratton in BERKELEY SQUARE, Sir Nathaniel Curzon in Curzon Street, Lord Grosvenor in GROSVENOR SQUARE and Lord Burlington in Burlington Gardens, for example. Wealthy residents attracted services, leading to the growth of exclusive retail facilities such as jewellery in BOND STREET and tailoring in SAVILE ROW, so commercial premises have always been present. During the twentieth century, however, these infiltrated further as families found large homes increasingly difficult to maintain, particularly as they could no longer afford servants. Many people moved out, leaving their successors to turn houses into small HOTELS, night clubs, restaurants, offices, banks and other activities that wanted the social cachet of a Mayfair address. In addition, large international hotel groups opened premises (such as the 228-room Inn on the PARK) at the fringe of the area. As a result, few of the great houses survive in their original state (even though planners have affected the pace and nature of change by controlling the façades and heights of properties) but the aura of wealth is still clearly evident.

MAYHEW, HENRY (1812–1887)

One of several authors who drew attention to the living conditions of the city's manual workers during the second half of the nineteenth century (see, for example, CHARLES BOOTH), Mayhew is best remembered for *London Labour and the London Poor*, a series of letters and articles that originally appeared in the *Morning Chronicle*. The son of solicitor Joshua Dorset Joseph Mayhew, he was born in London and educated at WESTMINSTER School but ran away to sea rather than complete his studies. After a period in Calcutta (India), he returned to England to work with his father for three years before turning his hand to writing. In 1831, he launched (with Gilbert à Becket) a weekly journal entitled *Figaro in London*, then, in 1834, wrote his first play – *The Wandering Minstrel* – which was performed at the Royal Fitzroy Theatre. In 1841, he started the satirical magazine *Punch*, which he co-edited with Mark Lemon for two years, then, until his death in BLOOMSBURY on 25

A street seller of dog collars, a coffee stall and an oyster stall. Illustrations of Victorian London streets from an edition of Henry Mayhew's *London Labour and the London Poor*.

July 1887, published a variety of stories, biographies, dramas and songs. Mayhew's articles on London were written in a lively but sympathetic prose that demonstrated more than superficial understanding of the men and women he described. Focusing on city tradesmen and their families, he drew partly on experience and partly on anecdote in an attempt to conform with the *Chronicle*'s policy of covering the important social issues of the day. The writings were collected in three volumes published in 1851, with a fourth (written with John Binny and concentrating on the prison system) added in 1862. A single revised volume appeared in 1864.

MAYOR

See LORD MAYOR; MAYOR OF LONDON.

MAYOR OF LONDON

The post of Mayor of London was created by the GREATER LONDON AUTHORITY ACT in 1999. That legislation made provision for the election of a Mayor who would head the GREATER LONDON AUTHORITY, assuming an executive role and developing strategies for the city's cultural, economic and social development. The responsibilities include control of environmental issues, fire and EMERGENCY SERVICES, healthcare, police, TRANSPORT, and urban regeneration and also the marketing of London's strengths as a cultural and financial capital. As part of the task, the Mayor appoints the boards of the London Development Agency (whose aim is to improve the city as a focus for business) and TRANSPORT FOR LONDON (which provides bus, river and rail services). He or she also sets the annual spending limits of the Greater London Authority, the London Development Agency, the LONDON FIRE BRIGADE, and Transport for London. The first Mayor – KENNETH ROBERT LIVINGSTONE – was elected on 4 May 2000 and took office on 23 July. He serves a four-year term and controls a budget of some £5 billion, more than that of many members of the United Nations. (See also LONDON ASSEMBLY.)

MEDICINE

See CHARING CROSS; CHARING CROSS HOSPITAL; CUSTOM HOUSE; GREAT ORMOND STREET HOSPITAL FOR SICK CHILDREN; GUY'S HOSPITAL; LONDON HEALTH EMERGENCY (LHE); MIDDLESEX HOSPITAL; ROYAL COLLEGE OF PHYSICIANS OF LONDON; ROYAL COLLEGE OF SURGEONS OF ENG-

LAND; ROYAL FREE HOSPITAL; ROYAL LONDON HOSPITAL; ROYAL MARSDEN HOSPITAL; ST BARTHOLOMEW'S HOSPITAL; ST GEORGE'S HOSPITAL; ST MARY'S HOSPITAL; ST THOMAS'S HOSPITAL; UNIVERSITY COLLEGE HOSPITAL; WESTMINSTER HOSPITAL; SNOW, JOHN.

MERTON

Merton lies towards the outskirts of London, some 7 miles south-east of CHARING CROSS. The land was acquired in 1114 by Gilbert the Knight, who established an Augustinian priory; there, in 1236, the English barons met to sign the Statute of Merton, which allowed Lords of the Manor to enclose common lands and is sometimes said to be the first Act of Parliament. The priory was dissolved in 1538 and the masonry carried off to build NONSUCH PALACE but the secular community survived and was later augmented by HUGUENOT immigrants, who established a calico bleaching and printing industry. In the early nineteenth century, Edmund Littler founded a textile printing business that was acquired by LIBERTY's in 1904 and printed that company's fabrics until 1974. Also, William Morris, one of the leaders of the arts and crafts movement, worked from premises he set up in Merton in 1881. The only home Lord Horatio Nelson ever owned was at Merton Place (south of the present High Street), where he lived with his mistress, Emma Hamilton, and her husband from 1801 until his death at the Battle of Trafalgar in 1805. However, most building has occurred since 1871, when horticulturalist and businessman John Innes began to lay out streets in which ARCHITECTURE and trees blended to produce a pleasing urban landscape. The arrival of the LONDON UNDERGROUND in 1926 added to the pace of development, turning the area into a residential suburb. The settlement was part of the County of Surrey until 1965, when it gave its name to the new LONDON BOROUGH OF MERTON. Its name may be derived from the Old English *mere* and *tun*, meaning 'the homestead by the pool'.

MERTON, LONDON BOROUGH OF

Merton's 15 square miles are covered largely by suburban housing. The borough was formed in 1965 through the merger of MERTON, MITCHAM, MORDEN and WIMBLEDON, all of which were previously part of the County of Surrey. The Wimbledon area is one of the most affluent parts of London, with high proportions of professional and managerial workers who use the southern terminus of LONDON UNDERGROUND's DISTRICT LINE to commute to jobs in the central city (nearly two of every three employed people living in Merton have jobs outside the borough, reflecting the limited industrial and commercial base). Elsewhere, manual and clerical workers in TRANSPORT, retailing and public service predominate, with about one in every four citizens drawn from non-white ethnic groups. The population numbered 187,900 in 2001.

METROLAND

The term Metroland was invented by METROPOLITAN RAILWAY advertising staff in 1915 as part of a campaign designed to encourage Londoners into the countryside. The company had built track to HARROW-ON-THE-HILL, Pinner, Chesham, Aylesbury and other settlements at the fringe of the city, had purchased land close to its stations, and had encouraged housing developments. Through its property guide, it presented an image of large homes surrounded by woodlands and fields but accessible to the city centre through cheap fares. The Poet Laureate John Betjeman (1906-84) caught the essence of the place in his work (with references to 'autumn-scented Middlesex' and to 'sepia views of leafy lanes in PINNER') and in a nostalgic, but very successful, documentary produced by the BBC in 1973. The name is still regularly used in advertising and is sometimes employed as a shorthand term for middle-class suburbia.

METROPOLITAN BOARD OF WORKS

By the 1850s, a number of services (such as policing and SEWAGE DISPOSAL) were administered on a London-wide basis, but many others were organized locally. More than 300 bodies (some with very vague powers) exercized authority in a wide variety of areas, including road maintenance and healthcare. ST PANCRAS alone had sixteen different committees dealing with street paving and carrying out duties required by twenty-nine Acts of Parliament. Arguments favouring centralization were frequently countered by local leaders, frightened of losing power, who claimed that the city was too diverse to be ruled by one council because people in the suburbs had little in common with those in the centre of the urban area, but the case for reform was compelling and, in 1855, the Metropolitan Board of Works was established by Parliament under the terms of a Metropolis Management Act.

The board had forty-five members, appointed by the CITY OF LONDON's COURT OF COMMON COUNCIL and by thirty-eight newly created District Boards (defined on a territorial basis) rather than by city residents. Its powers were limited (in deference to the critics) and concerned largely with civil engineering matters. The requirements that all projects costing over £50,000 should get government approval and all those over £100,000 Parliamentary approval greatly inhibited its freedom of action but the GREAT STINK from the RIVER THAMES during the summer of 1858 proved a powerful ally and the go-ahead was given for construction of a new drainage system. In less than ten years, Chief Engineer JOSEPH WILLIAM BAZALGETTE supervised the laying of 82 miles of sewer that would carry the city's effluent to outlets east of the city. Also, a major road-building programme was undertaken, involving construction of lengthy sections of the embankment along the Thames and the building of streets, including CHARING CROSS ROAD and SHAFTESBURY AVENUE. The new thoroughfares undoubtedly improved access and introduced opportunities for a variety of new businesses, but their introduction required the demolition of much inexpensive housing and thereby added to problems of overcrowding in other slum areas. As the evidence of the interrelationship between housing and poverty mounted, radical pressure groups maintained that private enterprise could not solve the problems of London's poor on its own and, by the 1880s, they had convinced the politicians of the need for a new authority with wider powers and responsibilities. As a result, in 1888 the Board of Works was superseded by the LONDON COUNTY COUNCIL. (See also LONDON FIRE BRIGADE; PLUMSTEAD.)

METROPOLITAN CATTLE MARKET

In 1855, trading in live cattle was moved from Smithfield (see SMITHFIELD MEAT MARKET) to a new location, known as the Metropolitan Cattle MARKET, in Copenhagen Fields at HOLLOWAY. Animals were bought and sold on Mondays and Thursdays, leaving the rings available for a more general market on Fridays. As animal sales declined, the other business (known as 'The Caledonian' because of its proximity to Caledonian Road) increased, with over 2,000 stalls present during the 1930s, but the Second World War brought trading to an end for good. For over twenty-five years, the site was unused, then, in 1965, it was covered by a local authority housing estate.

METROPOLITAN DRINKING FOUNTAIN AND CATTLE TROUGH ASSOCIATION

The Association was founded, in 1859, by Member of Parliament Samuel Gurney, who hoped that it would decrease the incidence of CHOLERA and drunkenness in the city. The first fountain was erected outside the Church of the Holy Sepulchre (in HOLBORN Viaduct), where it still stands. Drinking troughs for animals were built from 1867 and are still maintained by the organization.

METROPOLITAN LINE

The route of the world's first underground passenger RAILWAY, opened in 1863 and running from Farringdon (in the CITY OF LONDON) to PADDINGTON, is still followed by LONDON UNDERGROUND's Metropolitan Line services. Construction of the first track (by cut and cover methods, which involve digging trenches from the road surface rather than tunnelling) took three years and was funded by the Metropolitan Railway. Despite the smoke from the steam engines, the services (priced at a flat fare of threepence, fourpence or sixpence depending on the passenger's preferred class of travel) proved popular, with well over 9 million journeys made during the first twelve months. Commercial success led to extension of the line, initially to HAMMERSMITH (in 1864) then to MOORGATE (1865) and ALDGATE (1876). The route north-west of BAKER STREET (known as the Metropolitan Extension) was the result of co-operation between the Metropolitan (which saw the potential for exploiting the growing suburbs) and the Manchester, Sheffield and Lincolnshire Railway (which wanted to link the Midlands and the North of England to the capital). Publicizing the attractions of 'Metroland' from 1915, the Metropolitan Railway promoted urban development (and thus created its own market), as it extended its track to Chesham (1889), Aylesbury (1892), UXBRIDGE (1904), Watford (1925) and STANMORE (1932).

The company bitterly fought plans to convert the city's TRANSPORT services to public ownership, arguing that it was providing main line services, but lost the battle in 1933 (see LONDON TRANSPORT). The years since then have brought a truncation of its network: the Stanmore route was taken over by the BAKERLOO LINE in 1939, the last trains to destinations north of Amersham ran in 1961, and the track from Hammersmith to BARKING became the HAMMERSMITH AND CITY LINE in 1990. Current services run from Aldgate to Amersham and Chesham, taking just over an hour. Trains are repaired in depots at WEMBLEY PARK and NEASDEN. In 2003, maintenance of the line's infrastructure was franchised to Metronet, a consortium of private businesses, but London Underground remained responsible for providing the services. (See also EARL'S COURT; EAST LONDON LINE; KILBURN; METROLAND; RUISLIP; SWISS COTTAGE.)

METROPOLITAN POLICE

Until the early nineteenth century, nobody had sole responsibility for maintaining law and order in London. In the CITY OF LONDON, the peacekeeping process evolved over time into a geographically based system of 200 precincts, each with its own constable. In addition, every WARD had unpaid watchmen who were supposed to prevent illegal activities. WESTMINSTER adopted a similar arrangement in 1584 but, as in the City, each territorial unit guarded its individuality, so there was little co-operation across boundaries. By the eighteenth century, corruption was rife as professional thief-catchers worked for rewards and posts such as Keeper of NEWGATE PRISON were auctioned to the highest bidder, who then attempted to recoup his expenditure by whatever means was available, including extortion. Moreover, the constables could not be relied on to carry out their duties (for example, during the GORDON RIOTS of 1780 many sympathized with the rebellion and made no attempt to prevent looting or destruction of property). In 1812, 1816 and 1818, Parliamentary committees recommended change, but the public objected, fearing that reform might bring a loss of freedom; the City, in particular, mounted strong opposition because it did not want to see its police force controlled by the HOUSE OF COMMONS (see PALACE OF WESTMINSTER).

In Tudor London parish constables patrolled the streets at night and provided the only law enforcement.

In 1829, however, Home Secretary Robert Peel negotiated a compromise that allowed the CORPORATION OF LONDON to make its own arrangements but created a Metropolitan Police force to co-ordinate crime prevention and detection throughout the rest of London, with administrative headquarters at SCOTLAND YARD. Peel's name gave rise to the slang terms 'bobby' and 'peeler' for a police officer. Initially, wages were low and citizens hostile so manpower wastage was considerable but by mid-century the tide of opinion was changing and the police were becoming an accepted part of London life. A Criminal Investigation Department was formed in 1878 to co-ordinate detective work, a Special Branch in 1885 to investigate acts of terrorism and a Central Finger Print Bureau in 1901 to provide a database of criminals. During the First World War, a women's unit was formed to carry out the work of policemen serving with the armed forces; initially, it was intended to be a temporary body but, in 1919, it was absorbed within the main force. Since then, the emphasis has been on increasing specialization to meet more sophisticated forms of crime. In part, that is reflected in the multiplication of special units, such as the Bomb Squad, Flying Squad, Drug Squad and Fraud Squad. The force has also increased the number of its specialists in computers, video surveillance cameras and other high-technology equipment. However, the rising cost of crime prevention, coupled with pressure on finances, was reflected in manpower. In 2000, the Metropolitan Police had 24,600 officers (over 7,000 fewer than in 1991) and, according to its commissioner, Sir John Stevens, was facing a major recruitment crisis after a series of press reports about corruption and racism. Unlike the rest of the country, where local police forces are headed by a Chief Constable responsible to the relevant county or metropolitan council, the Met is headed by a

Commissioner responsible directly to the Home Office.

The City of London eventually reformed its policing system in 1839 but remains a separate force. It is organized on similar lines to those of the Metropolitan Police but has only about 800 officers. Because of the City's relatively small resident population, much of its work relates to fraud and to security at the large number of financial institutions in the SQUARE MILE. (See also BOW STREET RUNNERS; LONDON PLAN; RIVER POLICE; SIEGE OF SIDNEY STREET; TRAFALGAR SQUARE.)

MIDDLESEX COUNTY CRICKET CLUB

The Middlesex club was formed in 1864 (although several teams naming themselves after the county had played matches from the middle of the previous century). Since 1877, it has been based at LORD'S CRICKET GROUND, home of the MARYLEBONE CRICKET CLUB (MCC), but some First XI games are played at the Walker Ground in SOUTHGATE, in the LONDON BOROUGH OF ENFIELD, and the Second XI often uses EALING Cricket Club's facilities. Middlesex was one of the eight sides which met at Lord's on 16 December 1889 and agreed to organize a league competition for the English counties. Since then, it has won, or shared, the Championship on twelve occasions, most recently in 1990 and 1993. It has also won the Benson and Hedges Cup twice (the 4-run victory over Essex in 1983 and the 2-run victory over Kent in 1986 were among the most exciting in the history of the event). In 1999, however, the team finished sixteenth out of eighteen in the County Championship and was allocated to the Second Division of the new league structure for the 2000 season.

MIDDLESEX HOSPITAL

The Middlesex Hospital was founded in 1745 and opened the following year, providing eighteen beds that could be used by the people of SOHO. Initially known as the Middlesex Infirmary and located in Windmill Street, it assumed its present name in 1755 when (partly through the proceeds of performances by the actor DAVID GARRICK and the composer Georg Frideric Handel) it was able to expand on to an adjacent site. It added a cancer ward (funded by the brewer Samuel Whitbread) in 1791 and a medical school in 1835. In 1935, as the property increasingly fell into disrepair, the hospital closed down but a public appeal led by Lord Webb-Johnson (President of the ROYAL COLLEGE OF SURGEONS) provided money for rebuilding and the new facilities accepted patients in 1935. After the Second World War, several specialist units (such as the Bland-Sutton Institute of Pathology and the Courtauld Institute of Biochemistry) were added, often as a result of donations by individual or group benefactors. In 1982, the Middlesex united with UNIVERSITY COLLEGE HOSPITAL, a merger that resulted in the closure of some facilities, such as the casualty department. In 1994, further reorganization led to the creation of the University College London Hospitals National Health Service Trust, which plans to open a new hospital in Euston Road from 2005 and thus bring many of its sites under a single roof.

MIDDLE TEMPLE

See INNS OF COURT.

MILE END

Mile End is a largely working-class suburb lying 4 miles east of CHARING CROSS. Open land until the late Middle Ages, it was built over from the fifteenth century. The western section, close to SPITALFIELDS, developed particularly rapidly during the late 1600s and became known as Mile End New Town. During the eighteenth and nineteenth centuries, it was an important focus of small industrial and processing activities, including sugar refining, fish curing, saw milling and dyeing. To the east, Mile End Old Town became a centre for Jewish IMMIGRANTS after they were allowed into England in 1657 (the Jews' first burial ground in London was established there). Later, in the Victorian period, religious groups and individual philanthropists concentrated much of their charitable work in the area (in 1868, at Mile End Waste, WILLIAM BOOTH held some of the first meetings from which his Salvation Army developed and, two years later, THOMAS JOHN BARNARDO opened a home for orphan children near BEN JONSON Road). By the early twentieth century, Mile End was densely populated, with residents finding employment in the DOCK and other local industries, such as brewing. The bombs of the BLITZ caused much loss of life and damage to property but did allow local authorities to clear land and erect modern homes after the Second World War. The suburb was incorporated within the LONDON BOROUGH OF TOWER HAMLETS when London's local government was reorganized in 1965. (See also ROYAL LONDON HOSPITAL; TURNPIKES.)

MILLENNIUM BRIDGE

At the end of the twentieth century, a footbridge was built across the RIVER THAMES in an attempt to link the open space around ST PAUL'S CATHEDRAL (in the CITY OF LONDON) to the GLOBE THEATRE and TATE GALLERY developments at BANKSIDE (on the northern edge of SOUTHWARK). London's first river crossing for over a century (and the sole crossing in the central city available only to pedestrians), it was designed by a consortium consisting of architects Foster and Partners, sculptor Sir Anthony Caro and engineers Ove Arup and Partners, who won the contract in an international competition that attracted 227 entries. The structure, which cost over £14 million, was opened in June 2000 but immediately closed because it rocked violently from side to side as 100,000 people tried to cross it. Repairs designed to eliminate the movement cost £5 million but allowed the bridge to reopen in March 2002.

MILLENNIUM DOME

The dome was built on a site close to the RIVER THAMES at GREENWICH to mark the beginning of the twenty-first century and opened on 31 December 1999. Fraught with problems from its inception, it cost £758 million, about half of which was raised through the National Lottery and the rest through private sponsorship. Much of the exhibition area consisted of thirteen themed zones (including the Body Zone, Home Planet and the Play Zone) with the remainder designed to accommodate public performances for large audiences. The plans were criticized by many people who felt that the money invested would have been better used on improvements to educational provision and healthcare. Also, religious leaders (including the Archbishop of Canterbury, head of the Church of England) argued that a monument built to mark the passage of 2,000 years since the birth of Christ should have a religious theme (press reports indicated that Tony Blair had refused to allow the Archbishop to hold a service at midnight on New Year's Eve because it would spoil the party atmosphere). Prince Charles claimed that the building looked like a monstrous blancmange, many guests invited to the opening ceremony failed to arrive because their invitations had been mailed late and hundreds of those who did turn up waited several hours for public transport to the site because limited car parking was available. Then, after only five weeks of operation, the Chief Executive of the New Millennium Experience Company was fired because visitor numbers were well below expectations. Government plans to sell the dome to a private concern after twelve months' operation produced further complaints that the site should be used for some public purpose. The exhibitions closed at the end of 2000, and, three years later, the government and the MAYOR OF LONDON announced that the area around the Dome would be earmarked for the construction of

35,000 houses in an attempt to reduce the shortage of homes in south-east England. (See also JUBILEE LINE.)

MILL HILL

Mill Hill lies on the north-west fringe of London, some 10 miles from CHARING CROSS. From the seventeenth century until after the First World War, it was a fashionable place in which to establish a country home; three LORD MAYORS – John Wilkes (1774), John Anderson (1797) and Charles Flower (1808) – had houses there, as did Peter Collinson (1694–1768), the botanist who introduced the yucca and the hydrangea to Britain, and William Wilberforce (1759–1833), who campaigned in the HOUSE OF COMMONS (see PALACE OF WESTMINSTER) for the abolition of slavery. It also attracted a number of educational institutions, including Mill Hill School (built in 1907 for the children of nonconformists) and St Joseph's College (opened in 1871 to train Roman Catholic missionaries). During the 1920s, however, it became less exclusive as LONDON UNDERGROUND'S NORTHERN LINE extended into the area, attracting commuters willing to travel to office jobs in the city and encouraging developers to lay out streets of detached and semi-detached homes. Although much open space remains nearby (partly as a result of the designation of the GREEN BELT in 1938), Mill Hill is a typical interwar suburb. It was incorporated within the LONDON BOROUGH OF BARNET in 1965 and gets its name from a mill which once stood in the north of the area. (See also EDUCATION.)

MILLWALL

Millwall occupies the western half of the ISLE OF DOGS, taking its name from the structures that pumped water out of the marshes that line the north shore of the RIVER THAMES. It was industrialized during the nineteenth century, attracting port activities such as food processing and shipbuilding (when the *Great Eastern*, designed by ISAMBARD KINGDOM BRUNEL, was launched from John Scott Russell's yard in 1859, it was the largest ship ever built in Britain). The 36-acre Millwall DOCK opened in 1868, dealing largely in grain, and MILLWALL FOOTBALL CLUB was founded in 1885, providing a Saturday afternoon recreational facility for the largely working-class population. As migrants moved in, looking for homes near their jobs, the area suffered increasingly from overcrowding, but extensive damage during the BLITZ and the progressive closure of London's docks from the 1960s enabled local authorities and private interests to undertake major redevelopment programmes. Much of the land is now occupied by offices and by newspaper printing works, but some housing has been built along the riverfront. The area was included within the LONDON BOROUGH OF TOWER HAMLETS when the city's local government was restructured in 1965.

MILLWALL FOOTBALL CLUB

In 1885, workers at J.T. Morton's jam-making factory, on the ISLE OF DOGS, formed a football team which they called MILLWALL Rovers. Many of those workers were expatriate Scots so, quite naturally, they adopted club colours (blue) and a badge (a lion rampant) that reminded them of their homeland. The team, later known as Millwall Athletic and then as Millwall, played at several grounds in the EAST END and GREENWICH before settling at The Den, in Cold Blow Lane, NEW CROSS, in 1910. They remained there until 1992, when they transferred to a new stadium, now seating 20,146 spectators and known as The New Den, only a few hundred yards away at Senegal Fields.

Millwall was elected to the Third Division (South) of the Football League in 1920. By 1939, it had won the championship twice (in 1928 and 1938) and become the first Third Division side to reach the semi-finals of the FA Cup (in 1937), but the team struggled in the years after the Second World War and by

1959 it was playing in the League's Fourth Division. The 1960s brought a resurgence of footballing fortunes as the club fought back to the Second Division and, in 1965/66, played fifty-nine League games without defeat, but the decade also saw the start of a history of football violence that was to plague the side for the next forty years. The troubles began in the spring of 1966, when fans invaded the QUEENS PARK RANGERS pitch at Loftus Road in an attempt to get a game abandoned because Millwall was losing heavily, and continued at the next home match, when smoke bombs were thrown. They resurfaced in the late 1970s and early 1980s, culminating in a riot on 13 March 1985, following an away game at Luton, as supporters tore seats from the stands and used them as missiles, injuring eighty-one people, thirty-one of them policemen.

The club won promotion to the Second Divison that season but a £7,500 fine imposed by the Football League, coupled with the need to invest £1 million in safety improvements at The Den, left the coffers bare. Chairman Alan Thorn sold players (such as John Fashanu) in an attempt to recoup funds so by the summer of 1986 there were only eight professionals on the books, but debts still amounted to £4.9 million. After complex negotiations, a new board, headed by investment consultant Ray Burr, saved the business from bankruptcy and attempted both to reconstruct the playing staff and to solve the hooliganism problem through close involvement with the local community.

The efforts to rebuild the team were relatively successful as a carefully constructed side of young players, inexpensively acquired, won promotion to the First Division (for the first time in the club's history) in 1988 and has maintained a place in the First or Second Division ever since (albeit in a League reconstructed in the early 1990s). The campaign to eliminate hooliganism brought more limited returns. The LONDON BOROUGH OF LEWISHAM became the first British local authority to sponsor a professional football team, tickets for home games were distributed to elderly and needy residents living close to the ground and players led coaching sessions at local schools, but Millwall was regularly stereotyped in the press as one of the centres of violence in English football and a section of fans seemed to revel in the attention. In May 2002, following a 1-0 defeat by Birmingham City, over 900 supporters went on the rampage, setting fire to cars and throwing paving stones which injured forty-seven policemen and twenty-six police horses. Although there was no violence inside the ground, the directors were forced to take drastic action. During the 2002/03 season, all supporters from six other clubs were banned from The Den and local people could watch home games only if they bought season tickets or were members of the official supporters' club. As a result, average gates fell from 13,000 to some 7,500, threatening further financial problems.

MILNER HOLLAND REPORT (1965)

In the early 1960s, amidst public concern about the lack of properties available for rent in London and the activities of unscrupulous landlords (see RACHMANISM), the government in 1963 formed a Committee of Enquiry, led by Sir Milner Holland, to assess the situation and recommend solutions to the problem. The Committee's report, published in 1965, reported that many residents were living in substandard conditions (some 200,000 people had no fixed bath or shower, for example), that a shortage of accommodation (coupled with high rents) prevented poor families from finding homes at prices they could afford and that some tenants were living in fear of physical and psychological abuse by property owners. Recommendations included increased provision of housing by local authorities and other agencies, a system of controlled rents which would bring landlords an economic return on their investment without exploiting tenants, increased security for those tenants and introduction of legislation designed to prevent abuse by landlords.

MITCHAM

Mitcham, 8 miles south-west of CHARING CROSS, was farmed before the Roman invasion of Britain and was well populated by Anglo-Saxon times (excavation of a graveyard near Ravensbury PARK revealed over 200 bodies interred during the period, along with numerous brooches and other artefacts). During the Middle Ages, a community developed around the Church of St Peter and St Paul (established during the thirteenth century) and wealthy Londoners acquired country estates nearby. Calico bleaching and printing developed in the seventeenth and eighteenth centuries, augmenting farming incomes, as did the growing of medicinal herbs, market gardening and the cultivation of watercress. Inns were also built along the road to the capital and, by 1732, an annual fair was being held every August. From the later 1800s, however, the area was converted from a rural village into a metropolitan suburb as TRAMS and RAILWAYS improved access to the central city and attracted commuters who wanted a home near the country. The area became increasingly developed, but the 460-acre common was preserved as open space and, although partially converted into sports fields, is now managed as an ecological resource. In 1934, as the population rose, Mitcham was accorded borough status, but when London's local government was reformed in 1965 it was incorporated within the LONDON BOROUGH OF MERTON.

MITHRAEUM

See TEMPLE OF MITHRAS.

MONASTERIES

Although most monastic groups preferred the peace of rural areas to the hustle and bustle of English towns during the medieval period, London attracted several major religious foundations, including the Bene-dictine community at WESTMINSTER ABBEY, the Carthusians at CHARTERHOUSE, the Dominicans at BLACKFRIARS and the Franciscans at GREYFRIARS MONASTERY. In addition, many smaller groups dedicated themselves to the care of the urban poor, establishing hospitals as well as chapels. From 1532, all of these orders were required to accept the Acts of Supremacy, which recognized the monarch (rather than the Pope) as head of the Church in England. Many refused and paid the price; their buildings were torn down, their property was confiscated, their monks and nuns were executed or imprisoned and their communities were dispersed. Those believers who were willing to take oaths supporting the legislation were given pensions. The Dissolution of the Monasteries is frequently regarded by scholars as the end of the Middle Ages in London because of its social impact, clearing the city of the cassocked clergy and leaving it with too few hospitals and places of worship for its needs. (See also ABBEY WOOD; BARKING; BARTHOLOMEW FAIR; BEDLAM; BERMONDSEY; CANONBURY; CLERKENWELL; COVENT GARDEN; DULWICH; EDGWARE; EPPING FOREST; ERITH; GREENWICH; HOUNSLOW; ILFORD; KILBURN; KNIGHTS HOSPITALLER; MERTON; MUSWELL HILL; ORPINGTON; REGENT'S PARK; ST BARTHOLOMEW-THE-GREAT CHURCH, SMITHFIELD; ST MARYLEBONE; SHOREDITCH; SPITALFIELDS; STANMORE; STRATFORD; STREATHAM; SYON HOUSE; WANSTEAD; WATER POLLUTION; WHITEFRIARS; WOODFORD.)

MONUMENT

In 1666, Parliament approved the rebuilding of those areas of the CITY OF LONDON that had been destroyed by the GREAT FIRE and authorized the erection of a monument 'to preserve the memory of this dreadful Visitation.' CHRISTOPHER WREN and his friend, Robert Hooke, prepared the plans, proposing a single shaft of PORTLAND STONE surmounted by a bronze urn and a gilded ball of flame. The 202-foot-high structure (still the tallest isolated stone column in the world) was completed in 1671. Inside, a spiral staircase with 311 steps leads to a balcony, which, in 1842, was enclosed in an iron cage after six people had thrown themselves to their deaths. At the base, inscriptions in Latin describe the conflagration (a sentence attributing it to 'Popish frenzy' was removed in 1831), note the contribution of Charles II and his Parliament to the rebuilding and list the LORD MAYORS of the time. Also, a bas-relief by Caius Gabriel Cibber depicts the king commanding his courtiers to give help to the distressed area. If the monument toppled eastwards, the urn would land exactly at the location of the baker's premises where the fire began.

MOORGATE

The Moorgate area of the CITY OF LONDON gets its name from the postern gate that was built in 1415 to give access to the rough marshlands outside the medieval settlement. The gate was rebuilt after the GREAT FIRE of 1666 but demolished in 1762. The street which now bears the name runs for just under ½ mile northwards from the BANK OF ENGLAND and was laid out during the 1840s as part of a development designed to improve access to JOHN RENNIE's LONDON BRIDGE, which was built in 1832. Initially, the road was lined by the homes of wealthy merchants but these have long been replaced by banks, offices and the classrooms of London Metropolitan UNIVERSITY's business school, though the gardens in FINSBURY Circus, at the northern end, survive as an oasis of green space. One of the worst accidents in the history of the LONDON UNDERGROUND occurred at Moorgate Station on 28 February 1975, when a train crashed in a dead-end tunnel at the height of the morning rush hour, killing forty-three people. (See also METROPOLITAN LINE; NORTHERN LINE.)

MORDEN

Morden lies some 9 miles south-west of CHARING CROSS. Although there is evidence of Roman occupation of the area and records show that the land was granted to the monks of WESTMINSTER ABBEY by King Edgar in AD 968, the settlement remained a small village, focusing on the manor house and the Church of St Lawrence (founded by the beginning of the thirteenth century), until 1926, when the southern terminus of the NORTHERN LINE was built nearby. The improved access to central London encouraged the development of private and public housing, including the LONDON COUNTY COUNCIL's St Helier Estate, built in the 1930s with the streets all named after religious establishments in alphabetical order from Abbotsbury Road in the north-east to Woburn Road in the south-west. Morden Hall, the former manor house, is now owned by the National Trust but is used as offices by the local authority. A seventeenth-century building, it was stuccoed in the 1840s. The PARK provides an important recreational facility in a heavily urbanized area and is managed to promote wildlife. Morden was included within the LONDON BOROUGH OF MERTON when local government in the metropolitan area was reorganized in 1965. The name may be derived from the Old English words *mor* (meaning moor or marshland) and *dun* (meaning hill).

MORRISON, HERBERT STANLEY

(1888–1965)

Although Morrison is best remembered for his prominent role in national politics from 1945 to 1959, his work in London between the two world wars had more lasting impact. Born in BRIXTON on 3 January 1888, the youngest of seven children in the family of Police Constable Henry Morrison and his wife, Priscilla, he left school at the age of fourteen and worked in a series of jobs before becoming Secretary of the London Labour Party in 1915. Realizing that electoral success depended on finding suitable candidates and training them to manipulate committees, he introduced organizational reforms that resulted in major Labour successes in the LONDON BOROUGHS and LONDON COUNTY COUNCIL (LCC) elections in 1919. He was elected Mayor of HACKNEY the same year then, in 1922, gained an LCC seat himself. By wooing voters on the rapidly expanding local authority housing estates, he won a surprise victory for Labour in the council elections in 1934, establishing a foundation that (aided by the movement of more wealthy residents to suburban areas beyond the LCC boundary) resulted in socialist government in the city for the next thirty-one years.

By creating a new Public Relations Department, Morrison skilfully fed the local press with stories and pictures that created the image of an administration bent on improving conditions for all Londoners. Work began on a new bridge at WATERLOO in 1934, programmes of slum clearance and house building were implemented within the inner city (under Morrison's direction, Labour built new homes for over 34,000 people during its first three years in office), the regulations preventing married women from working as schoolteachers were swept away in 1935 and a GREEN BELT, which preserved open space by restricting the outward extension of urban development, was established in 1938.

In 1923, Morrison was elected Member of Parliament for Hackney South and, six years later, was made Minister of TRANSPORT by Prime Minister Ramsay MacDonald. Arguing that the LONDON UNDERGROUND and other mass transit services in the city needed unified management, he introduced the London Passenger Transport Bill to the HOUSE OF COMMONS (1931). The subsequent legislation created the London Passenger Transport Board (see LONDON TRANSPORT), a public corporation that, at the time, was the world's largest transport authority.

Morrison lost his Parliamentary seat in 1931 but regained it four years later and led a campaign, strongly supported in London, for new laws that would curb the activities of pro-Nazi groups in the city. The principal results – gained through the passage of the Public Order Act in 1936 – were a ban on the wearing of uniforms for political ends and additional powers enabling the police to stop marches that might result in violence. When the national government was formed in 1940, some months after the outbreak of the Second World War, Morrison was initially made Minister of Supply but, after a few months, was appointed Home Secretary, forming a nationwide Fire Service to ensure co-ordination in efforts to reduce the effects of enemy AIR RAIDS. In 1945, he put his experience of political party organization to good effect, receiving much of the credit for Labour's landslide victory in the first post-war General Election. (In 1997 his grandson, Peter Mandelson, gained the same plaudits following the even greater victory of Tony Blair's Labour Party after eighteen years of Conservative rule.) Prime Minister Clement Attlee appointed Morrison Lord President of the Council, with responsibility for the reconstruction of the British economy but he never fully grasped the issues involved and, after two years, concentrated solely on piloting the government's contentious legislation on the nationalization of industries through the HOUSE OF COMMONS (a task that allowed him to make full use of his administrative skills). For a few months in 1951, he was at the Foreign Office, but, a Londoner at heart, he lacked the knowledge and understanding of other cultures necessary for such a diplomatic position and was not a success.

When Attlee retired from the post of Leader of the Labour Party in 1955, Morrison was one of the candidates for the position but, at the age of sixty-seven and unable to win Attlee's support, lost to Hugh Gaitskell. He was awarded a peerage in 1959 then served as president of the British Board of Film Censors. Following his death at Sidcup on 6 March 1965, he was cremated and his ashes scattered on the RIVER THAMES.

MORTLAKE

Mortlake lies on the SOUTH BANK of the RIVER THAMES between BARNES and KEW. It was part of the Archbishop of Canterbury's estate during the Middle Ages and, by the end of the sixteenth century, had evolved into a substantial village. From 1619, when James I provided premises for a community of fifty HUGUENOT weavers, the settlement earned a reputation for producing the finest tapestries in Europe, then, following the closure of the business in 1703, became widely known for its market gardens, pottery workshops and BREWERIES. It escaped the nineteenth-century industrialization that transformed other riverside areas of London and remains predominantly residential, with several eighteenth-century properties surviving (as at The Limes, built in the 1720s for the Countess of Stafford). J.F. Bentley (architect of WESTMINSTER CATHEDRAL) and explorer Richard Burton are buried at St Osmond's Roman Catholic Church, Burton in an unusual tomb resembling a desert nomad's tent fashioned in stone. Mortlake was included within the LONDON BOROUGH OF RICHMOND when London's local government was restructured in 1965. The origin of the name is unclear. It is cited as *Mortlage* in the DOMESDAY BOOK (1086), leading some writers to suggest that it is derived from *Morta* (an Old English personal name) and *lacu* (a word for 'stream'), which dates from the same period. Others claim that the first element may come directly from *mort*, an Old English word for 'young salmon'. (See also CHISWICK BRIDGE; UNIVERSITY BOAT RACE.)

MOST VENERABLE ORDER OF THE HOSPITAL OF ST JOHN OF JERUSALEM

See KNIGHTS HOSPITALLER.

MOTORWAY BOX

See GREATER LONDON DEVELOPMENT PLAN (1969).

MOUSETRAP, THE

Agatha Christie's mystery, *The Mousetrap*, opened at the Ambassador's THEATRE on 25 November 1952 and was still attracting audiences, after nearly 20,000 performances, at the end of the millennium, by which time it was the world's longest-running play. The production, watched by a total audience of over 10 million, has starred some 350 actors and actresses, including David Raven (who appeared 4,575 times as Major Metcalfe) and Nancy Seabrooke (who understudied the role of Mrs Boyle for 6,240 performances and appeared on only seventy-two occasions). In 1973, the play transferred to St Martin's Theatre but the set has changed only twice, in 1963 and 1999. On the latter occasion, props were auctioned to provide funds for Denville Hall, a residential nursing home for retired actors and actresses.

MUSEUM OF LONDON

In 1976, Guildhall Museum (established in 1826 by the CORPORATION OF LONDON) and the London MUSEUM (founded by Viscount Esher and Viscount Harcourt in 1912) merged collections illustrating the city's history to form a single Museum of London. Housed in the BARBICAN development, the museum combines modern technology with artefacts from the past (such as a Roman pavement, Elizabethan jewellery, eighteenth-century goldsmith's goods and a Victorian barber's shop) to explain how a small settlement beside the RIVER THAMES evolved into a major metropolis. It also supports archaeological excavations designed to further understand the capital's development.

MUSEUM OF MANKIND

In 1970, the BRITISH MUSEUM, lacking sufficient space to exhibit ethnographic material at its Great Russell Street site, opened the MUSEUM of Mankind in Burlington Gardens, taking over a building erected in 1869 for the University of London. Collections from Africa, the Americas, Australasia, Eurasia and the Pacific Islands were housed in galleries that emphasized education rather than mere display, with items as disparate as a crystal skull fashioned by Aztec craftsmen and masks once worn by tribal groups in New Guinea. In recent years, some of the material has been a focus of controversy because foreign governments claim the return of artefacts, which, they argue, were stolen by British colonialists (Ghana would like to see the Ashante regalia returned to West Africa, for example). From 1995 the exhibits were returned to new galleries at the main British Museum in BLOOMSBURY and in 1997 the Museum of Mankind closed.

MUSEUM OF THE MOVING IMAGE

The MUSEUM of the Moving Image was located next to the NATIONAL FILM THEATRE underneath the arches of WATERLOO Bridge (both institutions were managed by the British Film Institute, which was formed in 1933 to develop film as an art form). Opened in 1988, the museum told the story of the evolution of moving images from the days of Javanese shadow puppets, which entertained audiences 4,000 years ago, to the computer-generated special effects of productions such as *Star Wars*. Visitors could read the news on television, submit to interviews and, like Mary Poppins, fly over London. There were also posters, props, stills and other illustrative material as well as space for temporary exhibitions. In the evening, the National Film Theatre took over the premises to show full-length movies. The museum closed in 1999, ostensibly for refurbishment, but has not reopened.

MUSEUMS AND GALLERIES

Although kings and courtiers amassed *objets d'art* with which to impress their subjects and aristocratic visitors, the concept of museums and galleries as centres of learning and public EDUCATION did not develop in London until the eighteenth century. Visitors to the BRITISH MUSEUM, when it opened in 1759, were strictly controlled; only thirty were allowed in each day and then only if they had applied in writing and received the approval of the Principal Librarian. Within a few decades, however, rich merchants and professional men were bequeathing their private (and often very eclectic) collections to the nation (see, for example, SIR JOHN SOANE'S MUSEUM) and events such as the GREAT EXHIBITION were fuelling interest in the unusual and exotic. Also, the need for an educated workforce encouraged investment in the dissemination of knowledge. At the instigation of PRINCE ALBERT, the site of the Great Exhibition in south KENSINGTON was developed to extend 'the influence of Science and Art upon productive industry' through the erection of museums, concert halls and premises for learned societies; the NATURAL HISTORY MUSEUM, the SCIENCE MUSEUM and the VICTORIA AND ALBERT MUSEUM became the nineteenth-century equivalents of Animal Planet and the Discovery Channel. At the same time, great works of art were increasingly brought from private collections and offered to a wider audience; the NATIONAL GALLERY opened in 1824 after the Tory government purchased thirty-eight old masters from the estate of John Julius Angerstein, the NATIONAL PORTRAIT GALLERY followed in 1859 (also partly because of Prince Albert's enthusiastic support) and the TATE GALLERY (the gift of sugar refiner Sir Henry Tate) widened the range of paintings further in 1897.

During the twentieth century, increased leisure time and the spread of literacy widened the market for museums and galleries, but the cost of maintaining large, all-embracing collections rose markedly. Although the major institutions continued to flourish, they had to keep apace with the times by employing up-to-date technology (as with the BLITZ Experience at the IMPERIAL WAR MUSEUM) and, during the 1980s (amidst great controversy), to charge admission in an attempt to defray expenses. Also, they found themselves competing with growing numbers of smaller, specialist museums such as the CABINET WAR ROOMS, the LONDON TRANSPORT MUSEUM and the BETHNAL GREEN MUSEUM OF CHILDHOOD. As a result, the city now has a great range of premises presenting exhibits of enormous variety using techniques that range from mounting artefacts in traditional glass cases to hands-on examinations and computerized multimedia experiences. (See also BAKER STREET; BANK OF ENGLAND; BANQUETING HOUSE; BELFAST, HMS; BRENTFORD; CAMBERWELL; CLERKENWELL; CLINK PRISON; COURTAULD INSTITUTE OF ART; DESIGN MUSEUM; DICKENS' HOUSE MUSEUM; DOCKS; DULWICH; EPPING FOREST; FREUD'S HOUSE; GEFFRYE MUSEUM; GEOLOGICAL MUSEUM; GOLDERS GREEN; GUNNERSBURY; HAYWARD GALLERY; HENDON; HORNIMAN MUSEUM; JEWISH MUSEUM; JOHNSON'S HOUSE, DR; KEATS' HOUSE; KENSINGTON PALACE; KENWOOD HOUSE; KNIGHTS HOSPITALLER; LONDON DUNGEON; MADAME TUSSAUD'S WAXWORKS; MARBLE HILL HOUSE; MARYLEBONE CRICKET CLUB (MCC); MUSEUM OF LONDON; MUSEUM OF MANKIND; MUSEUM OF THE MOVING IMAGE; NATIONAL ARMY MUSEUM; NATIONAL MARITIME MUSEUM; OLD KENT ROAD; RANGER'S HOUSE; ROYAL ACADEMY OF ARTS; ROYAL COLLEGE OF SURGEONS OF ENGLAND; ROYAL LONDON HOSPITAL; ST BRIDE'S CHURCH, FLEET STREET; ST THOMAS'S HOSPITAL; SERPENTINE; SLOANE, HANS; SOHO; SOMERSET HOUSE; STOCKWELL; SYON HOUSE; THEATRE MUSEUM; TOTTENHAM; TOWER BRIDGE; TOWER OF LONDON; TOYNBEE HALL; WESLEY'S CHAPEL; WHITECHAPEL; WILLIAM MORRIS GALLERY; WIMBLEDON; WOOLWICH.)

MUSIC HALLS

The music hall was a popular place of entertainment for working-class Londoners from about 1850 until the period between the First and Second World Wars. Drawing on the fairground performers' tradition of mixing acrobatic acts, songs and dances, the halls developed from 1843, when the Theatres Act allowed public houses to offer cheap entertainment. By the mid-1860s, about 200 were operating, seating audiences of up to 2,000, but the introduction of increasingly strict fire prevention regulations from 1878 caused many of the smaller businesses to close and entrepreneurs to build larger auditoriums. Bawdy humour, songs with rousing choruses and an ability to make patrons forget their troubles combined to make entertainers such as Dan Leno, Marie Lloyd, George Robey and Vesta Tilley household names, despite efforts by the temperance movement and other protectors of moral rectitude to deplore the drunkenness and sexual license with which the halls were often associated. By the early 1900s, however, fashions were changing. Performers forsook the music halls, with their procession of individual acts and sketches, for more sophisticated musicals and revues. Then, in the 1920s, cinemas began to attract the customers who had previously frequented the halls and, although THEATRES such as the HACKNEY Empire, the London Palladium and the Victoria Palace kept the genre alive, young people were looking for other forms of entertainment. The music hall tradition survives (most notably in the annual Royal Command Performance, attended by Elizabeth II and other members of the royal family) but its most enduring legacy is probably the image of the COCKNEY as the archetypal, cheerful, indomitable, working-class Londoner portrayed by characters such as Eliza Doolittle in George Bernard Shaw's *Pygmalion* (first performed in 1913) and in the countless productions of the Alan Jay Lerner and Frederick Loewe musical *My Fair Lady* (1956), which is based on Shaw's play. (See also BRIXTON; CLAPHAM; GOLDERS GREEN; HOXTON; OLD VIC; OLD KENT ROAD; SADLER'S WELLS; SOHO.)

MUSWELL HILL

During the twelfth century, the Augustinian community at St Mary's Priory in CLERKENWELL acquired land at Muswell Hill, 6 miles north of CHARING CROSS, for pasturing cattle and producing milk. The estate included a mossy well whose waters were believed to have healing qualities and which gave its name to the area. Apart from a few villas erected in the eighteenth century, the land remained agricultural until, in the two decades from 1896, James Edmundson and W.J. Collins laid out a typically late Victorian suburb of solid homes and shops built with stone-dressed brick. The spire of St James's Church (which was designed by J.S. Alder, opened in 1901 and constructed of Ancaster stone with Bath stone facings) provides a prominent landmark. Muswell Hill became part of the LONDON BOROUGH OF HARINGEY when the local government in the metropolitan area was reorganized in 1965. It probably gets its name from the Old English *meos* (meaning 'mossy') and *wella* (meaning 'spring').

N

NASH, JOHN (1752–1835)

Nash had a major impact on London's townscape, converting the open lands of royal estates west of the CITY OF LONDON into the residential development and spacious lawns of REGENT STREET and REGENT'S PARK. Born in 1752 (possibly in London but perhaps in Wales), he was trained by architect Robert Taylor before going into business on his own account as a builder and house designer. When that venture failed in 1783, he moved to Carmarthen but continued to practice ARCHITECTURE and built up a strong list of clients as he concentrated on the preparation of plans for country houses and institutional structures (such as Cardigan jail).

When he returned to London in the late 1790s, working in an informal partnership with landscape gardener Humphry Repton, Nash's work attracted the attention of several aristocratic patrons, including George, Prince Regent, who, in 1811, commissioned him to present a scheme for the conversion of Marylebone PARK into a place for public recreation. The development, now known as Regent's Park, included the REGENT'S CANAL, gardens and a lake, with shopping arcades and housing designed for artisan as well as for middle-class families. Regent Street, built to link the park to the Prince's residence at Carlton House, was completed between 1820 and 1825, with All Soul's Church (which has an unusual circular portico and a conical spire) erected at Langham Place to add impact to the view. Nash was also responsible for the Royal Opera Arcade (erected in 1816 and 1818 and one of the earliest arcades in the city), the layout of parts of the CHARING CROSS area (including Suffolk Place and Suffolk Street in 1820), the conversion of BUCKINGHAM PALACE from country mansion to royal palace (1820–30), the redesign of ST JAMES'S PARK (1827–9) and the building of the Theatre Royal, HAYMARKET (1831). His last years in business were marred by disputes over the cost and structural quality of the Buckingham Palace programme. Dismissed from the project following George IV's death in 1830, he retired to East Cowes Castle (on the Isle of Wight) which he had built in 1798 and where he died on 13 May 1835. (See also ARCHWAY; CLARENCE HOUSE; MARBLE ARCH; OXFORD STREET; PORTLAND PLACE; ROYAL MEWS; TRAFALGAR SQUARE; WOOLWICH.)

NATIONAL ARMY MUSEUM

The MUSEUM, originally located at the Royal Military Academy Sandhurst (in Surrey), was moved to its present site beside CHELSEA HOSPITAL in 1971. Its displays outline English and British military history from the early sixteenth century, with additional exhibits relating to the armies of the Commonwealth of Nations. An extensive library of books, photographs and related material is available to researchers.

NATIONAL FILM THEATRE (NFT)

In 1953, the British Film Institute (founded in 1933 and primarily concerned with the promotion of film as an art form) built a cinema on the SOUTH BANK of the RIVER THAMES near WATERLOO Bridge. Known as Telekinema, it concentrated on demonstrating technical developments in movie production and proved so successful that a new building – the National Film Theatre – was built under the arches of the bridge five years later. A second auditorium was opened in 1970 and the screen at the MUSEUM OF THE MOVING IMAGE commandeered for evening performances from 1988. Altogether, about 2,000 films are shown every year, including early silent movies as well as recent releases. In addition, the NFT hosts the annual London Film Festival. Shows are open only to members, but visitors can purchase day membership for a small charge.

NATIONAL GALLERY

The gallery, located on the north side of TRAFALGAR SQUARE, holds one of the world's most important art collections. Its nucleus was the thirty-eight paintings acquired by the government from the estate of Russian-born merchant John Julius Angerstein in 1824. As private collectors gifted other works, the gallery rapidly outgrew its initial home in Angerstein's PALL MALL house so William Wilkins was commissioned to design the present building, which was erected on the site of the WHITEHALL PALACE stables in 1838 and has since been extended several times, most recently in 1991 when a wing (funded by the Sainsbury family) was added to the west. The gallery's principal strength is its fine selection of paintings by representatives of the various mainland European schools, including Flemish and Dutch masters such as Rembrandt and Rubens, the principal Italian Renaissance artists (Giotto and Leonardo da Vinci, for example), French painters of the seventeenth, nineteenth and early twentieth centuries (notably Poussin and Cézanne), and Spanish canvases by Velázquez, Goya and El Greco. The gallery, which receives some 5 million visitors every year, has its own conservation department and presents a regular lecture programme. In 2003, work was completed on a terrace which linked the Gallery to Trafalgar Square. (See also GIBBONS, GRINLING; TATE GALLERY.)

NATIONAL MARITIME MUSEUM

The MUSEUM, which opened in 1937, is based at GREENWICH in a complex of buildings with naval connections and considerable architectural interest. Its main centre is the QUEEN'S HOUSE, designed by INIGO JONES and originally intended as a residence for Anne of Denmark, wife of James I. The museum uses it as a gallery for its Elizabethan and Stuart collections. Other buildings, commissioned in 1807 to commemorate Lord Nelson's victory at the Battle of Trafalgar two years earlier, are connected to the Queen's House by colonnades. In addition, there are exhibits in the former ROYAL NAVAL COLLEGE and the ROYAL OBSERVATORY. In total, the twenty-nine galleries comprise the world's largest maritime museum and include marine art (Joshua Reynolds' early study of Commodore Keppel, painted in 1749, is on display), water transport (there is a section dealing with emigration from Britain to North America) and archaeology (with an emphasis on the replica of a seventh-century burial ship discovered at Sutton Hoo, Suffolk, in 1939) as well as naval material and biographical data on individuals such as Captain James Cook, who added many territories to the British Empire during the eighteenth century. One of the most popular foci for visitors is the jacket Nelson was wearing when he was shot at Trafalgar: the hole where the fatal musket ball entered his body is clearly evident.

NATIONAL PORTRAIT GALLERY

The gallery was opened in 1859 following pressure on the government from historian Philip Earl of Stanhope, who convinced PRINCE ALBERT, Queen Victoria's husband, to support his cause. Its initial collection of fifty-seven paintings was regularly augmented by gifts and purchases, necessitating a series of moves to bigger and better accommodations, which culminated in the building of its present home, behind the NATIONAL GALLERY, in 1890–5. Currently, the gallery has about 10,000 works, selected on the basis of subject rather than artistic qualities, which depict men and women who have graced the stage of English history. Some of the canvasses are by renowned artists (such as Holbein, who painted Henry VII, Henry VIII and Thomas More). Others are crude by any standards but important nonetheless (for example, the portrait of Jane Austen by Cassandra, her sister, is the only likeness of the novelist completed while she was alive). Since 1968, the paintings, drawings and sculptures have been augmented by an archive of photographs, which now contains over 500,000 pictures. In recent years further building and refurbishment have enhanced the displays. In 2000 Elizabeth II opened the Ondaatje Wing. Erected largely through funding provided by Christopher Ondaatje, it houses the Tudor galleries and incorporates a balcony with images of late twentieth-century celebrities. Also, a redesign of the Victorian and early-twentieth-century galleries has unblocked windows and given a lighter feel to the previously enclosed space. The collection attracts about a million visitors every year.

NATIONAL THEATRE

See ROYAL NATIONAL THEATRE.

NATIONAL WESTMINSTER TOWER

In 1959, the National Provincial Bank (which merged with the Westminster Bank in 1968) purchased property adjoining its premises at 15 Bishopsgate and applied to the LONDON COUNTY COUNCIL for planning permission to allow it to demolish the newly acquired buildings and erect offices. The council felt that the old structures had sufficient architectural and historical interest to merit retention and requested revised proposals, which were approved. However, in 1964, before work started, the government passed legislation limiting the size of office developments in London so the plan was postponed again. At the end of the decade, as opinions about urban design changed, the CORPORATION OF LONDON gave the go-ahead for a skyscraper development that would act as a focal point in the city centre. Construction of the fifty-two-storey, 600-foot-high tower began in 1971 and was completed in 1981. Until CANARY WHARF was finished a decade later, it was the tallest building in London.

NATURAL HISTORY MUSEUM

One of a complex of educational institutions in south KENSINGTON, the MUSEUM was opened in 1881 when natural history exhibits were transferred from the BRITISH MUSEUM in an attempt to relieve congestion. The building, designed by Alfred Waterhouse, has a large central hall (deliberately reminiscent of a cathedral because the museum would display the works of the Creator) and a typically Victorian ornate exterior. Several of the galleries were destroyed by bombing during the Second World War, but new accommodations were constructed after the conflict ended, providing (in 1959) facilities for the library, lecture theatre, reference collections, a Botanical Gallery (finished in 1963) and an additional wing built in 1977.

Initially, the museum's core exhibits were those collected by physician HANS SLOANE during the first half of the eighteenth century, but these were augmented by purchases and donations such as the botanical collection of Sir Joseph Banks (president of the ROYAL SOCIETY from 1778 to 1820). Currently, new additions are made at a rate of about 300,000 every year so the museum can show only a fraction of its 65 million specimens. For that reason, it has concentrated, since the 1970s, on displaying a series of self-contained exhibitions in an attempt to attract more visitors; for example, computer technology is employed to enable children to find things out for themselves, and one gallery of arthropods is labelled 'creepy crawlies'. The resultant tension between scholars and accountants led one writer to *The Spectator* to claim, in 1991, that there were, in effect, two institutions, one consisting of the community of research scientists who have little or no influence on what is displayed in the public galleries and the other the museum, with themed displays viewed by some 1.7 million people every year.

NEASDEN

Neasden, 7 miles north-east of CHARING CROSS, lies in the centre of the LONDON BOROUGH OF BRENT. An agricultural village until late in the nineteenth century, it was transformed by improved accessibility to the central city. The first changes occurred in the 1880s, when the Metropolitan RAILWAY Company built houses for employees while laying its lines. Then, in the period between the First and Second World Wars, the construction of the North Circular Road around inner London initiated a second phase of development, turning the area into a residential suburb. Its supposed lack of individuality has made it the butt of many jokes, particularly in the satirical magazine *Private Eye*. It may get its name from the Old English *neosu* and *dun*, indicating a 'nose-shaped hill'. (See also DISTRICT LINE; EAST LONDON LINE; HAMMERSMITH AND CITY LINE; METROPOLITAN LINE.)

NELSON'S COLUMN

See TRAFALGAR SQUARE.

NEW CROSS

As late as the seventeenth century, the New Cross area, some 4½ miles south-east of CHARING CROSS, was covered in forest. In 1614, however, much of the land was purchased by the Haberdashers (one of the City LIVERY COMPANIES) and by the eighteenth century travellers were paying tolls to use the London to Dover road, which passed through the woodlands. The hostelry at the toll gate was known as the New Cross Inn so, gradually, the growing community assumed that name. A RAILWAY station opened in 1839 and a second followed ten years later (both were confusingly called New Cross until 1923, when the first was renamed New Cross Gate). The Royal Naval School, for the sons of naval officers, took its first pupils in 1843 (the building is now occupied by Goldsmith's College, part of the UNIVERSITY of London) then, from the 1870s, the Haberdashers developed housing on the 200-acre Hatcham Manor Estate (and, in 1875 and 1891, opened schools for both sexes). By the end of the First World War, New Cross was absorbed within the metropolitan area. It became part of the LONDON BOROUGH OF LEWISHAM when the city's local government was reorganized in 1965. (See also EAST LONDON LINE; MILLWALL FOOTBALL CLUB; RENNIE, JOHN.)

NEWGATE

Archaeological evidence suggests that Newgate was one of the principal entries in the western sector of the defensive wall built around LONDINIUM by the Romans during the late second century. The gate was rebuilt in 1555–6, 1628–30 and 1672, but demolished in 1767.

NEWGATE PRISON

By the twelfth century, a PRISON had been established near the NEWGATE entrance to the CITY OF LONDON, but that structure was completely destroyed during the GREAT FIRE of 1666. Although a new building opened in 1672, contemporary records indicate that conditions for the inmates were primitive, with inadequate water supplies or ventilation.

The smell was overwhelming, outbreaks of infectious disease were common and warders supplemented their incomes by selling candles or letting wealthy prisoners occupy cells in the least oppressive areas. In 1770–8, a replacement jail was erected to designs by GEORGE DANCE THE YOUNGER but damaged in 1780 during the anti-Catholic GORDON RIOTS and rebuilt in 1780–3 (one of its first occupants was Lord George Gordon, who was convicted on charges of libel in 1787 and kept in the cells until his death six years later). In 1783, public hangings were transferred from TYBURN to a gibbet outside the prison, continuing there until Parliamentary legislation in 1868 brought them to an end. Newgate was demolished in 1902 to provide space for the erection of the CENTRAL CRIMINAL COURT (the Old Bailey). Its inmates had included Quaker leader William Penn, Daniel Defoe and Rob Roy MacGregor (clan chief and cattle thief). Elizabeth Fry visited in 1813 and was appalled by the sight of women, many drunk and starving, lying on floors with no bedding. She proposed a series of administrative changes (including the separation of prisoners by sex, provision for religious and other EDUCATION, employment for inmates, and female warders for female convicts), which were increasingly adopted throughout Europe during the nineteenth century. CHARLES DICKENS, probably as a result of his childhood experiences when his father was constantly in and out of debtor prisons, also admitted to a fascination with Newgate, describing it in chilling detail in *Sketches by Boz* (1835–7). (See also CATO STREET CONSPIRACY; DANCE, GEORGE (1700-1768); WHITTINGTON, RICHARD 'DICK'.)

NEWHAM, LONDON BOROUGH OF

Newham was formed in 1965 through the merger of EAST HAM and WEST HAM with parts of BARKING and north WOOLWICH. It has all the economic and social hallmarks of inner-city areas, with high proportions of manual workers, above average rates of unemployment, significant concentrations of non-white ethnic minorities (which together account for over 60 per cent of the 243,900 population) and an unenviable reputation as one of the most deprived areas in the United Kingdom. In recent years, local authorities have co-operated with national government and local businesses to invest in regeneration schemes. These focus primarily on STRATFORD (proposed as the site for a railway station that would provide a terminus for lines linking Britain to France, attracting commercial interests and providing clerical and managerial employment) and the former Royal DOCKS (on the north bank of the RIVER THAMES), where a 56-acre business park has been developed in an effort to provide facilities for research companies. The southern part of the borough is well served by east-west road links but lacks good LONDON UNDERGROUND connections. (See also BECKTON; CUSTOM HOUSE; DOCKLANDS; EXCEL; MANOR PARK.)

NEW SCOTLAND YARD

From AD 959 until the early sixteenth century, Scotland's monarchs occupied property close to WHITEHALL PALACE during their visits to London, so the buildings in the area became known as Little Scotland Yard, Middle Scotland Yard and Great Scotland Yard. In 1829, the headquarters of the new METROPOLITAN POLICE force was based at 4 WHITEHALL Place, which had been formed by merging the first two of these yards, but the rear of the premises was converted into a police station with an entry from Great Scotland Yard and, very quickly, the formal title of Metropolitan Police Office was simplified to Scotland Yard in common parlance. The name stuck so in 1890, when office staff were moved to another site near WESTMINSTER BRIDGE, James Munro (the Commissioner of Police) decided to recognize the usage by calling the accommodation New Scotland Yard. That name was retained in 1967, when a further transfer was made to a twenty-storey block in Broadway that houses nearly 700 offices and covers 11 acres. Great Scotland Yard is now occupied by the Civil Service Club and the first New Scotland Yard (now renamed Norman Shaw Building, in honour of its architect) is used as offices by Members of Parliament.

NINE ELMS

A working-class area on the eastern edge of BATTERSEA, Nine Elms takes its name from a row of trees that grew by the roadside during the first half of the seventeenth century. It developed as an industrial area with brewing, flour milling, lime production and DOCKyard activities all providing sources of income. The economy was boosted in 1838, when the London and Southampton RAILWAY opened its terminus. Although the station functioned for only a decade, it attracted goods yards, sidings and other facilities, which remained after the company moved its base to WATERLOO, providing an attractive location for manufacturing plants until after the Second World War. During the 1950s and 1960s, reorganization of rail TRANSPORT led to the closure of many of the yards and economic change put several factories out of business, but the relocation of the COVENT GARDEN fruit and vegetable MARKET to the derelict premises in 1974 fuelled a resurgence in activity. The market (the largest wholesale source of fresh produce in Britain) occupies a 68-acre site, with the flower trade located on the site of the former station. The area forms part of the LONDON BOROUGH OF WANDSWORTH.

NONSUCH PALACE

In 1538, Henry VIII cleared the population from Cuddington Village, near CHEAM, and built a hunting palace that was named Nonsuch because it was without equal. The building was small by standards of the time

Nonsuch Palace.

but opulently decorated in Renaissance style, with stucco reliefs along the south front and around the inner of two courtyards. Ornate towers, surmounted by cupolas, were erected at either end of the 150-yard-long structure and gardens laid out with the studied formality required by Tudor taste. James I continued to use the palace as a base for hunting but his grandson, Charles II, presented it to a mistress, Barbara, Countess of Castlemaine, who sold it to Lord Berkeley in 1682. Shortly after, the new owner demolished the structure, using some of the stone to erect a house near EPSOM. The location of the building was lost until 1959, when excavations allowed archaeologists to reconstruct its ground plan. The land is now used as a public PARK. (See also WORCESTER PARK.)

NORTH DOWNS

A range of chalk hills, known as the North Downs, marks the southern edge of the LONDON BASIN. Rising to 965 feet at Leith Hill, near Dorking, it is heavily wooded and characterized by steep-sided valleys. London's suburbs spread onto the northern slopes but much of the land is protected from urban development by GREEN BELT and similar legislation. (See also CROYDON; EPSOM.)

NORTHERN LINE

LONDON UNDERGROUND's Northern Line is based on routes developed by the City and South London Railway (C&SLR) and the CHARING CROSS, Euston and Hampstead Railway (CCE&HR) during the late nineteenth and early twentieth centuries. When it carried its first passengers in 1890, the C&SLR line, which ran for 3 miles from STOCKWELL (now in the LONDON BOROUGH OF LAMBETH) to King William Street (in the CITY OF LONDON), was the world's first electric TUBE railway, taking south London workers to jobs in the financial heart of the capital. Capacity was limited (the tunnels were narrow and the power system inadequate) but the three-carriage trains provided a clean, fast and cheap form of transport so the venture was a commercial success, encouraging entrepreneurs to consider construction of other tube systems. The CCE&HR link between Hampstead and CHARING CROSS was authorized in 1893 but the company had problems attracting speculative capital and, in 1900, it was bought by CHARLES TYSON YERKES, an American investor, who planned a northern extension to the then undeveloped area of GOLDERS GREEN, operating the first trains in 1907.

In 1913, the C&SLR was added to Yerkes' TRANSPORT empire and the track was extended further out from the city centre, reaching EDGWARE in 1924 and MORDEN in 1926. In 1937, four years after the UNDERGROUND system was taken into public ownership (see LONDON TRANSPORT), the two systems were combined as the Northern Line and in 1940 a new northern terminus was established at High Barnet. An additional tentacle between FINSBURY PARK and MOORGATE, opened by the Great Northern and City Railway, was linked to the two main branches of the Northern Line after the formation of the LONDON PASSENGER TRANSPORT BOARD and was known as the HIGHBURY Branch. It was transferred to British Rail's main line network in 1975.

During the Second World War, many of the stations were used as air-raid shelters and, in 1951, Goodge Street was converted into a hostel for visitors to the FESTIVAL OF BRITAIN. The line gained a reputation for delays and cancellations in the 1980s but improvements to trains and signals the following decade brought relief to long-suffering commuters. The trains are serviced at four depots – Edgware, Golders Green, HIGHGATE and Morden. In 2002, responsibility for the line's infrastructure was franchised to Tube Lines, a consortium of private businesses, but London Underground remained responsible for providing the services. (See also BELSIZE PARK; FINSBURY PARK; JUBILEE LINE; MILL HILL; WATERLOO.)

NORTHOLT

The Northolt area, some 12 miles west of CHARING CROSS, was settled by Anglo-Saxon times (in the middle of the eleventh century it belonged to Ansgar, who fought against the invading Norman force at the Battle of Hastings in 1066). It developed as an agricultural village, producing hay and grain for the London market, with brick-making also contributing to the local economy, particularly during the nineteenth century. Changes began in 1907 with the arrival of the RAILWAY, continued with the opening of an aerodrome in 1915 and speeded up following the First World War as construction firms erected row upon row of small properties to meet the demands of office workers willing to commute daily from a home in a semi-rural environment to an office job in the City. After 1945, local authorities took advantage of greenfield sites to add to the stock of public housing and alleviate overcrowding in the inner city. In spite of the building, however, the centre of the small settlement (including the village green and the Church of St Mary the Virgin, which measures only 44 feet by 25 feet) survived comparatively unscathed and is now protected by conservation legislation. When local government in the metropolitan area was reorganized in 1965, Northolt was included within the LONDON BOROUGH OF EALING. Its name was noted as *Northala* in the DOMESDAY BOOK (1086) and may be derived from the Old English *north* and *halh*, meaning 'a northern nook of land'.

NOTTING HILL

Notting Hill forms the northern section of the ROYAL BOROUGH OF KENSINGTON AND CHELSEA. It evolved during the Middle Ages as an agricultural village, with gravel pits providing additional employment from the seventeenth century. From the 1830s, however, the farmland was eroded by housing development as London expanded and, within fifty years, had vanished altogether. The new residents formed a heterogeneous community, with rich and poor living next door to each other. In addition, during the 1950s, the area became a focus for Trinidadian IMMIGRANTS, who brought their festive traditions and, in 1966, founded the exuberant Notting Hill Carnival. The event, which was almost closed after groups of young black people rioted in 1976, is held each year on the Sunday and Monday of the August Bank Holiday and, with 500,000 participants, claims to be Europe's largest street festival. Such racial harmony has not always been the case. There were significant race riots in the 1950s and 1960s, when the area was viewed as a rundown suburb and the inhabitants were exploited by unscrupulous landlords. The gentrification of the area in recent years is portrayed in the award-winning film *Notting Hill*. The area's name has been a rich source of debate among linguists. Some argue that 'Notting' is a corruption of an Old English personal name and the suffix *ing*, and thus indicates 'a place associated with Cnotta'. Others believe that it may be the family name of incomers from Knotting in Bedfordshire. More romantically, it has also been suggested that local people once collected nuts (branches from hazel trees) on the eve of May Day (as in the nursery rhyme *Here we go gathering nuts in May*). (See also RACHMANISM; RILLINGTON PLACE.)

O

OLD BAILEY

See CENTRAL CRIMINAL COURT.

OLD CURIOSITY SHOP

A bric-a-brac store in Portsmouth Street (near LINCOLN'S INN FIELDS), the Old Curiosity Shop was built in 1567 and claims to be the oldest in London. It takes its name from CHARLES DICKENS' novel, published in 1841 (the shop was the home of Little Nell, the story's heroine).

OLDE CHESHIRE CHEESE, YE

Throughout the eighteenth and nineteenth centuries, the Cheshire Cheese (in Wine Office Court, off FLEET STREET) was a favourite PUBLIC HOUSE for London's men of letters. SAMUEL JOHNSON, JAMES BOSWELL, Thomas CARLYLE, Thomas Hood, Alfred Lord Tennyson and William Makepeace Thackeray all gathered beneath the oak beams to drink ale and dine on puddings made with beef, larks, oysters, kidneys, mushrooms and spices. More recently, the building (erected in 1667) has become a tourist haunt, but even so, the oak-panelled interior retains some of the atmosphere of the past and steak pie is still on the menu.

OLD JEWRY

By the twelfth century, the area of the CITY OF LONDON now known as Old Jewry was settled by Jewish IMMIGRANTS, who built a synagogue where they could meet for worship but suffered greatly for their beliefs (in 1262, for example, over 500 Jews were murdered because one moneylender charged more than the legal rate of interest). Replaced as the city's chief financiers by Italian and French Christians, they were driven out of England by Edward I in 1290 and remained in exile until Oliver Cromwell sanctioned their return in 1656. From then, they re-established themselves in their former area and became a significant force in city finance companies, although their businesses were marginalized by the growth of the central banks during the early twentieth century.

Jews in England suffered greatly for their beliefs. Here a Jew is represented with three faces to indicate the more than double dealing with which Jews were credited at the time (from a late thirteenth-century manuscript).

OLD KENT ROAD

One of Britain's ancient thoroughfares, the Old Kent Road runs for 3½ miles along the line of WATLING STREET, which connected the Roman settlement of LONDINIUM to the port at Dubris (Dover). Geoffrey Chaucer's pilgrims made their way along the track as they left London, stopping for refreshment at the shrine of St Thomas a Watering (now the site of the Thomas à Becket public house) as they journeyed to Canterbury. A gallows was built beside the path, with the bodies of criminals hanging as a deterrent to would-be wrongdoers. Travel increased from late Georgian times as technological change made transport easier: horse-drawn buses began to ply the route in 1829, the UNDERGROUND railway (now part of the EAST LONDON LINE) arrived in 1866 and motorized buses were introduced in 1904. By the eighteenth century, the road was lined with houses (some Georgian terraces still survive nearby) and, in 1890, Sir George Livesey founded a library (now the Livesey MUSEUM, the building houses interactive displays and workshops for children under twelve). The raucously popular Victorian MUSIC HALL song *Wotcher* (better known as *Knocked 'em in the Old Kent Road*) was recorded by Shirley Temple in 1939 and is still much sung.

OLD VIC

In 1818, a new playhouse, designed by Rudolph Cabanel and named the Royal Coburg Theatre, opened in Waterloo Road, attracting such distinguished actors as Edmund Kean. Fifteen years later, it changed its name to the Royal Victoria Theatre in honour of the fourteen-year-old Princess (later Queen) Victoria, reduced prices and staged more down-market productions for a local clientele. The interior was redesigned in 1871 then again in 1880, when Emma Cons, a champion of social reform and the first woman member of the LONDON COUNTY COUNCIL, converted it into the Royal Victoria Coffee MUSIC HALL, where working-class people could enjoy wholesome entertainment without the temptation of alcohol to divert them from the pleasures of the stage. After her death in 1912, the property (which became widely known as the Old Vic) was acquired by her niece, violinist and teacher Lilian Bayliss, who attempted to raise artistic standards by presenting WILLIAM SHAKESPEARE's plays, along with operas and dance. In 1931, the Vic-Wells Ballet Company was formed under Ninette de Valois (see ROYAL BALLET), and from 1963 to 1976 the building was the home of the National Theatre (see ROYAL NATIONAL THEATRE). In 1981, the Old Vic was bought by Edwin Mirvish, a Canadian businessman, who restored it to its late-Victorian splendour, then, in 1998, it was sold to a charitable trust dedicated to preserving it as a home for serious THEATRE in London.

OLYMPIA

With over 500,000 square feet of display space, Olympia is one of London's major venues for exhibitions, indoor sports events and, more recently, conferences. Designed by architect Henry E. Coe and set in 5.5 acres of garden, it opened as the National Agricultural Hall in 1884, assuming its present name two years later. Since then, it has staged major circus performances, motor shows, ideal home exhibitions, international showjumping competitions, boxing matches and other entertainments. A New Hall (now known as the National Hall) was added in 1923 and was followed six years later by the art deco Empire Hall (renamed Olympia 2 in the post-colonial years after the Second World War). Conference facilities were built into the complex in 1987. (See also CIRCLE LINE.)

ORCHESTRAS

See LONDON PHILHARMONIC ORCHESTRA (LPO); LONDON SYMPHONY ORCHESTRA (LSO); PHILHARMONIA ORCHESTRA; ROYAL PHILHARMONIC ORCHESTRA (RPO).

ORPINGTON

Orpington, on the south-east outskirts of London, has been settled since Neolithic times but remained an agricultural village until the early twentieth century. During the First World War, a hospital was built to treat Canadian servicemen then, in the 1920s and 1930s, housing estates were erected to meet the needs of commuters. Further private and local authority developments since the 1950s have turned the area into a metropolitan suburb. Most industry is concentrated at nearby St Mary Cray, whose location beside the River Cray helped further manufacturing activities, such as bell-making and paper works. Orpington Priory, founded during the thirteenth century as a hostelry for the priors of Christ Church, Canterbury, was restored with public funds in 1974–5 and converted for use as a MUSEUM, library and office complex. When London's local government was reformed in 1965, Orpington was included within the LONDON BOROUGH OF BROMLEY. Its name may be derived from a combination of the Old English *ing* and *tun*, along with a personal name, and mean 'the place of Orped'.

OSTERLEY HOUSE

Osterley, one of the finest country houses in the London area, lies north of HOUNSLOW. It was built in 1576 for Sir THOMAS GRESHAM, a wealthy merchant, but substantially remodelled from the late 1750s by brothers Robert and Francis Child, who commissioned WILLIAM CHAMBERS, then (from 1761) ROBERT ADAM, to prepare the plans. Adam radically altered the structure, enlarging the property and changing its Tudor features to meet Georgian tastes for classical ARCHITECTURE. A double screen of Ionic columns, approached by an imposing flight of steps, was erected across the east front and windows were moved on all four sides of the building to emphasize symmetry. In the front hall, state rooms and long gallery, great care was invested in the selection of sumptuous furniture, paintings, carpets and wall hangings, which would complement ceiling, frieze and pilaster decorations. The work was completed in 1780 and the house remained a private residence until 1949, when the Earl of Jersey (a descendant of Robert Child) presented it to the nation. The National Trust manages the building and the PARK, which contains a conservatory, gardens and butterfly house.

OUTER LONDON

See GREATER LONDON.

OVAL, THE

The headquarters of the SURREY COUNTY CRICKET CLUB (which was formed in The Horns, a local PUBLIC HOUSE, in 1845), the Oval, like much other property in the area, is leased from the Duchy of Cornwall. Until the first half of the nineteenth century, cricket was played on the nearby KENNINGTON Common, but as that open space was converted to urban uses alternative pitches became increasingly necessary. The Montpelier Cricket Club obtained a lease on a former market garden site in 1845 and, the following year, a match between the Gentlemen and the Players of Surrey took place on the grounds. A pavilion was erected in 1858 and the first Test match against Australia was held on 6–8 September 1880 (England won by five wickets). It has become the traditional venue for the final Test match of each summer. In 1938 Len Hutton scored his then record Test score of 364 runs, and it was here too that Don Bradman was bowled for 0 in his last Test innings, resulting in his Test average failing by 4 runs to be 100 for his Test career. The Oval has also been used for other sports, including RUGBY and FOOTBALL (it staged many of the FA Cup final matches between 1870 and 1892, for example), and was requisitioned to provide accommodation for German prisoners during the Second World War.

OXFORD CIRCUS

See OXFORD STREET.

OXFORD STREET

Oxford Street, one of London's principal retailing centres, stretches westwards for 1¼ miles from the northern end of CHARING CROSS ROAD to MARBLE ARCH, following the line of a Roman road that once ran from the South Coast of England to East Anglia. It gets its name from Edward Harley, Earl of Oxford, who owned land on the north side of the street during the eighteenth century. Until 1739, the thoroughfare was flanked by fields, but from that year development spread from the urban area in the east, so by 1800 it was lined with houses and shops as far as HYDE PARK. Towards the end of the nineteenth century, DEPARTMENT STORES began to oust shoemakers, furniture-makers and other specialist trades, turning the street over to mass market sales in nationwide stores such as Boots, John Lewis, and Marks and Spencer. The older tradition survives, however, partly through the fruit carts, which seem to be parked at every corner, and partly through the itinerant vendors who offer cheap souvenirs and other low-price goods.

Oxford Circus (the intersection of REGENT STREET and OXFORD STREET) was laid out by JOHN NASH in 1816–24, but the present buildings (consisting of four quadrants with identical façades) were designed by Sir Henry Tanner; the south-east sector was erected in 1913, the north-east in 1923, the south-west in 1925 and the north-west in 1928. Because of its location at the crossroads of major east-west and north-south highways in an area of considerable commercial importance, the junction generates very heavy road traffic. In addition, three LONDON UNDERGROUND lines (the BAKERLOO LINE, CENTRAL LINE and VICTORIA LINE) interconnect below street level, disgorging 250,000 passengers every day and making the station one of the busiest on the network. However, pedestrian flows in the street fell by 34 per cent between 1987 and 1999 as shoppers transferred their allegiance to huge new out-of-town malls so at the turn of the century retailers were considering plans to woo the public back by banning traffic, providing more restaurants and offering play areas for children.

P

PADDINGTON

Paddington lies on the north-west edge of central London, bounded by Bayswater Road in the south, Edgware Road in the east, MAIDA VALE in the north and NOTTING HILL in the west. Its name is probably derived from that of Padda, an Anglo-Saxon leader who settled in the area following the Roman withdrawal in AD 410. Until the Industrial Revolution, the economy was based on agriculture, although HUGUENOT refugees from France introduced craft industries (such as textile working) during the eighteenth century. Urban development began in 1801 (when the Grand Junction Canal connected London with the Midlands and attracted commerce to its terminus at Paddington Basin) then flourished after the Great Western RAILWAY opened in 1838 (see PADDINGTON STATION). Landowners and speculative builders laid out extensive estates (such as that at Ladbroke, named after a family that had held property in the area for several generations); many built expensive homes for wealthy families (in BAYSWATER, for instance), others designed more modest houses for manual workers and tradesmen (particularly near KILBURN). Attracted by employment in the building industry and by the cheap accommodation, IMMIGRANT labour arrived from other parts of the British Isles and from abroad, creating a cosmopolitan residential neighbourhood (for example, Queensway and the southern end of the Edgware Road have become significant Arab business areas and there is a large Irish community). By the mid-twentieth century, however, many of the buildings had become slums and unscrupulous landlords were charging exorbitant rents to incomers desperate for living space (see RACHMANISM). Since then, redevelopment programmes, coupled with laws that improved the rights of tenants, have raised living standards while retaining the best of the Victorian ARCHITECTURE. The area is now largely residential and commercial, with few industrial premises, but has retained its distinctive ethnic mix. The Paddington Basin area is currently the focus of a major urban regeneration project. (See also BUSES; DISTRICT LINE; HAMMERSMITH AND CITY LINE; LONDON UNDERGROUND; METROPOLITAN LINE; ST MARY'S HOSPITAL.)

PADDINGTON STATION

The station at PADDINGTON opened in 1838 as the London terminus of the Great Western RAILWAY. Four years later, Queen Victoria arrived at the end of her first train journey; the 17-mile trip from Slough took 23 minutes at an average 44 miles per hour, a speed PRINCE ALBERT (her husband) felt was excessive. The present building, designed by ISAMBARD KINGDOM BRUNEL, was completed in 1854 and covers 13 acres, with a roof of glass and steel. The platforms are 700 feet long. However, in 2000, Railtrack (the company that operated the station) announced plans for a major redevelopment that would include a 673-foot-high skyscraper with over 900,000 square feet of office space, additional platforms and demolition of train sheds. Paddington is still the principal London station for services to Wales and south-west England.

PALACE OF WESTMINSTER

In the middle years of the eleventh century, Edward the Confessor built a palace on the north bank of the RIVER THAMES at WESTMINSTER, providing an alternative focus of development to that of the CITY OF LONDON. For 463 years (and twenty-five reigns), it was the centre of the English court, losing its prestige only when Henry VIII moved to GREENWICH PALACE in 1529. The King's Council met in WESTMINSTER HALL, which was added to the palace in 1097 and evolved into the HOUSE OF LORDS and the HOUSE OF COMMONS, forming the home of Britain's Parliamentary system of government. However, on the night of 16 October 1834, most of the structure was destroyed by fire, only the Great Hall, the thirteenth-century undercroft of St Stephen's Chapel and the Jewel Tower surviving. The government immediately announced a competition to design a replacement building, which would be known as the New Palace of Westminster and would be constructed in Elizabethan or Gothic style. CHARLES BARRY's entry was considered the best of the ninety-seven that were submitted and construction began in 1837, with AUGUSTUS WELBY NORTHMORE PUGIN commissioned to assist. Barry was most at ease with Renaissance ARCHITECTURE, Pugin with Gothic, but (despite some bickering about who should take the greatest credit) the two collaborated well, the former producing the overall plan and the latter adding the exuberant decoration of the interior. The House of Lords was opened in 1847 and the HOUSE OF COMMONS completed four years later. Work on the Clock Tower (commonly known as BIG BEN) ended in 1858 and the Victoria Tower (336 feet high) was roofed in 1860 (a flag flying from the Victoria Tower by day and a light shining from the Clock Tower by night indicate when Parliament is sitting).

The interior of the House of Lords, c. 1646.

Between September 1940 and May 1941, during the BLITZ, the building was damaged by German bombs on eleven occasions, most seriously on 10 May, when the HOUSE OF COMMONS was destroyed. It was reconstructed in 1945–50 to plans prepared by GILES GILBERT SCOTT, who retained Barry's overall design but (to the annoyance of some critics) subdued the flamboyance of Pugin's decoration. (See also ALBERT, PRINCE; GREAT STINK; GUNPOWDER PLOT.)

PALL MALL

When, in 1603, James VI of Scotland succeeded to the English throne (as James I), he moved his court south from Edinburgh, introducing to London a French game – pallo a

The burning of the Houses of Parliament, 16 October 1834.

maglio – which was similar to croquet. The sport proved popular with aristocrats and particularly with Charles II (James's grandson), who enjoyed playing it with his mistresses in ST JAMES'S PARK. Unfortunately, activities were frequently disrupted by passing carriages so in 1662 the traffic was moved to a new road built immediately to the north. Although formally named Catherine Street (after Catherine of Braganza, Charles's queen), it was popularly known as Pall Mall and that vernacular name survived. Because of the road's royal associations, the properties that lined it were much sought after, becoming the homes of aristocratic families (and ELEANOR 'NELL' GWYN, one of Charles's favourite paramours). During the eighteenth and nineteenth centuries, its status declined as shops and COFFEE HOUSES were established and writers and artists moved in (Jonathan Swift, author of *Gulliver's Travels*, took up residence in 1710, Laurence Sterne in 1760 and Thomas Gainsborough in 1774, for example). Now, it is entirely commercial, best known for its GENTLEMEN'S CLUBS, notably the Travellers' Club (founded in 1819), THE ATHENAEUM (1824) and the REFORM CLUB (1836). (See also BARRY, CHARLES; GAS; LONDON LIBRARY; MALL, THE; REGENT STREET; ROTHMAN'S OF PALL MALL; ROYAL ACADEMY OF ARTS; STREET LIGHTING.)

PARK LANE

Park Lane runs for ¾ mile along the eastern edge of HYDE PARK, linking MARBLE ARCH to HYDE PARK CORNER. The first buildings were erected during the eighteenth century, but the area did not become fashionable until about 1820, when new properties were constructed and older ones extensively refurbished (for example Londonderry House, designed by James Stuart for the Earl of Holdernesse, was built in the 1760s but much altered in 1825–8 by Benjamin and Philip Wyatt for the Marquess of Londonderry). By 1850, its residents were all affluent aristocrats or merchants, but in the second half of the century their peace was increasingly disturbed by a growing volume of traffic and the use of HYDE PARK for public assemblies, such as the demonstration against a Sunday Trading Bill that attracted 150,000 protesters in 1855. From the 1920s, as families left for more peaceful environments, homes were converted into offices or demolished and replaced by HOTELS, such as the DORCHESTER HOTEL, which opened in 1931. Park Lane is the only tree-lined dual carriageway in central London.

PARKS

London has about 400 parks of 20 acres or more and hundreds of smaller open spaces. In the central city, the largest of these were originally royal hunting grounds located outside the medieval town walls but engulfed by urban expansion during the nineteenth and twentieth centuries; although still owned by the Crown, they are now open to the public (see ROYAL PARKS). Others (such as VICTORIA PARK, in the EAST END) were established as the municipal authorities in the Victorian city responded to campaigns encouraging them to provide recreational facilities in the burgeoning residential areas (and particularly in working-class communities). Also, the construction of embankments (see BAZALGETTE, JOSEPH WILLIAM) along the RIVER THAMES during the 1860s and 1870s presented an opportunity for providing gardens, such as those at the northern end of HUNGERFORD BRIDGE (close to CHARING CROSS and the STRAND), which are often used by office workers on summer lunch breaks. Many common lands, where tenants had a right to collect firewood and graze animals, survived the building boom as well (although sometimes the space had to be fought for, as at WANDSWORTH, where wealthy residents attempted to enclose it for their own purposes); as a result, extensive areas of land, such as the 1,100 acres of WIMBLEDON Common are retained in a form that still has an element of wildness. In addition, local councils sometimes acquired formerly private estates (at AVERY HILL, for example) and were able to make the grounds available to neighbourhood residents. During the second half of the twentieth century, planning policies have required inclusion of PARKland within building developments so that residents are provided with sports facilities, land where children can play informally and places where families can walk. (See also ABERCROMBIE PLAN (1943–44); ALEXANDRA PALACE; BATTERSEA PARK; BURIAL GROUNDS; BUSHY PARK; CLAPHAM COMMON; CUPER'S GARDENS; DULWICH; EPPING FOREST; ERITH; FINSBURY PARK; GREEN PARK; GREENWICH PARK; GUNNERSBURY; HAMPSTEAD HEATH; HERNE HILL; HOLLAND HOUSE; HORNIMAN MUSEUM; HYDE PARK; KENNINGTON; KENSINGTON GARDENS; LAMBETH PALACE; LEA, RIVER; LINCOLN'S INN FIELDS; MARBLE HILL HOUSE; MORDEN; NONSUCH PALACE; OSTERLEY HOUSE; PECKHAM; PRIMROSE HILL; REGENT'S PARK; RICHMOND PARK; ROYAL BOTANIC GARDENS; ST JAMES'S PARK; SERPENTINE; SYDENHAM; VAUXHALL; WALWORTH.)

PARLIAMENTARY CONSTITUENCIES

The metropolitan area took its modern form in 1965, when the GREATER LONDON COUNCIL replaced the LONDON COUNTY COUNCIL. At that time, the city sent 103 representatives to the HOUSE OF COMMONS (see PALACE OF WESTMINSTER) but boundary revisions over the next three decades brought reductions as residents moved out of the urban area. The most recent change occurred in 1997, when the number of constituencies fell from eighty-four to seventy-four. In the General Election that year, the Labour Party won fifty-seven of the seats (gaining 49.5 per cent of the total vote), the Conservative Party eleven (with 31.2 per cent of the vote), and the Liberal Democrats six (with 14.6 per cent of the vote). Conservative support was confined to affluent suburbs such as BECKENHAM and ORPINGTON and to such wealthy inner-city areas as the CITY OF WESTMINSTER. The Liberal Democrats were at their strongest in the south-west, where they had built strong bases of support at the local council level. The new Members of Parliament included eleven women, ten representing Labour seats and one representing the Liberal Democrats.

PEABODY, GEORGE (1795–1869)

In the mid-nineteenth century, Peabody's largesse was responsible for significant improvements in the quality of life of large numbers of London's least affluent citizens. Born on 18 February 1795 into a poor Puritan family living in South Danvers (Massachusetts), he had little formal education. However, the tenets of hard work, considered use of resources and concern for others that dominated the values of his home stood him in good stead when he began to earn a living. In 1814, along with Elisha Riggs (who provided financial backing), he opened a dry goods warehouse at Georgetown in Washington, D.C. It relocated to Baltimore the following year and, by 1822, had branches in Philadelphia and New York. In 1827, business interests took him to London, where he settled ten years later, then, in 1843, founded a bank. From 1862 until his death at a friend's home in Eaton Square on 4 November 1869, he made gifts amounting to some £500,000 to his adopted city, with the specification that the money should be used 'to ameliorate the condition of the poor and needy of this great metropolis and promote their comfort and happiness'. The authorities met the condition by building 'cheap, cleanly, well-drained and healthful dwellings' (known as Peabody Buildings) for the working class. The first opened at SPITALFIELDS in 1864 but others followed rapidly, so by 1890 some 5,000 homes had been made available. The exteriors were austere (architectural historian Nikolaus Pevsner condemned one block as 'detestable'), but they undoubtedly did much to alleviate overcrowding in central London and the EAST END. Peabody also promoted Anglo-American relations, encouraging meetings between prominent figures from both nations and used his considerable wealth to support charitable causes in the United States (for example, from 1866 to 1869 he donated US$3.5 million to groups promoting education for all races in the Deep South). In 1868, the name of his birthplace was changed to Peabody, in his honour. The trust that now manages the properties he financed in London controls some 12,000 apartments on over seventy sites. In recent years, it has undertaken much refurbishment, improving provisions internally and renovating external brickwork.

PEABODY BUILDINGS

See PEABODY, GEORGE.

PEARLY KINGS AND QUEENS

During the nineteenth century, London's costermongers (the people who sold fruit, vegetables and other goods from barrows in the street or at MARKETS) appointed representatives to protect their rights, fend off competitors and act as bodyguards. So that they could be identified, these individuals (who rapidly attained an elite status among the traders) decorated their clothes, in flamboyant Victorian style, with pearl buttons. Today, they still dress up for functions such as the costermongers' Harvest Festival, held in ST MARTIN-IN-THE-FIELDS CHURCH. In 1911, they formed a Pearly Kings' and Queens' Association, which devotes much energy to charitable causes.

PEASANTS' REVOLT

In 1381, rural dwellers were provoked to rebellion by a combination of the food short-

A London costermonger.

ages that followed a series of bad harvests, actions taken by landowners to counteract the labour shortages caused by the BLACK DEATH, and the poll tax levied to provide funds for war with France. The boy king Richard II decided to confront Wat Tyler (one of the rebel leaders) at BLACKHEATH but was unable to reach the meeting place because of the large crowds. Frustrated, Tyler marched on London, killing a number of lawyers, destroying legal records and setting inmates free from PRISONS. On 14 June, Richard made concessions, granting demands for an easing of restrictions on land sales, an end to feudal service and the introduction of a right to rent property but Tyler continued to terrorize the city, beheading the Archbishop of Canterbury (Simon of Sudbury) and setting fire to the TOWER OF LONDON. Taking the law into his own hands, William Walworth, the LORD MAYOR, attacked and killed Tyler during a meeting at Smithfield (see SMITHFIELD MEAT MARKET). Robbed of direction, the peasants drifted back to the countryside. The event – the first large-scale public protest recorded in England – had little long-term impact but did succeed in ending the poll tax until Margaret Thatcher's disastrous attempts to re-introduce it in the late 1980s. (See also INNS OF COURT; JACK STRAW'S CASTLE; KNIGHTS HOSPITALLER; LAMBETH PALACE; MARSHALSEA PRISON.)

PECKHAM

Peckham lies south of the RIVER THAMES between CAMBERWELL and DEPTFORD. It was settled during Anglo-Saxon times and, for over a millennium, functioned as an agricultural village where incomes from farming were supplemented by market gardening and by provision of pasturage, accommodation and refreshments for drovers taking cattle to the London MARKETS. The Grand Surrey Canal, which was intended to link the Thames DOCKS to MITCHAM, was the first spur to urban development, arriving in 1826, and was soon lined with houses and industrial premises such as the South Metropolitan GAS Company's works. An omnibus service from the Adam and Eve Inn to the WEST END furthered contacts with the central city from 1851 and from 1872 the London, Chatham and Dover RAILWAY allowed commuters to live in the area but work elsewhere. The improved access encouraged speculative builders to develop housing estates, replacing green fields with brick terraces, but some open space remained, notably the 54-acre Nunhead Cemetery (laid out in 1840), the 64-acre Peckham Rye Common (which was bought by Camberwell Vestry in 1868 and converted into sports fields) and the 49-acre Homestall Farm (which became a public PARK in 1890). After the Second World War, and particularly from 1960, many of the poorer-quality Victorian properties were demolished and replaced by local authority housing, mainly consisting of high-rise flats immortalized in the BBC television comedy *Only Fools and Horses*. The canal, having outlived its usefulness, was closed in 1971. Peckham forms part of the LONDON BOROUGH OF SOUTHWARK. The name is probably derived from the Old English *peac* and *ham*, meaning 'the homestead in the hills'. (See also DOMESDAY BOOK; PECKHAM EXPERIMENT.)

PECKHAM EXPERIMENT

In 1935, Dr Scott Williamson opened a three-storey building in St Mary's Road, PECKHAM, with the intention of conducting investigations into the biology of human beings. The glass and concrete structure, designed by Sir E. Owen Williams, contained a cafeteria, games rooms, a gymnasium, a swimming pool and a THEATRE. Families were encouraged to become members through payment of a weekly subscription and submission of an undertaking to attend regular physical examinations in the clinic on the site. The project was interrupted by the Second World War (when a munitions plant took over the accommodation) and abandoned in 1950 when funds were exhausted.

PENTONVILLE

The area east of KING'S CROSS was one of London's first planned suburbs, laid out from 1773 on 134 acres of farmland owned by Thomas Penton, the Member of Parliament for Winchester. Initially, it was popular with craftsmen working in the CITY OF LONDON but, during the second half of the nineteenth century, shops and small industrial premises infiltrated the residential area and the estate gradually turned into an urban slum. After the Second World War, local authorities demolished most of the properties, replacing them with higher standard public housing. Pentonville PRISON, which opened in 1842, was designed as an institution where male offenders would be taught a trade then transported to work in the colonies. Modernized in the late twentieth century, it now holds men convicted of civil offences and others awaiting sentence. The area forms part of the LONDON BOROUGH OF ISLINGTON. (See also RILLINGTON PLACE.)

PEPYS, SAMUEL (1633–1703)

Pepys's diary is an important source of information on London life during the 1660s, a turbulent decade that included the GREAT PLAGUE (1664–6), the GREAT FIRE (1666) and the restoration of the English monarchy following Oliver Cromwell's Puritan rule. Pepys was born in the city on 23 February 1633, one of eleven children in the family of tailor John Pepys and his wife, Mary. He was educated in Huntingdon and at St Paul's School (London) before attending Cambridge University, where he was awarded a BA degree in 1650 and an MA in 1660. The considerable influence of his cousin, Sir Edward Montagu, secured him a post as Clerk to the King's Ships, from which relatively lowly status he rose to become the most respected of the country's naval administrators, combining his talents for diplomacy and hard work with a business acumen that endeared him to Parliament and the monarchy. He survived accusations of treason and of support for Roman Catholicism in 1679 to become president of the ROYAL SOCIETY (1684) and first Master of TRINITY HOUSE (1685), dying at CLAPHAM on 26 May 1703.

Pepys's diaries are notable partly because of the writer's eye for detail, partly because of the importance of the events of the time and partly because of his honest observation. They begin on 1 January 1660 and end on 31 May 1669, by which time failing eyesight had made recording a painful task. The pain of the plague years is clearly evident; on 16 October 1665, Pepys noted that he 'walked to the town; but, Lord! How empty the streets are, and melancholy, so many poor, sick people in the streets full of sores; and so many sad stories overheard as I walk, everybody talking of this dead, and that man sick, and so many in this place, and so many in that.' The following summer, he saw London burn, writing on 2 September that he went to an alehouse in BANKSIDE where he watched the conflagration spread 'as far as we could see up the hill of the City, in a most horrid, malicious, bloody flame, not like the fire flame of an ordinary fire.' He took good care, however, to protect his own property as far as possible because two days later he dug a pit in his garden to bury wine and parmesan cheese so that they would not be destroyed.

The diaries also tell of family joys and sorrows. On 18 March 1664, Pepys went to ST BRIDE'S CHURCH to make funeral arrangements for Thomas, his brother. The negotiations with the gravedigger proved shocking. 'To see how a man's tombes are at the mercy of such a fellow, that for sixpence he would, as his own words were, "I will jostle them together but I will make room for him;" speaking of the fulness of the middle aisle, where he was to lie; and that he would, for my father's sake, do my brother, that is dead, all the civility that he can; which was to disturb other corps that are not quite rotten, to make room for him.' Other days proved more pleasurable. Pepys was clearly attracted by ladies, making frequent reference to their looks; on 18 August 1667, he records that, while attending a service at ST DUNSTAN-IN-THE-WEST CHURCH, FLEET STREET, he 'stood by a pretty, modest maid whom I did labour to take by the hand and the body, but she would not, but got further and further from me, and at last I could perceive her to take pins out of her pocket to prick me if I should touch her again.' Domestic arrangements, relationships with superiors and social engagements are all faithfully recorded, providing a fertile source of material for scholars. (See also ALDERSGATE; EPSOM; FLOOD CONTROL; HYDE PARK; ROYAL NAVAL DOCKYARDS; ST MARGARET'S CHURCH, WESTMINSTER; ST OLAVE'S CHURCH, HART STREET; VAUXHALL.)

PETTICOAT LANE

One of London's principal STREET MARKETS, Petticoat Lane (in WHITECHAPEL) probably derived its name from the shopkeepers who sold second-hand clothes in the area during the sixteenth century. The road was renamed Middlesex Street in 1830 in a puritanical attempt to avoid reference to ladies' underwear, but popular usage retained the earlier title for the MARKET, which was established by the mid-eighteenth century. Attempts were made to stop trading on Sunday mornings but, in 1936, Parliamentary legislation confirmed rights to operate. Although stalls are open every day of the week, they are busiest by far on Sunday, when over 800 booths are set up to sell clothes, leather goods, records, fruit, vegetables, confectionery, flowers, kitchen knives and other goods. Buyers banter with the EAST END salesmen, who rely on crowd reaction to promote trade.

Petticoat Lane street market, c. 1830s.

PHILHARMONIA ORCHESTRA

The Philharmonia was formed in 1945, primarily to make recordings of classical music. It made its first European tour in 1952 and visited the United States in 1955, then suffered a period of administrative disharmony before becoming a self-governing entity, administered by a Council of Management, in 1964. For some years after that, it was threatened by serious financial problems but survived to become one of the world's leading orchestras. During the 1990s, it developed major bases at Bedford, Paris, the ROYAL FESTIVAL HALL (where it became resident in 1996), Leicester and Athens. It has played under most major conductors during the second half of the twentieth century, including Herbert von Karajan, Otto Klemperer and Richard Strauss, presenting about forty concerts in London each year and (since 1992) making a commitment to commission works from leading composers.

PICCADILLY

Piccadilly is one of central London's principal routeways, stretching for about a mile from PICCADILLY CIRCUS to HYDE PARK CORNER in the CITY OF WESTMINSTER. In the early seventeenth century, it was no more than a country lane but, as traffic from the west increased, it became the major highway to the CITY OF LONDON, attracting housing development. One of the first residents was tailor Robert Baker, who made picadils (a trimming for collars then very fashionable among aristocrats); he built a mansion named Piccadilly Hall, after the source of his wealth and, over the next 150 years, the name was applied to the whole street. With the exception of BURLINGTON HOUSE, the earliest buildings have been swept away by more recent developments. A number of the present properties date from 1760–1850, when wealthy citizens gained status by owning homes located close to the city but with semi-rural surroundings (for example, Apsley House, designed by ROBERT ADAM and built in 1771–8, was the residence of the Duke of Wellington and, since 1952, has housed the WELLINGTON MUSEUM collections). Further building occurred during the late nineteenth and early twentieth centuries but since then most private residents have moved away and their houses have been converted for use as GENTLEMEN'S CLUBS, shops, airline offices and HOTELS, particularly in the east. Only GREEN PARK has escaped the developers, providing an important recreational space for workers and shoppers close to the heart of the city. (See also CHAMBERS, WILLIAM; CHURCHILL, WINSTON SPENCER; FORTNUM AND MASON; JACKSON'S OF PICCADILLY; PICCADILLY LINE; RITZ HOTEL; ST JAMES'S CHURCH, PICCADILLY; WREN, CHRISTOPHER.)

PICCADILLY CIRCUS

With its coloured neon lights and the statue of Eros, this busy meeting point of several major thoroughfares symbolizes the heart and vitality of the West End. It was first formed in 1819, when REGENT STREET was designed to link with PICCADILLY and the frontages at the intersection were set back to enhance the sense of space. SHAFTESBURY AVENUE, constructed during the 1880s, brought further traffic then in 1893 the statue of Eros (designed by Alfred Gilbert and placed in the centre of a fountain) was erected at the crossroads as a memorial to the seventh Earl of Shaftesbury, who had advocated education for the poor and other social reforms. (Eros represents the angel of Christian charity, not the god of love, and was the first statue in London to be cast in aluminium.) Between 1900 and 1910, electrically illuminated billboards were placed on the buildings forming the north-east sector of the Circus, which, by mid-century, had become a brash mixture of shops, restaurants and offices, particularly busy after dark as playgoers made their way to the nearby THEATRES. Since the end of the Second World War, there have been intermittent debates about how to improve the area, which lacks architectural impact (particularly during the day) and attracts homeless young people, but there has been little action although access to Eros has improved and the LONDON UNDERGROUND station was refurbished in 1989.

PICCADILLY LINE

In 1901, CHARLES TYSON YERKES bought the rights to three sections of UNDERGROUND railway where construction had not yet begun and combined them to form the Piccadilly Line. The first services ran between HAMMERSMITH and FINSBURY PARK in 1906 (the year after his death) and, at EARL'S COURT, introduced escalators to the city's TRANSPORT network. A branch line from HOLBORN to ALDWYCH opened the following year but the Great Northern RAILWAY was able to prevent extensions northwards until 1932, when a station was built at Arnos Grove. The terminus at COCKFOSTERS was completed in 1933. In an attempt to relieve congestion on the DISTRICT LINE, Piccadilly Line tracks were laid from Hammersmith to South Harrow in 1932, then from South Harrow to UXBRIDGE and from ACTON TOWN to HOUNSLOW West in 1933. Finally, in 1977, the Hounslow route was extended to HEATHROW AIRPORT. Trains (most of which date from the 1970s and provide luggage space for airline passengers) are maintained at depots near Cockfosters and Northfields. In 2002, responsibility for the line's infrastructure was franchised to Tube Lines, a consortium of private businesses, but LONDON UNDERGROUND remains responsible for providing the services. (See also FINSBURY PARK; KING'S CROSS FIRE; PICK, FRANK; SOUTHGATE.)

PICK, FRANK (1878-1941)

As commercial manager of the Underground Electric Railways Company (UERL), then chief executive officer of the LONDON PASSENGER TRANSPORT BOARD (LPTB), Pick exerted great influence over the development of train, tram and bus services in the city during the first forty years of the twentieth century. The eldest child of Francis Spalding (a draper) and his wife, Fanny, Frank was born in Spalding on 23 November 1878 and educated at St Peter's School in York and at the University of London, ultimately graduating in 1903 with an LLB degree. He had found employment with the North-Eastern Railway the previous year and was given experience in several departments before joining the staff of Sir George Gibb, the general manager. In 1906, Gibb was appointed to a post with the Metropolitan District Railway (part of CHARLES TYSON YERKES' UERL empire) and he persuaded Pick to move with him.

As UERL aggressively expanded, Pick gained control over tram and bus interests as well as UNDERGROUND railways and, in 1912, became commercial manager of the company. By 1933, when the capital's TRANSPORT services were taken into public ownership, his reputation as an administrator made him the obvious candidate for the post of chief executive officer of the LPTB, which ran the integrated system.

Pick was a shy man with an ability to grasp detail quickly. He believed that the LTPB could integrate different forms of travel to provide mass transit which genuinely met the needs of residents and visitors and, as a devout member of the Congregational Church, he felt that motivation to serve the public came from roots other than bonuses, awards and recognition. In particular, he argued that the visual arts were a civilizing influence and went to great lengths to ensure that design was elegant and attractive as well as functional. He commissioned the bar and circle logo which still identifies the LONDON UNDERGROUND, asked calligrapher Edward Johnston to design an easily read alphabet for signs, concerned himself with the detail of station architecture (as with Charles Holden's plans for Arnos Grove, SOUTHGATE and other stops on the PICCADILLY LINE) and employed unknown as well as famous artists to paint posters. As a result, Kenneth Clark, the Director of the National Gallery, was able to claim that, in another age, Pick 'might have been a sort of Thomas Aquinas'.

Frank Pick retired in 1940 and died on 7 November the following year. The LONDON TRANSPORT MUSEUM has a collection of his notes, journals and letters that is an important resource for historians of art as well as researchers studying the evolution of the city's travel facilities.

PIMLICO

Pimlico occupies the north bank of one of the RIVER THAMES' southerly meanders, with BELGRAVIA to the west and WESTMINSTER to the east. The origin of the name is unknown; some writers suggest that it is derived from Ben Pimlico (an innkeeper during the sixteenth century), others that it recognizes a connection with the Pamlaco tribe of American Indians who traded with England during the 1600s, or that it is the name of a local drink whose ingredients are now unknown. During the seventeenth century, the area was acquired, through marriage, by Sir Thomas Grosvenor (see GROSVENOR ESTATE) but was undeveloped until THOMAS

CUBITT replaced the marshes and market gardens with rows of terraced houses from 1835. The properties were less grand than those in Belgravia so Pimlico never acquired the same social status as its neighbour but, even so, became popular with the middle class. During the twentieth century, many of the homes were converted into small HOTELS, and other commercial properties infiltrated the area, but it still retains a predominantly residential character with a slightly bohemian reputation stemming from its popularity with artists and literary groups. The suburb forms part of the CITY OF WESTMINSTER. (See also VAUXHALL.)

PINNER

Although its name is derived from Old English (the words *pinn* and *ora* mean 'the pointed ridge' or 'the pointed bank'), the settlement is not recorded in documents until 1321. An affluent middle-class residential suburb in the north-west of the LONDON BOROUGH OF HARROW, it consists largely of substantial, red-brick family homes erected during the 1930s and clustering around the fifteenth-century flint and freestone church of St John the Baptist. Many older buildings (including two sixteenth-century half-timbered PUBLIC HOUSES in High Street) are protected from development by conservation area legislation but Headstone Manor (constructed in 1344 for the Archbishop of Canterbury) serves as a local history MUSEUM and other properties are used as shops or offices. A fair is held every spring; originally founded as a cattle MARKET in 1336, it is now devoted entirely to the pursuit of pleasure, with merry-go-rounds and ferris wheels. (See also METROLAND.)

PLANETARIUM

See MADAME TUSSAUD'S WAXWORKS.

PLUMSTEAD

Plumstead, on the SOUTH BANK of the RIVER THAMES in the LONDON BOROUGH OF GREENWICH, was settled before the Roman invasion and thrived as an agricultural village, noted for sheep grazing and fruit growing, until the nineteenth century. The arrival of the RAILWAY (in 1849) and industrial expansion at neighbouring WOOLWICH increased demands for building land and resulted in rapid population increases that transformed the area into a metropolitan suburb. The community resisted much of the development, rioting when open spaces were acquired for military training in the 1870s and forcing the METROPOLITAN BOARD OF WORKS to purchase Plumstead Common and Winns Common, which were protected from further encroachment and preserved for public recreation. Plumstead's name is probably derived from the Old English *plume* and *stede*, suggesting that it was 'a place where plum trees grow'.

POET'S CORNER

See WESTMINSTER ABBEY.

POLLUTION

See AIR POLLUTION; GREAT STINK; SEWAGE DISPOSAL; WATER POLLUTION.

POOL OF LONDON

The Pool stretches along the RIVER THAMES from LONDON BRIDGE downstream to Limekiln Creek. Shipping has made little use of the section above TOWER BRIDGE in modern times (though some cruise liners tie up alongside HMS BELFAST) but the reaches provided most of the city's harbour facilities from the Roman period until the advent of large container vessels, which necessitated a move closer to the deep waters of the river mouth during the late 1960s. Faced with the decline in traffic, the East India DOCKS closed in 1967; WAPPING (1968), St Katharine's (1969), Surrey (1970), West India (1980), MILLWALL (1980), George V (1981), Royal Albert (1981) and Royal Victoria (1981) all followed, leaving extensive areas of derelict land on both banks of the river. Many of the nineteenth-century warehouses, built to hold cargoes from around the world, were demolished as development programmes were introduced but the DOCKLANDS urban regeneration scheme retained some elements of the old port in its marinas, retail complexes and offices.

POPLAR

For most of its existence, the EAST END suburb of Poplar (lying on the north bank of the RIVER THAMES some 5 miles east of CHARING CROSS) has had close links with the sea. During the medieval period, it developed as a fishing village, then, from the sixteenth century, expanded as ships increasingly utilized harbour facilities at nearby BLACKWALL, attracting repair, construction and supply businesses. The opening of the West India DOCKS in 1802, followed by the East India Docks four years later, brought an influx of merchants, administrators, seamen, craftsmen, tradesmen and labourers who swelled the POPULATION from 4,500 in 1801 to over 55,000 in 1881. During the twentieth century, however, the port facilities declined and the middle-class element left for more attractive residential environments, turning Poplar into one of the poorest areas in London. In such conditions, the Labour Party's socialist philosophies found fertile ground (see, for example, POPLARISM) and produced a continuing stream of left-wing politicians both at the local government and at the Parliamentary levels. The area suffered greatly during the BLITZ but once the land was cleared of damaged properties when the Second World War ended in 1945 extensive public housing programmes effected major improvements in living conditions. With the closure of the docks from 1967, the maritime industries disappeared. Small engineering firms and a host of small textile manufacturers and retailers (many from Bangladesh, India and Pakistan) provide employment but levels of wealth are still low. In 1965, when the local authorities in the metropolitan area were reorganized, Poplar was included within the LONDON BOROUGH OF TOWER HAMLETS. The area probably gets its name from the poplar trees which flourished in the damp soils alongside the river. (See also AIR RAIDS; DOCKLANDS LIGHT RAILWAY (DLR).)

POPLARISM

During the 1920s, residents of POPLAR (in London's EAST END) campaigned for national and local government policies that would ease the plight of the city's poor. Led by GEORGE LANSBURY, the local councillors declined to levy the property taxes that would pay the borough's contribution towards the running costs of the LONDON COUNTY COUNCIL, the Metropolitan Asylums Board and the METROPOLITAN POLICE. Thirty of them were imprisoned for insisting on maintaining the protest, but fear of public unrest in the East End forced the government to release them after six weeks and to introduce Parliamentary legislation that transferred much of the cost of caring for the least well off to the Ministry of Health. As a result, official efforts to help the disadvantaged became widely known as Poplarism.

POPULATION

All figures for London's population prior to 1801 (when the first official census was carried out in Great Britain) are educated guesses because no authority was responsible for collating statistics of births, deaths and population migration. Moreover, assessments of change over time are complicated by periodic revisions of local authority boundaries. It is believed, however, that numbers during the Roman occupation reached 45,000–50,000 in the third century but declined after the invaders' withdrawal because the economy of the Anglo-Saxon peoples who replaced them was rural, rather than urban, in character. Evidence of occupation from the fifth until the eleventh centuries is limited; modern Londoners march to work along streets (such as CHEAPSIDE) that have Old English names, and the Venerable Bede wrote, at the beginning of the eighth century, that London was 'the mart of many nations resorting to it by sea and land,' but, in the absence of suitable data, few scholars venture estimates of the city's size.

Several writers claim that, in the period immediately following the Norman conquest in 1066, London had 15,000–20,000 residents, only returning to Roman levels in the middle of the thirteenth century at a time of considerable prosperity. From then, growth was limited until (for reasons that are still unclear but were probably related more to IMMIGRATION from other parts of England than to changes in the birth rate or death rate) the citizenry increased from 50,000 souls to over 200,000 during the last fifty years of Tudor rule (which ended in 1603) then to around 600,000 by the time the Hanoverian monarchs replaced the ill-fated Stuarts in 1714.

The 1801 census indicated that the area now covered by the thirty-two LONDON BOROUGHS had 1,096,784 residents (though some writers suggest that the real total was as much as 5 per cent higher). Within forty years, they doubled to 2,207,653, then, over the next forty, doubled again to 4,713,441 as medical and environmental improvements lengthened life expectancy and as migrants arrived in droves (as many as 30,000 a year in 1841–71) to seek work. The spread of the RAILWAY network from 1836 encouraged speculative builders to erect housing near TRANSPORT links, speeding up the rate of urban growth and hastening the evolution of dormitory suburbs – a trend continued by the expansion of BUS routes and ownership of private cars during the twentieth century. Before the outbreak of the Second World War in 1939, London's population reached 8.6 million but, by 1981, numbers had fallen to 6.7 million as parents chose to raise families in the countryside rather than the city and as government urban renewal policies resulted in the transfer of council house and slum tenants to newly built properties, with a high standard of amenity, in surrounding counties. Since then, however, the total has climbed again, reaching just under 7.2 million in 2001, largely as a result of relatively high rates of natural increase.

Population densities are highest in the inner city (the ROYAL BOROUGH OF KENSINGTON AND CHELSEA has nearly 34,000 people per square mile) and lowest in the suburbs (for example, in the LONDON BOROUGH OF BROMLEY and the LONDON BOROUGH OF HILLINGDON densities fall below 5,500 per square mile). Residents are younger than the British average (42.7 per cent are aged 20–44, compared to 35.2 per cent nationally). As a result of that youthfulness, the birth rate (about fifty-nine births annually per 1,000 women aged 15–44) is slightly higher than the national average (fifty-five per 1,000) and death rates are slightly lower (9 of every 1,000 residents die every year compared to 11 per 1,000 nationally). (See also ABERCROMBIE PLAN (1943–44).)

PORTLAND PLACE

Named after the Duke of Portland, who owned the land on which it was built, Portland Place was laid out to the east of CAVENDISH SQUARE by ROBERT ADAM and his brother, James, from 1774. Forty years later, JOHN NASH (who believed that it was the finest road in London) used it as a northern extension of REGENT STREET, linking REGENT'S PARK to PALL MALL. Originally entirely residential, it became increasingly commercialized after the opening of the LANGHAM HOTEL in 1865. As developers moved in, many of the original properties (most of which were designed by James Adam) were demolished or substantially altered, so, although it retains some of its original style, the street has lost much of its architectural impact. Modern occupants of the buildings have included several national institutions, notably the BRITISH BROADCASTING

CORPORATION (in Broadcasting House at No. 10), the Royal Institute of Public Health and Hygiene (No. 28), the Royal Institute of British Architects (No. 66) and the CITY AND GUILDS OF LONDON INSTITUTE (No. 76, once the home of novelist and Governor General of Canada John Buchan). (See also ST MARYLEBONE.)

PORTLAND STONE

For centuries, Portland stone was much prized as building material for churches and other important structures in London. A strong, attractive, easily carved limestone, which rings like a bell when struck with a chisel, it consists of material laid down in a subtropical sea during the Jurassic period (some 120–140 million years ago) and now exposed in near horizontal strata at England's South Coast on the Isle of Portland. The rock, first quarried by the Romans, was introduced to London architects in the early seventeenth century by INIGO JONES then used by CHRISTOPHER WREN to rebuild ST PAUL'S CATHEDRAL after the GREAT FIRE of 1666 (he transported it to the city in a fleet of barges routed along the English Channel and up the RIVER THAMES) and by WILLIAM CHAMBERS in the construction of SOMERSET HOUSE (1776–86). It is also found in the BANQUETING HOUSE, MANSION HOUSE, the ROYAL COURTS OF JUSTICE and many of the government offices that line WHITEHALL. (See also BARRY, CHARLES; BUCKINGHAM PALACE; CENOTAPH; CENTRAL CRIMINAL COURT; CHISWICK BRIDGE; COUNTY HALL; MONUMENT; REGENT STREET; RICHMOND BRIDGE; ST BENET'S CHURCH, PAUL'S WHARF; ST JAMES'S CHURCH, PICCADILLY.)

PORTOBELLO ROAD MARKET

From 1870, Portobello Road (in north KENSINGTON) became a popular location for trade in horses. As business increased, other merchants set up their stalls in an attempt to attract customers for other goods, so, in 1929, a formal license for street trading was issued by the local authorities. The MARKET continued to flourish after the Second World War, drawing tourists as well as Londoners to the growing number of booths offering antiques. It is open every day except Sunday but is busiest on Saturdays, when bargain hunters throng the mile-long street. The street got its un-English-sounding name when, in 1739, the British captured Porto Bello, a Spanish settlement on the East Coast of Central America, and a local farmer renamed his farm in honour of the achievement.

PORT OF LONDON

See DOCKLANDS; DOCKS; POOL OF LONDON; PORT OF LONDON AUTHORITY (PLA).

PORT OF LONDON AUTHORITY (PLA)

In 1902, a Royal Commission reported that London's harbour facilities were inefficient, poorly equipped, expensive, managed by too many organizations and likely to become increasingly uncompetitive. It recommended the creation of a single authority to manage the DOCK, but because of bickering between vested interests and claims by some politicians that the proposal was a step towards socialism, the new body – the Port of London Authority – was not established until 1909. It took over responsibility for the tidal area of the RIVER THAMES from Teddington (west of the metropolis) to the mouth of the estuary, a distance of about 100 miles, and, by 1939, had dredged a 50-mile-long channel, 30 feet deep at low water, so that large ships could sail upriver. In addition, it had built 6 miles of quay and enclosed 80 additional acres of dock water. As a result, the annual weight of cargo passing through London rose by 50 per cent to 60 million tons and the percentage of the United Kingdom's sea-borne trade handled by the port rose from 29 to 38 per cent. Further improvements were made immediately after the Second World War, partly in order to repair damage but also to facilitate the rebuilding of the country's economy. In particular, container-handling equipment was installed at Tilbury, some 20 miles downstream of the city centre. During the last quarter of the twentieth century, the PLA became heavily involved in the redevelopment of the harbour area closest to TOWER BRIDGE (see DOCKLANDS), occupying a site at the showpiece St Katharine DOCK as its own headquarters. Also, in 1987 it assumed responsibility for pilotage on the river.

The PLA (which moved, in 2000, to offices in Bakers' Hall, Harp Lane) is unusual amongst Britain's harbour management agencies because it is wholly independent of the commercial cargo-handling operations that use the port. It functions as a public trust, funded by charges on vessels using the docks, and is governed by a board consisting of a chairman supported by seven non-executive members (all of whom are appointed by the Secretary of State for Transport) along with four executive members (chosen by the board itself). In addition to its general oversight of port activities, it licenses certain craft (such as tugs) and the people who work on them. It can also veto any proposal to build on, over or under the riverbed if navigation would be impaired.

POSTAL DELIVERIES

The first regular system of postal deliveries to private citizens began in 1635, when arrangements were made to carry letters along the main routes out of the CITY OF LONDON as part of the Royal Mail service organized by the General Post Office (GPO). Local carriage had to be arranged privately until, in 1680, William Dockwra offered to transport letters and packages within the urban area at a cost of one penny, paid by the sender. Business was so great that, in 1682, his enterprise was taken over by the government and incorporated within the GPO. During the early nineteenth century, reforms (initiated by Edward Johnson of the Postmaster General's Office) speeded up deliveries but, in 1801, a price increase (to twopence) put the service beyond the means of many households. Campaigns for reform resulted in the introduction of a national delivery service in 1840, with the basic penny cost reinstated. The introduction of the postage stamp by Sir Rowland Hill created the economies of scale which allowed this universal tariff. As the originator of the postage stamp, the United Kingdom retains the privilege of being the only country not to display the country of origin on its stamps. In London, the great bulk of the mail is still delivered by the Post Office, with prices based on weight, but there is also a large fleet of private motorbike riders (couriers) who carry parcels and documents between commercial concerns.

POST OFFICE TOWER

See BRITISH TELECOM TOWER.

PRIME MERIDIAN

The meridian is the line of 0° longitude that passes through the ROYAL OBSERVATORY at GREENWICH. Until the Observatory published the *British Nautical Almanac* in 1767, sailors tended to use the capital city of their home country as the base for calculating longitude. From the late eighteenth century, however, the *Almanac* was increasingly used by mariners of all nations as an aid to navigation, so, in 1884, an international conference held in Washington, D.C., confirmed the Greenwich meridian as the reference point from which all longitudes should be measured. World time zones are measured from the same place, with every 15° east or west of Greenwich representing an hour (though there are many local deviations). The meridian's location is marked by a brass rod, set in concrete, beside the Observatory. (See also GREENWICH MEAN TIME (GMT).)

PRIMROSE HILL

Lying just north of REGENT'S PARK, Primrose Hill, which is 206 feet high, is an ideal site for viewing a city skyline extending from TOWER BRIDGE in the east to beyond the HOUSES OF PARLIAMENT (see PALACE OF WESTMINSTER) in the west. During the medieval period, it was forestland (the hill probably got its name from the primroses that bloomed in the woodlands in spring) but the trees were cleared during the second half of the sixteenth century and the land was converted to meadow. By the 1800s, it had become a popular location for duelling and also as a gathering ground for protest groups, such as the Chartists. During the Second World War it housed an anti-aircraft battery. The hill, now an open space hemmed in by urban development, is managed by the ROYAL PARKS Agency. (See also SARACENS FOOTBALL CLUB.)

PRINTING HOUSE SQUARE

By the seventeenth century, printing shops had concentrated on the former site of the Dominican monastery at BLACKFRIARS so the area became known as Printing House Square. Bonham Norton and John Bill (who produced official documents for Charles I) had a press in operation by 1627, publishing the first edition of the LONDON GAZETTE on 5 February 1666. In 1784, John Walter bought the building and, the following year, founded the *Daily Universal Register*, which changed its name to THE TIMES in 1788. Now the longest surviving national newspaper in England, *The Times* was a financial success, expanding into neighbouring properties and earning the nickname of 'The Thunderer' with impassioned editorials during debates on Parliamentary reform in 1830. When production moved to Gray's Inn Road in 1974, the Printing House Square premises were occupied by *The Observer* (a Sunday paper first published in 1791). *The Times* was absorbed by Rupert Murdoch's publishing empire in 1981 and is now printed at WAPPING. *The Observer* has also left, taking over part of the CANARY WHARF site in the 1990s.

PRISONS

See BRIDEWELL; BRIXTON; CLINK PRISON; CRIPPLEGATE; FLEET PRISON; HOLLOWAY PRISON; MARSHALSEA PRISON; NEWGATE PRISON; PENTONVILLE; TOWER OF LONDON; WORMWOOD SCRUBS.

PROMS, THE

In 1895, Robert Newman, manager of the Queen's Hall in Langham Place, appointed Henry Wood conductor of an orchestra he was forming and asked him to introduce a series of promenade concerts that would interest the public in classical music. At the time, the only other permanent orchestra in the metropolitan area was based south of the RIVER THAMES at CRYSTAL PALACE and Wood mixed the familiar with the innovative, presenting talented young solo performers who introduced audiences to works by new composers, so the events were a considerable success. However, by 1927 costs had risen and the future was uncertain so the BRITISH BROADCASTING CORPORATION, which had been formed five years earlier with a mandate to educate and entertain, assumed organizational control, retaining Wood as conductor but using its own symphony orchestra, founded in 1930, to provide much of the music. Following the destruction of the Queen's Hall by German bombs on 10 May 1941, during the BLITZ, The Proms moved to the ALBERT HALL and are still held there every summer, a highlight of the city's musical season. Traditionally, the last night is a noisy, ebullient affair with a regular programme of sea shanties and a promenaders' chorus of *Rule Britannia*.

PUBLIC HOUSES

Pubs have been a feature of British life ever since the Roman conquest, which began in AD 43. As the invaders spread through the islands, they established a series of *tabernae* – inns where travellers could be assured of food and shelter from the elements. As London grew, taverns opened up to meet the needs of city residents as well as visitors (see, for example, ANCHOR INN, GEORGE INN and YE OLDE CHESHIRE CHEESE) but the growth in popularity of the public house dates primarily from the nineteenth century, as hot and dusty labour in mills and factories produced millions of thirsty workers. Water was often unpalatable and usually polluted, so beer became the preferred alternative, particularly for the working class. Public houses became important components of the landscape of the DOCKS, of manufacturing areas and of the neighbourhoods where the workforce lived. Often, they carried a sign that aided identification by a largely illiterate population. From the early twentieth century, many of these independent businesses were acquired by BREWERIES intent on providing a guaranteed market for their products but since the 1960s changing fashions have led to closures as patrons have found other leisure time activities. In response, many of the 7,000 pubs in the city began to provide food as well as drink and, in addition, attempted to attract a particular clientele, adapting their decor and providing entertainment (such as music, strippers or quizzes) to meet the perceived tastes of office workers, commuters, young people or other social groups. (See also ANGEL, THE; ARSENAL FOOTBALL CLUB; BATTERSEA PARK; BLACKFRIARS; CHIGWELL; COCKFOSTERS; COFFEE HOUSES; EDGWARE; EDMONTON; EGHAM; ELEPHANT AND CASTLE; FLEET MARRIAGES; HARROW-ON-THE-HILL; HOUNSLOW; JACK STRAW'S CASTLE; KRAY TWINS; LEADENHALL MARKET; LONDON WASPS RUGBY FOOTBALL CLUB; MAIDA VALE; NEW CROSS; OLD KENT ROAD; OVAL, THE; RED LION SQUARE; SOUTHWARK; SPANIARDS, THE; SURREY COUNTY CRICKET CLUB; SWISS COTTAGE; TOTTENHAM HOTSPUR FOOTBALL CLUB.)

A sixteenth-century engraving of Staple Inn, Holborn.

Hogarth's famous engraving *Beer Street*, 1751.

PUBLIC RECORD OFFICE (PRO)

Until the middle of the nineteenth century, official government documents were stored at several locations, including the TOWER OF LONDON and WESTMINSTER ABBEY. However, in 1838, an Act of Parliament established a Public Record Office responsible for collating and storing the papers. A mock Tudor building, designed by Sir James Pennethorne, was erected in CHANCERY LANE and records were deposited following its completion in 1856. By the end of the century, several extensions to the property had expanded storage space, but, even so, the accommodation proved inadequate and after the First World War administrators had to erect sheds and huts nearby in order to cope with the growing volume of paper. In 1977, however, a new facility was opened at KEW to hold documents from modern government departments. Legal material and state papers dated prior to 1782 remained at the central London site until an extension at Kew was completed in 1995. By the end of the following year, the Chancery Lane site was vacated, with microfilm records of births, marriages, deaths, wills and nineteenth-century census material transferred to a new Family Records Centre at 1 Myddelton Street in the LONDON BOROUGH OF ISLINGTON. Among its most prized documents, the PRO has copies of the DOMESDAY BOOK (William the Conqueror's survey of his English estates, carried out in 1085-6), the Magna Carta (a charter of liberties, restricting royal rights, signed by King John in 1215) and WILLIAM SHAKESPEARE's will (in which he left his wife his second best bed). In 2003 the PRO joined with the Historical Manuscripts Commission to form the National Archives. (See also GREAT EXHIBITION.)

PUBS

See PUBLIC HOUSES.

PUDDING LANE

The GREAT FIRE of London began in Farynor's bakery, in Pudding Lane, on the night of 2 September 1666 and spread throughout the city, destroying eighty-nine churches and 13,200 houses. The street, on the north bank of the RIVER THAMES east of LONDON BRIDGE, probably got its name from the animal entrails (or puddings) carried down the road from butchers' premises to refuse disposal boats during the Middle Ages.

PUGIN, AUGUSTUS WELBY NORTHMORE (1812–1852)

Although CHARLES BARRY designed the exterior of the PALACE OF WESTMINSTER, Pugin was responsible for the exuberant neo-Gothic decoration that characterizes the interior. The only child of Augustus and Catherine Pugin, he was born in the family home at 34 Store Street, BLOOMSBURY, on 1 March 1812. He attended Christ's Hospital School, then worked in the architect's practice owned by his father, who had fled to London to escape the consequences of the French Revolution in 1789. In 1827, Pugin was awarded a commission to design furniture for the royal palace at Windsor, then, in 1831, he prepared the scenery for *Kenilworth*, a ballet performed at the THEATRE ROYAL, DRURY LANE, but he did not prosper financially and, the same year, was imprisoned for debt. He became a Roman Catholic in 1835, a year before he published the polemical *Contrasts*, a work in which he argued that the quality of a society's ARCHITECTURE was a reflection of its cultural values.

The next decade was to be the most productive and influential period in Pugin's career. He was a prominent critic of the work of John Soane (see SIR JOHN SOANE'S MUSEUM) and James Wyatt, designers of the PALACE OF WESTMINSTER, so when the building burned down on 16 October 1834 he wept few tears. The competition to design a new meeting place for the nation's Parliament was won by Charles Barry, with Pugin preparing the drawings that accompanied the entry. In 1836, he presented further sketches of fixtures and fittings then, in 1844, was called upon to make additional plans for decoration. In all, historians suggest, he completed over 2,000 pictures of furniture, hangings, metalwork, tiles, wallpaper and woodcarvings. His involvement in such a prestigious development inevitably earned him much attention and brought many commissions, including those for St Alban's Church (Macclesfield), St Chad's Church (Birmingham), Downside Priory (Bath), St Giles Church (Cheadle), St Mary's Church (Stockton-on-Tees), St Mary-on-the-Sands Church (Southport) and St Oswald's Church (Liverpool). In London, he worked on St Joseph's School (Cadogan Street, CHELSEA), St Thomas's Church (Rylston Road, EALING) and St George's Roman Catholic Cathedral, SOUTHWARK (most of which was destroyed by German bombs in 1941, during the BLITZ). He also prepared the altarpiece for the CHURCH OF THE IMMACULATE CONCEPTION in Farm Street, MAYFAIR, planned additions to Alton Towers (the Staffordshire home of the Earl of Shrewsbury), published several books, married three times and fathered eight children. By 1851, he was suffering from overwork and the following year he spent some time in the BEDLAM mental asylum. On 14 September 1852 (only a few months after his fortieth birthday), he died at his home in Ramsgate, Kent, exhausted physically and mentally. The government awarded his widow an annual pension of £100 in recognition of his contribution to British architecture. (See also ALBERT, PRINCE.)

PUNK

Punk was an assertive, confrontational fashion that took root among young working-class people during the second half of the 1970s. Although it flourished for a time in cities of the United States, it was replaced in North America by disco, leaving London as the focus of the trend. There, its followers adopted aggressive clothing (such as leather jackets emblazoned with provocative slogans), body piercing (such as nose rings and lip rings, sometimes linked by chains) and unconventional, gaudily coloured hairstyles. Politically, punks were frequently associated with right-wing political movements such as the National Front and musically they favoured the SEX PISTOLS, the Clash and other rock bands that challenged accepted orthodoxies through the profanity of their language and the decadence of a lifestyle focusing on sex and drugs. During the 1980s, young people turned away from the excesses of the movement but several of its attributes (such as the acceptance of tattoos on women, earrings on men and lip studs on both sexes) were absorbed by mainstream society.

PURCELL ROOM

See QUEEN ELIZABETH HALL.

PUTNEY

Putney lies on the SOUTH BANK of the RIVER THAMES about 5 miles from CHARING CROSS. Archaeological evidence suggests a lengthy period of settlement, dating from the Iron Age, but the economy was based on farming and fishing until the early sixteenth century, when wealthy noblemen and merchants (such as Thomas Cromwell, adviser and later Chancellor to Henry VIII) began to acquire property and give it an up-market reputation. Growth occurred rapidly (given the standards of the time) during the seventeenth and eighteenth centuries and was enhanced by the opening of a bridge across the Thames to FULHAM in 1729 (see PUTNEY BRIDGE), but modern Putney is largely a product of Industrial Revolution expansion. In 1846, the opening of a RAILWAY station on the London and South-Western Railway's line to WATERLOO allowed office workers to move out of the central city and buy a terraced or semi-detached home in the fashionable riverside town, which rapidly became a suburb of London as open spaces were acquired by builders. However, the cost of land and the greater attraction of areas closer to the city for commercial and industrial developers allowed Putney to retain its essentially residential nature. The lack of construction since the 1920s (by which time most of the former fields and market gardens were built over) emphasizes the Victorian and Edwardian ARCHITECTURE of the area, which is now part of the LONDON BOROUGH OF WANDSWORTH. The origin of the place name is unclear. The second element may be from the Old English *hyth*, or 'landing place'. The first is probably a corruption of *Putta*, a personal name from the same period, but *putta* may also be a word for 'hawks'. (See also DOMESDAY BOOK; UNIVERSITY BOAT RACE.)

PUTNEY BRIDGE

The first BRIDGE across the RIVER THAMES between PUTNEY and FULHAM was a wooden edifice, designed by Jacob Ackworth and opened in 1729. Until 1750, when WESTMINSTER BRIDGE was built, it was the closest crossing to the CITY OF LONDON west of LONDON BRIDGE but its twenty-six spans (varying in size from only 14 feet to 32 feet) proved an increasingly serious impediment to navigation so in 1882–6 it was replaced by the present granite structure, designed by JOSEPH WILLIAM BAZALGETTE, which has five spans. The bridge has been the starting point of the annual boat race between Oxford and Cambridge Universities since 1845 (see UNIVERSITY BOAT RACE). The lattice-girder RAILWAY bridge, which lies a few yards to the east, was erected for the London and South-Western Railway in 1887–9.

Q

QUEEN ELIZABETH HALL

Built immediately east of the ROYAL FESTIVAL HALL in the arts complex on the SOUTH BANK of the RIVER THAMES close to WATERLOO BRIDGE and named after Elizabeth II, the concert hall opened in 1967. It seats about 1,100 people and initially presented programmes by small orchestras. However, the stage has since been adapted for the performance of musicals and opera. The Purcell Room, part of the same building and erected at the same time, is more intimate, holding audiences of up to 370 for concerts by solo artists and chamber music groups. The LONDON COUNTY COUNCIL Architect's Department was responsible for the design of the complex and prepared its plans at a time when stark, multi-level, concrete buildings were fashionable. The result, to modern critics, looks bare and functional, with exterior bridges and stairways that present considerable problems to elderly and other physically challenged patrons.

QUEEN'S HOUSE

In 1616, James I commissioned INIGO JONES to build a house for his wife, Anne of Denmark, in GREENWICH PARK. Anne died, three years later, before much work was done but the building was completed during the 1630s for Henrietta Maria, consort of Charles I. The first English residence built in the Palladian style, it was constructed in the form of the letter H, straddling the WOOLWICH to DEPTFORD road, with the two sides connected by a bridge. The queen loved it, calling it her 'house of delight'; ousted when her husband was dethroned during the Civil War, she returned when the monarchy was restored in 1660 and spent most of her last years there. During the 1690s, CHRISTOPHER WREN (at the insistence of Mary II) ensured that his plans for the construction of the ROYAL NAVAL COLLEGE maintained a clear view of the building from the RIVER THAMES. For the next century, it continued to serve as a home for aristocrats but, in 1806, was converted for use as a school and, by 1933, when the educators moved out, was in a dilapidated condition. After improvements had been made, it was handed over to the NATIONAL MARITIME MUSEUM in 1937 as a gallery for its Elizabethan and Stuart exhibits, then, from 1984 to 1990, was returned to its seventeenth-century condition at a cost of £5 million. The first-floor apartments have been furnished in the style of a royal palace of the period and are open to the public.

QUEENS PARK RANGERS FOOTBALL CLUB (QPR)

QPR was formed in 1886 through the merger of two west London youth teams (St Jude's and Christchurch Rangers). It adopted its present name the following year (because most of the players lived in the Queen's PARK area of the city) and played at several grounds in Kensal Rise and KILBURN before settling at Loftus Road, where it has remained ever since apart from two short spells at the WHITE CITY in 1931–33 and 1962–63. The club turned professional in 1898 and joined the Third Division (South) of the English League in 1920. For over forty years, it remained on the lower rungs of the ladder, the championship of the Third Division (South) in 1948 its only significant honour. However, from the mid-1960s its impact increased as it won the Third Division championship and the League Cup (beating West Bromwich Albion 3-2 in the final) in 1967, worked its way through Division Two, was narrowly beaten into the runners-up place in the First Division in 1975, and entered European competition for the first time in 1977 (when it got to the quarter final of the UEFA Cup then lost on penalties after throwing away a 3-0 lead against AEK Athens).

The successes continued into the 1980s as the side reached the FA Cup final in 1982 (but lost 1-0 to TOTTENHAM HOTSPUR in the replay which followed a 1-1 draw), won the Second Division championship in 1983 and appeared in a League Cup final for the second time in 1986 (losing 3-0 to Oxford United). However, the achievements of the players were dogged by off-field controversy. In 1967/68, a merger with BRENTFORD FOOTBALL CLUB was mooted by directors but dropped when fans protested vociferously and in 1981/82 the installation of a plastic pitch (the first at a major English club) brought claims that QPR would have an unfair advantage at home games because other clubs would not be used to the vagaries of an artificial surface. A second merger, this time with FULHAM FOOTBALL CLUB, was proposed in 1987 (when the business was bought by Marler Estates) but met the same fate as its predecessor.

By the late 1990s hopes were high that QPR would maintain both independence and financial solvency. Chris Wright, who bought the club for £10 million in 1997, purchased LONDON WASPS RUGBY FOOTBALL CLUB, replaced Loftus Road's plastic pitch with a surface more suited to the handling code so that the two sports could share the ground and floated his company on the stock market, allowing fans to purchase a share in their team and using the income to pay off loans and buy new players. However, spending greatly exceeded income so, in April 2001, the club was placed in the hands of the receivers, with debts amounting to £11 million. Forbidden to enter the transfer market and forced to put its stars up for sale, the club relied heavily on wealthy supporters for donations and investigated another merger proposal, this time with WIMBLEDON FOOTBALL CLUB and again with total lack of success. The receivership restrictions were lifted in May 2002 but QPR's ambitions remained constrained as it languished in Division Two, well below its previous League heights. (See also MILLWALL FOOTBALL CLUB.)

QUEEN VICTORIA MEMORIAL

Soon after Queen Victoria's death in 1901, a committee was formed to devise a means of commemorating her reign. Part of its plan was a programme of 'architectural and scenic' change in the neighbourhood of BUCKINGHAM PALACE, with a statue of the monarch forming the centrepiece. Thomas Brock was commissioned to prepare the sculpture, which consists of a 13-foot-high representation of Victoria facing eastwards down THE MALL from a richly ornamented pedestal, which clearly demonstrates the Edwardians' passion for allegorical figures such as Truth, Constancy and Motherhood, who compete for attention with Charity, War, Architecture, Peace and Manufacture. Carved from a single 2,300-pound block of marble, the statue was unveiled in 1911 by George V (the queen's grandson), who knighted Brock during the ceremony. Later, critic Osbert Sitwell, disrespectfully but memorably, described the sculpture as 'tons of allegorical females in white wedding cake marble, with whole litters of their cretinous children.' The memorial (which is a favourite grandstand for the more athletic members of the crowds that turn out to see members of the royal family make public appearances on the palace balcony) is surrounded by flowerbeds.

R

RACHMANISM

In the mid-1950s, demand for privately rented accommodation in London greatly exceeded supply, partly because the rents of unfurnished rooms were controlled and landlords had difficulty getting a reasonable return on their investment. The Conservative government, in an effort to alleviate the situation, slackened the controls in 1957, allowing property owners to increase rents when sitting tenants moved out, but some unscrupulous landlords took advantage of the new laws and attempted to bully families into leaving. The most notorious of these was Perec (or Peter) Rachman.

Rachman was born in Poland in 1920. Despite his Jewish background, he escaped persecution by the Nazis but spent much of the Second World War in a Russian labour camp before moving to London in 1946. He found a job in a SHEPHERD'S BUSH estate agency before branching into business on his own, buying properties in NOTTING HILL and neighbouring areas of west London. When he acquired a building, he offered sitting tenants a financial inducement to move out. If that failed, he made life difficult (by arranging for loud music to be played throughout the night in neighbouring flats, for example). And if that failed, he cut off water supplies, disconnected ELECTRICITY and threatened families with violence.

Faced with the abuse, most tenants eventually left. Rachman then packed the rooms with IMMIGRANTS, many of them from the Caribbean, too poor to get better housing, too new to know their rights and too recently arrived to qualify for local authority homes. The rents for the squalid, dilapidated slums were extortionate and Rachman lived well on the proceeds, with a mansion in HAMPSTEAD, a Rolls Royce and a reputation for throwing lavish parties. His activities were largely unknown until, in 1963, the year after his death, the press followed up disclosures that John Profumo, the Defence Secretary, had been involved with Christine Keeler, a high-class prostitute who included Eugene Ivanov, the Soviet Naval attaché in London, among her clients. Mandy Rice-Davis, a friend of Keeler and also a prostitute, was one of Rachman's mistresses.

Ben Parkin, the Member of Parliament for PADDINGTON North, coined the term Rachmanism to describe the tactics adopted to intimidate tenants and advocated legislative changes to prevent exploitation of some of the weakest and most vulnerable of London's citizens. In response, the government established an independent committee (see MILNER HOLLAND REPORT) to investigate the housing situation in the city and make proposals designed to improve conditions.

RAG FAIR

A second-hand clothes MARKET, the Rag Fair was probably established during the Stuart monarchy in the seventeenth century and flourished during the Victorian period, when penniless slum dwellers had few options but to buy other people's cast-offs (commentators of the time refer to the goods on offer as mere 'shreds and patches'). Held in Rosemary Lane (which was renamed Old Mint Street in 1905), it was managed principally by Jewish IMMIGRANTS and thrived on the custom of poor citizens from nearby neighbourhoods, many of them Irish incomers who had made their way to London to find work. The fair survived into the twentieth century but disappeared before the outbreak of the First World War.

RAILWAYS

London's railways are a product of the Victorian era, with the core of the network taking shape between 1836 and 1876. The first line, from BERMONDSEY to DEPTFORD, was authorized by Parliament in 1833 and ran its first services three years later. Other connections quickly followed – EUSTON STATION to Birmingham in 1837, LONDON BRIDGE Station to CROYDON in 1839, FENCHURCH STREET STATION to BLACKWALL in 1841 and London Bridge to Brighton in the same year. PADDINGTON STATION opened in 1838, providing connections to the west (Queen Victoria made her first rail journey, from Slough to Paddington, in 1842, averaging a speed of 44 miles an hour, which PRINCE ALBERT, her husband, felt was much too fast). KING'S CROSS STATION became the terminus of the Great Northern Railway in 1852, attracting traffic from Edinburgh, Newcastle and York. VICTORIA Station brought services from the south-west over the RIVER THAMES in 1860 and LIVERPOOL STREET STATION was designated the Great Eastern Railway's base in 1874.

Most of the termini were located towards the edge of the city's urban area but provided a focus for warehouses, HOTELS, shops and other services, thereby contributing significantly to the expansion of the metropolis. Also, the construction process drastically altered patterns of social segregation because middle-class families bought homes in environmentally attractive locations, leaving the dirty, smoky, noisy sites beside the lines to those who could afford nothing better. In addition, many homes in poorer areas were demolished to make way for track and sidings (estimates of the numbers of people made homeless vary but they were probably in the region of 37,000 from 1857 to 1869 and 76,000 from 1850 to 1900). During the last quarter of the nineteenth century, routes reached towards the outer suburbs as the city spread its bricks and mortar, with much of the suburban house building actively promoted by the railway companies. The LONDON UNDERGROUND system, which opened in 1863, complemented those lines that brought workers from the outskirts to downtown jobs.

The first half of the twentieth century brought further improvements; additional connections filled gaps in provision and the nationalization of the system by the Labour government in 1947 allowed the newly formed British Railways to plan timetables as a whole. Since the 1960s, however, passenger numbers have declined, resulting in the closure of many branch lines and reductions in the frequency of services elsewhere. The only significant construction in recent years has been the DOCKLANDS LIGHT RAILWAY, which linked the south-east of the CITY OF LONDON to the redeveloped DOCK area at CANARY WHARF in 1987. During the 1990s, the Conservative government under John Major privatized the railways and created Railtrack, the private company which ran the railways' infrastructure. Following a number of serious accidents with fatalities and a decline in the standard of service, the Labour government withdrew Railtrack's subsidy, forcing it into liquidation. A non-profit-making body – Network Rail – was set up to replace it in 2003; it has announced that the state of the railway infrastructure is so poor that 95 per cent punctuality will not be achieved until 2010. However, government approval of the Crossrail project (also announced in 2003) will eventually result in easier travel between the east and west of the city. (See also ABBEY WOOD; ACTON; AIRPORTS; BALHAM; BARKING; BARNES; BATTERSEA; BATTERSEA BRIDGE; BLACKFRIARS; BRIDGES; BRONDESBURY; CANNING TOWN; CANNON STREET STATION; CATFORD; CHALK FARM; DRAIN, THE; DULWICH; EARL'S COURT; EAST LONDON LINE; EDMONTON; HOLBORN; HORNSEY; HOUNSLOW; KILBURN; KING'S CROSS FIRE; LEYTONSTONE; MANOR PARK; METROLAND; NEW CROSS; PICCADILLY LINE; PICK, FRANK; ST PANCRAS; ST THOMAS'S HOSPITAL; SOUTHALL; SOUTHGATE; STOCKWELL; STRATFORD; SURBITON; TRANSPORT; UXBRIDGE; WANDSWORTH; WATERLOO; WILLESDEN; YERKES, CHARLES TYSON.)

RANGER'S HOUSE

One of a series of buildings associated with GREENWICH PALACE, the Ranger's House was erected in 1699–70 for Captain Francis Hosier and enlarged forty years later by Philip Earl of Chesterfield. In 1815, it became the official residence of the Rangers (or guardians) of GREENWICH PARK (the first holder of the post was Princess Sophia Matilda) but in 1902 was bought by the LONDON COUNTY COUNCIL, which turned it into a cafeteria. Restoration work was carried out in 1959–60 then, in 1974, it was converted to an art gallery housing the Suffolk Collection of seventeenth-century portraits (one of the most important exhibitions of Jacobean and Stuart family paintings in the country) and the Dolmetsch collection of musical instruments. The grand salon is used regularly as a concert venue.

RECORDER OF LONDON

The Recorder is the CORPORATION OF LONDON's principal law officer. He is appointed by the Corporation's ALDERMEN (formally, he is elected to the position of Recorder of London and High Steward of SOUTHWARK) but, because he is the senior judge at the CENTRAL CRIMINAL COURT, he must have the Crown's approval before taking up his post. In addition to his court duties, the Recorder has important ceremonial roles (at the election of the LORD MAYOR, for example). The long line of incumbents dates at least from 1298. (See also COMMON SERJEANT.)

REDBRIDGE, LONDON BOROUGH OF

Redbridge lies on the north-eastern outskirts of the London conurbation. When local government in the area was reorganized in 1965, the borough was created through the merger of WOODFORD and WANSTEAD with ILFORD, parts of DAGENHAM and sections of CHIGWELL. All of the new authority (which covers just under 22 square miles and takes its name from a red-brick bridge that crossed the River Roding during the eighteenth century) was previously within the County of Essex. About one-third (mostly in the north and west, including stretches of EPPING FOREST) is GREEN BELT where urban development is restricted. The population of 238,600 (2001) includes a large Asian community (the majority of whom live in the south of the area).

RED LION SQUARE

As a result of the GREAT FIRE in 1666, London suffered a chronic shortage of housing, so speculative developers, sensing profit, bought rights to build homes on land that had previously been open space. One of these entrepreneurs – Nicholas Barbon – laid out Red Lion Square, in 1684, on a 17-acre paddock in HOLBORN, incurring the wrath of the lawyers at nearby GRAY'S INN (the august members of the legal profession objected to the loss of their rural vistas and attempted to take the law into their own hands, unsuccessfully attacking Barbon and his workmen). During the eighteenth and nineteenth centuries, the square became popular with the city's radicals, including pre-Raphaelite painter Dante Gabriel Rossetti, who, in 1851, rented No. 17, accepting a lease that required that 'the models are kept under gentlemanly restraint as some artists sacrifice the dignity of art to the baseness of passion.' William Morris, one of the founders of the arts and crafts movement and a friend of Rossetti, lived in the same house in 1856–9 and opened a showroom for his fabric designs at No. 8. The area's nonconformist links are still evident; the National Secular Society (established in 1886) has its headquarters at No. 26 and the South Place Ethical Society (which formed in 1793) is based at Conway Hall, whose rooms are rented for gatherings of left-wing political groups, gay book fairs and similar events. John Harrison, inventor of the marine chronometer, which, from the 1770s, allowed seamen to determine longitude accurately, occupied a property on the site where the Cable and Wireless Company's offices now stand. The square gets its name from a local tavern.

REFORM CLUB

The Reform Club was founded in 1836 as a GENTLEMEN'S CLUB with radical political views, attracting most leading members of the Whig Party during the nineteenth century. Its rooms at 104–105 PALL MALL, in the heart of London's clubland, were designed by CHARLES BARRY and are opulently furnished (Phineas Fogg was in the smoking room when he accepted the bet that took him on the journey described by Jules Verne in *Around the World in Eighty Days*, published in 1873). During the twentieth century, the club gradually moved away from its roots and is now almost entirely a social organization. It amended its rules in 1981 so that ladies could join.

REGENT'S CANAL

Regent's Canal, which opened in 1820, links PADDINGTON Basin to the RIVER THAMES at LIMEHOUSE, where a DOCK was constructed to allow ships to load and unload cargoes. It formally closed for industrial traffic in 1969, having lost the competition for trade with road and rail transport. However, large sections of the towpath still survive, providing an important recreational resource in the heavily urbanized EAST END. At Camden Lock (in CAMDEN TOWN) a weekend STREET MARKET, popular with young people, sells antiques, books, records and bric-a-brac. Farther east, the area around the junction with the GRAND UNION CANAL is known as Little Venice (a name apparently conferred by Robert Browning and Lord Byron but not popularly used until the second half of the twentieth century) as a result of the increase in popularity of living in houseboats on the canal. The tree-lined walkways have attracted artists (such as Lucian Freud) as well as tourists, who take narrowboat trips through REGENT'S PARK. In the west, the area around Paddington Basin is the focus of a major urban regeneration project.

REGENT'S PARK

Covering 487 acres, Regent's PARK is a major open space close to the centre of London. In 1539, the land (which had been owned by Barking Abbey) was acquired by Henry VIII, who set aside a large portion as hunting territory. A survey in 1649 showed that it still had over 16,000 trees, but these were felled soon after (partly to build ships for the Royal Navy) and the estate was converted to farmland, which provided milk and other produce for the city markets. As the urban population expanded, however, buildings increasingly encroached on the fields, so in 1811, John Fordyce, Surveyor General for Crown Lands, held a competition designed to produce a plan that would increase profits from the area. The winner – JOHN NASH – presented a scheme for a garden city, with detached homes and terraced houses carefully located in a setting that emphasized countryside rather than town.

Although critics raised objections to the proposal, the Prince Regent (later George IV) vehemently supported Nash, exerting a royal influence that enabled work to begin in 1812. Because costs rose, the architect's vision was never fully realized (only eight of the suggested fifty-six villas were completed, for instance) but, by 1840, a large element was in place, with the elegant terraces (such as Cumberland Terrace, named after the Duke of Cumberland, George's younger brother) greatly admired.

Unfortunately, a combination of AIR POLLUTION and, during the Second World War, neglect led to deterioration, so, by 1945, the buildings required considerable rehabilitation, which was undertaken by the Crown under the guidance of architect Louis de Soissons, who completed the work during the 1970s. The PARK now includes an open air THEATRE (where WILLIAM SHAKESPEARE's plays have been performed on summer evenings since 1900), sports facilities (including tennis courts, football pitches and an athletics track), bandstands, children's playgrounds and the LONDON ZOO. It is maintained by the ROYAL PARKS Agency and has been used as a model for public park provision at sites around the world. (See also CHALK FARM; GRAND UNION CANAL, REGENT STREET.)

REGENT STREET

Designed by JOHN NASH in 1813–6, Regent Street was intended to link Carlton House (home of George, the Prince Regent) to the new developments at REGENT'S PARK, alleviate traffic congestion at CHARING CROSS and increase the value of royal lands at HAYMARKET and PALL MALL. Just under a mile long, it involved construction of OXFORD CIRCUS and PICCADILLY CIRCUS in order to accommodate road junctions and, at its southern end, required an eastward curve (known as The Quadrant) to avoid the fashionable aristocratic area around ST JAMES'S PALACE. Nash sought to achieve a visual balance with the buildings that would line the route, managing to preserve an element of architectural unity even though the development was funded by private individuals, who had their own views about property façades. The area north of OXFORD STREET was intended to be residential but, farther south, the plans provided for exclusive shops catering to an affluent clientele. For most of the nineteenth century the stores thrived, but by 1900 an increasingly demanding public, seeking fashionable goods at low prices, was threatening the security of several of the businesses, which frequently had too many customers crowding into limited retail space. As a result, rebuilding was undertaken when leases ran out, replacing Nash's stucco frontages with more prosaic PORTLAND STONE. Also, in 1925 the local traders founded the Regent Street Association to promote their commercial interests and help members facing financial difficulty. As a result, the road has retained its commercial importance, with shops such as Mappin and Webb's jewellery premises and Dickins and Jones' DEPARTMENT STORE complementing music publisher Boosey and Hawkes and the Veeraswamy Indian restaurant. All the properties are owned by the Crown Estate, which, in 1999, announced proposals to pedestrianize the street over a period of ten years. (See also CAFÉ ROYAL.)

RENNIE, JOHN (1761-1821)

Rennie was an imaginative engineer, who devised creative solutions to construction problems and, in the process, had a considerable impact on London's landscape. The son of Mr and Mrs James Rennie, he was born at Phantassie, near Edinburgh, on 7 June 1761 and educated at Dunbar High School and Edinburgh University. While still a child, he had shown an aptitude for mechanical tasks and in 1784 visited James Watt, developer of the steam engine, at his works in Soho, Staffordshire. Watt offered the young Rennie a job, which he accepted, and in 1789 he was sent to London to supervise the construction of machinery for the Albion Flour Mills at BLACKFRIARS. That task earned him much recognition so, in 1791, he was able to set up his own business in Holland Street, near the Albion works. From that base, he undertook many civil engineering projects associated with the developing canal system, the drainage of the Lincolnshire fens, harbour construction and bridge building.

In London, his first major responsibilities were as engineer at LONDON DOCKS (which opened in 1801) and West India Docks (1802), and as consultant to the East India Dock scheme (1806), jobs that involved planning warehouse space as well as quays. In 1809, he supervised the digging of the CROYDON Canal, which from 1808 provided a waterway from Croydon to the Grand Surrey Canal at NEW CROSS (South Norwood Lake was once a reservoir for the system). His major achievements, however, were three bridges spanning the RIVER THAMES. The first was WATERLOO Bridge, built of Dartmoor granite between 1811 and 1817. A refinement of a design he had used at Kelso, in the south of Scotland, fifteen years earlier, it was radically different from earlier structures because it was flat from bank to bank rather than rising to a peak at the centre of the crossing. It had nine elliptical arches, with pairs of Doric crosses at the piers, and was described by sculptor Antonio Canova as 'the noblest bridge in the world'. The structure survived for over 100 years but in 1923 two of its piers moved so, in 1936, it was demolished, despite much public protest. SOUTHWARK BRIDGE – a three-arch cast-iron bridge – was erected between 1814 and 1819 in order to link Blackfriars to the south side of the Thames and was described by the engineer Robert Stephenson as 'unrivalled'. It was replaced between 1912 and 1921. Finally, LONDON BRIDGE was built to Rennie's designs between 1823 and 1831. In the early 1970s, it was dismantled and re-erected at Lake Havasu City, Arizona.

Rennie died in his home at 18 Stamford Street on 4 October 1821 and was buried in ST PAUL'S CATHEDRAL, close to Sir CHRISTOPHER WREN. His sons George and John both became distinguished engineers in their own right. John supervised the building of London Bridge after his father's death and George took charge of production at the Holland Street plant, where he produced the first biscuit-making machinery. (See also MOORGATE.)

RICHMOND

During the twelfth century, the Kings of England frequently moved their court 9 miles from London to the manor house at Shene, on the SOUTH BANK of the RIVER THAMES, so that they could enjoy hunting in the surrounding forests. A small village grew up around the house, which became a favourite resort for aristocrats and developed as the number of courtiers increased. When the residence burned down in 1499, Henry VII, previously Earl of Richmond in Yorkshire, decided to rebuild on the same site and named his new palace 'Rychemonde' after his northern estates (see RICHMOND PALACE). Since then, the settlement has retained its status and evolved as a service centre rather than an industrial community. The palace was largely destroyed after the execution of Charles I in 1649 but, during the early eighteenth century, the town continued to attract visitors, who came to drink the waters at the wells in the grounds of Cardigan House. A THEATRE opened in the 1760s and, ever since, has presented productions featuring Britain's leading actors (Edmund Kean actually became lessee in 1831 and was buried in the churchyard two years later).

The road BRIDGE, which opened in 1777 (see RICHMOND BRIDGE), brought additional population, as did the RAILWAY some seventy years later, but there are still extensive areas of public open space, as at RICHMOND PARK and the ROYAL BOTANIC GARDENS. Even the village green, where Henry VII held a jousting tournament in 1492, has survived and is still used for sporting events by the local cricket team. During the 1980s, the riverside area was redeveloped to provide offices, shops, restaurants and apartments. Many of the Georgian and Victorian frontages were retained and the façades of the new buildings designed to blend with the old. Some critics have claimed that the result is an unattractive pastiche, but others (such as Prince Charles) argue that it is a successful attempt to retain the best of the old in a modern townscape. Many of Richmond's residents commute to work in the CITY OF LONDON, but the quality of the urban environment has helped to attract the British headquarters of the Compaq computer company and educational institutions such as the US-based Richmond College. (See also DISTRICT LINE; LONDON WELSH RUGBY FOOTBALL CLUB; RICHMOND UPON THAMES, LONDON BOROUGH OF.)

RICHMOND BRIDGE

The graceful five-span bridge of PORTLAND STONE, which links RICHMOND (on the east bank of one of the RIVER THAMES meanders) with TWICKENHAM (on the west), was designed by James Paine and built in 1774–7. It is the oldest road crossing of the waterway in the London area. Downstream, the steel RAILWAY bridge, designed by J.W. Jacomb Hood, was erected in 1908. It replaced a cast-iron structure that had carried the tracks of the Windsor, Staines and South-Western Railway from Richmond to Windsor since 1848.

RICHMOND PALACE

From the reign of Henry I, during the twelfth century, England's monarchs used the manor house at Shene, some 9 miles south-west of CHARING CROSS, as a base for hunting. It became a favourite haunt of Richard II, Henry V, Edward IV and Henry VII in particular but, in 1499 (by which time it was known as Shene Palace), it was destroyed by fire. Henry VII erected a new building on the site, naming it 'Rychemonde' Palace after his estates at Richmond in Yorkshire, and died there a decade later (reputedly leaving a fortune in gold hidden under the floors and in the walls). Catherine of Aragon lived at Richmond from 1502 until she married Henry VIII in 1509, Anne of Cleves received the palace as part of her divorce settlement from the same monarch, Elizabeth I entertained Walter Raleigh and other courtiers there during the summer, and the ill-fated Charles I gave it to his bride (Henrietta Maria of France) as a wedding present in 1625. Following Charles's execution in 1649 most of the structure was destroyed, but a single gatehouse (bearing the arms of Henry VII) survives and, in Old Palace Yard, part of the Tudor building (with eighteenth-century alterations) was converted into three houses during the 1950s.

RICHMOND PARK

The largest of the ROYAL PARKS in London, Richmond Park's 2,360 acres were first enclosed, in 1637, by Charles I, who used the land as a hunting forest. Its vegetation remains semi-natural, consisting largely of ancient oak woodland and acidic grassland, with areas of bog and bracken. Deer still roam the area (which was classified as a Site of Special Scientific Interest by English Nature – one of the government's conservation agencies – in 1992) but are fed in winter to ensure their survival. Pen Ponds, built during the eighteenth century, attract fishermen seeking pike, bream, carp and roach. In 1894, the future Edward VIII (who chose to abdicate his throne rather than give up the American divorcee he loved) was born in the White House, built in 1727–9 by the Earl of Pembroke towards the south-east of the park. The building is now used by the Royal Ballet School and closed to the public, but visitors can find refreshment at another Georgian property, Pembroke Lodge, where Lord John

Russell (who derived no pleasure from London social life) lived while he was Prime Minister during the 1840s and 1850s. The park has two golf courses and is popular with horse riders. Cars are confined to the perimeter of the area so most of the estate's features are accessible only on foot.

RICHMOND UPON THAMES, LONDON BOROUGH OF

The only one of the LONDON BOROUGHS to span the RIVER THAMES, Richmond was created in 1965 by the merger of TWICKENHAM (on the western side of the waterway) with RICHMOND (on the east). Largely residential, Richmond has one of the highest proportions of professional and managerial residents of any local authority area in England and a low proportion of children. Twickenham is similarly affluent, though with a greater proportion of its workforce in technical posts. Much of the borough's 21 square miles are open space, used for recreation (see, for example, BUSHY PARK, RICHMOND PARK and the ROYAL BOTANIC GARDENS), but there is a significant commercial and industrial presence, with retailing, publishing and a growing high technology sector attracted by good road and rail links to central London. In 2001, the resident population was 172,300. (See also BARNES; KEW; MORTLAKE.)

RILLINGTON PLACE

In 1950, Timothy Evans (who had the intellectual capacity of a ten-year-old child) was executed in PENTONVILLE Prison after confessing to the murder of his wife and baby daughter at 10 Rillington Place, NOTTING HILL. Three years later, the bodies of three women were found in a cupboard at the flat below, occupied by John Reginald Halliday Christie. A police search discovered the body of Christie's wife under the kitchen floorboards and the skeletons of two more women in the garden. Under questioning, Christie admitted to murdering all eight females. He was tried then hanged at Pentonville in 1953. Evans's death fuelled the campaign for the abolition of the death penalty in the United Kingdom. He was given a full pardon (though not until 1966) and Rillington Place was demolished.

RITZ HOTEL

The Ritz has become a byword for opulent luxury, contributing *ritzy* to the vocabulary of the English language. It was erected in PICCADILLY for the Blackpool Building and Vendor Company Ltd, on a site previously occupied by the Walsingham House and Bath Hotels, and opened in 1906. The first major steel-framed building in London, it was designed by architects Charles Frederic Mewès and Arthur Joseph Davis to the specifications of Swiss businessman César Ritz, who had made a great success of the Carlton hotel in HAYMARKET. Furnished in the style of Louis XVI's reign in France, with rooms decorated in blue, peach, pink and yellow, the hotel was bought from the Trafalgar House group by private individuals in 1995 and refurbished in stages using French craftsmen and suppliers. Room prices start at around £300 a night.

RIVER POLICE

By the end of the eighteenth century, about two-thirds of Britain's imports and exports were passing through London's DOCK, but secure facilities for storing commodities were limited so theft was common. In 1798, Patrick Colquhoun and John Harriott attempted to reduce the losses by forming a 200-strong force of river policemen, who frequently suffered violent attacks as they attempted to arrest thieves and pirates. In 1839, the force was incorporated within the METROPOLITAN POLICE.

ROEHAMPTON

Roehampton lies east of RICHMOND PARK, some 6½ miles south-east of CHARING CROSS in the LONDON BOROUGH OF WANDSWORTH. It was established during the late thirteenth century by incomers from PUTNEY, then developed, from about 1630, as a fashionable place for wealthy nobles and merchants to build a country mansion. From the Victorian period, however, many families moved farther away from the city, selling their estates to speculative builders and their homes to medical and educational interests (thus, for example, Roehampton House, which was designed by Thomas Archer, erected in 1710–2, and expanded by Sir Edwin Lutyens in 1912, was converted for use as a hospital in 1915). The LONDON COUNTY COUNCIL also utilized much of the open space for public housing after the Second World War, diversifying the social composition of the area, which has a mix of residential and institutional uses. The area's name is probably derived from the Old English *hroc* and *ham-tun*, describing 'a home farm where rooks are found'. (See also CHAMBERS, WILLIAM.)

ROOKERIES

London's nineteenth-century slums were known as rookeries. Black from accumulations of soot, overcrowded, fetid and noisy, they were considered by middle-class Victorians to be the hiding place of humanity's dregs, ridden with CRIME and permeated by disease. Many had a high proportion of Irish-born residents, adding to the fear of the unknown for outsiders. The most notorious was St Giles, a zone of cramped, winding alleys bounded by Great Russell Street, Crown Street (now CHARING CROSS ROAD), Long Acre and DRURY LANE. There, according to the 1851 census, over 50,000 people lived at a density of twelve to a house (100 years earlier, William Hogarth had condemned it as a place of debauchery and vice in *Gin Lane* and other prints). Saffron Hill, a similarly poor environment between Smithfield and Clerkenwell Green, was made the home of the Artful Dodger and Fagin in CHARLES DICKENS' *Oliver Twist* (1838) and much of the EAST END and the areas close to the DOCKS were also impoverished. The suggestion that these places were sources of disease was undoubtedly justified because the high-density living led to the spread of infection. However, the allegation that they were occupied by criminals may have been overstated, according to some modern scholars. They were removed by large-scale slum clearance programmes (many designed to make way for the railways) from the 1840s but the demolition simply shunted the poverty to other parts of the city as tens of thousands of people were thrown out of their homes without any compensation or alternative accommodation.

ROTHERHITHE

Rotherhithe is located on the marshy southern shore of the RIVER THAMES in the LONDON BOROUGH OF SOUTHWARK, 4 miles east of CHARING CROSS. By the fourteenth century, although isolated from the CITY OF LONDON, it had developed a shipbuilding industry, shaping a relationship with the sea that was to last for over 700 years. In 1620, the *Mayflower* left the harbour to carry the Pilgrim Fathers to the Americas; Christopher Jones, her captain, was a native of the community and lies buried in St Mary's churchyard. Seventy-nine years later, the Howland, London's earliest enclosed DOCK, was opened, the first of nine that would extend over 300 acres by the beginning of the twentieth century and be jointly known as Surrey Commercial Docks. In 1823, Marc Brunel began work on the first tunnel under the Thames, linking Rotherhithe to WAPPING. He took twenty years to complete the project, assisted by his son, ISAMBARD KINGDOM BRUNEL, but revolutionized engineering by employing a novel shield that left only a small part of the advancing excavation exposed to workers and thus reduced the danger that the soft clays would collapse as the shaft advanced. Originally used by pedestrians, the tunnel was converted for the East London RAILWAY's trains in 1869 and is now part of the LONDON

UNDERGROUND system. A second tunnel, which linked the area to SHADWELL from 1908, involved much demolition of property as new streets were built to provide access for vehicular traffic. Following the closure of the docks in 1970, most of the harbour areas were filled in and sold to developers. By the late 1990s, over 6,000 new homes had been built, along with budget accommodation for students and young people (Rotherhithe has London's largest youth hostel as well as housing for undergraduates at the University of Westminster). In addition, some of the old warehouses were converted into flats and new BUS routes integrated the area with the central city. But, in the process, the links with the sea were severed as the employment base and social composition of the community changed. The origin of the area's name is unclear. The second element is probably Old English *hyth*, or 'landing place', and the first may be from *redhra* (which means 'sailor') or *hryther* ('cattle'). (See also EAST LONDON LINE.)

ROTHMAN'S OF PALL MALL

In 1890, Louis Rothman (an immigrant from the Ukraine) opened a tobacconist's shop at 55 FLEET STREET. Each day, after his store closed, he sat for hours, making cigarettes for sale to the reporters who worked in the newspaper businesses nearby. Ten years later, as his reputation spread and his profits grew, he moved to a more prestigious site in PALL MALL. Royal warrants from Edward VII of Britain (1905) and Alfonso XIII of Spain (1910) brought additional business from the courts of Europe and allowed him to develop larger factory premises, where workers continued to roll the cigarettes manually until, after the outbreak of the First World War, he introduced a machine that made Virginia blends. Rothman died in 1926 and, three years later, his business became a limited company. In 1999 (by which time it had expanded into luxury goods, with interests in Montblanc and Cartier), the firm was taken over by British American Tobacco for US$7.55 billion. The merged producer was expected to control about 16 per cent of the world cigarette market.

ROTTEN ROW

During the last decade of the seventeenth century, William III rode regularly between his residences at KENSINGTON PALACE and ST JAMES'S PALACE. The track he followed became known as the *route du roi* (French for 'the King's road'), which, in time, was corrupted into Rotten Row. The 1,500-yard path, at the southern edge of HYDE PARK, was the first street in England to be lit at night because the king, determined to frighten off highwaymen, arranged for 300 lamps to be hung from nearby trees. A fashionable place to promenade during Georgian and Victorian times, Rotten Row is still used by horse riders, though stabling, once common, is no longer available.

ROYAL ACADEMY OF ARTS

Reputably the oldest British society devoted to the fine arts, the academy was founded in 1768. Joshua Reynolds served as the first president, the architect WILLIAM CHAMBERS was the first treasurer, Thomas Gainsborough was one of the leading members and George III announced that he would be the institution's patron. Originally based in the STRAND, with exhibitions held at a property in PALL MALL, the academy moved to its present location in BURLINGTON HOUSE in 1868. For much of its history, it has been criticized as a bastion of artistic conservatism, failing to support individualistic talent, but its elitism has made it a powerful lobby in business and political circles. It mounts frequent, often controversial, exhibitions, the best known being the summer show, which has been held annually for 200 years. The academy owns an important collection of works gifted by artists such as John Constable and J.M.W. Turner – a collection destined to grow because its regulations require each newly elected Academician to present 'a picture, bas-relief or other specimen of his abilitie.' (See also DANCE, GEORGE (1741–1825); ROYAL COLLEGE OF ART; ROYAL SOCIETY OF ARTS (RSA).)

ROYAL ACADEMY OF DRAMATIC ART (RADA)

The academy – the oldest school of drama in England – was founded by actor-producer Sir Herbert Beerbohm Tree in 1904. Two years later, a council was formed to facilitate management, then, in 1908, associates, all distinguished in aspects of the theatre, were appointed as advisers. The Prince of Wales (later Edward VIII) became patron in 1921 and in 1931 the institution's Gower Street headquarters was remodelled to incorporate a THEATRE. As RADA's activities have expanded (it has become the country's principal training ground for young actors and actresses) it has required further space so workshops and rehearsal rooms are now housed in a Chenies Street annex.

ROYAL ACADEMY OF MUSIC

The academy was founded in 1823, largely through the influence of a group of aristocrats headed by Lord Burghersh. Although George IV agreed to act as patron, the institution's early years were dogged by financial problems but fortunes improved from 1868, following a decision by William Gladstone's Liberal government to award an annual grant. In 1926, it moved to its present premises in Marylebone Road, adding a theatre and lecture room in 1926, a library (funded by a public appeal) in 1968 and a concert hall in 1977. The academy is the oldest organization undertaking advanced musical training in the United Kingdom. (See also ROYAL COLLEGE OF MUSIC.)

ROYAL AIR FORCE MUSEUM

See HENDON.

ROYAL ALBERT HALL

See ALBERT HALL.

ROYAL ARSENAL

Until the early eighteenth century, the principal gun-casting works in south-east England was located in the CITY OF LONDON but, in 1713, following an explosion that killed seventeen people, it was moved to more spacious premises at WOOLWICH, close to the ROYAL NAVAL DOCKYARD. Originally known as The Warren (after the site where it was located), the depot was renamed the Royal Arsenal by George III in 1805. By the time of the First World War, it had extended to over 1,200 acres and employed nearly 80,000 people, but output declined from the mid-twentieth century and the works was closed in 1967. For thirty years the site stood derelict but, in 1996, plans were announced to develop the area as a complex of MUSEUMS, workshops for small businesses, sports facilities and halls of residence for students at the UNIVERSITY of Greenwich. In 1886, a works FOOTBALL team was formed at the arsenal. In 1914, it moved to HIGHBURY in north London and, as the ARSENAL FOOTBALL CLUB, has become one of Europe's leading teams.

ROYAL BALLET

The ballet was founded in 1956, when the Sadler's Wells Company (originally formed by Dame Ninette de Valois in 1931 at the OLD VIC) was awarded a royal charter. It is based at the ROYAL OPERA HOUSE (in COVENT GARDEN), where it has mounted productions with most of the world's leading dancers. During the 1990s, the ballet suffered from a series of artistic and financial crises as lacklustre productions led to disaffection among dancers and to the departure of leading talents. However, the refurbishment of the company's Royal Opera House headquarters in 1998–9 and the appointment of Australian Ross Stretton as director in 2000 offered the prospect of greater stability and a return to world-class status. The Royal Ballet School (also a product of Dame Ninette's enterprise) provides both general education and dance training for young people. Those aged eleven to sixteen are taught at White Lodge (RICHMOND PARK) and older students at a property in Talgarth Road (West KENSINGTON), which was originally acquired with an Arts Council grant in 1947. Most members of the country's leading ballet companies have attended the school.

ROYAL BOTANIC GARDENS

One of the world's major centres of botanical research, the gardens are located about 7 miles west of CHARING CROSS in the suburb of KEW (and so are popularly known as Kew Gardens). They were originally laid out by Augusta, the widow of Frederick, Prince of Wales, in 1759, but extended by her son, George III, then landscaped by Capability Brown during the 1770s. Under the unofficial direction of botanist Sir Joseph Banks (who was president of the ROYAL SOCIETY from 1778 to 1820), they built a reputation as a site for the scientific study of plant life during the early nineteenth century. That reputation lay partly in the extent of the collections (as Britain acquired an empire, the gardens acquired species brought by explorers from all corners of the world), but now rests on expertise in conservation and in the economic exploitation of species (scientists from Kew introduced bread fruit trees to the West Indies and rubber trees to Malaya, for instance). In addition, researchers have access to a library of over 120,000 monographs and a seed bank, which concentrates, in particular, on wild plants of Great Britain and the arid tropics.

Since 1840, when the estate was donated to the nation following a Royal Commission report, the 300-acre grounds have also had an important recreational and educational function. Hurricane-force gales on 15 October 1987 caused havoc, destroying many trees, but Kew still has an enormous collection of plants. The Alpine House alone contains over 3,000 upland species and the Grass Garden over 600. Also, many of the buildings are of considerable architectural merit. The ten-storey Orangery, designed by WILLIAM CHAMBERS and built in 1761, has been converted into a MUSEUM and book stall, but Decimus Burton's glass and iron Temperate House (which was started in 1860 but took thirty years to complete) and his Palm House (the latter designed in conjunction with engineer Richard Turner during the 1840s) retain their original function (the Temperate House was restored in 1980). In 2003 the gardens were designated a World Heritage Site.

Another of Chambers' buildings – the Great Pagoda, which was inspired by a visit to Canton – was built in 1761–2 in the south-east corner of the gardens, providing an easily identifiable landmark. In the north, the red-brick Kew Palace (which measures only 70 feet long by 50 feet wide and is the smallest of the royal residences) dates from 1631. It was built by Samuel Fortey, a merchant of Dutch parentage (and so it is sometimes known as the Dutch House) but it was leased by Queen Caroline in 1728 and became the favourite home of George II. The garden behind the palace (named the Queen's Garden after Elizabeth II) is laid out in seventeenth-century style, with an emphasis on herbs. Kew Gardens was designated a World Heritage Site by the United Nations in 2003.

ROYAL COLLEGE OF ART

In 1837, following a Parliamentary inquiry into art education, a School of Design was established at SOMERSET HOUSE, with classes emphasizing the practicalities of industrial draughtsmanship rather than mastery of the fine arts. Four years later, the government founded similar institutions in other parts of the country so the school began a programme of teacher training. In 1896, it was renamed the Royal College when Queen Victoria granted it permission to award diplomas and, in 1967, it was given a charter empowering it to grant masters and doctoral degrees. The college is now based in Kensington Gore, housed in a stark 1960s building (designed by H.T. Cadbury-Brown, Sir Hugh Casson and R.Y. Gooden), which contrasts with the nineteenth-century ebullience of the ALBERT HALL, its immediate neighbour. (See also ROYAL ACADEMY OF ARTS.)

ROYAL COLLEGE OF MUSIC

In 1882, largely as a result of the influence of the Prince of Wales, the Royal College was established in Kensington Gore. It moved to its present site in Prince Consort Road during 1894, occupying a building (designed by Sir Arthur Blomfield) that was extended in 1964 and 1973. The college owns a collection of old musical instruments – including Joseph Haydn's clavichord – which was presented to it by Sir George Donaldson in 1894, and numbers composers Benjamin Britten and Ralph Vaughan Williams among its former students. (See also ROYAL ACADEMY OF MUSIC.)

ROYAL COLLEGE OF PHYSICIANS OF LONDON

The college – the oldest of England's medical organizations – was founded in 1518, largely due to the efforts of Thomas Linacre, Henry VIII's doctor. Its headquarters in St Andrew's Place (close to REGENT'S PARK) house an important library of historical textbooks, some 140 of them survivors of the GREAT FIRE of 1666, others bequeathed by the Marquess of Dorchester in 1680. Along with the British Medical Association and the ROYAL COLLEGE OF SURGEONS OF ENGLAND, the college forms a powerful lobby for healthcare interests in the United Kingdom.

ROYAL COLLEGE OF SURGEONS OF ENGLAND

Although the college was founded in 1800, it can trace its roots to a Guild of Surgeons that functioned in the CITY OF LONDON during the medieval period (see LIVERY COMPANIES). That guild was amalgamated with the Barbers in 1540, but members sought to regain their independence in 1745, breaking away to form a Company of Surgeons. In 1797, the organization obtained property at LINCOLN'S INN FIELDS, extending the premises on several occasions over the past 200 years to provide exhibition galleries, laboratories and facilities for the Nuffield College of Surgical Sciences, which trains graduate students. The College of Surgeons has a library of over 120,000 books and houses the Hunterian MUSEUM, a collection of over 6,000 anatomical specimens, most of which were acquired by Scottish surgeon John Hunter (1728–93) for use with his pupils. It has a strong research orientation and lists most of the distinguished English surgeons of the past two centuries among its membership. (See also MIDDLESEX HOSPITAL; ROYAL COLLEGE OF PHYSICIANS OF LONDON.)

ROYAL COMMISSION ON THE DISTRIBUTION OF THE INDUSTRIAL POPULATION (1937–1939)

See BARLOW COMMISSION.

ROYAL COMMISSION ON LONDON TRAFFIC (1903-1905)

In 1901, CHARLES TYSON YERKES, an American financier, began to invest heavily in companies providing UNDERGROUND RAILWAY services in London. The following year, London United Tramways, backed by the J.S. Morgan Bank of New York, published plans for a service running from SOUTHGATE (in the north of the city) to HAMMERSMITH (in the south-west). The possibility that the capital's public TRANSPORT system could be shaped by competition between two powerful transatlantic interests led Parliament to establish, in 1903, a Royal Commission that would examine the state of mass transit in London. Its report, published two years later, concluded that residents were suffering because the system was unco-ordinated, expensive and subject to long delays. Commission members suggested that streets could be widened so that electric TRAMS could cover the whole metropolitan area, that new (and wider) roads should be built, that further underground railways should be constructed using cut and cover methods (which involved digging up roads, building a tunnel, laying track, covering the tunnel and re-laying the road surface) rather than deep tube technology, and that a Traffic Board should be created to plan transport provision for an area greater than that administered by LONDON COUNTY COUNCIL. The government responded by forming a London Traffic Branch within the Board of Trade but its impact was limited. Yerkes bought a controlling interest in London United Tramways and his company (the Underground Electric Railways Company of London) dominated passenger transport provision in the city until the LONDON PASSENGER TRANSPORT BOARD (LPTB) was established in 1933. (See also M25 MOTORWAY.)

ROYAL COURTS OF JUSTICE

Until the late nineteenth century, the principal English courts dealing with civil litigation had no central base they could use throughout the year, so, in 1871, an area on the north side of the STRAND was cleared of slums and work begun on a new building that would allow all non-criminal cases to be heard at a single location. The plans were approved by 1874, but bad weather, problems over financing and disputes with the workforce meant that the Victorian Gothic structure was not opened until 1882 (architect George Edmund Street died of a stroke in 1881, allegedly worn out by attempts to complete the project). Built of brick and faced with PORTLAND STONE, it has over 1,000 rooms arranged round a central hall that is 230 feet long. Initially, there were nineteen courts but extensions in 1911 and 1968 added a further sixteen. The Supreme Court of Justice, which uses most of the facilities, consists of the Court of Appeal, the High Court and the Crown Court, with the High Court subdivided into the Court of Chancery (which considers matters related to property issues), the Family Division (which rules on domestic disputes) and the Queen's Bench Division (which deals principally with wrongs that can be compensated by an award of damages). The Court of Appeal hears appeals on civil and criminal matters and the Crown Court hears trials on indictment. In addition, the Bankruptcy Court and Companies Court have separate premises to the north of the complex and a number of criminal trials are held there because of pressure on the space at the CENTRAL CRIMINAL COURT. In addition to its formal title, the building is often referred to simply as the Law Courts.

ROYAL EXCHANGE

In 1565, a group of London merchants, led by Sir THOMAS GRESHAM, purchased a site at the junction of CORNHILL and THREADNEEDLE STREET, with the intention of erecting a meeting place where they could buy and sell. Most of the building materials for the four-storey structure were imported from Antwerp (Belgium), where the Merchant Adventurers (who controlled more than half of England's foreign trade) had their headquarters. Grasshoppers – an element of the Gresham family crest – adorned the bell tower and the walls around the inner courtyard were decorated with statues of England's monarchs. Space was provided for about 100 shops, including goldsmiths, milliners and booksellers. The building was opened in 1568 and, on 23 January 1570, received a visit from Elizabeth I, who decreed that it should be named the Royal Exchange 'and so to be called from henceforth and not otherwise,' but it survived only until 1666, when it was destroyed in the GREAT FIRE.

A second Exchange, designed by Edward Jarman and built on the same site, was opened on 28 September 1669, but storekeepers proved unwilling to rent all of the sites made available to them and eventually much of the property was taken over by Royal Exchange

The Royal Exchange, as built by Sir Thomas Gresham, c. 1640.

Assurance and LLOYD'S OF LONDON. Some offices were occupied by the LORD MAYOR'S court, and the EAST INDIA COMPANY stored pepper in the vaults.

On 10 January 1838, another fire (which is thought to have begun in Lloyd's premises) destroyed the Exchange for a second time, so a third edifice, designed by Sir William Tite, was erected, with Sir CHRISTOPHER WREN'S St Benet Fink Church demolished to make way for it. Eight Corinthian columns support a pediment with an elaborate sculpture, by Richard Westmacott, which shows Commerce attended by the Lord Mayor and merchants from around the world. The internal courtyard contains the pavement from the original Exchange and the walls are adorned with scenes from London's past. When Queen Victoria officially opened the building on 28 October 1844, she echoed her royal predecessor with an announcement that 'It is my royal will and pleasure that this building be hereafter called the Royal Exchange.' It ceased to function as a place for general business dealings in 1939, many of its original commodities having developed specialist markets, such as the LONDON METAL EXCHANGE, with their own premises. Since then, most of the facilities have lain unused, although a number of the rooms have been occupied by an insurance company, legal firms, small shops and a restaurant. Also, for a number of years in the 1980s and early 1990s, the trading floor was occupied by the LONDON INTERNATIONAL FINANCIAL FUTURES AND OPTIONS EXCHANGE (LIFFE).

ROYAL FESTIVAL HALL

The Festival Hall was the first building erected at the SOUTH BANK arts complex near WATERLOO and is used for concerts, ballets, choral events and films. Opened in 1951 as part of the FESTIVAL OF BRITAIN celebrations, it was designed by Robert Matthew and J.L. Martin and much praised for the quality of its acoustics. The concrete exterior looks bleak to some observers but the interior is spacious, with a 3,000-seat auditorium and an open network of foyers and staircases. Since 1988, the hall has housed the Arts Council's Poetry Library, whose archives and readings are open to visitors. (See also PHILHARMONIA ORCHESTRA; ROYAL PHILHARMONIC ORCHESTRA (RPO).)

ROYAL FREE HOSPITAL

In 1828, William Marsden, a Yorkshire doctor, found a young woman dying on the steps of ST ANDREW'S CHURCH, HOLBORN, because she could not afford to pay for treatment at a hospital. Touched by the experience, he persuaded members of the Cordwainers'

Company (one of the City LIVERY COMPANIES) to found a medical service which would be available to everybody, regardless of their means. Initially based at 16 Greville Street (near HATTON GARDEN) and known as the London General Institution for the Gratuitous Care of Malignant Diseases, it gained much public recognition in 1832, when it was the only London hospital to accept patients suffering from CHOLERA. It changed its name to the Royal Free Hospital in 1837, when Queen Victoria accepted the role of patron, then, in 1843, it leased more spacious premises at the former barracks of the Light Horse Volunteers in Gray's Inn Road. In 1877 it became a teaching hospital, allowing students from the London School of Medicine for Women to train in its wards (at the time, it was the sole hospital in the city to accept female trainee doctors and it was only in 1938 that men were admitted), in 1889 it established a school of nursing and in 1895 it continued its pioneering approach to healthcare by appointing an almoner, one of the earliest experiments in medical social work. In 1921, it opened an obstetrics and gynaecology unit (becoming the first English hospital to provide such facilities) and in 1926-30 it added the Eastman Dental Hospital.

With the introduction of the National Health Service (NHS) in 1948, the Royal Free was united with the Children's Hospital, HAMPSTEAD, the Elizabeth Garrett Anderson Hospital, the Hampstead General Hospital and the London Fever Hospital (the Coppetts Wood and New End Hospitals were added to the group in 1968 and Queen Mary's Maternity Home four years later but the Elizabeth Garrett Anderson was transferred to the North-West Metropolitan Regional Hospital Board in 1972). Unable to expand in central London (where, in any case, the population was declining), it relocated to Pond Street, Hampstead, in 1974, despite vociferous objections from local residents, who feared intrusion by noise and traffic. In 1991, the Royal Free was one of the first hospitals to establish a trust under the provisions of the NHS and Community Care Act, passed the following year, and in 1998 its medical school united with University College London, creating one of Europe's largest training centres for healthcare workers. By the end of the decade, the trust had some 1,000 beds and was treating 500,000 patients every year. (See also ROYAL MARSDEN HOSPITAL.)

ROYAL GEOGRAPHICAL SOCIETY

Since its foundation in 1830, the Royal Geographical Society has fostered exploration, supporting expeditions such as those by David Livingstone to Africa in the middle years of the nineteenth century, Robert Falcon Scott to the polar lands in the early twentieth century and John Hunt to Mount Everest in 1953. In the process, it has accumulated the largest privately owned collection of maps in the world and a 150,000-volume library. It also has a large archive of photographs donated by travellers. In recent years, the 13,000-member society has favoured interdisciplinary research studies in sparsely populated areas and small-scale projects mounted by educational organizations. During the 1990s (and not without some acrimony), it united with the Institute of British Geographers (formerly the professional academic body for geography professors and graduate students at British UNIVERSITIES) in order to provide a stronger voice in public debate at a time when government policies were reducing the time available for the discipline in schools. The society's offices at Lowther Lodge in Kensington Gore were designed by Norman Shaw and built in 1874.

ROYAL HORTICULTURAL SOCIETY

See CHELSEA FLOWER SHOW

ROYAL HOSPITAL, CHELSEA

See CHELSEA HOSPITAL.

ROYAL INSTITUTE OF INTERNATIONAL AFFAIRS

After the First World War, a group of influential academics, politicians and journalists (including Viscount Cecil and THE TIMES Editor Geoffrey Dawson) agreed to form a British Institute of International Affairs in order to provide a forum for discussions about issues affecting the world community. In 1923 the organization purchased premises at 10 St James's Square (the former home of William Pitt the Elder, the Earl of Derby and William Gladstone) and in 1926 it was given a royal charter by George V. An independent body, it conducts research and encourages publication on international issues. Membership is by election.

ROYAL INSTITUTION

The institution was founded in 1799 by Benjamin Thompson as a means of 'diffusing the knowledge and facilitating the general introduction of useful mechanical inventions and improvements.' It acquired premises in Albemarle Street (close to PICCADILLY), which it converted into office, laboratory and lecture facilities, and was awarded a royal charter by George III in 1800. In 1802, it appointed chemist Humphry Davy (inventor of the miners' safety lamp) as its first professor. Eleven years later, Michael Faraday was engaged as Davy's assistant, a position that enabled him to conduct the series of experiments that established the nature of electromagnetic induction in 1831. Since then, many influential scientists, including T.H. Huxley and Lord Rutherford, have held positions at the Institution, which has restored Faraday's workroom and mounted an exhibition of his instruments. During the winter, it holds a series of lectures designed to present research findings in terms understandable by a general audience.

ROYAL LONDON HOSPITAL

The hospital was founded at a meeting in the Feathers Tavern, CHEAPSIDE, on 23 September 1740, when seven men, led by John Harrison (a twenty-two-year-old surgeon), decided to improve healthcare in the city. Initially based in Featherstone Street, near FINSBURY Circus, and known as the London Infirmary, it moved to Prestcot Street (close to the ROYAL MINT) in 1741 and was renamed the London Hospital in 1748. In 1757, it transferred to what was then a rural site in WHITECHAPEL. Its medical school, founded by Sir William Blizard in 1785, was the first in London to be attached to a hospital. During the nineteenth century, the premises expanded and medical facilities reflected the advancement of science (for example, the first microscope was bought in 1849, the first obstetrician appointed in 1854 and an outpatient department for treating illnesses of the ear, nose and throat established in 1866). A major rebuilding was undertaken during the 1890s and further improvements were made in the 1920s and 1930s, most of them funded through the efforts of Viscount Knutsford, chairman of the governors. Because of its proximity to London's DOCKS, the hospital suffered badly during the Second World War, but, since then, it has been at the forefront of medical advance (in 1964, for instance, it became the first hospital in London to purchase a computer). In 1967, it merged with two other EAST END hospitals – the MILE END Hospital and St Clement's Hospital – and in 1990, when the Queen visited the wards to commemorate its 250th anniversary, the group was renamed the Royal London Hospital. The following year, it reorganized administratively as a National Health Service Trust, adding ST BARTHOLOMEW'S HOSPITAL and the London Chest Hospital in 1994 and the Queen Elizabeth Hospital for Children in 1996. The Royal London now serves a wide area of east London, specializing in cardiology, cardiovascular surgery, nephrology, neurology, neurosurgery, radiotherapy and treatments for newborn babies and patients suffering from haemophilia. It also houses a MUSEUM, refurbished in 2002, which displays a series of exhibits relating to the history of the hospital and to healthcare in the East End. Former staff and students at the Royal London include THOMAS JOHN BARNARDO (founder of Dr Barnardo's Homes), nurse Edith Cavell (who, in 1915, was executed by the German Army for helping British soldiers to escape from occupied Belgium to neutral Holland) and William Grenfell (who provided medical care to the fishing communities in the rugged environment of Labrador and Newfoundland for forty years).

ROYAL MARSDEN HOSPITAL

The Royal Marsden was the first hospital in the world to concentrate solely on the treatment of cancer. It was founded in 1851 by William Marsden, five years after his wife, Elizabeth-Ann, had died of the disease and twenty-three years after he had founded the ROYAL FREE HOSPITAL. Although Queen Victoria initially refused any association with the institution because cancer patients were already being treated at other, general, hospitals, the unit flourished. It initially operated as a dispensary for outpatients from a house at 1 Cannon Row, but, in 1862, it moved to its present site in FULHAM Road and became known as the Cancer Free Hospital. It was given its regal prefix by Edward VIII, assumed its present name in 1954 and, eight years later, opened a second base at SUTTON in order to meet a growing need for its specialist services. It reorganized itself as a National Health Service Trust in 1994. From its earliest days, the Marsden has been an important centre for cancer research (Marsden himself insisted on meticulous record-keeping). It is now the largest hospital in Europe dealing with the disease and has a reputation for pioneering advances in patient care as well as in treatment. During the 1990s, an appeal for funds, supported by Princess Diana, allowed it to open a new clinical block at Fulham Road and a children's facility at Sutton. (See also ST GEORGE'S HOSPITAL.)

ROYAL MEWS

The Mews (or stables) were an integral part of JOHN NASH's plans for BUCKINGHAM PALACE and were built in 1824–5. They still house the royal family's carriage horses and about 100 carriages, including the Gold State Coach (built for George III in 1762 and used at coronations ever since), the Irish State Coach (made in Dublin in 1852 and acquired by Queen Victoria for use at STATE OPENINGS OF PARLIAMENT) and the Glass State Coach (bought by George V in 1910 for royal weddings). The Mews is administered by the Crown Equerry, who is also responsible for the coachmen and grooms.

ROYAL MILITARY ACADEMY

See WOOLWICH.

ROYAL MINT

It seems certain that a mint was founded in London some 200 years before the Norman Conquest of 1066 and that, by the beginning of the fourteenth century, it was based in the TOWER OF LONDON. In 1811, because of pressure on space, it was moved to a building in Little Tower Hill then in 1968, as part of the Labour government's attempt to decentralize official functions to the British regions, to Llantrisant in South Wales.

ROYAL NATIONAL THEATRE

The suggestion that Britain should have a national THEATRE was first made by London publisher Effingham Wilson in 1848 but no steps were taken to build one until the mid-twentieth century. Meetings were held, appeals proposed and sites recommended but nothing concrete was achieved until 1944, when the LONDON COUNTY COUNCIL promoted the amalgamation of the Shakespeare Memorial National Theatre Committee (formed in 1907 as a vehicle to promote works by aspiring playwrights as well as productions of classical drama) and the OLD VIC Theatre (which opened in 1818 and, by the

1940s, was the principal stage for presentations of WILLIAM SHAKESPEARE's plays in the nation's capital). Parliament approved funds for a new theatre in 1949 and, two years later, the foundation stone was laid at a site just east of WATERLOO Bridge on the SOUTH BANK of the RIVER THAMES. Little further work was done for several years but, in 1962, a National Theatre Board was established, with Viscount Chandos (formerly Oliver Lyttleton) as the first chairman and Sir Laurence Olivier as artistic director. The board built up a National Theatre Company, based at the Old Vic, which presented its first production (Shakespeare's *Hamlet*, with Peter O'Toole in the leading role) the following year. Serious work on the new theatre, designed by Denys Lasdun, began during the late 1960s and was completed in 1976. The building has three auditoriums. The Olivier (named after Sir Laurence) is the largest, with about 1,100 seats placed around an open stage. The Lyttleton (honouring the first chairman of the company) is a conventional proscenium theatre seating an audience of 900 and the Cottesloe (taking its name from a former chairman of the Arts Council, which promotes drama and other arts through government grants) has 300 seats that can be removed to allow actors to mingle with paying customers in experimental theatre. There are also rehearsal rooms big enough to allow actors to work with a full set, as well as costume shops and facilities for making scenery. Free performances are staged in the foyer. The company presents Shakespeare regularly but has also developed a reputation for its wide range of works by modern writers. In 1988 it was given permission by Elizabeth II to add the prefix 'Royal' to its title.

ROYAL NAVAL COLLEGE

The college buildings, designed by CHRISTOPHER WREN, were built on the site of GREENWICH PALACE and originally used as a home for disabled and elderly seamen. Wren's first plans were controversial because they hid the view of the QUEEN'S HOUSE from the RIVER THAMES so they were redrawn at the specific request of Mary II. There are four ranges: King Charles Building (completed in 1694) and King William Building (built in 1704 but with a façade on the west front, designed by John Vanbrugh, added in 1728) lie to the east, Queen Anne Building (finished in 1728) and Queen Mary Building (opened in 1742) to the west.

SAMUEL JOHNSON was unimpressed, claiming that the structures were 'too much detached to make one great whole' and the hospital residents, too, were unenthusiastic (in 1771, a Captain Baillie complained that 'Columns, colonnades and friezes ill accord with bully beef and sour beef mixed with water'). However, modern scholars suggest that the complex is Wren's finest work after ST PAUL'S CATHEDRAL and praise James Thornhill's decoration of the Great Hall, where, after his death at the Battle of Trafalgar in 1805, Lord Nelson lay in state under a painted ceiling that shows William III and Mary II delivering peace and liberty to Europe. During the first two decades of the nineteenth century, the hospital housed as many as 3,000 patients. However, by the 1860s the number had declined significantly, so, in 1873, the Royal Naval College was transferred to the premises from Portsmouth in order to ensure that the space was fully utilized. For over a century, young officers from Britain and abroad attended lectures at the site but, in 1994, the government decided to concentrate training for all armed forces at one location. GREENWICH was considered too small for the purpose. As a result, in 1996, arrangements were made for the buildings to be taken over by the UNIVERSITY of Greenwich and Trinity College of Music. (See also HAWKSMOOOR, NICHOLAS.)

ROYAL NAVAL DOCKYARDS

England's first royal DOCKyard was built at Portsmouth, on the South Coast. That town had the advantage of a strategic location commanding ship movements through the English Channel but was a considerable distance from London, where cannons were made, so, in 1512, Henry VIII established a second dockyard at WOOLWICH, on the SOUTH BANK of the RIVER THAMES and therefore closer to the source of armaments. Its first task was to build *Great Harry* as the flagship for his Navy. A third yard was opened 3 miles upriver at DEPTFORD the following year. Both sites were close to GREENWICH PALACE, so the king could watch his vessels take shape. The yards, run by a Navy Board, attracted ancillary activities (such as rope-making, coopering and sail manufacture), so they became foci for industrial development and urban expansion. Although SAMUEL PEPYS, Secretary to the Board, found 'much evidence of neglect' during a visit in 1661, Woolwich and Deptford were at the centre of the country's maritime activities for three centuries. Elizabeth I ordered Francis Drake to Deptford to receive his knighthood in 1581 following his circumnavigation of the world in the *Golden Hind*. From Woolwich, Walter Raleigh set off for the Americas and John Franklin for the Arctic. However, during the nineteenth century, the yards failed to adapt to the new technologies brought by the Industrial Revolution and suffered as the river deposited silt in their harbours. Housing hemmed in port activities, leaving little room for expansion, so in 1869 both were closed. The CORPORATION OF LONDON purchased most of the Deptford site and converted it for use as a cattle MARKET (the only original building left standing is the master shipwright's house, which was erected in 1704). At Woolwich the yards are covered by housing built by the LONDON BOROUGH OF GREENWICH during the 1970s. (See also ROYAL ARSENAL.)

ROYAL OBSERVATORY

Britain's oldest government-funded scientific establishment, the Royal Observatory was built in 1675 to designs prepared by CHRISTOPHER WREN. It is located in GREENWICH PARK and was originally charged with improving navigation on the high seas by developing techniques that would allow sailors to fix their position. In 1767 it began to publish the *British Nautical Almanack*, which rapidly became so widely used that, at an international conference held in Washington, D.C. in 1884, delegates agreed that the 0° line of longitude should pass through the building (see PRIME MERIDIAN). In 1833 a large red ball was built on a turret and is still lowered at 1 p.m. every afternoon so that mariners in the RIVER THAMES can set their chronometers accurately. By the later nineteenth and early twentieth centuries, however, the industrialization of south-east England was seriously interfering with astronomical observations, so, in 1948, the observatory's scientific work was moved to the clearer skies of rural Herstmonceux, in Sussex. The NATIONAL MARITIME MUSEUM took over the old buildings, where visitors can see the top-floor Octagon Room, which Wren designed for Sir John Flamsteed, the first Astronomer Royal. There is also a fine collection of early astronomical equipment, including a 28-inch refracting telescope (one of the largest in the world), which was installed in 1857.

ROYAL OPERA HOUSE

In 1732 entrepreneur John Rich (see BEEFSTEAK CLUB) built a lavish new THEATRE in DRURY LANE (near COVENT GARDEN). It opened with William Congreve's *Way of the World*, which was followed, over the next seventy years, by a string of successes, including George Frideric Handel's *Judas Maccabeus* (1747), Oliver Goldsmith's *She Stoops to Conquer* (1773) and Richard Sheridan's *The Rivals* (1775). In 1808 the building was destroyed by fire, but a second theatre was erected the following year, presenting the first performances in English of Wolfgang Amadeus Mozart's *Don Giovanni* (1817) and *The Marriage of Figaro* (1819), and of

Gioacchino Rossini's *The Barber of Seville* (1818), before experiencing financial difficulties, which were relieved only after a public appeal for funds in 1829. In 1855 that theatre, too, burned down, leaving a gutted site that remained empty until 1858, when the present structure, designed by E.M. Barry, was built.

Initially known as the Covent Garden Theatre, it was renamed the Royal Opera House in 1892, reflecting the policy of the management, which mounted the English premieres of Richard Wagner's *Lohengrin* (1875), Giuseppe Verdi's *Aida* (1876), Giacomo Puccini's *Tosca* (1900) and Richard Strauss's *Der Rosenkavalier* (1913). In 1946 the SADLER'S WELLS Ballet and the Covent Garden Opera Company made it their base and, in 1956 and 1968 respectively, were granted royal charters. Renamed the ROYAL BALLET and the Royal Opera, they mounted a series of high-cost productions, turning the 'House' into the principal British focus for both art forms but experiencing mounting criticism over costs. In particular, a £260 million refurbishment and considerable friction between management and artists fuelled press complaints that it was an over-funded institution serving a minority group (see EYRE REPORT). However, when Michael Kaiser (formerly of the American Ballet Theater) was appointed executive director in 1998, the Arts Council agreed to raise its annual grant to £20 million in return for introduction of policies (such as reduced price seats), which would attract larger audiences, and understandings were reached with the performers' trade unions. By 2000, when Kaiser decided to move on, media reports were suggesting that the House's public image, and its financing, had improved significantly.

ROYAL PARKS

Several of London's largest PARKS were originally land that was designated for hunting by Henry VIII during the early sixteenth century or as deer farms for animals that would later be used as game. Over time, attitudes towards hunting changed and the protected ground was surrounded by urban expansion, limiting the sporting opportunities. Gradually, the public was allowed access to the expanses of grass and woodland, which are now major recreational resources in the city although still owned by the Crown. The parks are maintained by the Royal Parks Agency, which also looks after other open spaces in the city, including Parliament Square. (See also BUSHY PARK; GREEN PARK; GREENWICH PARK; HYDE PARK; KENSINGTON GARDENS; PRIMROSE HILL; REGENT'S PARK; RICHMOND PARK; ST JAMES'S PARK.)

ROYAL PHILHARMONIC ORCHESTRA (RPO)

The orchestra was founded in 1946 by Sir Thomas Beecham, who guided its fortunes until his death in 1961. In its early days, its finances were derived largely from recording contracts with US companies, but it also played regularly in London and at the Glyndebourne summer opera season (where it was resident from 1948 until 1963). When Beecham died, the orchestra restructured itself as a limited company, with each member a shareholder. It formed its own record business in 1986, then, in 1987, created a concert orchestra to cater to audiences interested in light classical music. Plans to merge the Royal Philharmonic with the LONDON SYMPHONY ORCHESTRA were abandoned in 1995 after a report by management consultants suggested that the likely financial savings could not justify the artistic turmoil that would ensue. The RPO now divides its time between London (where it plays at the Royal ALBERT HALL) and Nottingham. It has undertaken to provide 125 compact discs for Tring International – the largest contract ever signed between a single orchestra and a record company.

ROYAL SOCIETY

Britain's oldest scientific organization was officially established in 1660 (although scholars had been meeting informally to discuss matters of common interest since 1648). Properly known as the Royal Society of London for the Promotion of Natural Knowledge, it depended heavily on Puritan sympathizers for its early support but, as knowledge of the natural sciences improved, it gained rapidly in influence and funds. In 1768 it organized the first scientific expedition from Europe to the Pacific in order to observe the planet Venus; led by Captain James Cook, the group also charted the East Coast of Australia and claimed it for Britain. Other activities included sponsorship of the ill-fated attempt by John Franklin to find the Northwest Passage through the Arctic from the Atlantic Ocean to the Pacific Ocean in 1845 (all 130 explorers died) and, more successfully, the confirmation of Albert Einstein's Theory of Relativity through field observations in the Gulf of Guinea in 1919. It also advises the government on scientific matters when required, awards medals to those who have made particularly significant contributions to knowledge and (since 1665) has published academic papers in its *Philosophical Transactions*. The Royal Society (based in Carlton House Terrace, near ADMIRALTY ARCH, since 1967) has about 1,000 members (known as Fellows) who must be proposed for election by existing Fellows prepared to attest to the candidate's scientific achievements. Former presidents have included CHRISTOPHER WREN (1681–3), Isaac Newton (1703–27) and the Nobel prize-winning nuclear energy researcher Ernest Rutherford (1925–30). (See also BRITISH ACADEMY.)

ROYAL SOCIETY OF ARTS (RSA)

The RSA was founded in 1754 by William Shipley, a Nottingham art teacher, as the Society for the Encouragement of Arts, Manufactures and Commerce. It adopted its present title by permission of Edward VII in 1908 and occupies premises at 8 John Adam Street, which was part of ROBERT ADAM's ADELPHI development. The Society organized the country's first art exhibition in 1760, the first photographic exhibition in 1852 and (in conjunction with the ROYAL ACADEMY OF ARTS) the first major exhibition of industrial design in 1935. Each year, it awards its Albert Medal (named after PRINCE ALBERT, Queen Victoria's consort and president of the Society from 1843 to 1861) to an individual who has made distinguished contributions to commerce, the arts or science; recipients have included Michael Faraday (1866) and Ernest Rutherford (1928), Joseph Lister (1894), Barnes Wallis (1968), Laurence Olivier (1976) and Lord Sainsbury (1989). In 1856, the RSA introduced a series of examinations designed to enable working-class students to gain qualifications in vocational skills. The certificates gained widespread acceptance among employers, so by 1989, when the Examinations Board became an independent body with charitable status, nearly a million candidates were presented annually. The organization has over 20,000 members (known as Fellows) and, since 1996, has made strenuous efforts to increase the number of young people, women and representatives of ethnic minorites in its ranks.

RUGBY

See BRENTFORD FOOTBALL CLUB; HARLEQUINS RUGBY FOOTBALL CLUB; LONDON IRISH RUGBY FOOTBALL CLUB; LONDON SCOTTISH FOOTBALL CLUB; LONDON WASPS RUGBY FOOTBALL CLUB; LONDON WELSH RUGBY FOOTBALL CLUB; OVAL, THE; SARACENS FOOTBALL CLUB; TWICKENHAM.)

RUISLIP

Ruislip, some 13 miles north-east of CHARING CROSS, forms the northern part of the LONDON BOROUGH OF HILLINGDON. It was an agricultural settlement until 1904, when the METROPOLITAN RAILWAY arrived, attracting urban development, which, by the end of the century, had turned the township into a city suburb. Many of the older buildings survived the change, however. St Martin's Church, a flint rubble building dating from about 1250, has medieval wall paintings, a fifteenth-century roof and sixteenth-century pews. Next to Manor Farmhouse, a timber-boarded, aisled Great Barn, erected during the late thirteenth century, is said by some scholars to be the oldest barn in England. Its neighbour – the Little Barn (with a roof dating from around 1600) – has been converted into a public library and High Street has been sympathetically planned to incorporate modern shops whilst restoring older structures. In addition, much of the former open space has been preserved, including PARK Wood, a source of timber for construction work in the TOWER OF LONDON and the PALACE OF WESTMINSTER during the fourteenth century. Ruislip's name is said to derive from the Old English *rysc* and *hlyp*, or 'a rushy place where one can leap across the river'.

RUSSELL SQUARE

One of the principal features of the BLOOMSBURY townscape, Russell Square was laid out in 1800 and given the family name of the Duke of Bedford, owner of the property. Traditionally, it has attracted men from the professions and the arts: painter Sir Thomas Lawrence maintained a studio at No. 62 from 1805 to 1830, lawyer Lord Denman lived at No. 50 from 1818 to 1834 and Sir George Williams (founder of the Young Men's Christian Association) made his home at No. 13 from 1880 until his death in 1905. Although architect James Burton would recognize several of the houses he designed for the west side of the square, those to the north and south have been much altered and those on the east were demolished in 1898 to make way for the Russell HOTEL. In addition, there has been significant infiltration of institutional uses associated with the University of London (see UNIVERSITIES).

S

SADLER'S WELLS

Although Sadler's Wells, in Rosebery Avenue, is one of London's best-known THEATRES, it has suffered a series of vicissitudes since its foundation in 1683, when Thomas Sadler advertised the medicinal qualities of a spring flowing just beyond the northern boundary of the CITY OF LONDON and, encouraged by the response (some 500 visitors a day), provided musical entertainment for his customers. The business was acquired by Thomas Rosoman, who, in 1765, built a permanent theatre where Joseph Grimaldi (later to develop a reputation as a clown) first performed (as a child dancer) in 1781 and where Edmund Kean appeared (while still a boy) in 1804.

During the second half of the nineteenth century, trading conditions proved difficult so performances ceased in 1871 and an attempt to revive fortunes by catering to MUSIC HALL audiences was successful only from 1893 until 1906. In 1931, hopes of a more secure future encouraged construction of a new building, which would be a permanent base for ballet and opera companies. However, performances were suspended during the Second World War. Then, in 1946, the ballet dancers left for the ROYAL OPERA HOUSE in COVENT GARDEN. Two decades later, the opera singers also departed, transferring to the Coliseum Theatre in 1968. In 1997–8, however, a £48 million refurbishment was undertaken, with most of the money coming from the proceeds of Britain's National Lottery and the design placing an emphasis on facilities for dance. In the process a bore was sunk to the original well, providing water that would be sold to patrons and used in the air conditioning system. A new auditorium, with 1,600 seats, is the focus of an artistic complex, which includes a second theatre (the 200-seat Lilian Baylis), an education centre, a lecture room, film facilities and space for archives.

ST ALFEGE'S CHURCH, GREENWICH

Considered one of NICHOLAS HAWKSMOOR's finest works, St Alfege's stands in Greenwich High Road on the site where the saint (appointed Archbishop of Canterbury in 1005) was allegedly murdered by invading Danish forces in 1012 when he refused to approve payment of the ransom that would have saved his life. After an earlier building was destroyed by a storm in 1710, parishioners asked Parliament to provide them with a new place of worship. The result of their petition was legislation, passed the following year, that sanctioned the building of fifty new churches in London, with the construction financed by a tax on coal. Hawksmoor's structure was erected in 1711–8, but a tower (an early version of the pepperpot style) was added by John James in 1730. The interior was destroyed by German bombs in 1941, during the BLITZ, but restored in 1952 under the direction of Albert Richardson. St Alfege's was the christening place of Prince Henry (later Henry VIII) in 1491 and of Charles Gordon (one of Britain's most distinguished nineteenth-century military leaders) in 1833. Thomas Tallis (sometimes referred to as 'the father of English church music') was buried beneath the chancel of the old church in 1585 and General James Wolfe in the family vault at the new church in 1759, following his death fighting the French at Quebec.

ST ANDREW'S CHURCH, HOLBORN

St Andrew's is the largest of the parish churches built by CHRISTOPHER WREN, standing on a site that was occupied by a Christian chapel in AD 951. Erected in 1684–90, it is 105 feet long and 63 feet wide. In 1896 the construction of Holborn viaduct, across the valley of the FLEET RIVER, resulted in the loss of the churchyard and, during the BLITZ of 1941, German bombs caused much damage but the church was restored to its original condition by John Seely (later Lord Mottistone) and Paul Paget in 1960–1. During the winter of 1827, Dr Richard Marsden found a young woman dying in the precincts because she had been unable to get treatment at any of the London hospitals. Marsden was so affected that he persuaded the Cordwainers' Company (one of the City LIVERY COMPANIES) to found the ROYAL FREE HOSPITAL, the first clinic to provide treatment to all-comers, regardless of their ability to pay. Two future Prime Ministers, Henry Addington and Benjamin Disraeli (although of Jewish background), were christened in St Andrew's in 1757 and 1817 respectively.

ST ANDREW UNDERSHAFT CHURCH, LEADENHALL STREET

The church is first mentioned in records dating from 1147, when it was known as St Andrew CORNHILL. It gets its present name from the extremely tall maypole that overshadowed the steeple when it was erected during May Day celebrations in the fifteenth and early sixteenth centuries (the festivities were discontinued after 1517 following attacks by LIVERY COMPANY apprentices on foreign residents). The present building, erected in1520–32, has been restored and renovated on several occasions. Its organ (by Renatus Harris) dates from 1696 and its altar rails (by Jean Tijou) from 1704. St Andrew also contains a statue of JOHN STOW (the first historian of London), who was buried in the church when he died, a pauper, in 1605. The monument is inscribed with the motto *Aut scribenda agere, aut legenda scribere* ('Either do something worth writing about, or write something worth reading') and includes a real quill pen in Stow's hand. Each year, at a memorial service, the LORD MAYOR removes the pen, hands it to the school pupil adjudged to have written the best essay on the city and replaces it with a new one.

ST BARTHOLOMEW'S HOSPITAL

In 1123, Rahere (a courtier attending King Henry I) returned to London at the end of a pilgrimage to Rome. During his journey, he had fallen ill and, as an act of thanks for his recovery, he founded a hospital dedicated to St Bartholomew and charged with serving the needs of the CITY OF LONDON's poor. Initially, it was attached to an Augustinian priory but since 1539, when the religious establishment was dissolved by Henry VIII, it has functioned independently. It survived the GREAT FIRE of 1666 and was rebuilt to the designs of JAMES GIBBS between 1729 and 1770. (Gibbs planned the structure as four separate blocks, set around a square, because it was believed that such a layout would encourage the circulation of air and thus help reduce the spread of infectious disease.) During the nineteenth century, its development was shaped partly by advances in medical knowledge and technologies – dental facilities were provided in

1836, an anaesthetist was appointed in 1875, a pathologist joined the staff in 1893, a special unit treating skin diseases opened in 1908 and in 1954 Bart's was the first British hospital to use mega-voltage radiotherapy in the treatment of cancers. In addition, new buildings were added, reflecting changing approaches to healthcare and provision for staff (an outpatients' department was added in 1842, for example, and a nurses' home was erected between 1921 and 1929).

In 1994, Bart's joined the ROYAL LONDON HOSPITAL in a National Health Service Trust and now provides the city's largest trauma service along with specialist facilities for treating cancer, cardiac diseases and renal disorders.

ST BARTHOLOMEW-THE-GREAT CHURCH, SMITHFIELD

The oldest parish church building in London, St Bartholomew is the only remaining part of an Augustinian priory founded in 1123 by Rahere, a courtier of Henry I. In 1539, during the Reformation, it was sold to Sir Richard Rich (see WANSTEAD), who demolished the nave. During the seventeenth and eighteenth centuries, much of the structure was put to secular use. The crypt served as a coal and wine store and the Lady Chapel (which had been rebuilt in 1336) was redesigned as private residences then became a print shop (where Benjamin Franklin, one of the founding fathers of the United States, worked as an apprentice in 1725). The cloisters were turned into stables, the south triforium into a school, the sacristy into a hop store and the north transept into a blacksmith's forge. However, in 1887, the rector (Reverend Borrodail Savory) initiated restoration work, aided by architect Sir Aston Webb. The porch was rebuilt, the west front refaced before the end of the century and a choir screen (by Frank Beresford) erected in 1932. Because of its great age, St Bartholomew has a particularly rich collection of funeral monuments dating from the sixteenth century.

ST BENET'S CHURCH, PAUL'S WHARF

St Benet's, erected in 1683 on the site of a twelfth-century chapel destroyed in the GREAT FIRE, serves London's Welsh-speaking Anglican community. Built of red brick, with alternate courses of PORTLAND STONE at the corners, it was designed by CHRISTOPHER WREN, who departed from his normally plain style by decorating the window frames with stone garlands. INIGO JONES, a fellow architect, was buried in the old church in 1652 and, in 1747, Henry Fielding demonstrated a disdain of middle-class values by marrying Mary, his first wife's former maid, in the new church.

ST BOTOLPH'S CHURCH, ALDGATE

St Botolph, a patron saint of travellers, has several churches dedicated to his name in London. That at Aldgate may have been founded before the Norman Conquest of 1066 and was certainly in use by 1115. The present brick building was designed by GEORGE DANCE THE ELDER and erected in 1741–4 but has been much altered internally since then, principally by John Francis Bentley (architect of WESTMINSTER CATHEDRAL) in 1887–91. In addition, from 1958 to 1966, Rodney Tatchell supervised repairs necessitated by Second World War bomb damage and an unexplained fire in 1965. St Botolph's organ was built by Renatus Harris in 1676 and its peal of eight bells cast by Lester and Pack in 1744. Daniel Defoe, who was married in the church in 1683, records how, at the time of the GREAT PLAGUE, 5,136 people were interred at the BURIAL GROUND in only sixteen weeks. The crypt now serves as a centre for homeless people and as a youth club.

ST BRIDE'S CHURCH, FLEET STREET

Archaeological excavations suggest that St Bride's occupies the site of London's first church, founded by St Bridget during the sixth century. The building was originally designed by CHRISTOPHER WREN and erected in 1671 after its fifteenth-century predecessor was destroyed in the GREAT FIRE five years earlier. A spire, added in 1701, was the only substantial part of the structure to survive German bombing on 29 December 1940, during the BLITZ, but restoration work (supervised by Godfrey Allen and financed largely by donations from the national and international press) retained much of Wren's plan, including the tunnel-vaulted nave. The crypt, which incorporates a MUSEUM of London west of the FLEET RIVER, displays remains of the earlier buildings and other relics. St Bride's is still the parish church of London's newspaper industry even though most of the presses have moved away from the area. Its spire had been the inspiration for wedding cake designs ever since a local pastry cook hit on the idea of associating the church's dedication with the marriage ceremony in the late eighteenth century. (See also PEPYS, SAMUEL.)

ST CLEMENT DANES CHURCH, STRAND

The origins of St Clement's are obscure, though writers have suggested that it takes its name from a ninth-century Danish settlement in the area (some scholars believe that it may be the burial place of Harold Harefoot and other Scandinavian leaders). A church erected on the site in the late tenth or early eleventh century survived the GREAT FIRE of 1666 but was considered unsafe in 1679 and demolished. A new building, designed by CHRISTOPHER WREN and completed in 1682, survived until German bombs destroyed it during the BLITZ of 1941. It was restored in 1955–8 by Anthony Lloyd, with much of the funding contributed by the Royal Air Force (RAF), which designated it as a memorial church commemorating the 125,000 members of the service who were killed in the Second World War. Over 700 badges of RAF units were cut from Welsh slate and laid in the side aisles. Under the north gallery, a book of remembrance lists the names of American airmen who died while based in Great Britain between 1941 and 1945. The peal of bells, which was hung in 1957, sometimes plays the tune associated with the nursery rhyme *Oranges and Lemons*, but the St Clement's Church mentioned in the verses is probably that at EASTCHEAP, where citrus fruits were unloaded from cargo boats arriving from Mediterranean countries. (See also GIBBS, JAMES.)

ST DUNSTAN-IN-THE-WEST CHURCH, FLEET STREET

Although St Dunstan's is not mentioned in written records until 1185, it was probably founded before the Norman Conquest of 1066. William Tyndale (translator of the first Bible to be printed in English) worked there as a preacher (1523), John Donne was rector (1624–31) and Izaak Walton (author of the *Compleat Angler*, published in 1653 by Richard Marriott, whose business operated from the churchyard) was scavenger, questman and sidesman (1629–44). The building escaped destruction in the GREAT FIRE of 1666 and was refurbished in 1701 but by 1829 it was so dilapidated that it had to be demolished. Its replacement (built on the site of the former BURIAL GROUND so that nearby streets could be widened) was an octagonal structure, designed by John Shaw and opened in 1831. An early example of Gothic Revival ARCHITECTURE, it has a yellow freestone tower modelled on that at All Saints' Pavement Church in York and a clock that was originally placed on the old church in 1671. The timepiece, the first in London to have a minute hand, was a notable city landmark, mentioned in Oliver Goldsmith's *Vicar of Wakefield* (1766), Walter Scott's *The Fortunes of Nigel* (1822) and CHARLES DICKENS' *Barnaby Rudge* (1841). In 1954, St Dunstan's was designated a Guild Church so its parish was merged with that of ST BRIDE'S CHURCH, FLEET

STREET, and the building closed on Saturdays and Sundays, but during the week it holds services and other meetings for CITY OF LONDON office workers. (See also PEPYS, SAMUEL.)

ST ETHELBURGA-THE-VIRGIN-WITHIN-BISHOPSGATE CHURCH, BISHOPSGATE

The CITY OF LONDON's smallest church, measuring some 60 feet by 30 feet, St Ethelburga's is dedicated to the daughter of Aethlebert I, King of Kent from AD 560 to AD 616 and the first Anglo-Saxon ruler to accept the Christian faith. The first stone building on the site was probably erected during the thirteenth century but there was considerable restructuring 200 years later and much alteration and refurbishment since then, including the addition of a south gallery in 1629 and a bell turret in 1775. St Ethelburga's was designated a Guild Church in 1954; its parish was amalgamated with that of St Helen Bishopsgate Church, and instead of serving a declining population of local residents on Sundays, it introduced weekday services for office workers, with special emphasis on healing. In 1993, it was badly damaged by an IRA bomb that exploded in a nearby street but, six years later, the Bishop of London launched an appeal for funds that would support a rebuilding programme using the original fabric and incorporating a centre for peace and reconciliation.

ST ETHELDREDA'S CHURCH, HOLBORN

In 1876, when St Etheldreda's was acquired by the Fathers of Charity, it became the first place of worship in England to revert to Roman Catholic use after the Reformation. Originally built towards the end of the thirteenth century as a private chapel for William de Luda, Bishop of Ely (where Etheldreda had been an abbess some six centuries earlier), it was badly damaged during the BLITZ but renovated after the Second World War. The east and west windows contain stained glass, by Joseph Nuttgens and Charles Blakemen, which commemorates martyrs who refused to renounce their faith and were put to death at TYBURN. On 3 February each year, when a service is held in memory of St Blaise (who saved a boy who was choking to death on a fishbone), candles are lit near worshippers suffering from throat diseases. (See also ELY PLACE.)

ST GEORGE'S HOSPITAL

During the 1720s, the governors of WESTMINSTER Infirmary became increasingly convinced that they needed larger premises if their institution was to cater properly to the needs of the local population. Most of them favoured a site in Broad Sanctuary, which opened as WESTMINSTER HOSPITAL in 1734, but a minority preferred Lanesborough House, at HYDE PARK CORNER, because it was a less urban location and thus could provide patients with country air. St George's was established at the Lanesborough House site in 1733, with thirty beds, but it expanded rapidly, catering for 250 in-patients within twelve years. In 1827–9, it was rebuilt to meet growing demand for healthcare and in 1869 a convalescent home was built at WIMBLEDON using funds bequeathed by Atkinson Morley (a governor and owner of the Burlington HOTEL). By the 1930s, it was evident that a major refurbishment was necessary because of changed practices in patient care and advancements in medical science. Funds were raised by public subscription but the Second World War broke out before any work could be done and by the late 1940s government ministers were convinced that the Hyde Park Corner site was too small. In 1951, St George's began a move to a site in TOOTING occupied by the Grove Fever Hospital. It now covers some 36 acres, with most of the buildings erected from 1980. In 1993, it was reorganized administratively as a National Health Service Trust. Since then, it has linked with the ROYAL MARSDEN HOSPITAL to provide specialist facilities for the treatment of cancer and has transferred its neurosurgery unit from the Atkinson Morley to Tooting. The list of distinguished alumni includes Henry Gray, whose *Anatomy* has been on sale in bookshops since 1858.

ST GILES-IN-THE-FIELDS CHURCH, ST GILES HIGH STREET

In 1101, Matilda (wife of Henry I) built a leper hospital in the fields beyond the western wall of the CITY OF LONDON and dedicated it to St Giles, the patron saint of outcasts. The hospital chapel, which also served as a parish church, was rebuilt in 1623 (largely through the largesse of Alicia, Duchess Dudley) and again (to designs prepared by Henry Flitcroft) in 1733. Since then it has changed very little apart from interior alterations made in 1875 and 1896. Henry Pelham (a future Prime Minister) was baptized in St Giles in 1694 and DAVID GARRICK was married there (to Eva Maria Veigel) in 1749. Poet Andrew Marvell was buried in the church in 1678, Luke Hansard (printer to the HOUSE OF COMMONS (see PALACE OF WESTMINSTER)) in 1828, and John Soane (see SIR JOHN SOANE'S MUSEUM) in 1837. Because the GREAT PLAGUE began in St Giles Parish in 1665, the churchyard also provided a last resting place for many of its victims. (See also TYBURN.)

ST JAMES'S CHURCH, PICCADILLY

St James's, the last of the London churches designed by CHRISTOPHER WREN and the only one built on a new site, was part of a fashionable suburban development promoted by Henry Jordan, Earl of St Albans. The brick building, with PORTLAND STONE quoins and dressings, was consecrated in 1684 and

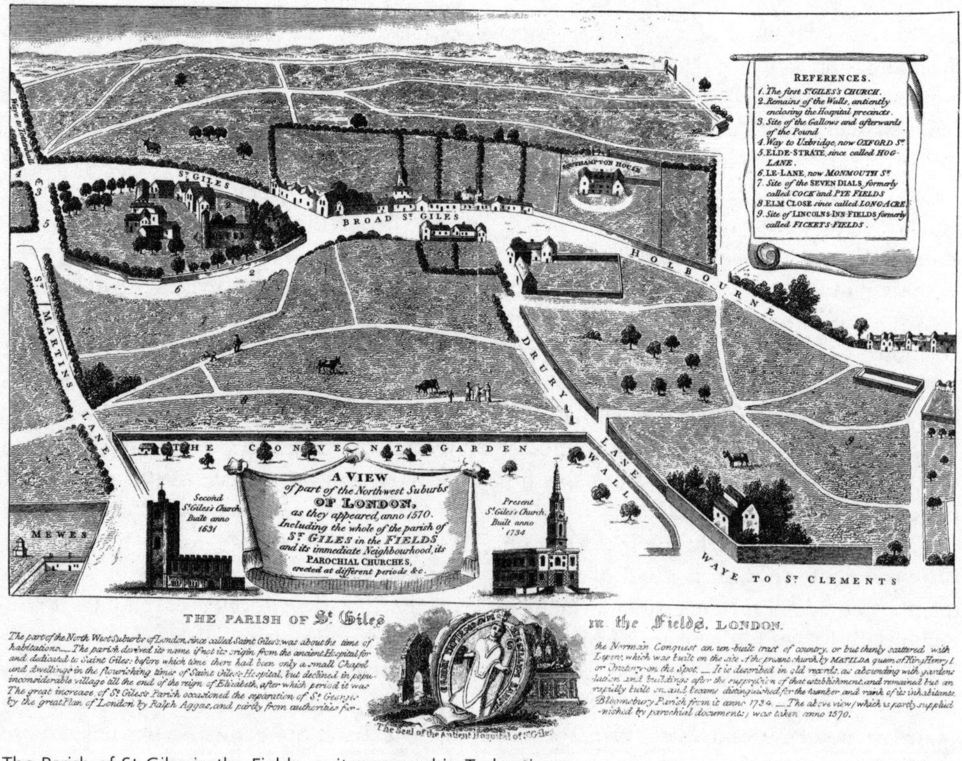

The Parish of St Giles-in-the-Fields, as it appeared in Tudor times.

Hogarth's engraving of drunken debauchery, *Gin Lane*, 1751. Hogarth set Gin Lane in St Giles, by then a notorious borough for gin-fuelled drunkenness.

designed so that everyone in a congregation of 2,000 could hear the preacher clearly. It suffered badly during the BLITZ but was renovated under the direction of Sir Albert Richardson after the Second World War. Fitments that had survived the damage (including the reredos and the marble font, both carved by GRINLING GIBBONS) were retained and the BURIAL GROUND turned into a garden of remembrance to commemorate the courage of Londoners during the German AIR RAIDS.

ST JAMES'S FAIR

For seven days from the eve of St James's Day, medieval Londoners held a fair outside the leper hospital at the site on which ST JAMES'S PALACE now stands. It was clearly a boisterous event because it was closed in 1664 on the grounds that it promoted riotous behaviour and loose living, reopened in 1689, closed again (for the same reasons) in 1708 and revived in 1738. During the 1760s, according to John Carter, there were booths for prize fighters, jugglers and exotic animals. Moreover, 'the sports under cover were mountebanks, ass-racing, dice-ditto, ups-and-downs, merry-go-rounds, bull-baiting, running for a shift, hasty pudding eaters, eel-divers and an infinite variety of other pastimes.' The fair closed for good in 1764 because the Earl of Coventry, who had a residence in nearby PICCADILLY, complained about the noise.

ST JAMES'S PALACE

Standing at the western end of PALL MALL, where GREEN PARK and ST JAMES'S PARK adjoin, the palace is located on the site of a medieval leper hospital built outside the walls of the CITY OF LONDON. Henry VIII bought the property in 1531, gave the inmates a pension, demolished the buildings and erected a small residence in their place. It has been much used by royalty ever since. Mary Tudor died there in 1533, Elizabeth I slept there while the Spanish Armada sailed up the English Channel in 1588, Charles I stayed there in 1649 the night before he was taken to the be executed, Charles II made it his principal home (refurbishing it after Oliver Cromwell had turned it into a prison so that he could provide rooms for his several mistresses) and William III employed CHRISTOPHER WREN to design new apartments of state. From 1698 (when WHITEHALL PALACE was destroyed by fire) until 1837 (when Queen Victoria moved into BUCKINGHAM PALACE) it was the principal royal palace in Britain (and, legally, remains so, which is why foreign ambassadors are accredited to the Court of St James). Queen Anne and her successors (George I, George II and George III) spent much time there and George III's son (the future George IV) was married there in 1795 (his bride, Queen Caroline, reported that he was so drunk after the wedding celebrations that he collapsed, stupefied, into a fireplace and lay there until morning).

St James's Palace in the seventeenth century.

A large part of the structure was destroyed by fire in 1814 but immediately rebuilt. It is now the London residence of Prince Charles and of Princess Alexandra and Sir Angus Ogilvy. Also, it houses the offices of the Lord Chamberlain (who is responsible for the management of the monarch's domestic staff) and the Prince of Wales's administrative staff. With the exception of the Chapel Royal (where services are held on Sunday mornings from October until the week before Easter) and the Queen's Chapel (where they are held from Easter Sunday until the end of July), none of the rooms – which contain fine carvings by GRINLING GIBBONS, door cases by William Kent (see KENSINGTON PALACE) and tapestries woven for Charles II – is open to the public. (See also ST JAMES'S FAIR.)

ST JAMES'S PARK

A ROYAL PARK covering 90 acres in the heart of London, St James's PARK is bounded by THE MALL to the north, BUCKINGHAM PALACE to the west, BIRDCAGE WALK to the south and the government buildings of WHITEHALL to the east. It takes its name from St James's leper hospital, which stood at the north-western edge of the area during the fifteenth and early sixteenth centuries on the site now occupied by ST JAMES'S PALACE. Henry VIII bought the estate in 1531, drained the marshes where the lepers had grazed their pigs and used the land as a deer farm. Over the next fifty years, many of the trees were cut down, so James I, after his accession to the English throne in 1603, was able to lay out formal gardens, build a small zoo and construct an aviary. During the second half of the seventeenth century, Charles II (advised by André Le Nôtre, the French landscape gardener who had been responsible for the design of the grounds at the Palace of Versailles, near Paris) planted fruit trees, built an avenue surfaced with powdered cockle shells and linked a series of small ponds into a single length of water (known as the Canal), but after his death in 1685 the grounds were little cared for, becoming a favoured location for prostitutes to ply their trade. Improvements, which shaped the present structure of the area, were made in 1827 by JOHN NASH, who remodelled the Canal, introduced new walks and planted more trees. Other features (such as an iron suspension bridge across the water) were added later in the century but most have since been removed. By the late twentieth century, the PARK had become a popular place for feeding wildfowl (which have frequented the lake since Charles II's day) and listening to summer band concerts. The views across to Whitehall are mentioned in almost every guidebook to city sights. In 1982 a bomb, planted in the bandstand by the IRA, exploded as a detachment of the Household Cavalry (see HOUSEHOLD DIVISION) was passing; four soldiers and seven horses were killed.

ST JAMES'S SQUARE

In the late eighteenth century, St James's Square (north of PALL MALL) was the most desirable residential area in London. It was laid out in 1665 by Henry Jermyn, Earl of St Albans and a staunch supporter of Charles II, who had returned from exile the previous year. Plots were leased to speculative builders willing to build houses for aristocratic families seeking homes close to ST JAMES'S PALACE and red-brick residences were erected on the north, east and west sides of a central piazza. However, over the next 100 years, most of the properties were demolished or extensively redesigned, then, during the first half of the nineteenth century, many were taken over by commercial interests as private individuals moved west to BELGRAVIA so little of the original fabric remains and the buildings are almost entirely devoted to business or institutional purposes. Residents have included three Prime Ministers (William Pitt the Elder, the Earl of Derby and William Gladstone, who lived at No. 9 in 1751–61, 1837–54 and 1890 respectively). General Dwight D. Eisenhower established his headquarters at No. 31 during the Second World War and architect ROBERT ADAM considered No. 20 (built in 1771–5) one of his best works. (See also LONDON LIBRARY.)

ST JOHN'S CHURCH, CLERKENWELL

See KNIGHTS HOSPITALLER.

ST JOHN'S WOOD

The residential area to the north-west of REGENT'S PARK takes its name from the Knights of St John of Jerusalem (see KNIGHTS HOSPITALLER), who owned it from 1312 until the Reformation. Largely forested until the early nineteenth century, it succumbed to urban development following the construction of the REGENT'S CANAL in 1812–20 and an artillery barracks in 1832. The building of the Great Central RAILWAY during the 1890s added to the pressures on land then, during the 1920s and 1930s, apartment blocks were erected for city workers. 'The Wood' experienced considerable damage during the BLITZ but, since the end of the Second World War, many of the older properties have been restored and development has taken the form of town houses rather than apartments. The relatively inexpensive but well-designed semidetached villas built during the Victorian period attracted middle-class groups, including painters, authors and scientists (for example, George Eliot lived at 21 North Bank with critic G.H. Lewes and naturalist T.H. Huxley at 48 Marlborough Place). The artists (who became known as the St John's Wood Clique) concentrated on dramatic, frivolous or pathetic scenes and included W.F. Yeames, best known for *And When Did You Last See Your Father?* Perhaps because of its somewhat secluded environment, the area also became a favourite place for wealthy men to provide accommodation for their mistresses (Napoleon III of France made a home for Elizabeth Anne Howard at 23 Circus Road, for instance). (See also BRONDESBURY; DOMESDAY BOOK; MARYLEBONE CRICKET CLUB (MCC).)

ST MARGARET'S CHURCH, WESTMINSTER

St Margaret's – the parish church of the HOUSE OF COMMONS (see PALACE OF WESTMINSTER) – was founded in the early twelfth century but the present building dates from 1486. Since then it has been altered and refurbished on many occasions. It narrowly escaped demolition in 1549, when the Duke of Somerset ordered that it be knocked down to provide stone for his new palace (see SOMERSET HOUSE). However, the parishioners refused to give up their chapel, attacked the workmen and chased them away. SAMUEL PEPYS was married in the church in 1655, John Milton in 1656 and WINSTON CHURCHILL in 1908. William Caxton was buried there in 1491 (though the site of his tomb is unknown) and the headless body of Sir Walter Raleigh was placed under the high altar following his execution in 1618.

ST MARTIN-IN-THE-FIELDS CHURCH, TRAFALGAR SQUARE

St Martin-in-the-Fields is located at the north-east corner of TRAFALGAR SQUARE. A chapel stood on the site as early as 1222 (when it really was surrounded by fields) but the present structure, designed by JAMES GIBBS, was erected in 1722–6 to serve the area west of COVENT GARDEN, which was developing as a fashionable suburb. The building is a simple rectangular hall with a portico of six Corinthian columns surmounted by a pediment and a high steeple. Church members have a long tradition of helping the homeless, dating from the days when the crypt was used to shelter soldiers returning from the First World War. They have also seen many famous men and women buried in the grounds, including courtesan ELEANOR 'NELL' GWYN in 1687, Joshua Reynolds in 1762, Thomas Chippendale in 1779 and surgeon John Hunter (see ROYAL COLLEGE OF SURGEONS OF ENGLAND) in 1793. In 1987 the bells (which were making the steeple structurally unstable) were sent to the University of Western Australia in exchange for 20 tons of copper and tin, which were fashioned into a new (and lighter) peal. A new organ, with 3,637 pipes, forty-eight stops and three manuals, was installed in 1990, continuing the church's long tradition as a focus of fine music. (See also PEARLY KINGS AND QUEENS.)

ST MARY ABCHURCH CHURCH, ABCHURCH LANE

Of all the London churches designed by CHRISTOPHER WREN, St Mary's is the least altered. Erected in 1686 on the site of a twelfth-century chapel, it forms a square, some 63 feet long and 60 feet broad, under a shallow dome, which rests on eight arches and is lit by oval lunettes. The quality of the interior decoration is outstanding; the dome was painted by William Snow, the wood pulpit carved by William Grey and the marble font sculpted by William Kempster. The reredos – the only one in the CITY OF LONDON known to be by GRINLING GIBBONS – was blasted into more than 2,000 pieces when the church was damaged by German bombs in 1940 but was restored between 1948 and 1953. Under the terms of legislation approved by Parliament in 1952, St Mary's was made a Guild Church, closing its doors on weekends but providing services and other activities for office workers from Monday to Friday.

ST MARYLEBONE

The St Marylebone area lies north of OXFORD STREET (the name is derived from the Church of St Mary by the bourne, or stream, and is often listed simply as Marylebone). During the Middle Ages, the land was held by the KNIGHTS TEMPLAR, KNIGHTS HOSPITALLER and BARKING Abbey but it was acquired by the Crown when Henry VIII dissolved the English MONASTERIES from 1532. Much of the northern section became royal hunting forest and was later converted into REGENT'S PARK. Other sections were acquired, in 1553, by the Portman family (which still owns large tracts in the area). The remainder of the estate was leased to a variety of tenants before being sold by James I to Edward Forsett (a Justice of the Peace) in 1611; after passing through several hands, it was acquired (through inheritance) by the Earl and Countess of Oxford, who developed it from 1717 in an attempt to emulate the successful housing ventures in MAYFAIR. The focus of building was CAVENDISH SQUARE, the centre of a gridiron pattern of streets differing markedly from the wandering alleys of the CITY OF LONDON. In 1741, the land passed to Oxford's daughter, Margaret, who later married William Bentinck, Duke of Portland, and continued the expansion process (see, for example, PORTLAND PLACE). By the end of the eighteenth century, the area was extensively built up, with the final open spaces covered soon afterwards. Since the end of the Second World War, commercial uses have increasingly infiltrated but distinct communities still thrive, focusing on local shopping centres such as Marylebone High Street. (See also HOLMES, SHERLOCK; SARACENS FOOTBALL CLUB.)

ST MARY-LE-BOW CHURCH, CHEAPSIDE

See BOW BELLS.

ST MARY'S HOSPITAL

St Mary's Hospital opened in 1851. It was built to provide medical care for the rapidly growing population around PADDINGTON and, although there were some structural problems (it closed in 1875, and again in 1886, so that the drains could be relaid), it was enlarged over the next fifty years to include a medical school (founded in 1854), an accident ward (added in 1857), an outpatient department (which took its first patients in 1882) and other specialist facilities. The improvements continued through the early twentieth century with the construction of a nurses' home (1936) and a wing for private patients (1937). Following the foundation of the National Health Service (NHS) in 1948, St Mary's united with other hospitals in order to widen the range of provision (by providing convalescent and geriatric facilities, for instance). It was reconstituted as an NHS Trust in 1992 and now supplies a comprehensive healthcare service to west central London. The Trust has major plans for rebuilding the hospital as part of a major programme of urban improvements in Paddington. The hospital has a long association with the royal family. Queen Victoria and Prince Albert became patrons in 1846 and the Queen Mother was a patron from 1930 until her death in 2002. As a child, King George VI received treatment for typhoid, and Princes William and Harry were born in the Lindo Wing in 1982 and 1984 respectively. The list of eminent doctors who have worked with the patients includes Nobel prize winners Alexander Fleming and Rodney Porter.

ST NICHOLAS COLE ABBEY CHURCH, DISTAFF LANE

See COLE ABBEY CHURCH, DISTAFF LANE.

ST OLAVE'S CHURCH, HART STREET

St Olave's is the last survivor of five London churches dedicated to King Olaf of Norway, who fought alongside Aethelred II of England against the invading Vikings in 1014 and was canonized for his services to the Christian faith. The original wooden church was erected during the eleventh century, replaced 200 years later with a more substantial stone structure then rebuilt in Perpendicular style (see ARCHITECTURE) around 1450. It survived the GREAT FIRE of 1666 but was badly damaged by bombs in 1941, during the BLITZ, and restored under the supervision of E.B. Glanville, reopening in 1954. SAMUEL PEPYS was a regular worshipper during the seventeenth century, describing several of the services in his diaries. His wife, Elizabeth, was buried there in 1669 (aged only twenty-nine but having been married for fourteen years). The parish register records that, in 1586, a Mother Goose was interred in the churchyard, which also contains the remains of Mary Ramsay, who allegedly introduced the GREAT PLAGUE to London in 1664.

ST PANCRAS

The St Pancras area is one of the oldest centres of Christian worship in England, with a church established by the early seventh century, only a few years after St Augustine arrived from Rome, charged by Pope Gregory I with the task of converting the Anglo-Saxons. Most of the land remained under the control of the Church until Henry VIII's reign, when it was divided into a number of agricultural estates administered by rich barons. Urban development began during the Georgian period, as the CITY OF LONDON expanded, and speeded up after the RAILWAYS arrived in the nineteenth century. St Pancras Station was opened in 1868 as the terminus of the Midland Railway, which had previously shared the Great Northern Railway's facilities at KING'S CROSS. Designed by W.H. Barlow, it was built on the site of Agar Town, one of mid-Victorian London's worst slums, which CHARLES DICKENS described as 'A complete bog of mud and filth with wretched hovels, the doors blocked up with mud, heaps of ashes, oyster shells and decayed vegetables,' adding that 'The stench of a rainy morning is enough to knock down a bullock.' An enormous glass and iron hall, 640 feet long, 249 feet wide and 100 feet high, it earned much praise from architectural critics of the time. Above it, the former Midland Hotel (built to George Gilbert Scott's plans, opened in 1872 and closed in 1935) presents a Gothic façade of towers and spires to Euston Road. In recent years, local authorities have swept away many of the older properties, replacing them with modern institutional buildings, such as the BRITISH LIBRARY (which moved to the site in 1997) and a youth hostel (opened in 1997 to provide budget accommodation for young tourists). Also, the resident population has declined as the railway industry has contracted and property values have risen.

ST PAUL'S CATHEDRAL

St Paul's is the cathedral church of the CITY OF LONDON and the site of most religious ceremonies of state in the United Kingdom (the major exception is the coronation of the monarch, which takes place in WESTMINSTER ABBEY). The present building is the fifth Christian place of worship on the site, succeeding a wooden chapel erected early in the seventh century but destroyed by fire, a stone edifice that replaced it in AD 685 but was ransacked by Viking invaders in AD 962, a late tenth-century structure and a Norman cathedral begun in 1087 after the last Saxon church burnt down. During the medieval period, St Paul's was more than a religious focus; Londoners met there to socialize and do business, a law school was established in the precincts, booksellers traded in the churchyard and major public announcements were made from the steps. However, by the time James I succeeded to the throne in 1603 much of the fabric was decaying. An extensive programme of renovation began in 1638 but was halted during the Civil War of 1642–9, when the nave was used as a barracks for Oliver Cromwell's anti-royalist troops. Then, in 1663, CHRISTOPHER WREN was asked to prepare plans for further refurbishment but in September 1666, less than a week after his proposals were

The west front of St Paul's in London from an early fourteenth-century manuscript.

Preaching at Paul's Cross, St Paul's Cathedral. Educated Londoners flocked to hear sermons at the open-air pulpit in the cathedral churchyard.

approved, the cathedral was destroyed by the GREAT FIRE.

Not entirely unhappy at the prospect of designing a completely new building, Wren drew up a further set of drawings and began work on the construction of the present cathedral in 1675, altering details as he progressed and completing the project in 1710. The main entrance is by the steps and two-storey portico of the west front. Inside, the dominating feature is the baroque dome, decorated by James Thornhill with scenes from the life of St Paul and rising 218 feet above the floor. At its base, it is encircled by the Whispering Gallery, where softly spoken words by a visitor on one side can be picked up by a listener on the other, 107 feet away. In the crypt, one of the largest in Europe, the remains of Admiral Horatio Nelson lie immediately underneath the dome in the cask of spirits that preserved his body during the journey back to England from the battle of Trafalgar in 1805. Wren himself is buried nearby, his tomb bearing the Latin inscription *Lector, si monumentum requiris, circumspice* ('Reader, if you seek a monument, look around you'). Despite its size, the cathedral survived the BLITZ with little damage, partly because an army of volunteers risked their lives to defuse unexploded bombs that fell nearby. The Jesus Chapel, behind the High Altar, was struck in 1940 but refurbished as the American Chapel, a tribute to the 20,000 US citizens based in Great Britain who lost their lives during the Second World War. In 1997, amidst much con-

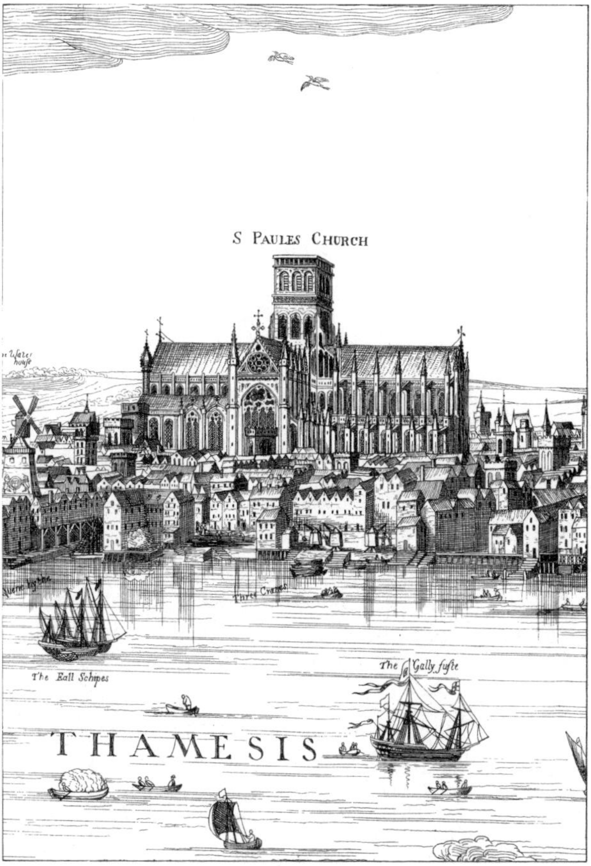

St Paul's dominated the Tudor skyline of London even after (as in this engraving) it had lost its great medieval spire.

troversy, the cathedral appointed Lucy Winkett as its first female priest. (See also BRONDESBURY; DANCE, GEORGE (1741–1825) GIBBONS, GRINLING; GUILDHALL; HAWKSMOOR, NICHOLAS; JONES, INIGO; PORTLAND STONE; RENNIE, JOHN.)

ST PAUL'S CHURCH, COVENT GARDEN

The first Anglican church to be built on a new site in London after the Reformation, St Paul's was designed by INIGO JONES, who had been commissioned by Francis Russell, Earl of Bedford, to plan a housing development at COVENT GARDEN in 1627. Construction was completed in 1633, parish boundaries drawn up in 1645 and major renovations undertaken in 1788, 1795 (following a fire) and 1871. The church is located on the western side of the piazza, which formed the centre of Jones's scheme, with the main entrance opening onto the square. However, the Church of England hierarchy insisted that the altar should be placed in its traditional place against the east wall, so the door at that point is a sham and entry is gained from the rear of the building. The 1795 fire destroyed most of the original structure but it was faithfully rebuilt to Jones's designs by Thomas Hardwicke. St Paul's is very closely associated with the entertainment community because several THEATRES are located nearby and, for three centuries, actors have found accommodation in neighbouring lodgings. Thomas Arne (composer of *Rule Britannia*) was buried there in 1778, as was actress Ellen Terry in 1928. Inside there are memorials to Ivor Novello and others who have contributed to the London stage. George Bernard Shaw set the opening scene of *Pygmalion* (published in 1916) in the church portico, which is still used as an impromptu stage by street musicians. (See also GIBBONS, GRINLING.)

ST STEPHEN'S CHURCH, WALBROOK

St Stephens was originally founded in the second half of the eleventh century. The present church, regarded by many critics as CHRISTOPHER WREN's finest achievement (David Piper claimed that it surpasses ST PAUL'S CATHEDRAL), was built during the 1670s. Its principal feature is a large Roman dome, lit centrally and supported by eight Corinthian columns. Arches, outer columns and angled clerestory walls combine to produce changing patterns of light, shade and differing perspectives as visitors move about the church. Furnishings survived the BLITZ so the pulpit, reredos, rails and font are Wren's originals, but the altar is a highly controversial Henry Moore sculpture of travertine stone placed under the dome in 1987 following a series of bitter court battles. Property developer Peter Palumbo financed much restoration work within the building and commissioned the new altar. Traditionalists likened the rock to a lump of cheese and argued that it moved the focus of worship from the east end of the church (where the pulpit stood) to the centre but the judges ultimately ruled for the modernizers.

ST THOMAS'S HOSPITAL

In 1106, two of Henry I's knights – William Pont de l'Arche and William Dauncey – founded a priory, which they named St Mary Overie, at a site in SOUTHWARK just south of LONDON BRIDGE. The Augustinian monks and nuns who lived there were required to look after the sick so they established a hospital dedicated to Thomas Becket (though that dedication cannot have been made before 1175, when Thomas was canonized by Pope Alexander III). At the beginning of the thirteenth century, the priory was destroyed by fire and rebuilt, with the hospital relocated to a site beside Borough High Street. During the fifteenth century, the healthcare facilities were expanded through the provision of a lying-in ward for unmarried women (the funds were endowed by RICHARD 'DICK' WHITTINGTON). In 1540, the priory was dissolved by Henry VIII and the hospital was closed.

In 1552, however, Edward VI gave the buildings to the CITY OF LONDON, which reopened the hospital under the same name but, this time, dedicated it to St Thomas the Apostle because Thomas Becket had been decanonized by Henry VIII. Between 1693 and 1709, Sir Robert Clayton (a former LORD MAYOR) funded a major redesign and reconstruction (which was carried out by Thomas Cartwright, later Master Mason to CHRISTOPHER WREN at ST MARY-LE-BOW CHURCH, CHEAPSIDE) then, in 1859, the site was sold to the CHARING CROSS RAILWAY, which used it to build London Bridge station. (One of the strongest advocates of the sale was Florence Nightingale, who opened a training school for nurses at St Thomas's in 1860 in an effort to make nursing a respected profession for women.) In 1871, a new hospital opened in LAMBETH PALACE Road and the decades that followed brought both an increasing range of medical specialisms and additional building. In 1993, St Thomas's united, administratively, with GUY'S HOSPITAL in a National Health Service Trust. A MUSEUM illustrating the life of Florence Nightingale opened in one of the hospital buildings in 1989.

SALVATION ARMY

See BOOTH, WILLIAM.

SARACENS FOOTBALL CLUB

Saracens was formed in 1876 by a group of RUGBY-playing former pupils of the Philological School in MARYLEBONE, taking its name from the Islamic warriors renowned in the twelfth century for their endurance and mobility. Perhaps appropriately, the club merged with the Crusaders, a neighbouring side, two years later. It played its first games at PRIMROSE HILL and quickly built up a strong fixture list which included the major London clubs and strong teams from south and south-west England, but it failed to produce an internationalist until J.H. Steeds was selected as hooker for England in 1949. The side was at its strongest in the 1880s (it lost only one try in the 1885/86 season), the period immediately after the Second World War (it was unbeaten at home in 1946/47) and again in the 1970s. However, following the introduction of a national league system in 1988, it seesawed between the First and Second Divisions until, in 1995, businessman Nigel Wray provided the financial backing that allowed it to attract players of the quality of Michael Lynagh (who scored over 900 points in 65 appearances at fly half for Australia) and François Pienaar (captain of South Africa's World Cup-winning side). The following year it moved from Bramley Road, where it had been based since 1939, to the Enfield Football Club ground then, in 1997, a pitch-sharing arrangement with WATFORD FOOTBALL CLUB took it out of London altogether.

SAVILE ROW

Connecting Burlington Gardens with Conduit Street, towards the eastern edge of MAYFAIR, Savile Row takes its name from Lady Dorothy Savile, wife of the Earl of Burlington, who developed the road on land behind his PICCADILLY house during the 1730s (see BURLINGTON HOUSE). Originally, the properties were occupied by families (residents included physician Richard Bright – who identified Bright's Disease of the kidney – who lived at No. 11 from 1830 to 1858 and Richard Brinsley Sheridan who lived at No. 14 from 1813 until his death in 1816). However, from 1843 (when Henry Poole and Company started trading), gentlemen's tailors increasingly set up business, attracted by the affluent Mayfair market and willing to pay rents that private individuals could not match. By the end of the twentieth century, the street was entirely commercial, its name an international byword for fine clothing. Gieves and Hawkes are at No. 1, Hardy Amies at No. 14, Welsh and Jefferies at No. 35. Maxwell and Company, the shoemaker at No. 11, was founded as a manufacturer of spurs in 1756.

In 1998, Margaret Howells became the first woman to open a store in what had previously been an exclusively male domain (she stocked designer menswear).

SCIENCE MUSEUM

The MUSEUM holds the scientific collections of the VICTORIA AND ALBERT MUSEUM, which was founded in 1857 and based in Marlborough House, PALL MALL. Initially, the sciences were represented by exhibits from the GREAT EXHIBITION of 1851 and the museum of the Royal School of Practical Art (created in 1852), along with items acquired from a variety of other sources. In 1864, a collection of naval models, donated by THE ADMIRALTY, was added, then, in 1883, a science library was established. The following year, the Patent Office Museum was incorporated, bringing Richard Arkwright's spinning machine (which enabled the production of cotton yarn to become a factory industry) and George Stephenson's *Rocket* (the locomotive that revolutionized steam power and led to the expansion of the RAILWAY industry). As the exhibits increased in number, display space became a scarce resource, so, in stages from 1913 (when the east front was built) until 1977 (when an east block extension was completed), the acquisitions were moved to the present premises in Exhibition Road, behind the NATURAL HISTORY MUSEUM. There, displays focus on three major themes – industry, science and society – with a concentration on the inventions that led to Britain's nineteenth-century technological prowess as well as on international scientific achievement during the twentieth century (including the development of computers and advances in medicine). The museum, which receives about 1.5 million visitors every year, also presents regular lectures and houses a library of over 500,000 volumes.

SCOTLAND YARD

See NEW SCOTLAND YARD.

SCOTT, GILES GILBERT (1880–1960)

Scott, designer of several of the most important buildings erected in London during the first half of the twentieth century, came from a long line of architects; his grandfather (George Gilbert Scott) prepared the plans for the ALBERT MEMORIAL and his father (also named George Gilbert Scott) played a considerable part in promoting the Gothic Revival movement in Victorian Britain. Giles Scott was born in HAMPSTEAD on 9 November 1880 and educated at Beaumont College in Old Windsor. He achieved prominence in 1902 when he won the competition to design a Church of England cathedral for Liverpool, a success that caused the organizers some embarrassment because he was hardly out of his teens and, furthermore, a Roman Catholic.

Further church commissions followed (including St Albans in GOLDERS GREEN) but he did not restrict himself to religious structures. In 1932, he was appointed architect for WATERLOO Bridge, proposing a five-arch combination of concrete and steel with comparatively little decoration. Also, he was responsible for the imposing brick design of BATTERSEA POWER STATION, opened in 1933. Following the Second World War, Scott was invited to carry out remedial work on a number of old buildings. The most important was the PALACE OF WESTMINSTER, where the HOUSE OF COMMONS had been badly damaged by bombs so the architectural challenge was to reconstruct the debating chamber in its original form but without the exuberance of AUGUSTUS WELBY NORTHMORE PUGIN's decoration. Reconstruction of the GUILDHALL in the CITY OF LONDON involved replacement of the roof while maintaining such masonry and timber as remained. Scott was knighted in 1924, served as president of the Royal Institute of British Architects from 1933 to 1935 and was awarded the Order of Merit in 1944. He died in London on 8 February 1960. (See also DENMARK HILL.)

SELFRIDGES

One of London's largest and best-known department stores, Selfridge's stands near the western end of OXFORD STREET. It was opened in 1909 by Henry Gordon Selfridge, a native of Ripon (Wisconsin) who had worked in the retail trade in Chicago before seeking his fortune in Europe and said that his new shop was a place where 'women can realize some of their dreams'. The building, with a façade of Ionic columns, occupies a complete block on the north site of the street and is considered an outstanding example of Edwardian commercial ARCHITECTURE. Its design was the result of a transatlantic collaboration; originally conceived by Daniel Burnham and Frank Swales in the United States, it was built under the supervision of British architects R.F. Atkinson and John Burnet. The store brought American sales methods to London, using eye-catching window displays to attract customers inside and showing stock to its best advantage. In 2002, Selina Clark and Matthew Birkby, of Benson in Oxfordshire, were married in the shop – the first British couple to hold their wedding ceremony in a department store. They made their vows in the lower ground atrium, close to an escalator. In 2003, the Canadian billionaire Galen Weston bid £598 million for the firm.

SERPENTINE

The 28-acre lake in HYDE PARK was built at the suggestion of Caroline of Ansbach, wife of George II. From the windows of KENSINGTON PALACE, she could see a string of small ponds, separated by marshland, which she believed could be linked to form a single, curving stretch of water by damming the Westbourne River. The work was carried out in 1730–1 and the lake used by the royal family for yachting. A bridge (designed by George Rennie), which provides fine views of WESTMINSTER ABBEY, was built in 1826 and an Italian water garden added at the northern end in 1861. On the west side, in KENSINGTON GARDENS, George Frampton's bronze statue of Peter Pan (the little boy who never grew up) was erected in 1912, paid for by an anonymous admirer of J.M. Barrie, who created the character. The lake is still used for boating as well as fishing and swimming (one group of masochists insists on taking a dip every New Year's Day). The Serpentine Gallery, a showcase for contemporary art and sculpture, was designed in 1972, not far from Rennie's bridge, in a building opened as a tea house in 1907.

SEWAGE DISPOSAL

Until the second half of the nineteenth century, little provision was made for the disposal of London's sewage, which was allowed to flow freely into the RIVER THAMES and its tributaries. In 1858, however, Parliament passed legislation designed to reduce WATER POLLUTION in the river and, the following year, work began on plans, prepared by JOSEPH WILLIAM BAZALGETTE, to provide a drainage system for the city. A 1,300-mile network of brick tunnels was built in three layers leading to outfalls 11 miles downstream from LONDON BRIDGE. Initially, the sewage was disgorged straight into the Thames, with the result that much reappeared in central London at high tide, but, even so, as construction neared completion in 1875 it was clear that the incidence of diseases such as CHOLERA, contracted through contaminated drinking water, was declining rapidly. In 1879, the system was augmented by some 12 miles of storm sewer and, after 1887, waste was treated chemically, with much taken by boat for disposal in the North Sea. Further improvements were made by the LONDON COUNTY COUNCIL between 1900 and 1935. From 1936 small treatment plants were increasingly replaced by larger and more efficient units, culminating in the opening of the BECKTON works (the largest in Europe) in 1975. The previous year, responsibility for sewage disposal had been transferred from local government to the Thames Water

Authority, which was privatized by the Conservative government in 1989 and concentrates its purification processing at Beckton and at Crossness (where plants that use bacteria to purify sewage have operated since 1964). (See also GREAT STINK; HUNGERFORD BRIDGE.)

SEX PISTOLS

During the late 1970s, the Sex Pistols rock band was the musical focus of the PUNK movement. Its members, all Londoners, were Paul Cook, Steve Jones, John Lydon (who adopted the stage name of Johnny Rotten), Glen Matlock and John Ritchie (better known as Sid Vicious). Brought together in 1976 by Malcolm McLaren to promote Sex, a store that sold clothing favoured by extremist political movements, they adopted a musical style that mixed the rhythms of such nonconformist stars as Iggy and the Stooges with the influences of groups such as The Who and the Small Faces, who had dominated British popular music a decade earlier. *Anarchy in the UK*, their first single, released in 1976, shocked orthodox society with its violent, aggressive imagery but appealed to many rebellious, urban, working-class youngsters, particularly in London. Confrontational stage performances, persistent profanities in television interviews and nihilistic lyrics led to bans by the media and local authorities but despite official disapproval their records sold well, *God Save the Queen*, *Pretty Vacant*, *Holidays in the Sun* and *Never Mind the Bollocks, Here's the Sex Pistols* all reaching the top ten in the charts during 1977 through sophisticated manipulation of the press and television. By late that year, however, the group's momentum had slowed. An unsuccessful tour of the United States led to a split in 1978, then, in February 1979, Vicious died of a heroin overdose in New York while on bail awaiting trial on a charge of murdering his girlfriend, Nancy Spungen. The remaining members of the band reformed for a reunion tour in 1996 but, by that time, punk had been replaced by other fashions and the Pistols were a fond memory in the minds of middle-aged parents rather than contemporary musical hell-raisers who seemed to be threatening the fabric of British society.

SHADWELL

Shadwell lies north-east of WAPPING on the marshy north bank of the RIVER THAMES, in the heart of London's DOCKLANDS. It developed from the mid-seventeenth century, when Thomas Neale erected St Paul's Church, opened a waterworks, established a MARKET and built houses to accommodate workers in tanneries, rope-making works, BREWERIES and other small industries. Within two centuries, the community had grown to nearly 12,000 people, although that number declined during the 1850s, when many buildings were demolished to make way for improved harbour facilities at Shadwell Basin. Construction of the King Edward VII Memorial PARK in 1922 resulted in further slum removal. The area, still characterized by industry and by a largely working-class population, was incorporated within the LONDON BOROUGH OF TOWER HAMLETS when the city's local government was reorganized in 1965. (See also ROTHERHITHE.)

SHAFTESBURY AVENUE

During the last quarter of the nineteenth century, JOSEPH WILLIAM BAZALGETTE (the METROPOLITAN BOARD OF WORKS' Engineer) planned a series of new roads in order to reduce traffic congestion in central London. A critical element of that strategy, Shaftesbury Avenue, was built during the 1880s to facilitate movement between PICCADILLY CIRCUS and BLOOMSBURY. In addition, its construction allowed the authorities to demolish some of the city's most notorious slums (the street was named after the seventh Earl of Shaftesbury, a social reformer who had done much to ease the plight of poor families living in the area). Much of the new property was taken over by

THEATRES; the Lyric was the first, opening in 1888, but it was soon followed by the Palace (established as the Royal English Opera house in 1891), the Apollo (1901), the Globe (1906), the Queen's (1907), the Shaftesbury (1911) and later by the Saville (1931). The Shaftesbury was damaged by bombs in 1941, during the BLITZ, and later demolished but cinemas and other forms of entertainment continued to move in after the Second World War, turning the street into the heart of the WEST END.

SHAKESPEARE, WILLIAM (1564–1616)
Shakespeare, acknowledged by most literary scholars as the world's greatest playwright, was born in Stratford-upon-Avon to merchant John Shakespeare and his wife, Mary. The child was baptized in Holy Trinity Church on 26 April 1564; his birth date is unknown but traditionally recognized as 23 April. John Shakespeare was a significant figure in Stratford – a burgess who was appointed bailiff (a post similar to that of mayor) in 1568 – so his son almost certainly attended the local grammar school.

Late in 1582, he married Anne Hathaway, who bore him a daughter (Susanna) in May of the following year and twins (Hamnet and Judith) in 1585. His activities over the next seven years or so are less certain. There are stories that he ran away from Stratford when he got into trouble for poaching deer, that he served as a soldier and that he worked as a schoolmaster but there are no records to authenticate any of these claims. By 1594, however, he was certainly in London and attached to the Lord Chamberlain's Company, which presented entertainments at BANKSIDE and SHOREDITCH. He also, apparently, attracted the attention of the nobility because his first published poems (*Venus and Adonis* (1593)) and *The Rape of Lucrece* (1594)) were dedicated to Henry, Earl of Southampton. In 1596 he was living in Bishopsgate (see BISHOP'S GATE) close to the two THEATRE districts and in 1599 at SOUTHWARK, near the newly built GLOBE THEATRE. By 1604, he was lodging in CRIPPLEGATE with the Mountjoys, a HUGUENOT family, and in 1613 he bought his first London home, the gatehouse at BLACKFRIARS, where the former monastery hall had been converted into a playhouse.

Although it is not possible to produce an accurate chronology of Shakespeare's texts, the comments of contemporaries indicate that his reputation grew and that he was highly regarded by his peers (BEN JONSON, for example, wrote that he was 'not of an age but for all time'). Although he made little effort to devise plots (for example, *The Comedy of Errors* is based on the plays *Menaechmi* and *Amphitruo* by Plautus, a Roman author), he was adept at reworking tales in order to heighten characterization and increase the dramatic effect of a story's climax. Early dramas, such as *The Taming of the Shrew* (1593–4) and *Romeo and Juliet* (1594–5) (both of which were performed when he was still in his twenties), were simply the precursors of a great range of historical plays, tragedies and comedies that drew audiences from all social classes and earned him enduring fame. He also collaborated with other writers, as when he worked with John Fletcher on *The Two Noble Kinsmen*, but these contributions were often unattributed, leaving later scholars to debate the true extent of his influence on Elizabethan and Jacobean drama in London. After 1613, he produced no new work, though he may have continued to act. He returned to Stratford in 1614 and died there on 23 April 1616, allegedly from an illness that developed after a drinking session with Jonson and other cronies. (See also GEORGE INN; OLD VIC; PUBLIC RECORD OFFICE (PRO); REGENT'S PARK; ROYAL NATIONAL THEATRE; SOUTHWARK CATHEDRAL; WESTMINSTER ABBEY.)

SHENE PALACE
See RICHMOND PALACE.

SHEPHERD'S BUSH

Best known as the site of the BRITISH BROADCASTING CORPORATION's Television Centre, Shepherd's Bush is located between NOTTING HILL (which lies to the east) and ACTON (to the west). It developed during the nineteenth century, as the expansion of the RAILWAY network encouraged suburban housing growth, but retained some open space because 8 acres of common land (once known as Gabblegoose Green) were protected by Parliamentary legislation in 1872 and 30 acres of PARKland owned by the Manor of Ravenscourt were acquired by the METROPOLITAN BOARD OF WORKS in 1887 and converted into playing fields. In 1914 an outdoor MARKET opened near Goldhawk Road; surviving serious damage during the BLITZ and threats of closure after the Second World War, it expanded from the 1950s, drawing custom from nearby IMMIGRANT communities by offering fruit, vegetables and household goods with a strong West Indian emphasis. The origin of the area's name is unclear but may be derived from the family name of some local residents. (See also CENTRAL LINE; RACHMANISM; STREET MARKETS.)

SHERIFF

The Sheriff is one of the principal officers of the CORPORATION OF LONDON, second only to the LORD MAYOR in status. The post dates from 1132, when Henry I awarded the CITY OF LONDON a charter empowering it to appoint a Sheriff (or Shire Reeve) for the County of Middlesex as well as for its own area. Until 1189, when a Mayor was first appointed, they ran the city as the monarch's representatives, collecting taxes and administering justice. The Local Government Act of 1888 removed their jurisdiction over Middlesex but allowed the city of London to retain two Sheriffs, who are now appointed annually by the members of the city LIVERY COMPANIES on Midsummer Day (24 June) and take their oath of office on Michaelmas Eve (28 September). Usually, one Aldermanic Sheriff is appointed from the ranks of the ALDERMEN (only those who follow this route can become Lord Mayor). A second official (known as the Lay Sheriff) may be an Alderman or a member of the COURT OF COMMON COUNCIL or neither (though if he does not hold one of these positions, he must retire from the Corporation at the end of his year of office). The Sheriffs accompany the Lord Mayor on official occasions, attend sessions at the CENTRAL CRIMINAL COURT and may present petitions from the City of London to Parliament. (See also COMMON SERJEANT.)

SHOREDITCH

By the early twelfth century, a settlement had formed at Scoredich (or Sceorf's Ditch), where two Roman routeways met outside the north-east walls of the CITY OF LONDON. For much of the medieval period, the land was owned by the Roman Catholic Church but following the Dissolution of the English MONASTERIES from 1532 it fell into secular hands and in 1576 became the site of The THEATRE, the first playhouse built in England (several Elizabethan entertainers are buried nearby in St Leonard's Church, including Gabriel Spencer, who was killed in a duel with BEN JONSON in 1598). From the late seventeenth century, the area was increasingly developed, evolving into a densely populated inner-city suburb. During the twentieth century, many of the older properties were removed to make way for housing that would meet modern standards but some older buildings remain, notably the former Georgian almshouses in Kingsland Road that house the GEFFRYE MUSEUM. In 1965, when local government in the metropolitan area was reorganized, Shoreditch was included within the LONDON BOROUGH OF HACKNEY. (See also DANCE, GEORGE (1700–68).)

SIEGE OF SIDNEY STREET

On 16 December 1910, a group of Latvian IMMIGRANTS tried to rob a HOUNDSDITCH jeweller's shop by tunnelling into the property from an adjacent building. A local resident, hearing the noise, called the police, who attempted to arrest the burglars but the gang escaped, leaving four constables shot dead. Early the following year, an informer told the Metropolitan Police that two of the culprits – William Joseph and Fritz Svaars – were hiding in a house at 100 Sidney Street, in London's EAST END. The area was cordoned off and armed officers were stationed at strategic locations. Later, marksmen from a unit of Scots Guards garrisoned in the TOWER OF LONDON were brought to reinforce the police and Home Secretary WINSTON CHURCHILL arrived to take charge of operations. An inspector who knocked on the door of the house was driven back by gunfire and for ten hours the robbers held the law at bay. Then, around midday, smoke was seen rising from the upper floor windows and soon it was clear that the whole of the top floor was ablaze. The fire spread and at about two o'clock in the afternoon the shooting stopped. Soon afterwards, the walls of the house caved in. Later, two bodies were found – one man, on the upper floor, had clearly been shot and the other, on the ground floor, had been suffocated by the smoke and fumes. The siege was a salutary lesson for the police, whose firearms were greatly inferior to the Mauser pistols carried by the robbers. Shortly afterwards, more effective weapons training programmes were introduced and equipment was improved.

SIR HENRY WOOD PROMENADE CONCERTS

See PROMS, THE.

SIR JOHN SOANE'S MUSEUM

A thoroughly personal collection of *objets d'art*, the MUSEUM holds the lifetime acquisitions of John Soane (1753–1837). The son of a bricklayer, Soane established himself as an architect in 1781 and was responsible for designing many important London buildings during the late eighteenth and early nineteenth centuries, including the BANK OF ENGLAND, the Law Courts in WESTMINSTER, the library at the HOUSE OF LORDS (see PALACE OF WESTMINSTER) and some of the WATERLOO CHURCHES. Many of these have been demolished or radically altered, but his home (erected in 1658 and extensively renovated under his direction in 1792) still stands in LINCOLN'S INN FIELDS, housing his eclectic purchases. Soane's wealth was supplemented by that of his wife, the heiress of a rich builder, so he was able to indulge an interest in painting, manuscripts, sculpture, precious stones and other artefacts. He took over neighbouring houses in order to provide space for his acquisitions then, in 1833, made arrangements for everything to be preserved as a public museum. The exhibits include the eight canvasses of William Hogarth's *Rake's Progress* (1735), paintings by Antonio Canaletto, books from architect ROBERT ADAM's library and fifty-five volumes of drawings from his office, CHRISTOPHER WREN's watch, Napoleon Bonaparte's pistols, the sarcophagus of the Egyptian pharaoh Seti I (who died in 1290 BC), a thirteenth-century Bible and many other treasures. (See also CHELSEA HOSPITAL.)

SLOANE, HANS (1660–1753)

The plants, rocks, animals and other objects collected by Hans Sloane provided the foundation for the BRITISH MUSEUM's collections. The seventh son of tax collector Alexander Sloane and his wife, Sarah, Hans was probably born in Killyleagh, Ireland, on 16 April 1660. He studied medicine in London, Paris, Montpellier and Orange, graduating in 1683. Through an association with Thomas Sydenham, one of the most renowned physicians of the late seventeenth century, he built up a large practice, supported by wealthy clients and earned a scientific reputation that won him Fellowships of the ROYAL SOCIETY

(1685) and the ROYAL COLLEGE OF PHYSICIANS OF LONDON (1687). In 1687 he travelled to Jamaica as doctor to the island's governor, the Duke of Albermarle, but returned when his employer died the following year, was appointed physician to Queen Anne in 1712, created a baronet in 1718, was made Physician General to the Army in 1722, accepted the post of Physician in Ordinary to George II in 1727 and served as president of the Royal Society from 1727 to 1741. In 1712, he bought the Manor of CHELSEA and settled there when he retired from practice in 1741. He died on 11 January 1753.

Sloane's interest in natural history dated from his childhood and was pursued at university alongside his medical studies. When he returned from Jamaica, he carried over 800 plant species with him (he also tried, but failed, to transport a live crocodile, an iguana and a 7-foot snake). In his herbarium, he included a sample of *Theobroma cacao*, which Jamaicans used to make a drink Sloane found unpalatable. However, in the spirit of experiment, he mixed the liquid with milk and thus became the father of the chocolate industry.

As affluent patients flocked to his surgery in BLOOMSBURY Square, Sloane used the fees he collected to add books, medals, coins, mathematical instruments and other artefacts to his collection. In 1749 he made a will bequeathing the acquisitions to the nation in return for a sum of £20,000 paid to his family. Six months after his death, the gift was accepted by an Act of Parliament and trustees were appointed to manage it. In 1754 they purchased Montague House, not far from his Bloomsbury practice, and merged his collections with the LIBRARIES of Sir Robert Bruce Cotton (1571–1631) and Edward Harley, Earl of Oxford (1689–1741), to form the British MUSEUM. Sloane is commemorated in several London street names, including SLOANE SQUARE and Hans Road, which runs alongside HARRODS. (See also CHELSEA PHYSIC GARDEN; NATURAL HISTORY MUSEUM.)

SLOANE RANGER

See SLOANE SQUARE.

SLOANE SQUARE

A busy traffic junction towards the eastern end of KING'S ROAD, the square is named after HANS SLOANE, president of the ROYAL SOCIETY from 1727 to 1741 and Lord of the Manor of CHELSEA from 1712 until his death in 1753. It was developed as a residential area from 1771 but was increasingly infiltrated by commercial interests during the nineteenth century and redesigned just before the Second World War to improve the circulation of traffic. Peter Jones, one of London's principal department stores, has stood on the west side of the square since 1877 and the Royal Court Theatre (which has developed a reputation for avant-garde productions) on the east since 1887. During the 1980s, the area became a fashionable shopping haunt for affluent, young professionals who became known as 'Sloane Rangers' or 'Sloanes', terms still used to describe the Barbour jacket-wearing, Land Rover-driving, polo-playing upper middle class.

SMITH, W.H., LTD

In 1792 Henry Walton Smith opened a small newsagent's shop in Little Grosvenor Street. Although he died shortly afterwards, the business flourished under the management of his family and, in 1828, assumed its present name when his son, William Henry, took full control. By the middle of the century, the firm had developed a reputation for speedy distribution of newspapers (it chartered a special boat to carry reports of the death of George IV to Irish readers in 1830) and had opened bookstalls to cater for travellers at railway stations. When contracts to trade on the platforms were terminated, W.H. Smith established shops nearby, building up a nationwide chain by the 1940s. It became a public company in 1948 and subsequently acquired interests abroad, opening over 500 stores in the United States alone, principally at airports and luxury hotels. In 1998 it bought the retail interests of John Menzies.

SMITHFIELD MEAT MARKET

London's largest wholesale meat MARKET grew up on the 'smooth field' just outside the walls of the CITY OF LONDON. From at least the twelfth century, sales of horses, sheep, pigs and other animals were held alongside BARTHOLOMEW FAIR (which initially specialized in cloth). These were formally recognized in 1638, when the CORPORATION OF LONDON established a cattle market on the site under the terms of a royal charter, but problems arose over the next 200 years as the urban area expanded; drovers took a perverse pleasure in the disruption caused by driving herds through confined streets, beasts were slaughtered in the open, blood flowed along drainage channels and entrails were dumped on the ground to rot. In 1855 Bartholomew Fair was closed because it was accompanied by drunkenness and public disorder, sales of live animals were moved to the METROPOLITAN CATTLE MARKET in ISLINGTON and the field was converted for trade in slaughtered meat. A covered hall, designed by Horace Jones, was opened in 1868, with additions in 1875 and 1899 extending the area to over 10 acres. During the second half of the twentieth century, there were continual rumours of Smithfield's demise as retailers changed buying practices and other major markets (notably BILLINGSGATE FISH MARKET and COVENT GARDEN fruit and vegetable market) moved to new sites away from the city centre. However, major rebuilding in the 1960s (following a fire in the poultry section in 1958) and refurbishment during the 1990s have upgraded facilities, providing better refrigerated storage and improved hygiene. Nearby there is a wide range of public houses, cafés and restaurants that cater to the needs of early morning workers. Smithfield employs about 1,000 people and sells about 150,000 tons of meat each year.

SNOW, JOHN (1813–1858)

For forty years during the nineteenth century, cholera was one of London's killer diseases. Introduced from India as British ships expanded their trading contacts, it caused a series of epidemics in 1831–2, 1848–9, 1854 and 1856, with over half of the sufferers dying. Its decline during the second half of the century was a direct result of John Snow's willingness to follow up his belief that the disease was transmitted by water. Born into a farming family in York on 15 March 1813, Snow was educated at a private school in the city before taking up an apprenticeship with Newcastle surgeon William Hardcastle in 1827. Nine years later, he moved to London in order to study medicine formally and, in 1838, became a member of the ROYAL COLLEGE OF SURGEONS OF ENGLAND and a licentiate of the Society of Apothecaries. He graduated from the University of London (see UNIVERSITIES) with the degree of Doctor of Medicine in 1844, then, in 1850, was made a licentiate of the ROYAL COLLEGE OF PHYSICIANS OF LONDON. In 1849 Snow published a monograph suggesting that cholera (then a little-understood illness) was water-borne, a view that was challenged by Dr Robert Baker (who believed that it was associated with slum conditions) and Dr Henry Acland (who felt that marshy conditions were the cause). During the late summer of 1854, an outbreak of the disease in SOHO caused at least 500 deaths over a period of ten days. Snow, who had a practice in the area at Golden Square, prepared a map showing the location of the house where each victim lived, adding the pumps that were the only source of drinking water at the time. The map depicted a distinct cluster of deaths close to a pump in Broad Street, so the authorities removed the handle. Within days, the epidemic was over but sceptics argued that it was on the wane anyway, so some years passed before Snow's thesis was fully accepted.

The use of anaesthetics in London hospitals also owes much to Snow's advocacy. In 1846 he was one of the first doctors in the city to use ether while treating patients. He also did much to promote acceptance of chloroform by employing it when Queen Victoria gave birth to Prince Leopold in 1853 and Princess Beatrice in 1858. He died on 16 June 1858 and was buried at BROMPTON Cemetery. Although he was a lifelong teetotaller (as well as a vegetarian and non-smoker), he is commemorated by a pub that bears his name at the corner of Broadwick Street (the Broad Street of Snow's day) and Lexington Street. (See also WESTMINSTER HOSPITAL.)

SOHO

The Soho area of the CITY OF WESTMINSTER is one of London's principal entertainment centres, bounded by OXFORD STREET to the north, REGENT STREET to the west, SHAFTESBURY AVENUE to the south and CHARING CROSS ROAD to the east. The land was used by aristocrats for hunting during the medieval period ('So-ho!' was a common cry when hares were roused) but was increasingly built over during the seventeenth century, particularly around Soho Square, which was laid out by builder Richard Frith during the 1680s and attracted such noble residents as the Duke of Monmouth and Viscount Preston. The area also proved attractive to foreign IMMIGRANTS, including HUGUENOTS fleeing persecution (in 1739 William Maitland wrote that 'Many parts of this parish so greatly abound with French that it is an easy Matter for a Stranger to imagine himself in France'). They were followed by writers and artists, giving this section of the city a distinctively cosmopolitan, bohemian character. Around the middle of the nineteenth century, THEATRES and MUSIC HALLS became increasingly common, attracting restaurants, drinking places, prostitutes and other services in their wake. Waiters and other workers, many from abroad, crammed into small rooms, forcing population densities up and facilitating the spread of infectious disease (see SNOW, JOHN).

From the 1960s, the area's reputation as a red light district flourished, with strip clubs, sex shops and sellers of pornographic books boosting a tourist trade seeking the risqué and salacious, but, in 1972, members of the Soho Society (which represented local residents) initiated a campaign designed to reverse the growth of the industry. Several police officers were found guilty of corruption and the ensuing publicity led Parliament to introduce licensing programmes for firms selling sex; as a result, the number of premises involved fell six-fold during the 1980s. In the decade that followed, the social composition of Soho changed radically. A housing association was formed to erect homes for families to rent, the proportion of school-age residents rose, a new parish church and community hall were built, and a MUSEUM was opened to improve knowledge of the neighbourhood's history. (See also CHINATOWN; MIDDLESEX HOSPITAL; WARDOUR STREET.)

SOMERSET HOUSE

During the medieval period, the London residences of the Bishops of Chester and Worcester occupied the site in the STRAND where Somerset House now stands. In 1547–50, these buildings were swept away and replaced by England's first Renaissance palace, erected for Edward Seymour, Duke of Somerset and Lord Protector of England during the reign of Edward VI. After Seymour's execution in 1552, the mansion passed to the Crown, which, over the next 200 years, used it as a residence for members of the royal family and as government offices. It was demolished in 1775 and replaced, between 1776 and 1786, by a structure, designed on classical lines by WILLIAM CHAMBERS, which is set around a courtyard measuring 350 feet by 310 feet and faced with PORTLAND STONE. An 800-foot-long façade fronts the RIVER THAMES, which flowed past the south terrace until embankments were built during the late nineteenth century (see BAZALGETTE, JOSEPH WILLIAM). Initially, the

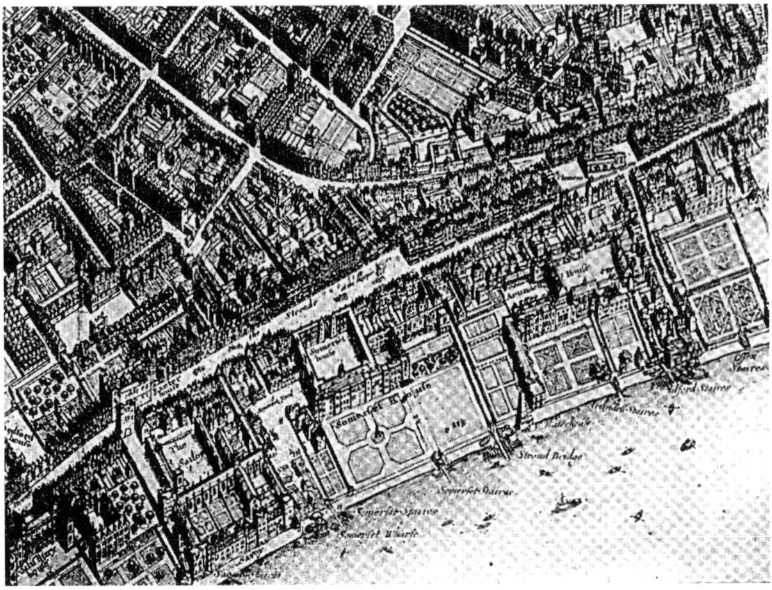

Hollar's 1658 bird's-eye plan of Somerset House.

ROYAL ACADEMY OF ARTS, the ROYAL SOCIETY and the Society of Antiquaries were housed in the north wing, the Royal Navy in the west and part of the south wings and government officials in the remaining areas. Since then, occupants have included the COURTAULD INSTITUTE OF ART, the Inland Revenue and the General Register of Births, Marriages and Deaths. In 1997 a trust was formed to prepare plans for the conservation of the building, oversee refurbishment and provide housing for a collection of European decorative art gifted to the nation by Mr Arthur Gilbert. (See also ATHENAEUM, THE; KNIGHTS HOSPITALLER; ROYAL COLLEGE OF ART; ST MARGARET'S CHURCH, WESTMINSTER; UNIVERSITIES.)

SOTHEBY'S

In 1744 Samuel Baker, a London bookseller, began a series of annual auctions. A decade later he embarked on a more regular series of sales from premises near COVENT GARDEN, expanding the firm and taking on additional employees, including (in 1776) his nephew, John Sotheby. Expansion also necessitated moves to more capacious accommodation near the STRAND in 1818 and then, in 1917, to the present address at 34–35 New BOND STREET. From the 1860s until 1913 the firm concentrated on books but, from the First World War, increasingly challenged CHRISTIE'S as a major auctioneer of fine art, finally surpassing its rival in 1954 and remaining ahead for forty-three years. Sotheby's opened a New York base in 1955 and now has over 100 offices throughout the world. Its interests extend to international property sales and financial advising, with turnover amounting to some £1.25 billion annually. In 2000, it became the first international art auction house to hold auctions on the internet but, two years later, its reputation suffered when Alfred Taubman, a former chairman of the company, was convicted of illegal price-fixing in the United States and jailed for a year.

SOUTH BANK

From the late 1940s the derelict properties that lined the south bank of the RIVER THAMES between HUNGERFORD BRIDGE and WATERLOO BRIDGE were swept away. In their place, one of the world's largest art complexes was built, beginning with the ROYAL FESTIVAL HALL, erected for the FESTIVAL OF BRITAIN in 1951. The NATIONAL FILM THEATRE followed five years later, two concert venues – the Purcell Room and the QUEEN ELIZABETH HALL – in 1967 and the HAYWARD GALLERY (which houses art exhibitions) in 1968. The ROYAL NATIONAL THEATRE opened in 1976 and, most recently, the MUSEUM OF THE MOVING IMAGE was added in 1988. Some commentators have complained that the concrete structures are unnecessarily bleak but others have praised the views across the water to the CITY OF LONDON. In 2000 plans were unveiled for a £150 million facelift for the area. The project would involve construction of a 1,400-seat amphitheatre underneath a 6-acre landscaped PARK but would retain much of the concrete and would be supervised by American architect Rick Mather. (See also ABERCROMBIE PLAN (1943–44).)

SOUTHGATE

The suburb of Southgate lies some 9 miles north of CHARING CROSS. Sited on high ground overlooking the valley of the RIVER LEA, it got its name because it was at the southern edge of ENFIELD Chase, once a royal hunting forest. Local people used the woodlands for timber and firewood but population was limited until the development of the RAILWAY system in the second half of the nineteenth century. By the 1930s, trees and fields in the Bowes PARK, Palmers Green and Winchmore Hill areas had all vanished under bricks and mortar and wealthy families were fleeing their large homes for more secluded sites in the countryside. The arrival of LONDON UNDERGROUND's PICCADILLY LINE in 1933 provided a further catalyst for development because it provided easy access to jobs in the city centre. The west of the area, in particular, experienced considerable housing development in the years just before the Second World War and the new residents required services, adding to demands for building space (Chase Side became a major focus for retailers and is still a significant regional shopping area). Modern employment is largely in the service sector, including a call centre, market research and publishing.

Administratively, Southgate was part of EDMONTON until 1881, when it was given its own Board of Health after a long campaign by local people. It was made an urban district under the terms of the Local Government Act of 1894 and achieved borough status in 1933. In 1965, it merged with Edmonton and Enfield to form the LONDON BOROUGH OF ENFIELD. (See also PICK, FRANK; ROYAL COMMISSION ON LONDON TRAFFIC (1903–05).)

SOUTHALL

Southall lies close to HEATHROW AIRPORT, in the LONDON BOROUGH OF EALING and 12 miles west of CHARING CROSS. For most of its history, it has been an agricultural settlement but the arrival of the Great Western RAILWAY in 1838 heralded change. Factories were built close to the line and attracted workers from as far afield as Wales and Ireland. By the early twentieth century, industry was the major employer and the range of products manufactured was wide, including commodities as disparate as margarine, pottery and London buses. In a buoyant economy, labour was often in short supply and, during the 1950s, Woolfe's rubber factory mounted a recruitment campaign in India. Most of the early IMMIGRANTS were Sikh men from the Punjab (the first Sikh temple opened in 1957) but, within a few years, their families followed and by the end of the century some 60 per cent of the population was of Indian, Pakistani or Bangladeshi origin. With so many local shops stocking ethnic goods, the local cinema showing Bollywood films and Punjabi as common as English, the area is widely known as Little India. Periodically, trouble flares between communities (as in 1979, when teacher Blair Peach was killed during demonstrations against a National Front gathering) and social workers report that hard drugs, such as heroin, are widely used by young people but many of the immigrants have built up successful careers and the area houses several millionaires. The area's name may be derived from the Old English *suth* and *halh*, meaning 'southern nook of land'.

SOUTHWARK

As the Romans established control of their new British colony during the first century AD, they built a bridge across the RIVER THAMES to provide access to their settlement at LONDINIUM. Southwark developed at the southern end of that bridge, evolving into a significant market town, with a fair held annually from 1462 until petty crime and prostitution forced the authorities to ban the event in 1763. Because of its position at the southern end of LONDON BRIDGE, for centuries the only bridge into the city, all southbound traffic had to pass through it. Consequently, it housed many taverns (including the Tabard, where poet Geoffrey Chaucer describes the gathering of his pilgrims in *The Canterbury Tales*, published *c.* 1387–1400) and, at the end of the sixteenth century, became London's principal entertainment area, with playhouses (such as the GLOBE THEATRE) attracting large audiences. Many of the buildings were destroyed by fire in 1676 but, even so, the land was heavily developed by the end of Queen Anne's reign in 1714. The completion of WESTMINSTER BRIDGE in 1750 and BLACKFRIARS Bridge in 1769 hastened the development process so by the mid-nineteenth century Southwark had become part of central London, with a host of small industries, particularly brewing, food processing and leather-making. After the Second World War, it was made the focus of several urban renewal programmes (as at ELEPHANT AND CASTLE) and in 1965, when local government in the metropolitan area was reorganized, gave its name to the LONDON BOROUGH OF SOUTHWARK. By the tenth century, the area was known as *Suthriganaweorc*, a name derived from the Old English *suth* and *weorc*, meaning 'the fort of the southerners'. (See also BANKSIDE; CLINK PRISON; GEORGE INN; HENSLOWE, PHILIP; MARSHALSEA PRISON; PUGIN, AUGUSTUS WELBY NORTHMORE; RECORDER OF LONDON; ST THOMAS'S HOSPITAL; SOUTHWARK BRIDGE; SOUTHWARK CATHEDRAL; THEATRE; WALWORTH.)

SOUTHWARK, LONDON BOROUGH OF

Southwark was created, following the dissolution of the LONDON COUNTY COUNCIL in 1965, by the merger of the formerly independent

Southwark Fair, a satirical print by Hogarth, 1733.

authorities of BERMONDSEY, CAMBERWELL and SOUTHWARK. Lying on the SOUTH BANK of the RIVER THAMES, opposite the CITY OF LONDON, it covers 11 square miles and has a population of 245,000 (2001). The 3-mile river frontage is a complex mixture of old and new, with the thirteenth-century SOUTHWARK CATHEDRAL sitting close to modern office developments and the re-created GLOBE THEATRE. Much of the remainder of the borough is covered by rows of nineteenth-century terraced housing and modern local authority estates occupied by clerical and manual workers, although DULWICH, at the southern tip, has a high proportion of professional and managerial families. The area is one of the poorest in the United Kingdom, with a considerable black population (largely from Africa but also from the Caribbean) and unemployment rates generally above the city average. Moreover, the urban landscape is often bleak, with few open spaces for recreation and several places (such as ELEPHANT AND CASTLE) where road improvements have taken precedence over community development. However, the local authority has invested heavily in regeneration programmes, tearing down high-density high-rise blocks built in the 1960s and replacing them with conventional housing. Also, improved access during the 1990s (notably through the extension of LONDON UNDERGROUND'S JUBILEE LINE and the opening of the international rail terminal at nearby WATERLOO) has helped to attract such new business as the £1.4 billion office complex planned for a site between LONDON BRIDGE and TOWER BRIDGE by the CIT Group. (See also BANKSIDE; DOCKLANDS; KENNINGTON; PECKHAM; ROTHERHITHE.)

SOUTHWARK BRIDGE

Erected despite protests that it would interfere with navigation on the RIVER THAMES, the first Southwark Bridge, designed by JOHN RENNIE, linked BANKSIDE (on the south shore of the river) to the CITY OF LONDON (on the north). It was built in 1814–9, with three arches and a 240-foot central span, the largest ever made of cast iron. The structure was replaced by the present five-span steel BRIDGE, constructed to Ernest George's plans, in 1912–21.

SOUTHWARK CATHEDRAL

The cathedral occupies a site, south-west of LONDON BRIDGE, that has been a Christian place of worship for 1,400 years. According to tradition, the first chapel was built by a ferryman early in the seventh century but destroyed by fire and replaced in about 852 under the supervision of St Swithun, Bishop of Winchester. That structure, too, burned down (in 1106) and was rebuilt by Augustinian monks but survived for only a century before succumbing to another blaze. Work on a new church, dedicated to St Mary Overie, began in 1220 and continued until the tower was completed in 1520. London's first example of religious ARCHITECTURE in Gothic style, it is considered (with WESTMINSTER ABBEY) to be one of the two most important medieval properties remaining in the city. The building was extensively refurbished during the nineteenth century (in particular, the nave was declared unsafe and, in 1890–7, replaced to plans prepared by Sir Arthur Blomfield) then elevated in status from parish church to cathedral, with a dedication to St Saviour and St Mary Overie, in 1897 (a decision that reflected the growing population south of the RIVER THAMES). The building is particularly noted for its monuments, the earliest of which, dating from about 1275, is an effigy of a knight. A memorial to WILLIAM SHAKESPEARE (who lived in Southwark from 1599 until 1604) stands in the south aisle underneath a stained-glass window, designed by Christopher Webb and erected in 1954, which shows characters from the plays. The Harvard Chapel, adjoining the north choir aisle, was built in 1907 as a memorial to John Harvard, who was baptized in the church in 1607, emigrated to North America and, when he died, left his books and property to the

Massachusetts college that later became Harvard University. In 2000 the church celebrated the millennium by forming London's first cathedral girls' choir and embarking on a £10 million restoration programme.

SPANIARDS, THE

A sixteenth-century weather-boarded building, The Spaniards, in Hampstead Lane, is one of the best-known PUBLIC HOUSES in London. The origin of its name is contested; some writers believe that it was the home of the Spanish ambassador to the court of James II during the seventeenth century, others that it was owned by two Spanish brothers who killed themselves in a duel over a woman. More certainly, it was used by highwayman Dick Turpin, who stabled Black Bess, his mare, on the other side of the road. In 1780 rioters on their way to destroy nearby KENWOOD HOUSE were delayed by the landlord, who plied them with alcohol until soldiers arrived to arrest them. The pub's location on the edge of HAMPSTEAD HEATH made it a popular haunt of the literary men who frequented Hampstead village during the nineteenth century. Lord Byron, John Keats (see KEATS' HOUSE) and Percy Bysshe Shelley were regular visitors and CHARLES DICKENS clearly knew the place because, in *The Pickwick Papers* (1836–7), he describes how Mrs Bardell and her friends met there to plot against Mr Pickwick. (See also JACK STRAW'S CASTLE.)

SPEAKERS' CORNER

At the north-eastern edge of HYDE PARK, Speakers' Corner stands close to TYBURN, where criminals were hanged in public from 1388 until 1783. Condemned men and women were allowed to make a statement from the gallows before they were executed and, over the years, that privilege was extended to more general acceptance of a right to free speech at the site. During the 1850s and 1860s a series of mass meetings in the PARK sometimes led police to arrest inflammatory orators, but, since 1872, the authorities have accepted both that crowds have a right to assemble and that speakers have a right to address them on any subject they choose provided there is no blasphemy or obscenity and no incitement to cause a breach of the peace. Traditionally, the soap-boxes are brought out on Sunday mornings and passers-by listen to impassioned arguments on all matter of religious, political and social themes. Heckling is common but most speakers have a quick wit, readily turning criticisms to their own advantage.

SPITALFIELDS

About 1197 Walter and Rose Bruno founded an Augustinian priory, known as St Mary Spital, on land to the east of the CITY OF LONDON. The fields nearby remained open until the seventeenth century, when proximity to the main urban area encouraged building. From 1685, when Louis XIV of France revoked legislation giving French Protestants freedom of worship, HUGUENOT refugees flooded into the area, attracted by its reputation as a nonconformist heartland. They brought with them a heritage of silk weaving, re-establishing their businesses in England and turning Spitalfields into a centre of textile production (houses in Fournier Street still have the large attic windows that the IMMIGRANTS built in order to provide sufficient light for them to work their looms). The industry's reputation attracted dyers, weavers, bobbin-makers and other workers, creating an interdependent complex of small companies that still characterizes the suburb even though silk has long been superseded by artificial fibres. The growing population led to a rash of church building (see, for example, CHRIST CHURCH, SPITALFIELDS) but the economics of the trade meant that most workers were poor so much of the religious bodies' effort was concentrated on charitable work. During the eighteenth and nineteenth centuries, employment opportunities diversified with the growth of the Black Eagle BREWERY (which was founded in 1660 and produced a popular black stout) and the Spitalfields MARKET (established in 1682 to sell vegetables). The ethnic composition also changed with an influx of Jewish migrants from about 1880. The most recent incomers are the Bengalis, who arrived in the early 1960s and have established themselves in the clothing industry and retail services. Spitalfields was incorporated within the LONDON BOROUGH OF TOWER HAMLETS when the metropolitan area's local government system was reformed in 1965 and, since then, has benefited from slum clearance programmes and conservation efforts that have retained much of the early Georgian housing. (See also PEABODY, GEORGE.)

SQUARE MILE

The CITY OF LONDON, with its complex of financial services, is sometimes referred to as 'The Square Mile' because it covers an area of 677 acres, just over 1 square mile.

STAMFORD HILL

Stamford Hill, in the LONDON BOROUGH OF HACKNEY, has one of the largest concentrations of ultra-Orthodox Jews (known as Hasidim) in London. The only Jewish community in Britain to use the Yiddish language extensively, it has its roots in eighteenth-century Poland, where Ba'al Shem Tov led a charismatic movement that emphasized a non-intellectual relationship with God and a strict code of personal conduct. The black frock coats and wide-brimmed fur hats worn by the Polish nobility were adopted as the distinctive form of dress, making the men easily identifiable in the north London community. The women wear wigs, believing that only their husbands should see their real hair, and mix only with males to whom they are related. Divorce is unusual and disputes are solved according to traditional rules rather than by the tenets of English law. Stamford Hill developed during the eighteenth century, when it was popular with City bankers and financiers, many of whom had a Jewish background. The pace of expansion increased with the arrival of the RAILWAY in 1872 and the social composition of the area altered with the construction of flats specifically for working-class families in the period between the two world wars but, since then, the suburb has altered little. Jewish worshippers meet at a synagogue in Egerton Road and buy bread, groceries and other goods at shops catering to their needs in the commercial heart of the area at the crossroads of Stamford Hill and Amhurst PARK. In the thirteenth century, the area was known as *Saundfordhull*. The Old English roots of that name (*sand*, *ford*, *hyll*) suggest that it was once a ford by a sandy hill.

STANMORE

Stanmore, on the north-west fringe of the metropolitan area in the LONDON BOROUGH OF HARROW, was settled by Neolithic times and was the location of a battle between the Celtic Catuvellauni people and an invading Roman army in 54 BC. Ranulf de Glanville, Chief Justiciary of England, founded a priory in the area in 1170, but development was limited until the twentieth century, when the proximity of the CHILTERN HILLS and the restrictions on building imposed by GREEN BELT legislation attracted successful City bankers and stockbrokers. The Church of St John the Evangelist dates from Saxon times, but the present building, designed by Henry Clutton, was erected in 1850; Lord Aberdeen (Prime Minister from 1852 to 1855) is buried in the vaults of its brick predecessor, which stands nearby, and the remains of Sir W.S. Gilbert, poet and writer of comic operas, lie in the churchyard. Known in the eighth century as *Stanmere*, the area probably derives its name from the Old English *stan* and *mere*, suggesting that the place was once known for its stony pond. (See also BAKERLOO LINE; JUBILEE LINE; METROPOLITAN LINE.)

STANSTED AIRPORT

See AIRPORTS.

STATE OPENING OF PARLIAMENT

In a ceremony little changed since Elizabethan times, the monarch rides in procession from BUCKINGHAM PALACE to WESTMINSTER PALACE, usually in November each year, to declare each session of Parliament open. Since 1852 kings and queens have travelled to the event in the Irish State Coach (bought by Queen Victoria specifically for the occasion), flanked by heralds and pursuivants. The Foot Guards and cavalry of the HOUSEHOLD DIVISION form a guard of honour for dignitaries, who include the Earl Marshal, a hereditary post (held by the Dukes of Norfolk) that involves responsibility for all state ceremonial events. When the royal party reaches the HOUSES OF PARLIAMENT (see PALACE OF WESTMINSTER), it enters by the Victoria Tower then makes its way to the Robing Room before processing to the HOUSE OF LORDS. Members of Parliament are summoned from the HOUSE OF COMMONS by the Gentleman Usher of the Black Rod, who has the door slammed in his face three times as a reminder of the elected body's independence, then, when the whole group is assembled (with the MPs standing and the Lords seated), the sovereign reads a speech that is written by the government and outlines its intentions for the coming session.

STEELYARD

The London centre of the Hanseatic League stood on the north bank of the RIVER THAMES, taking its name from the large scales used to weigh imports. The League was created from 1241 as the Hansas (groups of German merchants trading with foreign countries) formed alliances with the ports from which they operated in order to further their commercial interests and restrict piracy. It reached the height of its power during the fourteenth century but was much resented by Londoners, partly because members of the League did not mix with representatives of other business interests in the city and partly because they had privileges not accorded to local people (they did not have to pay rent on the Steelyard, for example). In 1551, Edward VI confiscated their property and revoked the privileges, then, in 1598, Elizabeth I expelled them. The Steelyard was converted into a storehouse for the Royal Navy and burned down in the GREAT FIRE of 1666. In 1865, CANNON STREET STATION was built on the site.

STEPNEY

Stepney forms part of London's working-class EAST END, lying some 3½ miles from CHARING CROSS. Although settled by the Romans, the area remained agricultural until the sixteenth century, when buildings spread along the north bank of the RIVER THAMES as the CITY OF LONDON expanded beyond its defensive walls. From 1802, when the West India DOCK opened on the ISLE OF DOGS, the area experienced a rapid influx of IMMIGRANTS from other parts of the British Isles as well as from abroad, many of them unskilled and poor. The clothing industry was also an important source of employment but wages were low, so workers crammed into small, overcrowded houses, where infectious disease spread easily and educational standards were low. German attempts to bomb riverside industries during the BLITZ caused much damage to residential property (one in three homes was destroyed) but left many sites available for redevelopment when the Second World War ended. Stepney was incorporated within the LONDON BOROUGH OF TOWER HAMLETS when the metropolitan area's local government was reorganized in 1965 and, since then, has been the focus of many urban renewal programmes, which have reduced populations and replaced nineteenth-century slums with modern housing. At the end of the first millennium, the area was known as *Stybbanhythe*. The Old English word *hyth* means 'landing place' so the settlement may at first have been 'Stybba's quay'. (See also ABERCROMBIE PLAN (1943–44).)

STOCK EXCHANGE (LSE)

The origins of the London Stock Exchange – the most important in the world for international business – lie in the city's seventeenth- and eighteenth-century COFFEE HOUSES, where brokers sold stocks and shares to private buyers. In 1773, a group of these brokers purchased a THREADNEEDLE STREET building, which they called the Stock Exchange, opened it to members (who paid a daily subscription) and organized regulatory committees. Disputes over the rules led, in 1801, to a breakaway movement, which involved some 500 traders, who established their own Exchange at Capel Court (off Old Broad Street, in the CITY OF LONDON), with its own governing bodies. The capital generated by the Industrial Revolution contributed to their success so, by 1850, their numbers had grown to well over 800 and, by 1905, to more than 5,500. In addition, regional cities established their own exchanges around Britain.

The twentieth century brought a series of alterations to operating procedures, including the admission of women as members (in 1973) and the amalgamation of London with the provincial United Kingdom exchanges and the Dublin exchange as the International Stock Exchange of the United Kingdom and the Republic of Ireland (also in 1973). In 1979 the abolition of foreign exchange controls enabled British savings institutions to invest money overseas in non-UK securities, initiating competition with foreign brokers, then, during the 1980s, following government pressure, major changes to the rules were made in order to increase trade (and alter the widely held public view that the institution was a GENTLEMEN'S CLUB that had adopted a whole range of restrictive practices). In particular the LSE was converted, in 1986, from an association of members into a nonprofit-making limited company, with individual firms becoming shareholders, each with a single vote. The separation between brokers (who bought or sold on behalf of clients) and jobbers (who acted as middlemen between brokers) was ended, promoting mergers of financial services companies, and outside concerns were permitted to take over member businesses, enabling them to increase their capital base. Also in 1986, the traditional face-to-face dealing on the trading floor was replaced by a computerized technology (known as SEAQ – the Stock Exchange Automated Quotations service), which allowed quotes to be displayed on screens and deals to be confirmed by telephone.

In 1991 the governing council was replaced by a Board of Directors, with a membership drawn from several sources, including the LSE's customers. Then, in 1995, in response to a European Union directive that each state must have its own statutory regulation, Dublin business was redirected to a new exchange in the Irish Republic. In combination, the reforms swept away much of the excitement and tradition (including the attendants, who had been known as waiters since the coffee house days) but they introduced up-to-date business practices. In 1998, the Exchange announced an alliance with the Deutsche Börse in Frankfurt but plans for a full merger proved controversial and were abandoned two years later. A major shake-up of the board, the appointment of Clara Furse (formerly of Crédit Lyonnais Rouse) as chief executive and a decision to list the Exchange on its own market followed in 2001. (See also BIG BANG.)

STOCKWELL

Until the nineteenth century, Stockwell (which lies some 2 miles south of CHARING CROSS) was a cluster of houses around a village green close to St Andrew's Church (built in 1767) and the manor house. However, from the 1830s, with wealthy families seeking country homes on the fringe of the urban area, speculative builders erected large villas in areas such as Stockwell PARK. The arrival of the London, Chatham and Dover RAILWAY in 1863 and the NORTHERN LINE of the UNDERGROUND in 1890 added to the pressures on land and, as affluent residents moved to more rural locations, older houses were subdivided and terraced properties constructed for incomers with more limited funds. The area was much damaged by German bombs during the Blitz but the destruction allowed local authority planners to design housing with more modern amenities (as at the Studley Estate, erected in the 1950s). In recent years, a significant Portuguese community has moved into the area, opening cafés and other small businesses. The National MUSEUM of Type and Communication, opened in 1991 at 100 Hackford Road, has one of the world's most comprehensive typographical collections. Stockwell was included in the LONDON BOROUGH OF LAMBETH when the city's local government was reorganized in 1965. Its name, derived from the Old English *stocca* and *wella*, means 'the spring beside the tree stump'. (See also ELECTRICITY; TUBE.)

STOKE NEWINGTON

Archaeological studies suggest that Stoke Newington, located 4 miles north-east of CHARING CROSS, was populated as early as Palaeolithic times. The site of a Saxon settlement, it was (according to legend) given by King Aethelstan to the monks of ST PAUL'S CATHEDRAL in AD 939. By the eighteenth century, it had evolved into a sizeable agricultural village, providing a particular attraction for nonconformists, who were not allowed to take up residence in the CITY OF LONDON because they refused to worship in the Church of England. One of them – Daniel Defoe – went to school in Stoke Newington and gave the surname of Thomas Cruso, his classmate, to the hero of the novel, *Robinson Crusoe*, published in 1719. Isaac Watts (who wrote *When I Survey the Wondrous Cross* and other hymns), essayist William Hazlitt and Edgar Allan Poe were also educated in the area, which still retains its dissenting tradition. During the eighteenth century, London began a process of encroachment that would ultimately engulf the community. In the early phase a series of substantial mansions were built to house affluent families then, from 1830, THOMAS CUBITT erected large villas in the Greek Revival style popular at the time and, after 1860, developers designed more modest terraced homes, filling the remaining open spaces. In the second half of the twentieth century, local authorities undertook a number of urban renewal programmes and the area became the focus for small groups of IMMIGRANTS from the Caribbean, India and the Turkish sector of Cyprus. Stoke Newington was included within the LONDON BOROUGH OF HACKNEY when local government in the metropolitan area was reformed in 1965. The first part of the name is probably derived from the Old English word *stoccen*, which can mean 'by the tree stumps' or 'made of logs'. The second part of the name may date from the same period and be a corruption of *niwe* ('new') and *tun* ('homestead' or 'estate'). Stoke Newington may, therefore, have originated as a new settlement in a woodland clearing. (See also KRAY TWINS.)

STOW, JOHN (*c.* 1525–1605)

Stow's *Survey of London*, published in 1598, provides scholars with a detailed account of the city's buildings and businesses in the late Elizabethan period of transition from medieval to modern. Stow lived his entire life in London. Born in the parish of St Michael, CORNHILL, he is known to have had an address in ALDGATE in 1549 and then to have moved to Leadenhall Street, where he remained for the rest of his life. Nothing is known of his parents, though some writers conjecture that his father was a tailor because Stow followed that trade, establishing a prosperous business until, from about 1560, he turned increasingly to writing and to collecting documents dealing with English history. In 1561, he published an edition of the works of Geoffrey Chaucer, then, in 1565, completed a *Summarie of Englyshe Chronicles*, which included the names and periods in office of 'all the Bylyffes, Maiors, and Sheriffes of the Citie of London Sens the Conquest' and was regularly updated over the next forty years. The 1598 *Survey* (which was revised and enlarged in 1603) described the city's foundation and growth, listed details of monuments and buildings, outlined urban customs, and provided insights into the habits and occupations of the citizenry. Modern historians regard the painstaking work as accurate but, at the time, Stow's honesty and diligence were much impugned by rivals. In 1562, for example, Richard Grafton, with a pun designed to deceive nobody, scoffed (in his *Abridgement of the Chronicles of England*) at the 'memories of superstitious foundations, fables, and lyes foolishly stowed together.' Stow was well able to defend himself, however, responding in 1567 with a similarly obvious swipe at the 'thundering noise of empty tonnes and unfruitful graftes of Momus' offspring.'

As his passion for history and for recording the events of his day consumed more and more of his time, Stow wandered the country, collecting texts and talking to the great men of the period, including BEN JONSON and Archbishop of Canterbury Matthew Parker (who employed him to edit some medieval papers). Inevitably his business suffered and he became increasingly dependent on charity. Moreover, his Roman Catholic leanings led to accusations of disloyalty by government officials sworn to defend the reformed Church of England so he was called, on several occasions, to face courts of inquiry. He appears, however, to have accepted the vicissitudes with good grace and survived to see the succession of James I when he was nearly eighty. Stow died on 6 April 1605 and was buried in ST ANDREW UNDERSHAFT CHURCH near his Leadenhall Street home.

STRAND

Running for ¾ mile westward from the ROYAL COURTS OF JUSTICE to TRAFALGAR SQUARE, the Strand links London's commercial core in the City to the political complex at WHITEHALL. Originally a path running alongside the RIVER THAMES, it attracted residential development as early as the twelfth century and, by the Elizabethan period, was lined with the mansions of bishops and courtiers (see, for example, SOMERSET HOUSE). By the time George I ascended the throne in 1714, it had become well known for its COFFEE SHOPS, many of them frequented by the metropolitan literati, such as JAMES BOSWELL, who picked up his prostitutes from the plentiful supply in neighbouring alleys. Redevelopment began around CHARING CROSS in the 1830s and spread along the street to include construction of HOTELS such as the Savoy (1884), several restaurants (including Simpson's, opened in 1904) and numerous THEATRES, of which only the Vaudeville (which presented its first performance in 1870), the Savoy (which was originally built in 1881) and the ADELPHI (now in a building dating from 1930) remain. During the second half of the twentieth century, further reconstruction involved the erection of administrative accommodation for commercial, government and educational interests, but the road is still lined with cafeterias and specialist shops (such as the stamp dealer Stanley Gibbons). (See also ALDWYCH; JUBILEE LINE; ST CLEMENT DANES CHURCH, STRAND; WATERLOO; YERKES, CHARLES TYSON.)

STRATFORD

A mixed residential and industrial area in the north-west of the LONDON BOROUGH OF NEWHAM, Stratford takes its name from Stratford Langthorne Abbey, which was founded by William de Montfichet in 1135 and became one of the richest Cistercian MONASTERIES in the country. The processing and manufacturing activities were begun by the monks, who built mills along the banks of the RIVER LEA, and continued after the abbey's dissolution in 1538 with the development of gunpowder works, distilleries, textile printing shops and porcelain furnaces. Then, in the nineteenth century, the Eastern Counties RAILWAY made Stratford its major centre for locomotive and rolling stock maintenance (1847) and facilitated the growth of a fruit and vegetable MARKET from 1879. These sources of employment attracted a large working-class population, who found accommodation in densely packed streets of terraced houses (many of which were erected by the railway company). Little evidence of the area's early history remains (the abbey site is now covered by factories, for example), though a plaque in St John's Church commemorates eighteen Protestant martyrs burned at the stake in 1555–6 for refusing to give up their beliefs. In recent years, the area has seen the growth of a major shopping centre for east London. Stratford has also been proposed as the location of the terminus for fast rail links via the Channel Tunnel to France. In 2003 the government gave its support to a London bid for the 2012 Olympic Games on condition that many of the required stadiums, athletes' accommodation and other buildings be built on waste ground in the north of the area.

The suburb is probably now best known for its THEATRE Royal, which was founded in 1884 despite complaints from local ministers that it would not 'tend to the moral elevation of the people of the neighbourhood'. It concentrated on popular dramas for most of its first forty years but fell on hard times during the period between the wars as it suffered from competition from the cinemas and the economic recession in the EAST END. For over twenty years from 1953, when the Theatre Workshop took a lease on the building and presented a repertoire of classical and contemporary plays under the direction of Joan Littlewood, it gained national prominence for its adventurous (and often left-wing) productions. More recently, it has developed a strong educational ethic and a reputation for providing opportunities to Black and Asian writers and actors. In 2003, Stratford was earmarked by the government as a site for the construction of new homes in an attempt to reduce the housing shortage in south-east England. (See also DOCKLANDS LIGHT RAILWAY (DLR); JUBILEE LINE.)

STRAWBERRY HILL

In 1747 Horace Walpole, Earl of Oxford, acquired a small property overlooking the RIVER THAMES at TWICKENHAM. For over forty years, he worked on the building, converting it into a Gothic castle with battlements, moulded ceilings and quatrefoil windows. To assist him, he appointed a Committee of Taste, which scoured pictures of other structures, identified architectural features that seemed attractive and adapted them to suit his needs. Thus, one of the chimney pieces was modelled on details of Edward the Confessor's tomb in WESTMINSTER ABBEY and another on that of Archbishop Wareham in Canterbury Cathedral. Friends were commissioned to find appropriate furnishings and detailed inventories were kept of all acquisitions. In 1757, Walpole installed a printing press in the house and published many of his own works (notably the novel *Castle of Otranto* in 1765) as well as those of other writers, such as poet Thomas Gray's Pindaric *Odes* (1757). After his death the estate passed through the hands of several owners before it was inherited by Frances, Countess Waldegrave in 1846. She enlarged the building to make it more appropriate for grand receptions then, for thirty years, held gatherings attended by the major political figures of the mid-Victorian era. In 1923, the house was bought by the Catholic Education Council and turned into a teacher training college, which was later integrated with the University of Surrey.

STREATHAM

Streatham lies towards the southern end of the LONDON BOROUGH OF LAMBETH. During late

Saxon times it was the property of the Abbey of Chertsey but, after the Norman Conquest in 1066, was given to Richard of Tonbridge (a cousin of William I), who gifted it to the Benedictine order. Although Streatham gained the right to hold a fair in the thirteenth century, the small settlement experienced little development until 1659, when a ploughman discovered a spring with waters, which, doctors declared, had medicinal qualities. Crowds flocked to the village, which developed a considerable reputation as a spa, attracting HUGUENOT weavers fleeing persecution in France and London merchants seeking suitable locations for their country homes. The latter included the Thrales, who had made their wealth from BREWERIES and, in 1740, built Streatham Place, which became a favourite haunt of DAVID GARRICK, SAMUEL JOHNSON (who conducted chemistry experiments in an oven in the garden), Oliver Goldsmith, Joshua Reynolds and other representatives of the arts. During the Georgian and Victorian periods, TRANSPORT links improved, encouraging further immigration, notably after the opening of the RAILWAY station in 1856. By 1881, the population had reached 20,000 and, by 1901, had soared to 70,000. Agricultural land was covered by houses, roads and commercial properties, a process that has continued into the twenty-first century as Streatham earned a reputation as an entertainment focus (with an ice rink as well as a dance hall, a THEATRE and cinemas) and became a suburb within the metropolitan area rather than an independent community. The area's name is probably derived from the Old English *straet* and *ham*, suggesting that the settlement originated as 'a homestead beside a paved road'.

STREET LIGHTING

Until the early nineteenth century, the darkness of the London night was relieved only by candles flickering in windows, oil lamps suspended over doorways and the glimmer of the moon. In 1804, however, Frederick Winsor (a German immigrant) formed the New Light and Heat Company and, three years later, provided a demonstration of GAS lighting on the north side of PALL MALL in celebration of the birthday of the Prince of Wales (later George IV). The prince gave his enthusiastic support to advocates of the new fuel, a patronage that helped lead to the formation of the Gas Light and Coke Company, which, in 1812, received the rights to light streets in the CITY OF LONDON, SOUTHWARK and WESTMINSTER. Lamps were placed on WESTMINSTER BRIDGE in 1814 and the rest of the central city soon followed. By 1840, a dozen firms employed an army of 380 lamplighters to light the burners at dusk and shut them off at dawn, though some communities (such as the aristocratic residents of GROSVENOR SQUARE) resisted the newfangled technology. Initially the lamps were simply open flames that were frequently blown out by winds, but, from 1885, changes in design greatly improved the efficiency of the system. By that time, however, gas was giving way to ELECTRICITY. Westminster Bridge was lit by electricity as early as 1858 but its use was limited until vacuum bulbs with incandescent carbon filaments were introduced in 1878–82. During the twentieth century, gas lighting was gradually superseded by the more reliable, and increasingly sophisticated, electric systems, though some lamps in the area near TEMPLE CHURCH were hand lit as late as 1986.

STREET MARKETS

Until the second half of the nineteenth century, most Londoners did their shopping at street MARKETS or with street traders. As late as 1851, the census showed that more than 30,000 people in the city earned a living as costermongers, selling fish, vegetables, meat and other products from barrows. Usually, they announced their presence with shouted cries or some other noise (such as the handbell of the muffin man). The markets, where traders congregated, developed from the tradition of fairs (such as BARTHOLOMEW FAIR), which were sanctioned by the authorities from as early as the twelfth century but suppressed from the Georgian period, often because of CRIME and other antisocial behaviour with which they became associated. The Industrial Revolution dealt a further blow, introducing mass-produced products more easily sold in DEPARTMENT STORES than at roadside stalls. And, more recently, a welter of legislation governing food hygiene has forced many of the barrow boys out of business. However, the hot chestnut man still sells his wares during the winter months, office workers buy their lunch from street traders in OXFORD STREET throughout the year and Tubby Isaac's whelk bar offers jellied eels in Goulston Street. The open-air market tradition has also survived, supported by increasing numbers of bargain-seeking tourists. PETTICOAT LANE, with its COCKNEY traders, offers a wide range of fruit, vegetables, clothing and domestic goods, as does East Street (near ELEPHANT AND CASTLE). BRIXTON and SHEPHERD'S BUSH have become well known for their West Indian products, PORTOBELLO ROAD MARKET and the New Caledonian Market in BERMONDSEY Square for antiques, Leather Lane for crockery, Columbia Road for house plants and Camden Lock (see CAMDEN TOWN) on the REGENT'S CANAL for bric-a-brac, including books and records. (See also LAMBETH WALK; RAG FAIR.)

STROUD GREEN

See FINSBURY PARK.

SURBITON

Surbiton, located some 12 miles south-west of CHARING CROSS, owes its existence to the RAILWAY. When local authorities in KINGSTON UPON THAMES refused to allow railway developments, the transport companies swung their routes south, opening a station at rural Surbiton in 1838. The improved access to the CITY OF LONDON attracted wealthy businessmen and -women, who built substantial villas in the area, earning it a reputation for affluence that it still retains. The suburb expanded rapidly, gaining borough status in 1938 and becoming part of the LONDON BOROUGH OF KINGSTON UPON THAMES in 1965. During the second half of the twentieth century, many of the larger houses were converted into offices, but in the churches of St Andrew, St Mark, St Matthew and St Raphael it retains some of the best small-scale Victorian church ARCHITECTURE in the city. Also, a number of residential neighbourhoods are protected from development by conservation legislation. The area's name may be derived from the Old English *suth* and *beretun*, meaning 'the outlying farm in the south'. (See also BARNARDO, THOMAS JOHN.)

SURREY COUNTY CRICKET CLUB

In 1844, the Montpelier Cricket Club was ousted from its south London pitch because the site was bought for development. On 22 August the following year, several members gathered at The Horns (a PUBLIC HOUSE in KENNINGTON) and agreed to form a new organization that would draw support from the whole of the County of Surrey (which, at the time, included much of London south of the RIVER THAMES). They were granted permission to play at THE OVAL on land owned by the Duchy of Cornwall and brought turf from TOOTING Common to create a new wicket (thirty years later, Edward, Prince of Wales and Duke of Cornwall, allowed the club to incorporate the feathers, which adorn his crest, in its badge).

The Surrey club has a distinguished history. It has won the county championship twenty-two times (including a run of six successive victories from 1887 to 1892 and seven from 1952 to 1958), the Benson and Hedges Cup three times (1974, 1997 and 2001), the NatWest Trophy once (1982) and the Sunday League Championship once (1996). It has also carried out considerable refurbishment at The Oval over the past two decades, providing hospitality boxes and other facilities.

SUTTON

Sutton, some 10 miles south-west of CHARING CROSS, was probably settled by Saxon immigrants during the sixth or seventh century (its name is derived from the Old English *suth* and *tun*, or 'southern settlement') but remained an agricultural village until the RAILWAY spurred urban development from 1847. During the second half of the nineteenth century, developers built housing for all classes of society and private benefactors contributed to the establishment of institutions such as Thomas Wall's adult and nursery schools, opened in 1895 and 1909 respectively. Residential growth continued into the twentieth century so, in 1965, when the town became the administrative heart of the new LONDON BOROUGH OF SUTTON, a major programme of urban reconstruction was initiated, with a new civic centre, offices and retail units opening in 1965 and an additional shopping mall added in 1991. As a result, little evidence of the old village remains, but St Nicholas Church, founded in the seventh century, has survived, although it was substantially rebuilt to Edwin Nash's designs in 1862–4. (See also ROYAL MARSDEN HOSPITAL.)

SUTTON, LONDON BOROUGH OF

The London Borough of Sutton lies on the southern rim of the London conurbation. Created in 1965, when local government in the metropolitan area was reformed, it consists of a series of small towns and villages covering some 17 square miles of what was previously part of the County of Surrey. Although there are several big employers (such as Reed Business Publishing, Canon and Securicor), the borough is largely residential, with a high proportion of white-collar workers, particularly in SUTTON and in CHEAM. For many of the 179,800 residents (2001), the principal attraction is the quality of life, with regular rail services to central London, easy access to the M25 motorway and Gatwick AIRPORT and large areas of open space (including the NORTH DOWNS) within easy reach.

SWEENEY TODD

Sweeney Todd is probably a mythical figure who set up a barber's shop at 186 FLEET STREET then killed his customers, passing their bodies to his neighbour, Mrs Lovett, who used them as the principal ingredient for meat pies, which earned a reputation as the best in London. The character first appears in the story 'A String of Pearls', which was printed in *The People's Periodical and Family Library* in 1846. A dramatized version of the tale was staged at the Britannia Theatre the following year and caught the public imagination, so, in succeeding decades, the details of the enterprising business were fashioned and refashioned in various forms. For over a century, Sweeney was presented as an unlovely individual but, in 1973, Christopher Bond recast him in a more sympathetic light, suggesting that he was the victim of society because his wife and daughter were taken from him by a lecherous judge and that he was cast into jail unjustly. That version of the story was turned into a musical by Stephen Sondheim, Harold Prince and Hugh Wheeler in 1979, winning eight Tony awards but, by Broadway standards, failing at the box office. It is not known whether the original character was solely a figment of a penny dreadful writer's imagination, but, in 1880, when houses at the western end of Fleet Street were demolished during an urban renewal programme, piles of human bones were discovered in a pit beneath No. 186.

SWISS COTTAGE

The area north-west of PRIMROSE HILL, on the fringe of central London, developed from 1826 when a turnpike road was opened to link REGENT'S PARK to HAMPSTEAD. An alpine-style inn, erected beside the tollgate, gave the area its name. As transport links improved, the largely agricultural landscape was increasingly urbanized, particularly after a BUS terminus was established in 1859 and a station for the LONDON UNDERGROUND'S METROPOLITAN LINE was built in 1868. Expansion continued during the twentieth century, enmeshing the suburb in the metropolitan area, so in 1965 it was absorbed by the LONDON BOROUGH OF CAMDEN. Still essentially residential, it houses the Hampstead Public Library, designed by Basil Spence and constructed in 1964. Sigmund Freud, who developed the science of psychoanalysis, lived nearby at 20 Maresfield Gardens (see FREUD'S HOUSE.)

SWORDBEARER

The Swordbearer, the senior of the LORD MAYOR's three principal personal staff, is responsible, along with the other ESQUIRES, for ensuring that public engagements are efficiently organized. The post dates back to 1419, when 'a man well bred' was appointed to carry the Lord Mayor's sword ahead of him in processions (a duty still carried out on ceremonial occasions). When the holder retires, he is succeeded by the CITY MARSHAL. (See also COMMON CRYER AND SERJEANT-AT-ARMS.)

SYDENHAM

Sydenham lies some 6 miles south-east of CHARING CROSS. Throughout the Middle Ages it had low populations, serving largely as grazing land and a source of firewood. From the mid-seventeenth century, however, the allegedly medicinal properties of local springs attracted crowds of visitors, many of whom built country homes in the area. In 1810, as agricultural practices changed, the open common was enclosed by hedges then increasingly sold to builders. Lower Sydenham developed as a working-class area, with Upper Sydenham, higher on the hill slopes, attracting more wealthy families, particularly after 1854, when the erection of the CRYSTAL PALACE to the south enhanced its fashionable status. Ernest Shackleton lived at 12 Westwood Hill and John Logie Baird (the first man to transmit television pictures) at 3 Crescent Wood Road, but, as the twentieth century progressed and the metropolitan area expanded, many of the more affluent families moved further into the countryside and Sydenham evolved into a residential suburb with a high proportion of residents commuting to work in central London. Office accommodation and retail developments increasingly infiltrated after the Second World War and local authorities used some of the remaining open space for public housing while the site of the wells that originally promoted urban growth was converted into a municipal PARK. Sydenham was incorporated within the LONDON BOROUGH OF LEWISHAM in 1965. Its name probably derives from a personal name and the Old English *ham*, meaning 'Cippa's homestead' or 'Cippa's enclosure'. (See also CRYSTAL PALACE FOOTBALL CLUB.)

SYON HOUSE

Syon House overlooks the west bank of the RIVER THAMES near BRENTFORD, in west London. It stands on the site of a Bridgettine MONASTERY, which was founded by Henry V in 1415 but appropriated in 1534 by Henry VIII, who confined his fifth wife, Catherine Howard, in the building before her execution in 1542. Five years later, while Henry's body was lying in state overnight at Syon, his coffin burst open and, some hours later, dogs were discovered consuming his remains. When Edward VI succeeded to the throne in 1547, the estate passed to Edward, Duke of Somerset (who erected a house), then, following his execution in 1552, it was acquired by John Dudley. It was there, the following year, that Lady Jane Grey, Dudley's daughter-in-law, was offered the Crown of England, beginning a reign that lasted for only nine days. In 1594 Syon was leased to the Percy family, heirs to the dukedom of Northumberland, who have made it their home ever since.

Under successive dukes, the house has taken the form of a block, some 140 feet square, built round an open courtyard and with a turret at each corner. INIGO JONES designed an arcade for the east side in 1632 then, from 1761, ROBERT ADAM transformed the interior by creating a suite of rooms, which included a great hall, a dining room, a drawing room (with crimson silk wall hangings) and a gallery that runs for the full length of the east front. Further alterations were made during the nineteenth century, when a conservatory was added and the north front rebuilt then faced with Bath stone. Many of the furnishings, which include seventeenth-century portraits of members of the royal family, were brought from a Percy property, demolished to make way for the construction of Northumberland Avenue. The gardens, laid out between 1767–73 by Capability Brown, were opened to the public in 1834 and now house a large motor MUSEUM (which contains British vehicles dating from 1895) and a butterfly exhibition. (See also LONDON TRANSPORT MUSEUM.)

T

TATE GALLERY

The Tate was opened in 1897, when sugar refiner Sir Henry Tate gifted his collection of sixty-five paintings to the nation and financed the construction of exhibition rooms at Millbank (on the north shore of the RIVER THAMES near VAUXHALL Bridge amidst the middle-class homes erected by THOMAS CUBITT during the 1840s). An additional wing was provided by art dealer Sir Joseph Duveen for J.M.W. Turner's works, which had previously hung at the NATIONAL GALLERY. Extensions to the property were added in 1926 and 1937 (both funded by Duveen's son, who was later made Lord Duveen of Millbank), in 1979 (when the Gulbenkian Foundation paid a large part of the building costs) and in 1987 (when donations from the family and charitable foundation of the property developer Charles Clore provided cash for new halls in which the Turners could be displayed). The gallery housed a British Collection (which included paintings, drawings, engravings and sculptures from *c.* 1550 to *c.* 1900) and a Modern Collection (which concentrated on British artists working from about 1880 and foreign artists from the time of the French impressionists in the late nineteenth century). Initially, the two collections were considered distinct but, in 1989, the exhibits were rearranged into a single chronological sequence tracing the development of British art and its associations with foreign schools during the twentieth century. In 2000, however, they were separated again when the representatives of modern art from 1900 (including Matisse, Picasso, Salvador Dalí and the Cubists) were rehoused in the former BANKSIDE Power Station, which was renamed Tate Modern. The British painters (including William Hogarth, Joshua Reynolds, Thomas Gainsborough, William Blake, John Constable, Edwin Landseer and the pre-Raphaelites) remained at the Millbank site, which was rechristened Tate Britain. In its last full year on a single London site, the Tate attracted 1.8 million visitors.

TAXIS

In 1897, mechanically driven taxicabs began to compete with the horse-drawn carriages that had transported city dwellers for hundreds of years. Powered by ELECTRICITY, they could travel for about 30 miles before their batteries needed recharging but were extremely unreliable. Tyres quickly wore out and vibration caused both an uncomfortable ride and mechanical problems so, within three years, they had vanished. However, the disappearance provided only a temporary stay of execution for the horses. From 1904, petrol-driven vehicles became increasingly popular (there were 8,397 registered in 1914), gradually replacing the slower, more uncomfortable hansom cabs, which finally disappeared in 1947. In 1906 the METROPOLITAN POLICE drew up a set of regulations for the new form of transport. One of these rules stipulated that taxis must have a turning circle of no more than 25 feet; that regulation is still in force and accounts for the legendary manoeuvrability of the vehicles. Before they are allowed to pick up passengers, drivers must undergo exacting tests on 'the knowledge' – a corpus of information that involves map-like understanding of street patterns and destinations within 6 miles of CHARING CROSS. They are also required to be physically fit and to meet high character standards. Over 20,000 of those who have qualified are active, using about 17,000 taxis, most of them diesel-powered. In recent years, to the annoyance of traditionalists, many of the vehicles have replaced the traditional black colouring with advertisements. (See also HACKNEY CABS; TRANSPORT.)

TEA AUCTIONS

See LONDON TEA AUCTIONS.

TELEVISION CENTRE

See BRITISH BROADCASTING CORPORATION (BBC).

TEMPLE BAR

Temple Bar marks the western limit of the CITY OF LONDON, taking its name from nearby land formerly owned by the KNIGHTS TEMPLAR. Records from the later thirteenth century indicated that it was originally a simple chain attached to wooden posts but by 1351 a larger gateway had been constructed. It was repaired on several occasions then rebuilt in the 1670s to designs prepared by CHRISTOPHER WREN and, from 1684 until 1746, used to mount the heads of traitors. By 1878, complaints about traffic congestion led to the dismantling of the obstruction and its transfer to the Hertfordshire estate of Sir Henry Bruce Meux. A memorial marking the original site of Temple Bar was erected in 1880. In 1588, when Elizabeth I was on her way to a service in ST PAUL'S CATHEDRAL, where she gave thanks for the defeat of the Spanish Armada, her entourage passed through the gate. Ever since, when a monarch has had to enter the City on state occasions, a ceremony has been held at the site; the sovereign asks for permission to pass through, the LORD MAYOR presents his sword as a token of loyalty and the weapon is returned to indicate that the head of the realm is under his protection.

Temple Bar, as depicted by Hogarth's satirical engraving, *c.* 1726.

TEMPLE CHURCH

In 1185, the KNIGHTS TEMPLAR erected a circular church on the north shore of the RIVER THAMES, just under a mile east of CHARING CROSS. According to some scholars, the design reflects that of the church of the Holy Sepulcher in Jerusalem; others claim that the Dome of the Rock was a more likely model. Dedicated to the Blessed Mary, the building was consecrated by Heraclius (Roman Catholic Patriarch of Jerusalem) at a service attended by Henry II. It made much use of Purbeck marble (the first time the stone had been used extensively in London) and was extended in 1220–40 by the addition of a rectangular choir and a small chapel with a crypt where initiation rights were performed. When the Knights were disbanded in 1312, the land was given to the KNIGHTS HOSPITALLER, who leased it to lawyers. It was acquired by the Crown during the reign of Henry VIII but, in 1608, James I gave the freehold jointly to the Inner Temple and the Middle Temple (see INNS OF COURT) on condition that they maintained the fabric and the religious services for all time. The church, a mixture of Norman and Gothic styles, was badly damaged on 10 May 1941, the last night of the BLITZ, but restored under the direction of Walter Godfrey after the Second World War. Technically, it is a Royal Peculiar, a status that makes its clergy answerable to the monarch and the Archbishop of Canterbury rather than to the Bishop of London.

TEMPLE OF MITHRAS

In 1889, suspicions that a temple might lie under the streets of the CITY OF LONDON were aroused when a relief of Mithras, the Persian god of light, was discovered in the WALBROOK. Those suspicions were confirmed in 1954, during redevelopment of a section of Queen Victoria Street, when excavations by Professor W.F. Grimes revealed a temple known as the Mithraeum and built by the Romans during the second century. Mithras was an important rival to Jesus Christ in the Roman world but, even so, his place of worship bears a distinct resemblance to a Christian church, with an entrance to the east, a nave and a raised sanctuary. Its discovery so caught the public's imagination that the building was reconstructed in front of Bucklesbury House, the office block built on the site. It is on permanent view to visitors but an unreliable guide to the original (the floor is modern paving rather than earth, for example, and the open location is the antithesis of the original, underground sanctum). Sculptures and other artefacts (including a silver incense box) found during the excavation are on display in the MUSEUM OF LONDON.

THAMES, RIVER

The Thames, which flows through the centre of London, rises in the Cotswold Hills and flows eastward for 210 miles to the North Sea. Only the final 65 miles are tidal. The river was named Tamesis by Julius Caesar but is variously spelled in documents, with Tamis, Tamisa and Tamensim common (the origin of these names is unclear but some writers suggest that they are derived from a Celtic word meaning 'river' or 'dark one'). The banks consist largely of clays and unconsolidated sediments, leaving only one point – on the SOUTH BANK at SOUTHWARK and on the north bank immediately opposite – where the technology available to the Romans allowed bridge construction along the tidal stretch. Roads converged at the wooden crossing point, a small port developed and the settlement eventually evolved into LONDINIUM. In 1197, the CORPORATION OF LONDON paid Richard I a sum of 1,500 marks for the right to control the river then, for centuries, entrepreneurs siphoned off the flow, filled containers and sold water from door to door along the city streets. Boats carried goods of all kinds from sellers to buyers, with barges able to travel as far upriver as Oxford by 1624.

Navigation improved with the construction of locks between Staines and Teddington in 1810–5 but disputes were common, particularly over fishing rights. The friction came to a head during the 1830s, when the Crown claimed ownership of the riverbanks and bed between the ebb and flow of the tides. The city initially disputed the claim but eventually conceded defeat, enabling Parliament to enact legislation forming a Board of Conservancy in 1857. Nine years later, that body was reformed as the Thames Conservancy Board and given authority over the entire navigable area of the river. Further change in 1908 awarded the PORT OF LONDON AUTHORITY control from Teddington to the river mouth and the Conservancy Board responsibility for the remainder of the waterway. Both, however, lost some of their power following the passage of the Water Act (1973), which created the Thames Water Authority (TWA), giving it supremacy over other organizations in the river's 5,000-square mile catchment and requiring it to manage the entire water cycle, making provision for supply, SEWAGE DISPOSAL, prevention of WATER POLLUTION, and recreational facilities. The same legislation established a National Rivers Authority, whose Thames Region deals with drainage, navigation, fisheries and FLOOD CONTROL.

Until the twentieth century, the river was a major route, developing extensive DOCKS, particularly downriver from LONDON BRIDGE. However, most of the ferries have vanished (the exceptions are those which ply between Woolwich and North Woolwich, and between Gravesend and Tilbury), as has the bulk of the local industrial traffic. A water-bus service takes passengers from GREENWICH to PUTNEY, stopping at piers en route, but an increasing number of the boats are recreational. Yachts crowd into St Katharine's Marina in the redeveloped DOCKLANDS and, particularly during the summer months, larger vessels take tourists on outings to centres such as KEW. (See also ABERCROMBIE PLAN (1943–44); BRIDGES; DOGGETT'S COAT AND BADGE RACE; BRUNEL, ISAMBARD KINGDOM; FROST FAIRS; GREAT STINK; RENNIE, JOHN; ROYAL NAVAL DOCKYARDS; WATER SUPPLY.)

THAMES BARRIER

See FLOOD CONTROL.

THAMESMEAD

Shortly after its formation in 1965, the GREATER LONDON COUNCIL (GLC) prepared plans to drain 1,600 acres of marshland on the SOUTH BANK of the RIVER THAMES near ABBEY WOOD and create a new suburb that could house 100,000 people, with transport links to the central city and extensive provision for community activities. The first homes, however, were built of precast concrete blocks in high-rise developments, which proved hard to maintain and were prone to dampness. Although advertised as 'the city of the twenty-first century,' they seemed soulless to many critics (and certainly to Stanley Kubrick, who used Thamesmead as the location for *A Clockwork Orange*, the violent futuristic movie filmed in 1971). By 1974, only 12,000 residents had moved in, so planners abandoned high-rise construction and made greater use of brick in an attempt to produce a more welcoming environment. At the dismemberment of the GLC in 1986, administrative responsibilities passed to a private company but new management failed to cure the malaise as complaints about high rents and poor provision of services mounted so, in 1999, the town was split into three units, each run by an Estate Management Board. At the end of the century, the population numbered only 30,000 and the yachting marina, commuter boat service and other facilities envisaged in the early plans had still not materialized. However, in 2003, the government announced that Thamesmead would be the focus of a major house-building programme, which would help reduce the shortage of homes in south-east England. (See also BEXLEY, LONDON BOROUGH OF; JUBILEE LINE.)

THEATRE

London's first playhouse (known as The Theatre) was built at SHOREDITCH in 1576 (prior to that, dramatic performances had been presented at alehouses or churches). A second (The Curtain) opened nearby the following year but the regulations imposed by the CORPORATION OF LONDON encouraged managers to move across the RIVER THAMES to the more liberal environment of SOUTHWARK. By 1600, a sizeable entertainment complex had evolved in BANKSIDE, with the GLOBE THEATRE, the Rose and the Swan attracting large audiences to performances of works by WILLIAM SHAKESPEARE and his contemporaries. All of the buildings were made of wood and operated as theatres in the round, with tiered rows of seats facing inward to a central stage. Mid-century Puritan authorities, led by Oliver Cromwell, enforced their closure but from about 1660 they began to reappear north of the river, particularly around COVENT GARDEN (see, for example, THEATRE ROYAL). Revivals of Shakespeare's plays and dramatizations of works by popular authors such as Walter Scott created a large Victorian demand for popular entertainment, resulting in the construction of new playhouses and refurbishment of the old. As a result, many of London's largest commercial theatres date from the late nineteenth or early twentieth century, including the Criterion (which has an 1870s interior), the Albery (which opened in 1903 and has a distinctive Edwardian design) and the Palladium (which presented its first performance in 1910). More recently, the ROYAL NATIONAL THEATRE (completed in 1976) and the BARBICAN Centre (opened in 1982) have added modern venues. About forty companies present plays regularly in the WEST END, with countless other repertory groups, amateur dramatic societies and pub players adding to the variety in other parts of the city. Many suburban locations, such as RICHMOND and WIMBLEDON, have their own theatres, which are usually subsidized by local authorities and present plays before they appear in the big cities. (See also ALDWYCH; BLACKFRIARS; CHALK FARM; GOLDERS GREEN; HAYMARKET; HENSLOWE, PHILIP; HOXTON; LEICESTER SQUARE; MOUSETRAP, THE; MUSIC HALLS; OLD VIC; REGENT'S PARK; ROYAL ACADEMY OF DRAMATIC ART (RADA); SADLER'S WELLS; SHAFTESBURY AVENUE; STRAND; STRATFORD; THEATRE MUSEUM; TODD, SWEENEY.)

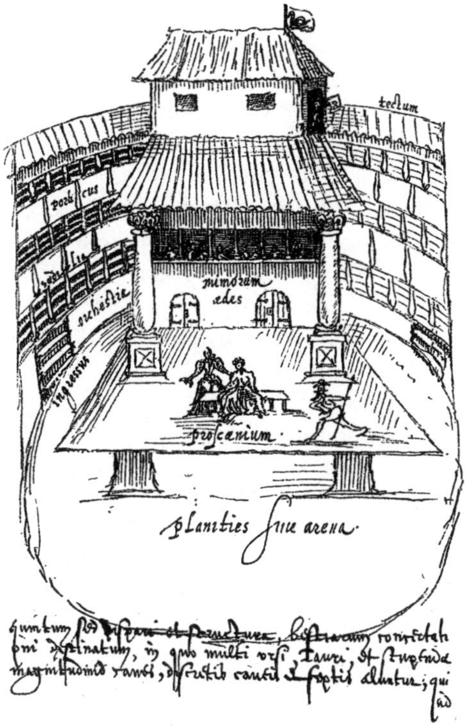

De Witt's early seventeenth-century drawing of the Swan Theatre, Southwark.

THEATRE MUSEUM

Proposals for a MUSEUM displaying the story of British THEATRE were first advanced by Laurence Irving (grandson of actor Henry Irving) in 1955. Following a series of donations, displays were mounted at a site in KENSINGTON in 1963. The exhibits were taken over by the VICTORIA AND ALBERT MUSEUM eight years later then, in 1987, transferred to the basement of the former COVENT GARDEN flower MARKET in Tavistock Street. The core of the collection is the Irving Archives, the Gabrielle Enthoven collection of playbills and programmes (which include items from the 1920s), and material from the Richard Buckle Museum of Performing Arts. Paintings, scripts, costumes, stage designs, prompt copies and other material are used to illustrate the development of London's entertainment complex and the contributions of individual actors, producers and impresarios.

THEATRE ROYAL, DRURY LANE

In 1663, a THEATRE was built in DRURY LANE (near COVENT GARDEN) but it survived for only nine years before being burned down. Its replacement, designed by CHRISTOPHER WREN, provided the stage where, in 1742, DAVID GARRICK made his debut. Over the next thirty years it built a reputation for Shakespearean drama (Sarah Siddons made a less successful first appearance as Portia in *The Merchant of Venice* in 1775). In 1776, Garrick retired and dramatist Richard Brinsley Sheridan took over, commissioning Henry Holland to redesign the building in 1794. On 24 February 1809, that structure, too, was destroyed by fire. (Sheridan sat in a nearby COFFEE HOUSE philosophically drinking port; 'Surely,' he said, 'a man may take a glass of wine by his own fireside.') The fourth building, which still stands, was modelled on the theatre in Bordeaux (France), designed by Benjamin Wyatt and completed in 1812. James Spiller added a porch in 1820 and Samuel Beazley gave the eastern front a colonnade of pillars in 1831. During the twentieth century, it has become best known for its musicals (*My Fair Lady* ran for 2,281 performances from 30 April 1958). The maximum audience is 2,188 people and one ghost, which appears in the Circle at matinees (it is believed that the apparition dates from 1840, when the skeleton of a man with a knife in his ribs was discovered behind a wall). In 2000 the venue was acquired by Andrew Lloyd Webber through the purchase of the Stoll Moss company. (See also DOGGETT'S COAT AND BADGE RACE; PUGIN, AUGUSTUS WELBY NORTHMORE.)

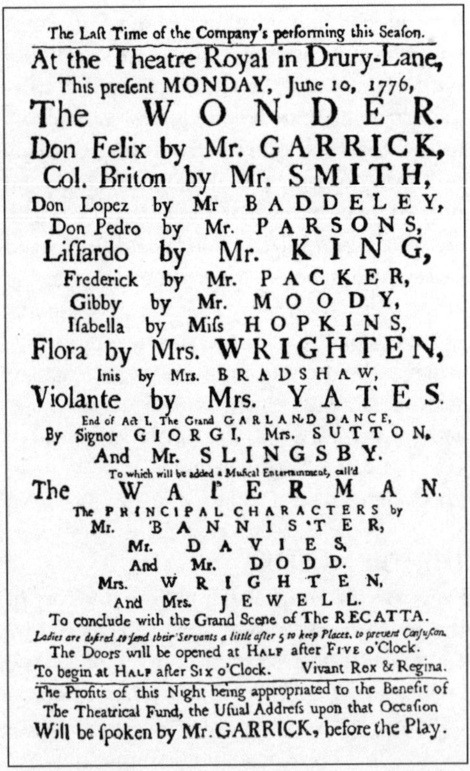
The Laſt Time of the Company's performing this Seaſon.
At the Theatre Royal in Drury-Lane,
This preſent MONDAY, June 10, 1776,
The WONDER.
Don Felix by Mr. GARRICK,
Col. Briton by Mr. SMITH,
Don Lopez by Mr BADDELEY,
Don Pedro by Mr. PARSONS,
Liſſardo by Mr. KING,
Frederick by Mr. PACKER,
Gibby by Mr. MOODY,
Iſabella by Miſs HOPKINS,
Flora by Mrs. WRIGHTEN,
Inis by Mrs. BRADSHAW,
Violante by Mrs. YATES.
End of Act I. The Grand GARLAND DANCE,
By Signor GIORGI, Mrs. SUTTON,
And Mr. SLINGSBY.
To which will be added a Muſical Entertainment, call'd
The WATERMAN.
The PRINCIPAL CHARACTERS by
Mr. BANNISTER,
Mr. DAVIES,
And Mr. DODD.
Mrs. WRIGHTEN,
And Mrs. JEWELL.
To conclude with the Grand Scene of The REGATTA.
Ladies are deſired to ſend their Servants a little after 5 to keep Places, to prevent Confuſion.
The Doors will be opened at HALF after FIVE o'Clock.
To begin at HALF after SIX o'Clock. Vivant Rex & Regina.
The Profits of this Night being appropriated to the Benefit of The Theatrical Fund, the Uſual Addreſs upon that Occaſion Will be ſpoken by Mr. GARRICK, before the Play.

An advertisement for a performance of *The Wonder* at the Theatre Royal, Drury Lane, featuring David Garrick in June 1776.

THREADNEEDLE STREET

This 500-yard-long street in the heart of the CITY OF LONDON is best known as the home of the BANK OF ENGLAND. The road may get its name from the needle and thread used by the Merchant Taylors and the Needlemakers (two of the LIVERY COMPANIES). In 1243, a community of French Protestants, known as the Hospital of St Anthony, was established on the north side of the street to give aid to travellers and collect alms. A school was attached to the site 200 years later (Sir Thomas More, Lord Chancellor of England from 1529 to 1532 and

Henry VIII's man for all seasons, was educated there) but the buildings (apart from the chapel) were destroyed in the GREAT FIRE of 1666. The south-western end of the street was occupied by the ROYAL EXCHANGE (whose first two premises were also burned down) in 1565, the STOCK EXCHANGE moved into offices farther to the east in 1733 and the Bank of England built its headquarters near the junction of Threadneedle and Princes Streets in 1734, expanding its location in 1765. Financial concerns now line most of the remainder of the pavement. (See also BALTIC EXCHANGE.)

TIMES, THE

England's oldest national daily newspaper was founded on 1 January 1785 by John Walter, a coal dealer and insurance underwriter who acquired the rights to use logotypes (fonts of words rather than letters). In an attempt to popularize the system he bought a disused printing shop in BLACKFRIARS and established the *Daily Universal Register.* The failure of the printing process encouraged him to concentrate on the broadsheet newspaper, which he renamed *The Times* in 1788. Under Thomas Barnes, editor from 1817 to 1841, it flourished, adopting an avowedly liberal political stance and earning a reputation as '*The Thunderer*' because of its impassioned advocacy of Parliamentary reform. In 1853, it employed the world's first war correspondent (William Howard Russell) but by the end of the century was in considerable financial trouble, surviving only through the intervention of Alfred Harmsworth, Viscount Northcliffe, in 1908. Journalistic standards also left much to be desired until William Haley (then Director General of the BRITISH BROADCASTING CORPORATION) was appointed editor in 1952 and adopted a more lively reporting style (which included replacing front page advertisements with news in 1966).

The acquisition of new production technologies provoked a lengthy dispute with the print unions, which resulted in suspension of publication in 1978–9. The bitterness continued after the business was acquired, in 1981, by Rupert Murdoch, who attempted to replace hot metal with computers in the publishing process. At the time, the newspaper industry was heavily overmanned and printers were able to command wages well beyond those of other employees in skilled trades. However, employers allowed the situation to continue because the high costs of production kept potential competitors from entering the industry. Murdoch changed the situation one weekend in January 1985 when he moved *The Times* from its headquarters near FLEET STREET to a new plant at WAPPING, where journalists could compose their stories on computer screens. The action provoked a violent response from the printers, who besieged the new site in a year-long dispute marked by bitter clashes with the police, but were eventually forced to concede defeat (see WAPPING DISPUTE). Since then, the newspaper has aggressively challenged its rivals in a price war. In addition to its conventional paper editions, it also publishes on an Internet site. (See also HAMMERSMITH AND CITY LINE.)

TOOTING

Throughout the Middle Ages, Tooting (which lies 6 miles south of CHARING CROSS) was owned by aristocratic and monastic interests. The economy was primarily agricultural until well into the nineteenth century, though wealthy Londoners built country mansions in the area from about 1715. Villa developments were common by 1850, encouraged by improving TRANSPORT links with the central city, but urban expansion was limited until the LONDON COUNTY COUNCIL erected a housing estate at Totterdown in the 1890s. Private construction companies followed, throwing up rows of small houses for working-class families. As the urban area expanded, Tooting was enmeshed in the metropolis, becoming part of the LONDON BOROUGH OF WANDSWORTH in 1965, but some of the open space has survived, notably the 150 acres of Tooting Bec Common, where villagers once dug gravel and cut firewood. The origins of the area's name are unclear, though most writers suggest Old English roots. Some believe that the second element of the word is derived from *ingas* and that the meaning was 'the settlement occupied by Tota's followers'. Others argue that the first element comes from *tot* rather than a personal name, so the name would mean 'the people of the lookout place'. Yet another group claims that it is a corruption of *theou* and *ing*, which would make it 'the dwelling of the slaves' or 'the dwelling of the villeins'. The name of the common reflects its former ownership by the Norman abbey of Bec-Hellouin. (See also ST GEORGE'S HOSPITAL; SURREY COUNTY CRICKET CLUB.)

TOTTENHAM

A suburb of densely packed, largely working-class housing located amidst pockets of light industrial activity, Tottenham lies some 6 miles north of CHARING CROSS. It was probably settled during Saxon times; the DOMESDAY BOOK, William I's record of property, indicates a population of about sixty farmers in 1086 and some scholars suggest that All Hallows Church was founded before the Norman Conquest twenty years earlier. The village developed during the Middle Ages and, by the early seventeenth century, had evolved into a relatively prosperous agricultural community but that rural economy was swept away by the Industrial Revolution. In 1840, the Great Eastern RAILWAY laid a line through the area then, in 1872, publicized its services by offering workmen cheap transport to LIVERPOOL STREET STATION. That promotion resulted in a vast increase in demand for houses, which builders satisfied by erecting rows of small terraced homes. These were followed by manufacturing premises, institutional developments (such as the Prince of Wales Hospital, opened in 1868) and recreational services (notably TOTTENHAM HOTSPUR FOOTBALL CLUB, formed in 1880 and now one of the great powers of English football) so, by 1920, the area was totally urbanized, leaving very limited open space. Tottenham was incorporated within the LONDON BOROUGH OF HARINGEY when local government in the metropolitan area was reorganized in 1965. Since then, the local authority has undertaken several urban renewal projects, including the construction of public housing. Bruce Castle, a thirteenth-century structure originally owned by King Robert the Bruce of Scotland but confiscated by Edward I of England in 1306, was bought in 1827 by Rowland Hill (who invented adhesive stamps and founded the penny post system in 1840, see POSTAL DELIVERIES); it now functions as a MUSEUM of local and postal history and as the regimental museum of the Middlesex Regiment, which was raised in 1755, saw service in the Peninsular War (1808–14), the Zulu War (1879) and the Boer Wars (1880–1 and 1899–1902) but was absorbed in the Queen's Regiment in 1967. The last element of the area's name may be derived from the Old English *ham* and the first from a personal name of the same period, making this 'Totta's homestead'. (See also WOOD GREEN.)

TOTTENHAM HOTSPUR FOOTBALL CLUB

Spurs was formed in 1882 and has a conspicuous record, winning the FA Cup eight times (in 1901, 1921, 1961, 1962, 1967, 1981, 1982 and 1991), the League Cup three times (1971, 1973 and 1999), the First Division Championship twice (1951 and 1961), the UEFA Cup twice (1972 and 1984), and the European Cup-Winners Cup once (1963). The original players were north London schoolboys but the club expanded quickly and turned professional in 1898 when it moved to its present ground at White Hart Lane (the first pitch was on the site of a former MARKET garden close to the White Hart PUBLIC HOUSE). In 1901, it became the only non-League club to win the FA Cup (beating Sheffield United

3-1 in the replay which followed a 1-1 draw) and in 1908 it joined the Second Division of the Football League. Its major successes came in the 1960s and early 1970s as teams studded with internationalists dominated the major English competitions, emphasizing their power by winning the double – the League Championship and FA Cup – in 1961 (the first club in the twentieth century to manage the feat) and earning recognition as the first English side to win a European competition by beating Atlético Madrid in the final of the European Cup-Winners Cup in 1963.

More recent years have brought fewer trophies, with only a League Cup victory in 1999 adding to the silverware between 1992 and 2002, and the lack of success on the field has been accompanied by financial and legal troubles off it. The problems surfaced in 1982, when Irving Scholar, a property developer, bought a controlling interest in the business although its debts amounted to £5.5 million. He had plans to develop White Hart Lane into a stadium ranking with the best in Europe but the budget was more than the club could afford and, as costs mounted, additional borrowing was required. Then, works to the East Stand were carried out unsatisfactorily and further money was needed for remedial work. As a result, by 1990 the club was £12 million in debt and dealings in its shares were suspended by the LONDON STOCK EXCHANGE.

In 1992, Scholar sold his interest to Alan Sugar (chairman of the Amstrad computer company) and Terry Venables (a player and manager). Initially, the duo were seen as a 'dream team' capable of returning Tottenham to its previous heights but Sugar proved unpopular with fans because he allegedly saw his investment primarily as a business deal and Venables, who assumed the role of chief executive, made ill-judged appointments to his administrative staff. One of those appointments was Eddie Ashby, a bankrupt banned from senior posts in public companies. When Sugar found out about Ashby's situation, he sacked both him and Venables. Venables took his case to the High Court and lost (later, in 1996, he and his publisher, Michael Joseph, were ordered by the courts to pay Sugar damages amounting to £100,000 as a result of remarks made in his autobiography). Following a Football Association investigation, Spurs was fined £600,000, banned from the FA Cup for a season and told that 12 points would be deducted from its League total. Sugar protested successfully, the ban was rescinded and the points penalty was reduced to 6 – decisions which pleased supporters even though the fine was more than doubled to £1.5 million. The chairman's actions did little to endear him to fans over the long term and, in 2001, he sold his shares to ENIC, an international sports company with interests in such other major football clubs as FC Basle and Glasgow Rangers. (See also ARSENAL FOOTBALL CLUB; CHARLTON ATHLETIC FOOTBALL CLUB; QUEENS PARK RANGERS FOOTBALL CLUB.)

TOWER BRIDGE

The first and, until the Elizabeth II Bridge was completed at Dartford in 1991, the only BRIDGE to be built downstream of LONDON BRIDGE, Tower Bridge is one of London's best-known landmarks. Designed by architect Horace Jones (who died before the work was completed) and engineer John Wolfe-Barry, it was opened in 1894, linking the commercial and industrial area around the TOWER OF LONDON to the BERMONDSEY DOCKS. Constructed of stone, with a steel skeleton, the bridge has two 200-foot-high Gothic towers, one at each end. Two walkways connect them 142 feet above high tide level. Underneath, bascules (in effect, a double drawbridge) can be raised to allow ships into the upper area of the POOL OF LONDON (this operation was electrified in 1976 but the original steam-powered machinery has been preserved). Suspension spans at the sides connect the towers to the riverbanks. In 1982, a MUSEUM was opened inside the bridge, allowing visitors to inspect the Victorian engines and view the river from the walkways, which have been enclosed in glass. (See also GREATER LONDON AUTHORITY; TRANSPORT.)

TOWER HAMLETS

During the medieval period, the garrison in the TOWER OF LONDON was responsible for the safety of surrounding communities. In 1564, a militia from the villages was formed in order to secure the settlements' defence, then, in 1605, the area north of the RIVER THAMES and east of the CITY OF LONDON was formally named Tower Hamlets for military purposes. A Parliamentary borough with the same title was created in 1832 but secessions brought boundary changes and the unit was dissolved in 1918. However, when local government within the metropolitan area was reorganized in 1965, the traditional nomenclature was resurrected for the LONDON BOROUGH OF TOWER HAMLETS.

TOWER HAMLETS, LONDON BOROUGH OF

The borough lies immediately east of the CITY OF LONDON, covering 8 square miles of the EAST END. It was created in 1965 through the merger of BETHNAL GREEN, POPLAR and STEPNEY, all of which were independent authorities during the LONDON COUNTY COUNCIL's jurisdiction. The great majority of the 196,100 residents (2001) are semi-skilled or unskilled and many have immigrant backgrounds because this is a traditional home for newcomers to Britain; the Bangladeshi community, 65,500 strong, is the largest in Europe and there are sizeable groups of Bengalis, Chinese, Jews, Somalis and West Indians. Since the 1960s, the local economy has undergone radical change, with the closure of the DOCKS leaving large acreages of vacant land and many derelict buildings, which were transformed by the injection of £6 billion of public and private capital. CANARY WHARF, on the ISLE OF DOGS, has derived much of the benefit but the lower valley of the RIVER LEA (traditionally an industrial area) and the western fringe of the borough adjoining the City have also undergone considerable transformation. However, most of the investment has concentrated on office building and the provision of a TRANSPORT infrastructure, which has attracted a skilled workforce who leave for suburban homes every evening. The residents are among the most deprived in the country, with unemployment rates often twice the national average, only 29 per cent of homes owner-occupied (the lowest figure for any English local authority) and levels of educational attainment significantly below those of more

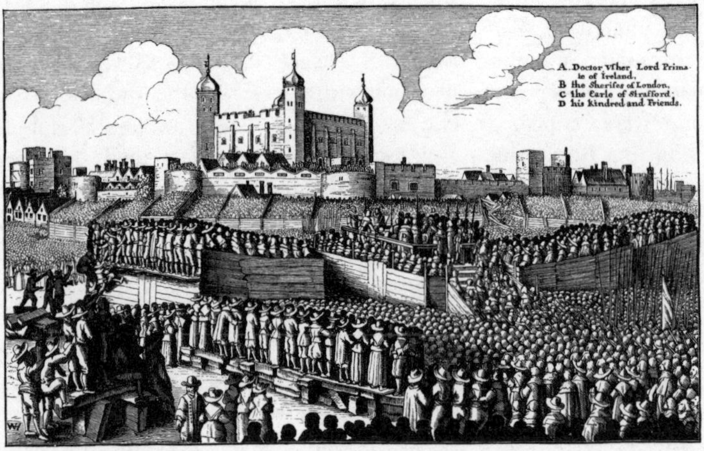

An execution on Tower Hill.

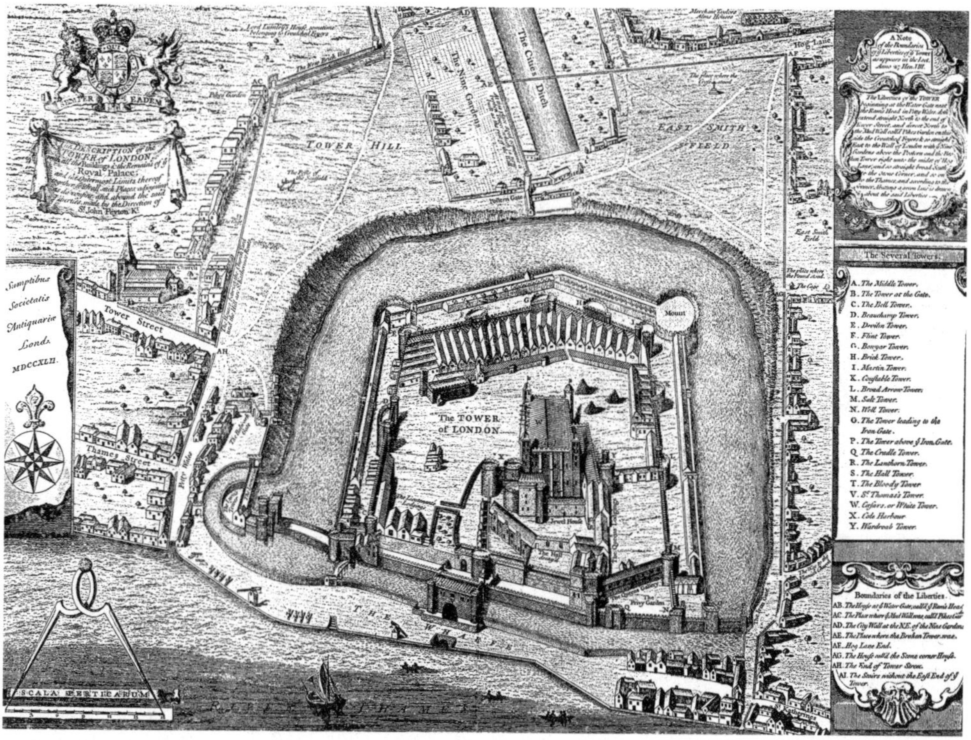

A plan of the Tower of London, *c.* 1597.

affluent suburbs. (See also BETHNAL GREEN; BLACKWALL; BOW; CUBITT TOWN; DOCKLANDS; ETHNIC GROUPS; LIMEHOUSE; MILE END; MILLWALL; SHADWELL; SPITALFIELDS; TOWER HAMLETS; VICTORIA PARK; WAPPING; WHITECHAPEL).

TOWER HILL

Most prisoners in the TOWER OF LONDON who were condemned to death met their fate outside the 'Bloody Tower' on Tower Hill. A total of seventy-five men and women were executed, including Sir Thomas More (Lord Chancellor of England) in 1535, Thomas Cromwell (one of the architects of the English Reformation) in 1540 and William Laud (Archbishop of Canterbury) in 1645. In 1747, so many spectators gathered to see the death of Lord Lovat, a Jacobite supporter, that a wooden grandstand collapsed, killing several of the crowd. A plaque at the western end of the Trinity Square gardens marks the site of the executions, the last of which took place in 1780.

TOWER OF LONDON

Work on the Tower of London was begun by William I in 1078, following the Norman invasion, and finished during the reign of Edward I, more than 200 years later (by which time it covered more than 18 acres and consisted of a series of concentric defences). Originally erected as a fortress designed to provide security for the invaders, dominate access along the RIVER THAMES and impress the conquered people, it has also served as a royal palace, prison, mint, astronomical observatory and record office. The oldest structure is the White Tower (which gets its name from the whitewash applied during the thirteenth cen-

The Tower of London from Visscher's *Panorama of London*, early seventeenth century.

tury). Probably completed about 1100, it has walls 90 feet high and 15 feet thick and is now used as a MUSEUM of arms and armour. Other principal buildings include the Bell Tower (where Thomas More was kept prisoner before his execution in 1535), the Bloody Tower (by tradition, the place where Edward V and his brother, Richard, were murdered on the orders of Richard III in 1483), Traitor's Gate (the principal entrance to the castle from the river during the Middle Ages) and the Chapel of St Peter ad Vincula (under the floor of which lie the bodies of Anne Boleyn and Catherine Howard, the second and fifth wives of Henry VIII). King Stephen, in 1140, was the first monarch to use the place as a royal residence; from then, it was popular with England's kings and queens until James I became more interested in WHITEHALL PALACE.

Involuntarily, many prisoners spent time there, though dungeons and cells were never an integral part of the building. Captives were simply placed in whatever rooms were available (one in the White Tower was only 4 feet square). The first person incarcerated was Ranulf, Bishop of Durham, who was confined in 1101 for selling benefices, but many others followed, including, during the twentieth century, traitor Roger Casement and Nazi fugitive Rudolf Hess. Frequently, supervision of captives was lax so many escaped, including the Welsh baron Roger Mortimer, who was helped to freedom in 1324 by his mistress, Isabella (wife of Edward II), and Jacobite Lord Nithsdale, who disguised himself as a maid and walked out with his wife the day before his scheduled execution in 1716.

For over 600 years, the Tower also housed a menagerie, which provided both amazement and amusement for the royal court. It originated in 1235 with a gift of three leopards from the Holy Roman Emperor to Henry III (leopards adorned the coat of arms of England's Plantagenet rulers). A polar bear (presented by the king of Norway) arrived in 1252 (the CORPORATION OF LONDON was ordered to provide it with a long chain so that it could catch fish in the Thames) and an elephant house was added in 1255. James I enjoyed watching dogs fight lions but later monarchs took less interest in the collection so, by 1822, all that remained was a bear, an elephant and a few birds. In that year, however, Alfred Copps was appointed Royal Keeper and set about rebuilding the menagerie, which numbered fifty-nine species by the time it was transferred to LONDON ZOO in 1839 after lions had attacked some passers-by. The only remaining non-human residents are ravens; there is a legend that when these birds leave the country will fall so the authorities keep their wings clipped rather than tempt fate.

Although the Tower is located within the area of the CITY OF LONDON, it is considered outside the jurisdiction of the LORD MAYOR. A permanent garrison is maintained, headed by a Constable (who always holds the rank of field marshal) and a resident Governor. Queen Victoria restored many parts of the fortress and opened it to the public. During the 1990s, further restoration work was carried out, particularly in the thirteenth-century Wakefield Tower, built by Henry III as a private lodging. (See also BEEFEATER; CEREMONY OF THE KEYS; CROWN JEWELS; DOCKLANDS LIGHT RAILWAY; SIEGE OF SIDNEY STREET; TOWER HILL.)

TOYNBEE HALL

In 1884 Samuel Barnett (vicar at St Jude's Church in WHITECHAPEL) established Toynbee Hall, in Commercial Street, as a centre where he could 'educate citizens in the knowledge of one another' as well as 'provide teaching for those willing to learn and recreation to those who are weary.' These were ambitious goals because the Hall (named after social philosopher Arnold Toynbee) was located in one of London's poorest districts but, aided by UNIVERSITY students who shared his ideals, he provided a programme of educational and cultural activities that spawned nationwide organizations such as the Workers' Educational Association and the Workers' Travel Association. Locally, the art exhibitions he organized led to the establishment of Whitechapel Art Gallery in 1901. During the twentieth century, Barnett's work was continued by resident workers, who included Clement Attlee (Prime Minister from 1945 to 1951), social reformer William Beveridge (architect of Britain's welfare state) and philosopher R.H. Tawney. (See also HAMPSTEAD GARDEN SUBURB.)

TRAFALGAR SQUARE

Trafalgar Square is central London's only large public square, so it has become a place where people congregate for political rallies and national celebrations. Located on a site used to stable royal horses during the sixteenth century and as an army barracks during the seventeenth, it was originally proposed, in 1812, as part of JOHN NASH's urban renewal scheme for CHARING CROSS but not completed (to CHARLES BARRY's plans) until 1840. Nelson's Column, 172 feet 2 inches high, dominates the space. One of London's best-known landmarks, it was designed by William Railton, shaped from Devonshire granite and erected in 1839–42. The 17-foot-high statue of Admiral Horatio Nelson that stands at the top of the column is the work of Edward Hodges Baily. At the base, four bronze reliefs (cast from captured French cannon and finished in 1849) depict scenes from Nelson's victories at Cape St Vincent (1797) and the Nile (1798), his bombardment of Copenhagen (1801) and his death at Trafalgar (1805). The four bronze lions that guard the column were designed by Edwin Landseer, cast by Baron Carlo Marochetti and completed in 1867.

The fountains that form the other main features of the square were originally erected in 1845 but remodelled by Edward Lutyens in 1939 as memorials to two First World War naval commanders – Admiral Earl David Beatty and Admiral Earl John Jellicoe. The oldest of the statues is the bronze of Charles I, which was cast in 1633. In 1649, Parliamentarian authorities ordered brazier John Rivett to destroy it so that the metal could be used for armaments, but he buried it in his garden instead. It was later acquired by Charles II and placed in its present position in 1675: the Royal Stuart Society places a wreath beside it on 30 January, the anniversary of Charles I's execution. At the south-east corner of Trafalgar Square, the smallest police station in Britain is located in a lamp-post. Each December, the people of Norway provide a

Christmas tree for the Square and on New Year's Eve there is a lively party atmosphere. During the year, visitors derive much pleasure from feeding the pigeons that flock on the open ground. On occasion the authorities have tried to limit the practice because of the nuisance caused by the birds but it has survived all efforts to eliminate it although, early in 2001 Bernard Rayner (whose family had sold pigeon seed at a site on the square for half a century) was persuaded to close his booth and accept compensation for loss of livelihood from the GREATER LONDON AUTHORITY. Plans to close the area in front of the NATIONAL GALLERY to traffic and create a pedestrian piazza were announced in 2000; work on the project completed three years later. (See also JUBILEE LINE; ST MARTIN-IN-THE-FIELDS CHURCH, TRAFALGAR SQUARE.)

TRAMS

The first tramcars appeared on London's streets in 1861, when George Francis Train introduced a service between Victoria Street and Bayswater Road. The vehicles were supposed to capitalize on the more limited friction between wheels and metal rails than between wheels and the normal road surface used by horse BUSES, but actually created friction because pedestrians, and other traffic, found the tracks (which projected above the street level) a considerable hazard. In 1869, however, three tramways were built on the outskirts of the city and, with rails sunk into macadamized roads, proved a popular form of travel that was speedily replicated elsewhere. In 1899, most of the network was taken over by the LONDON COUNTY COUNCIL, which, four years later, began an extensive development programme. The local authority found the venture highly profitable, despite a low-fare policy, but failed to invest either in track or in vehicles so, when all public transport was handed over to the London Passenger Transport Board (see LONDON TRANSPORT) in 1933, it seemed more economical to replace the 2,500 trams with trolleybuses, which used overhead power lines. Also, from 1945, diesel engine buses became increasingly popular so, by the end of 1952, the trams had been phased out. (See also ROYAL COMMISSION ON LONDON TRAFFIC (1903–05); YERKES, CHARLES TYSON.)

TRANSPORT

The earliest forms of transport in the London area were probably by water along the RIVER THAMES and by horse along the marshy shores. Until comparatively recently, the river was an important thoroughfare. Archaeological evidence shows that the Romans and Saxons used it extensively (the remains of a Roman ship were discovered during excavation for the site of COUNTY HALL, for example) then, during the medieval period, DOCKS developed for sailing ships as trading contacts expanded and ferries conveyed travellers (and even wagons) across the water. The horse dominated land travel though the poor had little option but to walk. Public transport along city streets was introduced during the late sixteenth century with the arrival of the hackney cab, named from the French *haquenée* (meaning 'a slow moving old nag'). The hackney was an exclusive way of getting around – two horses drew a carriage, which contained two seats, one of which was occupied by the driver – but it quickly became popular, threatening the incomes of those who made their living moving people by boat.

In 1711, the sedan chair provided a further alternative, favoured by those who did not want to be exposed to the elements as they made their way from a cab to their home. Sedans survived for over a century (there are reports of their use in HAMPSTEAD and MAYFAIR during the 1830s and 1840s) but their sedate rate of progress made them less attractive as the city spread. Wealthy Londoners preferred coaches, some maintaining their own, others hiring from local stables (the hire business survived until the 1920s). Additionally, public stagecoaches offered a means of getting around the city during the late eighteenth and early nineteenth centuries. Carriages normally carried six people in relative comfort inside, with an additional three on top, but, from 1829, were challenged by the horse-drawn omnibus (which could carry up to eighteen passengers).

The foundations of the modern mass transit system were laid from 1836, with the development of the RAILWAY network. The LONDON UNDERGROUND extended its route system from 1863, then, in 1897, the first motorized BUSES appeared, making commuting a way of life by the turn of the century. The private car revolutionized movement during the twentieth century, with over 1.1 million arriving in central London each day by the 1990s, causing congestion in a road system designed for the horse and cart age. Also, the growth of air travel following the opening of HOUNSLOW aerodrome in 1919 (and particularly after the end of the Second World War) attracted increasing numbers of tourists from throughout the world. In the modern city, public transit systems remain extremely important, primarily because of the lack of parking facilities for motorists and the rush-hour traffic jams that slow drivers' journeys. Every weekday, LONDON TRANSPORT'S UNDERGROUND network carries 2.5 million passengers in 470 trains along 254 miles of track and the buses move a further 1.2 million. (See also ABERCROMBIE PLAN (1943–44); AIRPORTS; ARCHWAY; BLACKFRIARS; BRIDGES; CANNON STREET STATION; CONGESTION CHARGES; DOCKLANDS LIGHT RAILWAY; DRAIN, THE; EGHAM; ENFIELD; FINSBURY PARK; GRAND UNION CANAL; GREATER LONDON DEVELOPMENT PLAN; HACKNEY CABS; LONDON PLAN; LONDON REGIONAL PASSENGERS' COMMITTEE (LRPC); M25 MOTORWAY; MAYOR OF LONDON; PICK, FRANK; POOL OF LONDON; PORT OF LONDON AUTHORITY (PLA); REGENT'S CANAL; ROYAL COMMISSION ON LONDON TRAFFIC (1903–05); TAXIS; TRAMS; TUBE; TURNPIKES; VICTORIA; WANDSWORTH; WATERLOO; YERKES, CHARLES TYSON.)

TRANSPORT FOR LONDON

See LONDON TRANSPORT (LT).

TREASURY BUILDINGS

The British government's principal finance officers work in the Treasury Buildings on the western side of WHITEHALL. Originally erected in 1845 (to designs by CHARLES BARRY) on a site previously occupied by WHITEHALL PALACE's cock-fighting pit, the offices were redesigned in 1960–4 (when construction work revealed the walls of the Tudor palace's tennis courts). An underground passage (known as Cockpit Alley) runs beneath the property, linking DOWNING STREET with HORSE GUARDS PARADE, but is closed for security reasons.

TRINITY HOUSE

From Trinity Square, near the TOWER OF LONDON, Trinity House manages the lighthouses along the coastlines of England, Wales and the Channel Islands. The organization has its origins in the DEPTFORD Guild of Mariners, which, in 1514, was granted a royal charter authorizing it to provide pilotage on the RIVER THAMES. The charter was renewed in 1547, when the guild was renamed The Corporation of Trinity House on Deptford Strand, and again in 1553, 1558, 1604 and 1685 (the last of these documents, drafted by SAMUEL PEPYS, is the basis of Trinity House's modern responsibilities). The first lighthouse was built at Lowestoft (the easternmost point in England) in 1609 and the first light vessel anchored in The Nore (an area of the Thames estuary some 4 miles south-east of Shoeburyness) in 1732. Control of all English and Welsh lighthouses was assumed in 1836. In addition, the corporation has responsibility for providing navigation aids such as buoys and beacons as well as for making assistance available to sailors suffering financial hardship. Its policies are determined by a board consisting of Elder Brethren (that is, senior members of the corporation) and representatives of commercial interests. The lighthouse service has a separate committee.

TROOPING THE COLOUR

One of the most popular of London's annual ceremonies, the Trooping of the Colour takes place at HORSE GUARDS PARADE to honour the monarch on his or her official birthday in early June. It has its roots in the practice of medieval military commanders, who paraded banners in front of their armies before battle, so that soldiers would be familiar with the colours that would be their rallying point, and was first held as a formal event in 1755. One of the five regiments of Foot Guards in the HOUSEHOLD DIVISION is the focus of the parade, with the monarch (who wears the uniform of that regiment) taking the salute. The other regiments and the Household Cavalry, with their massed bands, add bustle and music. Over 1,400 infantrymen and 200 mounted horsemen participate, demonstrating intricate and precise marching manoeuvres. Demand for seats vastly exceeds supply, so tickets for the event are allocated by ballot; unsuccessful applicants line THE MALL to watch the procession to and from Horse Guards.

TUBE

Although the term 'Tube' is usually used loosely as a synonym for the whole of the LONDON UNDERGROUND system, it is most properly applied to the 85 miles of deep track on the central city sections of the WATERLOO AND CITY, BAKERLOO, CENTRAL, JUBILEE, NORTHERN, PICCADILLY and VICTORIA LINES. The name was first applied to the City and South London RAILWAY, which opened in 1890 with services from King William Street (near the BANK OF ENGLAND) to STOCKWELL (south of the RIVER THAMES). Designed by James Greathead, it incorporated tubular tunnels built 40 feet under the ground (earlier track had been constructed using a 'cut and cover' method, which simply involved digging up a road, laying track, providing roofing and then replacing the street). Modern tube trains travel at an average depth of 80 feet but reach over 221 feet on the Northern Line at Holly Bush Hill and HAMPSTEAD. Hampstead, 192 feet at its lowest point, is the deepest station. (See also ROYAL COMMISSION ON LONDON TRAFFIC (1903–05); YERKES, CHARLES TYSON.)

TUFNELL PARK

Tufnell Park lies east of KENTISH TOWN some 3 miles north of CHARING CROSS, taking its name from the Tufnells, a brewing family who owned large estates in the area. In the years prior to the Industrial Revolution, the land supplied milk and other dairy products to London's growing population but from the second quarter of the nineteenth century much of the pasture was used for villa developments. Initially, these were sold to well-to-do families. By 1900, however, many of the wealthy had left, leaving homes that were subdivided for poorer occupiers. In 1965, the suburb was incorporated within the LONDON BOROUGH OF ISLINGTON, which introduced several local authority housing projects but retained the essentially Victorian character of the area.

TULSE HILL

A residential suburb located south of BRIXTON, Tulse Hill takes its name from the Tulse family, which owned estates in the area during the seventeenth century (Sir Henry was LORD MAYOR of London in 1683). By 1800, much of the land was controlled by Dr Thomas Edwards, who saw potential for urban development as city residents sought homes with access to the countryside. Plots were leased to wealthy business and professional people, who built large residences, which could house an entourage of servants as well as members of the family, and in 1856 Holy Trinity Church, designed by T.D. Barry, was completed. However, such an exclusive estate inevitably attracted growth on its fringes (a growth hastened by the construction of a RAILWAY station in 1869), so, by the end of the nineteenth century, many of the richer occupants were moving farther out to sites that retained some semblance of rural life and provided greater privacy. Since then, apartment blocks have replaced several of the older properties, particularly in the north of the area. Tulse Hill was incorporated within the LONDON BOROUGH OF LAMBETH in 1965.

TURNPIKES

By the late eighteenth century, many roads in and around London (as elsewhere in England) were in a state of disrepair. Legally, parishes were responsible for their upkeep but few authorities considered the task important so Parliament eventually passed a series of acts creating Turnpike Trusts, which were empowered to charge tolls to travellers using the routeways under their control, with the funds invested in highway maintenance. These bodies undoubtedly wrought considerable improvement (building bridges and raising the standard of drainage, for example) but, over the years, much of the income was siphoned into the pockets of members rather than used for upkeep. Profits were high and the potential for fraud was considerable so trusts, which could be bought and sold, were attractive commodities even though some forms of traffic (such as soldiers in uniform and ministers carrying out parish duties) were exempt from payment. Those at ELEPHANT AND CASTLE, MILE END Road, Tottenham Court Road, HYDE PARK CORNER, ISLINGTON and TYBURN proved particularly lucrative but users complained bitterly about the prices charged and, from 1864, they were phased out. The gates at Mile End, London's last major turnpike, were removed in 1866, although some smaller trusts survived into the twentieth century.

TWICKENHAM

Modern Twickenham is a predominantly residential suburb 10 miles south-west of CHARING CROSS. Until the mid-nineteenth century, it was a village located well outside London with an economy based largely on agriculture, fishing and ferry services for travellers requiring transport across the RIVER THAMES. Wealthy courtiers built grand mansions on their estates (see, for example, MARBLE HILL HOUSE) and there was something of a tourist trade because steamers from the city carried parties upriver for picnics on Eel Pie Island (CHARLES DICKENS describes a typical outing in *Nicholas Nickleby*, published in 1839). In 1848 however, the Windsor, Staines and South-Western RAILWAY laid track through Twickenham to RICHMOND and Windsor. The London and South-Western Railway added lines to KINGSTON in 1863 and the District Railway to HOUNSLOW in 1883 (see DISTRICT LINE), making the area's open spaces attractive to builders providing homes for commuters keen to work in central London but raise families near the countryside. In addition, some 17 acres were acquired by the RUGBY Football Union for its headquarters in 1907 (England plays its home international matches at the stadium, which now has a capacity of 57,400 spectators). Also, in 1933, a BRIDGE (the first in Britain to use three-hinged reinforced concrete arches) was built to carry the Great Chertsey Road across the Thames to Richmond. In spite of the surge of development during the late nineteenth and early twentieth centuries, much of the older property survived, particularly towards the south of the area. The church of St Mary the Virgin was built in 1714–5 but incorporates elements of previous places of worship on the site, including the west tower, which dates from the fourteenth century. Alexander Pope, who lived in Twickenham from 1719 to 1744, was buried in the church and the graveyard contains a memorial to Thomas Twining, founder of the firm of tea merchants. Alfred Lord Tennyson and Walter de la Mare had homes in Montpelier Row, a brick terrace erected as a speculative development in 1720, and, in 1747–91, STRAWBERRY HILL (now occupied by

An execution at Tyburn.

St Mary's College) was converted from a cottage to a Gothic castle by Horace Walpole.

The origins of Twickenham's name are unclear, though most writers agree that it has its roots in Old English. Some believe that it is derived from *Twicca* (an Anglo-Saxon personal name) and *ham* (which has several meanings, one of which is 'land within a river meander'). Others claim that the first element comes from *twice*, which means 'a fork in a river'. (See also HARLEQUINS RUGBY FOOTBALL CLUB; RICHMOND UPON THAMES, LONDON BOROUGH OF.)

TYBURN

From 1388 until 1783, public executions were carried out at Tyburn (the name is taken from a small stream that ran nearby), now the site of Marble Arch. These events were public holidays (the authorities believed that watching men being hanged would deter members of the audience from committing crimes), so crowds of up to 200,000 people congregated around the gallows. Condemned prisoners dressed for the occasion, travelling from NEWGATE PRISON in an open cart but stopping at ST GILES-IN-THE-FIELDS CHURCH for a last mug of ale and at St Sepulchre Church, HOLBORN, (where the bellman asked citizens to pray for the soul of the felons). After the death, the hangman claimed the victim's clothes and onlookers pressed forward to touch the corpse in the belief that it had the power to cure illnesses. The site of the gallows (which was sometimes known as Tyburn Tree) is marked by a stone in the traffic island at the junction of Bayswater Road and Edgware Road. Those dispatched included Perkin Warbeck (who claimed he was heir to the English throne and mounted two invasions to prove his case but was put to death in 1499), Oliver Plunket (who died in 1681, the last Englishman to be martyred for his religious convictions) and highwayman Jack Sheppard (1714). After Charles II was restored in 1660, the bodies of Oliver Cromwell and two of his supporters were exhumed from their graves, hanged at Tyburn, then beheaded and buried beneath the gallows. (See also CHARTERHOUSE; KETCH, JACK.)

U

UNDERGROUND

See LONDON UNDERGROUND.

UNDERGROUND ELECTRIC RAILWAYS COMPANY OF LONDON

See CHARLES TYSON YERKES.

UNIVERSITIES

The first centre of higher EDUCATION in London was University College, founded in 1826 by poet Thomas Campbell and other religious non-comformists who wanted to provide classes for students barred from Oxford and Cambridge, which only admitted members of the Church of England. The Anglicans responded in 1828 by creating King's College then, in 1836, the Whig government established a University of London, with a charter in which William IV declared that it was a duty of his royal office 'to hold forth to all classes and denominations of his faithful subjects an encouragement for pursuing a regular and liberal course of education.' University College, King's College and other institutions presented male students for examination by the new body from 1838 but women were unable to graduate for a further forty years. Under the terms of the University of London Act (1898) the institution, originally based in SOMERSET HOUSE but now in Malet Street, is governed by a senate consisting of fifty-five members.

A second university was founded in 1962 when Brunel College of Advanced Technology (which took its name from ISAMBARD KINGDOM BRUNEL) was renamed Brunel University and allowed to award its own degrees. Four years later, City University (with particular strengths in the arts, business studies and the social sciences) was formed around Northampton Polytechnic. At the same time, the Labour government amalgamated groups of technical colleges to create nine polytechnics designed to specialize in vocational subjects and award degrees through a Council for National Academic Awards. Under the terms of the Further and Higher Education Act of 1992, these institutions were allowed to call themselves universities and confer their own degrees so, by the end of the decade, London had fourteen independent universities (including the London Business School and the ROYAL COLLEGE OF ART). Together they taught some 265,000 students. The largest was the University of London, where 93,600 undergraduates and postgraduates attended forty-seven colleges as disparate as the LONDON SCHOOL OF ECONOMICS AND POLITICAL SCIENCE, the COURTAULD INSTITUTE OF ART and the School of Slavonic Studies. In 2002, London Guildhall University and the University of North London merged to become London Metropolitan University. (See also AVERY HILL; BARNET, LONDON BOROUGH OF; BLOOMSBURY;

CUSTOM HOUSE; DEPTFORD; GREAT ORMOND STREET HOSPITAL FOR SICK CHILDREN; KINGSTON UPON THAMES, ROYAL BOROUGH OF; LORD MAYOR; MOORGATE; NEW CROSS; ROTHERHITHE; ROYAL ARSENAL; ROYAL COLLEGE OF SURGEONS OF ENGLAND; ROYAL NAVAL COLLEGE; RUSSELL SQUARE; UXBRIDGE.)

UNIVERSITY BOAT RACE

In 1829 crews from Oxford and Cambridge Universities held a race along the RIVER THAMES from Hambledon Lock to Henley (Oxford won). Sixteen years later, the event was held over a course of 4 miles 374 yards from PUTNEY to MORTLAKE, a route used ever since. The race became an annual competition in 1856, attracting crowds of onlookers. While interest declined in the post-war years, more recently the number of spectators has increased as a result of sponsorship and the higher profile of rowing generally through the Olympic successes of Steve Redgrave and Matthew Pinsent. In 1998, Cambridge broke the course record (with its heaviest crew ever) in a time of 16 minutes 19 seconds. By 2003, that university had seventy-seven wins, six more than Oxford. The 1912 race was the most sensational because both eights sank.

UNIVERSITY COLLEGE HOSPITAL

In 1834, University College (which had been founded eight years earlier), established a healthcare unit called the North London Hospital. The name was changed to University College Hospital (UCH) in 1837 and in 1846 a new facility was opened following a public appeal for funds. In 1906, a major rebuilding was completed, funded by furniture salesman Sir John Blundell Maple (who was greatly impressed by the cruciform plan of the wards, a layout designed to improve drainage, lighting and ventilation) and, during the twentieth century, the hospital expanded through the construction of additional space (such as a wing for private patients in 1937 and an out-patient department in 1970) and by the opening of specialist units (the Hospital for Tropical Diseases became part of University College Hospital in 1948, for instance). The hospital's reputation has been greatly enhanced by its surgeons, including Robert Liston (who, in 1846, carried out the first British operation to use ether), Joseph Lister (who pioneered the use of antiseptics from 1867), neurologist Sir William Gowers and Sir Rickman Godlee (Lister's nephew and the first man to remove a cerebral tumour). In 1994, UCH merged with the MIDDLESEX HOSPITAL in a National Health Service Trust, which has since expanded to include the Eastman Dental Hospital, the Elizabeth Garrett Anderson and Obstetric Hospital, the Heart Hospital, the National Hospital For Neurology and Neurosurgery, and the Royal London Homoeopathic Hospital, making it one of the largest in the country. The Trust is building a new £422 million, 725-bed hospital in Euston Road so that many of its widely spread components can be brought under a single roof.

UXBRIDGE

Uxbridge is the commercial heart of the LONDON BOROUGH OF HILLINGDON. Probably settled in Saxon times (the name is said to derive from a tribe known as the Wixan), it was an established MARKET centre by the twelfth century, building up a considerable trade in arable crops during the Middle Ages. Flour mills were built to the west of the settlement using streams and rivers as a source of water power and beginning a process of industrialization enhanced by the opening of the Grand Junction Canal, which linked the community to PADDINGTON in 1801 and to the Midlands in 1805. The arrival of the Great Western RAILWAY in 1838 promoted further development, encouraging the establishment of market gardens supplying fresh fruit, vegetables and flowers to London's rapidly growing urban population. During the twentieth century the creation of additional TRANSPORT links (including the opening of HEATHROW AIRPORT in 1946) attracted international as well as British businesses, including light manufacturing interests (such as makers of precision instruments) and offices. Brunel UNIVERSITY (named after ISAMBARD KINGDOM BRUNEL, the Great Western's engineer) was erected on a site south of the town in 1966–7, building on local skills by concentrating on engineering disciplines and developing strong research links with the incoming firms. As the town expanded, much open space made way for buildings (the university is located on 150 acres of former horticultural land, for example) and many of the older properties were demolished to facilitate the construction of a new civic centre, designed by Robert Matthew, Johnson-Marshall and Partners, which opened in 1979. However, part of High Street, with structures dating from the late fifteenth century, is protected by conservation area legislation and Treaty House, where Parliamentary and Royalist factions unsuccessfully attempted to resolve their differences in 1645, still stands (panelling taken from the house in 1929 to line walls in New York's Empire State Building was returned in 1955, as a gift to Elizabeth II, and reinstalled). (See also METROPOLITAN LINE; PICCADILLY LINE.)

V

VAUXHALL

Although it is now an urban area in the north of the LONDON BOROUGH OF LAMBETH, Vauxhall retained all the characteristics of a village until the beginning of the nineteenth century. The area derives its name from an early thirteenth-century mansion built by Falkes de Breauté and variously known as Fulke's Hall, Faukeshall or Foxhall. Although it was a popular location for the country homes of the rich (Sir Noel Caron, English Ambassador to Holland, built a mansion there in the early sixteenth century, for example), its main attraction from about 1660 until 1859 was the New Spring Garden (renamed Vauxhall Gardens in 1785), which was a major recreational resource for city residents. SAMUEL PEPYS admired the facilities, writing on 18 May 1667 of the pleasure of listening to 'the nightingales and other birds, and here fiddles and there a harp, and here a jews trump, and here laughing.' At night, the walkways were lit by hundreds of lights. Although they were accessible only by river until 1750, the gardens became very fashionable; Frederick, Prince of Wales, attended a ball on the site in 1732, SAMUEL JOHNSON and JAMES BOSWELL were frequent visitors, and a grand fête was held to celebrate the Duke of Wellington's victory over the French at Vitoria (Spain) in 1813.

In 1816, the opening of a BRIDGE to PIMLICO (the first iron structure across the RIVER THAMES in London) added to the traffic entering the little settlement and encouraged development, as did the construction of the terminus of the London and Southampton Railway in 1838 and the building of THE OVAL as the headquarters of the Surrey County Cricket Club during the 1840s. Then, in 1859, Vauxhall Gardens was closed, despite various attempts to resuscitate them after the owners went bankrupt in 1840, and the site was built over. With the demise of the gardens the area lost its social prestige and, during the second half of the nineteenth century, became one of the less affluent parts of the city as the working-class poor crowded in, attempting to find jobs at the railway depot and with the host of small industries – such as glove-making, chemical production and laundering – that sprang up nearby (St Peter's Church, designed by John Loughborough Pearson, one of the most distinguished church architects of the time, was built at Kennington Lane in 1863–4 specifically to cater to these largely illiterate and lowly paid immigrants).

From 1895 to 1906, the Thames bridge was replaced by a structure with five steel arches and granite piers, designed by Alexander Binnie, in order to improve transport but, during the twentieth century, the area retained its reputation as one of the more rundown parts of London, with a mixture of housing and commercial concerns. However, the transfer of

Vauxhall Gardens, 1751.

COVENT GARDEN market to NINE ELMS, at the western edge of Vauxhall, has led to some regeneration of industrial activity.

VICTORIA

The Victoria area, 1¼ miles south-west of CHARING CROSS in the CITY OF WESTMINSTER, is one of London's major termini for both rail and road TRANSPORT. Until the early nineteenth century, it was an extensive marsh forming the north bank of the RIVER THAMES but, in 1816, when Vauxhall Bridge was opened to provide a connection between WESTMINSTER and LAMBETH, builders grasped the opportunity to provide homes along the approach road. The Grosvenor Canal, originally built in 1725, was upgraded in the 1820s, encouraging industrial concerns (such as engineering works) to locate alongside, then, two decades later, THOMAS CUBITT developed land to the south. By 1851, slums were being cleared to make way for Victoria Street (named after Queen Victoria), which linked the area to the HOUSES OF PARLIAMENT (see PALACE OF WESTMINSTER), encouraging the appropriately named American businessman, George Train, to lay TRAM lines along it.

In 1860, the London, Brighton and South Coast RAILWAY built the Grosvenor Bridge (the first rail BRIDGE over the Thames in London) to bring the line from PIMLICO to the rapidly expanding WEST END and constructed a new station at the western end of Victoria Street. At the same time, the London, Chatham and Dover Railway opened an adjacent terminus (which, within weeks, became the point at which most travellers from Europe entered the city). Shortly afterwards the LONDON UNDERGROUND arrived and, inevitably, HOTELS, PUBLIC HOUSES, cafeterias, restaurants and shops were established to serve the transient clientele as the area flourished.

Development during the twentieth century further improved transport with the two railway termini functioning as a single unit from 1921 and a coach station built only 400 yards away. Also, the VICTORIA LINE, central London's first TUBE route since 1907, was tunnelled from BRIXTON to WALTHAMSTOW in 1962–71, intersecting the CIRCLE and DISTRICT LINES at Victoria, which is now one of the busiest stations in the system with over 86 million passengers every year.

In the process of change, many of the nineteenth-century buildings were swept away. Few remain along the route to VAUXHALL Bridge, most of the original Victoria Street is gone (including the Stag BREWERY, which was demolished in 1959, after 318 years in the same location, to make way for a twenty-seven-storey office block) and the shops in front of WESTMINSTER CATHEDRAL have been knocked down to create the open space of a piazza. (See also BAZALGETTE, JOSEPH WILLIAM; BUSES.)

VICTORIA AND ALBERT MUSEUM (V&A)

Part of a complex of MUSEUMS, learned societies and educational institutions in the BROMPTON area of south KENSINGTON (see, for example, NATURAL HISTORY MUSEUM, ROYAL COLLEGE OF ART, ROYAL GEOGRAPHICAL SOCIETY, SCIENCE MUSEUM), the V&A concentrates on the fine and applied arts of all periods and societies. It was founded in 1857 when the collections of the School of Design (created in 1837) and the Museum of Manufactures (established in 1852) were merged. Initially, exhibits were housed in wooden sheds and an enormous cast-iron and glass structure, built by William Cubitt, which was quickly christened 'the Brompton Boilers' (see BETHNAL GREEN MUSEUM OF CHILDHOOD). As acquisitions accumulated, through purchase and donation, the V&A became, in the words of former director Roy Strong, 'an extremely capacious handbag' exhibiting an eclectic range of artefacts with no obvious thematic link. Paintings (including a fine collection of works by British artists, donated by textile manufacturer John Sheepshanks in 1857) competed for space with the National Art Library (opened in 1884), the contents of the India Museum (transferred from the India Office) and individual items such as Raphael's Tapestry Cartoons (lent by Queen Victoria).

As space ran out, a competition, held to choose plans for new exhibition galleries, was won by Aston Webb (who was responsible for the Natural History Museum, erected in 1881). The foundation stone of the present 12-acre building, constructed to his designs, was laid in 1899 by Queen Victoria (performing the last major public engagement of her reign), but the flamboyant terracotta-brick edifice, with its central tower shaped to resemble an imperial crown, was not completed until 1909. During the twentieth century, the collection continued to grow (the Nehru Gallery of Indian Art was opened in 1990, for example), so the V&A authorities have attempted to solve display problems by dispersing material to other sites, such as the Museum of Childhood at Bethnal Green, the Wellington Museum (see HYDE PARK CORNER) and the THEATRE MUSEUM in COVENT GARDEN. However, the Kensington site still houses an enormous variety of artwork, with particular strengths in the early medieval, Gothic and Renaissance periods; regional emphases on India and the Far East; and thematic concentrations on continental and decorative arts prior to 1825, English furniture and decorative arts from 1500 to 1860, and portrait miniatures and costumes.

In 1988, the museum's new director, Elizabeth Esteve-Coll, incurred the wrath of traditionalists when she announced plans to make the institution more accessible to the public. Sir John Pope-Hennessey, one of her predecessors, claimed that proposals to mount more exhibitions focusing on popular culture and employ advertising agents who marketed the place as 'An ace café with quite a nice museum attached' were vulgar. A restructuring of senior staff responsibilities caused further problems, leading to job losses and serious internal tensions. However, visitor numbers increased markedly, particularly among young people, who numbered only 10,000 in 1990 but totalled 100,000 in 1994. Alan Borg, appointed to succeed Esteve-Coll in 1995, introduced further changes to operating practices (including imposition of admission charges and a reduction in the number of volunteer helpers) and, in 1998, announced plans for a major refurbishment of the British Galleries. Some 950,000 people now tour the exhibits every year. (See also HAM HOUSE.)

VICTORIA LINE

When the Victoria Line opened in the late 1960s, it was the first new UNDERGROUND RAILWAY to serve central London for over sixty years. Even before the outbreak of the Second World War, it was clear that peak hour bus and train services in the inner city were under strain and that VICTORIA and CHARING CROSS stations, main line railway termini at the southern fringe of the area, required better connections to KING'S CROSS and EUSTON stations further north. The new route was finalized in 1953, construction began in 1962, the first services ran between WALTHAMSTOW Central and HIGHBURY and ISLINGTON in 1968, and the line was extended south to BRIXTON in 1971. The tunnelling was relatively straightforward but construction of interchanges (particularly at the busy OXFORD CIRCUS station) was more complex, adding to the time taken to complete the work (connections can be made with other UNDERGROUND lines at nine of the sixteen Victoria Line stations). Provision of facilities for maintaining trains proved to be a problem because of lack of land on which to build a depot: as a result, an engineering base was erected beside Northumberland PARK main line station and connected, by two special tubes, to Seven Sisters underground station. In 2003, responsibility for the line's infrastructure was franchised to Metronet, a consortium of private businesses, but LONDON UNDERGROUND remains responsible for providing the services.

VICTORIA PARK

During the middle years of the nineteenth century, central and local authorities were placed under increasing pressure to alleviate social conditions in the working-class areas of London by providing public PARKS. In 1842, Robert Peel's Conservative government used the funds acquired through the lease of LANCASTER HOUSE to buy 290 acres of land in the EAST END, including the former site of STEPNEY Manor House. James Pennethorne (who also designed BATTERSEA PARK) was employed to landscape the area, which opened in 1845 as Victoria Park. Lakes were added the following year and an open-air swimming pool built in 1936. The park, which lies on the boundary of the LONDON BOROUGH OF HACKNEY and the LONDON BOROUGH OF TOWER HAMLETS, has frequently been used for mass demonstrations designed to attract support from the manual workers who dominate the eastern side of the city (as early as 1848, for example, a crowd of over 1,000 gathered to support the Chartist claims for universal adult male suffrage).

W

WALBROOK

The Walbrook rose in FINSBURY and flowed south to the RIVER THAMES, providing a WATER SUPPLY for the Roman occupants of LONDINIUM, who built the TEMPLE OF MITHRAS nearby. Following the Norman Conquest of England in 1066, several Christian churches were erected close to the stream, notably ST STEPHEN's (founded before 1096), St Mildred's (first mentioned in documents dating from 1175) and St Margaret's (built by 1197), all of which were destroyed during the GREAT FIRE of 1666 and re-erected to designs prepared by CHRISTOPHER WREN. However, the watercourse was only about 14 feet wide, too narrow for navigation and too easily polluted by refuse as the CITY OF LONDON expanded. As a result, it was covered over in 1440. A street of the same name, running from MANSION HOUSE to CANNON STREET STATION, follows the former east bank.

WALLACE COLLECTION

During the late eighteenth and nineteenth centuries, the Seymour-Conway family (Marquesses of Hertford) amassed a fine private collection of European art. The initial works were acquired by the first marquess, patron of Joshua Reynolds (1723–92) and Allan Ramsay (1713–1834). His son added several family portraits and his grandson (a flamboyant socialite on whom William Thackeray modelled the sinister Marquis de Steyne in *Vanity Fair*, published in 1848) contributed a series of Dutch cabinet paintings as well as *Perseus and Andromeda* by Titian (*c.* 1488–1576), and portraits by Anthony Van Dyck (1599–1641) and Thomas Gainsborough (1727–88). The fourth marquess was a recluse, who lived at the Château Bagatelle in the Bois de Boulogne, outside Paris, and devoted himself entirely to his collection, concentrating on French art at a time when it was very unfashionable. With the help of Richard, his illegitimate son (the product of a relationship with Mrs Agnes Jackson), he purchased canvasses by François Boucher (1703–70), Jean-Honoré Fragonard (1732–1806) and Antoine Watteau (1684–1721), along with several seventeenth-century Dutch masterpieces (including Frans Hals' *Laughing Cavalier*, painted in 1624) and select pieces of Sèvres china. Richard (who, in 1842, adopted Wallace, his mother's maiden name, as his own surname) inherited the entire collection, adding Renaissance gold, armour and Italian majolica. When he died in 1890 (having been knighted in recognition of his services to British nationals living in Paris during the Franco-Prussian War in 1870–1), the works passed to his wife, Julie, who (in accordance with her husband's wishes) bequeathed them to the nation in 1897. The collection was opened to the public three years later at Hertford House, the Wallaces' eighteenth-century home in Manchester Square. In 2000, the rooms were remodelled by American architect Rick Mather.

WALTHAM FOREST, LONDON BOROUGH OF

Waltham Forest, like the other LONDON BOROUGHS, was created in 1965, when the LONDON COUNTY COUNCIL was dissolved and replaced by a new structure of local government. In the process CHINGFORD, LEYTON and WALTHAMSTOW – all previously part of the County of Essex – were grouped together to form Waltham Forest, which took its name from the woodlands that once covered the area. Its 15 square miles are dominated by housing, though there is considerable open space in the north of the authority's territory. Chingford is the most affluent community, with relatively high proportions of clerical and skilled manual workers who own their own homes. However, some two-thirds of the 218,300 population (2001) live in Leyton and Walthamstow, which occupy the southern half of the borough. There, the workforce is less highly trained, more likely to live in rented properties and composed, to a considerable extent, of people from ethnic minorities (Waltham Forest has large Caribbean and Pakistani communities, each of which accounts for about 8 per cent of the resident population). Unemployment is higher than the OUTER LONDON average and concentrated among the young and non-white groups. (See also LEYTONSTONE.)

WALTHAMSTOW

The hamlet of Walthamstow developed as a farming community about 7 miles north-east of CHARING CROSS on the road from the CITY OF LONDON to Waltham Abbey. Settlement dates from the Bronze Age but, although wealthy incomers were attracted from about 1500 (George Monoux, LORD MAYOR of London in 1514, endowed a school, for example), there was little growth until the Industrial Revolution transformed the local and national economies during the nineteenth century. The marshes to the west were flooded to create reservoirs sufficient to supply water to expanding commercial interests as well as to meet domestic demands (see WATER SUPPLY). The arrival of the RAILWAYS led to speculative housing developments and entrepreneurs took advantage of the new technologies to establish manufacturing plants (the Brewer car – the first British automobile to use the internal combustion engine – was built in Walthamstow in 1892–5). Population increased as workers moved to jobs and commuters took advantage of houses less expensive than those in the increasingly congested city centre. Improved road access in 1930 fuelled construction (particularly in the north of the area) and local authority building added to the provision of homes. In the process, many of the older properties were destroyed but, following Walthamstow's incorporation within the LONDON BOROUGH OF WALTHAM FOREST in 1965, conservation orders were placed on several of those that remained (including the chapel at Forest Road School, which has stained-glass windows designed by the local craftsman and socialist William Morris in 1875–80). Walthamstow still has one of the largest street markets in the capital, and the BBC soap opera *EastEnders* is based on the area ('Walford' being a combination of Walthamstow and ILFORD, in the neighbouring LONDON BOROUGH OF REDBRIDGE). The Walthamstow Stadium, to the north of the area close to Chingford Road, is one of the largest greyhound racing venues in the country, holding up to 5,000 spectators. It was established in 1933 by William Chandler (who had previously earned an illegal living as a bookmaker) and is still run by his family. The area's name may be derived from the Old English *wilcuma* and *stow*, meaning 'a welcoming place' or 'the holy place of a woman called Wilcuma', (See also PARKS; VICTORIA LINE; WILLIAM MORRIS GALLERY.)

WALWORTH

A working-class, inner-city residential area, Walworth lies 2 miles south-east of CHARING CROSS. Archaeological evidence suggests that it was settled in prehistoric times but the population was low until, in the late eighteenth and early nineteenth centuries, the construction of BRIDGES over the RIVER THAMES allowed Londoners to move south of the river to the edge of the countryside, where farmers grew fruit and vegetables for the urban market. By 1850, the area had developed a reputation as a place for recreation, partly due to the establishment (during the 1830s and 1840s) of the Surrey ZOOLOGICAL GARDENS, which offered tableaux of famous military engagements, fireworks displays and floral displays, as well as animals, to fascinate its visitors. However, the zoo closed in 1855 and in 1877 its site was sold to developers as more and more people crowded into the area. Census reports show that Walworth had 14,800 residents in 1801 but 122,200 a century later, most of them forced out of the CITY OF LONDON as offices, RAILWAY stations, warehouses and banks vied for space there. Churches and philanthropic organizations attempted to alleviate the worst effects of the poverty but there was little impact until after the Second World War. Because Walworth was close to the DOCKS, German bombing destroyed many buildings during the BLITZ, allowing planners to introduce green space at locations such as Burgess PARK and undertake major urban regeneration projects, most significantly at ELEPHANT AND CASTLE, in the north-west of the suburb. The area was included in the LONDON BOROUGH OF SOUTHWARK when the city's local government was reorganized in 1965. Its name may be derived from the Old English *walh* and *worth*, meaning 'enclosure of the Britons'. (See also BOOTH, WILLIAM.)

WANDSWORTH

Wandsworth lies on the SOUTH BANK of the RIVER THAMES about 4½ miles south-west of CHARING CROSS. Water from the River Wandle, which flows into the Thames just west of the bridge that links the settlement to FULHAM (see WANDSWORTH BRIDGE), provided the power for a series of small mills and these, in turn, acted as a focus for the development, as early as the thirteenth century, of an industrial community that concentrated on flour-making, bleaching and dyeing, brewing, metalworking and sewing hats (officials of the Roman Catholic Church at the Vatican bought their headgear from Wandsworth companies, earning the area a European reputation for craftsmanship). The factory owners used their firms' profits to build substantial homes but their attempts to acquire land were not always successful; during the eighteenth century they tried to appropriate Wandsworth Common but were effectively resisted by other residents so the area is still a public open space incorporating a CRICKET ground.

The nineteenth century brought considerable expansion, much of it a result of the development of the RAILWAYS. In 1803 the Surrey Iron Railway – a horse-drawn system – began to carry goods along the Wandle Valley, connecting factories along the route. Later, the London and Southampton Railway brought its lines through Wandsworth as it introduced services to NINE ELMS in 1838 and then to WATERLOO a decade later. In addition to attracting commuters who wanted to live outside the city centre but relatively close to their work, the accessibility provided by the railway, coupled with the availability of land for building, led to the establishment of a series of institutions, such as the prison (opened in 1851) and an asylum (which admitted its first inmates in 1857). A five-span lattice-girder bridge connected the settlement to Fulham in 1870–3 (see WANDSWORTH BRIDGE), enhancing the TRANSPORT infrastructure, but, even so, the area avoided becoming a wholly working-class community of the kind that evolved at BATTERSEA (David Lloyd George, who became Prime Minister in 1916, lived at 3 Routh Road while he was president of the Board of Trade, for example). Most of the pre-Industrial Revolution buildings were, nevertheless, swept away during the building boom of the late nineteenth and early twentieth centuries, with the exception of All Saints' Church (largely built in 1779–80 but incorporating the tower erected for an earlier place of worship in 1630) and a terrace of six early eighteenth-century houses nearby in Wandsworth Plain. The community is now part of the LONDON BOROUGH OF WANDSWORTH. The area may derive its name from the Old English *worth*, together with a contemporary personal name, and mean 'Waendel's enclosure'. (See also HUGENOTS.)

WANDSWORTH, LONDON BOROUGH OF

The authority was created, in 1965, as part of a restructuring of local government within the city. One-third of the administrative area of WANDSWORTH, as it had existed under the LONDON COUNTY COUNCIL, was incorporated within a new LONDON BOROUGH OF LAMBETH; the remainder joined with BATTERSEA to form the LONDON BOROUGH OF WANDSWORTH. Although considered part of the inner city, it has a relatively large amount of open space, incorporating BATTERSEA PARK along with extensive areas of CLAPHAM COMMON, Putney Heath and other recreational land within its 13 square miles. Some traditional manufacturing industry survives along the RIVER THAMES frontage but local employment is now based primarily on service industries (including the fruit and vegetable MARKET at NINE ELMS) and over 60 per cent of the resident workforce commutes to jobs elsewhere, notably in central London. During the 1980s, Wandsworth aggressively supported the Conservative government's policy of reducing local council expenditure and, partly as a result, attracted growing numbers of well-paid, young professionals to its rows of terraced housing (Battersea, in particular, experienced a process of gentrification that increasingly confined manual workers to the local authority estates). However, lack of investment in infrastructure during that period left many areas somewhat shabby, encouraging the development of urban regeneration projects in more recent years, notably in Wandsworth town centre. In 2001, the borough (which includes ROEHAMPTON and parts of BALHAM and CLAPHAM) had a population of 260,400. (See also BATTERSEA POWER STATION; TOOTING.)

WANDSWORTH BRIDGE

The first BRIDGE connecting WANDSWORTH (on the SOUTH BANK of the RIVER THAMES) to FULHAM (on the north) was a lattice-girder structure with five spans, built in 1870–3. It was replaced in 1936–40 by the present cantilever bridge, which has three spans and was designed by T. Peirson Frank.

WANSTEAD

A relatively prosperous suburb on the fringe of London, Wanstead lies some 8 miles north-east of CHARING CROSS. It was settled at least by Roman times and was owned by religious interests from the Saxon period until the late Middle Ages, but is best known for the sixteenth-century mansion built by the aptly named Sir Richard Rich, who, in 1544 (following the Dissolution of the Monasteries by Henry VIII), acquired the buildings attached to the church of ST BARTHOLOMEW-THE-GREAT. The house, which was visited frequently by members of the royal family and courtiers such as Sir Philip Sidney, was extended by the Earl of Leicester (a favorite of Elizabeth I) then purchased, in 1667, by Sir Joseph Child, chairman of the EAST INDIA COMPANY. In 1715, his son, Richard, demolished the building and erected a new home, designed by Colen Campbell in Palladian style, which would influence a whole generation of architects, including John Wood the Elder, who was responsible for much of the layout of Georgian Bath. The luxurious interior is evident in William Hogarth's picture of

Sir Richard and his family with their guests in the main salon, painted in 1729 and now owned by the Philadelphia Museum of Art. Unfortunately, within a few generations, the Childs' wealth was dissipated and the building knocked down so that the fabric could be sold as building stone. Only the stables survive, converted for use as a clubhouse for golfers and lawn bowlers. During the eighteenth and nineteenth centuries, several other large villas were erected in the area but these, too, have vanished. Wanstead has developed, since the arrival of the RAILWAY in 1856, as a largely residential community close to EPPING FOREST and with areas of open space laid out for FOOTBALL AND other sports. It was incorporated within the LONDON BOROUGH OF REDBRIDGE when the metropolitan area's local government system was reorganized in 1965. Wanstead's name probably comes from Old English roots (possibly from *waenn* or *waen* and *stede*) and means either 'the place by a tumour-like mound' or 'the place where wagons are kept'.

WAPPING

A riverside suburb on the north bank of the RIVER THAMES, some 3 miles east of CHARING CROSS, Wapping has seen its social and economic structures transformed since the end of the Second World War. The settlement grew from the sixteenth century as London's maritime importance increased and ship repairers, mast-makers, suppliers of goods to seagoing vessels, sailors and prostitutes vied for employment in a rough, working-class community where, along High Street alone, there were thirty-six drinking establishments in 1750. During the nineteenth century, many of these small businesses were pushed out as large companies erected warehouses close to the DOCKS then, in the twentieth century, bomb damage and the decline of the harbour industries led to further-out migration and an increasingly derelict fabric. However, following the reorganization of local government, which placed Wapping in the LONDON BOROUGH OF TOWER HAMLETS from 1965, and the establishment of the London DOCKLANDS Development Corporation in 1981, major urban regeneration projects were initiated. Buildings were demolished or renovated as housing estates were built, leisure facilities were laid out and commercial concerns (such as News International, publishers of THE TIMES) were attracted to the area. In the process, many of the remaining working-class groups moved away, to be replaced by more affluent office workers seeking homes close to the facilities of the central city. The area's name is probably Old English in origin, deriving from a personal name coupled with either *ingas* or *ing*, meaning 'the settlement of Waeppa's followers' or simply 'Waeppa's place'. (See also BRUNEL, ISAMBARD KINGDOM; EAST LONDON LINE; ROTHERHITHE; WAPPING DISPUTE.)

WAPPING DISPUTE

In the early 1980s, restrictive practices by printing unions led to heavy over-employment in the newspaper industry's production units and allowed printers to command wages many times higher than those of other craft workers. Most newspaper proprietors acquiesced, knowing that the resultant high costs deterred rival publishing firms from entering the market. However, when Rupert Murdoch acquired *THE TIMES* in 1981 he faced the unions head-on in an attempt to replace traditional printing methods (such as typesetting by compositors and the use of hot metal) with computerized technologies and built a plant at WAPPING to replace the paper's cramped central London site off FLEET STREET. The printers were incensed by the contracts proposed to members who were offered jobs at the new site, resisting clauses that insisted on total flexibility of labour in the workplace, no strikes and management power to hire, and fire, at will. Undaunted by threats of disrupted production, Murdoch, under the guise of recruiting for a new paper (the *London Post*), which he had no intention of publishing, hired journalists, executives and printers sympathetic to his cause. Then, over a weekend in January 1985, he moved the entire production process to Wapping, where writers could compose their copy on computer screens. Furious, the print workers besieged the plant for a full year, clashing violently with the police and accusing them of supporting Margaret Thatcher's plans to crush union powers. In 1986, they were forced to concede a defeat that led to considerable job losses and lower wages in the industry.

WARD

As with other English metropolitan areas, London's local government areas (see CITY OF LONDON and LONDON BOROUGHS) are subdivided into wards, each of which elects representatives to the Borough Council. In the City of London, these units date from the period following the Norman Conquest in 1066, when William the Conqueror made London his capital. By 1206, there were twenty-four wards. In 1394, Farringdon was divided in order to simplify its administration but, since then, the pattern has remained unchanged (with the exception of Bridge Ward, which was created in 1550 to provide a sinecure post for former LORD MAYORS but abolished in 1978). Formerly, beadles were appointed in each ward to ensure that the law was observed, trading practices maintained and sanitation rules kept, but these posts are now entirely ceremonial. Annual meetings (known as WARDMOTES) are held on the first Friday of September, providing an opportunity for voters (who include residents qualified to vote at Parliamentary elections and all other people who own or rent property in the area) to choose representatives for the COURT OF COMMON COUNCIL. (See also CORPORATION OF LONDON.)

WARDMOTE

On the first Friday of September each year, electors in the WARDS of the CITY OF LONDON meet to select their representatives to the COURT OF COMMON COUNCIL, the CORPORATION OF LONDON's principal local government committee. The number of individuals chosen varies from one to four, according to the population of the ward. All adults entitled to vote at Parliamentary elections may attend, along with those who rent or own property in the area. Wardmotes (which can be held at other times if a vacancy for an ALDERMAN arises) also provide an opportunity for citizens to petition their Common Council members.

WARDOUR STREET

Wardour Street, which runs from north to south through SOHO, is considered by cinema enthusiasts to be the centre of the British film industry. It was originally built in the 1680s and named after Edward Wardour, a local landowner. During the eighteenth century, it became a focus for London's cabinet-making industry (Thomas Sheraton was a resident during the 1790s) and for antique dealers, but the trade declined during the Victorian period and was replaced, in the early 1900s, by entertainment interests. In 1906, architect Frank Loughborough Pearson designed Nos 152–160 as a headquarters for music publisher Novello and Company, modelling the building on the Renaissance Rathaus in Bremen (Germany). At the same time, theatre costumier Willy Clarkson moved into Nos 41 and 43, and firms making musical instruments occupied other premises. The movie companies established themselves from the 1930s, taking over many of the buildings and lining the street with stills from their latest productions.

WASPS RUGBY FOOTBALL CLUB

See LONDON WASPS RUGBY FOOTBALL CLUB.

WATERLOO

The north-east corner of the LONDON BOROUGH OF LAMBETH gets its name from the bridge that first linked the area to the STRAND, on the northern bank of the RIVER THAMES. Built of granite to JOHN RENNIE's designs, the structure had nine elliptical arches and a pair of Doric columns at each end. It was opened on 18 June 1817 and was named by Parliament to commemorate the Duke of Wellington's victory over Napoleon Bonaparte's troops at Waterloo (near Brussels, Belgium) exactly two years earlier. In 1848, the London and South-Western RAILWAY built a station at the southern end then, in 1864, the South-Eastern Railway added a second, bringing commuters pouring in from the growing suburbs. By the early 1890s, more than 10,000 of the 50,000 passengers who arrived at the platforms every weekday morning were heading for work in the CITY OF LONDON so a track, known as THE DRAIN, was built to link the BANK OF ENGLAND to Waterloo, emphasizing the area's growing importance as a TRANSPORT focus. The opening of the BAKERLOO LINE of the UNDERGROUND in 1906 and the CHARING CROSS to KENNINGTON section of the NORTHERN LINE in 1937 added to the traffic, attracting office developers (in 1922, for example, the LONDON COUNTY COUNCIL moved into purpose-built headquarters at nearby COUNTY HALL) and encouraging the establishment of shops, PUBLIC HOUSES and other services for travellers. In 1923, however, two of the piers supporting Rennie's bridge proved unsound so it was demolished and replaced by a five-span concrete structure designed by GILES GILBERT SCOTT (Scott's bridge, opened in 1945, was built largely by women because of the lack of male labourers during the Second World War). The railway station itself was much damaged during the BLITZ and significantly redeveloped afterwards (including a major extension designed by Nicholas Grimshaw and opened in 1993 to accommodate the trains serving the continent of Europe through the Channel Tunnel); as a result, little of the original fabric remains. Also, the neighbouring areas of LAMBETH were greatly altered in the process of reconstruction after the war, with semi-derelict Victorian property along the riverside removed and replaced by the SOUTH BANK arts complex and the twenty-five-storey office accommodation in the Shell Centre. (See also CARDBOARD CITY; JUBILEE LINE; WATERLOO AND CITY LINE; YERKES, CHARLES TYSON.)

WATERLOO AND CITY LINE

The Waterloo and City Line was built by the Waterloo and City Railway and opened in 1898 to provide commuters with easy access from the main line terminus at WATERLOO station to offices in the CITY OF LONDON. Known as 'THE DRAIN' to its users, it runs a shuttle service between Waterloo and Bank UNDERGROUND station, beside the BANK OF ENGLAND, throughout the working week but is closed on Saturday evenings and on Sundays. Because it was considered an extension of the main line service, it was excluded from the LONDON PASSENGER TRANSPORT BOARD's purview when the capital's mass transit system was taken into public ownership in 1933 but was transferred to LONDON UNDERGROUND in 1994. Maintenance of the rolling stock, which dates from 1992, is carried out in a depot at Waterloo. In 2003, responsibility for the line's infrastructure was franchised to Metronet, a consortium of private businesses, but London Underground remained responsible for providing the services. (See also TUBE.)

WATERLOO CHURCHES

In 1818, Parliament passed a Church Building Act that authorized expenditure of over £1 million for building places of worship as a thanksgiving for Britain's victory over Napoleon Bonaparte's French armies at the Battle of Waterloo. In London the thirty-eight that were erected became popularly known as the Waterloo churches. They include St John on BETHNAL GREEN and St Peter Walworth, both of which were designed by Sir John Soane (see SIR JOHN SOANE'S MUSEUM).

WATERMEN

While the RIVER THAMES was an important route, watermen had a monopoly over the carriage of passengers. The business was regulated by various Acts of Parliament and by the CORPORATION OF LONDON, which, from 1555, introduced a system of licensing and an apprenticeship-training programme. In the second half of the sixteenth century, the 40,000 watermen formed a LIVERY COMPANY to represent their interests and, in particular, to protect members from abduction for service in the Royal Navy. They united with the LIGHTERMEN in 1700 but lost power as the river was spanned by BRIDGES (reducing the demand for ferries), as land journeys became increasingly safe and comfortable (encouraging people to travel by coach), and as steam ships replaced sail (carrying more passengers and reducing demand for the watermen's services). By the beginning of the twentieth century, they had almost vanished, although a few survive to represent the ancient trade and the Watermen's Company still accepts apprentices. (See also WESTMINSTER BRIDGE.)

WATER POLLUTION

Although, during Roman times, the RIVER THAMES contained salmon, trout and other fish, population growth and the lack of sewers combined, by the early nineteenth century, to turn the waterway and its tributaries into a polluted sewer in which little life could survive. By 1290, the monks of the Carmelite priory in FLEET STREET were complaining that the stench from the FLEET RIVER had caused the death of several of their number and, during the seventeenth century, Paul Hentzner (a German visitor to the city) claimed that his clothes never lost the smell of slime after they had been washed in water from the Thames. Even by the 1850s, the CITY OF LONDON had only 15 miles of sewer. Most houses had their own cesspits, which contaminated water percolating through the ground towards the wells from which people drew their supplies for drinking and washing. As a result, outbreaks of such infectious diseases as CHOLERA were frequent and devastating (see SNOW, JOHN). In 1858, Parliament was forced into action, passing legislation, designed to clean up the Thames, which allowed JOSEPH WILLIAM BAZALGETTE to prepare plans for the construction of a SEWAGE DISPOSAL system ultimately completed in 1875. The improvements were considerable but, until the 1960s, discharges from vessels using the DOCKS and from the industrial premises that lined the banks proved difficult to control, causing continuing deoxygenation. From 1965, however, the closure of most of the harbour facilities and their associated factories, coupled with stricter environmental standards, resulted in major improvements in water quality. Salmon and trout returned to the Thames, along with flounder, prawns and eels, bringing birds such as heron, cormorant and grebe, which depend on them for food. Under the terms of the Water Act of 1973, the Thames Water Authority was made responsible for pollution control throughout the river basin. (See also AIR POLLUTION; GREAT STINK; HUNGERFORD BRIDGE.)

WATER SUPPLY

During the early stages of its development, London drew most of its water from the RIVER THAMES or from wells. However, as the city grew, these became increasingly tainted by industry (such as tanneries) and by human refuse (see WATER POLLUTION) so, from 1245, conduits were constructed in an attempt to transport purer supplies from further afield (for example, between 1439 and 1471, the CORPORATION OF LONDON built a pipeline in order to divert the flow from springs at PADDINGTON to consumers in FLEET STREET). The new channels helped to meet demand as the medieval city expanded but were limited by technology, relying solely on the force of gravity and therefore needing a source that was at a higher elevation than the user.

Seasonal variations in the flow caused problems as well so, from 1581, pumps were developed in order to widen the sources of supply then, following the GREAT FIRE in 1666, private companies began to provide water to wealthy householders and commercial concerns. These firms undoubtedly enhanced provision (although consumers had access to water for only a few hours each day) but also posed problems because they made little attempt to consult with one another over plans to install their wood and lead pipes. As a result, roads were sometimes dug up by one supplier, relaid then dug up by another shortly afterwards. Also, as more and more water companies were established, particularly during the first decade of the nineteenth century, competition became intense, prices dropped and profits fell. Desperate to avoid bankruptcy, the companies reached agreements that created monopoly suppliers in specific areas of the city. A committee of the HOUSE OF COMMONS registered concern in 1821, fearing that users would face escalating costs, and claimed that water supply should not be determined by market forces but, in the absence of legislation, the providers took little notice. Nine years later, another Parliamentary committee, unhappy that most of London's water was being taken from the heavily polluted Thames, considered the possibility of using other sources of supply but, again, failed to have any legislative impact (partly because many Members of Parliament were shareholders in the water companies).

By mid-century, however, the tide of educated opinion was forcing change. In 1849, a pamphlet published by JOHN SNOW convinced many Londoners that CHOLERA was caused by contaminated drinking water and, the following year, Edwin Chadwick (of the General Board of Health) argued that the city should find new sources of water, with public authorities taking responsibility for supply. Parliament was nudged into action and, in 1852, passed a Metropolitan Water Act, which stopped companies from taking supplies from the heavily polluted tidal area of the Thames below Teddington. They were also prevented from turning down requests for provision and made to cover all reservoirs within a 5-mile radius of ST PAUL'S CATHEDRAL. The SEWAGE DISPOSAL system designed by JOSEPH WILLIAM BAZALGETTE (and completed in 1875) contributed greatly to an improvement in the quality of drinking water – so much so that a Parliamentary Commission was able to report, in 1893, that 'the water supplied to the consumer in London is of a very high standard of excellence and of purity' – but, even so, the suppliers remained unpopular, much criticized for their unwillingness to make provision available in the poorer parts of the city and for the speed with which they cut off water if payments were late.

Ultimately, in 1897, Parliament appointed the Llandaff Commission to investigate the complaints and, as a result of its recommendations, passed the Metropolis Water Act, which created a Metropolitan Water Board in 1902. The board (consisting of sixty-six members appointed by the CORPORATION OF LONDON, the LONDON COUNTY COUNCIL and other local authorities) took over responsibility for water supply in London and initiated an extensive programme of reservoir construction in order to meet the needs of a growing population with increasing living standards. In 1974, its duties were assumed by the Thames Water Authority, which was required to manage the full water cycle within the Thames' 5,000-square-mile catchment area. The Authority, privatized by the Conservative government in 1989, uses a mixture of natural sources and reservoirs to meet the industrial and domestic needs of the metropolis. During the 1980s and 1990s, it undertook a £250-million replumbing scheme designed to improve the supply of water to its 6 million customers by building a 50-mile ring main underneath the city. Water from five main treatment works is fed into the ring, which connects reservoirs at Teddington (in the west) with others along the valley of the RIVER LEA (in the east). As the treated water drops 130 feet down a shaft from the works to the 7½-foot ring main, it moves the rest of the water round the system. Twelve pumping stations lift it back to the surface and feed it into distribution systems beneath the streets for supply to customers. (See also CHINGFORD; LONDON WETLANDS CENTRE; WALTHAMSTOW.)

WATFORD FOOTBALL CLUB

Although Watford lies outside London, its football club draws much of its support from the north-western suburbs of the metropolitan area. The side was formed (as Watford Rovers) in 1881, began to pay its players in 1897 and adopted its present name in 1898. It joined the Football League in 1920 but languished in the lower divisions until well after the Second World War, distinguishing itself only by reaching the sixth round of the FA Cup in 1932. A brief period of success in 1969 brought promotion to the Second Division and, the following year, an appearance in the FA Cup semi-final, but by 1975 the club was once again propping up the League in the Fourth Division. Its salvation was the pop singer, and long-time supporter, Elton John, who became chairman in 1976 and appointed Graham Taylor as manager, with Bertie Mee to assist him. An injection of cash for new players resulted in 'Elton John's Taylor-made army' winning promotion to the Third Division in 1978, to the Second in 1979 and, for the first time in its history, to the First in 1982. It finished the 1982/83 season as runner-up in the League Championship, earning a UEFA Cup place, and 1983/84 took it to the FA Cup final, which it lost to Everton. However, with Elton John's increasing concentration on other matters and Taylor's move to Aston Villa in 1987, the side slumped. In 1988, it was relegated to the Second Division and for nearly a decade it functioned outside the top ranks of English football. In 1996, however, Taylor was brought back and, despite very limited spending on new players, took the club to the Premiership in 2000. In 2002, Elton John resigned from the chairmanship, claiming that, in difficult financial times, the business needed somebody who could devote all his energies to the job. The club's stadium in Vicarage Road has been its base since 1922. (See also SARACENS FOOTBALL CLUB.)

WATLING STREET

Watling Street was built by the Romans to link the port of Dubris (Dover) with LONDINIUM (London), Verulamium (St Albans), Viroconium (Wroxeter) and north Wales. The name is derived from the Old English *atheling*, which means 'noble way'. Modern routes (such as the OLD KENT ROAD) follow the line of the ancient track but there is no evidence that the Watling Street in the CITY OF LONDON, east of ST PAUL'S CATHEDRAL, was ever part of the original Roman road. (See also KILBURN; EDGWARE.)

WELLINGTON ARCH

See HYDE PARK CORNER.

WELLINGTON MUSEUM

See HYDE PARK CORNER.

WEMBLEY

Despite evidence of settlement before the Norman Conquest of 1066, Wembley (some 8 miles north-west of CHARING CROSS) remained largely agricultural until after the First World War. Moreover, the RAILWAY, which led to rapid growth in other suburbs, did little to encourage development when it arrived in 1844. Towards the end of the century, however, the TRANSPORT companies began to promote recreational travel by advertising the attractions of the Wembley PARK Leisure Gardens, with their CRICKET and FOOTBALL pitches, running track, flowerbeds, fountains and waterfalls. Interest in the area's residential possibilities increased when the TRAMS improved access in 1908 and expanded further as a result of the publicity surrounding the BRITISH EMPIRE EXHIBITION of 1924–5 so, by the beginning of the Second

World War in 1939, terraced houses, small detached villas and light industry had replaced the fields. In 1965, when metropolitan local government was reorganized, Wembley became the administrative heart of the new LONDON BOROUGH OF BRENT.

The major building in the area is Wembley Stadium, designed in concrete by Sir John Simpson and Maxwell Ayerton, with Owen Williams as consultant engineer. The stadium, built as the centrepiece of the Empire Exhibition, opened on 28 April 1923 in time to stage the Football Association (FA) Cup final between Bolton Wanderers and WEST HAM UNITED, an event that proved memorable for reasons other than soccer as an estimated 200,000 people crammed over the terraces and spilled onto the pitch. With cancellation of the game a real possibility, Police Constable George Storey on Billie, his white horse, gently pressed the crowd back from the playing area so that the match could begin, earning national celebrity as the public read of his actions in the press and watched news film in cinemas. In the years that followed, the 80,000-seat arena became the home of England's national football team and housed other major sports competitions (such as the 1948 Olympic Games) and pop concerts. An indoor arena was added in 1933–4 (when it was known as the Empire Pool) and a conference centre in 1973–6. From 2000, the stadium was demolished. 30 September 2003 marked the first anniversary of the beginning of the construction of the the new Wembley Stadium.

The area probably gets its name from the Old English *leah* and a personal name, meaning 'Wembla's clearing in the woods'. (See also METROPOLITAN LINE; WHITE CITY.)

WESLEY'S CHAPEL

The chapel, which is built on a site in City Road where more than 50,000 tons of rubble were dumped before CHRISTOPHER WREN could begin work on ST PAUL'S CATHEDRAL, was opened by John Wesley (co-founder of the Methodist faith with his brother, Charles) in 1778. Between 1972 and 1978, it was substantially renovated following an international appeal for funds that raised nearly £1 million. Wesley is buried behind the chapel. The house next door, where he lived in 1779–91, has been converted into a MUSEUM that displays his furniture, books and other personal items. The church crypt is devoted to a display depicting the history of Methodism.

WEST END

In the northern hemisphere, the prevailing winds blow from west to east. As a result, the growth of coal-fired industry and the expansion of population from the late eighteenth century intensified concentrations of smoke and other forms of AIR POLLUTION towards the east of cities and wealthy citizens tended to gather in the more environmentally attractive west. London's distinctive West End emerged in just such conditions, coalescing around residential districts such as MAYFAIR and exclusive shopping areas such as BOND STREET. Since then, the term has evolved to refer also to the THEATRE and restaurant district, focusing on LEICESTER SQUARE, which flourished as a result of its proximity to affluent families with money to spend on entertainment. In 2000, the CITY OF WESTMINSTER issued a series of regulations designed to stem the proliferation of clubs and bars in the area and to restrict high-rise developments. (See also HAYMARKET; SHAFTESBURY AVENUE.)

WEST HAM

West Ham, lying 6 miles east of CHARING CROSS in the LONDON BOROUGH OF NEWHAM, was an early centre of industry in the London area, with flour, oil and timber milling, gunpowder production, distilling, leather-making, textile printing and porcelain production all evident by the eighteenth century. From 1802, the expansion of the DOCKS alongside the RIVER THAMES brought further employment then the RAILWAY, which arrived in 1839, improved accessibility and attracted additional business. In 1844, the Metropolitan Buildings Act enhanced the growing manufacturing complex by confining 'offensive trades' such as sulphuric acid, paint and soap production to a limited number of sites (notably places where dirty, odorous or noisy firms already operated) but also emphasized West Ham's working-class character by attracting relatively unskilled labour to the area. Small, terraced houses mixed with coal-burning factories in an environment that bred socialist sentiment; the London Co-operative Society was established in 1862 by railway workers in West Ham, one of the earliest of the modern labour unions (now the large General, Municipal, Boilermakers and Allied Trades Union) was founded in 1889, and JAMES KEIR HARDIE was elected to represent the southern part of the community in the HOUSE OF COMMONS in 1892, becoming one of the first two representatives of the Labour Party to win a Parliamentary constituency in London. Strongly paternalistic local authorities embarked on major house-building programmes between the two world wars in an attempt to alleviate some of the effects of poverty resulting from the world trade recession, and the decline in harbour industries from the 1950s provided space for urban renewal projects, but the population is still heavily dominated by manual groups with strong left-wing sympathies.

The area's name is probably derived from the Old English *ham*, which has several meanings, including 'an enclosure', 'land in a river meander', 'land surrounded by marsh' and 'river meadow'. (See also WEST HAM UNITED FOOTBALL CLUB.)

WEST HAM UNITED FOOTBALL CLUB

In 1895, Thames Ironworks founded a company football team. Five years later, the club turned professional, renamed itself West Ham United to capitalize on local support and moved to a ground, built on a former MARKET garden at Upton PARK, which it has occupied ever since (properly known as the Boleyn Ground, it takes its name from a house in nearby Green Street). It was elected to the Second Division of the Football League in 1919 but, since then, has been better known for its cup exploits than for its League performances (its best placing was third in the First Division in 1986). It appeared in the first FA Cup final at WEMBLEY in 1923 (losing 2-0 to Bolton Wanderers after a crowd estimated at 200,000 spilled onto the pitch) but its best years were from the late 1950s until the early 1980s. In 1958, the Hammers won the Second Division championship and in 1964 they won the FA Cup, beating Preston North End when Ronnie Boyce headed a goal in the last minute. In 1965, they took the European Cup-Winners Cup with a 2-0 victory over TSV Munich and in 1975 they won the FA Cup for a second time with a 2-1 win over FULHAM FOOTBALL CLUB. Their third FA Cup win, in 1980, was the most surprising because, as Second Division underdogs, they beat their London neighbours ARSENAL 1-0.

The following year, West Ham won the Second Division championship but, since then, they have achieved little apart from taking the Intertoto Cup, one of the less important European competitions, in 1999. The early 1990s brought financial worries as attempts were made to finance ground improvements through a bond issue which guaranteed fans seats at discount prices but the £19 million scheme was massively undersubscribed. In 1991/92, as crowds fell and fans made their feelings known, the side was relegated to the Second Division. In 1992/93, however, it fought its way into the new Premier League and, aware that its small ground significantly reduced income at the turnstiles, the club embarked on a series of stadium improvements which have increased capacity to 35,647. (See also CHARLTON ATHLETIC FOOTBALL CLUB.)

WEST LONDON EXTENSION BRIDGE

See BATTERSEA BRIDGE.

WESTMINSTER

Scholars suggest that Sebert (King of the East Saxons) founded a MONASTERY on a marshy island in the RIVER THAMES west of the former Roman settlement of LONDINIUM during the first half of the eighth century. In 1060, Edward the Confessor (King of England from 1042 to 1066) moved his palace to the site and ordered the building of a new abbey dedicated to St Peter (see WESTMINSTER ABBEY), thereby establishing a politico-ecclesiastical focus that would eventually rival the commercial centre of the CITY OF LONDON in power. Because of their importance, Church and court promoted urban expansion as lodging houses and services were established to meet the needs of visiting dignitaries. However, the wealthy residents attracted the poor, who hoped for charity and were particularly in evidence when monarchs moved their entourage (and, therefore, the affluent citizens) to other parts of England, so by the nineteenth century much of the area was a pestilential slum, with homeless beggars, overcrowded rooms and a high incidence of infectious disease. However, the construction of new roads from 1850 and the building of Parliament Square as an approach to the PALACE OF WESTMINSTER in 1868 cleared away many of the worst properties. During the twentieth century, government offices increasingly infiltrated WHITEHALL and a growing tourist industry brought souvenir shops in its wake. Westminster was given city status in 1900 and became one of the LONDON BOROUGHS in 1965 (see CITY OF WESTMINSTER). (See also ALDWYCH; DISTRICT LINE; ST GEORGE'S HOSPITAL; WESTMINSTER BRIDGE; WESTMINSTER CATHEDRAL; WESTMINSTER HALL; WESTMINSTER HOSPITAL.)

WESTMINSTER, CITY OF

Westminster was designated as one of the LONDON BOROUGHS (when London's local government was reformed in 1965) by merging the formerly independent authorities of PADDINGTON, ST MARYLEBONE and WESTMINSTER. Its 8

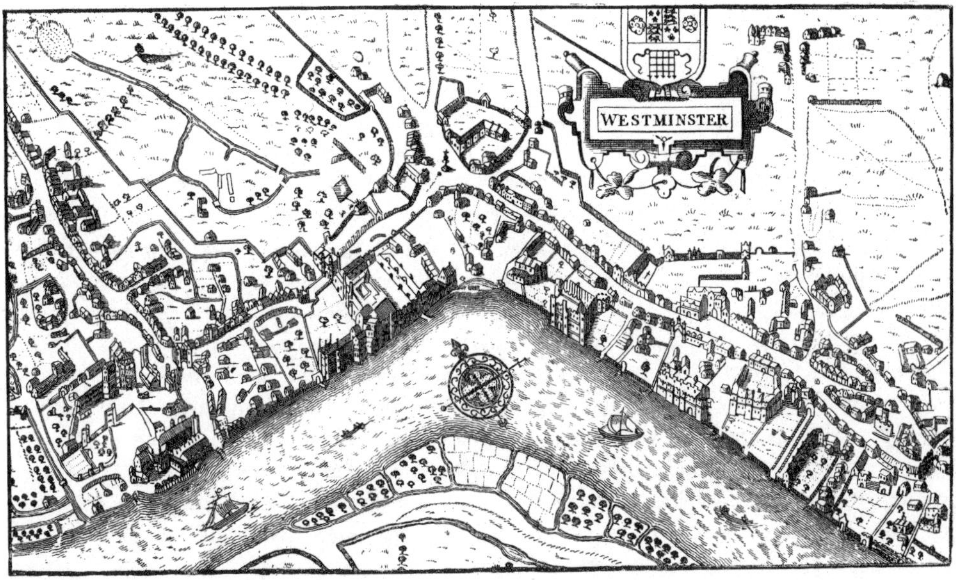

A plan of the City of Westminster at the time of Elizabeth I.

The coronation of Charles II in Westminster Abbey.

square miles include many of the attractions that draw tourists to the capital, including BUCKINGHAM PALACE, HARRODS, MADAME TUSSAUD'S WAXWORKS, the NATIONAL GALLERY, the NATIONAL PORTRAIT GALLERY, the PALACE OF WESTMINSTER, the ROYAL OPERA HOUSE, TRAFALGAR SQUARE, the WEST END and over one-fifth of all the historic buildings in London considered sufficiently important to be given legal protection against insensitive development. Some 90 per cent of the adults in the 181,300 population (2001) are employed in service industries, particularly banking and other financial activities, the HOTEL trade, retailing and public administration. Most of those residents are professional and managerial workers, nearly two-thirds of them living in rented accommodation. About a quarter are members of non-white ethnic minorities, though as a result of the long history of immigration by Chinese, south Asians, Arabs, Africans and Caribbeans, no single group dominates. The borough includes the districts of BAYSWATER, BELGRAVIA, CHARING CROSS, COVENT GARDEN, MAYFAIR, PICCADILLY, PIMLICO, REGENT STREET, SOHO, the STRAND, VICTORIA and WHITEHALL.

WESTMINSTER ABBEY

Westminster ABBEY stands close to the PALACE OF WESTMINSTER on the north bank of the RIVER THAMES. The first church on the site (probably founded by Sebert, King of the East Saxons, in about AD 750) was replaced in 1065, when Edward the Confessor (England's sovereign) authorized the construction of an abbey dedicated to St Peter. These early structures have vanished under the present buildings, begun by command of Henry III in 1245 and completed nearly three centuries later in 1532. The basic design is French Gothic (the apse is modelled on the church at Amiens, for example), but it incorporates typically English features (such as a double aisle) and makes use of local building materials (notably Reigate stone and Purbeck marble). The nave, 103 feet high, is taller than any other in the country. Over the past three centuries the fashion for erecting funerary and memorial monuments has detracted somewhat from the simple architectural line of the interior but, even so, these structures have their own interest.

A shrine dedicated to Edward the Confessor (who died on 5 January 1066, just eight days after his church was consecrated) stands behind the high altar, close to the marble tomb of Henry III, and Henry VII's chapel (built in 1503–12) contains the remains of Henry himself, Edward VI, Mary I, Elizabeth I, Mary Queen of Scots, James I, Charles II, William III, Mary II, Queen Anne and George II. Commoners, buried in the building from the reign of Richard II in the last quarter of the fourteenth century, include such notable politicians as William Pitt the Elder, William Pitt the Younger and William Gladstone. The south transept is widely known as Poet's Corner because, following Geoffrey Chaucer's interment in 1400, other prominent writers requested that they be laid close to the same spot. In fact, few poets found their last resting place there, though BEN JONSON, John Dryden, SAMUEL JOHNSON and Alfred Lord Tennyson were accorded that honour. Others (such as Robert Burns and WILLIAM SHAKESPEARE) are commemorated only by tablets, often erected long after the writers died because their lifestyles did not appeal to conservative clergy. Elsewhere in the abbey, tombs and inscriptions laud British citizens who made significant contributions to their country's history, including David Livingstone, Michael Faraday, Isaac Newton and architect ROBERT ADAM.

Since the fourteenth century, English monarchs have been crowned in the abbey on the oak Coronation Chair fashioned by Master Walter of Durham. The Stone of Scone, the coronation stone of Scottish sovereigns, which was seized by Edward I in 1297, lay underneath it until 1996, when it was returned to Edinburgh. In recent years, the rising number of tourists has led to access restrictions in certain areas (such as the garden) and, more controversially, to the introduction of admission charges. Eyebrows were also raised in 1999 when James O'Donnell was appointed Organist and Master of the Choristers, the most senior musical post in the Church of England. O'Donnell is the first Roman Catholic to win the job since the Reformation. Technically the abbey is a Royal Peculiar, and therefore under the jurisdiction of the monarch rather than the Church of England, but several Members of Parliament have argued that the ecclesiastical authorities should have more influence on management. (See also ARCHITECTURE; BARRY, CHARLES; CHAMBERS, WILLIAM; COVENT GARDEN; GARRICK, DAVID; GIBBONS, GRINLING; GIBBS, JAMES; HENDON; HOLBORN; HYDE PARK; MONASTERIES; MORDEN; PUBLIC RECORD OFFICE (PRO); ST PAUL'S CATHEDRAL; STRAWBERRY HILL; WESTMINSTER.)

WESTMINSTER BRIDGE

By the early eighteenth century, LONDON BRIDGE was still the only road crossing between the north and SOUTH BANKS of the RIVER THAMES in the vicinity of the city. Proposals for a second structure further upstream had been consistently sabotaged by the protests of WATERMEN who made a living by ferrying travellers over the river, shopkeepers who sold their wares on London Bridge and the CORPORATION OF LONDON, which controlled access to the settlement. However, as a result of increased traffic, caused by the growth of WESTMINSTER, and the promise of financial compensation for ferry operators, the arguments of the Earl of Pembroke and other advocates for improved TRANSPORT eventually prevailed. Construction began in 1738, when Swiss engineer Charles Labelye was appointed engineer to the project, and was completed in 1750. Built of stone, the new edifice incorporated fifteen arches and had its piers founded in chambers knows as caissons (the first time the technique had been employed in Britain). Londoners were proud of their new bridge – so much so that dogs were not allowed on it (in case they fouled it) and anyone caught decorating the sides with graffiti could be sentenced to death without a priest in attendance. JAMES BOSWELL, the Scottish commentator on social life in the capital, called it a 'noble edifice' and, in 1768, was sufficiently impressed to pick up 'a strong, jolly young damsel' in HAY-

MARKET and make love to the lady above the arches while the Thames rolled, uncaring, beneath them. In 1802, William Wordsworth, less vigorously but more romantically, observed that 'Earth hath not anything to show more fair' than the view of London, wearing 'the beauty of the morning,' from Westminster Bridge. However, there were continual technical problems with the foundations and Parliament decided that a replacement was needed. Thomas Page was appointed to design the crossing, with CHARLES BARRY as a consultant, and, in 1862, the present bridge, with seven arches resting on granite piers, was opened to traffic. It is 84 feet wide – extremely large by mid-nineteenth-century standards. (See also ALBERT, PRINCE; BOADICEA; BRIDGES; GAS; LONDON MARATHON; STREET LIGHTING.)

WESTMINSTER CATHEDRAL

Westminster Cathedral, dedicated to the Precious Blood of Our Lord Jesus Christ, is the mother church of the Roman Catholic faith in Great Britain. Construction work began in 1896 at a site, near VICTORIA Station,

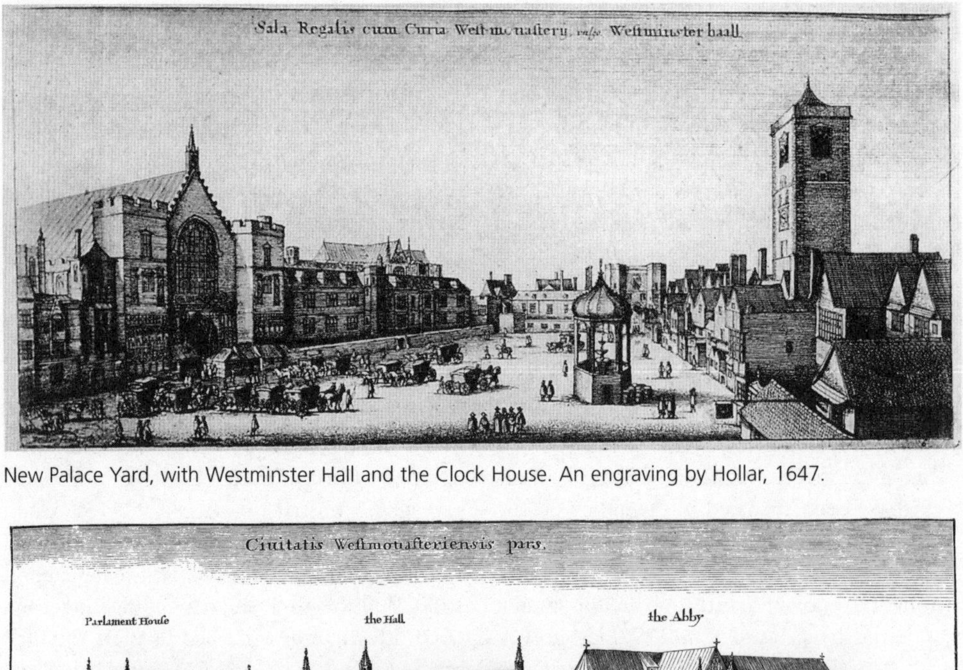

New Palace Yard, with Westminster Hall and the Clock House. An engraving by Hollar, 1647.

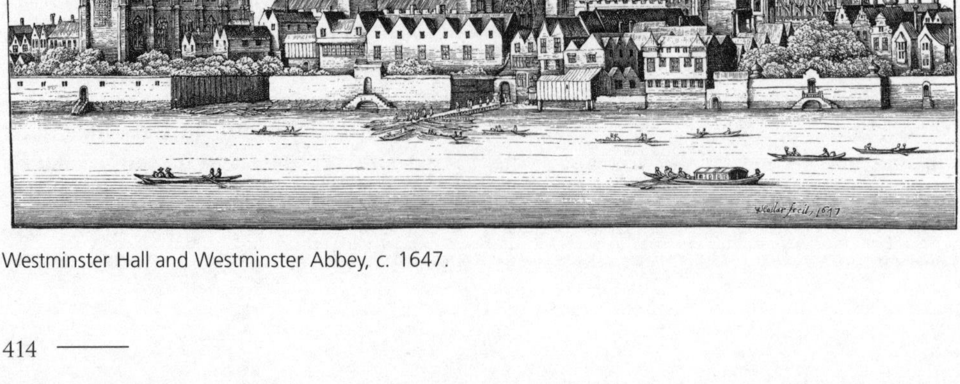

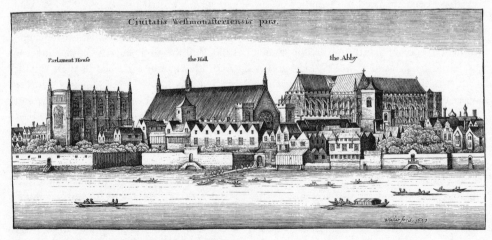

Westminster Hall and Westminster Abbey, c. 1647.

which was previously occupied by a women's PRISON, and was completed in 1903. Designed by John Francis Bentley, it is constructed of brick in Byzantine style (the more traditional Gothic was rejected so that the building would not look like a poor relation of nearby WESTMINSTER ABBEY) and parts are deliberately left unfinished so that the financial burden of decoration can be assumed by worshippers of the future. The interior, described by architectural historian Nikolaus Pevsner as 'one of the most moving of any church in London' is 342 feet long, 156 feet wide and 117 feet high. Marble brought from over 100 sites around the world adorns the walls and the aisles are lined with chapels. The Fourteen Stations of the Cross were carved on the piers of the nave by Eric Gill and the Metropolitan throne (gifted by the English Bishops in memory of Cardinal Herbert Vaughan, who initiated the building programme) was placed in the Sanctuary, close to an altar fashioned from Cornish granite. The body of John Southworth, hung for his faith at TYBURN in 1654, was brought from France in 1930 and now lies in the Chapel of St George. Visitors to the cathedral can take the lift to the top of the 273-foot-high campanile, which provides a magnificent view over central London.

The trial of Charles I in Westminster Hall, 1649.

WESTMINSTER HALL

Westminster Hall, built in 1097–9 by William Rufus (son of William the Conqueror), is the only substantial surviving fabric of the original PALACE OF WESTMINSTER. In 1394–1401, a hammer-beam roof, covering the 68-foot width of the room in a single span, was installed by Henry Yevele (Master Mason to Richard II) and Hugh Herland (the Master Carpenter). Initially the building provided space for banquets but, from the thirteenth century, it was used for administrative purposes, housing law courts, meetings of Parliament and other formal gatherings. William Wallace (leader of Scotland's struggle for freedom from English rule during the thirteenth century), Thomas More (who defied the edicts of Henry VIII), Guy Fawkes (implicated in the GUNPOWDER PLOT) and Charles I (convicted of treason against his people) were all tried and condemned to death in the Hall, which was also the site of coronation festivities until 1882. Today, it is used primarily for ceremonial events.

WESTMINSTER HOSPITAL

In 1715, banker Henry Hoare encouraged Patrick Cockburn (a minister), Robert Witham (a brewer) and William Wogan (a writer) to help him found a place at which they could provide care for 'the Sick and Needy and Other Distressed Persons' in WESTMINSTER, where poor diets, overcrowded living conditions and the damp, marshy environment combined to produce a high incidence of disease. In 1720, they rented a property in Petty France and opened a hospital, which, in 1724, they relocated to Great Chapel Street and named the Westminster Infirmary. In 1831, a site was purchased for a new building in Broad Sanctuary, on the opposite side of the street from WESTMINSTER ABBEY, and in 1834 the first patients moved into the new, state-of-the-art, Westminster Hospital, where the doctors included JOHN SNOW, who qualified in 1838, pioneered the use of anaesthetics and confirmed that CHOLERA was spread through the wells used to supply drinking water in the city. In 1933, as medical demands and social needs changed, the hospital moved to premises in Horseferry Road, where it remained for sixty years until, at a time of much reorganization of healthcare in the city, it amalgamated with St Stephen's, St Mary Abbot's, Westminster Children's and the West London Hospitals at a site in FULHAM Road. In 1994, the group reorganized administratively as the CHELSEA and Westminster Healthcare National Health Service Trust. (See also ST GEORGE'S HOSPITAL.)

WHITECHAPEL

The Whitechapel area of London's EAST END lies close to the CITY OF LONDON, taking its name from the white stone walls of the thirteenth-century chapel of St Mary Matfelon and developing as a centre for trades that were considered a nuisance in the City because of their noise or other pollution (the Whitechapel Bell Foundry moved from Houndsditch in 1583, for example; its products include BIG BEN and the United States' original Liberty Bell). Because of the suburb's location on the main road to Essex, residents also earned an income from coaching inns and MARKETS but wages in these trades were low so the area was characterized by poverty, attracting IMMIGRANTS because of the cheap housing and becoming widely known for its high crime rates (see, for example, JACK THE RIPPER). In an attempt to improve conditions, Samuel Barnett (vicar at St Jude's Church) founded TOYNBEE HALL in 1884 and the Whitechapel Art Gallery in 1901 but the area retained its reputation throughout the twentieth century. Since the 1970s, finance houses have expanded into the western fringe of the area from The City, replacing derelict property with office blocks, and services, such as PUBLIC HOUSES, have responded by upgrading facilities for the middle-class lunchtime trade. Also young, single people have purchased some of the cheap housing and carried out improvements. However, Whitechapel remains predominantly working class, with a large Bangladeshi community. In 1965, it was incorporated within the LONDON BOROUGH OF TOWER HAMLETS. The area's former residents include Jack Cohen, the son of an IMMIGRANT Polish tailor. Cohen earned a living by trading from a stall at Well Street Market in HACKNEY, where, in the years after the First World War, he offered damaged and salvaged goods at low prices. Needing a name for bags of tea, he combined his supplier's initials (TES) with the first two letters of his own surname and founded Tesco, now one of Britain's largest supermarket chains. (See also BOOTH, CHARLES; HAMMERSMITH AND CITY LINE; KRAY TWINS; PETTICOAT LANE; ROYAL LONDON HOSPITAL.)

WHITE CITY

In 1908, impresario Imre Kiralfy staged an exhibition at SHEPHERD'S BUSH in an effort to cement a political *entente* between Britain and France. Because the displays were housed in light-coloured buildings, the site became known as 'White City', a name still used to refer to the area. The athletics events at the fourth modern Olympic Games were held in a specially constructed stadium erected in the same year as the exhibition. The climax was the marathon, held over a 26-mile route from Windsor Castle and establishing the length of the event until a further 385 yards were added at the WEMBLEY games in 1948 so that the finishing line would be in front of the royal box.

White City forms part of the LONDON BOROUGH OF HAMMERSMITH AND FULHAM. (See also CENTRAL LINE; QUEENS PARK RANGERS FOOTBALL CLUB.)

WHITEFRIARS

The Whitefriars area of the CITY OF LONDON takes its name from the mantle of the Carmelite monks, who established a priory in the area during the second half of the thirteenth century. When Richard, Duke of Cornwall and brother of Henry II, returned from a visit to the Holy Land in 1241 he was accompanied by a group of hermits whom the Saracens had expelled from a monastery on Mount Carmel. It proved impossible for them to observe strict rules of silence and exclusion in England so, in 1247, Pope Innocent IV decreed that they could live in urban areas provided they were dependent on charity for their survival. A church was erected at the City site, close to ST PAUL'S CATHEDRAL, in 1253 and, over the next 300 years, numerous wealthy patrons (including John of Gaunt, Regent of England while Richard II was too young to rule) contributed to their welfare. When Henry VIII broke up Roman Catholic religious houses from 1536, much of the property (which extended from FLEET STREET to the RIVER THAMES and included a cemetery and a garden) was taken over by the Royal Armourer and the Royal Physician. The Great Hall, for a period during late Elizabethan and early Jacobean times, served as a playhouse. Most of the fabric of the priory has now vanished but excavations in 1927 revealed a fourteenth-century crypt and the paving of the cloister walk.

WHITEHALL

Whitehall runs for some 600 yards from TRAFALGAR SQUARE towards the HOUSES OF PARLIAMENT (see PALACE OF WESTMINSTER), getting its name from WHITEHALL PALACE, which stood on its western side from 1529 until 1698. It took its present form in the eighteenth century, when neighbouring buildings were demolished in order to widen the roadway and improve traffic flow. Over the past 200 years, as the duties of Parliament have multiplied, workplaces for ministers and civil servants have replaced the homes that formerly stood on the site (so much so that 'Whitehall' is now a synonym for 'government administration'). THE ADMIRALTY, the Foreign and Commonwealth Office, the Ministry of Agriculture, the Ministry of Defence, the Scottish Office, the TREASURY BUILDINGS, the

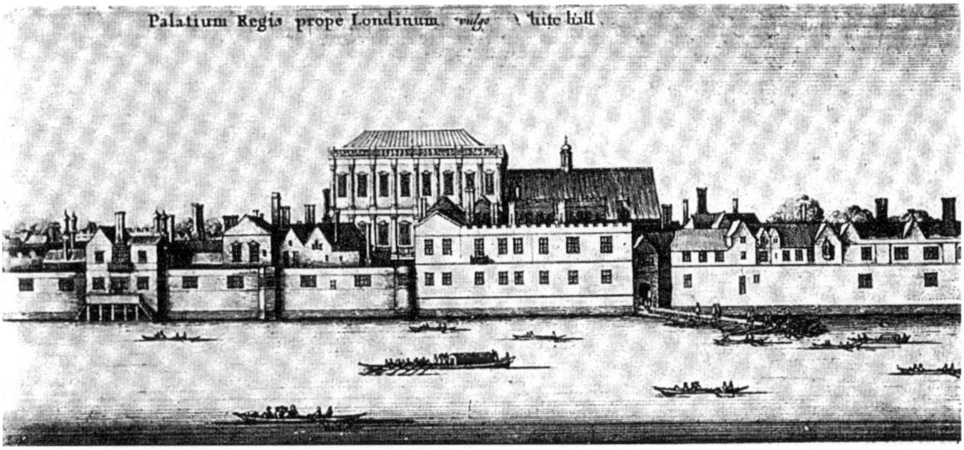

Whitehall from the river. Engraving by Hollar, c. 1650.

Welsh Office and other departments all have entries from the street or nearby. Also, the official homes of the Prime Minister and the Chancellor of the Exchequer are in DOWNING STREET, an alley leading off Whitehall. The area lies within the CITY OF WESTMINSTER. (See also BANQUETING HOUSE; CENOTAPH; PORTLAND STONE.)

WHITEHALL PALACE

In 1529, Henry VIII acquired property (previously owned by Thomas Wolsey, his former Lord Chancellor), which stood on the bank of the RIVER THAMES just south of the present TRAFALGAR SQUARE. Dissatisfied with his ageing palace at WESTMINSTER, he set about converting the premises into a new residence named Whitehall (probably because it was fashionable at the time to accord that title to any place given over to feasting and celebration but possibly also because of the light colour of the stonework). A 2,000-room warren of corridors and staircases, with gardens, orchards, a real tennis court, a tiltyard for jousting and a cockpit, it became the fulcrum of social life for the Tudor and Stuart monarchs. Henry celebrated his marriages to Anne Boleyn and Jane Seymour there in 1533 and 1536 respectively, Elizabeth I used the Great Hall as a theatre, James I commissioned INIGO JONES to build the BANQUETING HOUSE, Charles I acquired an extensive collection of paintings during the second quarter of the seventeenth century, Oliver Cromwell ruled from Whitehall as Lord Protector of England from 1653 until his death five years later, Charles II installed his mistresses as soon as he regained the Crown in 1660 and in 1688 the Roman Catholic James II sneaked out of the palace to seek safety in France from his Protestant persecutors. In 1689, however, William III, believing that the AIR POLLUTION in London was affecting his asthma, moved the royal court to KENSINGTON PALACE. Nine years later, the building burned to the ground, apparently because a servant woman left clothes drying too close to a fire. (See also DOWNING STREET; HORSE GUARDS PARADE; NATIONAL GALLERY; TREASURY BUILDINGS.)

WHITE'S

White's is the oldest, and probably the most prestigious, of London's GENTLEMEN'S CLUBS. It takes its name from White's Chocolate House, which opened for business in 1693 on the site now occupied by BOODLE'S at 28 St James's Street. Because it was one of the more expensive establishments, it attracted affluent customers who were willing to risk their wealth in wagers but in 1733 a fire broke out in the gaming room (which was known as Hell), destroying the premises and forcing patrons to relocate. By the time the clientele moved back into the refurbished building three years later, they had formed themselves into a private club, with eighty-two members who continued the betting tradition. In 1755, the club moved into its present home at 37-38 St James's Street and in 1811 a bow window was built into the façade (Beau Brummel was quick to take advantage, regularly sitting there with his dandy friends so that he could be seen from the street and comment on passers-by). The club has long been a haunt of the aristocratic and privileged. All prime ministers from Robert Walpole to Robert Peel were members, as were George IV, William IV and Edward VII. Prince Charles held his stag night at the club before his wedding to Lady Diana Spencer in 1981.

WHITTINGTON, RICHARD 'DICK'

(*c.* 1358–1423)

One of the most enduring children's tales in the English language tells how Dick Whittington, a poor orphan, went to seek his fortune in London. He found a job as a kitchen boy in the home of a rich merchant, who allowed his servants to include articles for sale with his own goods in the ships he dispatched abroad. Dick's only possession was his beloved cat so he sent that – a decision that made his fortune because the animal devoured the mice and rats at a foreign potentate's court, persuading the ruler to purchase it for an enormous sum. Unaware of his unexpected income, Dick had forsaken the merchant's house, driven out by the constant criticism of a nagging cook. He headed north but, as he rested at HIGHGATE, heard BOW BELLS ring out, telling him to return because he would be LORD MAYOR of London one day. He retraced his steps, learned of his new wealth, married Alice, the merchant's daughter, and lived happily ever after, serving as Lord Mayor three times.

The story, which evolved during the early seventeenth century, is completely unsubstantiated by evidence though Whittington was real enough. He was the son of wealthy parents – Sir William Whittington and his wife, Joan – but knowledge of his childhood and youth are scanty, though records show that he was living in London by 1379 and earning a living as a mercer. He played a part in the government of the city, serving as an ALDERMAN for Broad Street in 1393 and as a SHERIFF in 1393–4 before being appointed Lord Mayor in 1397, when the previous incumbent died. He held the post again in 1406–7 and 1419–20 but was distinguished more by the size of the loans he made to Richard II and Henry IV than by his impact on urban affairs. Whittington died, childless, in March 1423, predeceased by his wife (who really was called Alice). His estate was used to rebuild NEWGATE PRISON and support other civic developments. (See also ST THOMAS'S HOSPITAL.)

WILLESDEN

A traditionally working-class residential suburb within the LONDON BOROUGH OF BRENT, some 6 miles north-west of CHARING CROSS, Willesden became urbanized during the second half of the nineteenth century as a result of the expansion of the RAILWAY system. Stations opened near the village of Harlesden (1842), at Willesden Junction (1866) and at Willesden Green (1880), with the result that the population grew from less than 800 in 1811 to over 100,000 in 1901. The first houses were occupied by well-to-do CITY OF LONDON businesspeople (in Nicol Road, for example), but these were quickly outnumbered by rows of semi-detached and terraced homes built for families with lower incomes. Churches (mainly nonconformist) were erected to minister to spiritual needs and shops established to meet secular wants. Such open space as remains has been developed by local authorities for recreational use (as at Roundwood PARK) or is used as BURIAL GROUNDS (notably at the Jews' Cemetery, consecrated in Pound Lane in 1873). The area's name is probably derived from the Old English *wiell* and *dun*, suggesting 'a down with a spring'. (See also EAST LONDON LINE.)

WILLIAM MORRIS GALLERY

An artist, designer, poet and socialist, Morris (1834–96) believed that human potential could be realized through development of good craftsmanship. His wallpaper, textiles, tapestry and typefaces revolutionized design during the second half of the nineteenth century and are still widely used. In 1950, Water House, his home in WALTHAMSTOW from 1848 to 1856, opened as a MUSEUM, with rooms displaying examples of his own work and that of his associates, notably Edward Burne-Jones and Frank Brangwyn. There is also an extensive collection of pre-Raphaelite paintings gifted by Brangwyn as a memorial to Morris. (See also KELMSCOTT PRESS.)

WIMBLEDON

The remains of an Iron Age fort indicate that Wimbledon, some 7 miles south-west of CHARING CROSS, was settled in Prehistoric times. In the medieval period it was owned by the Archbishops of Canterbury, developing as a small hilltop village close to St Mary's Church. During the nineteenth century, it spread downhill towards the RAILWAY station, which opened in 1838, then expanded in the 1870s and 1880s as it attracted office workers willing to commute to jobs in central London. However, despite the urban encroachment, over 1,000 acres of common remains as rough grassland, providing an important open space for recreation. The area is well provided with sporting facilities, with WIMBLEDON FOOTBALL CLUB founded in 1889 and an extensive golf course, but is best known for the tennis championships held each June at the All England Club in Church Road. The club was founded by croquet enthusiasts in 1869, adding lawn tennis eight years later. There are nineteen grass courts and ten clay, with the former used only during the championship tournament. A MUSEUM, opened in 1977 (the centenary of the championships), contains exhibits illustrating the history of the sport and an extensive library. Wimbledon was incorporated within the LONDON BOROUGH OF MERTON in 1965, when the metropolitan area's local government was reorganized.

In the middle of the tenth century, the area's name was recorded as *Wunemannedune*. It is probably derived from a personal name coupled with the suffix *dun*, meaning 'Wynnmann's hill'. (See also BAZALGETTE, JOSEPH WILLIAM; DISTRICT LINE; EAST LONDON LINE; EPSOM; ST GEORGE'S HOSPITAL; WIMBLEDON FOOTBALL CLUB.)

WIMBLEDON FOOTBALL CLUB

In 1889, a group of young men formed an amateur football club known as Wimbledon Old Centrals, which played its matches on WIMBLEDON Common. In 1905, they changed the name to Wimbledon Football Club then, in 1912, moved to a ground in Plough Lane. In 1919, as football was restructured at the end of the First World War, Wimbledon joined the Athenian League but it remained there for only two years before transferring to the Isthmian League, where it had considerable success, winning the Championship ten times over the next forty-three years and reaching the Amateur Cup final in 1935, 1947 and 1963 (it lost on the first two occasions but won on the third). In 1964, the club turned professional and in 1977, following a run of giant-killing FA Cup victories over Burnley, Leeds and Middlesbrough, it was elected to the Fourth Division of the Football League. In 1979, it won promotion to the Third Division and in 1981 it was bought by Sam Hamman, a civil engineer who made his fortune as a building contractor in the Middle East but moved to London in 1975 so that his wife could have her second child in an environment free from the civil unrest which troubled his Lebanese homeland.

Under Hamman, the success continued for over a decade. Wimbledon was promoted to the Second Division in 1983 and to the First Division in 1986. In 1988, very much the underdog, it won the FA Cup, beating Liverpool 1-0 (Lawrie Sanchez headed the goal and 'keeper Dave Beasant saved a penalty), and in 1992 it earned a place in the new Premier League when the Football League structure was reorganized.

However, despite the achievements, the side never achieved the glamour status of teams such as ARSENAL and CHELSEA, gates were low and funds for new players limited. In an attempt to change the situation, and in spite of vociferous opposition from supporters, Hamman negotiated a ground-sharing agreement at Selhurst PARK with south London neighbours CRYSTAL PALACE FOOTBALL CLUB in 1991. Over the next few years, other options were mooted, including a move to Dublin and merger with QUEENS PARK RANGERS, then, in 1997, Hamman sold the business to the Norwegians Kjell Rokke and Bjoern Gjellsten for a reported £28 million. In 1998, the Plough Lane site was purchased by Safeway.

The new owners, faced with relegation to Division One in 2000 and aware that the club needed its own ground and a regular attendance of around 30,000 at home games if it was to survive, applied to the Football League for permission to move to Milton Keynes. Initially, the application was rejected but in 2002 an FA Commission approved the relocation on the grounds that the club was at risk of bankruptcy (the operating loss in 2000/01 was £6.6 million and by autumn of the following year the owners claimed it was losing £20,000 a day). Not surprisingly, the fans were incensed. Many boycotted the games at Selhurst Park (only 849 people turned up to watch a game against Rotherham in October 2002) and, in June 2003, the club was forced to place its affairs in the hands of the administrators.

WOODFORD

The suburb of Woodford occupies the north-western section of the LONDON BOROUGH OF REDBRIDGE. It developed as an agricultural village during the Middle Ages, when it was controlled by the monks of Waltham Abbey, then became a popular site for the country homes of rich gentry after the estate was broken up in 1540 as part of Henry VIII's campaign to dissolve the English MONASTERIES. The arrival of the RAILWAY in 1856 presaged the sale of the farms and PARKS to urban developers, who paid large sums for the right to build homes suitable for workers willing to commute to office jobs in the CITY OF LONDON. As a result, by the early twentieth century, Woodford was absorbed within the metropolitan area. Sir WINSTON CHURCHILL represented the constituency in the HOUSE OF COMMONS (see PALACE OF WESTMINSTER) from 1924 to 1964.

WOOD GREEN

The suburb of Wood Green lies 7 miles north of CHARING CROSS, adjoining HORNSEY, TOTTENHAM and EDMONTON. It derived its name from its origins as an agricultural village, with a green, located below a forested hill. The small community earned its living from farming until the second half of the nineteenth century, when the arrival of the RAILWAY (in 1859) improved access and promoted urban development, absorbing the settlement within the metropolitan area. It now functions as an important regional retail centre and houses the administrative headquarters of the LONDON BOROUGH OF HARINGEY, in which it was included when the city's local government was reorganized in 1965.

WOOLWICH

Woolwich developed as a fishing village on the SOUTH BANK of the RIVER THAMES about 8 miles east of CHARING CROSS. It was settled at least by Roman times but grew significantly from 1512, when Henry VIII converted the small harbour into a ROYAL NAVAL DOCKYARD specifically to build *Great Harry* as the flagship for his fleet. In subsequent years, the port was a focus for much maritime activity – from Woolwich, Walter Raleigh set off for the Americas and Martin Frobisher for the Arctic – so ancillary industries such as rope-making flourished nearby, along with glass production, brass manufacture and other activities that benefited from a location where raw materials could easily be imported by sea. In 1715 the ROYAL ARSENAL (where armaments were made and tested) was transferred from the CITY OF LONDON, in 1716 two regiments of artillery were formed at the base, then, in 1719, a school for officers was opened. A flourishing reputation for turning cadets into commanders led, in 1741, to the school's designation as a Royal Military Academy, which, over the next two centuries, trained many of Britain's military leaders, including General Charles Gordon and Earl Kitchener.

By the mid-nineteenth century, Woolwich was a prosperous working-class town, its wealth indicated by the establishment of the Woolwich Building Society, founded in 1847 and now one of the United Kingdom's largest financial institutions. Since then, however, the local economy has changed significantly. The DOCKyard closed in 1869 (most of the site is now covered by local authority housing built during the 1970s). Much of the Royal Arsenal depot has also been cleared and the land used for homes. The Military Academy merged with its sister institution at Sandhurst in 1947 and part of the barracks was turned into a MUSEUM for the Royal Regiment of Artillery, with an extensive research library. Nearby, the Rotunda – a tent-like structure designed by JOHN NASH – houses Britain's most comprehensive collection of guns in a display that traces the development of ordnance since the thirteenth century. Modern Woolwich is predominantly an administrative and educational centre, serving as the focus of local government for the LONDON BOROUGH OF GREENWICH. The administrative headquarters of the building society (which surrendered its mutual status and became a public limited company in 1997) dominate the small town square, the UNIVERSITY of Greenwich has a local campus and technical skills are taught at Woolwich College. A free ferry (which first opened in 1889) provides vehicles and pedestrians with a link to communities on the north shore of the Thames. In 2003, the government announced that Woolwich would be the focus of a major house-building programme designed to help alleviate the shortage of homes in south-east England. The area's name is probably derived from the Old English words *wul* and *wic*, indicating 'a port from which wool was shipped'. (See also ARSENAL FOOTBALL CLUB; CHARLTON ATHLETIC FOOTBALL CLUB.)

WOOLWICH ARSENAL
See ROYAL ARSENAL.

WOOLWICH DOCKYARD
See ROYAL NAVAL DOCKYARDS.

WORCESTER PARK
The residential suburb of Worcester Park, on the borders of the ROYAL BOROUGH OF KINGSTON UPON THAMES and the County of Surrey, lies on land that was once part of the NONSUCH PALACE estate. It takes its name from Worcester House, built by the Earl of Worcester when he was keeper of the palace PARK in the seventeenth century and later the farmhouse base for pre-Raphaelite artists John Everett Millais and William Holman Hunt (Hunt painted *The Light of the World*, which brought his work to public attention in 1854, in the orchard). Residential development began with the arrival of the RAILWAY in 1865 and continued until after the Second World War.

WORLD HERITAGE SITES
Governments may nominate locations within their boundaries for listing as World Heritage Sites by the United Nations Educational, Scientific and Cultural Organization (UNESCO). Before formal recognition is granted, candidates must have demonstrated their adherence to Article 4 of the 1972 World Heritage Convention, which requires them to conserve their natural and cultural environments. In London, four areas of the city have been designated – the neighbourhood of the PALACE OF WESTMINSTER, WESTMINSTER ABBEY and ST MARGARET'S CHURCH (which was recognized in 1987); the TOWER OF LONDON (also listed in 1987); maritime GREENWICH (1997); and KEW GARDENS (2003).

WORMWOOD SCRUBS
One of Britain's largest jails, the 'Scrubs' was designed by Edmund Du Cane (an advocate of PRISON reform) and built by convict labour in 1874–80. Originally it housed criminals of both sexes but, since 1902, has accommodated men only, normally taking about 1,000 inmates, many of whom are serving the initial stages of life sentences. After spy George Blake escaped from the premises in 1966 and made his way to the Soviet Union, security was tightened, but the strict regime, coupled with the inevitable lack of privacy and other problems in a building erected during the Victorian era, led to riots by the prisoners in 1979. There

was further controversy in 1999 when Sir David Ramsbotham, the Chief Inspector of Prisons, claimed that the Scrubs was a hotbed of racism in which prison officers were destructive and self-seeking, over-influencing management decisions. The name of the area in which the prison stands was recorded as *Wermeholte* at the beginning of the thirteenth century. That would indicate it may be derived from the Old English words *wyrm* and *holt*, which suggest that it was once 'a woodland with snakes'.

WREN, CHRISTOPHER (1632–1723)
Following the GREAT FIRE, which destroyed much of the CITY OF LONDON in 1666, Wren greatly influenced the way in which the urban area was rebuilt through his plans for ST PAUL'S CATHEDRAL and other places of worship. Born in East Knowle (Wiltshire), he was the son of the local rector, also called Christopher, and his wife, Mary. He showed considerable aptitude for the sciences while he was at Westminster School and continued to pursue these interests at Oxford University, where he graduated in 1653. After a further four years of research, he was appointed lecturer at Gresham College (see THOMAS GRESHAM), but in 1661 he returned to Oxford as Savilian Professor of Astronomy. Initially, he investigated the planet Saturn, carried out experiments designed to evaluate the moon's influence on barometric observations (the use of the barometer as a means of predicting weather is often attributed to Wren) and worked out a graphical method of explaining solar and lunar eclipses. He also played a large part in the discussions that led to the formation of the ROYAL SOCIETY, which he later served as president in 1681–3, but, from the early 1660s, became increasingly involved in architectural work (possibly because he had a reputation for preparing very precise drawings).

In 1663–5, Wren designed a new chapel for Pembroke College, Cambridge, and, in 1664–9, he was involved in preparing plans for the Sheldonian Theatre at Oxford. On 12 September 1666, less than a week after the Great Fire had burned itself out, he presented Charles II with proposals for the rebuilding of the city. That grand scheme was never fully put into effect but, even so, he was made a member of the commission responsible for planning the new London and is usually credited with designs for the replacement for St Paul's as well as those for fifty-one parish churches, thirty-six LIVERY COMPANY halls, the CUSTOM HOUSE and many private homes.

The reconstruction of the new cathedral was the most complex of these undertakings in terms both of ARCHITECTURE and of politics. The Church of England clergy clearly wanted a church built in traditional medieval style. Wren, however, had visited Paris in 1665 and preferred the domed structures he had seen there. As a result, drawings were constantly changed and refined in an attempt to satisfy both tastes so it was not until 1675 that a satisfactory compromise was reached. At other sites, he was able to impose more of his own preferences, relying, for his interiors, on simple shapes adapted and moulded to suit the needs of site and congregation, as at ST MARY ABCHURCH CHURCH. By contrast, the exteriors were often more flamboyant, with elaborately crafted spires that heightened individuality and made the churches conspicuous from a great distance (the steeple at ST BRIDE'S CHURCH, FLEET STREET, was the inspiration for the design of the traditional tiered wedding cake). Major secular commissions included the open courtyards of CHELSEA HOSPITAL (1681–91), the reconstruction of Cardinal Wolsey's Tudor palace at HAMPTON COURT (1689–94), the conversion of KENSINGTON PALACE into a residence for William III and Mary II (1689–1702), the erection of a Royal Naval Hospital at GREENWICH (from 1696) and additions to WESTMINSTER ABBEY (where he was appointed Surveyor in 1698). Outside London, he was responsible for repair work to Salisbury Cathedral (1668), the design of Trinity College library at Cambridge University (1676–84), the building of a new chapel at Queen's College, Oxford, and other works.

In 1669, Wren was appointed Surveyor General for London. Four years later, he was knighted by Charles II. He retained the patronage of the Stuarts through the reigns of William and Mary and of Queen Anne but the accession of the first Hanoverian monarch, George I, in 1714 allowed his enemies to plot his downfall. He was replaced as Surveyor General in 1718 and spent most of his remaining years at Hampton Court. On a visit to his London house at St James's Street, PICCADILLY, early in 1723 he caught a cold and on 23 February he died. He was buried in St Paul's, where an inscription in his honour, at the entrance to the choir, finishes with the words *Lector si monumentum requiris, circumspice* ('Reader, if you seek a monument, look around you').

In recent years some scholars have questioned traditional attributions of church and other designs to Wren, claiming that he could not have achieved everything credited to his name. For example, the more baroque parts of St Paul's, according to some critics, were the work of NICHOLAS HAWKSMOOR and ST BENET'S CHURCH, PAUL'S WHARF, that of Robert Hooke. (See also ADMIRALTY, THE; BANQUETING HOUSE; BLACKFRIARS; BOW BELLS; BUSHY PARK; COLE ABBEY CHURCH, DISTAFF LANE; CORNHILL; GUILDHALL; JONES, INIGO; LOMBARD STREET; BOROUGH HOUSE; MONUMENT; PORTLAND STONE; QUEEN'S HOUSE; ROYAL OBSERVATORY; ST ANDREW'S CHURCH, HOLBORN; ST CLEMENT DANES CHURCH, STRAND; ST JAMES'S CHURCH, PICCADILLY; ST JAMES'S PALACE; ST STEPHEN WALBROOK CHURCH, WALBROOK; ST THOMAS'S HOSPITAL; SIR JOHN SOANE'S MUSEUM; TEMPLE BAR; THEATRE ROYAL, DRURY LANE; WALBROOK.)

Y

YEOMAN WARDER OF THE TOWER

See BEEFEATER.

YEOMEN OF THE GUARD

The Yeomen of the Guard are reputed to be the world's oldest surviving company of royal bodyguards. Formed by Henry VII in 1485, their tasks are now largely ceremonial. Members, who wear a scarlet uniform of Tudor design, with royal emblems embroidered in gold, all formerly served with the armed forces. (See also HONOURABLE CORPS OF GENTLEMEN AT ARMS)

YERKES, CHARLES TYSON (1837–1905)

Yerkes transformed London's UNDERGROUND RAILWAY system at the beginning of the twentieth century. Born in Philadelphia on 25 June 1837, he left school at the age of seventeen and got a job as a clerk with a company dealing in grain. In 1859, he established a brokerage firm then, in 1862, founded a bank specializing in the sale of government bonds. Nine years later, when the bond market collapsed, he lost his entire capital and was imprisoned, ostensibly for embezzlement but the prosecution was certainly influenced by his decision not to give the City of Philadelphia priority as he repaid his debts. In 1873, pardoned by the state governor, he began to invest in TRANSPORT companies, particularly in Chicago, where he employed imaginative, and wholly illegal, methods to obtain competitive advantage (for example, he used prostitutes to seduce city officials then blackmailed the men into supporting his applications for franchises). In the 1890s, he was the principal architect of The Loop, Chicago's inner-city rail transport system, but accusations of shoddy workmanship, cash-flow problems and allegations of bribery encouraged him to sell his interests in 1900.

With the profits from that sale, Yerkes embarked on a process of acquisition in London, buying TRANSPORT companies that had developed piecemeal during the second half of the nineteenth century. In 1901, he purchased the Metropolitan District Electric Traction Company, the Great Northern and Strand Company, and the Baker Street and Waterloo Company, merging them into the Underground Electric Railways Company of London (UERL) and providing a foundation for provision of an integrated public transport service in the capital. Backed largely by American financiers, he promoted electrification of the network, expansion of lines beyond the suburbs to areas where housing development could follow the railway, and construction of deep level TUBES (rather than cut and cover tunnelling, which simply involved digging up a road, building the tunnel, laying track, covering the tunnel and replacing the road). He also ensured that stations were attractive and that trains were well equipped, making journeys as pleasant, safe and regular as possible.

Yerkes died in New York City on 29 December 1905, leaving an estate valued at US$4 million and many unhappy colleagues. The passenger numbers that he had predicted for his underground railways failed to materialize, partly because competition from BUSES and electric TRAMS kept fares low, so returns on investment were limited. However, in 1912, UERL initiated a second phase of aggressive expansion, buying the London General Omnibus Company, the Central London Tube Company and other businesses so that, within a year, it controlled the bulk of the city's mass transit provision, giving residents a relatively low-cost service above and below ground. (See also BAKERLOO LINE; DISTRICT LINE; NORTHERN LINE; PICCADILLY LINE; ROYAL COMMISSION ON LONDON TRAFFIC (1903–05).)

Z

ZOOLOGICAL GARDENS

See CHESSINGTON; LONDON ZOO; TOWER OF LONDON; WALWORTH.

London, c. 1560.

APPENDICES

HISTORICAL EVENTS

In the following list, entries for each year are listed in alphabetical order.

***c.* 55 BC**
According to legend, Julius Caesar leads his Roman Army across the River Thames at Brentford.

54 BC
An invading Roman Army battles with native Celtic Catuvellauni people at the site of modern Stanmore.

AD 43
The Romans invade the British Isles.

60
Londinium (with a population of about 30,000 people) becomes the capital of Roman Britain.

61
Boadicea attacks the Roman settlement at Londinium.

***c.* 100–*c.* 400**
The first London Bridge is built.

179
The Romans erect a basilica in Londinium.

190–220
The Romans encircle Londinium with a defensive wall.

410
The Romans abandon Londinium and the city's population falls.

457
Invading Jutes defeat native Britons in battle at Crayford.

604
Ethelbert, the first Christian king of Kent, founds St Paul's Cathedral.

605
The Bishopric of London is established.

***c.* 666**
St Erkenwald founds Barking Abbey.

685
The first stone church is erected on the site of St Paul's Cathedral.

***c.* 750**
Sebert, King of the Saxons, builds a church on the site now occupied by Westminster Abbey.

787
Offa, King of Mercia, holds a synod on the site of present-day Chelsea.

800–900
Danish invaders pillage London.

1030
Waltham Abbey is founded as a collegiate church of secular canons.

1060
Edward the Confessor builds a palace on the site of modern Westminster and orders the construction of an abbey dedicated to St Peter. Waltham Abbey is rebuilt by Harold, son of Earl Godwin of Wessex and future king.

1066
The Normans invade England and make London their administrative centre.

1078
Work begins on the construction of the Tower of London.

1091
London Bridge is destroyed by a storm but rebuilt.

1097
William Rufus (son of William the Conqueror) orders the building of Westminster Hall.

1099
According to the *Anglo-Saxon Chronicle*, the River Thames floods, causing much damage.

***c.* 1100**
London's population reaches 14,000–18,000.

1101
Matilda (wife of Henry I) builds a leper hospital in the fields beyond the western wall of the City of London.

1106
St Thomas's Hospital is founded.

1114
Gilbert the Knight acquires land at Merton and endows an Augustinian priory.

1120
St Margaret's Church is built at Westminster.

1123
Rahere, a courtier of Henry I, founds an Augustinian priory named in honour of St Bartholomew at Smithfield.

1132
Henry I grants the City of London a charter empowering it to appoint a sheriff.

1133
Henry I gives St Bartholomew's Priory the right to hold an annual fair for three days from St Bartholomew's Eve (24 August). The event survived until 1855.

1135
William de Montfichet founds Stratford Langthorne Abbey for the Cistercian order.

1136
London Bridge is burned down but rebuilt in elm wood.

1160–1185
Temple Church is built.

1170
Ranulf de Glanville, chief justiciary of England, founds a priory at Stanmore. Waltham Abbey is refounded as a community of Augustinian monks.

1176
Work begins on replacing the wooden London Bridge with a stone structure.

1178
Lesnes Abbey is founded for Augustinian monks by Richard de Luci as a penance for supporting Henry II in a dispute that led to the murder of Thomas Becket.

1185
The Knights Templar build a church on the north bank of the River Thames close to present-day Charing Cross.

1189
Henry FitzAilwyn is appointed first Lord Mayor of London.

1197
The Corporation of London pays Richard I the sum of 1,500 marks (£1,000) for rights of control over the River Thames.

***c.* 1197**
Walter and Rose Bruno found an Augustinian priory, St Mary Spital, to the east of the City of London.

1200
A Court of Aldermen is formed to provide local government for the City of London.

_c_. 1200
London's population reaches 20,000–25,000.

1221
Dominican monks found a monastery at Shoe Lane, in the area now known as Blackfriars.

1224
Franciscan friars establish a monastery on land gifted by John Travers, sheriff of London.

1236
The Statute of Merton, signed at the Augustinian priory and sometimes said to be the first Act of Parliament, gives lords of the manor power to enclose common lands.

1237
The City of London appoints its first city chamberlains.

1243
A community of French Protestants, the Hospital of St Anthony, is established north of Threadneedle Street.

1245–1532
Westminster Abbey is built in its current form.

1253
Carmelite monks build a priory in the City of London.

1273
London's first customs house is erected at Old Wool Quay.

1290
The Bishops of Ely establish a London residence at Ely Place.

1291
The heart of Queen Eleanor, wife of Edward I, is buried by the altar at Greyfriars Monastery.

1297
The Stone of Scone, coronation stone of Scotland's monarchs, is seized by Edward I of England and placed in Westminster Abbey.

_c_. 1297
Work begins on the construction of Lambeth Palace.

1300
St Etheldreda's Church is built in Holborn. Work begins on the construction of Eltham Palace.

1348
Edward III establishes the Order of the Garter (the oldest knighthood in Europe) at Eltham Palace.

1348–49
The Black Death (bubonic, pneumonic and septicaemic plague) ravages London, killing about half of the city's population.

***c.* 1350**
London's population reaches 40,000–50,000.

1370
The Legal Society of Lincoln's Inn is formed. Sir Walter Manny founds a Carthusian monastery at what is now Charterhouse Square.

1381
During the Peasants' Revolt, Wat Tyler leads a group of protesters into London, where they set fire to the Tower and behead the Archbishop of Canterbury at Lambeth Palace.

1388
Tyburn becomes a site for public executions.

1390
Construction of the nave in Westminster Abbey is completed.

1397
Richard Whittington is appointed Lord Mayor of London.

1400
Geoffrey Chaucer is buried in the south transept of Westminster Abbey, an area later known as Poet's Corner.

***c.* 1400**
Lincoln's Inn is built.

1410–20
The Bishop's Palace is built at Fulham.

1411–39
A Guildhall is built for the Corporation of London. After the Great Fire of 1666, it was the only pre-seventeenth-century stone structure left standing in the City of London.

1415
Henry V founds a Bridgettine monastery on the land later occupied by Syon House.

1426
Humphrey, Duke of Gloucester and brother of Henry V, builds Bella Donna, later known as Greenwich Palace.

1433
Greenwich Park is created as walls are built around the Bella Donna estate.

1480
Edward IV establishes a Franciscan monastery at Greenwich.

1484
Richard III founds the College of Arms.

1485
Henry VII creates the Yeomen of the Guard.

1497
Henry VII builds Richmond Palace.

1500–6
Henry VII rebuilds Greenwich Palace.

1503–12
Henry VII's chapel is built at Westminster Abbey.

1509
Henry VIII founds the Honourable Corps of Gentlemen at Arms.

1512
Henry VIII creates England's second Royal Naval Dockyard at Woolwich (the first was at Portsmouth).

1513
A third Royal Naval Dockyard is built at Deptford.

1514
The City of London's Court of Aldermen establishes an order of precedence for livery companies. The Deptford Guild of Mariners is granted a royal charter authorizing it to provide pilotage on the River Thames. Thomas Wolsey begins building Hampton Court Palace, intending that it will be the finest residence in England.

1515–20
Henry VIII builds Bridewell Palace.

1518
The Royal College of Physicians of London is founded.

1520–32
The Church of St Andrew Undershaft is erected.

1529
Henry VIII orders the building of Whitehall Palace. Thomas Wolsey gives him Hampton Court Palace.

1531
Henry VIII buys a leper hospital outside the western walls of the City of London, gives each inmate a pension, and builds St James's Palace in its place.

1536–41
English monasteries, including those in London, are dissolved and their assets transferred to the Crown.

1537
The Fraternity or Guild of Artillery of Longbows, Crossbows and Handguns (now the Honourable Artillery Company) is formed.

1538
The area now occupied by Bushy Park and Hampton Court Park is enclosed as a hunting forest by Henry VIII. The king builds Nonsuch Palace.

1539
A court of law is built beside Newgate Prison in a street named Old Bailey.

1547
The Corporation of London buys the buildings of St Mary Bethlehem Priory (known as Bedlam) and converts them into an asylum for the mentally ill. The Deptford Guild of Mariners is renamed the Corporation of Trinity House on Deptford Strand.

1551
Edward VI confiscates the property of the Hanseatic League.

1552
Edward VI gives estates at Covent Garden to John, Earl of Bedford.

1553
The City of London Corporation accepts Bridewell Palace as a gift from Edward VI and converts it into a prison. Edward VI establishes a school on the site of Greyfriars Monastery. (Now known as Christ's Hospital, the institution moved out of London in 1897.)

1557
The inmates at Bedlam asylum are moved to Moorfields and become a popular attraction for city residents.

1564–65
The River Thames freezes over. Archery contests are held on the ice.

1567
The Old Curiosity Shop is built on Portsmouth Street. Still functioning, it is claimed to be the oldest store in London.

1568
The Royal Exchange opens as a meeting place for merchants.

1572
John Lyon founds Harrow School.

1576
Sir Thomas Gresham buys Osterley Park House. The Theatre, London's first playhouse, opens at Shoreditch.

1577
Francis Drake sets off from Deptford on his circumnavigation of the world. A theatre opens in Blackfriars, attracting the city's literati and making the area a fashionable place to live.

1579
Thomas Gresham endows Gresham College, creating seven lecturerships in arts and sciences.

1587
Philip Henslowe builds the Rose Theatre, the first playhouse at Bankside.

1595
A Marshal is appointed to maintain order in the City of London.

1596
The Swan Theatre opens at Bankside.

1598
Playwright Ben Jonson kills actor Gabriel Spencer in a duel. Queen Elizabeth expels merchants of the Hanseatic League from London.

1598–99
Cuthbert and Richard Burbage build the Globe Theatre at Bankside.

1600
The East India Company is founded. Philip Henslowe builds the Fortune Theatre, the largest of its day, at Bankside.

***c.* 1600**
London's population reaches 200,000–250,000.

1603
James VI of Scotland enters London, by way of Aldersgate, to claim the throne of England as James I. A plague epidemic kills 30,000 people.

1605
Actor and theatre manager Edward Alleyn endows a college at Dulwich for twelve poor scholars. A group of Roman Catholic conspirators attempts to blow up the Houses of Parliament. Guy Fawkes (the explosives expert) is found in a cellar packed with gunpowder and, under torture, reveals the names of his colleagues, all of whom are executed. The River Thames freezes over.

1606
Settlers leave Blackwall to found the first permanent English colony in N. America at Virginia. Walter Cope, Chancellor of the Exchequer, builds Cope Castle (now known as Holland House) in Kensington.

1608
England's first golf club is formed on Blackheath.

1610
Sir Thomas Vavasour builds Ham House.

1611
Thomas Sutton buys the former Carthusian monastery at Charterhouse and converts it into a school (for boys) and hospital (for gentlemen).

1613
The Globe Theatre is destroyed by fire but rebuilt. Philip Henslowe opens the Hope Theatre at Bankside.

1616
Inigo Jones is commissioned to build the Queen's House at Greenwich for Anne of Denmark, wife of James I.

1620
The *Mayflower* leaves Rotherhithe for the Americas.

1621
Poet John Donne is appointed Dean of St Paul's Cathedral.

1622
The Banqueting House, designed by Inigo Jones, opens with a performance of Ben Jonson's *Masque of Angers*.

1630
Frances Russell, Earl of Bedford, commissions Inigo Jones to plan a development at Covent Garden.

1631–35
The Earl of Leicester erects a mansion on the north side of what is now Leicester Square, initiating urban development on agricultural land.

1633
St Paul's Church, Covent Garden (the first Anglican place of worship to be built in London after the Reformation), is completed.

1635
The first postal deliveries to private citizens in London are made as part of the Royal Mail service. Hyde Park is opened to the public.

1637
Charles I encloses Richmond Park as hunting forest.

1638
A cattle market is formally established at Smithfield by the Corporation of London (but the site had been a focus for trade in animals since the early twelfth century). William Newton develops Lincoln's Inn Fields for housing, despite the objections of the Inn.

1642
Puritan authorities close the Globe Theatre. Royalist troops defeat a Parliamentarian force at Brentford and advance (temporarily) on London.

1644
The Globe Theatre is demolished.

1649
Charles I is executed at the Banqueting House, and England becomes a republic.

1652
The Fleet River is clogged with rubbish and impassable to boats.

1657
Jews are allowed into England and settle in Mile End.

1660
The Earl of Southampton lays out Southampton (now Bloomsbury) Square. The English monarchy is restored, and Charles II's court returns to London. The Society of London for the Promotion of Natural Knowledge is founded.

1660–69
Samuel Pepys records the minutiae of London life in his *Diary*.

1661
At Blackwall, the East India Company builds a wet dock, the first with gated access to the River Thames.

1662
Charles II grants a royal charter to the Society of London for the Promotion of Natural Knowledge, founded in 1660. The organization is now known as the Royal Society.

1663
Diarist Samuel Pepys records that the River Thames flooded Whitehall.

1665
London suffers an epidemic of plague. Henry Jermyn begins to develop St James's Square.

1666
The Great Fire kills nine people and destroys over 13,000 buildings (including eighty-nine churches) in the City of London. The *London Gazette* is first published.

1669
Christopher Wren is appointed Surveyor General for London. The Royal Exchange reopens in new premises (its previous building was destroyed by the Great Fire of 1666).

1670
The Earl of Bedford obtains a royal charter entitling him to hold a daily fruit and vegetable market on his estate at Covent Garden. Leicester Square is laid out.

1670–83
St Mary-le-Bow Church is built to Christopher Wren's designs.

1671
A 202-foot-high monument is built to commemorate the Great Fire of 1666. Diarist John Evelyn introduces woodcarver Grinling Gibbons to the royal court.

1671–1703
St Bride's Church is built to designs prepared by Christopher Wren.

1672
John, Earl of Lauderdale, converts Ham House into one of the most sumptuous mansions in England.

1672–1717
St Stephen Walbrook Church is built to Christopher Wren's designs.

1675
An astronomical observatory, established by royal warrant, is built at Greenwich.

1675–1710
St Paul's Cathedral is rebuilt.

1676
The Apothecaries' Company establishes Chelsea Physic Garden so that its members can conduct research into the properties of medicinal plants. Fire destroys much of Southwark.

1676–84
St James's Church, Piccadilly, designed by Christopher Wren, is erected.

1677–83
St Benet's Church, Paul's Wharf, is built to Christopher Wren's designs.

1679–82
Christopher Wren rebuilds St Clement Dane's Church.

***c.* 1680**
Edward Lloyd's coffeehouse, a popular meeting place for ship masters and merchants, becomes the best place in London at which to arrange insurance deals. From these beginnings, Lloyd's of London evolves into one of the world's principal insurers.

1681
Soho Square is laid out.

1681–86
Christopher Wren rebuilds St Mary Abchurch Church.

1682
Charles II founds Chelsea Hospital as a home for soldiers who are no longer able to undertake military duties. Nonsuch Palace is bought, and demolished, by Lord Berkeley, who uses the stone to build a mansion at Epsom (Surrey).

1683
Abraham Boydell Cuper (gardener to the Earl of Arundel) opens Cuper's Gardens as a place of recreation for Londoners. A spa, with entertainment for visitors, opens at Sadler's Wells.

1683–84
When the River Thames freezes over, stall holders set up booths on the ice. Charles II attends the Forst Fair with his family.

1684
Nicholas Barbon lays out Red Lion Square.

1684–90
Christopher Wren designs the Church of St Andrew, Holborn.

1685
Islington Spa attracts Londoners to its supposedly health-giving waters. Louis XIV of France revokes legislation giving French Protestants freedom of worship. As a result, Huguenot refugees flee to London.

1685–95
St. Andrew by the Wardrobe, Christopher Wren's last church in the City of London, is erected.

1689
William III moves the royal court from Whitehall Palace to Kensington Palace because air pollution in central London is affecting his asthma. Christopher Wren is commissioned to refurbish and extend the building, which was previously known as Nottingham House.

1691
Nicholas Hawksmoor is appointed Clerk of Works at Kensington Palace.

1692
John Campbell founds the bank now known as Coutts and owned by the Royal Bank of Scotland, which holds the account of Queen Elizabeth II.

1694
Scotsman William Paterson founds the Bank of England at Mercers' Hall.

1696
Howland Great Dock is built at Rotherhithe to accommodate 120 merchant ships. In the nineteenth century, when it is known as the Greenland Dock, it becomes part of the Surrey Commercial Docks development.

1696–1702
Christopher Wren, Nicholas Hawksmoor, John Vanbrugh and other architects build Greenwich Hospital (which became the Royal Naval College in 1873) on the site of Greenwich Palace.

1697
The first tea auctions are held in London.

1698
Fire destroys much of the interior of Whitehall Palace and the Banqueting House. As a result, the royal family makes St James's Palace its principal residence. Parliamentary legislation abolishes the cartel controlling sales at Billingsgate Fish Market.

1699–1700
The Ranger's House is erected at Greenwich.

***c.* 1700**
London's population reaches 575,000–670,000.

1701
Development of a spa attracts fashionable Londoners to Hampstead.

1702
The *Morning Chronicle*, London's first newspaper, is published.

1704
The first houses are built in Queen Anne's Gate.

1705
The Queen's Theatre (now known as Her Majesty's Theatre) opens in Haymarket under the management of architect John Vanbrugh (who designed the building) and dramatist William Congreve.

1707
William Fortnum and Hugh Mason found the grocery store that still bears their names.

1709–11
Marlborough House, designed by Christopher Wren, is built next to St James's Palace for Sarah, Duchess of Marlborough.

1711–18
St Alfege's Church, Greenwich, is rebuilt to Nicholas Hawksmoor's designs.

1713
Thomas Doggett leaves a will requiring that a portion of his estate be used to provide a coat and badge for the winner of a sculling race on the Thames. The race is now the oldest fixture in Britain's sporting calendar.

1714
Architect James Gibbs sets up practice in London and wins a commission to design St Mary-le-Strand Church.

1715
Following an explosion which kills seventeen people, the Royal Arsenal (then known as The Warren) moves from the City of London to Woolwich.

1715–16
The River Thames freezes over. Booths are set up by retailers and entertainments held on the ice.

1717
The Bank of England is made responsible for the management of government securities. Cavendish Square, the first urban development north of Oxford Street, is laid out by John Prince.

1719
A school for prospective Army officers is established at Woolwich. Westminster Hospital is founded.

1720
Haymarket Theatre opens.

1722
Drainage works initiate a process of land improvement on Clapham Common.

1722–26
James Gibbs builds St Martin-in-the-Fields Church.

1724–29
Marble Hill House is built for Henrietta Howard, Countess of Suffolk and mistress of the Prince of Wales.

1725
Guy's Hospital is founded.

1725–29
Richard Boyle, Earl of Burlington, builds Chiswick House, fuelling a resurgence of interest in classical architecture.

1725–31
Grosvenor Square (the second largest square in London) is built as the focus of the Grosvenor Estate's Mayfair development.

1729
Christ Church, Spitalfields, regarded by many critics as Nicholas Hawksmoor's masterpiece, is consecrated. A wooden bridge built across the River Thames links Putney (on the south bank) to Fulham (on the north).

1730–31
The Serpentine is created in Hyde Park at the suggestion of Caroline of Ansbach, wife of George II.

1731–33
St Giles-in-the-Fields Church is rebuilt to the designs of Henry Flitcroft.

1732
Entrepreneur John Rich builds a lavish new theatre in Drury Lane, opening with a performance of William Congreve's *Way of the World*. No. 10 Downing Street becomes the Prime Minister's official residence.

1733
George's Hospital is founded.

1734
The Bank of England moves to Threadneedle Street.

1735
John Rich (founder of the Covent Garden Theatre) and George Lambert (a scene painter) form the Beefsteak Club, a society for twenty-four gentlemen of noble birth.

1738
George Dance the Elder is appointed architect and surveyor to the Corporation of London.

1738–50
Westminster Bridge is built.

1739
Work begins on the development of Berkeley Square.

1739–40
The River Thames freezes. As in 1715–16, stall holders set up booths on the ice.

1739–52
The Mansion House, official residence of the Lord Mayor of London, is built to the designs of George Dance the Elder.

1740
The London Hospital is founded.

1741
Actor David Garrick makes his first appearance (as Harlequin) on the London stage. The Army officer training school at Woolwich is given the status of Royal Military Academy.

1741–44
St Botolph's Church is built to plans prepared by George Dance the Elder.

1742
Thomas Coram founds a children's hospital at Lamb's Conduit Fields.

1744
Samuel Baker, a London bookseller, opens the auction house that becomes Sotheby's.

1745
The Middlesex Hospital is founded.

1747
Actor David Garrick leases Drury Lane Theatre in partnership with James Lacy. London's first Corn Exchange is built at Mark Lane.

1747–76
Author Horace Walpole buys a small property at Strawberry Hill and appoints a Committee of Taste to advise on its conversion into a Gothic castle.

1748
Novelist Henry Fielding is appointed magistrate at Bow Street and forms the Bow Street Runners.

1750–60
Horse Guards Parade is laid out by John Vardy to William Kent's designs.

1751
The Bank of England assumes responsibility for administering the national debt.

1753–56
John Brooks perfects the art of printing transfers on porcelain, selling the resulting products as Battersea China.

1754
William Shipley, a Nottingham teacher, founds the Society for the Encouragement of Arts, Manufactures and Commerce. The organization was renamed the Royal Society of Arts in 1908 by permission of Edward VII.

1755
The first Trooping the Colour ceremony is held.

1757
Horace Walpole installs a printing press at his home in Strawberry Hill and publishes many of his own works, as well as those of other writers (such as poet Thomas Gray).

1758
Architect Robert Adam establishes a practice in London.

1758–59
A wooden bridge is erected across the River Thames between Kew and Gunnersbury.

1758–62
Houses are removed from London Bridge and the structure's arches strengthened.

1759
The British Museum opens to the public (but visitors are admitted only if they request permission in writing). The Royal Botanic Gardens are laid out by Augusta, widow of Frederick, Prince of Wales.

1760
Bishop's Gate, the point at which the Romans' Ermine Street entered London, is demolished, along with Cripplegate (one of the Romans' northern entrances to the city), so that the road system can be improved. Cuper's Gardens close and a vinegar distillery is built on the site. Ludgate, originally an entry to the western areas of Roman London, is demolished. The Society for the Encouragement of Arts, Manufactures and Commerce holds Britain's first art exhibition.

1760–69
A new bridge is built across the River Thames between Blackfriars and Southwark to provide the only crossing between Westminster Bridge and London Bridge.

1761
Aldgate (the site of the eastern entry to Roman London) and Aldersgate (one of the northern entries) are demolished. Portman Square is laid out. Rivals Robert Adam and William Chambers are appointed architects to George III.

1761–62
William Chambers builds the Great Pagoda at Kew Gardens.

1761–68
Robert Adam redesigns Syon House for Hugh, Duke of Northumberland.

1762
Edward Boodle founds Boodle's as an apolitical gentlemen's social club based in Pall Mall.
John and Francis Baring establish a merchant bank in the City of London.

1763
James Boswell and Samuel Johnson meet for the first time.

1763–67
Robert Adam is commissioned to remodel Osterley Park House.

1764
Robert Adam is commissioned to remodel Kenwood House.

1765
Thomas Roseman builds a theatre at Sadler's Wells.

1766
Midshipman James Christie establishes an auction house in Pall Mall.

1767
Newgate, originally one of the western entry points to Roman London, is demolished.

1767–73
The gardens at Syon House are laid out by Capability Brown.

1768
Captain James Cook leaves from Deptford to search for 'Terra Australis'. George Dance the Younger succeeds his father as architect and surveyor to the Corporation of London. Robert, James and John Adam begin work on the Adelphi development. The Royal Academy of Arts is founded.

1770
The discovery of a spring with allegedly health-giving properties leads to the establishment of a spa at Bermondsey.

1770–78
Newgate Prison is rebuilt to the designs of George Dance the Younger. Robert Adam finalizes plans for Apsley House (now the Wellington Museum).

1771–72
A wooden bridge is built across the River Thames between Chelsea and Battersea.

1771–81
The cutting of wood for fuel reduces the area of Epping Forest from 9,000 to 3,000 acres.

1773
A group of brokers forms a stock exchange in Threadneedle Street.

1774
The first cricket match in England is held between Kent and an All-England team at a site in City Road. The River Thames is bridged at Richmond.

1775
Dr Samuel Johnson publishes his two-volume *Dictionary of the English Language*.

1775–80
Thomas Crewer and William Scott lay out Bedford Square, one of London's finest Georgian developments.

1776
Manchester Square is developed.

1776–86
Somerset House is built to William Chambers' designs.

1777
Charles and John Wesley, founders of Methodism, visit Bethnal Green, in the East End, and declare that the area is scarred by 'such poverty as few can conceive without seeing it'. George Dance the Younger lays out Finsbury Square.

1780
Lord George Gordon leads a series of protests designed to prevent the Tory government from repealing anti-Catholic legislation. During the disturbances, the Bank of England is stormed and several prisons (including Newgate) ransacked. Public executions at Tower Hill are abolished.

1783
Public hangings are transferred from Tyburn to a gallows outside Newgate Prison.

1784
The City Day Police are formed to maintain law and order in the City of London during daylight hours. General William Roy establishes, at Hounslow, a baseline for the mapping of the British Isles.

1785
John Walter publishes the *Daily Universal Register.*

1787
Marylebone Cricket Club is formed.

1788
The *Daily Universal Register* is renamed *The Times.*

1788–89
The River Thames freezes and a fair is held on the ice.

1790
Violinist and impresario Johan Peter Salomon commissions the music now known as the *London Symphonies* from Joseph Haydn.

1791
Flogging of women prisoners at Bridewell is abolished. James Boswell's *Life of Samuel Johnson* is published.

1792
Henry Walton Smith opens a newsagent's store in Little Grosvenor Street. (The firm's name changed to W.H. Smith in 1828 and by 2000 the company had become the largest retailer of books and stationery in the United Kingdom.)

1798
Patrick Colquhoun and John Harriott form a force of river police.

1799
The Royal Institution is founded by Benjamin Thompson as a means of 'diffusing the knowledge and facilitating the general introduction of useful mechanical inventions and improvements'.

1800
Bedlam asylum for the mentally ill moves from Moorfields to Lambeth. Russell Square is laid out by architect James Burton.

1801
The first British census indicates that London has 959,310 citizens. Paddington Canal opens.

1802
The West India Company builds London's first large enclosed wet dock on the Isle of Dogs.

1803
The Surrey Iron Railway (the world's first public railroad service) links Wandsworth to Croydon.

1805
London Docks open at Wapping. No. 11 Downing Street becomes the official residence of the Chancellor of the Exchequer.

1806
The East India Docks at Blackwall are expanded. John Smith builds the Sans Pareil Theatre (now known as the Adelphi Theatre) in the Strand so that he can further his daughter's acting career.

1807
Frederick Winsor presents a display of gas lighting in Pall Mall to celebrate the birthday of George, Prince of Wales. Surrey Docks (the only enclosed docks on the south bank of the Thames in London) open at Rotherhithe.

1808
Addington Palace, Croydon, becomes the official London residence of the Archbishops of Canterbury.

1811
George, Prince Regent, commissions architect John Nash to convert Marylebone Park into a place for public recreation. The result is the Regent's Park development.

1813
The East India Company loses its monopoly rights to trade with India and with east and south-east Asia.

1813–14
The River Thames freezes over and a great fair is held on the ice.

1814
Dulwich Picture Gallery (now Britain's oldest public art collection) opens. The first Grand Union Canal is opened, linking London to the East Midlands. The Gas Light and Coke Company provides London's first permanent street lighting by placing lamps on Westminster Bridge. Much of St James's Palace is destroyed by fire but immediately rebuilt.

1814–19
The River Thames is bridged between Southwark and the City of London.

1815
Doulton and Watts begin porcelain production in Lambeth.

1815–17
William Montague lays out Finsbury Circus to the designs of George Dance the Younger.

1818
Charing Cross Hospital is founded. The passage of the Church Building Act (a thanksgiving for Britain's victory over the armies of Napoleon Bonaparte at Waterloo) leads to the construction of thirty-eight places of worship in London. Rudolph Cabanel builds the Royal Coburg Theatre (now known as the Old Vic).

1819
Piccadilly Circus takes shape as Regent Street links with Piccadilly.

1820

Conspirators meet in Cato Street to plot the assassination of the whole British cabinet but are betrayed and arrested. George III commissions architect John Nash to prepare plans for Buckingham Palace. Regent's Canal opens, allowing barges to move between Paddington Basin and the River Thames at Limehouse.

1820–40

Trafalgar Square is laid out.

1823

The Baltic Club is founded to regulate trade between London and the Baltic states. Marc Brunel begins work on the first tunnel underneath the River Thames, linking Rotherhithe to Wapping. The Royal Academy of Music is founded by a group of aristocratic arts patrons.

1823–31

The construction of a replacement for London Bridge improves the flow of the River Thames and prevents the channel from freezing over.

1823–47

A new home is built in Great Russell Street for an expanding British Museum.

1824

John Wilson Croker forms The Society (later known as the Athenaeum gentlemen's club) for scientists, writers and artists at Somerset House. The National Gallery opens, with thirty-eight old masters (purchased by the government from the estate of John Julius Angerstein) forming the nucleus of the collection.

1825

Builder Thomas Cubitt starts work on Belgrave Square, the focus of now fashionable Belgravia. The foundations of Lancaster House are laid.

1825–28

Clarence House is built.

1826

Poet Thomas Campbell and other religious dissenters found University College as a centre of learning for nonconformists excluded from Oxford and Cambridge.

1827

A new bridge across the River Thames links Hammersmith (on the north bank) to Barnes (on the south).

1828

London Zoo opens in Regent's Park. Marble Arch is erected as a gateway to Buckingham Palace. St Katharine's Dock, designed by Thomas Telford, opens. Supporters of the Church of England establish King's College as a rival to the nonconformist University College, created in 1826. The Wellington Arch is erected outside Apsley House.

1829

The first boat race between Cambridge University and Oxford University is held on the River Thames. Oxford wins. George Shillibeer introduces a service of horse-drawn carriages that transport passengers between the City of London and Paddington. The Mansion House is refaced with Portland stone. Robert Peel creates the Metropolitan Police force.

1829–32
The Travellers' Club, designed by Charles Barry, is built in Pall Mall.

1830
The hay market at Haymarket closes, and the land is colonized by the entertainment industry. The Royal Geographical Society is founded.

1831
The Duke of Sussex founds the Garrick Club. John Nash designs the Theatre Royal, Haymarket. The Royal Horticultural Society holds its first exhibition.

1832
The Carlton Club is founded (and later evolves into the social headquarters of the Conservative Party). The Society for the Encouragement of Arts, Manufactures and Commerce holds Britain's first exhibition of photography.

1833
Bank of England notes become legal tender. Individual fire brigades merge to form the Fire Engine Establishment. London's first commercial cemetery is laid out at Kensal Green by the General Cemetery Company. The Royal Coburg Theatre is renamed the Royal Vic in honour of the fourteen-year-old Princess (later Queen) Victoria. Sir John Soane arranges for his eclectic collection of curiosities, acquired over a lifetime, to be preserved in a museum. Using Boz as a pen name, Charles Dickens begins to publish stories that draw on his experiences of London.

1834
Much of the Palace of Westminster is destroyed by fire.

1835
Madame Tussaud opens a gallery of waxworks in Baker Street.

1835–60
The Palace of Westminster is rebuilt to designs prepared by Charles Barry and Augustus Welby Northmore Pugin.

1836
London's first steam-driven rail service connects Bermondsey to Deptford. The Reform Club is founded as a meeting place for gentlemen with radical political views. The Whig government creates a University of London, based at Somerset House.

1837
The Geological Museum is founded. The London and Birmingham Railway builds Euston Station. Queen Victoria moves the royal household from St James's Palace to Buckingham Palace. A school of design, predecessor of the Royal College of Art, is established at Somerset House.

1838
The Great Western Railway opens a London terminus at Paddington. The London and Southampton Railway opens a terminus at Nine Elms. The Public Record Office is created by an Act of Parliament.

The Royal Exchange is destroyed by fire. The University of London holds its first examinations (for twenty-three students).

1839
The Bow Street Runners are disbanded. The London Cemetery Company opens a burial ground at Highgate.

1839–42
Nelson's Column is built in Trafalgar Square.

1841
The City of London's first railway station is opened in Fenchurch Street by the London and Blackwall Railway. Following its destruction in the fire of 1838, the Royal Exchange is rebuilt to plans prepared by William Tate. The work involves the demolition of St Benet Fink Church, designed by Christopher Wren. The Royal Botanic Gardens, popularly known as Kew Gardens, are given to the nation by Queen Victoria.

1841–45
Hungerford Bridge is built, providing access to Hungerford Market from the south bank of the River Thames.

1842
Fleet Prison closes. Pentonville Prison accepts its first inmates. Robert Peel's Conservative government buys land on which to lay out Victoria Park, in the East End.

1845
Surrey County Cricket Club is formed, with headquarters at the new Oval ground. The Treasury Buildings are erected in Whitehall to Charles Barry's designs. Waterloo Bridge, designed by John Rennie, links Lambeth to the Strand.

1846
The character of Sweeney Todd makes his first appearance in a story published in the *People's Periodical and Family Library*. Parliament passes legislation authorizing construction of a public park on Battersea Common.

1846–49
Barnes Bridge is erected for the London and South-Western Railway.

1848
The London and South-Western Railway builds a station at Waterloo. A medical officer of health is appointed for the City of London. The Windsor, Staines and South-Western Railway builds a bridge to carry its services over the River Thames at Richmond.

1849
Bedford College (now part of the University of London) is founded specifically to provide a liberal education for women. Harrods store opens in Knightsbridge.

1850
Sir Robert Peel (founder of the police force) dies following a fall from his horse on Constitution Hill. Thomas Cubitt lays out Gordon Square, the last of the Bloomsbury Squares.

1851

Artist G.F. Watt moves into Holland House as a guest of Sara Prinseps and establishes the Holland House Circle. Dr Charles West founds the Great Ormond Street Hospital for Sick Children. The Great Exhibition attracts 6 million visitors to Hyde Park in fourteen weeks. Henry Mayhew's writings on *London Labour and the London Poor*, originally published in the *Morning Chronicle*, appear in a three-volume collection. Marble Arch is moved from Buckingham Palace to its present position at the junction of Oxford Street, Edgware Road, Hyde Park and Bayswater Road.

1851–58

A suspension bridge links Chelsea (on the north bank of the River Thames) to Battersea (on the south).

1852

At the instigation of Prince Albert, profits from the Great Exhibition are used to purchase a site for the construction of museums and educational institutions in south Kensington. Crystal Palace, centerpiece of the Great Exhibition, is dismantled and moved to Sydenham. The Great Northern Railway opens Britain's largest railroad station at King's Cross. Holloway Prison is built. The Palace of Westminster, much rebuilt after the fire of 1834, is opened by Queen Victoria.

1853

Battersea Park opens for public use. The University of London moves from Somerset House to Burlington Gardens.

1854

During an outbreak of cholera in Soho, Dr John Snow persuades the authorities to remove the handle from a water pump in Broad Street. The epidemic ends within days, confirming Snow's belief that the disease is carried by water. The premises of the small arms factory opened at Enfield in 1804 are expanded to facilitate production of the Enfield rifle.

1855

Bartholomew Fair, first held in 1133, is closed because of drunkenness and disorder. Bridewell Prison is closed and inmates are transferred to Holloway. Claridge's Hotel opens. A college for Jews is founded in Golders Green. The Metropolitan Board of Works, London's first citywide local authority, is appointed to replace a plethora of bodies, each dealing with a specific function. The Metropolitan Cattle Market moves from Smithfield to Holloway. The Royal Victoria, first of the Royal group of docks, is opened by Prince Albert.

1856

Joseph William Bazalgette is appointed surveyor to the Metropolitan Board of Works and initiates a programme of improvements to roads and sewage disposal systems. The Society for the Encouragement of Arts, Manufactures and Commerce introduces examinations designed to help young people from working-class families learn vocational skills. By 1989, when the Examinations Board became an independent body with charitable status, nearly a million students were being presented annually.

1857

The Science Museum is founded. The Victoria and Albert Museum is created through the merger of collections of fine and applied arts held by the School of Design and the Museum of Manufactures.

1858

Blackheath Football Club, the oldest public Rugby Union club in London, is formed. Covent Garden Theatre (renamed the Royal Opera House in 1892) opens on the site of the theatre built in Drury Lane by

John Rich in 1732. During an exceptionally hot summer, sewage carried by the River Thames emits a stench that becomes known as the Great Stink. The opening of the Alhambra Theatre proves to be the first step in the growth of an entertainment complex at Leicester Square. Westminster Bridge is lit by electricity.

1859
The chimes of Big Ben ring out over London for the first time. HMS *Warrior*, Britain's first iron-hulled battleship, is launched at the Thames Ironworks in Canning Town. A National Portrait Gallery opens, partly because of Prince Albert's enthusiastic support for the venture. Samuel Gurney founds the Metropolitan Drinking Fountain and Cattle Trough Association in an attempt to reduce levels of cholera and drunkenness.

1860
The Grosvenor (or Victoria) Bridge is built across the River Thames by the London, Chatham and Dover Railway to provide access to Victoria Station. Hungerford Market closes. The London, Brighton and South Coast Railway and the London, Chatham and Dover Railway open stations at Victoria. The Royal Victoria Dock, at Plaistow Marshes, is extended by construction of the Royal Albert Dock.

1861
Tramcars appear on London streets. A wrought-iron bridge is built across the River Thames between Battersea and Chelsea to give the West London Railway access to the station at Clapham Junction.

1862
The London Co-operative Society is founded by railway workers in West Ham. Westminster Bridge is replaced.

1863
Alexandra Palace is opened as an exhibition centre in north London. It is destroyed by fire after only two weeks but rebuilt. London's first underground railway company (the Metropolitan) offers services between Paddington and the City of London. A railway station, now Britain's busiest, opens at Clapham Junction. The Royal College of Art is founded.

1864
Completion of a wrought-iron bridge allows the London, Dover and Chatham Railway to carry passengers across the River Thames from Southwark to the Metropolitan Railway at Blackfriars. The first Peabody Buildings open at Spitalfields. The former Bridewell Prison is demolished. The Hungerford Railway Bridge links Charing Cross to the south bank of the River Thames. John Lewis, a buyer of dress fabrics, opens a shop in Oxford Street that evolves into a major national department store business. The South-Eastern Railway builds a station at Waterloo.

1864–65
The Langham, the first of London's luxury hotels, is built in Portland Place.

1865
Daniel Nicholas Thévenon, a Parisian wine merchant, opens the Café Royal in Glasshouse Street. Parliament approves legislation creating the Metropolitan Fire Brigade. William Booth establishes his first mission in Whitechapel.

1866
Bishops of the Church of England convene for the first Lambeth Conference. The gates at Mile End, London's last major turnpike, are removed. London's first blue plaque (honouring Lord Byron) is erected.

1867

The Hurlingham Club is formed. The Metropolitan Asylums Board is created and introduces a limited ambulance service.

1868

The construction of Parliament Square involves demolition of some of London's worst slums. A covered hall for meat trading is built at Smithfield Market. Millwall Dock opens. Parliamentary legislation ends the spectacle of public hangings in London. St Pancras Station opens as the terminus of the Midland Railway.

1869

The All England Croquet Club is formed at Wimbledon. The bridge over the River Thames between Blackfriars and Southwark is replaced. The Royal Naval Dockyards at Deptford and Woolwich are closed.

1870

Charles Dickens is buried at Westminster Abbey. Dr Thomas John Barnardo opens his first children's home in Mile End. The Gas Light and Coke Company builds a plant, designed to serve the whole of London, on the north bank of the River Thames at Beckton. A London School Board is appointed to provide education for children aged five to thirteen. The Vaudeville Theatre is built in the Strand, opening with performances of James Albery's *Two Roses*, a comedy that helped launch the acting career of Henry Irving.

1870–73

Wandsworth Bridge is built across the River Thames between Wandsworth and Fulham.

1871

Mary Tealby moves her home for unwanted cats and dogs from Holloway to Battersea. The Royal Albert Hall is opened by Queen Victoria.

1871–73

The Albert Bridge is built to carry traffic across the River Thames between Chelsea (on the north bank) and Battersea (on the south).

1872

Charterhouse School moves out of London to Surrey. The first London School Board institution opens in Berners Street.

1873

The East India Company is terminated. The Royal Naval College transfers from Portsmouth to Greenwich.

1874

The Criterion Theatre (one of the first to be constructed underground) opens. Liverpool Street Station opens as the London terminus of the Great Eastern Railway. Wormwood Scrubs Prison is built by convict labour.

1875

Liberty's Store opens in Regent Street. The rules of polo are formalized at the Hurlingham Club.

1876

The Albert Memorial, erected in Kensington Gardens as a tribute to Queen Victoria's late husband, is completed. St Etheldreda's Church, Holborn, becomes the first place of worship to revert to Roman Catholic use since the Reformation.

1877
The All England Croquet Club, founded in 1869, admits tennis players as members. The Corporation of London provides a trading hall for Billingsgate Fish Market. Peter Jones' department store opens for business at Sloane Square.

1878
Cleopatra's Needle is erected on the Victoria Embankment. The Corporation of London and the livery companies found the City and Guilds of London Institute to provide technical and scientific education. The Corporation of London takes control of Epping Forest in order to preserve it as a recreational amenity. A Criminal Investigation Department is formed to co-ordinate detective work within the Metropolitan Police. Parliamentary legislation creates a senate to act as governing body for the University of London. The University of London allows women to receive degrees. William Booth coins the phrase 'Salvation Army' to describe his growing band of missionaries in east London.

1879
Dan Harries Evans opens the D.H. Evans drapery store in Oxford Street, specializing in lace work. Fulham Football Club, the oldest still playing in the top flights of English football, is formed. The passage of the Thames Flood Act leads to construction of embankments alongside the river.

1880
The Corporation of London founds the Guildhall School of Music.

1881
The Comedy Theatre opens in Panton Street, presenting comic operas. The Natural History Museum opens. The Royal Albert Dock opens. The Savoy Theatre (the first public building in London to be lit by electricity) opens in the Strand.

1882
Electricity begins to challenge gas as a source of lighting in London after Parliament authorizes the use of overhead and underground cables as a means of providing power. The Playhouse Theatre is built in Northumberland Avenue by speculator Sefton Parry, who believed that the South-Eastern Railway would eventually purchase the site. The Royal College of Music is founded. The Royal Courts of Justice open in the Strand.

1882–86
The wooden bridge across the River Thames between Putney and Fulham is replaced by a granite structure, designed by Joseph Bazalgette.

1883
The Wellington Arch is moved to its present location at the west end of Constitution Hill. The world's first electricity generating station opens at Holborn Viaduct.

1883–87
The central span of Hammersmith Bridge is replaced.

1884
Construction of the Underground's Circle Line is completed. Delegates at an international conference in Washington DC, agree that the prime meridian (0° longitude) will pass through Greenwich. The footbridge across the River Thames at Teddington is completed. The National Agricultural Hall opens as an exhibition centre. The Prince of Wales becomes patron of Battersea Dogs' Home, setting a precedent for

royal support for the institution. The Prince's Theatre (later known as the Prince of Wales Theatre) opens in Coventry Street. Samuel Barnett founds Toynbee Hall as an educational centre in London's East End. The Savoy Hotel opens.

1886

A bridge is built across the River Thames from Southwark to St Paul's railway station for the Holborn Viaduct Station Company. The South-Eastern Railway opens a terminus at Cannon Street Station. Tilbury Docks open. Tower Bridge is built, linking the Tower of London to Bermondsey docks.

1886–90

New Scotland Yard, designed by R. Norman Shaw, is built as a headquarters for the Metropolitan Police.

1887

Arthur Conan Doyle creates the fictional detective Sherlock Holmes. The Imperial Institute (now the Commonwealth Institute) is founded to commemorate the Golden Jubilee of Queen Victoria's reign.

1888

Female employees at the Bryant and May match factory in Bow go on strike in the first British attempt to involve women in labour union activity. Jack the Ripper cuts the throats of six women in Whitechapel. The London Clearing House is formed. The London County Council replaces the Metropolitan Board of Works. The Lyric Theatre opens in Shaftesbury Avenue. The Royal Court Theatre is built in Sloane Square.

1889

The Garrick Theatre is built for lyricist W.S. Gilbert. London dockers strike and win concessions from managements, encouraging labour in other British industries to form trade unions in an effort to improve working conditions. Queen Victoria allows public access to the state apartments at Kensington Palace. Wyndham's Theatre is built in Charing Cross Road for Charles Wyndham (the only person whom the Marquis of Salisbury would allow to erect a playhouse on his estate).

1889–1903

Charles Booth, in his seventeen-volume *Life and Labour of the People of London*, draws attention to the extent of poverty in the city.

1890

A cast-iron bridge across the River Thames replaces the wooden structure linking Battersea to Chelsea. Electricity is used by the Underground for the first time on the line linking Stockwell to King William Street. Frederick Horniman provides the basis for the modern Horniman Museum by allowing the public to view the objects he has amassed during his travels. Louis Rothman opens a tobacconist's shop in Fleet Street. In 1999, the firm that developed from that inauspicious birth was acquired by British American Tobacco for US$7.55 billion.

1891

Arsenal is the first London football club to turn professional. The London Shipping Company is formed to serve the growing ocean liner industry. The Royal English Opera House (renamed the Palace Theatre in 1892) opens with performances of Arthur Sullivan's *Ivanhoe*.

1891–97

A 4,000-foot-long tunnel is built to link Blackwall (on the north side of the River Thames) with Greenwich (on the south).

1892
John Burns and James Keir Hardie win seats in Parliament, becoming the first members of working-class organizations to represent London constituencies in the HOUSE OF COMMONS. Covent Garden Theatre is renamed the Royal Opera House. The Royal English Opera House is renamed the Palace Theatre. The Trafalgar Square Theatre (now known as the Duke of York's Theatre) is the first playhouse to open in St Martin's Lane.

1892–95
The Brewer Car – the first British automobile to use an internal combustion engine – is built at Walthamstow.

1893
A statue of Eros is erected in Piccadilly Circus as a memorial to the seventh Earl of Shaftesbury.

1894
Lincoln's Inn Fields becomes a public park.

1895
A Jewish Cemetery is laid out at Golders Green. The London School of Economics is founded with funds from the estate of Henry Hunt Hutchison, a left-wing sympathizer.

1895–1903
The Roman Catholic Church builds Westminster Cathedral.

1897
The Anglican Church of St Saviour and St Mary Overie is raised in status, becoming Southwark Cathedral. Christ's Hospital School moves out of London to Horsham (Sussex). The Coburg Hotel (now the Connaught) is erected in Carlos Place. Frederick Temple, Archbishop of Canterbury, sells Addington Palace, London residence of the Primates of the Church of England since 1807. Horse-drawn carriages face their first competition from electric-powered taxis. Motorized omnibuses appear on London streets. The Tate Gallery, gift of sugar refiner Henry Tate, opens at Millbank.

1897–1906
University College Hospital is built.

1898
The Drain – the underground rail link between Waterloo Station and the City of London – is opened. The first London boroughs are created.

1899
The Hospital for Tropical Diseases is founded. The London County Council assumes responsibility for running the Metropolitan Fire Brigade.

1899–1909
Aston Webb designs a new façade for the Victoria and Albert Museum's Cromwell Road frontage.

1900
The Church of England donates nine acres of land at Lambeth Palace to the London County Council for use as a public park in an inner-city area with limited green space. The Wallace Collection of European art, bequeathed to the nation in 1897, is placed on permanent display in Manchester Square. Westminster is given city status.

1901

The Apollo Theatre opens in Shaftesbury Avenue as a venue for musicals. The Baltic Club and the London Shipping Company merge as the Baltic and Mercantile Shipping Exchange Ltd. The Bechstein Concert Hall (later known as the Wigmore Hall) opens with a performance by Evelyn Stuart. The census shows that the County of London has a population of 4,536,267. Electric trams are introduced in London. Frederick Horniman's museum (established in 1890) is acquired by the London County Council. The Metropolitan Police create a Fingerprint Bureau. Whitechapel Art Gallery opens.

1902

The British Academy is founded. A foot tunnel is built under the River Thames between Greenwich and the Isle of Dogs. The London County Council buys Marble Hill House (Twickenham) and the Ranger's House (Greenwich). A Metropolitan Water Board is created to manage London's water supplies. Newgate Prison is demolished to provide space for the erection of the Central Criminal Court.

1902–7

Buildings for the Central Criminal Court, designed by Edward Mountford, are erected at Old Bailey.

1903

The Abbey Theatre opens. The first Wolseley cars are manufactured at Crayford. The New Theatre (later known as the Albery Theatre) is built in St Martin's Lane for Charles Wyndham.

1904

Actor and producer Herbert Beerbohm Tree founds the Royal Academy of Dramatic Art. The Coliseum Theatre (also known as the London Coliseum) opens with a repertoire of variety shows. George Barker makes his first films at the Barker Motion Photography studios in Ealing. The London Symphony Orchestra is formed. Responsibility for children's education passes from the London School Board to the London County Council. Simpson's restaurant opens in the Strand. The Stephen family move into 46 Gordon Square, establishing the Bloomsbury Group.

1905

The Aldwych Theatre opens, featuring musical comedies. The Waldorf Theatre (now known as the Strand Theatre) opens with a repertoire of operas and dramatic productions.

1906

Admiralty Arch, designed by Aston Webb, is built across the eastern entrance to The Mall as part of the nation's memorial to Queen Victoria. The Baker Street and Waterloo Railway and the Great Northern, Piccadilly and Brompton Railway introduce underground services.

1907

The Charing Cross, Euston and Hampstead Railway introduces underground services. The Queen's Theatre opens in Shaftesbury Avenue. The Rugby Football Union makes Twickenham its headquarters. Wyldes Farm, in north London, is put on the market. Much of the land is purchased by a trust fund that develops it as Hampstead Garden Suburb.

1908

The cast-iron railway bridge across the River Thames at Richmond is replaced by a stronger steel structure. London's first escalator is installed at Harrods store. The Society for the Encouragement of Arts, Manufactures and Commerce is renamed the Royal Society of Arts. White City Stadium is erected.

1909
The Port of London Authority is created to manage the city's docks. Selfridge's store opens in Oxford Street.

1910
The London Palladium Theatre opens, featuring variety shows.

1911
Claude Graeme-White establishes Hendon as a centre of innovation in the infant aircraft industry. The Prince's (known from 1962 as the Shaftesbury) Theatre opens with a performance of *The Three Musketeers*. The Queen Victoria Statue, at the western end of The Mall, is unveiled. The University of London moves to a site in Bloomsbury. The Victoria Palace Theatre opens, providing music hall entertainment.

1911–22
County Hall is built, on the opposite side of the River Thames from the HOUSES OF PARLIAMENT, as the headquarters of the London County Council.

1912
The Baltic Exchange moves into new premises at St Mary Axe. George Frampton's statue of Peter Pan, the little boy who never grew up, is placed in Kensington Gardens. The University of London appoints its first female professor.

1912–21
The cast-iron bridge between Southwark and the City of London is replaced by a five-span steel structure designed by Ernest George.

1913
Aircraft manufacturer Handley Page builds a plant at Cricklewood. The Ambassadors Theatre opens in West Street, off Shaftesbury Avenue. Big Ben's winding gear is automated. The Royal Horticultural Society holds its first Chelsea Flower Show.

1914
The London County Council opens the Geffrye Museum.

1916
The last of the horse-drawn carriages, which provided a public transport service in London, disappear from the streets. St Martin's Theatre opens in West Street.

1919
Great Britain's first civil airport is opened on Hounslow Heath, providing services to Paris and Australia. The Palais de Danse (usually known as the Hammersmith Palais) opens on the site of a former tramcar garage in Shepherd's Bush Road. Parliamentary legislation (known as the Addison Act) provides government subsidies that allow London's local authorities to erect 27,000 low-rent homes.

1919–20
The Cenotaph, designed by Edward Lutyens, is erected in Whitehall as a memorial to servicemen and women of the British Empire and Commonwealth who were killed during the First World War.

1920
The Imperial War Museum is established by an Act of Parliament. London Airport is opened at Croydon.

1921

Construction of the George V Dock is completed. Hammersmith Palais is the first British dance hall to have a jazz band on stage. High construction costs result in the abandonment of the housing subsidies introduced by the Addison Act (1919).

1922

The British Broadcasting Corporation (BBC) makes its first radio transmissions from Savoy Hill.

1923

Horace Walpole's Gothic revival castle at Strawberry Hill is bought by the Catholic Education Council and turned into a teacher training college. Wembley Stadium opens in time to host the Football Association Cup final, attended by over 200,000 people.

1924

Legislation introduced by the Labour government re-establishes subsidies for local authority house building and results in the construction of 64,000 low-rent homes over the next decade.

1924–25

The British Empire Exhibition, held at Wembley, attracts over 27 million visitors.

1927

Lord Iveagh bequeaths Kenwood House to the London County Council.

1928

The airstrip at Croydon is officially named London Airport. Lloyd's of London moves from the Royal Exchange to Leadenhall Street. The River Thames floods.

1929

The Duchess Theatre opens in Catherine Street. Managers of London's tram, underground railway and bus companies agree to co-ordinate their services. A second Grand Union Canal is completed, linking London to Birmingham.

1930

The London County Council assumes responsibility for the city's ambulance service. The Phoenix Theatre opens with a performance of Noel Coward's *Private Lives*, featuring Coward himself in the cast. The Prince Edward Theatre opens. The Royal Bethlehem Hospital for the mentally ill (Bedlam) moves out of London to premises in Addington, Surrey. The Whitehall Theatre opens, featuring Walter Hackett in his own play, *The Way to Treat a Woman*.

1930–35

Embankments alongside the River Thames are raised in order to prevent further flooding.

1931

Chessington Zoo opens. The Dorchester Hotel opens in Park Lane. The Ford Motor Company starts car production at Dagenham. Industrialist Samuel Courtauld founds the Courtauld Institute of Art. Ninette de Valois creates a ballet company (later known as the Royal Ballet) at the Old Vic theatre. The Saville Theatre opens.

1932

The Jewish Museum is founded. Lambeth Bridge is replaced. Thomas Beecham creates the London Philharmonic Orchestra.

1933
Battersea Power Station opens. The city's transport service is nationalized and placed under the control of a London Passenger Transport Board.

1935–50
Dr Scott Williamson supervises the Peckham Experiment, conducting research into human biology in the south London community.

1936
The British Broadcasting Corporation builds the world's first television transmitter at Alexandra Palace and begins regular broadcasts. The Crystal Palace is burned to the ground. A pro-fascist rally led by Sir Oswald Mosley breaks up following violence between marchers and their opponents in Cable Street.

1936–40
The lattice-girder bridge across the River Thames between Fulham and Wandsworth is replaced by a cantilever structure designed by T. Pierson Frank.

1937
Earl's Court Exhibition Hall (the largest reinforced concrete structure in Europe at the time) opens. Lupino Lane popularizes the dance known as the Lambeth Walk. The National Maritime Museum opens at Greenwich. St Paul's railway station is renamed Blackfriars Station.

1938
A Green Belt of land protected from development is designated around London by Parliament. Michael Balcon acquires the former Barker Motion Photography site, renames it Ealing Studios, and, for more than a decade, produces a highly successful string of movies now known as the Ealing comedies.

1939
Building work is completed at the Bank of England in Threadneedle Street. Evacuation of schoolchildren begins after the United Kingdom declares war on Germany at the beginning of the Second World War. Irish terrorists make an unsuccessful attempt to blow up Hammersmith Bridge. The Royal Exchange ceases to function as a place for general merchant trading due to the development of specialist markets.

1939–45
John Rennie's Waterloo Bridge is replaced by a new structure designed by Giles Gilbert Scott.

1940–41
During the Blitz, an estimated 18,800 tons of explosive are dropped on London by German aircraft, killing 15,000 people and damaging 3.5 million homes.

1941
The Dorchester Hotel becomes General Dwight D. Eisenhower's British headquarters after the United States enters the Second World War. German bombs destroy the Queen's Hall, forcing the Henry Wood Promenade Concerts to move to the Albert Hall, where they have remained ever since.

1945
Walter Legge forms the Philharmonia Orchestra.

1945–50
The House of Commons is rebuilt following bomb damage suffered during the Second World War.

1946

The Bank of England is nationalized. The City of London (Various Powers) Act gives local councils the authority to create smokeless zones in an effort to reduce smog. Covent Garden Opera Company and Sadler's Wells Ballet make the Royal Opera House their base. The General Assembly of the United Nations holds its first meeting in Methodist Central Hall. Heathrow is recognized as London Airport and provides direct services to the United States. Thomas Beecham founds the Royal Philharmonic Orchestra.

1947

Hansom cabs disappear from London streets. The Royal Military Academy at Woolwich is merged with its counterpart at Sandhurst and part of its barracks converted into a museum for the Royal Regiment of Artillery.

1948

The Labour government nationalizes electricity supply and appoints a London Electricity Board to manage power distribution in the city. The London Passenger Transport Board is replaced by the London Transport Executive. The National Trust acquires Ham House. The Royal Observatory moves from Greenwich to the clearer skies of Herstmonceux (Sussex).

1949

The Earl of Jersey gives Osterley Park to the nation.

1950

Four Scottish nationalist students steal the Stone of Scone (the coronation stone of Scotland's first kings) from Westminster Abbey. It is recovered after four months (though rumours persist that the authorities were deceived into returning a replica to London). Timothy Evans is hanged at Pentonville Prison for the murder of his wife and daughter despite widespread doubts about his guilt. The event fuels the (ultimately successful) campaign to have capital punishment abolished in the United Kingdom.

1951

The Labour government promotes a Festival of Britain in an effort to raise public morale at a time of food rationing and economic reconstruction following the Second World War. The focus of the celebrations is on the dockside between Waterloo Bridge and Hungerford Bridge, where the Royal Festival Hall is built. Battersea Park is redesigned as part of the celebrations.

1952

The last trams are withdrawn from service. The London County Council buys Holland House and converts it for use as a youth hostel. *The Mousetrap*, the world's longest-running play (still being performed at the end of the millennium), opens at the Ambassador's Theatre. 112 people are killed, and 340 injured, when two express trains collide at Harrow and Wealdstone and a third runs into the wreckage. A smog lasting from 5 to 9 December leads to the deaths of 4,700 Londoners with respiratory diseases. The Wellington Museum opens.

1953

The British Film Institute builds a National Film Theatre on the South Bank.

1954

Cutty Sark, built in 1869 and one of the fastest of the tea clippers, is placed in dry dock at Greenwich as a tourist attraction. Excavations under Queen Victoria Street, in the City of London, uncover the remains of the Roman Temple of Mithras, built during the second century AD. The London Commodity Exchange is established.

1956
Big Ben's operating mechanism is overhauled. The BBC moves its television studios from Alexandra Palace to Shepherd's Bush. The Clean Air Act introduces tighter controls on sources of air pollution in London. The Royal Ballet is created through the award of a royal charter to the Sadler's Wells Company.

1957
Boutiques begin to appear in Carnaby Street, which becomes a symbol of 'swinging London' during the 1960s. A Royal Commission, chaired by Sir Edwin Herbert, is appointed to consider the reorganization of local government in London.

1958
The City of London Corporation buys the Barbican site by compulsory purchase order and commissions a new housing estate, with provision for public buildings such as premises for the Museum of London. Gatwick Airport is opened on farmland 25 miles south of central London to accommodate growing air traffic to the capital. A planetarium is built adjacent to Madame Tussaud's waxworks.

1958–61
The United States embassy is built at the western end of Grosvenor Square.

1959
Croydon Airport, increasingly hemmed in by urban development, is closed. The Mermaid Theatre, the first playhouse to open in the City of London for over three centuries, offers its first productions at Puddle Dock.

1960
The Royal Commission established to consider the reorganization of local government in London recommends formation of a Greater London Council and the creation of new boroughs with enhanced powers.

1960–67
A second tunnel is built under the Thames between Blackwall and Greenwich to relieve traffic congestion.

1961
The Royal Navy's victualling yard at Deptford closes. Steam engines are withdrawn from the London Underground railway.

1962
An Act of Parliament establishes the Covent Garden Market Authority to manage London's principal food and vegetable wholesalers. Brunel College of Advanced Technology is renamed Brunel University and given authority to award its own degrees. The Prince's Theatre is acquired by Charles Clore and EMI, who rename it the Shaftesbury Theatre. St Mary-le-Bow Church, originally designed by Christopher Wren, holds its first services after being largely rebuilt and refurbished following damage by German bombers during the Blitz.

1962–72
London Underground's Victoria Line is built between Stockwell and Walthamstow.

1963
Bankside power station is commissioned. The London Government Act creates the Greater London Council. The Mayfair Theatre is built as an extension to the Mayfair Hotel in Stratton Street. A Museum of the Theatre opens in Kensington.

1963–66
The British Telecom Tower is built. Over 600 feet high, it dominates central London's skyline and allows radio and television waves to travel above buildings.

1964
The London Boroughs Association is formed.

1965
London's local government is reshaped as the Greater London Council and thirty-two London boroughs replace the London County Council.

1966
The British Airports Authority assumes responsibility for the management of Gatwick and Heathrow Airports, initiating a series of improvements to runway and terminal facilities. City University is founded. Marble Hill House is converted for use as a museum of eighteenth-century art and furniture. Trinidadian immigrants hold the first Notting Hill carnival.

1967
Construction work begins at Thamesmead, which will house a community on land reclaimed from River Thames marshes. East India Docks close. The Hayward Art Gallery opens on the South Bank. A major rehabilitation scheme, designed to reduce pollution of the River Lea and convert the area into a regional park, is unveiled by local authorities. The Queen Elizabeth Hall (named after Queen Elizabeth II) opens on the South Bank. The Royal Arsenal at Greenwich closes. Thames Television is founded to provide programming for the London region.

1968
Covent Garden Opera Company is renamed the Royal Opera. St Katharine's Dock closes.

1968–72
London Bridge is replaced.

1969
The Beckton Gas Production Plant, opened in 1870, closes as natural gas from the North Sea replaces town gas as a source of fuel and power. The London Docks close. Regent's Canal is closed to industrial traffic. The Transport Act denationalizes the city's public transport system, transferring management responsibilities to the Greater London Council. Twins Ronald and Reginald Kray, leaders of London's major criminal organization, are convicted of murder at the Old Bailey.

1970
The British Museum, lacking space to exhibit ethnographic material at its Great Russell Street site, opens a Museum of Mankind in Burlington Gardens. Central London Polytechnic, City of London Polytechnic, Kingston Polytechnic, North-East London Polytechnic, South Bank Polytechnic and Thames Polytechnic are created in order to enhance opportunities for higher education in London. John Rennie's London Bridge is sold to American interests, transferred to the United States, and re-erected at Lake Havasu City, Arizona. Surrey Commercial Docks close. The Young Vic is founded as part of the National Theatre.

1971
HMS *Belfast*, the largest cruiser ever built for the Royal Navy, is berthed at Symon's Wharf as a tourist attraction. The National Army Museum moves from the Royal Military Academy, Sandhurst, to a site

beside Chelsea Hospital. North London Polytechnic is founded. Plans to convert London's declining docklands into office and commercial space are shelved in the face of a public outcry.

1971–72
Embankments along the River Thames are raised in an attempt to prevent flooding.

1971–81
The 600-foot-high National Westminster Tower is built. At the time, it was the tallest building in London.

1972
The Conservative government authorizes construction of a flood barrier across the River Thames at Woolwich. Hangars at the former airstrip in Hendon are converted for use as a Royal Air Force Museum. Soho residents initiate a campaign to change the area's image as the centre of London's sex industry.

1973
The British Museum Library, the National Central Library and the National Lending Library merge to form the British Library. The London Stock Exchange unites with the Dublin Exchange and those operating in provincial cities of the United Kingdom. It also admits women as members. Middlesex Polytechnic is founded. The Water Act creates a Thames Water Authority with responsibility for water supply, pollution control, sewage disposal and provision of recreational facilities in the Thames river basin.

1974
Covent Garden fruit and vegetable market transfers to Nine Elms. The old site is redeveloped as a tourist focus, with boutiques, stalls and outdoor cafés. The Ranger's House at Greenwich is converted into an art gallery and museum of musical instruments.

1976
Guildhall Museum and the London Museum merge to form the Museum of London. The London Docklands Strategic Plan proposes community-based development, including housing, in the city's former dock area. The Notting Hill carnival is marred by rioting. Work on the National Theatre is completed, twenty-five years after the foundation stone was laid.

1977
The Astoria Cinema, in Charing Cross Road, is converted for use as a theatre. The Bryant and May match factory at Bow is closed and redesigned as flats. Heathrow Airport is linked to the Underground railway system by an extension of the Piccadilly Line. The Public Record Office opens a new base at Kew.

1978–79
Disputes between management and labour at *The Times* lead to frequent disruption of printing schedules but end with the introduction of new working practices.

1978–86
Richard Rogers and Partners design the controversial steel and glass Lloyd's Building.

1979
The Bank of England is made responsible for the supervision of all banks based in the United Kingdom. London Underground's new Jubilee Line improves access between Bond Street and Charing Cross. The New Victoria Cinema is renamed the Apollo Victoria, refurbished, and opened as a theatre presenting musicals and pop concerts.

1980

Alexandra Palace is destroyed by fire for the second time. The last of Blackwall's docks closes. The London Transport Museum opens in a converted flower market building at Covent Garden. Millwall Docks and West India Docks close.

1981

Bankside power station is decommissioned. The London Docklands Development Corporation is established, with a brief to regenerate the former dock area of the city. The London Symphony Orchestra takes up residence at the Barbican Centre. Riots in Brixton lead to an official government inquiry into relationships between the Metropolitan Police and London's black community. The Royal group of docks (the Victoria, Albert and King George V) close, becoming the last of the nineteenth-century harbour developments to cease operations. Rupert Murdoch's publishing empire absorbs *The Times*.

1982

The Barbican Arts Centre opens. Billingsgate Fish Market moves to the Isle of Dogs. Construction of a flood barrier across the River Thames at Woolwich is completed. The London International Financial Futures and Options Exchange (LIFFE) opens as a trading base for companies whose transactions involve a considerable element of financial risk.

1983

Battersea power station is decommissioned. The Duchess Theatre is the first London playhouse to perform musicals regularly on Sundays (*Snoopy* was the initial production). London Health Emergency is formed to campaign against the Conservative government's plans to close hospitals in the city. Thirteen local authorities, all dominated by the Labour Party, withdraw from the London Boroughs Association and form the Association of London Authorities.

1984

London's public transport system is renationalized and a management body, known as London Regional Transport, created to oversee provision. Parliamentary legislation creates a London Regional Passengers' Committee to consider complaints about bus and rail services in the city.

1985

The Geology Museum and the Natural History Museum merge. Stansted is designated London's third airport.

1986

The Big Bang revolutionizes financial practices in the City of London. The London Planning Advisory Committee is created to advise the government and London boroughs on strategic planning issues and major development proposals. London Transport replaces some of the advertising on its Underground services with poems, a policy that meets with widespread approval from travellers and leads to the publication of a successful book series. London's last gas street lamps are extinguished at Temple. A major development of Liverpool Street railway station includes construction of offices, restaurants and shopping facilities. Part of Hampton Court Palace's south wing is destroyed by fire. Prime Minister Margaret Thatcher's government abolishes the Greater London Council. The Stock Exchange converts from an association of members into a non-profit-making limited company and replaces face-to-face dealing with a computerized system of trading.

1987

The Docklands Light Railway links the City of London to the Isle of Dogs. A fire at King's Cross Underground station kills thirty-one people. London City Airport opens in the Docklands. The London

Commodity Exchange renames itself London Fox, the Futures and Options Exchange. London's Corn Exchange business transfers to the Baltic Exchange. Plans are prepared for an 850-foot-high tower, incorporating offices, a concert hall and a railway station, at Canary Wharf. A special Act of Parliament allows the Great Ormond Street Hospital for Sick Children to continue receiving financial benefits from the copyright of J.M. Barrie's play, *Peter Pan*, after the normal period for receipt of royalties expires. The Tower of London and the area that includes Westminster Abbey, the Palace of Westminster and St Margaret's Church are declared World Heritage Sites by the United Nations Educational, Scientific and Cultural Organization (UNESCO).

1987–88
Excavations reveal the foundations of a Roman amphitheatre underneath Guildhall Yard.

1988
Alexandra Palace, rebuilt after a fire in 1980, is opened as a sports, leisure and exhibition centre. A Museum of the Moving Image opens on the South Bank.

1989
A Design Museum, showing the best of British manufacturing, opens in a former warehouse at London's Docklands.

1990
The Courtauld Institute of Art moves from Portman Square to Somerset House. The Inner London Education Authority is abolished by the Conservative government, with which it had frequently crossed swords. The London Philharmonic Orchestra is made the resident orchestra at the Royal Festival Hall. Thames Water Authority is privatized by the Conservative government.

1991
Electricity supply is denationalized, returning the industry to private companies. The London International Insurance and Reinsurance Market Association (LIRMA) is formed. The Queen Elizabeth II Bridge carries southbound traffic across the River Thames at Dartford (at the eastern edge of the metropolitan area) and relieves congestion at the Dartford Tunnel. The Roche Consortium, a development company that had received planning permission to convert the former Battersea power station into a theme park, runs out of money. West London Polytechnic is founded.

1992
An IRA bomb damages the premises of the Baltic Exchange but has little effect on trading. Commercial organizations create London First to co-ordinate public and private attempts to improve investment in the city, increase the quality of transport provision, encourage tourism, and reduce air pollution. The London International Financial Futures and Options Exchange (LIFFE) absorbs the London Traded Options Market. Parliamentary legislation allows the London polytechnics to call themselves universities.

1993
Buckingham Palace is opened to the public. Admission fees are used to pay for rebuilding work at Windsor Castle. County Hall, former headquarters of the Greater London Council, is bought by a development company and converted into a hotel, restaurant and entertainment complex.

1994
The Baltic Exchange moves to new premises in St Mary Axe. The Conservative government announces its decision to close the Royal Naval College at Greenwich. London Transport assumes responsibility for The Drain (the underground rail link between Waterloo Station and the City of London). Prime

Minister John Major vetoes a proposal by his defence secretary, Michael Portillo, to sell Admiralty Arch to a private developer who would develop its office potential.

1995

The Association of London Authorities and the London Boroughs Association merge as the Association of London Government. Barings, the oldest merchant bank in the City of London, collapses financially after one of its employees takes excessive risks with the firm's funds on the Singapore futures market. The Conservative government decides against construction of additional runways at Gatwick and Heathrow Airports. London bus services are denationalized, returning to private sector control. In response to a European Union directive, Dublin business on the London Stock Exchange is redirected to a new exchange in the Republic of Ireland.

1996

The IRA bombs Canary Wharf Tower, killing two people and injuring 100. Lloyd's of London reaches a £3.1 billion settlement with most of the names who alleged that losses experienced between 1987 and 1992 were, in part, due to bad management. London International Financial Futures and Options Exchange (LIFFE) absorbs London Fox. The Royal Philharmonia takes up residence at the Royal Festival Hall. The Stone of Scone, coronation stone of the early Scottish monarchs, is removed from Westminster Abbey and returned to Scotland.

1997

The Bank of England is given responsibility for altering interest rates, a task previously reserved for government. The British Library moves to a purpose-built site at St Pancras. Cars are banned from Hammersmith Bridge but buses, cyclists and pedestrians retain rights of access. Greenwich is designated a World Heritage Site by UNESCO. The new Globe Theatre opens its first season of plays. The newly elected Labour government announces plans to privatize part of the Underground railway system but later shelves them following internal disputes over funding. The Swansea to Paddington express train passes a red signal and crashes into a goods locomotive at Southall. Seven people are killed, 150 injured, and Great Western Trains (operators of the express service) are fined a record £1.5 million for breaching safety legislation.

1997–99

The British Film Institute builds a seven-story IMAX cinema (the largest in Europe) on a site near Waterloo Station.

1998

The Londons Dockland Development Corporation is dismantled and its powers transferred to the London boroughs. Tea auctions are held in London for the last time.

1999

The Millennium Dome opens at Greenwich amid complaints about its cost, design and management.

2000

Andrew Lloyd Webber buys the Stoll Moss theatre empire in the West End. Australian Ross Stretton is the first foreigner to be appointed director of the Royal Ballet. The Athenaeum, one of London's principal gentlemen's clubs, votes to admit ladies as members. London citizens elect Ken Livingstone, a left-wing MP, as their first mayor. The London Eye, a giant ferris wheel, is erected outside County Hall, allowing visitors a view of the city from 450 feet above the River Thames. The London International Financial Futures and Options Exchange (LIFFE) announces a joint venture with NASDAQ (the North American exchange for high technology stocks) to form a market for stock futures. The Real IRA bombs the

BBC's Television Centre, but damage is limited and only one person is injured. The Tate Gallery opens new exhibition rooms for its modern art collection in the former Bankside power station. The Underground's Jubilee Line is extended through the Docklands to Stratford.

2001

The Royal Shakespeare Company decides to move out of the Barbican Centre, leaving it without a permanent base in London. The Stock Exchange announces plans to list itself on its own market. English Heritage reveals plans to remodel Hyde Park Corner at a cost of £20 million. Fulham Football Club reports a loss of £24 million, a sum believed by some observers to be the largest annual deficit ever recorded in English football. The International Petroleum Exchange is taken over by Intercontinental Exchange. The London International Financial Futures and Options Exchange (LIFFE) is bought by Euronext (a consortium formed by the Belgian, Dutch and French stock exchanges).

2002

Following the Queen Mother's death, her home at Clarence House is refurbished at a cost of £4.5 million. Maintenance of some tube lines is franchised to a private consortium but London Underground remains responsible for providing services. Mayor Ken Livingstone unveils a London Plan, proposing construction of 130 new schools, increased provision of homes, improved public transport and a larger police force.

2003

Boxer Michael Watson, who suffered brain damage in a world title fight in 1991, completes the London Marathon, taking six days to cover the 26 miles 385 yards. The Canary Wharf development is threatened as several tenants consider giving up office space in an effort to cut costs. The government backs a bid to hold the 2012 Olympic Games in London and approves a Crossrail project which will allow trains to run from Ealing, in the west of the city, to Romford, in the east (though the line will not be ready by the time of the Games). Kew Gardens is awarded World Heritage Site status by the United Nations. Mayor Ken Livingstone introduces a £5 'congestion charge' designed to reduce levels of traffic in the city centre. Russian businessman Roman Abromovich buys a controlling interest in Chelsea Football Club and embarks on a multi-million pound spending spree in an attempt to strengthen the team.

LORD MAYORS OF LONDON

1189	Henry FitzAilwyn
1212	Roger FitzAlan
1215	Serlo le Mercer
	William Hardel
1216	James Alderman
1217	Salomon de Basing
1218	Serlo le Mercer
1222	Richard Renger
1227	Roger le Duke
1231	Andrew Buckerel
1238	Richard Renger
1239	William Joynier
1240	Reginald de Bungheye
1241	Ralph Ashwy
1244	Michael Tovy
1246	John Gisors
	Peter FitzAlan
1247	Michael Tovy
1249	Roger FitzRoger
1250	John Norman
1251	Adam de Basing
1252	John Tulesan
1253	Nicholas Bat
1254	Ralph Hardel
1258	William FitzRichard
1259	John Gisors
	William FitzRichard
1261	Thomas FitzThomas
1265	Hugh FitzOtho
	John Walerand
	John de la Linde
1266	William FitzRichard
1267	Alan la Zuche
1268	Thomas de Ippegrave
	Stephen de Eddeworth
1269	Hugh FitzOtho
1270	John Adrien
1271	Walter Hervey
1273	Henry le Waleys
1274	Gregory de Rokesley
1281	Henry le Waleys
1284	Gregory de Rokesley
1285	Ralph de Sandwich
1289	John le Breton
	Ralph de Sandwich
1293	John le Breton
1298	Henry le Waleys
1299	Elias Russell
1301	John le Blund
1308	Nicholas de Farndone
1309	Thomas Romeyn
1310	Richer de Refham
1311	John de Gisors
1313	Nicholas de Farndone
1314	John de Gisors
1315	Stephen de Abyndon
1316	John de Wengrave
1319	Hamo de Chigwell
1320	Nicholas de Farndone
1321	Robert de Kendale
	Hamo de Chigwell
1323	Nicholas de Farndone
	Hamo de Chigwell
1326	Richard de Betoyne
1327	Hamo de Chigwell
1328	John de Grantham
1329	Simon Swanlond
1330	John de Pulteney
1332	John de Prestone
1333	John de Pulteney
1334	Reginald de Conduit
1336	John de Pulteney
1337	Henry Darci
1339	Andrew Aubrey
1341	John de Oxenford
1342	Simon Frauncis
1343	John Hamond
1345	Richard le Lacer
1346	Geoffrey de Witchingham
1347	Thomas Leggy
1348	John Lovekyn
1349	Walter Turke
1350	Richard de Kislingbury
1351	Andrew Aubrey
1352	Adam Fraunceys
1354	Thomas Leggy
1355	Simon Frauncis
1356	Henry Picard
1357	John de Stodeye
1358	John Lovekyn
1359	Simon Dolseley
1360	John Wroth
1361	John Pecche
1362	Stephen Cavendisshe

1363	John Nott
1364	Adam de Bury
1366	John Lovekyn
1367	James Andreu
1368	Simon de Mordone
1369	John de Chichester
1370	John Bernes
1372	John Pyel
1373	Adam de Bury
1374	William Walworth
1375	John Warde
1376	Adam Stable
1377	Nicholas Brembre
1378	John Philipot
1379	John Hadle
1380	William Walworth
1381	John de Northampton
1383	Sir Nicholas Brembre
1386	Nicholas Exton
1388	Sir Nicholas Twyford
1389	William Venour
1390	Adam Bamme
1391	John Heende
1392	Sir Edward Dalyngrigge
	Sir Baldwyn Radyngton
	William Staundon
1393	John Hadle
1394	John Fresshe
1395	William More
1396	Adam Bamme
1397	Richard Whittington
1398	Drew Barentyn
1399	Thomas Knolles
1400	John Fraunceys
1401	John Shadworth
1402	John Walcote
1403	William Askham
1404	John Heende
1405	John Wodecok
1406	Richard Whittington
1407	William Staundon
1408	Drugo Barentyn
1409	Richard Merlawe
1410	Thomas Knolles
1411	Robert Chichele
1412	William Walderne
1413	William Crowmere
1414	Thomas Fauconer
1415	Nicholas Wotton
1416	Henry Barton
1417	Richard Merlawe
1418	William Sevenoke
1419	Richard Whittington
1420	William Cauntbrigge
1421	Robert Chichele
1422	William Walderne
1423	William Crowmere
1424	John Michell
1425	John Coventre
1426	John Reynwell
1427	John Gedney
1428	Henry Barton
1429	William Estfeld
1430	Nicholas Wotton
1431	John Welles
1432	John Perneys
1433	John Brokle
1434	Robert Otele
1435	Henry Frowyk
1436	John Michell
1437	William Estfeld
1438	Stephen Broun
1439	Robert Large
1440	John Paddesle
1441	Robert Clopton
1442	John Hatherle
1443	Thomas Catworth
1444	Henry Frowyk
1445	Simon Eyre
1446	John Olney
1447	John Gedney
1448	Stephen Broun
1449	Thomas Chalton
1450	Nicholas Wyfold
1451	William Gregory
1452	Geoffrey Feldynge
1453	John Norman
1454	Stephen Forster
1455	William Marowe
1456	Thomas Canynges
1457	Geoffrey Boleyn
1458	Thomas Scott
1459	William Hulyn
1460	Richard Lee
1461	Hugh Wiche
1462	Thomas Cooke
1463	Matthew Philip
1464	Ralph Jossleyn
1465	Ralph Verney
1466	John Yonge

1467	Thomas Oulegrave
1468	William Taillour
1469	Richard Lee
1470	John Stockton
1471	William Edward
1472	Sir William Hampton
1473	John Tate
1474	Robert Drope
1475	Robert Bassett
1476	Sir Ralph Josselyn
1477	Humphrey Hayford
1478	Richard Gardyner
1479	Sir Bartholomew James
1480	John Browne
1481	William Haryot
1482	Edmund Shaa
1483	Robert Billesdon
1484	Thomas Hill
1485	Sir William Stokker
	John Warde
	Sir Hugh Bryce
1486	Henry Colet
1487	William Horne
1488	Robert Tate
1489	William White
1490	John Mathewe
1491	Hugh Clopton
1492	William Martin
1493	Ralp Astry
1494	Richard Chawry
1495	Sir Henry Colet
1496	John Tate
1497	William Purchase
1498	Sir John Percyvale
1499	Nicholas Ailwyn
1500	William Remyngton
1501	Sir John Shaa
1502	Bartholomew Rede
1503	Sir William Capel
1504	John Wynger
1505	Thomas Kneseworth
1506	Sir Richard Haddon
1507	William Browne
1508	Sir Lawrence Aylmer
	Stephen Jenyns
1509	Thomas Bradbury
1510	Sir William Capel
	Henry Kebyll
1511	Roger Achleley
1512	William Copynger
1513	Sir Richard Haddon
	William Browne
1514	Sir John Tate
	George Monoux
1515	William Boteler
1516	John Rest
1517	Thomas Exmewe
1518	Thomas Mirfyn
1519	James Yarford
1520	John Brugge
1521	John Milborne
1522	John Mundy
1523	Thomas Baldry
1524	William Bayley
1525	John Aleyn
1526	Sir Thomas Semer
1527	James Spencer
1528	John Rudstone
1529	Ralph Dodmer
1530	Thomas Pargeter
1531	Nicholas Lambarde
1532	Stephen Pecocke
1533	Christopher Ascue
1534	Sir John Champneys
1535	Sir John Aleyn
1536	Ralph Warren
1537	Sir Richard Gresham
1538	William Forman
1539	Sir William Hollyes
1540	William Roche
1541	Michael Dormer
1542	John Cotes
1543	William Bowyer
1544	Sir Ralph Warren
	William Laxton
1545	Sir Martin Bowes
1546	Henry Huberthorn
1547	Sir John Gresham
1548	Henry Amcotts
1549	Sir Rowland Hill
1550	Andrew Judde
1551	Richard Dobbis
1552	George Barne
1553	Thomas Whyte
1554	John Lyon
1555	William Garrarde
1556	Thomas Offley
1557	Thomas Curtes
1558	Thomas Leigh
1559	William Hewet

1560	Sir William Chester	1606	Sir John Watts
1561	William Harper	1607	Sir Henry Rowe
1562	Thomas Lodge	1608	Sir Humphrey Weld
1563	John Whyte	1609	Sir Thomas Cambell
1564	Richard Malorye	1610	Sir William Craven
1565	Richard Champyon	1611	Sir James Pemberton
1566	Christopher Draper	1612	Sir John Swynnerton
1567	Roger Martyn	1613	Sir Thomas Middleton
1568	Thomas Rowe	1614	Sir Thomas Hayes
1569	Alexander Avenon	1615	Sir John Jolles
1570	Rowland Heyward	1616	John Leman
1571	William Allen	1617	George Bolles
1572	Lionel Duckett	1618	Sir Sebastian Harvey
1573	John Ryvers	1619	Sir William Cokayne
1574	James Hawes	1620	Sir Frances Jones
1575	Ambrose Nicholas	1621	Edward Barkham
1576	John Langley	1622	Peter Probie
1577	Thomas Ramsay	1623	Martin Lumley
1578	Richard Pype	1624	John Gore
1579	Nicholas Woodroofe	1625	Allan Cotton
1580	John Branche	1626	Cuthbert Hacket
1581	James Harvye	1627	Hugh Hammersley
1582	Thomas Blanke	1628	Richard Deane
1583	Edward Osborne	1629	James Cambell
1584	Thomas Pullyson	1630	Sir Robert Ducye
1585	Wolstan Dixie	1631	George Whitmore
1586	George Barne	1632	Nicholas Rainton
1587	George Bonde	1633	Ralph Freeman
1588	Martin Calthorp	1634	Thomas Moulson
1589	Richard Martin		Robert Parkhurst
	John Harte	1635	Christopher Clitherow
1590	John Allot	1636	Edward Bromfield
1591	Sir Rowland Heyward	1637	Richard Ven
	William Webbe	1638	Sir Morris Abbot
1592	William Rowe	1639	Henry Garraway
1593	Cuthbert Buckell	1640	Edmund Wright
1594	Sir Richard Martin	1641	Richard Gurney
	John Spencer	1642	Isaac Penington
1595	Stephen Slanye	1643	Sir John Wollaston
1596	Thomas Skinner	1644	Thomas Atkyn
	Henry Billingsley	1645	Thomas Adams
1597	Richard Saltonstall	1646	Sir John Gayer
1598	Stephen Soame	1647	John Warner
1599	Nicholas Mosley	1648	Abraham Reynardson
1600	William Ryder	1649	Thomas Andrewes
1601	John Garrarde		Thomas Foot
1602	Robert Lee	1650	Thomas Andrewes
1603	Sir Thomas Bennett	1651	John Kendricke
1604	Sir Thomas Lowe	1652	John Fowke
1605	Sir Leonard Halliday	1653	Thomas Vyner

1654	Christopher Pack
1655	John Dethick
1656	Robert Tichborne
1657	Richard Chiverton
1658	Sir John Ireton
1659	Thomas Alleyn
1660	Sir Richard Browne
1661	Sir John Frederick
1662	Sir John Robinson
1663	Sir Anthony Bateman
1664	Sir John Lawrence
1665	Sir Thomas Bludworth
1666	Sir William Bolton
1667	Sir William Peake
1668	Sir William Turner
1669	Sir Samuel Starling
1670	Sir Richard Ford
1671	Sir George Waterman
1672	Sir Robert Hanson
1673	Sir William Hooker
1674	Sir Robert Vyner
1675	Sir Joseph Sheldon
1676	Sir Thomas Davies
1677	Sir Francis Chaplin
1678	Sir James Edwards
1679	Sir Robert Clayton
1680	Sir Patience Ward
1681	Sir John Moore
1682	Sir William Prichard
1683	Sir Henry Tulse
1684	Sir James Smyth
1685	Sir Robert Geffrye
1686	Sir John Peake
1687	Sir John Shorter
1688	Sir John Eyles
	Sir John Chapman
1689	Thomas Pilkington
1691	Sir Thomas Stampe
1692	Sir John Fleet
1693	Sir William Ashurst
1694	Sir Thomas Lane
1695	Sir John Houblon
1696	Sir Edward Clarke
1697	Sir Humphrey Edwin
1698	Sir Francis Child
1699	Sir Richard Levett
1700	Sir Thomas Abney
1701	Sir William Gore
1702	Sir Samuel Dashwood
1703	Sir John Parsons
1704	Sir Owen Buckingham
1705	Sir Thomas Rawlinson
1706	Sir Robert Bedingfield
1707	Sir William Withers
1708	Sir Charles Duncombe
1709	Sir Samuel Garrard
1710	Sir Gilbert Heathcote
1711	Sir Robert Beachcroft
1712	Sir Richard Hoare
1713	Sir Samuel Stanier
1714	Sir William Humfreys
1715	Sir Charles Peers
1716	Sir James Bateman
1717	Sir William Lewen
1718	Sir John Ward
1719	Sir George Thorold
1720	Sir John Fryer
1721	Sir William Stewart
1722	Sir Gerard Conyers
1723	Sir Peter Delmé
1724	Sir George Merttins
1725	Sir Francis Forbes
1726	Sir John Eyles
1727	Sir Edward Becher
1728	Sir Robert Baylis
1729	Sir Robert Brocas
1730	Humphrey Parsons
1731	Francis Child
1732	John Barber
1733	Sir William Billers
1734	Sir Edward Bellamy
1735	Sir John Williams
1736	Sir John Thompson
1737	Sir John Barnard
1738	Micajah Perry
1739	Sir John Salter
1740	Humphrey Parsons
1741	Daniel Lambert
	Sir Robert Godschall
1742	George Heathcote
1743	Robert Westley
1744	Henry Marshall
1745	Richard Hoare
1746	William Benn
1747	Sir Robert Ladbroke
1748	Sir William Calvert
1749	Sir Samuel Pennant
1750	John Blachford
	Francis Cockayne
1751	Thomas Winterbottom

1752	Robert Alsop
	Crisp Gascoyne
1753	Edward Ironside
	Thomas Rawlinson
1754	Stephen T. Janssen
1755	Slingsby Bethell
1756	Marshe Dickinson
1757	Sir Charles Asgill
1758	Sir Richard Glyn
1759	Sir Thomas Chitty
1760	Sir Mathew Blakiston
1761	Sir Samuel Fludyer
1762	William Beckford
1763	William Bridgen
1764	Sir William Stephenson
1765	George Nelson
1766	Sir Robert Kite
1767	Thomas Harley
1768	Samuel Turner
1769	William Beckford
1770	Barlow Trecothick
	Brass Crosby
1771	William Nash
1772	James Townsend
1773	Frederick Bull
1774	John Wilkes
1775	John Sawbridge
1776	Sir Thomas Hallifax
1777	Sir James Esdaile
1778	Samuel Plumbe
1779	Brackley Kennett
1780	Sir Watkin Lewes
1781	William Plomer
1782	Nathaniel Newnham
1783	Robert Peckham
1784	Richard Clark
1785	Thomas Wright
1786	Thomas Sainsbury
1787	John Burnell
1788	William Gill
1789	William Pickett
1790	John Boydell
1791	John Hopkins
1792	Sir James Sanderson
1793	Paul le Mesurier
1794	Thomas Skinner
1795	William Curtis
1796	Brook Watson
1797	John Anderson
1798	Sir Richard Glyn
1799	Harvey Christian Combe
1800	Sir William Staines
1801	Sir John Eamer
1802	Charles Price
1803	John Perring
1804	Peter Perchard
1805	James Shaw
1806	Sir William Leighton
1807	John Ansley
1808	Charles Flower
1809	Thomas Smith
1810	Joshua Smith
1811	Claudius Stephen Hunter
1812	George Scholey
1813	William Domville
1814	Samuel Birch
1815	Matthew Wood
1817	Christopher Smith
1818	John Atkins
1819	George Bridges
1820	John Thomas Thorp
1821	Christopher Magnay
1822	William Heygate
1823	Robert Waithman
1824	John Garratt
1825	William Venables
1826	Anthony Brown
1827	Matthias Prime Lucas
1828	William Thompson
1829	John Crowder
1830	John Key
1832	Sir Peter Laurie
1833	Charles Farebrother
1834	Henry Winchester
1835	William Taylor Copeland
1836	Thomas Kelly
1837	John Cowan
1838	Samuel Wilson
1839	Sir Chapman Marshall
1840	Thomas Johnson
1841	John Pirie
1842	John Humphrey
1843	William Magnay
1844	Michael Gibbs
1845	John Johnson
1846	Sir George Carroll
1847	John Kinnersley Hooper
1848	Sir James Duke
1849	Thomas Farncomb
1850	John Musgrove

1851	William Hunter
1852	Thomas Challis
1853	Thomas Sidney
1854	Francis G. Moon
1855	David Salomons
1856	Thomas Finnis
1857	Sir Robert Carden
1858	David Wire
1859	John Carter
1860	William Cubitt
1862	William Rose
1863	William Lawrence
1864	Warren Hale
1865	Benjamin Phillips
1866	Thomas Gabriel
1867	William Allen
1868	James Lawrence
1869	Robert Besley
1870	Thomas Dakin
1871	Sills Gibbons
1872	Sir Sydney Waterlow
1873	Andrew Lusk
1874	David Stone
1875	William Cotton
1876	Sir Thomas White
1877	Thomas Owden
1878	Sir Charles Whetham
1879	Sir Francis W. Truscott
1880	William McArthur
1881	John Ellis
1882	Henry Knight
1883	Robert Fowler
1884	George Nottage
1885	Robert Fowler
	John Staples
1886	Sir Reginald Hanson
1887	Polydore de Keyser
1888	James Whitehead
1889	Sir Henry Isaacs
1890	Joseph Savory
1891	David Evans
1892	Stuart Knill
1893	George Tyler
1894	Sir Joseph Renals
1895	Sir Walter Wilkin
1896	George Faudel-Phillips
1897	Lieutenant Colonel Horatio Davies
1898	Sir John Moore
1899	Alfred Newton
1900	Frank Green
1901	Sir Joseph Dimsdale
1902	Sir Marcus Samuel
1903	Sir James Ritchie
1904	John Pound
1905	Walter Morgan
1906	Sir William Treloar
1907	Sir John Bell
1908	Sir George Truscott
1909	Sir John Knill
1910	Sir Thomas V. Strong
1911	Sir Thomas B. Crosby
1912	Colonel Sir David Burnett
1913	Sir Thomas V. Bowater
1914	Colonel Sir Charles Johnston
1915	Colonel Sir Charles Wakefield
1916	Sir William Dunn
1917	Charles Hanson
1918	Sir Horace Marshall
1919	Sir Edward Cooper
1920	James Roll
1921	Sir John Baddeley
1922	Edward C. Moore
1923	Colonel Sir Louis Newton
1924	Sir Alfred Bower
1925	Sir William Pryke
1926	Sir George R. Blades
1927	Sir Charles Batho
1928	Sir John E. K. Studd
1929	Sir William Waterlow
1930	Sir William P. Neal
1931	Sir Maurice Jenks
1932	Sir Percy Greenaway
1933	Sir Charles Collett
1934	Sir Stephen Killik
1935	Sir Percy Vincent
1936	Sir George Broadbridge
1937	Sir Harry Twyford
1938	Major Sir Frank Bowater
1939	Sir William Coxen
1940	Sir George Wilkinson
1941	Lieutenant Colonel Sir John Laurie
1942	Sir Samuel Joseph
1943	Sir Frank Newson-Smith
1944	Sir Frank Alexander
1945	Sir Charles Davis
1946	Sir Bracewell Smith
1947	Sir Frederick Wells
1948	Sir George Aylwen
1949	Sir Frederick Rowland
1950	Denys Lowson

1951	Sir Leslie Boyce
1952	Sir Rupert De La Bère
1953	Sir Noel V. Bowater
1954	H. W. Seymour Howard
1955	Cuthbert L. Ackroyd
1956	Sir Cullum Welch
1957	Sir Denis Truscott
1958	Sir Harold Gillett
1959	Sir Edmund Stockdale
1960	Sir Bernard Waley-Cohen
1961	Sir Frederick Hoare
1962	Sir Ralph Perring
1963	Sir James Harman
1964	Sir James Miller
1965	Sir Lionel Denny
1966	Sir Robert Bellinger
1967	Sir Gilbert Inglefield
1968	Sir Charles Trinder
1969	Lieutenant Colonel Sir Ian F. Bowater
1970	Sir Peter Studd
1971	Sir Edward Howard
1972	Rt Hon. The Lord Mais
1973	Sir Hugh Wontner
1974	Sir Murray Fox
1975	Sir Lindsay Ring
1976	Sir Robin Gillett
1977	Sir Peter Vanneck
1978	Sir Kenneth Cork
1979	Sir Peter Gadsden
1980	Sir Ronald Gardner-Thorpe
1981	Sir Christopher Leaver
1982	Sir Anthony Jolliffe
1983	Dame Mary Donaldson
1984	Sir Alan Traill
1985	Sir Allan Davis
1986	Sir David Rowe-Ham
1987	Sir Greville Spratt
1988	Sir Christopher Collett
1989	Sir Hugh Bidwell
1990	Sir Alexander Graham
1991	Sir Brian Jenkins
1992	Sir Francis McWilliams
1993	Paul Newall
1994	Christopher Walford
1995	John Chalstrey
1996	Roger Cork
1997	Richard Nichols
1998	Lord Levene of Portsoken
1999	Clive Martin
2000	David Howard
2001	Michael Oliver
2002	Gavyn Arthur
2003	Robert Finch

CHAIRMEN OF LONDON COUNTY COUNCIL

1889–1890	Earl of Rosebery
1890–1892	Sir John Lubbock
1892	Earl of Rosebery
1892–1895	Sir John Hutton
1895–1897	Sir Arthur Arnold
1897–1898	W.J. Collins
1898–1899	T. McKinnon Wood
1899–1900	Lord Welby
1900–1901	W.H. Dickinson
1901–1902	A.M. Torrance
1902–1903	Sir John McDougall
1903–1904	Lord Monkswell
1904–1905	J.W. Benn
1905–1906	Sir Edwin Cornwall
1906–1907	Evan Spicer
1907–1908	H. Percy Harris
1908–1909	R.A. Robinson
1909–1910	Sir R. Melvill Beachcroft
1910–1911	W. Whitaker Thompson
1911–1912	Sir Edward White
1912	Captain G.S.C. Swinton
1912–1913	Major-General Lord Cheylesmore
1913–1914	Cyril S. Cobb
1914–1915	Viscount Peel
1915–1916	Cyril Jackson
1916–1917	Alfred F. Buxton
1917–1918	Marquess of Crewe
1918–1919	R.C. Norman
1919–1920	Lord Downham
1920–1921	John W. Gilbert
1921–1922	Sir Percy Simmons
1922–1923	Francis R. Anderton
1923–1924	Henry C. Gooch
1924–1925	J. Herbert Hunter

1925–1926	Sir Oscar Warburg
1926–1927	Sir George Hume
1927–1928	J. M. Gatti
1928–1929	Lieutenant-Colonel Sir Cecil Levita
1929–1930	Lord Monk Bretton
1930–1931	Sir Robert Tasker
1931–1932	Ernest Sanger
1932–1933	Angus N. Scott
1933–1934	Ernest M. Dence
1934–1938	Lord Snell
1938–1939	Ewart G. Culpin
1939–1940	Eveline M. Lowe
1940–1941	A. Emil Davies
1941–1942	C.G. Ammon
1942–1943	J.P. Blake
1943	Sir Alfred Baker
1943–1944	Richard Coppock
1944–1945	Somerville Hastings
1945–1946	Charles Robertson
1946–1947	John Cliff
1947–1948	Lady Nathan
1948–1949	Walter R. Owen
1949–1952	J.W. Bowen
1952–1953	Edwin Bayliss
1953	Sir Arthur Middleton
1953–1954	Mrs Douglas Boulton
1954–1955	Victor Mishcon
1955–1956	Norman G.M. Prichard
1956–1957	Helen Bentwich
1957–1958	R. McKinnon Wood
1958–1959	A.E. Samuels
1959–1960	Sidney J. Barton
1960–1961	Mrs F.E. Cayford
1961–1962	Harold Shearman
1962–1963	Olive G. Deer
1963	A. Reginald Stamp
1963–1964	Arthur E. Wicks

CHAIRMEN OF GREATER LONDON COUNCIL

1964–1966	Harold C. Shearman
1966–1967	Herbert Ferguson
1967–1968	Sir Percy Rugg
1968–1969	Sir Louis Gluckstein
1969–1970	Leslie Freeman
1970–1971	Peter Black
1971–1972	Robert Mitchell
1972–1973	Frank Abbott
1973–1974	Arthur E. Wicks
1974–1975	Lord Pitt
1975–1976	Dame Evelyn Denington
1976–1977	Lord Ponsonby
1977–1978	Lawrence Bains
1978–1979	H.T. Mote
1979–1980	Robert Vigars
1980–1981	Bernard Brook-Partridge
1981–1982	John B. Ward
1982–1983	Sir Ashley Bramall
1983–1984	Harvey Hinds
1984–1985	Illtyd Harrington
1985–1986	Tony Banks

ACKNOWLEDGEMENTS

Some people have contributed to this book by supplying information, others by providing insight and others by offering support. I am indebted to every one of them. A volume such as this relies heavily on the value of its sources and, therefore, on the thoroughness of the compilers of statistical tables, designers of websites, authors of books, writers of newspaper articles and researchers of encyclopaedia entries who collated the information on which I have drawn. There are too many to name individually but I can assure them that working through their information was an unfailing source of pleasure. Also, I have greatly valued the help of librarians who facilitated access to their collections (notably at London Metropolitan Archives, Redhill Public Library and the library of the University of Southern Mississippi) and of Aubree Stewart, who assisted with data collection in the later stages of the work.

There is more to London than facts and figures, of course, and I owe a particular debt of gratitude to colleagues and friends who helped me to understand the city by asking questions, telling me of their own experiences and discussing their opinions (and their prejudices). In addition to the regulars on the 08.24 from Earlswood to London Bridge, I am especially grateful to Dr Peter Allen, Dr Martin Bridge, James Bromwich, Dr Lawrence Clinton, Dr Keith Cowlard, Dr Skeeter Dixon, Dr Andrew Haggart, Drs John and Ray Hall, Dr Tim Hudson, Dr Amy McCandless, Dr Gwyn Meirion-Jones, Dr Barrie Morgan, Dr Maureen Ryan, Dr Jim Schnur and Mary-Ann Schnur, Dr Peter Shoebridge, Frances and Phil Sudduth, and Dr Jerry Waltman. Most of all, perhaps, interest in London was stimulated by students of London Guildhall University and the University of Southern Mississippi who argued in tutorials, analysed census data in practical classes and trudged the streets doing fieldwork. Many of them continued the discussions long after graduation and I have benefited, in particular, from the friendship of Kirstin Howgate, Ros Mandil-Wade, Zarmina Moghal and Karen Rae.

The book itself is the product of a large group of people, many wholly unknown to me, who have used their considerable talents to turn a manuscript into a readable publication. The text was originally prepared for an American audience and published by Scarecrow Press (an imprint of the Rowman and Littlefield group). Jon Woronoff, editor of Scarecrow's *Historical Dictionaries of Cities of the World* series, suggested that the volume should be added to his list and allowed me to draw on his expertise throughout the process. His perceptiveness undoubtedly makes the work significantly better than it would have otherwise have been so he is as much a part of this *Companion* as I am. Jonathan Reeve had the vision to see that the American book could be adapted for a British readership and I have learned much through contact with him and with Becky Gadd, his congenial colleague at Tempus Publishing. Don Shewan, of City Cartographic, has also made an important, and very effective, contribution through his maps of London's growth and the London boroughs. I am also aware of the army of proofreaders, designers, printers and others, on both sides of the Atlantic, who used their skill to make the book both attractive and easy to use. I wish I had their talent.

I have been able to write this book only because I could draw on the kindness of friends and colleagues, who gave their support unstintingly. Tim Hudson, Provost at the University of Southern Mississippi, has been a colleague as well as a friend for over twenty years: we have spent many evenings together talking about London as we drained a bottle of Ardbeg and I have valued his acuity as well as his support. In addition to the others mentioned above, long-time friends Andrew Blackadder, Jock Brown, Donald McAlpine, Iain and Jean Nicolson, and

Alec and Rona Stevenson have been towers of strength in good times as well as in bad. I am also indebted to new-found friend Debbie Watson for her generosity and for her shortbread (though not necessarily in that order) as well as to Felicia Casey, Paula Mathis, Diane Miller and Dr Tom Richardson (my colleagues at the University of Southern Mississippi's Honors College) for the willingness with which they shouldered extra loads while I learned a new job and, simultaneously, tried to meet Tempus's deadlines.

All of these people played an important part in shaping this book, some directly, some indirectly, and I am deeply grateful to every one of them but I hope they will understand that the greatest of my debts is owed to my daughter, Mhorbhaine. My wife, who had been my anchor for nearly forty years, died in 2001 while the page proofs of the American volume were being edited and my mother died in 2002, while the British volume was nearing completion. Mhorbhaine shared the emotional upheavals and understood that putting the volumes together was a kind of therapy. We have leaned heavily on each other and it is to her that this book is dedicated, with love and with thanks.

LIST OF ILLUSTRATIONS

p.4/5 London in 1647 by Hollar (Tempus Archive).
p.6 The development of London from Roman times to the present (Don Shewan).
p.11 Southwark in 1543 by Wyngaerde (Tempus Archive).
p.12 A 1761 advertisement for a book publisher based in St Paul's courtyard (Jonathan Reeve).
p.14 Hollar's engraving of the Great Fire of 1666 (Jonathan Reeve).
p.28 A late seventeenth-century engraving of the Lord Mayor and the Court of Aldermen (Jonathan Reeve).
p.37 The Bank of England in the eighteenth century (Jonathan Reeve).
p.38 Bankside, c. 1560 (Tempus Archive).
p.39 Bankside was a den of iniquity in the 1640s, so the puritanical Oliver Cromwell closed the many pleasure palaces that littered the area, in an attempt to eradicate the squalid atmosphere (Jonathan Reeve).
p.40 Execution of Charles I in 1649 in front of the Banqueting Hall, Whitehall (Jonathan Reeve).
p.52 View of Bermondsey monastery in 1543 (Tempus Archive).
p.55 Billingsgate, c. 1598 (Jonathan Reeve).
p.56 Bishopsgate, 1599 (Tempus Archive).
p.58 The building of Blackfriar's Bridge, July 1766 (Jonathan Reeve).
p.60 A 1787 engraving of Bloomsbury Square (Jonathan Reeve).
p.68 Bridewell Place and the entrance to the Fleet River as they appeared in 1660 (Tempus Archive).
p.77 Henry VIII created Bushy Park as a hunting forest. Drawing by Hans Holbein (Tempus Archive).
p.85 The Cato Street conspirators surprised. A contemporary drawing by George Cruikshank (Tempus Archive).
p.88 The Coronation procession of Edward VI passing Charing Cross on its way from London to Westminster (Tempus Archive).
p.89 Plan of the Charing Cross area, c. 1554 (Jonathan Reeve).
p.93 The Lord Mayor's procession in 1761 passing down Cheapside (Jonathan Reeve).
p.93 Early seventeenth-century Cheapside before the Great Fire of 1666 (Jonathan Reeve).
p.98 A view of Chiswick, c. 1750, from an old print (Jonathan Reeve).
p.101 A plan of the City of London in the time of the Tudors (Tempus Archive).
p.107 A scene in a London coffee house, c. 1688, from a contemporary engraving (Jonathan Reeve).
p.112 The piazza in Covent Garden, an engraving by Hollar (Tempus Archive).
p.118 View of the Custom House, c. 1600 (Tempus Archive).
p.130 Eastcheap market, c. 1598 (Jonathan Reeve).
p.143 The yard at Fleet Prison, c. 1749 (Jonathan Reeve).
p.144 View of the Fleet River, c. 1750 (Jonathan Reeve).
p.147 Frost Fair on the Thames, 1683 (Jonathan Reeve).
p.153 The Globe Theatre in the early seventeenth century, from Visscher's Panorama of London (Tempus Archive).
p.157 Widespread sympathy was excited throughout the country following the Great Fire of London in 1666. Within a week of the news reaching Lyme Regis in Dorset, the townspeople raised and sent to London £100 to aid those affected (Jonathan Reeve).
p.158 Leake's exact survey of the streets contained within the ruins of the City of London, 1669 (Tempus Archive).
p.158 The Great Fire of London, 1666, from a contemporary print (Jonathan Reeve).
p.160 A contemporary woodcut of the plague of London (Jonathan Reeve).
p.162 Greenwich Palace from Wyngaerde's Panorama of London, 1543 (Tempus Archive).
p.167 The chief conspirators of the Gunpowder Plot, 1605 (Jonathan Reeve).
p.170 A seventeenth-century four-wheeled coach (Jonathan Reeve).
p.172 A woodcut of the flight of townspeople into the country to escape from the Great Plague of London (Jonathan Reeve).
p.173 Cardinal Wolsey began building Hampton Court Palace in 1514 (Tempus Archive).
p.174 Elizabeth I was very fond of hunting at Hampton Court. In this contemporary woodcut, she is depicted with her huntsman (Jonathan Reeve).
p.178 View of Harrow-on-the-Hill from the Thames, early in the seventeenth century (Jonathan Reeve).
p.190 The rules of polo were formalized by the Harlington Club at Ranelagh Gardens (Jonathan Reeve).